A Guide to the New ICC Rules of Arbitration

by

Yves Derains
Eric A. Schwartz

KLUWER LAW INTERNATIONAL
THE HAGUE / LONDON / BOSTON

Published by Kluwer Law International
P.O. Box 85889
2508 CN The Hague, The Netherlands

Sold and distributed in the USA and Canada by
Kluwer Law International
675 Massachusetts Avenue
Cambridge, MA 02139, USA

Sold and distributed in all other countries by
Kluwer Law International
Distribution Centre
P.O. Box 322
3300 AH Dordrecht, The Netherlands

A C.I.P. Catalogue record for this book is available from the Library of Congress

First reprint, 1998

Printed on acid-free paper

Cover design: Alfred Birnie bNO

ISBN: 9041105956

© 1998 Kluwer Law International

Kluwer Law International incorporates the publishing programmes of Graham & Trotman Ltd,
Kluwer Law and Taxation Publishers and Martinus Nijhoff Publishers

FOREWORD

The Rules of Arbitration of the International Chamber of Commerce ("ICC") are widely regarded as one of the world's leading sets of rules for the arbitration of international commercial disputes. After more than two years of work by the ICC's International Court of Arbitration and its Commission on International Arbitration, the ICC adopted new Rules in April 1997 which entered into force on January 1, 1998. The new Rules represent the first major revision of the ICC's Rules of Arbitration since 1975 and apply, in principle, to all new ICC arbitrations commenced since January 1, 1998.

In this book, we have undertaken to explain the principal characteristics of the new Rules, how they differ from the prior version and how they are expected to operate in practice. Because it was our wish to provide a practical guide to the new Rules that would be of assistance to users, whether as counsel or arbitrator, we have devoted our comments primarily to the operation of the Rules themselves rather than to broader issues of arbitration theory and practice, subjects that have been treated in depth by many others. Our commitment to a practical approach has also inspired the form of this book, which reviews the Rules on an article-by-article basis, principally in the light of our own experiences both inside and outside the ICC as administrators, arbitrators and counsel over the past 25 years.

Although each of us has served as Secretary General of the ICC's International Court of Arbitration (the "ICC Court") and participated in the drafting of the new Rules, this book is by no means intended as an official commentary. Nor are the views expressed herein necessarily representative of the attitudes of those presently charged with responsibility for the Rules' application. The ICC Rules have always been the subject of an evolving body of related practice and jurisprudence. Although the ICC Court and its Secretariat have developed a number of relatively settled practices over the years, which this book will hopefully help to illuminate, they are nevertheless not bound by their past decisions and policies, which are constantly subject to review and reconsideration. It should therefore not be assumed that simply because the ICC Court may have taken a certain position in the past, it will necessarily follow it in the future.

The ICC Court's ability to adapt to change through a diverse and increasingly substantial infrastructure has always been one of its strengths. With not only a new set of Rules, but also, since January 1997, a new Chairman and Secretary General, the Court can reasonably be expected in the years ahead to explore new paths. It is nevertheless hoped that this book will provide a useful roadmap to first-time users of the Rules and experienced practitioners alike in navigating their way through the changed landscape of ICC arbitration.

Finally, we wish to express our gratitude to all those whose assistance and support made this book possible, including, in particular, the International Chamber of Commerce, the ICC International Court of Arbitration and its current Secretary General, Horacio Grigera Naón, who graciously read and commented upon portions of the manuscript. The law firm of Salans Hertzfeld & Heilbronn also provided unstinting support, as did Rolf Johnson, Sophie Boca, Caroline Harris and Isabelle Stefani, who helped ready the manuscript for publication. Our thanks are, of course, also owed to our families, who had to cope with our devotion to this project.

Yves Derains
Eric A. Schwartz
Paris, February 1998

Table of Contents

CHAPTER 5
THE ARBITRAL PROCEEDINGS (Articles 13-23)

APPENDICES

Note on References

References are repeatedly made throughout this book to a certain number of publications on the subject of ICC and international arbitration as well as to other documents. For convenience, the following abbreviations have been used when referring to them:

BOOKS

Craig Park and Paulsson – Craig, Park and Paulsson, *International Chamber of Commerce Arbitration*, 2nd ed. (ICC Publishing/Oceana Publications 1990).

Fouchard Gaillard and Goldman – Fouchard, Gaillard and Goldman, *Traité de l'arbitrage commercial international* (Litec 1996).

Holtzmann and Neuhaus – Holtzmann and Neuhaus, *A Guide to the UNCITRAL Model Law on International Commercial Arbitration* (Kluwer 1989).

ICC Arbitral Awards 1974-1985 – Jarvin and Derains, eds., *Collection of ICC Arbitral Awards 1974-1985* (ICC Publishing/Kluwer 1990).

ICC Arbitral Awards 1986-1990 – Jarvin, Derains and Arnaldez, eds., *Collection of ICC Arbitral Awards 1986-1990* (ICC Publishing/Kluwer 1994).

ICC Arbitral Awards 1991-1995 – Arnaldez, Derains and Hascher, eds., *Collection of ICC Arbitral Awards 1991-1995* (ICC Publishing/Kluwer 1997).

ICCA Yearbook – van den Berg, ed., *Yearbook of Commercial Arbitration*, published annually since 1976 by the International Council for Commercial Arbitration ("ICCA").

Lalive Poudret and Reymond – Lalive, Poudret and Reymond, *Le Droit de l'Arbitrage Interne et International en Suisse* (Payot 1989).

Redfern and Hunter – Redfern and Hunter, *Law and Practice of International Commercial Arbitration*, 2nd ed. (Sweet & Maxwell 1991).

PERIODICALS

Am. Rev. Int. Arb.	*American Review of International Arbitration.*
Arbitration	*Arbitration*, the Journal of the Chartered Institute of Arbitrators.
Arb. Int.	*Arbitration International*, the Journal of the London Court of International Arbitration.
ASA Bull.	*Bulletin of the Swiss Arbitration Association.*
Clunet	*Journal du Droit International.*
ICC Ct. Bull.	*The ICC International Court of Arbitration Bulletin.*
J. Arb. Int.	*Journal of International Arbitration.*
Mealey's	*Mealey's International Arbitration Report.*
Rev. arb.	*Revue de l'arbitrage*, the Journal of the Comité Français de l'Arbitrage.

OTHER DOCUMENTS

New York Convention	The United Nations Convention of 1958 on the Recognition and Enforcement of Foreign Arbitral Awards
UNCITRAL Model Law	The UNCITRAL Model Law on International Commercial Arbitration
AAA International Arbitration Rules	The International Arbitration Rules of the American Arbitration Association (effective April 1, 1997).
LCIA Rules	The Rules of the London Court of International Arbitration (effective January 1, 1998).

WIPO Arbitration Rules   The Arbitration Rules of the World Intellectual Property Organization (effective October 1, 1994).

UNCITRAL Rules   The UNCITRAL Arbitration Rules.

Chapter 1
An Introduction to the New ICC Arbitration Rules

The ICC International Court of Arbitration was founded in Paris in 1923 by the ICC in order to place at the disposal of "financiers, manufacturers and business men of all countries" an international organization capable of settling international commercial disputes "without recourse to formal legal procedure."[1] Seventy-five years later, the ICC Court has administered nearly 10,000 international arbitration cases and become widely known as the leading institution for the arbitration of international commercial disputes.

THE INTERNATIONAL CHAMBER OF COMMERCE

The ICC is a non-profit, private association that was established in 1919, just after the close of the First World War, by prominent members of the business communities of Belgium, France, Italy, the United Kingdom and the United States.[2] The objective of its founders was to create an institution that would foster reconciliation and peace through the promotion of international commerce. But in order to achieve that goal, the ICC's founders recognized the need for the gradual harmonization of international trade practices and legislation and the development of internationally recognized commercial instruments and mechanisms, including mechanisms for the resolution of international commercial disputes. It was this vision that led to the creation of a Court of Arbitration (which was renamed the International Court of Arbitration in 1989).

Over the years, the ICC has grown into a far-flung international organization with members in approximately 150 countries and so-called National Committees in more than 60 of them, where membership in the organization is sufficiently large to justify the creation of local structures to represent the mem-

---

[1]   Rules of the Court of Arbitration of the International Chamber of Commerce adopted on July 10, 1922.
[2]   The ICC is established in France as an "association" under the law of 1901 governing non-profit associations.

1

bers in the governance and working bodies of the ICC.[3] The National Committees are autonomous organizations that each elect representatives to the ICC's Council, the ICC's supreme governing body. The Council in turn elects an Executive Board and the officers of the organization, including, in particular, a President as well as a Secretary General who oversee the work of the ICC's permanent Secretariat, which since 1919 has been based in Paris and today also includes a Hong Kong branch office opened in 1997. The President of the ICC serves for a two-year term and is always a prominent business leader. Past ICC Presidents have been drawn from many different nations around the world. The immediate past President is Rahmi Koç, the Chairman of one of Turkey's largest corporate groups. The current President (until December 31, 1998) is Helmut Maucher, the Managing Director of Nestlé.

It is also the task of the ICC Council, as discussed further below, to adopt rules issued by the organization, including arbitration rules, and to appoint the members of the International Court of Arbitration.

The work of the ICC, through more than two dozen different Commissions, encompasses a broad range of commercial, legal and economic issues relating to international trade. Among other things, ICC Commissions have developed the "Incoterms," uniform rules and practices for documentary letters of credit, standard forms of bank guarantees and corporate codes of conduct relating to bribery, environmental issues and other matters. The ICC is active in the fields of insurance, intellectual property, taxation, telecommunications, and transportation, among others. It developed and administers the "ATA Carnet" system to facilitate the clearance of goods through customs and maintains an ongoing dialogue with other international organizations, including the United Nations and its various working bodies, in order to convey the views of world business.

THE RULES OF ARBITRATION

Within this multifaceted, private international organization, arbitration has always occupied a special place. The ICC was a pioneer in developing modern, international commercial arbitration, and it played an important role in helping to bring about both relevant legislative change and the principal multilateral arbitration treaties of the twentieth century. The ICC's first Rules of Arbitration (and accompanying Conciliation Rules) were published in English and French, the ICC's two working languages, in 1922, immediately preceding the establishment of the first Court of Arbitration, and they were followed by new or amended Rules in 1927, 1931, 1933, 1939, 1947, 1955, 1975 and 1988 that were issued in response to the ICC's evolving arbitration experience and legal developments in the field. Notwithstanding their many different manifestations, however, the Rules have always shared a common vocation, that is, to be suitable for international use, consistent with the ICC's international character and mission. Thus,

---

[3] A list of the ICC's National Committees is set forth in Appendix 3.

although the ICC Court sits in Paris, ICC arbitrations may be conducted anywhere. Over the years, ICC arbitrations have been conducted in dozens of countries throughout the world, with arbitrators and parties of as many as 100 different nationalities.[4]

The Rules are therefore commonly said to have as one of their fundamental characteristics a "universal" character, meaning that they are intended for use in any country, under any law and in accordance with any system of legal procedure.[5] This has, in turn, influenced their basic style and structure. Indeed, because of the diversity of the participants in the process, the Rules have been drafted so as to provide only a general framework for the arbitration without impinging upon the right of the parties or the arbitrators to fashion procedures suitable for an individual case. The Rules have therefore also traditionally provided relatively little procedural detail and avoided imposing on the parties either a common or civil law (or other) procedural bias. In addition, the parties are accorded the greatest possible freedom in the selection of arbitrators – the ICC has no roster or panel of approved arbitrators. Indeed, with parties from so many different countries, it would be difficult, even with the considerable support that the Court receives from its network of National Committees, to maintain a roster of sufficient diversity.

The counterpart of so much flexibility and autonomy is a high degree of institutional involvement in the supervision of the arbitral process. Although no arbitral institution is in a position to guarantee completely the ultimate quality and efficacy of the process, the ICC, more than any other institution, has historically endeavored to do so through a combination of the efforts of its International Court of Arbitration and National Committees. The Court, first of all, is unique, both in its composition and in the role that it plays in monitoring the conduct of all ICC arbitrations. Composed of legal professionals of more than 50 nationalities, the Court, with the support of its permanent Secretariat in Paris, brings to bear on the decisions that it is its responsibility to make the collective and disparate knowledge and experience of a multinational body having a composition as diverse as that of the participants in the process. Its functions include deciding whether to accept an arbitration, whether to permit the joinder of arbitrations, designating arbitrators, reviewing and confirming the appointment of arbitrators nominated by the parties, fixing, if necessary, the place of arbitration, reviewing and deciding upon allegations of arbitrator bias or misconduct, extending time limits, fixing the fees of arbitrators, reviewing and approving, as necessary, the arbitrators' Terms of Reference, and, most notably,

---

4   For recent statistical information concerning ICC arbitration, *see* Appendix 6.

5   In order to permit the widest possible access to the ICC Rules, they have also been translated into a number of different languages, in addition to English and French (although only the English and French versions are "authoritative"). The previous Rules were, thus, available in Arabic, Bulgarian, Chinese, German, Hungarian, Italian, Japanese, Polish, Russian, Spanish, Turkish and Vietnamese. The ICC will presumably endeavor to translate the 1998 Rules into as many languages eventually.

reviewing and approving (as to their form), the arbitrators' Awards. The National Committees, meanwhile, appoint the members of the Court, assist in the selection of arbitrators and, from time to time, can be of assistance in obtaining voluntary compliance with an Award by a recalcitrant party.

When undertaking the reform leading to the 1998 Rules (the "New Rules"), the ICC wished to ensure that these essential features of the ICC arbitration system would not be disturbed.[6]

THE REFORM OF THE RULES

During the last few decades there has been unprecedented growth in the use of arbitration to resolve international commercial disputes. Spurred by the expansion of transnational trade and investment and shifting patterns of economic development, arbitration truly has become, as this century comes to a close, the normal method of finally resolving international commercial disputes. This has inevitably had a dramatic effect, both on the volume and nature of the ICC's caseload and on the related demands on the institution. In 1955, when the ICC undertook the first major reform of its Rules after the Second World War, the ICC Court received only 33 Requests for Arbitration. Forty years later, in 1995, the number of new cases exceeded 400, and, indeed, nearly three-quarters of the 10,000 cases administered by the ICC in the Court's 75-year history have been received during the last twenty years.

But apart from this increase in numbers, the participants in the process have also become much more diverse. For most of its early history, the ICC drew most of its users from the North Atlantic countries that founded the ICC and from Western Europe, in particular. The vast majority of ICC arbitrators were European, and nearly all ICC arbitrations took place in Europe, with France and Switzerland being the preferred venues. Over the years, the ICC, thus, acquired a strong European identity, even though its membership and vocation have long been global. In 1996, for the first time in the ICC's history, a majority of the parties in ICC arbitrations commenced during that year came from outside Western Europe, with large numbers of parties from Asia, Latin America and Central and Eastern Europe. Moreover, the wave of legislative reform in respect of international arbitration that has been sweeping the world in recent years has opened up

---

[6]   The Working Party established by the ICC Commission on International Arbitration to make proposals for the revision of the Rules identified the "fundamental characteristics" of ICC arbitration as: "... its universality, the existence of a Court of Arbitration, the support of the National Committees, the control of time limits and financial matters by the institution, its flexibility and adaptability to all types of procedure, the Terms of Reference, the scrutiny of draft Awards by the Court of Arbitration and ensuring that the guarantees to which users are accustomed in ICC arbitration are preserved." Proposed Mandate (October 4, 1995) of the Working Party on the Revision of the ICC Rules of Arbitration, ICC Doc. No. 420/342. Over the years, a substantial body of literature has emerged with respect to these and other features of the ICC arbitral process.

to ICC arbitration an increasing number of "arbitration-friendly" venues outside the traditional international arbitration centers of Western Europe. It is therefore not unusual today for ICC arbitrations to be held in places such as Mexico City and Hong Kong, and this is a trend that is likely to continue.

The increasing globalization of international arbitration has, among other things, created a correspondingly greater need for clear and accessible arbitration rules. First-time users of the Rules, wherever they may be, need to be able to apprehend easily how the process works. Quite apart from this, the transformation of international arbitration into the normal way of resolving international commercial disputes has inevitably resulted in a relatively less informal process. Indeed, many arbitrations today are hardly fought, high-stakes disputes. The possible imprecision or ambiguity of rules may be fatal in such cases. All arbitral institutions, moreover, are under pressure to provide services that are expeditious and cost-effective. The ICC, in particular, has, over the years, constantly had to combat the perception, which is largely undeserved, that ICC arbitration is slower and more costly than other forms of arbitration.

It is against this backdrop that the ICC began, in the spring of 1995, the process of examining the possible need to amend its Rules. Since the Second World War, there had previously been only two major reforms of the ICC Rules, first in 1955 and then in 1975. Each of those reforms was innovative, for its time, and served as a source of inspiration to others subsequently involved in drafting international arbitration rules and legislation. The 1955 Rules, for example, introduced the then controversial notion of "competence-competence" (*see* Article 6(2) *infra*), *i.e.,* the concept that the Arbitral Tribunal is competent to decide upon challenges to its own jurisdiction, while the 1975 Rules provided for the first time that the parties and the arbitrators should be free to conduct the arbitration procedure without reference to the procedural laws of any country, except, of course, to the extent that they may mandatorily apply (*see* Article 15(1) *infra*).

The 1975 Rules, to a large degree, conserved the basic structure and features of the Rules adopted in 1955 and, in turn, proved to be remarkably resilient. Nonetheless, it was recognized within the ICC as early as 1986 that the combination of the changing landscape for ICC arbitration and the continued expansion of the Court's caseload would eventually require an in-depth reexamination of the Rules. In September 1986, the Court's then Chairman, Michel Gaudet, thus, noted:

> On the one hand, the expansion of international commercial arbitration has engendered new situations with respect to the nature and extent of the disputes, the parties involved and the laws applicable. On the other hand, the recent arrival on the scene of carefully designed arbitration rules ... have contributed to clarifying certain problems and developing answers that the ICC Rules cannot fail to take note of. Lastly, the increasing emphasis placed on procedural questions by the parties' legal advisors calls

for the clarification of a number of the current provisions ... so as to meet the requirements of the wide variety of cases brought to the ICC ... .[7]

Soon thereafter, in 1988, certain, limited modifications were made to the Rules in order to correct "uncertainties that practice ha[d] shown to be particularly threatening."[8] In the years that followed, the considerations mentioned by Mr. Gaudet as well as persistent expressions of frustration concerning, in particular, the time required to conduct an ICC arbitration continued to nourish a lively debate both inside and outside the ICC regarding the need for and possible extent of required, further change to the Rules. In the meantime, however, substantial investments were made by the ICC in increasing the size and resources of the Court's Secretariat and in improving the efficiency of the Court's practices.

Ultimately, it was not the Court, but the ICC Commission on International Arbitration (the "Commission"), that took the initiative of launching a thorough reexamination of the ICC Rules at a meeting of the Commission in Paris on April 20, 1995. The Commission is a distinct consultative body, separate from the Court, that is composed of representatives of the ICC's National Committees, but in which the members of the Court also participate. Neither the Commission nor the Court has any authority to amend the Rules. This is the exclusive province of the ICC Council. However, the Council has traditionally deferred to the judgment of the Commission and the Court, who have generally endeavored to achieve a consensus in respect of proposals to be placed before the Council in this regard.[9] At its April 1995 meeting, the Commission decided to constitute a Working Party (the "Working Party") to make proposals to the Commission concerning the possible need for Rules changes.[10] The Working Party was, at the

---

[7]   Letter, dated September 8, 1986, to O. Glossner, then Chairman of the ICC Commission on International Arbitration, ICC Doc. No. 420/286.

[8]   *Id.* The changes concerned the provisions relating to the selection, challenge and replacement of arbitrators, the calculation of time limits and the advance on costs.

[9]   The Court's Statutes (Appendix I to the ICC Rules) provide, in this connection, that the Court is required to lay before the Commission any proposal for the amendment of the Rules. However, neither the Statutes, which, like the Rules, were modified as of January 1, 1998, nor any other document clearly provides who has the authority within the ICC to propose Rules changes to the ICC's governing bodies.

[10]   The Working Party was chaired by Yves Derains, and Stephen Bond, the Court's Secretary General from 1985-1991, was named vice-chairman. The other members of the Working Party were: Orhan Azizoglu (Turkey); Kamel Ben Salah (Tunisia); Marc Blessing (Switzerland); Michael Bühler (Germany); William Laurence Craig (U.S.A.); Bernardo Cremades (Spain); Mathieu de Boisséson (France); Antonias Dimolista (Greece); Horacio Grigera Naón (Argentina and later as Secretary General of the Court); Sigvard Jarvin (Sweden); Dominique Hascher (Secretary of the Commission and General Counsel of the Court); Robert Knutson (Canada); John Merrett (U.K); Renzo Morera (Italy); Carlos Nehring Netto (Brazil); Andreas Reiner (Austria); Luis D. Santos Jimenez (Mexico); David Sarre (U.K.); David Sutton (U.K.); Michael Schneider (Switzerland); Eric Schwartz (Secretary General of the Court); Youssef Takla (Lebanon); and René van Rooij (Netherlands).

same time, directed to comment on certain proposed additions to the Rules that had already been placed before the Commission by the Court.[11]

In October 1995, the Working Party reported to the Commission that it proposed to undertake a general examination of the ICC Rules with a view to suggesting revisions that would be capable of responding to the needs of practitioners for at least a decade, it being the general view that changes to a well-known body of rules, such as the ICC Rules, should not be made too frequently. The Working Party reported, in particular, that the objectives of the revision should be to "reduce delays ... [and] unpredictability ... rationalise costs ... [and] improve any defective rules, while respecting the fundamental characteristics of ICC arbitration ... ."[12] It further decided to consider the Court's proposals in the context of the Working Party's general examination of the Rules, given the Working Party's wish to avoid piecemeal revisions.

The decision to respect "the fundamental characteristics of ICC arbitration" enjoyed broad support within the Commission, although it was not entirely free from controversy. Indeed, certain of those "fundamental characteristics" – in particular, the Terms of Reference and the Court's role in scrutinizing arbitral Awards – had themselves been under attack for years in certain quarters on the ground that they unnecessarily prolonged the ICC arbitration process and, at the very least, ought to be made optional.[13] This proved, however, to be the view of a relatively small minority, not only within the Commission but among those practitioners throughout the world with whom the ICC's National Committees consulted. Indeed, notwithstanding past criticism of the Terms of Reference, increased familiarity with them on the part of many practitioners, and with international arbitration practice generally, appears to have enhanced their reputation as a useful tool (and, moreover, led to their importation into many non-ICC arbitrations). Similarly, the Court's scrutiny of Awards has widely come to be seen, by parties and arbitrators alike, as a valuable safeguard that distinguishes the ICC system and that should be retained.

During the course of the twelve months following the October 1995 meeting of the Commission, the Working Party prepared a number of draft texts of pos-

---

[11]   The Court had, as of that time, requested the Commission to comment on the proposed addition to the Rules of provisions in respect of a certain number of matters, including, in particular, the following: (i) the constitution of the Arbitral Tribunal in multi-party cases; (ii) the authority of the arbitrators to order interim measures; (iii) the correction and interpretation of arbitral Awards; (iv) the change by the Court of the agreed place of arbitration; (v) confidentiality; (vi) the extension by the Court of deadlines fixed by the parties; and (vii) the possibility for the Court to replace an arbitrator without requesting a new nomination from the party that had nominated the arbitrator being replaced.

[12]   Proposed Mandate of the Working Party on the Revision of the ICC Rules of Arbitration, ICC Doc. No. 420/342 (October 4, 1995).

[13]   Typical of such criticisms are those contained in Wetter, "The Present Status of the International Court of Arbitration of the ICC: An Appraisal," *Am. Rev. Int. Arb.*, Vol. 1, No. 1 (1990), p. 91, *and* Marriott, "ICC/UNCITRAL Arbitration," *Mealey's*, Vol. 8, No. 3 (1993), p. 34.

sible Rules revisions that were discussed among its members and, in the event of a consensus within the Working Party, forwarded to the ICC's National Committees for comment as well as to the Court. In addition, members of the Working Party participated in informal consultations with representatives of National Committees and other groups. The proposed revisions were the subject of both conferences and published comments.[14] In December 1996, a complete draft text of new Rules was submitted by the Working Party to the Commission for consideration. After taking account of the Commission's comments and decisions with respect to specific matters at that time, the Working Party prepared a revised draft that, after consultation, further revision and discussion, was finally approved by the Commission on February 27, 1997. Following the review and approval of the final draft by the Court at a special working session in March 1997, the Court's Chairman, Dr. Robert Briner, submitted the New Rules to the ICC's Executive Board and Council in Shanghai for approval on April 8, 1997.[15] Thereafter, amendments were also made to the three appendices accompanying the Rules (*i.e.,* the ICC Court's Statutes, its Internal Rules and the schedule of Arbitration Costs and Fees).

Consistent with the objectives that the Working Party originally fixed for itself, the New Rules do not fundamentally alter the ICC system of arbitration. However, many changes have been made, the most obvious of which is the Rules' presentation. In the manner of other modern arbitration rules, the Rules have been rearranged in an order intended to mirror the chronological progression of the arbitration process, from the submission of the Request for Arbitration to the making of the Award and the fixing of costs. This change alone should make the Rules easier to use and more comprehensible to the first-time participant in the ICC process. Apart from this, the changes in the New Rules are primarily intended to: (i) permit the acceleration of the arbitration process; (ii) fill gaps in the earlier version of the Rules or otherwise adapt them to modern practice in respect of a number of matters, such as interim measures, the appointment of arbitrators in multi-party cases, "truncated" arbitration tribunals, and the correction and interpretation of arbitral Awards; (iii) correct ambiguities and remove inconsistencies between the two official versions of the Rules, in English and French; and (iv) import into the Rules provisions previously contained in the Court's Internal Rules that concerned substantive obligations of the parties and that, properly speaking, were not really "internal" rules.

Although all of the changes made are discussed in detail in the chapters that follow, the principal modifications can be summarized as follows:

---

[14] *See, e.g.,* Kreindler, "Impending Revision of the ICC Arbitration Rules – Opportunities and Hazards for Experienced and Inexperienced Users Alike," *J. Arb. Int.,* Vol. 13, No. 2 (1996), p. 45.

[15] The Rules submitted for approval were in both English and French. The New Rules were, however, first drafted in English and then translated into French. Following their approval by the Council, they were then the subject of minor editorial changes made by the Court.

1. Changes Intended to Accelerate the Arbitration Process

One of the primary objectives of the Rules revisions was to reduce the delays that can occur between the commencement of the arbitration and the constitution of an Arbitral Tribunal and, subsequently, the transmission of the file to the tribunal by the ICC. The process of preparing the Terms of Reference, no matter how useful they may be, has also often been unnecessarily prolonged. In order to attempt to reduce these delays and also to impose greater discipline on the arbitrators in conducting the arbitration proceedings, the following changes have been made in the New Rules:

a. The Secretary General of the Court has been given the authority to confirm the appointment of arbitrators when there is no related dispute between the parties requiring a decision of the ICC Court (Article 9(2)). Under the former Rules, only the Court itself could confirm arbitrators, which meant awaiting a meeting of the Court, which, in turn, was a source of delay.

b. In addition, the Secretary General has been authorized to fix a provisional advance on costs sufficient to cover the costs of the arbitration through the Terms of Reference stage (Article 30). It is intended that this advance will normally be fixed upon the receipt of the Request for Arbitration and be payable by the Claimant immediately so that the ICC will be in a position to transmit the file to the Arbitral Tribunal as soon as it has been constituted. Previously, the advance would not usually be fixed until a later stage by the Court, in an amount required for the entire proceeding, and 50 per cent was to be paid – in equal shares by the Claimant and the Respondent – before the file could be sent to the arbitrators. Under the New Rules, once the Terms of Reference have been prepared, additional sums will be required to be paid by the parties on the basis of an advance to be fixed by the Court, as was previously the case. However, the payment of such sums is no longer a condition for the Terms of Reference to become operative. Thus, in the usual case, there should not be any reason for the delays that commonly occurred at this stage. The ICC Secretariat, together with the arbitrators, must ensure, however, that sufficient sums are on hand as the arbitration progresses so that both the arbitrators and the ICC are adequately remunerated.

c. The arbitrators no longer have the obligation, if they consider it inappropriate, to include in their Terms of Reference (Article 18) a definition of the issues to be determined, although the Terms of Reference continue to require that the parties' respective claims and requests for relief be described. The definition of the issues has often been a subject of contention and, as a result, a source of delay in the finalization of the Terms of Reference. Moreover, parties and arbitrators sometimes find it difficult to define the issues in a meaningful way at the Terms of Reference stage when the parties have not yet set out their cases fully, the Request for Arbitration and the Answer, in modern practice, often being relatively succinct. Finalization of the Terms of Reference has, in the past, also been delayed because, under the former Rules, new claims could not subsequently be introduced in the proceedings without the other party's consent. The New Rules (Article 19) now give the Arbitral Tribunal discretion to accept the introduction of new claims at a later stage of the arbitral proceedings. In cases of default, the New Rules also remove the requirement that the defaulting party be given a period of time in which to sign the Terms of Reference following their approval by the ICC Court.

d. Together with the Terms of Reference, the New Rules require the Arbitral Tribunal to submit to the ICC Court "a provisional timetable that it intends to follow for the conduct of the arbitration" (Article 18(4)). Although the timetable may subsequently be modified, it will nevertheless commit the tribunal "morally" to a schedule as from the outset.

e. In addition, upon the closing of the proceedings (Article 22), the Arbitral Tribunal, unlike under the former Rules, is required to indicate to the Secretariat of the ICC Court when it expects to submit a draft of its Award to the Court for scrutiny. This too will hopefully increase the pressure on arbitrators to complete their work expeditiously.

2. Other Substantive Changes and Additions of Importance

a. *Scope of Rules.* The New Rules make it clear that the ICC will accept an arbitration even when the dispute is not of an "international character" (Article 1). Although the Court's Internal Rules (Appendix II) long permitted this, they were framed in discretionary terms, which gave rise to uncertainty. It is still a requirement of the New Rules, however, that disputes be "business disputes," and it is therefore open to the ICC to refuse cases of a non-business nature.

b. *Communications.* Permissible means of notification and communication in the arbitration have been expanded (Article 3).

c. *Request for Arbitration.* The Request is no longer required to contain a "statement of the Claimant's case," a requirement that was inconsistent with the French version of the former Rules, but instead must describe "the nature and circumstances of the dispute" and indicate the relief sought (Article 4). In addition, under the New Rules, the Request must comment on the place of the arbitration, the applicable rules of law and the language of the arbitration.

d. *Effect of the Arbitration Agreement.* The New Rules (Article 6) specify that, unless the parties have agreed otherwise, they shall be deemed to have submitted to the Rules in effect on the date of commencement of the arbitration proceedings irrespective of the date of the arbitration agreement.

e. *Constitution of the Arbitral Tribunal.* A new provision (Article 10) has been added concerning the appointment of arbitrators in arbitrations involving more than two parties. It is intended to overcome the difficulties that have been encountered in past cases in this regard, in particular in the *Dutco* case, where an ICC Award was annulled by the French courts because of the practice followed by the ICC in constituting the Arbitral Tribunal.[16] Under the new provision, if the dispute is to be referred to three arbitrators and the parties are unable to agree on a method of appointing the arbitrators, the ICC Court has the power to appoint all of them, unlike under the former Rules, which do not confer any such power on the Court unless the parties agree.

f. *Challenge of Arbitrators.* Unlike under the former Rules, arbitrators are required to send to the parties a copy of any comments that they may submit to the ICC Court in respect of a challenge (Article 11(3)). This will increase the transparency of the challenge process. However, as under the old Rules, the Court will not be required to provide reasons for its related decisions.

g. *"Truncated" Tribunals.* The New Rules permit the Court to authorize fewer than all of the arbitrators to complete an arbitration when, subsequent to the closing of the proceedings, an arbitrator has died, resigned or otherwise been removed by the ICC Court (Article 12(5)). This is designed to save the parties the delay and expense of repeating all or part of the arbitration proceedings in appropriate circumstances. In deciding whether to so authorize the remaining arbitrators, however, the Court will be required to take account of relevant provisions of applicable law.

h. *Place of the Arbitration.* The New Rules recognize the right of the arbitrators to conduct hearings and meetings at places other than the place of the arbitration, unless the parties otherwise agree (Article 14).

i. *Applicable Law.* Like the former Rules, the New Rules (Article 17) permit the parties to choose the law to be applied to the merits of the dispute. However, in recognition of the increasing application in international arbitrations of rules of law drawn from more than a single national law, or of transnational legal rules, the prior references to "the law" have been replaced by the phrase "rules of law." In addition, where the parties have not agreed on the applicable "rules of law," the Arbitral Tribunal is given the power, under the New Rules, to apply the rules of law "which it deems to be appropriate," without, as was formerly the case, any need to refer to an appropriate rule of conflict (former Article 13(3)).

---

[16] *Sociétés BKMI et Siemens c/ société Dutco construction, Cour de cassation* (January 7, 1992), *Rev. arb.* (1992), p. 470.

j.   *New Claims.* The former Rules precluded the introduction of new claims in the arbitration after the Terms of Reference had been prepared, except if they remained "within the limits fixed by the Terms of Reference" or the other party consented. As this rule was frequently criticized as too rigid, the New Rules (Article 19) authorize the Arbitral Tribunal to exercise its discretion in this regard.

k.   *Interim Measures.* Although ICC arbitrators have long been considered to have the power to order conservatory and interim measures, the former Rules did not explicitly say so, and this was a source of uncertainty. That the arbitrators have such a power has now been made clear in the New Rules (Article 23).

l.   *Correction and Interpretation of Awards.* The absence of any provision in the former Rules authorizing an ICC tribunal either to correct or interpret its Award gave rise to uncertainties in this regard. The New Rules (Article 29) now specifically provide for the possible correction or interpretation of the tribunal's Award. The provision on correction is consistent with provisions to be found in all other major arbitration rules and most national laws. The matter of interpretation is more controversial, however, and is not dealt with in all arbitration rules, although it is provided for in some (*e.g.*, the UNCITRAL and AAA International rules).

m.   *Confidentiality.* A provision has been added (Article 20(7)) explicitly authorizing the Arbitral Tribunal to "take measures for protecting trade secrets and confidential information." However, the ICC rejected the option of including in the New Rules a general provision requiring the parties to respect the confidentiality of the arbitration. In this regard, the ICC Rules, like many other arbitration rules, have never explicitly obligated the participants in the arbitration (other than the ICC Court itself pursuant to its Internal Rules) to protect the confidentiality of the proceedings. Although the confidentiality of arbitration is often assumed, a number of recent court cases – most notably in the United States, the United Kingdom and Australia – have demonstrated that this cannot be taken for granted in all places and circumstances and that, in the absence of an express agreement to this effect, the parties do not necessarily have an absolute obligation to respect the confidentiality of the arbitration.[17] In the course of

---

[17]   *See, e.g., Esso/BHP* v. *Plowman,* High Court of Australia, *reprinted in Arb. Int.,* Vol. 11, No. 3 (1995), p. 235; *Hassneh Insurance Co of Israel & Others* v. *Stewart J. Mew,* [1993] 2 Lloyd's Rep. 243; *United States of America* v. *Panhandle Eastern Corp. et al.,* 118 F.R.D. 346 (D. Del. 1988). *But compare G. Aita* c/ *A. Ojjeh, Cour d'appel de Paris* (February 18, 1986), *Rev. arb.* (1986), p. 583. *See* more generally on this subject, Rogers and Miller, "Non-Confidential Arbitration Proceedings," *Arb. Int.,* Vol. 12, No. 3 (1996), p. 319; Neill, "The 1995 Bernstein Lecture: Confidentiality in Arbitration," *Arbitration,* Supplement, Vol. 62, No. 3 (1996), p. 1; Paulsson and Rawding, "The Trouble with Confidentiality," *ICC Ct. Bull.,* Vol. 5, No. 1 (1994), p. 48; Gaillard, *"Le principe de confidentialité de l'arbitrage commercial international,"* Recueil Dalloz-Sirey, 22ème Cahier-Chronique (1987).

reviewing the Rules, the ICC therefore was required to consider whether to introduce a provision on this subject, as certain other arbitral institutions have recently done.[18] After extensive consideration of this matter within the Working Party, however, it was decided not to propose a general confidentiality provision and, hence, to leave the matter, as it presently is, for the parties and, as necessary, local courts to deal with. Indeed, the Working Party was unable to arrive at a consensus regarding the appropriate formulation of any such rule, partly because of the many legitimate exceptions that may arise. In addition, as international arbitration increasingly becomes the normal forum for the final resolution of international commercial disputes, there are more and more participants in the process who question the conventional notion that, simply because it is private, arbitration must always be confidential. Arbitration assuredly provides the parties with the opportunity to provide for confidentiality. However, that this ought to be the rule in all, or even most, circumstances is not universally accepted.[19]

3. Changes Considered but Not Implemented

There are, in addition, a number of other important matters that, although the subject of considerable discussion within the Working Party, were ultimately not considered to warrant changes in the Rules.

First among these was the subject of "fast-track" arbitration, which has been a recurring theme of arbitration conferences and literature in recent years in the wake of the publicity surrounding a complex ICC arbitration conducted several years ago, on a "fast-track" basis, in less than three months.[20] Since that time, there have been further "fast-track" arbitrations at the ICC, and some arbitration institutions have adopted special rules or procedures for "fast-track," or expedited, arbitration. The Working Party did not consider, however, that it would be appropriate to add any special provisions to the ICC Rules on this subject, not out of an aversion to fast-track arbitration, but, rather, because of the difficulty of fashioning appropriate procedures for the variety of circumstances that may arise. Apart from this, the ICC Rules, unlike most other arbitration rules, already contain a relatively stringent six-month time-limit for the issuance of the arbitrators' Award. It was the view of the Working Party, and most ICC National Committees, that parties wishing to conduct arbitrations on a more accelerated basis would, thus, do better to adapt their arbitration agreements accordingly. For this reason, a new provision was added to the Rules (Article 32) that makes clear the parties' right to shorten the various time-limits in the Rules, subject to the conditions of that Article. Parties should nevertheless take care that fast-

---

[18] AAA International Arbitration Rules, Article 34; LCIA Rules, Article 30; WIPO Arbitration Rules, Articles 73-76.

[19] *See, e.g.,* "Expert Report of Dr. Julian D.M. Lew" (submitted in *Esso/BHP* v. *Plowman,* cited *supra,* note 17), *Arb. Int.,* Vol. 11, No. 3 (1995), p. 283; H. Smit, "Confidentiality in Arbitration," *Arb. Int.,* Vol. 11, No. 3 (1995), p. 337.

[20] *See* the series of articles on this subject in *ICC Ct. Bull.,* Vol. 3, No. 2 (1992).

track provisions are capable of operation in practice and that they do not unduly restrict the parties' ability to present their cases.

In respect of multi-party arbitration, it was also the Working Party's position that, apart from the change concerning the constitution of the Arbitral Tribunal, as mentioned above, it is best to leave matters in the hands of the parties when agreeing to arbitration. The failure of arbitration rules to cater to multi-party disputes is often characterized as a disadvantage of the arbitration process. However, parties are free to develop appropriate procedures, suitable for a particular transaction, and, on this basis, many multi-party proceedings have been conducted under the ICC Rules. In 1978, the ICC Commission established a working party to examine the various issues arising in this connection and to make recommendations. After more than fifteen years of study culminating in a final report issued in 1994, its conclusion was that it would not be proper "to deal with multi-party arbitration as if it were susceptible of simple and uniform treatment," given the variety and complexity of the situations that may be encountered.[21] The Working Party concurred with this view.

The Working Party also saw no reason to introduce into the Rules any special provisions on conciliation or mediation. With the subject of "ADR" very much in vogue, at least in certain parts of the world, it inevitably fell to the Working Party to consider whether any account ought to be taken of alternative dispute resolution mechanisms in connection with the arbitration process. But there was no significant support for this, given, in particular, that the ICC already has its own conciliation rules.[22] Although the ICC may wish to consider whether any renewed efforts ought to be made in order to breathe life into those rules, which are rarely used, there is strong resistance within the Commission to imposing them, or another conciliation process, on the parties during the course of an arbitration. Indeed, even though arbitrators often offer their good offices to parties in order to help them settle an arbitration, they will generally not pursue the matter unless this is what the parties all desire. The ICC conciliation rules, for their part, envisage the complete separation of the conciliation and arbitration processes because of the concern that conciliation cannot function effectively unless parties feel free to communicate information to a conciliator that they might fear would prejudice them if revealed in an arbitration. In addition, the disclosure of information on a confidential basis to a person acting as a conciliator could disqualify that person from acting subsequently as an arbitrator.

---

[21]   *See* "Final Report on Multi-party Arbitrations" of the ICC Commission Working Party on this subject (J.C. Delvolvé, Chairman), *ICC Ct. Bull.,* Vol. 6, No. 1 (1995), pp. 26, 41. More generally on this subject, *see Multi-party Arbitration* (ICC Publishing 1991).

[22]   The ICC Rules of Optional Conciliation are printed by the ICC together with the Rules of Arbitration. The present version of those rules, as reproduced in Appendix 8, entered into effect on January 1, 1988. The ICC also has Rules for Expertise that are administered by its International Centre for Expertise (*see* Appendix 9) and Rules for a Pre-Arbitral Referee Procedure (*see* Appendix 10). *See* Davis, "The ICC's Pre-Arbitral Referee Procedure in Context with Technical Expertise, Conciliation and Arbitration," *International Construction Law Review,* Vol. 9 (1992), p. 218.

There is, lastly, an issue that arises from time to time in ICC arbitration practice as to whether and, if so, to what extent, the parties may derogate from the Rules or whether they are otherwise mandatory. Certain provisions expressly contemplate their possible alteration by the parties. However, the Rules do not, for the most part, provide for this. Insofar as the ICC, by issuing its Rules, can be said to make an offer to the public to administer arbitrations in accordance therewith, the ICC can reasonably also take the position that it is not obligated to accept to administer cases where the parties have made alterations of the Rules that the Rules do not contemplate. Of course, the ICC is not necessarily precluded from accepting such cases either. It, thus, enjoys the discretion to determine what its policy ought to be in this respect. This is a matter as to which different institutions have taken different positions. Thus, for example, the International Arbitration Rules of the American Arbitration Association provide (Article 1(1)) that those rules shall apply "subject to whatever modifications the parties may adopt in writing." However, no such general provision has ever been included in the ICC Rules, and the ICC has, from time to time, refused to administer arbitrations where the parties have agreed to alterations of its Rules that the Rules do not themselves contemplate.

During the process of reviewing the Rules, the Working Party therefore took a fresh look at the question of whether the Rules, either in whole or in part, should be considered to be mandatory and, if so, whether this should be stated in the Rules. Ultimately, the Working Party decided, however, that the related issues of policy should be left to the ICC Court to resolve on a case-by-case basis. Although this may leave parties with a degree of uncertainty, the most prudent course for them, in the circumstances, would be to adopt the Rules without alteration unless they are otherwise able to obtain the ICC's assurance that a specific change will not raise a problem. In this regard, the Court's Secretariat has always been willing to provide advice and assistance to parties concerning the compatibility of proposed arbitration clauses with the Rules and the Court's practices.

The New Rules are the product of more than two years of work by the ICC Commission, its National Committees and the Court, based on years of experience of applying the former Rules and differing perspectives on the arbitral process. Like the product of any consensus, the Rules may not be regarded as perfect by any one audience. However, they perpetuate the fundamental characteristics of the ICC arbitration process – its universality, neutrality and flexibility – while taking account of the changes in international arbitration practice over the last two decades.

ICC arbitration has always been a distinctive form of supervised arbitration, and it will continue to be so. It is not necessarily the most suitable form of dispute resolution for all international commercial disputes. However, for those wishing the added security that the ICC's involvement in the arbitration process may bring, the New Rules should be viewed as a welcome and positive development.

Chapter 2
Introductory Provisions (Articles 1-3)

ARTICLE 1

International Court of Arbitration

Among the most important and distinctive features of the ICC arbitration process is the administering institution itself, the International Court of Arbitration (the "Court"). In their very first Article, the ICC Rules, unlike the rules of most other arbitral institutions, therefore set out the basic characteristics of the Court and draw attention to the additional, related provisions contained in the Court's Statutes and its Internal Rules, as set forth, respectively, in Appendices I and II to the Rules. Although little changed from the previous version of the Rules, Article 1 has nevertheless been the subject of various modifications, as have both the Court's Statutes and Internal Rules, as discussed below.

Article 1(1)

> *The International Court of Arbitration (the "Court") of the International Chamber of Commerce (the "ICC") is the arbitration body attached to the ICC. The statutes of the Court are set forth in Appendix I. Members of the Court are appointed by the Council of the ICC. The function of the Court is to provide for the settlement by arbitration of business disputes of an international character in accordance with the Rules of Arbitration of the International Chamber of Commerce (the "Rules"). If so empowered by an arbitration agreement, the Court shall also provide for the settlement by arbitration in accordance with these Rules of business disputes not of an international character.*

Nature and composition of the Court. As is well known to those familiar with ICC arbitration, the Court is not a "court," as that word is normally understood, but the administrative body charged with responsibility for overseeing the ICC arbitration process. As stated in the Court's Statutes, to which Article 1(1) now explicitly refers, the Court is composed of a Chairman, Vice-Chairmen and

17

other members appointed by the ICC's main governing body, the ICC Council, in which each National Committee of the ICC is represented. Except for the Chairman and Vice-Chairmen, who are appointed by the Council on the recommendation of the ICC's Executive Board and the Court's Chairman, respectively, the Court's members are appointed by the Council on the proposal of the ICC's National Committees.

As the number of ICC National Committees has grown over the years, so too has the size of the Court. At the beginning of 1998, the Court had 57 members from as many countries plus 8 alternate members, 10 Vice-Chairmen and, as its Chairman, Robert Briner, a prominent Swiss lawyer and arbitrator who previously served as President of the Iran-U.S. Claims Tribunal.[23] Dr. Briner assumed the Chairmanship of the Court on January 1, 1997 following the expiration of the term of Alain Plantey, a French Counsellor of State, who had served for the previous eight years. Dr. Briner is the first practicing arbitrator and arbitration lawyer to be elected to the Chairmanship of the Court in nearly 25 years. Like all of the other members of the Court, his term is for three years, expiring on December 31, 1999, and is renewable.

The Court's present membership includes a diverse group of legal professionals from every continent. Although there is no requirement in the ICC Rules or the Court's Statutes that its members must be lawyers – and, in fact, during the Court's early years, many of them were not – all of the Court's current members are drawn from the legal professions. Within their ranks are private practitioners, in-house counsel, law professors, retired judges and a judge of the International Court of Justice. With one exception (the ambassador of Uruguay in France), the Court does not, however, presently include any representatives of governments or civil servants. There is no prohibition in the Rules or the Court's Statutes against the appointment of such persons, and many have served on the Court in the past. However, the Court has generally wished in recent years to appear to be totally independent of any possible government influence, particularly as States are frequently parties in ICC arbitrations.

The members of the Court are not employed by the ICC, nor are they allowed to be remunerated by the ICC's National Committees, from which they are required to be independent. Although they receive certain very modest sums for attending Court sessions, their work as Court members is, for the most part, performed on a *pro bono* basis. The amount of work that the members of the Court are required to perform, however, is considerable and has increased dramatically over the last two decades together with the Court's caseload. Indeed, while the Court is served by a permanent, professional administrative staff (the "Secretariat," *see* the discussion of Article 1(5) *infra*), one of the particularities of the ICC arbitration system is that most of the decisions incumbent upon the arbitral institution under the ICC Rules are to be taken by the Court itself, as dis-

---

[23]   A list of the Court's members at January 1, 1998 is set forth in Appendix 2.

tinguished from its administrative staff. Parties and arbitrators in ICC cases, however, may only be dimly aware of this because they will not normally have any direct contact with the Court during the course of an ICC arbitration. Neither parties nor arbitrators are entitled to attend meetings of the Court, and all communications with it are required to be channeled through the Court's Secretariat, which is the public's only direct link with the arbitral institution.

The Court's decision-making role is nonetheless generally regarded by those close to the ICC as vital to the ICC arbitral system. Thus, during the work on the New Rules, there was widespread resistance within both the ICC Court and the ICC Commission to the suggestion, floated at any early stage of the revision process, that certain decisions required under the Rules to be taken by the Court itself might be delegated to the Secretariat. Those who were opposed to this considered that it is preferable for the Court to be the decision-maker because of the Court's much more diverse composition, the breadth of experience within the Court, and also because of the collective character of its decisions, which, it was felt, provides greater security to the parties and distinguishes the services provided by the ICC from those offered by other arbitral institutions.

For the purpose of taking decisions, the Court holds a monthly plenary meeting at ICC headquarters in Paris[24]. It also meets in Committees of three members (*see* the discussion of Article 1(4) *infra*) on a more frequent basis. In recent years, the number of Committee meetings has increased to three a month. The Chairman, or in his absence a Vice-Chairman, presides over the plenary sessions, which presently are ordinarily held on the fourth Wednesday of each month. Six court members must be present in order to constitute a quorum. Although Court members are not reimbursed for the cost of attending Court meetings, at a typical plenary session 15-25 members will be in attendance. They will usually have received from the Court's Secretariat during the week preceding the Court meeting one or more loose-leaf files containing the agenda and related materials for the matters to be considered by the Court. In addition, certain Court members will have been designated to report in writing on the matters to be discussed. As the Court's caseload has increased, the Court has been required to restrict the agenda of the plenary session only to the most important matters requiring the Court's decision and to refer all other matters to the thrice-monthly Committee sessions discussed further below in connection with Article 1(4). As a result, the Court's plenary sessions, in recent years, have generally been limited to the scrutiny of arbitral Awards (*see* Article 27 *infra*), the consideration of challenges of arbitrators or otherwise of an arbitrator's possible replacement (*see* Articles 11 and 12 *infra*), and the review of the existence of an ICC arbitration agreement (*see* Article 6(2) *infra*). Matters raising important, new issues for the Court may also be placed on the agenda of the plenary session together with questions that may previously have been referred to a

---

[24] For a description of such a meeting, and the Court's decision-making procedures, *see* R. Smit, "An Inside View of the ICC Court," *Arb. Int.*, Vol. 10, No. 1 (1994), pp. 53, 55-58.

Committee, but as to which the Committee was unable to reach a unanimous decision. The Court's current policies in this regard are discussed further below (*see* Article 1(4)).

In addition to its regular plenary sessions and Committee meetings, the Court holds a special working session once or twice a year to review and discuss matters of general policy. Those meetings are usually preceded by meetings of the Court's "Bureau," which is composed of the Chairman and Vice-Chairmen, assisted by the Secretary General and General Counsel. The Bureau formulates recommendations on policy that are then submitted for discussion to the Court as a whole. Examples of matters considered by the Bureau are the various notes published by the Secretariat, from time to time, on subjects such as the use of administrative secretaries and arbitration costs,[25] the publication of arbitration Awards, relationships with other arbitral institutions, and the internal functioning of the Court and its Secretariat. The Court has also established a number of regional arbitration groups (for Europe, the Arab countries, the Asia-Pacific region and Latin America) that bring together both Court members and others to discuss issues of particular interest to those involved in arbitration in the regions concerned.

The special role and responsibilities of the Court have required it to take special measures to preserve its impartiality and independence. Thus, meetings of the Court are open only to its members and to its Secretariat,[26] and the work of the Court is confidential.[27] Increasingly, moreover, the Court has taken pains to establish its autonomy and the confidential character of its work even with regard to the ICC itself, given that ICC members may be parties in ICC arbitration proceedings. In the Court's early years, the President and Secretary General of the ICC acted as the Court's Chairman and Secretary General, respectively. Although they long ago ceased to have any active involvement in the substantive work of the Court, the Court's Statutes nevertheless still provided, until their most recent amendment, for the participation in meetings of the Court of the ICC's Secretary General. This provision has now been eliminated.[28] In addition, a provision in prior versions of the Rules requiring the Court's Secretariat to bring Requests for Arbitration to the notice "of the National Committee concerned" has disappeared.[29]

---

[25] *See* Appendix 4. The Court's Internal Rules (Appendix II, Article 5(2)) now explicitly authorize the Secretariat, "with the approval of the Court," to issue "notes and other documents for the infomation of the parties and the arbitrators, or as necessary for the proper conduct of the arbitral proceedings."

[26] Article 1 of the Court's Internal Rules (Appendix II to the Rules).

[27] Article 6 of the Court's Statutes (Appendix I to the Rules) and Article 1 of the Internal Rules.

[28] *Compare* Article 4 of the Court's Statutes, prior to their amendment, with Article 2 of the new Statutes.

[29] *Compare* Article 3(1) of the former Rules with Article 4 of the New Rules, as discussed below.

Article 1(1), thus, states that the Court is "attached" to the ICC. The word "attached," which was introduced into the Rules in 1975, signifies that, while connected with the ICC, the Court is nevertheless a semi-autonomous body, consistent with its special functions. Although the Court does not have a legal personality of its own separate from that of the ICC, and its budget is required to be approved by the ICC, neither the Court nor its Secretariat are accountable to the ICC for decisions made with respect to specific arbitration cases.

In order to preserve the integrity of its work, the Court has also considered it necessary to place restrictions on the involvement of its members in ICC arbitration proceedings. Thus, members of the Court may not be appointed by the Court to act as arbitrators in ICC arbitrations. Except for the Chairman (and the staff of the Secretariat), members may nevertheless act as arbitrators on the proposal of parties or co-arbitrators or appear as counsel in ICC arbitrations.[30] But if they do so, they must recuse themselves from all work of the Court in connection with the arbitration in question, and, in such case, they will not receive any documentation or information relating to the same.[31] In addition, Court members are expected to recuse themselves from all matters in which they may have an interest, even if they are not directly involved in the arbitration.[32]

Because the members of the Court are not employees of the ICC and many of them have active professional careers, there is necessarily a risk that they will be interested, from time to time, in matters pending before the Court. However, the procedures put in place by the Court to exclude Court members in such cases from the Court's work have, thus far, appeared to operate satisfactorily and have not given rise to any significant problems.[33] Moreover, by permitting Court members, other than the Chairman, to act as arbitrators or counsel in ICC arbitrations, the ICC is better able to attract to the Court experienced arbitration

---

[30] Article 2 of the Court's Internal Rules (Appendix II to the Rules).

[31] *Id.*

[32] This is not expressly stated in the Court's Internal Rules, but has nevertheless been the Court's longstanding practice. It is for the Court's members themselves in individual cases to determine whether they have an interest warranting their exclusion from a particular matter.

[33] In a case brought before the Paris Court of Appeal and subsequently the French Court of Cassation in the 1970s, *Société Métal Profil c/ Société Intercraft, Cour de cassation* (March 31, 1978), *Rev. arb.* (1979), p. 457, a party to an ICC arbitration in Paris nevertheless challenged the competence of the Arbitral Tribunal on the ground that the counsel of the other party was a Vice-Chairman of the ICC Court and that this prevented the Court from administering the arbitration independently and impartially. The Court of Appeal and the Court of Cassation held, however, that the ICC Court's independence and impartiality were not affected insofar as the Vice-Chairman in question had been excluded from all sessions of the ICC Court in respect of this matter. This is the only instance, of which the authors are aware, in which an ICC arbitration was contested on this basis. Shortly thereafter, the Court adopted Internal Rules (*see* Article 1(2) *infra*) explicitly requiring Court members to recuse themselves in such circumstances, consistent with what had been the Court's existing practice. The Internal Rules were even more stringent, however, than the then prevailing practice as they forbade the Court's Vice-Chairmen from acting as counsel or arbitrators in ICC proceedings. This rule has now been eliminated, as discussed below.

practitioners who can contribute their expertise to the Court's work without having to give up all involvement in ICC arbitration.[34]

Scope of the Court's jurisdiction. Like the prior version of the Rules, the New Rules state that the Court's function is to "provide for the settlement by arbitration of business disputes of an international character in accordance with these Rules." However, the New Rules contain the additional statement that:

> If so empowered by an arbitration agreement, the Court shall also provide for the settlement by arbitration in accordance with these Rules of business disputes not of an international character.

The intention is to remove any possible uncertainty as to the willingness of the Court to accept an arbitration where the "international character" of a dispute may be in doubt. Indeed, what may be considered to be "international" may vary from country to country. In countries such as France and the United States, a dispute may be considered to be international even when it is between two domestic parties if it has related foreign elements. In other countries, however, a dispute may be regarded as domestic whenever both parties are domestic, even if one of the parties is partly or wholly foreign-owned.

For many years, it was the policy of the Court not to accept arbitrations unless they were of an "international nature," although the Court construed this requirement broadly.[35] During the course of the 1970s, however, the Court, from time to time, accepted cases that were not necessarily of an international character, and following the attempt of a party (which was ultimately unsuccessful) to have an ICC Award set aside on the ground that the arbitration was not "international,"[36] the Court included in the Internal Rules that it first published in 1980 (*see,* with regard to those rules, the discussion of Article 1(2) *infra*) a provision expressly recognizing its willingness to accept jurisdiction over cases of

---

[34]   It is for this reason that, in conjunction with the adoption of the New Rules, the Court has amended its Internal Rules (Article 4) to permit its Vice-Chairmen to act in ICC arbitrations, as was once the case. The restriction on the Chairman's participation in ICC arbitrations has been maintained, however, because he normally presides over meetings of the Court and, thus, should not be placed in the position of having to recuse himself from matters pending before the Court too frequently.

[35]   Thus, the *Guide to ICC Arbitration* issued by the ICC in 1972 stated, p. 15:
The following conditions must be fulfilled for the ICC Rules to be applicable:
– the dispute must be of an *international nature*. This phrase is construed in a wide sense so as to include any dispute which contains an international element, – for example, a contract between between two nationals of the same State, to be performed in some other country, or a contract between a company and a state, where it had been necessary for a foreign firm to form a company in the state concerned . . . .

[36]   *Japan Time* v. *Kienzle France, Cour d'appel de Paris* (July 11, 1980), as discussed in *Craig Park and Paulsson,* §11.03, note 3, pp. 188-89.

a non-international nature.[37] As that provision was merely of a permissive character, however, it did not provide the parties to contracts that might be regarded as non-international with the assurance that the Court would, in fact, accept jurisdiction over a related dispute if it arose. Because the Court has nevertheless always done so in the few instances where such disputes have been submitted to it in recent years, the ICC thus considered, when amending the Rules, that it was not desirable to allow any continuing uncertainty to persist in this regard. Under Article 1(1), it is therefore now clear that, although the ICC Court's vocation is primarily international, arbitrations will not be refused if the parties to a non-international contract provide for ICC arbitration.[38]

The Rules nevertheless continue, as they have since 1927, to describe the Court's function as limited to "business" disputes. Arguably, therefore, it is open to the Court to refuse to accept "non-business" disputes, and in at least one instance in the 1980s, the Court in fact refused, on the basis of this provision, to accept an arbitration relating to an inheritance dispute, although more recently it accepted jurisdiction over another such case. Thus, the existence of such language in the Rules has not been construed by the Court as necessarily preventing it from accepting non-business cases if the parties have agreed to ICC arbitration. The Court has, moreover, construed the term "business" in the broadest possible manner.[39] In particular, the word "business" is not intended to limit the Court's jurisdiction to matters of a "commercial" nature in the narrow sense in which "commercial" may be understood in certain legal systems (such as France, for example). Indeed, it is precisely for this reason that the Rules avoid any use of the word "commercial," either in English or in French.[40] Moreover, the reference in Article 1(1) to "business" disputes has not precluded the Court from accepting jurisdiction over large numbers of cases arising under contracts with governmental parties that might be regarded, in certain instances, as "admin-

---

[37] Article 1 of the Court's Internal Rules, thus, provided:
The International Court of Arbitration may accept jurisdiction over business disputes not of an international business nature, if it has jurisdiction by reason of an arbitration agreement.

[38] Parties should nevertheless take care that there are not possible legal impediments to the arbitration of non-international disputes. Thus, for example, French law does not recognize the validity of an agreement to arbitrate future disputes in the case of a non-"commercial" contract if it is not international within the meaning of French law. *See, e.g.,* Schwartz, "Going astray in Bordelais: a comment on a recent decision of the Court of Appeal of Bordeaux," *The Arbitration and Dispute Resolution Law Journal,* Part 2 (1997), p. 91.

[39] The *Guide to ICC Arbitration* published by the ICC in 1972 stated, for example:
[I]t is sufficient that the case arises out of a *"business transaction"* in the widest possible sense. As an example, the Court frequently entertains and deals with disputes which arise (a) between private persons and States or State controlled bodies, (b) out of contracts or concessions involving capital investments, (c) out of contracts for the construction of public works, and (d) out of contracts for the industrial equipment of new regions.

[40] Prior to 1975, the French version of the Rules referred to disputes *"d'ordre commercial"* (translation: "of a commercial nature"), but in 1975, this language was revised to refer, as the Rules still do, to disputes *"intervenant dans le domaine des affaires"* (translation: "arising in the area of business").

istrative" in nature. In addition, the Court has, on numerous occasions, accepted cases relating to the employment of international executives.

Lastly, by stipulating that the Court's function is to provide for the settlement of disputes "in accordance with these Rules," Article 1(1) establishes, from the outset, that the Court is not under any obligation to administer arbitrations if the parties have altered those Rules. Although the Court may nonetheless accept to administer cases where certain modifications have been agreed upon by the parties, it should not be assumed, when drafting an arbitration clause, that the Court will necessarily do so.[41]

Article 1(2)

> *The Court does not itself settle disputes. It has the function of ensuring the application of these Rules. It draws up its own Internal Rules (Appendix II).*

Function of the Court. The first two sentences of Article 1(2) are new. They replace the statement in the prior Rules that "[i]n principle, the Court meets once a month," a throwback to the days before the Court began meeting in Committees. The first sentence is merely intended to clarify that it is not the Court itself that decides the cases that are submitted to arbitration. This is, of course, the task of the arbitrators appointed in accordance with the Rules. The second sentence, meanwhile, has been imported into the Rules from the Statutes of the Court, which nevertheless also state (Article 1):

> The function of the International Court of Arbitration of the International Chamber of Commerce (the Court) is to ensure the application of the Rules of Arbitration and the Rules of Conciliation of the International Chamber of Commerce, and it has all the necessary powers for that purpose.

The above provision of the Statutes is broader than Article 1(2) insofar as it refers to the "Rules of Conciliation" (which are, in fact, called the "Rules of Optional Conciliation"). The reference to those Rules is odd, however, as the Court does not actually administer them. Rather responsibility for the administration of the Rules of Optional Conciliation is conferred by those Rules exclusively on the Court's Secretariat, as distinguished from the Court itself. The Rules of Arbitration, meanwhile, have never contained any reference to conciliation, and during the work on the New Rules, as already mentioned (*see* Introduction, "Changes Considered but Not Implemented," *supra*), no serious consideration was given to altering this situation, notwithstanding the increasing global interest in alternative forms of dispute resolution and subjects such as "med-arb" (the combination of mediation and arbitration). Indeed, the ICC's

---

[41] *See* Introduction, "Changes Considered but Not Implemented," *supra* p. 13, and note 44 *infra*.

Rules of Optional Conciliation, which were most recently amended in 1988, themselves envisage the complete separation of the conciliation and arbitration processes (in Article 10 thereof) insofar as they prohibit a conciliator from subsequently acting as an arbitrator unless the parties otherwise agree. There is, of course, nothing to prevent the parties from importing a conciliation (or mediation) procedure into an ICC arbitration if they so wish, nor is the Court's Secretariat prevented from drawing the parties' attention to the conciliation rules, as appropriate, although it has not generally sought to influence the parties in this regard in the past.[42] The ICC has nevertheless tried to encourage the greater use of those rules by printing them together with the Rules of Arbitration.[43]

As regards the Rules of Arbitration, the statement in Article 1(2), and in the Court's Statutes, that the Court "has the function of ensuring the[ir] application" is sufficiently broad to give rise to a number of potential issues, particularly when read in the light of the additional declaration in the Statutes that the Court "has all the necessary powers for that purpose." The most likely intention of the drafters was simply to affirm that the role of the Court is to administer the Rules and to confirm its authority, in so doing, to require that parties and arbitrators comply with their provisions. Thus, for example, the Court has, in the past, relied on this language in refusing to administer arbitrations where the parties have altered the Rules.[44]

The Court has generally been reluctant, however, to intervene directly in the conduct of the arbitration as much as it arguably might in order "to ensure the application of the Rules" or otherwise to ensure their consistent application. Indeed, except as necessary for the performance of its own administrative functions, the Court has not asserted any general power to interpret the requirements of the Rules where these might be uncertain or in doubt and has instead preferred to leave the Rules' interpretation to the arbitrators whenever possible.[45] The Court has, thus, permitted arbitrators to adopt differing, and even inconsistent, positions with respect to their powers under the Rules, or the parties' obligations, when the Rules may be subject to interpretation. It has also refused, on repeated occasions, to interfere with an arbitrator's conduct of an arbitration in the absence of a manifest violation of the Rules.

[42] For a discussion of the operation of the Rules of Optional Conciliation, *see* Schwartz, "International Conciliation and the ICC," *ICC Ct. Bull.,* Vol. 5, No. 2 (1994), p. 5.

[43] Until the New Rules were published, the ICC's standard arbitration clause also included a reference to the conciliation rules. However, it has now been eliminated. *See* Appendix 1.

[44] In several instances, the Court has, thus, refused to administer cases where the parties provided in their arbitration clauses for the appointment of two arbitrators and, in case of their disagreement, an umpire, on the theory that this is incompatible with the Rules (*see* Article 8(1) *infra*). The Court would most likely also adopt the same approach if the parties sought to exclude the Terms of Reference or the scrutiny of arbitral Awards by the Court, two essential features of the ICC arbitral system, as described further below.

[45] *See*, in support of such an approach, H. Smit, "The New International Arbitration Rules of the American Arbitration Association," *Am. Rev. Int. Arb.*, Vol. 2 (1991), pp. 1 , 33-34. *But cf.* R. Smit, *supra*, note 24, p. 57.

Internal Rules. The prior version of the Rules stated that the Court draws up its own "internal regulations." By substituting for those words a reference to the Internal Rules contained in Appendix II, the new Rules explicitly draw the parties' attention for the first time to the provisions of that Appendix. Although the prior reference to "internal regulations" dates back to the 1975 version of the Rules, Internal Rules for the Court were not drawn up until 1979 and first entered into effect on March 1, 1980.

The original purpose of the Internal Rules was to formalize practices and procedures relating to the Court's application of the ICC Rules and also to lay down rules relating to (i) the participation of ICC Court members in ICC arbitrations (*see* Article 1(1) *supra*) and (ii) the creation and functioning of the Court's Committee meetings (*see* Article 1(4) *infra*). Apart from the latter two subjects, however, many of the matters covered by the original Internal Rules had little or nothing to do with the internal functioning of the Court and much more to do with the rights and obligations of the parties and arbitrators under the Rules of Arbitration. In effect, the Court loaded its so-called Internal Rules with such provisions because it was more expedient at the time to put them there rather than to set in motion the machinery for the revision of the Rules of Arbitration themselves. The question then inevitably arose, however, as to whether the parties could be held to have agreed, in submitting to the ICC Rules of Arbitration, to the application of provisions contained in the Court's separate Internal Rules.[46] Although no particular difficulties were ever encountered by the Court in this regard, it was widely recognized that it would be desirable to import into the body of the Rules of Arbitration themselves those provisions of the Internal Rules that affected the substantive rights and obligations of the parties and the arbitrators.

The process of doing so, thus, began with the amendment of the Rules in 1988 and has been completed with the adoption of the New Rules and the accompanying new version of the Court's Internal Rules. The Internal Rules, as they now stand, consequently only deal with the internal functioning of the Court.[47]

---

[46]   *See* in this regard Jarrosson, *"Le rôle respectif de l'institution, de l'arbitre et des parties dans l'instance arbitrale,"* Rev. arb. (1990), pp. 381, 382-83.

[47]   For a discussion of the Internal Rules, *see* Grigera Naón, "The Appendixes to the 1998 ICC Arbitration Rules," *ICC Ct. Bull.,* Vol. 8, No. 2 (1997), p. 37. The Internal Rules deal with: (i) the confidential character of the Court's work (Article 1); (ii) the participation of Court members in ICC arbitration (Article 2); (iii) relations between Court Members and the National Committees (Article 3); (iv) the Committee of the Court (Article 4); (v) the Secretariat (Article 5); and (vi) the Court's scrutiny of arbitral Awards (Article 6). The Court has decided that the new Internal Rules are applicable to all pending cases as from January 1, 1998 (and not just new cases submitted as from that date), except that certain provisions of the former Internal Rules shall continue to apply to cases being conducted under the previous Rules. *See* Briner, "Implementation of the 1998 Rules," *ICC Ct. Bull.,* Vol. 8, No. 2 (1997), pp. 7-8.

Article 1(3)

> *The Chairman of the Court, or, in the Chairman's absence or otherwise at his request, one of its Vice-Chairmen shall have the power to take urgent decisions on behalf of the Court, provided that any such decision is reported to the Court at its next session.*

This provision, which was originally introduced into the Rules in 1955, remains virtually unchanged from its prior version. Only two small refinements have been made. In place of a former reference to the Chairman's "deputy," Article 1(3) now refers to the Court's Vice-Chairmen and further specifies that they may act on the Chairman's behalf "in the Chairman's absence or otherwise at his request."

The powers that the Chairman enjoys under this provision are considerable. In effect, by virtue of Article 1(3), the Chairman alone has the power to act on behalf of the Court in respect of any matter requiring the Court's decision. Somewhat anomolously, the Chairman enjoys even greater powers of decision under this Article than have, in the past, been delegated to the Committee of the Court, which is composed of the Chairman and two other members (*see* the discussion of Article 1(4) *infra*). Thus, for example, the Chairman may approve arbitral Awards in place of the Court, although the approval of Awards has, in the past, otherwise been the exclusive province of the Court's plenary session and outside the powers conferred upon the Court's Committee.[48] The same applies to decisions concerning the replacement of arbitrators. Of course, the Chairman's extraordinary powers under this Article only come into play if a matter is "urgent." But the Chairman enjoys a wide margin of appreciation in deciding whether a matter is sufficiently "urgent" for use to be made of his powers under Article 1(3).

In this connection, it can be argued that all decisions in nearly all arbitrations are "urgent." Usually, at least one of the parties, for any number of reasons, is impatient to be through with the arbitration and to have an Award in hand. The ordinary "urgency" that many parties may feel has not, however, sufficed for the Chairman of the Court to assume the exceptional powers reserved to him under this Article. Rather, to warrant exceptional treatment, exceptional circumstances have normally had to be present. These have, in the past, usually included cases where the Arbitral Tribunals themselves considered that there was a need for urgent action by the Court, *e.g.*, to approve an Award for emergency interim relief or to permit an Award to be delivered into the hands of a party in order to avert a possible bankruptcy or before the possible disappearance of the other party. In recent years, however, the Chairman has most frequently had recourse to Article 1(3) in cases of "fast-track," or accelerated, arbitrations, where the

---

[48] As discussed further below, however, this is now changing with respect to so-called "B" Awards.

parties had locked themselves into strict time limits, the non-respect of which would be fatal to the arbitration. In such circumstances, the Chairman has, thus, among other things, appointed arbitrators, fixed their fees, decided upon challenges and approved Awards, all on the basis of Article 1(3).[49]

When the powers granted to the Chairman under Article 1(3) were originally introduced into the Rules in 1955, the Court ordinarily met no more than once a month and, given the small number of cases then pending before the Court, there may well have been months when the Court did not meet at all. There was therefore a need for a mechanism permitting decisions to be taken, if required, during the relatively long intervals between sessions of the Court. However, with the development of the Court's Committee sessions, which are now ordinarily held three times a month, there is correspondingly less need for the Chairman's emergency powers, except with respect to matters normally requiring the approval of the Court's plenary session. In practice, in the case of such matters, the former Chairman, Mr. Plantey, would exercise his Article 1(3) powers only after convening, and obtaining the unanimous approval of, a special Committee of the Court. By extending the powers of the Committee, the Court could effectively achieve the same result and, thus, avoid the need for the burden of such decisions to weigh solely on the Chairman. As discussed below with respect to Article 1(4), the amendments recently made to the Court's Internal Rules allow the Court added flexibility in this regard.

Article 1(4)

> *As provided for in its Internal Rules, the Court may delegate to one or more committees composed of its members the power to take certain decisions, provided that any such decision is reported to the Court at its next session.*

This provision was one of the major innovations of the Rules changes made in 1975 and has only been the subject of minor, non-substantive revisions in the New Rules.

When first proposed in the 1970s, the concept of delegating decision-making from the Court as a whole to smaller groups of members was controversial. Among the representatives of the ICC's National Committees sitting in the ICC's Commission on International Arbitration at the time, many were deeply attached to the broad exchange of views that is possible in a plenary session of the Court as well as to the opportunity afforded by the plenary session for the expression of differing cultural sensibilities. There is, in fact, little question that the Court as a whole represents a rich resource for the ICC arbitral system, and that it is one of the truly distinctive features of that system, as distinguished from the

---

[49] *See* Davis, "Fast-Track Arbitration: Different Perspectives-The Case Viewed by a Counsel at the ICC Court's Secretariat," *ICC Ct. Bull.*, Vol. 3, No. 2 (1992), p. 4.

offerings of other arbitral institutions. Nonetheless, there was equally little question in 1975 that, with the increase of the Court's caseload by that time to approximately 200 new cases a year, it was simply no longer possible for all of the Court's business each month to be dealt with at a single plenary session. The solution ultimately adopted was the delegation, as appropriate, of decision-making powers to groups of Court members in between plenary sessions of the Court.

The 1975 Rules, no more than the New Rules, did not impose any specific restrictions on the nature of the decisions that could be delegated or on the modalities of delegated decision-making, except that decisions could not be delegated to a single Court member, and the Court was to be kept informed of all delegated decisions. Otherwise, the Rules have since 1975 left it to the Court to decide how its powers of delegation under Article 1(4) should be exercised. This the Court originally did when adopting the Internal Rules that entered into effect in 1980. Under those rules, a Committee of the Court was created with the power to take any decision within the jurisdiction of the Court, with the exception of decisions concerning challenges of arbitrators, allegations that an arbitrator is not fulfilling his functions and the approval of draft Awards other than consent Awards.[50] The Committee was to consist of the Chairman of the Court (or a Vice-Chairman) and two other members appointed from among the members of the Court; in principle, it was to meet twice a month; and all of its decisions were to be taken unanimously, failing which the matter in question was to be referred to the next plenary session of the Court. In practice, the Court members designated to serve on the Committee change with every Committee meeting so as to permit the burden of the Committee's work to be more evenly distributed among the Court's members. Not surprisingly, however, those Court members that reside in Western Europe bear the brunt of the Committee's work.

Since its inception, the Committee of the Court has operated essentially as just described. Over time, however, the number of monthly Committee meetings has been increased from two to three, and the Committee has taken on responsibility for the scrutiny of arbitral Awards, although it did not have the power to approve them under the Internal Rules formerly in place. Thus, the Committee would merely recommend the approval of Awards, as appropriate, to the plenary session, which would then normally approve them without any need for discussion. Awards submitted to the Committee for review are referred to within the Court as "B" Awards, as opposed to "A" Awards, which are Awards to be examined and discussed at the plenary session rather than the Committee.[51] It is the Court's Secretariat, possibly in consultation with the Chairman, that decides whether Awards should be classified as "A" or "B." In the past, "A" Awards have tended to be Awards that the Secretariat or the Chairman believe would most

---

[50] As a matter of practice, the Committee also would not ordinarily consider requests for decisions under Article 7 of the prior Rules relating to the *prima facie* existence of an arbitration agreement (*see* Article 6(2) *infra*).

[51] For more information about the scrutiny process, *see* the discussion of Article 27 *infra*.

benefit from exposure to the plenary session, possibly because of their length or complexity, the sums at stake, the issues raised or the identity of the parties. In addition, it has been the Court's general practice to classify Awards as "A" Awards when they are accompanied by dissenting opinions.

Although the creation of the Committee was an effective means of relieving the growing burden on the plenary session of the Court, and of permitting relatively routine matters to be dealt with more efficiently, the continued growth of the Court's caseload since the Committee system was instituted has placed increasing strains on the Court's ability to administer its caseload expeditiously. Indeed, since the late 1970s, when the Committee system was conceived, the number of cases filed with the ICC each year has more than doubled. During the work on the New Rules, the ICC Court and Commission therefore considered other possible means of dealing with the Court's escalating workload. This led, in turn, to the delegation of certain additional tasks to the Court's Secretariat, as discussed in connection with Article 9(2) below, as well as the reconsideration of the limitations on the powers of the Committee, as set forth in the Court's Internal Rules.

The new Internal Rules of the Court, thus, remove the rigid restrictions on the powers of the Committee that were contained in their prior version. Instead of excluding certain kinds of decisions from the scope of the Committee's authority, the new Internal Rules provide (Article 4(5)(a)) that:

> The Court shall determine the decisions that may be taken by the Committee.

On the basis of this provision, the Court decided at a special working session in September 1997 to expand the Committee's powers to include the approval of "B" Awards. As such Awards were effectively already approved by the Committee, it served little practical purpose to delay their formal approval until the next following plenary session. The Court also decided that all matters, other than the following, may be decided upon by the Committee:

> [Q]uestions dealing with the status of the arbitrator ... . This especially covers the challenge of arbitrators (Article 11(3)), acceptance of the arbitrator's resignation (Article 12(1)), replacement of an arbitrator when the Court, on its own initiative, decides, "that he is prevented *de jure* or *de facto* from fulfilling his functions or that he is not fulfilling his functions in accordance with the Rules or within the prescribed time limits" (Article 12(2)).

> Furthermore, decisions not to replace an arbitrator subsequently [*sic*] to the closing of the proceedings (Article 12(5)) will also be taken by the Court in Plenary Session.[52]

---

[52] *See* Briner, *supra*, note 47, at p. 9 (emphasis omitted).

In cases of particular difficulty, however, the Committee still has the option of referring matters to the plenary session.[53]

Occasionally, a party may insist that a particular matter be referred to a plenary session rather than the Committee. However, given the Court's powers of delegation under Article 1(4), no party has a right to request the submission to a plenary session of any matter that the Court is not explicitly required to refer to that session under its Internal Rules. Nor is a party entitled to the reconsideration by the plenary of any matter decided by the Committee, although nothing in either the Rules or the Court's Internal Rules explicitly precludes this (except in the case of Article 7(4), as discussed below). In general, the Court has been reluctant to reconsider its decisions – whether taken at a plenary session or at the Committee – in the absence of relevant new information that was not before the Court at the time of the initial decision. Indeed, the Court has long attached importance to the finality of its decisions in order to avoid the delay that would be caused to the arbitration process if the Court's decisions were routinely open to reconsideration.

In the years ahead, one of the important challenges for the Court will be to find ways of improving the efficiency of its decision-making. The monthly plenary session of the Court has been a long-standing and cherished ICC institution. However, with two new Requests for Arbitration, on average, now being submitted to the ICC every working day of the year, the trend towards delegated decision-making begun in 1980 is likely to accelerate, leaving for the plenary session only those matters of greatest moment.

It also remains to be seen for how much longer the Court will consider it necessary to require the physical presence of its members at its meetings, whether plenary or Committee, in order for decisions to be taken. The Court's practice, until now, of requiring the members' physical presence has restricted its spontaneity and hampered the ability of the Court's non-European members to contribute as much as they otherwise might to the Court's work.

---

[53] *See* Article 4(5)(c) of the new Internal Rules ("When the Committee cannot reach a decision or deems it preferable to abstain, it transfers the case to the next Plenary Session ... ."). In this regard, the Court has also decided that, "[w]hen dealing with matters which are for the first time expressly addressed in the 1998 Rules (*e.g.* multiple parties (Article 10), correction and interpretation of the award (Article 29)))," as well as with issues which under the New Rules are treated in a different fashion than they are now (*e.g.,* determination whether there exists a *prima facie* arbitration agreement (Article 6(2)), "the Committee will often want to submit the matter, together with its recommendations, to the next Plenary Session, at least until such time when clear guidelines have been established based on the practice of the Court." Briner, *supra*, note 47, at p. 9. In addition to removing the express restrictions on the Committee's powers, the new Internal Rules (Article 4(4)) permit the Committee to deliberate when only two members are present and also (Article 4(2)) permit the Committee to be chaired, "in exceptional circumstances," by a member of the Court other than the Chairman or a Vice-Chairman. The resulting additional flexibility ought to permit the Committee to adapt more easily to its growing workload.

Article 1(5)

> *The Secretariat of the Court (the "Secretariat") under the direction of its Secretary General (the "Secretary General") shall have its seat at the headquarters of the ICC.*

This Article introduces the Court's Secretariat, which is based in Paris and headed by a Secretary General.[54] As the members of the Court are not employed by the ICC, the Secretariat provides the Court with the full-time professional support that it requires in order to carry out its work. To this end, the Secretariat prepares all of the documentation required by the Court in order to take its decisions, communicates with both the parties and the arbitrators, as necessary during the course of the arbitration, receives and notifies the Request for Arbitration and other documentation prior to the constitution of the Arbitral Tribunal and, more generally, monitors the arbitrations on a day-to-day basis, bringing matters to the attention of the Court as necessary.[55] In addition, the New Rules attribute certain new responsibilities to the Secretariat, as discussed below. During the course of an arbitration, the parties and arbitrators will not have any contact with the Court directly. All of their contacts will be with the Secretariat.

From a small staff of only a handful of persons twenty years ago, the Secretariat has grown into an organization that today employs more than thirty persons. In addition, it receives administrative support and other services from other personnel of the ICC Secretariat in Paris as well as the ICC's National Committees around the world. Since January 1997, the Secretariat has also had a representative office in Hong Kong, which explains the minor modification in the New Rules of Article 1(5), which now provides that the Secretariat has its "seat" at ICC headquarters in Paris. Of the Secretariat's present staff, approximately half are lawyers. Those who are responsible for the administration of cases are organized into a number of different teams, each headed by a counsel, with at least one and in some cases two assistant counsels. Since 1991, the Secretariat has had six such teams, and the Secretariat has generally endeavored to ensure the greatest possible diversity in their composition. As at the beginning of 1997, the six counsels heading the teams were from Canada, Colombia, France, Germany, Switzerland and the United States. Their assistant counsels

---

[54] The present Secretary General, Horacio Grigera Naón, assumed his position in November 1996. He is originally from Argentina. His recent predecessors were Eric Schwartz (1992-1996), Stephen Bond (1985-1991) and Yves Derains (1977-1981). From 1982 until 1985, there was no Secretary General, but instead there was an Administrative Director (Tila Maria de Hancock) sharing responsibility with a General Counsel (Sigvard Jarvin). For a description of the operation of the Secretariat, *see* R. Smit, *supra*, note 24, pp. 58-60.

[55] At the conclusion of the arbitration, the Secretariat also retains certain (but not all) documents relating to the arbitration in its archives. *See* the Court's Internal Rules, Article 1(6)-(7).

were from England, France, Lebanon, Malaysia, Panama and Tunisia. All of the teams are capable of administering cases in both English and French. In addition, other teams can operate in German, Italian and Spanish or otherwise function, at least to some extent, in Arabic, Serbo-Croatian and Vietnamese.

When a Request for Arbitration is received by the Secretariat, the Secretary General assigns the case to one of the teams, and it is with the team that the parties and arbitrators thereafter deal. In making the assignment, the Secretary General takes into account, in particular, the language or possible languages of the arbitration, the nationalities of the parties and their counsel, the applicable laws and the caseloads of the teams. In 1997, each of the teams was responsible for the administration of approximately 150 pending cases. In order to assist the teams with the management of a caseload of that magnitude, the ICC has made substantial investments in recent years in the development of a computerized case management system and an accompanying data base of Court decisions and arbitral Awards for the internal use of the Court and its Secretariat. In addition, standardized letters have been prepared for the use of the teams in connection with the routine matters that arise in the course of an arbitration's administration. The letters are intended to reflect usual Court practices and policies, without, however, preventing the teams from adapting them, as appropriate, for individual cases.

Until the Court is required to take a decision in respect of an arbitration (*e.g.,* in order to appoint an arbitrator, fix the place of arbitration, or fix an advance on costs), the case is administered solely by the Secretariat. In ICC Court parlance, the Court has not yet been "seized" of the case during this initial phase. Once it is necessary for the Court to act, however, it has been the Secretariat's practice to invite it to "set the arbitration in motion," an ICC phrase that reflects the acceptance of jurisdiction inherent in the Court's willingness to take a decision for the first time in respect of a particular matter.[56]

Arbitrations being placed on the agenda of the Court for the first time have been referred to within the Court as "New Cases."[57] In this connection, the counsel in charge of the file within the Secretariat prepares a memorandum that is circulated to the Committee of the Court. The memorandum identifies the parties and their counsel, sets forth the arbitration clause and describes the circumstances of the case as well as the respective positions of the parties. It usually also presents financial information about the case – the amount in dispute and the possible fees and expenses of the arbitrators – before listing the issues to be decided by the Court and presenting the Secretariat's related recommen-

---

[56] Given that, under the New Rules, the Secretary General has the authority to confirm arbitrators and fix a provisional advance before the Court has been seized, it remains to be seen whether the Court will continue to be invited to "set the arbitration in motion." However, the actions of the Secretary General are not intended to prejudice any decision that the Court may subsequently make with respect to the jurisdiction of the ICC.

[57] But whether this will continue to be the practice remains to be seen in view of the new responsibilities of the Secretary General.

dations. Subsequently, each time in the life of a case that a decision is required of the Court, a similar memorandum is prepared, either for the Committee or the plenary session, as appropriate. When matters are presented to the plenary session, however, the Secretariat's memorandum is accompanied by the report of a Court member designated to act as a reporter.

Before the memoranda of counsel are distributed to the Court, they are reviewed in meetings of the Secretariat staff chaired by the Secretary General or, in his absence, the Deputy Secretary General, who is also the General Counsel.[58] The purpose of the staff meetings is to ensure the coherence of the Secretariat's recommendations, taking into account the Court's past practices, discuss new issues and develop new policy proposals. The staff meetings also permit the Secretary General to familiarize himself with the on-going work of the various teams. At any one staff meeting, memoranda concerning as many as 100 different cases may be reviewed.

In addition to assisting the Court, the Secretariat is available to the parties and arbitrators for information and advice with respect to ICC arbitration practice. Indeed, during the proceedings, a multitude of questions may arise concerning the procedures to be followed in constituting the tribunal, presenting arguments and evidence, making Awards and the like. As arbitration activity has become increasingly global, with more and more new participants in the process, this is today one of the Secretariat's most vital functions. It is, however, a delicate one, given the need for the ICC to maintain its neutrality as well as the appearance of neutrality, while at the same time providing information and advice to the parties and arbitrators that they may reasonably expect.[59]

There are a number of issues that arise in this connection, such as, for example, how to draw the line between advice that is "neutral" and advice that might be said to unduly advantage or disadvantage a party. In a sense, it can be argued that there is no such thing as "neutral" advice. Even the act of explaining to a Claimant party how to commence an arbitration, something that arbitral institutions routinely do, could be said to assist the Claimant and disadvantage the Respondent. However, it appears to be widely accepted that the institution does not violate any obligation of neutrality merely by explaining the requirements of its rules. On the contrary, this is part of the service that institutions are normally expected to provide. However, whenever advice goes beyond that to considerations of law or strategy outside the rules themselves, then questions may

---

[58] *See also*, with respect to the Deputy Secretary General/General Counsel, Article 5(1) of the Internal Rules ("In case of absence, the Secretary General may delegate to the General Counsel and Deputy Secretary General the authority to confirm arbitrators, to certify true copies of Awards and to request the payment of a provisional advance, respectively provided for in Articles 9(2), 28(2) and 30(1) of the Rules.").

[59] In recent years, the Secretariat has also established a site on the World Wide Web (www.iccwbo.org) on which information about ICC arbitration, seminars and publications is regularly posted. *See also* Article 5(2) of the Court's Internal Rules concerning the issuance by the Secretariat of notes and other documents "for the information of the parties and the arbitrators."

arise. For an institution, there will often be a temptation to provide advice to a party that will help to ensure that the arbitration will result in an Award that is enforceable. Indeed, many parties consider that this is one of the functions of an arbitration institution and that, as guardians of the arbitration process, institutions should actively preserve and protect its efficacy and credibility through not only advice but action, as required. There are necessarily limits, however, to what an institution should say or do consistent with the preservation of its own neutrality, and, arguably, it is not for the institution to save a party from itself if it is poorly advised.

Apart from giving advice, the Secretariat also assists the parties and arbitrators, as necessary, with logistical arrangements for the arbitration – locating hearing rooms, translators, reporters or the like. The ICC unfortunately has limited hearing facilities at its headquarters in Paris, which means that parties interested in using them must make arrangements for the same well in advance.

ARTICLE 2
Definitions

This is an entirely new Article, which was intended to simplify the drafting of the Rules and, at the same time, clarify certain concepts from the outset. Although it was at one time envisaged by the Working Party that certain additional terms might be defined, only the following three definitions were ultimately retained in this Article:

(i)   *"Arbitral Tribunal" includes one or more arbitrators.*

In drafting the new Rules, the Working Party preferred to use the term "Arbitral Tribunal" rather than the singular "arbitrator," as was the case in the prior version when referring to the tribunal. Article 2(2) of the former Rules stated in this regard that "the word 'arbitrator' denotes a single arbitrator or three arbitrators as the case may be." It will immediately be noticed that, apart from substituting the words Arbitral Tribunal for arbitrator, the new Rules replace the reference to one or three arbitrators by "one or more arbitrators." Although, as discussed in respect of Article 8 below, one or three arbitrators remain the norm in ICC arbitration, the intention of the drafters of the new Rules, consistent with the ICC's standard arbitration clause (see Appendix 1), was to indicate that the Rules do not preclude the parties from agreeing on another number of arbitrators, although this is extremely rare.

(ii)   *"Claimant" includes one or more claimants and "Respondent" includes one or more respondents.*

The prior version of the Rules did not explicitly refer to the possible multiplicity of Claimant and Respondent parties, except in one Article (Article 9) relating to the payment of the advance on costs. In all other respects, the Rules, like most other arbitration rules and legislation, were drafted as if there were only two parties to the arbitration, a Claimant and a Defendant (now called a "Respondent"). As a consequence, it was occasionally argued that multi-party arbitrations (i.e., proceedings involving more than two parties) were incompatible with the Rules and should not be allowed to proceed in the absence of the express agreement of all of the parties. In defining the Claimant and the Respondent so as to include a multiplicity of Claimant and Respondent parties, the Rules now make it clear that there is no obstacle per se to the conduct of a multi-party arbitration, and, indeed, in approximately 20 per cent of the cases submitted to the ICC in recent years there have been more than two parties.

This being said, the New Rules do not address many of the issues that may arise in a multi-party context, such as, for example, with respect to the joinder of parties not named in the Request for Arbitration or the filing of a cross-claim by one Respondent against another. Indeed, by referring only to "Claimants" and "Respondents," the Rules continue, as in their prior versions, to cater to disputes with no more than two sides (even though there may be a number of parties on either side). This does not mean that arbitrations involving three or more sides cannot be conducted under the ICC Rules. However, as discussed further with respect to Article 4(6) below, in the absence of appropriate provisions in the Rules, parties wishing to do so must be able to agree on the procedures to be followed or run the risk that the ICC Court will require separate arbitrations to be instituted in respect of the various disputes involved.

(iii)   "Award" includes, inter alia, an interim, partial or final Award.

Over the years, as arbitration has become more complex, there has been a growing tendency for arbitrators to decide issues during the course of the arbitration by means of separate Awards in advance of a final Award. Most modern arbitration rules and laws take account of this by expressly conferring on the arbitrators the power to issue "interim," "partial" or other (*e.g.,* "interlocutory") non-"final" Awards.[60] However, nowhere in the ICC Rules was there previously any reference to interim Awards, and the former Rules contained only one reference (in former Article 21 on the scrutiny of Awards) to the possible issuance of partial Awards. The above new definition therefore now brings the ICC Rules broadly into line with most other arbitration rules.

This being said, there are no internationally accepted definitions of the terms "interim" and "partial" in this context. In some jurisdictions (*e.g.,* England), Awards made in advance of the final Award are usually referred to as "interim" Awards; in others, such as France and Switzerland, the term "partial" is favored; and in still others (e.g., the Netherlands), both terms are used for different purposes.[61] Under the Rules, the arbitrators are free to use whatever designations

---

[60]   *See, e.g.,* UNCITRAL Rules, Article 32(1).
[61]   *See* Article 1051 of the Netherlands Arbitration Act 1986, which distinguishes between "interim" Awards and "partial final" Awards.

may appear to them to be appropriate in respect of such Awards, including other possible terms that are not explicitly mentioned in Article 2. Indeed, this is the reason for the inclusion in the definition of the term *"inter alia,"* thus permitting the arbitrators to refer to their Awards as "interlocutory" or to use other terminology if they may so choose.

In this connection, what is even more important is the absence in the Rules of any indication as to the kinds of decisions that need to take the form of an Award if rendered prior to the final Award. Although the Rules do not differ from other arbitration rules or most arbitration legislation in this regard – indeed, neither the UNCITRAL Model Law nor the New York Convention specifies what an "Award" is and, more particularly, which decisions of arbitrators should be treated as "Awards" – the question is especially important in ICC arbitration because of the requirement, set forth in Article 27 of the Rules (see infra), that all "Awards" must be scrutinized and approved by the Court. It may therefore be asked whether decisions as to matters such as the following are required to take the form of Awards:

(i)   the arbitrator's jurisdiction;
(ii) the rules of law to be applied by the arbitrator to the merits of the dispute;
(iii) the language of the arbitration;
(iv) procedural issues (*e.g.,* whether to appoint an expert);
(v)   other preliminary questions (*e.g.,* whether any or all of the claims are barred by statutes of limitation);
(vi) interim measures of protection; and
(vii) substantive claims in the arbitration.

Several years ago, a working party of the ICC Commission suggested that, when the Rules were next revised, the ICC should consider specifying the types of decisions that ought to take the form of an Award, and that, as a consequence, would be required to be scrutinized by the ICC Court.[62] Ultimately, however, this was not done, mainly because of the absence of any uniform rules or practices in this respect internationally.

Indeed, even within jurisdictions such as France and Switzerland – historically the two most important venues for ICC arbitration – there continue to be disagreements and uncertainties concerning the definition of an arbitral Award. Thus, it is the view of certain, but not all, Swiss authorities that no decision of an arbitrator that does not result in the final determination of a claim can be considered to be an Award.[63] In accordance with this view, for example, an Arbitral Tribunal's decision, by means of a preliminary ruling, that the claims submitted to arbitration are not barred by a statute of limitations would not be regarded as

---

[62]   *See* "Final Report on Interim and Partial Awards," of the ICC Working Party on this subject (M. Hunter, Chairman), *ICC Ct. Bull.,* Vol. 1, No. 2 (1990), p. 26.

[63]   *See, e.g., Lalive Poudret and Reymond*, pp. 405-08.

an Award (although a contrary decision normally would be). Nor would a decision on the principle of a party's liability (prior to consideration of the relevant damages claimed) constitute an Award unless the decision were that there was no liability.

Such a relatively restrictive view of what constitutes an Award is to be contrasted, however, with the decision of a French court of appeal in the case of *Société Industrialexport-Import c/ société GECI et GFC*.[64] In that case, which related to an *ad hoc* arbitration proceeding in Paris, the court found to be Awards susceptible to recourse before the French courts three "procedural orders" of the Arbitral Tribunal that: (i) decided that the Arbitral Tribunal was competent and had been correctly constituted; (ii) determined the applicable procedural rules; and (iii) rejected an application for the suspension of the arbitral proceedings. The French court found that all three orders were, in fact, arbitral Awards (although they did not purport to be) because they (translation) "constituted decisions of a jurisdictional nature" that finally settled litigious procedural issues between the parties. Even if the characterization of all of those decisions as "Awards" might reasonably be questioned, the judgment in that case illustrates the uncertainties that continue to prevail internationally.

Thus, it is ordinarily for the Arbitral Tribunal to decide in each case, depending upon all of the relevant circumstances, whether a particular decision is required to take the form of an "Award" or may be issued instead in the form of a procedural order.[65]

ARTICLE 3
Written Notifications or Communications; Time Limits

This Article, which corresponds to Article 6 of the former Rules, sets out the procedures to be followed in respect of written communications among the parties, the arbitrators and the Secretariat during the arbitration. The four sub-paragraphs of former Article 6 (the last of which was added to the Rules in 1988) have all been retained, although a number of modifications have been made, particularly in order to bring the new Article into line with modern practice.

The provisions of this Article may also be supplemented by such arrangements as the parties and the arbitrators may consider appropriate. Normally, when drawing up the Terms of Reference (*see* Article 18 of the Rules), the arbitrators will, thus, provide further details concerning the procedures to be followed in respect of notifications during the arbitration. At a minimum, the Terms of Reference are required to set out in this regard the addresses of the parties and arbitrators to which communications are to be addressed.

---

[64] *Cour d'appel de Paris* (July 9, 1992), Note Jarrosson, *Rev. arb.* (1993), p. 303.

[65] For a French court decision finding that this is the responsibility of the arbitrators, rather than the ICC Court, *see Société Cubic Defense System c/ Chambre de commerce internationale, Tribunal de grande instance de Paris* (May 21, 1997), *Rev. arb.* (1997), p. 417.

Article 3(1)

> *All pleadings and other written communications submitted by any party, as well as all documents annexed thereto, shall be supplied in a number of copies sufficient to provide one copy for each party, plus one for each arbitrator, and one for the Secretariat. A copy of any communication from the Arbitral Tribunal to the parties shall be sent to the Secretariat.*

Background. This provision formerly only concerned "pleadings and written communications" from the parties. It now also adds the express requirement – not otherwise set forth in the Rules – that the arbitrators must send copies of their communications with the parties to the Secretariat. This is intended to ensure that the Secretariat is in a position to monitor the arbitrators' conduct of the arbitral proceedings. In the past, the Secretariat routinely requested arbitrators to send it copies of their correspondence with the parties. However, on rare occasions, arbitrators questioned the Secretariat's authority to insist upon this. The addition of the new language now makes the Secretariat's authority clear.

The primary purpose of Article 3(1) is otherwise to ensure that all parties, the arbitrators and the Secretariat receive copies of all "pleadings and written communications" from the parties and that the party producing the document in question bears the burden of reproducing it. Thus, neither the ICC nor the arbitrators should be required to reproduce for others written submissions received from a party. In the early days of ICC arbitration, all communications were normally channeled through the ICC's National Committees or the Secretariat. Thus, copies of all documents were submitted by the parties to them, and the National Committees or Secretariat would ensure their distribution to the other parties concerned. Although not apparent from Article 3(1), as drafted, the ICC long ago abandoned this practice. Thus, while the communication of the Request for Arbitration, the Answer and the Reply, if any (*see* Articles 4 and 5 of the Rules), is still effected through the Secretariat, it is otherwise the Secretariat's practice to invite the parties to send copies of their communications directly to each other and, once the file has been transmitted to it, the Arbitral Tribunal, with a copy to the Secretariat. Article 3(1) does not expressly provide for this. However, the Secretariat's practice is not inconsistent with the terms of that provision and generally is in the interest of achieving the greatest possible expedition and efficiency.

Number of copies required. Although the number of copies required to be supplied under Article 3(1) may appear, at first glance, to be self-evident, this, in fact, depends upon the number of arbitrators for the arbitration. In many cases, of course, the number of arbitrators is not specified in the arbitration clause and is therefore not known until either the parties agree on the number or the Court decides the matter pursuant to Article 8 of the Rules. Until that time, therefore, the number of copies of pleadings and written submissions (including, notably, the Request for Arbitration and the Answer) required to be submitted under Article 3(1) will not be certain.

As a practical matter, the Secretariat has, in such circumstances, normally requested the parties to furnish a number of copies sufficient to provide one for each of the number of arbitrators that it proposes should be appointed. Thus, if the arbitration clause does not specify the number of arbitrators, a party requesting the appointment of three arbitrators should supply sufficient copies for all three. However, the Secretariat has generally been relatively flexible in applying this rule, and, indeed, it would not be reasonable of it to insist on the supply of copies for three arbitrators for as long as there remained any uncertainty as to the number of arbitrators to be appointed.[66]

Communications with the Secretariat. Neither Article 3(1) nor any other part of Article 3 lays down any requirements in respect of communications from the arbitrators to the Secretariat or, more generally, communications from the Secretariat to the arbitrators. Unless otherwise provided elsewhere in the Rules, the Secretariat is therefore free to decide whether to inform the parties of its communications with the arbitrators, and whether it does so is likely to depend upon the nature and purpose of the communication in question.

Article 3(1) also does not create any obligation for the Secretariat to inform all of the parties and arbitrators of all communications that it sends to a party in respect of an arbitration. However, insofar as it obliges the parties to supply copies of all "pleadings and written communications" in sufficient copies for the other parties, the arbitrators and the Secretariat, Article 3(1) raises the question of whether parties may make submissions to the Secretariat without copies being supplied to the other parties or the arbitrators and, moreover, whether and to what extent the Secretariat may be required, or should be permitted, to engage in *ex parte* communications with parties to ICC arbitrations.

In practice, it has long been the policy of the Secretariat to perform its administrative functions as transparently as possible, primarily because of the importance to the ICC of maintaining not only its impartiality but its appearance of impartiality with respect to the parties concerned. Thus, the Secretariat has ordinarily sought to ensure that the parties are fully informed of all communications of one of the parties with the Secretariat during the arbitration, and the arbitrators are generally informed of such communications as well. This is, moreover, clearly indispensable with respect to any matters as to which the Court may be required to make a decision.

There may nevertheless be circumstances in which parties should be permitted to communicate with the Secretariat on a confidential basis. In this connection, it has to be recognized that the Secretariat plays a fundamentally different role from the arbitrators in the arbitration process. Arguably, by dealing with parties on an *ex parte* basis in certain circumstances, the Secretariat can facili-

---

[66]   In fact, until 1975, the Rules expressly only required the supply by the parties of documents in triplicate, with the Secretariat having the power to require the supply of further copies as appropriate.

tate the process. Thus, for example, parties may be concerned about the conduct of an arbitrator, but may feel reluctant to disclose this. By allowing parties to air their concerns in confidence, the Secretariat may not only receive information that might not otherwise have come to its attention, but it may be in a position to defuse possible difficulties that could otherwise eventually disrupt the arbitration, *e.g.*, if the arbitrator were formally challenged. In the eyes of many parties, the Secretariat can, thus, serve as a useful screen between the arbitrators and themselves, or sometimes between the parties as well, when this may be in the interest of smoothing over or avoiding difficulties in the course of an arbitration. It is also arguably freer to play this role insofar as, even within the ICC, the Secretariat is not the ultimate decision-maker with respect to most matters. As already stated, this is the role of the Court, which does not, in contrast to the Secretariat, have any direct contacts with the parties.

Notwithstanding its apparent breadth, it is therefore doubtful that Article 3(1) was intended to preclude confidential communications between parties and the Secretariat. In fact, the present text of that provision has its origin in a proposal made during the drafting of the 1975 Rules that was originally entitled "Written Statements of Case."[67] The written statements that the drafters appeared to have in mind at the time were those intended for consideration by the Arbitral Tribunal in connection with the substance of the arbitration. Ultimately, the words incorporated in the 1975 Rules were "pleadings and written statements," which, in turn, have evolved into "pleadings and other written communications" in the New Rules. It remains to be seen how the Secretariat will construe this language in respect of communications that parties may seek to make to it on a confidential basis.

Article 3(2)

> *All notifications or communications from the Secretariat and the Arbitral Tribunal shall be made to the last address of the party or its representative for whom the same are intended, as notified either by the party in question or by the other party. Such notification or communication may be made by delivery against receipt, registered post, courier, facsimile transmission, telex, telegram or any other means of telecommunication that provides a record of the sending thereof.*

Background. As compared with the prior version of this provision in the former Rules, Article 3(2) greatly expands the permissible means of communications from the Secretariat and the arbitrators in connection with the arbitration. It is

---

[67] Article 6 of the draft arbitration rules submitted for consideration to the ICC Commission at its meeting on October 8, 1974, ICC Doc. No. 420/166. The draft of Article 6 was itself a revised version of Article 11 of the 1955 Rules, which was entitled "Written Statements of the Case."

to be noted, however, that neither this Article nor any other provision of the Rules concerns the means of communications that may be used by the parties during the arbitration.

Previously, the Rules required all notifications or communications from the Secretariat and the arbitrators to be made either by registered post or personal delivery against receipt. However, as communications technology has evolved, parties and arbitrators have come to expect that notifications and communications will be made by facsimile and, in the future, may wish to receive communications by still other means. It therefore became necessary to bring this provision into line with modern practice, as many other arbitral institutions had already done.[68]

As a practical matter, the Secretariat long ago began using the fax to communicate with parties and arbitrators in ICC arbitrations, except when notifying documents such as the Request for Arbitration, the Answer or the Award, all of which have always been notified either by registered mail, return receipt requested, or by personal delivery against receipt. When using faxes for other communications, the Secretariat would nevertheless generally also send a confirming hard copy, either by mail – often but not always registered, with return receipt requested – or by courier in order to satisfy the requirements of the Rules. However, the practices of all of the Secretariat's counsels have not always been consistent in this regard. Depending on the nature of the communication, and in particular whether proof of receipt was important, some might send a confirming copy by ordinary mail or possibly no confirming copy at all. Moreover, out of an understandable wish to expedite the proceedings, the Secretariat might occasionally use faxes to fix deadlines for action by parties commencing as from the date of receipt of the fax rather than the confirming hard copy, even though such a practice could arguably be said to be inconsistent with the former Rules. Arbitrators, for their part, have routinely had recourse to the fax as well, and, indeed, it has become standard practice in ICC arbitrations for the arbitrators, without any objection from the Court, to provide specifically for this in the Terms of Reference, in derogation from the former Rules.

The changes incorporated in Article 3(2) will therefore remove any doubt as to the validity of the use of faxes by both the Secretariat and the arbitrators and should also obviate the need for duplicate confirming copies to be sent of all communications. Although it may not be possible to systematically establish proof of receipt of all communications made by fax, the Secretariat and arbitrators will be in a position to select the appropriate means of notification when they require such proof in respect of a particular communication.

Addresses to which notifications are to be made. As a practical matter, the addresses to which notifications are to be made are usually agreed by the par-

---

[68] *See, e.g.,* AAA International Arbitration Rules, Article 18; WIPO Arbitration Rules, Article 4.

ties and arbitrators and set forth in the Terms of Reference (*see* Article 18(1) of the Rules). The related provision in Article 3(2) is therefore generally of relevance only to the notification of the Request for Arbitration by the Secretariat to the Respondent or to cases where a Respondent party does not appear in the arbitration.

In the cases just mentioned, it has long been the Secretariat's practice to use the addresses indicated by the Claimants for the purpose of notifications to Respondent parties. The Secretariat does not independently verify whether the addresses communicated by Claimants are correct. This is the Claimant's responsibility. In the event that a document notified by the Secretariat in accordance with a Claimant's instructions is returned because the Respondent is not at that address, the Secretariat normally requests the Claimant to furnish another address and will then renotify the document in question. If the Claimant is unable to provide the Secretariat with another address, then, insofar as a notification has been sent to the Respondent's last known address, the Secretariat usually leaves it up to the Claimant to decide whether it wishes the arbitration to proceed notwithstanding the lack of actual notice to the Respondent party.

In exceptional circumstances, a party's address may be known, but notification to that address may be impossible, such as, for example, in cases of civil disturbance or war. During the fighting in Bosnia-Herzogovina, for example, the ICC and arbitrators were unable, for several years, to notify documents to parties in Sarajevo. As a consequence, the proceedings were suspended.

Validity of notice. All that Article 3(2) requires is that notices be made to the "address" of the party in question (or its representative). There is no requirement that notices be made to any particular person; nor need the Secretariat or the arbitrators verify that the notice has been received by a duly authorized person at the place where the notice has been delivered, provided that it has been delivered to the proper address.[69]

Article 3(2) also does not require that any particular formalities be respected by the Secretariat or arbitrators in making notifications under the Rules other than as set forth therein. This has not always been the case, however. Indeed, until 1975, the Rules provided that the Secretariat and the arbitrators should observe any additional formalities that might be required by special provisions of law in the case of notifications concerning the arbitration.[70] But that requirement was dropped from the Rules when they were amended in that year. The ICC evidently considered that the requirements of the Rules relating to notifications were adequate to ensure the validity of any notifications made in accordance therewith. And, indeed, it is today widely accepted that parties should be free to agree on the requirements governing notifications and communications

---

[69] For an example of a judicial decision explicitly recognizing the validity of this rule, see *Bin Saud Bin Abdel Aziz* c/ *Crédit Industriel et Commercial de Paris, Cour d'appel de Paris* (March 24, 1995), *Rev. arb.* (1996), p. 81.
[70] 1955 Rules, Articles 15 and 17.

in an arbitration and, thus, need not respect any formalities other than as set forth in the relevant arbitration rules. This is reflected in modern arbitration legislation[71] and the judgments of courts in many jurisdictions.[72]

Article 3(3)

> *A notification or communication shall be deemed to have been made on the day when it was received by the party itself or by its representative, or would have been received if made in accordance with the preceding paragraph.*

Article 3(3) fixes as the effective date of any notification or communication from the Secretariat or the arbitrators the date of its receipt. As a consequence, both the Secretariat and the arbitrators must be in a position to establish the date of receipt of a communication sent by them whenever this may have any consequences for the arbitration. Of course, there are circumstances in which a communication may never actually be received by a party, in particular when a party no longer has a known address and notification has to be made to the party's "last known address" in accordance with Article 3(2). In such cases, the best that the Secretariat or arbitrators can do is to establish that the communication was sent to the address in question and the date of attempted delivery. It is in recognition of this that Article 3(3) provides that notifications shall be deemed to be effected on the day when, if not actually received, they "would" have been.

While a notification made to a party's "last known address" may be sufficient for the purpose of the Rules and may, thus, permit an ICC arbitration to proceed, Article V(1)(b) of the New York Convention, like many arbitration laws, provides that enforcement of an Award may be refused if the party "against whom the Award is invoked was not given proper notice of the ... arbitration proceedings." Notwithstanding the provisions of Article 3(3), parties should therefore do all that they reasonably can to ensure that notice of the arbitration is actually received as from the outset of the proceedings.[73]

In addition, it is to be noted that neither Article 3(3) nor any other provision of the Rules deals explicitly with the date upon which communications from the parties should be considered to have been effected. This is therefore a matter with which the parties and arbitrators may wish to deal when drawing up the Terms of Reference or otherwise during the arbitration.

---

[71] *See, e.g.,* UNCITRAL Model Law, Article 3.
[72] *See, e.g., Société Guangzhou Ocean Shipping Company c/ société générale des Farines, Cour d'appel de Paris* (January 17, 1992), Note Bureau, *Rev. arb.* (1992), p. 656, *and* cases cited by van den Berg in his "Consolidated Commentary" on cases relating to the New York Convention *in ICCA Yearbook* XXI (1996), pp. 394, 488.
[73] *See* van den Berg, *supra,* note 72, at 488.

Article 3(4)

> *Periods of time specified in, or fixed under the present Rules, shall start to run on the day following the date a notification or communication is deemed to have been made in accordance with the preceding paragraph. When the day next following such date is an official holiday, or a non-business day in the country where the notification or communication is deemed to have been made, the period of time shall commence on the first following business day. Official holidays and non-business days are included in the calculation of the period of time. If the last day of the relevant period of time granted is an official holiday or a non-business day in the country where the notification or communication is deemed to have been made, the period of time shall expire at the end of the first following business day.*

The Rules fix a number of time limits, *e.g.,* for the submission of the Respondent's Answer, the nomination of arbitrators, the establishment of the Terms of Reference and the making of Awards. In addition, the Court and the Secretariat have the authority to fix various time limits in administering the Rules, as do the arbitrators in carrying out their functions. This provision, which was originally added to the Rules in 1988, therefore serves the useful function of specifying how such time periods are to be calculated. Although it has not been the subject of any significant substantive changes, the first sentence has been redrafted in a manner that, unlike its prior version, would appear to make it applicable to time periods fixed by arbitrators as well as by the Court and the Secretariat.[74]

---

[74] Article 6(4) of the former Rules expressly applied only to periods of time "specified" in the Rules or the Internal Rules or set by the Court. Article 3(4) has now been broadly drafted to include all periods of time "fixed under" the Rules, which may include periods fixed by arbitrators in conducting arbitrations. However, the French version of the Rule is arguably narrower. Unlike the English version, it refers to periods "*dont la fixation est prévue dans le ... Règlement*" (translation: "the fixing of which is provided for in ... the Rules").

Chapter 3
Commencing the Arbitration (Articles 4-6)

ARTICLE 4
Request for Arbitration

An ICC arbitration is commenced by filing a Request for Arbitration with the Secretariat of the Court. Although all arbitration rules require some kind of filing in order to initiate an arbitration proceeding, the nature of the filing required is not always the same. Thus, for example, under many rules (such as, for example, the UNCITRAL Rules), an arbitration may be commenced by giving a "notice" of arbitration containing no more than a brief reference to the claim and the relief sought, with a full statement of the claim and supporting documents to be submitted at a later stage, usually after the constitution of the Arbitral Tribunal.

In the case of ICC arbitration, however, the Rules have always contemplated that more than a simple "notice" should be required to be given in order for an arbitration to commence. The Request for Arbitration, therefore, is intended to be a more substantial document than a mere "notice" and not only serves to initiate the arbitration, but also contains descriptive information concerning the nature and circumstances of the claim, as described further below. An important advantage of this is that the Court is more fully informed about the nature of the arbitration than it otherwise would be when called upon to make decisions concerning such matters as the constitution of the Arbitral Tribunal, the place of arbitration or the advance on costs for the arbitration. Of course, for the parties too, time may be saved subsequently in conducting the arbitration proceedings if a relatively full statement of the claim is produced as from the beginning of the arbitration. As discussed below, however, the Rules allow the parties considerable freedom in deciding how much detail they wish to provide in the Request about their claims.

Article 4 preserves the basic features of what was previously Article 3 of the Rules. Although there was some discussion, during the Rules revision process, of possibly altering the requirements relating to the Request so that it would more closely resemble an arbitration "notice," this was almost universally opposed. Certain modifications were nevertheless made to the previous version of this Article, as noted below.

Article 4(1)

> *A party wishing to have recourse to arbitration under these Rules shall submit its Request for Arbitration (the "Request") to the Secretariat, which shall notify the Claimant and the Respondent of the receipt of the Request and the date of such receipt.*

Background. As in the case of the previous Rules, Article 4(1) establishes the principle that the Request for Arbitration is submitted by the Claimant to the Secretariat rather than to the Respondent directly. Indeed, there is no requirement under the Rules that the Claimant inform the Respondent that it has filed a Request for Arbitration. It is the responsibility of the Secretariat pursuant to Article 4(5), as discussed below, to notify the Request to the Respondent.

When a Request for Arbitration is received by the Secretariat, the Secretary General will ordinarily almost immediately (within one to two days) acknowledge its receipt by sending a letter to the Claimant confirming the same. The Secretary General then assigns the new case to one of the Secretariat's counsels and also verifies whether the required filing fee and an adequate number of copies have been submitted together with the Request (*see* Article 4(4)). If so, the counsel in charge of the file notifies the Request to the Respondent, normally within a week of its receipt by the Secretariat. However, if either the filing fee or adequate copies have not been received, the Request is not notified. Rather, the Secretariat first requests the Claimant to furnish the missing fee or copies. Although the Secretariat normally insists on receiving the same within two weeks, failing which the file may be closed, there have occasionally been instances when the Secretariat has allowed the Claimant a longer period than that. In either case, however, the Secretariat may be in possession of the Request for Arbitration for a relatively long period of time before it is notified to the Respondent.

It is for this reason that Article 4(1) now contains the requirement, which is new, that the Secretariat must inform the Respondent, in addition to the Claimant, when receiving the Request. This new requirement is not to be confused with the actual notification of the Request by the Secretariat. That is provided for separately in Article 4(5), as discussed below. Article 4(1) is intended to ensure, rather, that as soon as a Request has been filed, but before it has been notified, the Respondent will be made aware of this. The Secretariat is also required to specify the date of the Request's receipt so that each of the parties will immediately know the date as from which the arbitration proceedings shall have been deemed to commence. As a practical matter, the Secretariat need only send to the Respondent a copy of the letter acknowledging the receipt of the Request that it has, in the past, systematically sent to the Claimant.

One issue that may arise, from time to time, as a result of the new requirement of Article 4(1), is whether the Secretariat should notify the Request to the

Respondent, prior to receiving the required filing fee and number of copies, if the Respondent requests it to. Presumably, however, the Secretariat would be reluctant to incur the expense of doing so, and it could, in addition, be expected to invoke the requirements of Article 4(5) (*see infra*) as a reason for not notifying the Request in such circumstances.

One other change that has been made in Article 4(1), as compared with the corresponding provision of the prior Rules, is the elimination of any reference to the ICC's National Committees. It was previously the case under the Rules that a party could submit a Request for Arbitration to the Secretariat "through its National Committee," if any, and if it chose to submit it to the Secretariat directly, the Secretariat was required to "bring the Request to the notice of the National Committee concerned." Indeed, in the early days of ICC arbitration – until 1955 – an ICC arbitration was normally commenced through a National Committee or a member of the ICC. It was only as from 1955 that parties had the option of filing a Request directly with the Secretariat in Paris. With the new Rules, this has now become the exclusive means of initiating an ICC arbitration.

As a practical matter, parties only very rarely made use, in recent years, of the possibility of filing a Request with a National Committee. Although this might have been more convenient and less costly, in certain cases, than sending the Request to Paris, the disadvantage was that, as was specified for the first time in the 1975 Rules, the arbitration is deemed to commence only when the Request is received by the Secretariat in Paris, and a party depositing a Request for filing with a National Committee could not be sure when this would occur. For their part, the National Committees did not actively encourage prospective parties in their countries to use their services for this purpose, presumably because they were not eager to assume the related costs of transmitting the Request to Paris.

But apart from considerations of this kind, the Court and Secretariat had grown increasingly uncomfortable over the years with the concept that National Committees should systematically be made aware of arbitrations initiated by parties from their countries, either by the parties themselves through the deposit of their Requests or otherwise by the Secretariat. In fact, several years before the new Rules' adoption, the Secretariat stopped bringing Requests to the notice of National Committees, notwithstanding the stipulation in the previous Rules that required it to do so. This is because the Secretariat was concerned to maintain the confidentiality of the Requests submitted to it, even in relation to the National Committees. Although, as discussed further below in respect of Article 9 of the Rules, the National Committees have an important role to play in the constitution of ICC Arbitral Tribunals, it has long been the policy of the Court otherwise to avoid communicating information to them about specific ICC cases, except possibly in order to solicit their assistance in obtaining a local party's voluntary compliance with an ICC Award.

How to file the Request. As already noted with regard to Article 3(2), the Rules do not lay down any requirements concerning the manner in which notifications or communications from the parties are to be made, except that a certain number of copies are to be supplied, and no further guidance with respect to this is provided in Article 4. As a practical matter, Requests are usually sent to the Secretariat by mail or special courier or otherwise personally delivered. The Secretariat always acknowledges receipt in writing, as already mentioned. However, if it is important to a party to have additional proof of receipt, the Secretariat will sign and return to it an additional copy of the Request provided for this purpose.

Occasionally, parties, under the pressure of time, have filed Requests for Arbitration by fax. The Secretariat has accepted such filings as valid, but subject to receiving within a reasonable time thereafter original hard copies in the number required by the Rules.[75] The Secretariat would normally only notify the Request to the Respondent upon receipt of the hard copies. It is surely only a matter of time before parties also begin seeking to file Requests by electronic mail. As in the case of submissions by fax, there is nothing in the Rules that explicitly precludes this. However, there are related issues of confidentiality that may be of concern to the parties and that the ICC will have to address.

More generally, the Rules do not require the completion of any particular formalities in connection with the submission of the Request. Thus, for example, when a Request is filed by a lawyer on behalf of a party, the Rules do not require that it be accompanied by a power of attorney. If appropriate, the authority of any person acting on behalf of a party can be verified subsequently by the Arbitral Tribunal, once constituted.

Article 4(2)

> *The date on which the Request is received by the Secretariat shall, for all purposes, be deemed to be the date of commencement of the arbitral proceedings.*

This rule, which has been expressly set forth in the Rules since 1975, fixes the date of commencement of the arbitration. This is of obvious importance with respect to relevant statutes of limitation and possibly also where, for other reasons, the arbitration is required to be commenced by a particular date.

By linking the commencement of the arbitration to the receipt of the Request by the Secretariat, the Rules ensure that the parties will have no difficulty either in commencing the arbitration or establishing the date of its commencement. Under certain other arbitration rules – the UNCITRAL Rules are a notable example – the proceedings are deemed to commence on the date of receipt of the Request by the Respondent. The disadvantage of this, however, is that it may be difficult, or even impossible, to locate the Respondent or to serve the Request

---

[75] *See*, in this connection, the extract from the ICC Award in Case No. 6784, *ICC Ct. Bull.*, Vol. 8, No. 1 (1997), pp. 53-54.

upon it, thus possibly delaying or preventing the commencement of arbitration proceedings. In addition, the actual date of receipt of the Request by the Respondent may occasionally be disputed. Although, under the ICC provision, arbitration proceedings may be deemed to commence before the Respondent is aware of this, the new version of Article 4(1) should, as already noted, help to ensure that the Respondent is notified as soon as possible of the commencement of such proceedings. Moreover, the time limit in the Rules for the Respondent's Answer to the Request (*see* Article 5(1)) only begins to run as from the Respondent's receipt of the same and not as from the date of commencement of the arbitration proceedings.

One issue that may arise in connection with Article 4(2) is whether the arbitral proceedings should be deemed to have commenced when a Request is submitted without the required advance payment or the number of copies required (*see* Article 4(4)). In this connection, Article 4(2) only refers explicitly to the Request itself, and the Secretariat has always construed this provision without regard to the receipt of any payment or additional copies of the Request. During the work on the revision of the Rules, the Working Party considered whether this provision should contain a reference to the payment and copies required to be filed together with the Request, but concluded that no such change should be made. The mere submission of a Request to the ICC Secretariat should therefore suffice for the "commencement of the arbitral proceedings," subject, however, to the possible closure of the file subsequently pursuant to Article 4(4) if the requirements of that provision are not respected.

Article 4(3)

> *The Request shall, inter alia, contain the following information:*
> a) *the name in full, description and address of each of the parties;*
> b) *a description of the nature and circumstances of the dispute giving rise to the claims;*
> c) *a statement of the relief sought, including, to the extent possible, an indication of any amount(s) claimed;*
> d) *the relevant agreements and, in particular, the arbitration agreement;*
> e) *all relevant particulars concerning the number of arbitrators and their choice in accordance with the provisions of Articles 8, 9 and 10, and any nomination of an arbitrator required thereby; and*
> f) *any comments as to the place of arbitration, the applicable rules of law and the language of the arbitration.*

Background. As already noted, the Request is intended to be more than a simple "notice" of arbitration. Indeed, in the early years of ICC arbitration, the Request not only served the function of initiating the arbitration proceedings, but also often represented the Claimant's only written submission in relation to its claim, thus permitting the swift resolution of the dispute following the constitution of the Arbitral Tribunal. Over time, however, as international arbitrations have become increasingly complex and more aggressively litigated, the Request, as well as the Respondent's Answer, as discussed further below, have more commonly been used by parties primarily to introduce their claims on the assumption that they will subsequently have an opportunity to make more detailed written submissions. The Rules do not specifically provide for subsequent exchanges of written submissions, but they do not exclude them either and, indeed, the exchange of one or more sets of pleadings following the establishment of the Terms of Reference has become standard practice in ICC arbitrations.

Because substantial written pleadings are now commonly produced by the parties following the Terms of Reference, the Working Party considered, during the early work on the New Rules, whether the Request ought to be recast, as under many other arbitration rules, as a simple notice of arbitration. However, there was strong resistance to this. It was, on the contrary, generally felt that the requirement of a more ample Request has a number of advantages, both for the ICC Court, in making the various decisions that are incumbent upon it at the outset of the arbitration proceedings, and for the parties.[76] This being said, the Rules have always allowed the Claimant considerable discretion in deciding how much detail to provide in the Request concerning the nature and circumstances of its claim, and the new Rules were not intended to make any substantive changes in this regard. Article 4(3) nevertheless differs from its prior version (Article 3(2)) of the former Rules) in a number of respects, as follows:

First, instead of requiring "a statement of the Claimant's case" (Article 3(2)(b) of the previous Rules), Article 4(3) requires "a description of the nature and circumstances of the dispute giving rise to the claims" (subparagraph b) and "a statement of the relief sought, including, to the extent possible, an indication of any amounts claimed" (subparagraph c). These changes were intended to describe the information to be provided with more specificity than the previous reference to "a statement of the Claimant's case," which, in addition to being vague and a source of confusion, was not consistent with the corresponding provision in the French version of the Rules (which called for an *"exposé des prétentions du demandeur,"* or literally, a description of the Claimant's claims). As reformulated, the requirements of Article 4(3), although more specific and contemplating the provision of a minimum amount of information, nevertheless

---

[76] The advantages of a substantial Request have been well-described in *Craig Park and Paulsson,* §10.04, pp. 178-79, in the following terms:

First of all, this approach enables the ICC to select a good chairman. The Secretariat's description of the case to the National Committee asked to propose a presiding arbitrator is based only on materials provided by the parties. Furthermore, the initial dossier communicated by the ICC Secretariat to the arbitrators is bound to leave an impression on them. As the tribunal is formed for the sole purpose of hearing a single case, its members will wish to be informed of the nature of the case prior to the first meeting with the parties and prior to drawing up the Terms of Reference.... Furthermore, a full statement of claims allows the defendant's Answer to be a more responsive pleading. Hence, there is both a real and a psychological advantage to filing an extensive Request; there are few disadvantages.

allow parties the freedom to decide how much detail to provide, both with respect to the facts and the legal or contractual basis of their claims, as was previously the case.[77] The Claimant is, however, requested to provide an indication of the amounts claimed "to the extent possible" because of the relevance of this information to the determinations that the ICC Court and its Secretary General are required to make in fixing advances on costs for the arbitration.[78]

Second, Article 4(3) does not require, as did Article 3(2) of the earlier Rules, that the Request contain "such documentation or information as will serve clearly to establish the circumstances of the case." The earlier Rule appeared to require that all relevant documentary evidence be submitted together with the Request. Although Requests are commonly submitted together with supporting documentation, only rarely are they accompanied by all, or even most, of the documentation upon which parties may seek to rely in the arbitration. Rather, the bulk of the documentary evidence in most ICC arbitrations today is produced later, often together with the more detailed written pleadings that have become commonplace following the preparation of the Terms of Reference. Of course, nothing precludes a Claimant from submitting as much supporting documentation as it may wish together with the Request. However, its only obligation under the New Rules is to submit with the Request "the relevant agreements and, in particular, the arbitration agreement."[79]

Third, the requirements of Article 4(3) have been expanded, as compared to the former Article 3(2), to require expressly (*see* Article 4(3)(e)) the "nomination of an arbitrator," as required by the provisions on the constitution of the Arbitral Tribunal (*see* Articles 8-10), and to invite (*see* Article 4(3)(f)) "any comments as to the place of arbitration, the applicable rules of law and the language of the arbitration."

The requirement concerning the nomination of an arbitrator was, in fact, already implicit in the requirement of the previous version of the Rules that the Request contain "all relevant particulars concerning the number of arbitrators

---

[77] In this connection, *see* Kreindler, *supra*, note 14, pp. 68-70. Mr. Kreindler speculates, for example, that "a truncated list of mere categories of claims, without more, might arguably" have failed to satisfy the requirements of the previous Rules. The same might be argued under the New Rules, although it is not clear that this would be considered as invalidating the Request (*see infra*, "Ensuring compliance with the requirements of Article 4(3)").

[78] It is to be noted that Article 4(3) does not explicitly require the statement of a "claim," in contrast to Articles 18 and 19, which, respectively, require the arbitrators to summarize "the parties' respective claims" and regulate the submission of new "claims."

[79] While this appears to assume that there is a written arbitration agreement between the parties, the Rules do not, in fact, explicitly require that the arbitration agreement be in writing. With respect to the possible need for a written agreement, *see* the discussion of Article 6(2) *infra*. In addition, even where there is no earlier arbitration agreement between the parties, the Court's Secretariat will notify a Request to the Respondent in order to give the latter an opportunity to state whether it agrees to submit to arbitration. In at least one reported case, an Arbitral Tribunal was asked, but refused, to decide that a Request submitted without a copy of the arbitration agreement was, for this reason, "inadmissible." *See* the extract from the final Award in ICC Case No. 6784 (1990), *supra*, note 75.

and their choice" in accordance with the provisions regarding the Arbitral Tribunal. In this connection, as in the case of Article 2(4) of the former Rules, Article 8(4) of the New Rules (*see infra*) explicitly requires the Claimant to nominate an arbitrator for confirmation by the Court in its Request "[w]here the dispute is to be referred to three arbitrators." This the Claimant must therefore obviously do when the parties' arbitration agreement provides for three arbitrators. However, neither Article 8(4) nor any other provision of the Rules clearly indicates whether the Claimant is required to nominate an arbitrator in its Request when there is not a prior agreement on the number of arbitrators, but the Claimant proposes the appointment of three arbitrators in its Request. For many years, it has been the position of the Secretariat that the Claimant is not required to nominate an arbitrator in its Request in such circumstances as, until either the Respondent agrees with the Claimant's proposal or the Court decides that there shall be three arbitrators, it will not be clear that the dispute "is to be referred" to three arbitrators.[80] But it is nevertheless in the Claimant's interest to nominate an arbitrator in its Request if it wishes to expedite the constitution of the tribunal and also possibly be in a position to argue that the Respondent, if it agrees with the proposal of three arbitrators, must nominate an arbitrator within 30 days from receipt of the Request (*see* the discussion of Article 5(1) and (2) *infra*).[81]

As regards the place of arbitration, the applicable rules of law and the language of the arbitration, the Claimant's comments are invited because of their relevance to the decisions that the Court may be required to make when setting the arbitration proceedings in motion. While parties usually comment on such matters – indeed, relevant provisions are often contained in the arbitration clause – there are nevertheless many occasions when they fail to do so, and time may be lost in setting the proceedings in motion while the Court's Secretariat undertakes to solicit their views. It is to be noted, however, that the new rule does not actually require the Claimant to comment on any of the foregoing matters. But if the Claimant fails to do so, it runs the risk that the Court will fix the place of arbitration and constitute the Arbitral Tribunal without regard to the Claimant's possible position on the matters set forth in Article 4(3)(f).

In practice, parties need to be careful when commenting on the place of arbitration, in particular. (For a discussion of the factors that the Court takes into account when fixing the place, *see* the discussion of Article 14 *infra*.) When the parties are unable to agree on a place and the Court is required to make the decision, the Court has ordinarily wished, in the past, to avoid appearing to favor either of the parties, and this has usually led it to refuse to fix as a place any place to which one of the parties may have objected, provided, however, that there are

---

[80]   For a concurring view, *see* Kreindler, *supra*, note 14, pp. 58-59. *But compare Craig Park and Paulsson*, §10.04, p. 179, where it is stated that the Claimant must nominate an arbitrator in the Request if it "requests a three-member tribunal."

[81]   It has nevertheless also been argued that it may be disadvantageous for the Claimant to nominate an arbitrator before it knows the Respondent's position on the number of arbitrators. *See* Kreindler, *supra,* note 14, p. 59.

satisfactory alternative venues. One party's objection to a place does not necessarily suffice to exclude it. But even where a party has not provided a compelling argument for its objection to a particular venue, the Court can be expected, in the ordinary case, to try to find another place that neither party has commented on negatively if it appears to the Court to be a suitable venue.

Insofar as the language of the arbitration is concerned (*see* Article 16 *infra*), Article 4(3) does not impose any particular requirements, apart from inviting the parties' comments. If the parties have agreed in the arbitration clause on the language of the arbitration, then the Request for Arbitration should ordinarily be submitted in that language (although Article 4(3) does not actually say so). If a Claimant fails to do so, however, the Secretariat may nevertheless notify the Request, as submitted, to the Respondent party in order to provide it with an opportunity to comment. Were the Respondent to insist that the Request be put into the agreed language of the arbitration, then the Secretariat could be expected to insist that the Claimant do so before requiring the Respondent to submit an Answer pursuant to Article 5, provided, however, that there had been a clear breach of the parties' arbitration agreement. On at least one occasion, the Secretariat was faced with the objection of a Respondent party that some of the documents appended as exhibits to the Request had not been translated into the agreed language of the arbitration, and the Respondent took the position that the Request was defective and that it would not submit an Answer in the circumstances. The Claimant itself then withdrew the Request and later filed a new one with the requested translations. However, it is unlikely that the Secretariat would, in such a case, have itself insisted upon this. It is more likely that it would have granted the Respondent a reasonable extension of time to submit an Answer and left it up to the Arbitral Tribunal to decide whether translations should be required, depending on all of the circumstances.[82]

Where, as is common, the parties have not agreed on the language of the arbitration, it is for the Arbitral Tribunal to determine the language or languages to be used (*see* Article 16 *infra*). Some other arbitration rules provide that, where the parties have not agreed on the language, the language of the arbitration shall be the language of the arbitration agreement or of the documents in which it is contained, unless or until the Arbitral Tribunal determines otherwise.[83] The ICC Rules do not, however, contain any such rule of default, and, consequently, until

---

[82] *See*, in this regard, the extract from the interim Award in ICC Case No. 6228, *ICC Ct. Bull.*, Vol. 8, No. 1 (1997), p. 53. In that case, the arbitration clause specified that English would be the language of the arbitration, but the Claimant submitted its Request in French. The Respondent was not required to submit its Answer until after an English translation had been provided. As the English translation was not signed, however, the Respondent argued that the arbitration proceedings had not been "properly initiated," a claim that the Arbitral Tribunal rejected as it considered that the Respondent's rights of defense had not been prejudiced in the circumstances. It should also be noted that the Rules do not themselves require the Request to be signed.

[83] *See, e.g.*, AAA International Arbitration Rules, Article 14; LCIA Rules, Article 17; WIPO Arbitration Rules, Article 17.

an Arbitral Tribunal has been constituted and is in a position to decide upon the language, the language of the proceedings will remain uncertain, in the event of a disagreement between the parties. This effectively permits the parties to use whatever language they may choose in preparing the Request, the Answer and other possible applications or submissions prior to a decision being made on the matter by the Arbitral Tribunal, which can severely inconvenience a party that does not understand the language used by the other. The Secretariat is neverthe-less not likely to require a party to provide translations of its submissions in such circumstances, nor should the Court, pending a determination by the arbitrators, be expected to fix a language for the arbitration provisionally. The Secretariat is free, however, to use whatever language it considers appropriate in its own cor-respondence with the parties and to request that the parties correspond with it in a language that is understood by the Secretariat's staff in order to facilitate the administration of the case by the ICC.[84] Ordinarily, unless the parties otherwise agree, the Secretariat can be expected to correspond with them in the language of the relevant contract (provided that it is able to do so) until the language of the arbitration is determined.

Ensuring compliance with the requirements of Article 4(3). When a document calling itself a Request for Arbitration is received by the Secretariat, the Secretariat reviews it in order to determine that it contains the information required to be included in a Request. Thus, for example, in those occasional instances in the past when the Secretariat has received a simple letter requesting the ICC to initiate arbitration proceedings against another party, or a request of a similarly abbreviated nature, the Secretariat has normally returned the letter together with an explanation that a Request for Arbitration is required to include the various items listed in the Rules, and as the document received did not include the required information, it did not constitute a Request for Arbitration.

This being said, the Secretariat has been reluctant to undertake to verify, thoroughly and systematically, the Claimant's compliance with all of the requirements of the Rules relating to the Request, and the Court has also gener-ally avoided having to decide whether all of the relevant requirements have been satisfied, in cases of disagreement. Thus, for example, in one case the Court was asked by a disgruntled Respondent party to determine whether the Claimant had provided a sufficient statement of its case, as required under the former Rules. The Court refused to decide the matter, however, and directed that the issue be considered by the Arbitral Tribunal. Indeed, as a general rule, neither the Court nor the Secretariat has wished to be responsible for deciding upon the sufficien-cy of a party's satisfaction of specific requirements of the Rules, in cases where this is disputed, except possibly where the alleged breach is manifest (*see* the discussion of Article 1(2) *supra*). Moreover, it has not generally been the

---

[84] At present, the Secretariat routinely corresponds with parties in English, French, German and Spanish.

position of either the Court, or those arbitrators who have been called upon to decide upon such matters, that a defect in a Request should have the consequence of invalidating it, provided that it is correctible.

Thus, for example, a fairly common violation of the Rules' requirements relating to the Request occurs when a party submits a Request without nominating an arbitrator, although the Rules explicitly mandate this when the arbitration clause provides for three arbitrators (*see* the discussion of Article 8(4) *infra*). Particularly now that Article 4(3)(e) expressly requires the nomination of an arbitrator in the Request in such circumstances, it might be argued that the Secretariat should refuse to accept the Request, or to notify it, when this requirement has not been satisfied. However, this has not been the Secretariat's practice. Rather, the Secretariat has generally accepted such Requests and notified them, while at the same time drawing the Claimant's attention to the requirements of the Rules and inviting it to nominate an arbitrator, failing which the Court would be invited to appoint an arbitrator in its stead. This is, in fact, consistent with Article 8(4) of the Rules (*see infra*), which specifically foresees the possible failure of a party to nominate an arbitrator in its Request and provides a remedy. It is, moreover, also consistent with the generally pragmatic wish of both the Secretariat and the Court (and ICC arbitrators) to "save" the Request and the arbitration whenever reasonably possible. Thus, for example, in a case where a Respondent contended that a Request was "inadmissible" because of the Claimant's failure to provide a complete statement of its case, to attach a copy of the arbitration agreement and simultaneously pay the ICC administrative fee, the Arbitral Tribunal held otherwise.[85] Another Arbitral Tribunal also refused to decide that ICC arbitral proceedings had been invalidly initiated where the Request was submitted in a language other than the agreed language of the arbitration, a translation having been furnished before the Respondent was required to submit its Answer.[86] It was the view of the Arbitral Tribunal in each of those cases that the Respondent had not been prejudiced.

Similarly, for as long as a Claimant fails to comply with its obligation to nominate an arbitrator, the Respondent should not have to nominate an arbitrator either (notwithstanding the requirements of Article 5, as discussed below), and the Secretariat has not ordinarily required that it do so. However, the Secretariat has not generally considered that a Claimant's failure to nominate an arbitrator in its Request excuses the Respondent from otherwise answering the Request.

Amendments of the Request. Neither Article 4(3) nor any other provision of the Rules addresses the issues that may arise when a party wishes to amend its Request for Arbitration. Generally, until the Terms of Reference have been estab-

---

[85] *See* the extract from the final Award in ICC Case No. 6784 (1990), *supra*, note 75.
[86] *See* the extract from the interim Award in ICC Case No. 6228 (1990), *supra*, note 82.

lished (*see* Articles 18 and 19 *infra*), a Claimant is free to amend its Request. Although it may occasionally be argued by Respondents that the submission of an amended Request is tantamount to the commencement of a new arbitration, or alternatively should be considered to restart the clock for the submission of the Respondent's Answer (if an Answer has not already been submitted), this has not been the position of the Secretariat. Rather, an amendment has ordinarily been regarded as a supplemental written submission, which the Claimant is free to make before the establishment of the Terms of Reference (*see* Article 18 *infra*).

The situation is likely to be more complicated, however, if the amendment concerns the parties to the arbitration and, in particular, the addition (or substitution) of one or more Claimant or Respondent parties. Whenever a new party is being joined, the arbitration is entirely new as far as the joined party is concerned, and an amended Request, like a new Request, must be formally notified to all of the Respondents, including any new Respondent party, by the Secretariat (*see* Article 4(5) *infra*). In addition, any new Respondent should be given the same opportunity as the other Respondents to submit an Answer, and the latter should also be entitled to reconsider their positions in the light of the joinder of a new party. This may also be the case when a Claimant party is added or changes, given the possible jurisdictional issues, among others, that may arise. Whether, in the circumstances, it is appropriate for the ICC to treat the amended Request as commencing a new arbitration, from an administrative point of view, will generally be for the Secretariat or the Court to decide.

A Claimant wishing to amend a Request to introduce a new party may have no alternative, in any event, but to begin a new arbitration if the original arbitration is already so advanced as to preclude the joinder of an additional party without the consent of the others. Thus, for example, once an Arbitral Tribunal has been constituted, the Claimant should no longer be free to join a Respondent without its consent as it will otherwise have been deprived of its right to participate in the tribunal's constitution.[87] More generally, the Court has, in the past, refused to permit the joinder of parties, in the absence of the parties' consent or an agreed procedure for deciding upon the permissibility of such joinder, once the Court has "set the arbitration in motion."[88] There is nothing in the Rules, however, that mandates such a strict position, and it can reasonably be questioned whether the possibility of joining a party should depend upon the administrative status of an arbitration within the Court. Arguably, the primary consideration ought to be whether there would be any possible prejudice to the rights of the parties if such a joinder were permitted.

---

[87]   *See* the discussion of Article 10 *infra*.

[88]   *See, e.g.,* "Final Report on Multi-party Arbitrations", *supra*, note 21, p. 34:
The claimant, as the person who initiated the proceeding, may extend its Request to other defendants not initially identified, before the Court decides upon setting the arbitration proceeding in motion.... Once the Court has taken its initial decisions to set the proceeding in motion, voluntary intervention or joinder of a third party by a claimant requires the agreement of all of the parties....

Article 4(4)

> *Together with the Request, the Claimant shall submit the number of copies thereof required by Article 3(1) and shall make the advance payment on administrative expenses required by Appendix III ("Arbitration Costs and Fees") in force on the date the Request is submitted. In the event that the Claimant fails to comply with either of these requirements, the Secretariat may fix a time limit within which the Claimant must comply, failing which the file shall be closed without prejudice to the right of the Claimant to submit the same claims at a later date in another Request.*

This is a new provision, although it does not alter the previous practices of the Court. The first sentence is merely intended to draw attention to the separate requirements of Article 3, which determines the number of copies of the Request to be submitted, and Appendix III to the Rules ("Arbitration Costs and Fees"), which sets forth the amount to be paid to the ICC together with the Request (U.S. $2,500 as from January 1, 1998).[89] The second sentence (which should be read together with Article 4(5)) formalizes what has, in fact, been the Court's practice for a number of years.

When this provision was first proposed for inclusion in the New Rules, the question arose, as already noted (*see* the discussion of Article 4(2) *supra*), whether, given its requirements, an arbitration should be deemed to have commenced pursuant to Article 4(2) if a Request is not accompanied by the required copies and payment. However, the commencement of the arbitral proceedings under Article 4(2) is, pursuant to its terms, dependent only upon the receipt of the Request itself, and Article 4(4) was deliberately drafted so as to make it clear that the copies and payment required are not part of the Request.[90]

When the Request is received without the number of copies and payment required, the Secretariat normally requests the Claimant to provide the same within a specified time limit, as indicated in Article 4(4). For several years, the counsels within the Secretariat have had standing instructions not to grant more than fifteen days for this purpose except, possibly, in exceptional circumstances (*e.g.,* where a payment is late due to a delay in obtaining governmental exchange control approval). Indeed, the Respondent ought not to have to await indefinitely to receive a Request insofar as, pursuant to Article 4(2), it has the effect

---

[89]   *See* Article 1(1) of Appendix III, which also specifies that the amount in question "is nonrefundable, and shall be credited to the Claimant's portion of the advance on costs."

[90]   This has not, however, always been the Court's interpretation of the Rules' requirements. A draft Secretariat Handbook prepared in 1987 stated, "The date of receipt of a request is the date when the request *and* the advance on costs was received." *But see,* in this connection, the extract from the final Award in ICC Case No. 6784 (1990), *supra*, note 75, in which the Arbitral Tribunal found that a party's failure to pay the required advance together with the Request did not affect the admissibility of the Request.

of commencing proceedings against it. Thus, as Article 4(4) now states express-ly, the Secretariat has the power to close the file if the required payment and cop-ies are not received within the time limit fixed.

As regards the copies required to be submitted, it has not generally been the Secretariat's practice, however, to close the file if some copies are missing, but there are sufficient copies to permit the notification of the Request to each Respondent, in accordance with Article 4(5), plus one for the Secretariat. In fact, the Secretariat does not really require the additional copies, which are for the arbitrators, until the arbitrators have been appointed, and in many cases the num-ber of arbitrators may not even be known when the Request is filed (*see* the dis-cussion of Article 3 *supra*). Understandably, however, the Secretariat wishes to have all of the necessary copies on hand in due course so as not to delay the transmission of the file to the Arbitral Tribunal once it has been constituted; but this is normally also in the Claimant's interest.

One issue that may arise with respect to the application of Article 4(4), and also other rules on payment (in particular Article 30(4), as discussed *infra*) is when a payment should be considered to have been "made." In this regard, the Secretariat's long-standing practice has to been to a consider that a payment is made on the date when, in the case of an interbank transfer, the funds are received in the ICC's bank account or on the date of receipt by the Secretariat of a corre-sponding check or cash. It is therefore not sufficient for a party, within the period fixed, to instruct its bank to make the payment or to put a check in the mail.

Article 4(5)

> *The Secretariat shall send a copy of the Request and the documents annexed thereto to the Respondent for its Answer to the Request once the Secretariat has sufficient copies of the Request and the required advance payment.*

Article 4(5) replaces Article 3(3) of the previous Rules. It is identical except that, as already discussed with respect to Article 4(4), the receipt by the Secretariat of sufficient copies of the Request and the required advance payment are now expressly stated to be conditions to the notification of the Request (which they already were in practice).

Once the Secretariat has received the required payment and copies, it endeavors to send the Request to the Respondent as quickly as possible, typical-ly within two to three days. The Request is transmitted to the Respondent by the counsel whom the Secretary General has assigned to the arbitration and is accompanied by a letter in a standardized Secretariat format together with a copy of the Rules and information about the costs of the arbitration. The letter draws the Respondent's attention to the requirements of the Rules that are rele-vant to the submission of its Answer, including, in particular, the constitution of the Arbitral Tribunal.

In sending the Request to the Respondent, the Secretariat is required to respect the requirements of Article 3(2). However, Article 3(2) allows the Secretariat a number of different options from which to choose in notifying the Request and does not mandate the use of a single, standard method of notification. Usually, the Secretariat uses the method that appears most reasonable in the circumstances, consistent with its wish to expedite the proceedings. Thus, the Secretariat has, for many years, routinely used special courier services for all notifications outside Europe. Within Europe, Requests have more commonly been notified by registered mail, return receipt requested, except where the postal service in the country of the addressee does not return postal receipts, is not considered to be sufficiently efficient or reliable or the mails are otherwise disrupted. The cost of notification, by whatever method (and irrespective of the number of Respondent parties), is borne by the ICC and is intended to be covered by the advance payment submitted together with the Request. Thus, parties are not separately charged for this, irrespective of the cost to the ICC.

Occasionally, the Secretariat is unable to use either the mails or special courier services because of embargoes or other circumstances. It has, thus, from time to time, had recourse to diplomatic channels or otherwise sought to find some other means of effecting delivery. In all cases, however, it seeks to ensure that it has evidence of the actual delivery of the Request so that it can verify when the time period for the submission of the Respondent's Answer (*see* Article 5) has begun to run.

Unlike the previous Rules, Article 3(2) now also permits the Secretariat to notify documents by fax and other means of telecommunication that "provide a record of the sending thereof." It is therefore now open to the Secretariat to notify Requests in this manner, although it remains to be seen whether, and to what extent, the Secretariat will make use of this possibility. Apart from possible difficulties in obtaining proof of receipt, many Requests are simply too voluminous for cost-efficient transmission by fax. Although the Secretariat may choose, in certain cases, to notify Requests by fax, followed by the transmittal by mail of a confirming hard copy, the question may then arise as to whether the date of receipt of the fax or of the confirming hard copy should be treated as the date of "receipt" for the purpose of the deadline fixed for the Respondent's Answer. Given the provisions of Article 3(2), however, there would not seem to be any reason why the date of receipt of the fax should not be the operative date, provided, however, that it can be established.

Article 4(6)

> *When a party submits a Request in connection with a legal relationship in respect of which arbitration proceedings between the same parties are already pending under these Rules, the Court may, at the request of a party, decide to include the claims contained in the Request in the pending proceedings, provided that the Terms of Reference have not been signed or approved by the Court. Once the Terms of Reference have been signed or approved by the Court, claims may only be included in the pending proceedings subject to the provisions of Article 19.*

Background. Article 4(6) is the only provision of the Rules that deals with the possible joinder (or consolidation) of arbitral proceedings. It has been imported into the New Rules, with only minor modifications, from the Court's Internal Rules, of which it had been a part since the original publication of the Internal Rules in 1980.

For many years, the subject of the joinder, or consolidation, of related arbitration proceedings has been a source of difficulty and controversy.[91] The orthodox view is that arbitration is a consensual process and that therefore the joinder or consolidation of arbitration proceedings should be permitted only with the consent of all of the parties concerned. However, there are circumstances in which it would be more efficient and economical, and also help to avoid inconsistent results, if related disputes were resolved in a single proceeding, although parties often do not take account of this when agreeing to arbitration. Indeed, the standard arbitration clauses of institutions such as the ICC (*see* Appendix 1 *infra*) do not provide for matters such as joinder or consolidation. In the circumstances, legislators and arbitral institutions have, from time to time, been called upon, in the interest of the efficient administration of justice, to provide mechanisms for the possible joinder or consolidation of related arbitrations. However, few have been willing to take up the call, primarily because of the variety and complexity of the different circumstances that may arise.[92] In the case of the ICC, Article 4(6) represents the most that the institution has been willing to provide for in the Rules on this subject, although it has long been the Court's position that the parties are free to agree to join or consolidate arbitra-

---

[91] *See, e.g.*, Jarvin, "Issues Relating to Consolidation," *Multi-party Arbitration* (ICC Publishing 1991), p. 199; Mustill, "Multipartite Arbitrations: An Agenda for Lawmakers," *Arb. Int.*, Vol. 7, No. 4 (1991), p. 393; Wallace, "Consolidated Arbitration in the United States," *J. Arb. Int.*, Vol. 10, No. 4 (1993), p. 5; Level, "Joinder of Proceedings, Intervention of Third Parties, and Additional Claims and Counterclaims," *ICC Ct. Bull.*, Vol. 7, No. 2 (1996), p. 36.

[92] *See, e.g.*, "Consolidation: The Second Report of the United Kingdom Departmental Advisory Committee on Arbitration Law," *Arb. Int.*, Vol. 7, No. 4 (1991), p. 389; *but cf.* Article 1046 of the Netherlands Arbitration Act 1986; *and* Section 6B of the Hong Kong Arbitration Ordinance 1982.

tions independently of Article 4(6). Article 4(6) therefore does not preclude alternative agreements of the parties.

Conditions of joinder. The joinder of more than one arbitration under Article 4(6) requires an affirmative decision of the Court. Thus, the arbitrators do not have any authority to decide to join arbitration cases, although, independently of Article 4(6), they may, pursuant to Article 19, admit new claims or counterclaims in a pending arbitration (*see infra*). The Court's authority to join an arbitration with another arbitration that is already pending depends, pursuant to Article 4(6), on the satisfaction of the following conditions:

– Joinder is requested by a party;
– The arbitration proceedings are between the same parties;
– They are "in connection with" the same "legal relationship"; and
– The Terms of Reference have not yet been signed or approved by the Court (or, if they have, the claims that are sought to be added must be admissible under Article 19 of the Rules).[93]

The consent of all of the parties, however, is not required as a condition for any such joinder.

The first observation that might reasonably be made about the above conditions is that they are very narrow. In fact, they are so narrow that it can legitimately be asked what purpose Article 4(6) actually serves. If a party wishes to pursue claims against a party with whom it is already engaged in an arbitration in connection with the same legal relationship, and Terms of Reference have not yet been signed or approved, then it should normally be free to introduce those claims in the already pending arbitration (*see* the discussion of Article 18 *infra*). It should not have to commence a new arbitration and request its joinder with the first, as contemplated by Article 4(6). Moreover, if Terms of Reference have already been established, a party is also free to apply to the Arbitral Tribunal in the already pending proceeding in order to have new claims included, pursuant to Article 19 of the Rules. If the Arbitral Tribunal denies the application, then joinder would not otherwise be permitted pursuant to the express terms of Article 4(6).

Article 4(6) would therefore only appear to serve a purpose when the party seeking the joinder is not the party making the claims that are sought to be joined; for, as just noted, a party asserting new claims should not normally be

---

[93] Of these conditions, only the first is new. The previous provision in the Internal Rules (Article 13) did not explicitly require that joinder be requested by a party and, theoretically, permitted the Court to decide to join two cases on its own initiative. However, it never did so in practice. As regards the final condition, the modification of Article 19 (as compared to Article 16 of the previous Rules) effectively means that, once the Terms of Reference have been established, joinder will depend upon the Arbitral Tribunal's willingness to allow the introduction of the new claims in question in the arbitration, although the Court is not required, even if the Arbitral Tribunal agrees, to provide for the joinder of the arbitrations concerned.

required to commence a new arbitration for that purpose if all of the conditions of Article 4(6) are satisfied. However, occasionally a party may decide to commence a new arbitration deliberately with respect to claims that it would be free to introduce in an already pending proceeding, usually for the purpose of gaining some perceived tactical advantage. It may, for example, be unhappy with the Arbitral Tribunal constituted for the already pending case or it may simply not wish, colloquially speaking, to "place all of its eggs in one basket." It may otherwise simply wish to make the process more complicated and expensive, to the extent possible, for its adversary. In these circumstances, Article 4(6) can serve a purpose, as the other party may apply to the Court to request that the new arbitration be joined with the arbitration already pending between the same parties in connection with the same legal relationship.

In recent years, however, the Court has generally been reluctant to order the joinder of two arbitrations over the objection of one of the parties.[94] This has had the effect of depriving the provision regarding joinder of any real utility as, for the reasons just given, the only situation in which such a provision is actually needed is where, by definition, one of the parties does not wish to include its claims in an already pending arbitration between the same parties. It remains to be seen whether the Court, in the future, will be more disposed towards making use of the limited powers that it has under Article 4(6) and in what circumstances.

In this connection, it has been suggested that a party introducing a second arbitration can prevent its joinder with an already pending case simply by proposing a different arbitrator from the one that it had chosen for the first arbitration.[95] However, there is no reason why the mere proposal of a new arbitrator should preclude the Court from deciding to join a new arbitration with a previous one. If, in such circumstances, the Court were to decide to join the arbitrations, the nomination would no longer serve any purpose and presumably would not be confirmed (*see* with respect to confirmation, the discussion of Article 9 *infra*), there no longer being a second arbitration. If, however, one or more arbitrators had already been confirmed or appointed by the Court for the second arbitration, this could dissuade the Court from joining the arbitrations as it would be required to cause the newly-appointed arbitrators to step down. Indeed, it has been asserted in this connection that once an Arbitral Tribunal has been constituted for a second arbitration, it "becomes impossible," at least without the agreement of all of the parties, to join the claims in that arbitration with another arbitration if the tribunals in the two cases are different.[96] However,

---

[94]   *See* Hascher, Note on Award in ICC Case No. 5989 (1989), *Clunet* (1997), pp. 1046, 1049.

[95]   Leboulanger, "Multi-Contract Arbitration," *J. Arb. Int.,* Vol. 13, No. 4 (1996), p. 43, 93; Kassis, *Réflexions sur le règlement d'arbitrage de la chambre de commerce internationale – Les déviations de l'arbitrage institutionnel* (LGDJ 1988), Nos. 403 *et. seq.*

[96]   "Final Report on Multi-party Arbitrations," *supra,* note 21, p. 35. *See also* Arnaldez, Note on Award in ICC Case No. 6719, *ICC Awards 1991-1995,* p. 567, and Hascher, *supra,* note 94. In one unusual case, at the request of the parties, the Court accepted to join two arbitrations with different tribunals on the condition that the tribunal for the joined cases would be composed of four arbitrators. *See,* in this regard, Article 8(1) *infra*.

Article 4(6) does not by its terms preclude this, provided that its conditions are otherwise satisfied. If, in such circumstances, the arbitration claims in the second case were joined to those in the first, the arbitrators in the second case would arguably be in no different a position than if the arbitration had been withdrawn and would presumably become *functus officio.*

One other possible source of difficulty in the application of Article 4(6) relates to the requirement that the arbitrations in question must concern the same "legal relationship." When two arbitrations concern the same contract, the "legal relationship" in each case is obviously the same. However, in choosing the broader term "legal relationship" (rather than "contract"), the drafters appear to have left open the possibility of joinder in other possible circumstances, *i.e.,* where it may have been the parties' intention to have disputes arising in connection with more than one contract resolved in a single arbitration proceeding. Such an intention may either be expressly stated in connection with a series of inter-related contracts, or it may otherwise be inferred from the circumstances of a particular case. Indeed, as discussed further below with respect to Article 6(2), there are circumstances in which inter-connected agreements have been found effectively to constitute a single relationship permitting the arbitration of all related disputes in one proceeding.

This being said, if the Court has any doubt as to the existence of a single "legal relationship" within the meaning of Article 4(6), it would not be likely to decide to join separate arbitrations. When an ICC arbitration is commenced by a party in respect of a multiplicity of allegedly related transactions, the Court can, in the event that the Respondent objects, allow the Arbitral Tribunal to decide whether all of the matters set forth in the Request for Arbitration fall within its jurisdiction (and arguably, it should normally do so)[97] (*see* the discussion of Article 6(2) *infra*). If the Arbitral Tribunal decides that the Claimant was wrong to start a single arbitration, then the Claimant is itself responsible for this. Where, however, two separate arbitrations are commenced in respect of separate, but allegedly inter-connected, agreements, and the other party asserts that the arbitrations should be joined on the basis that they, in fact, each concern the same "legal relationship," the Court might understandably not wish to assume responsibility for joining arbitrations as to which it might ultimately be found that joinder is improper.

ARTICLE 5
Answer to the Request; Counterclaims

Article 5 combines in a single provision Articles 4 and 5 of the former Rules concerning the Answer and Counterclaims, respectively. Apart from consolida-

---

[97] But for a contrary view, *see* Leboulanger, *supra,* note 95, pp. 95-96, where it is argued that the Court ought to take the initiative of requiring the separation of arbitral proceedings in certain circumstances. The Court has, in fact, done so from time to time. *See*, in this connection, Hascher, *supra*, note 94; Gravel, "Multiparty Arbitration and Multiple Arbitrations," *ICC Ct. Bull.*, Vol. 7, No. 2 (1996), pp. 45, 48.

ting those two provisions and making a certain number of drafting changes, intended primarily to take into account the changes made to Article 4, Article 5 does not substantively alter the Respondent's obligations in respect of its Answer and Counterclaims or the Secretariat's related practices, as described below.

Article 5(1)

> *Within 30 days from the receipt of the Request from the Secretariat, the Respondent shall file an Answer (the "Answer") which shall, inter alia, contain the following information:*
> *a) its name in full, description and address;*
> *b) its comments as to the nature of the circumstances of the dispute giving rise to the claim(s);*
> *c) its response to the relief sought;*
> *d) any comments concerning the number of arbitrators and their choice in light of the Claimant's proposals and in accordance with the provisions of Articles 8, 9 and 10, and any nomination of an arbitrator required thereby; and*
> *e) any comments as to the place of arbitration, the applicable rules of law and the language of the arbitration.*

Article 5(1) fixes the period of time within which the Answer must be submitted and sets forth its required contents.

Time period. Subject to obtaining an extension of time pursuant to Article 5(2), the Respondent is required to "file" its Answer within 30 days of its receipt of the Request from the Secretariat.[98] Article 5(1), like most, but not all, other arbitration rules, thus, makes the Respondent's receipt of the Request the operative event triggering the commencement of the time period for the submission of an Answer.[99] In addition, Article 5(1) resembles most other arbitration rules in limiting that period to 30 days.[100]

The 30-day period fixed in Article 5(1) was introduced into the Rules in 1927, and has survived ever since, even though it is an extremely short period

---

[98] Article 5(1) does not itself state that the Answer is to be filed with the Secretariat. However, this follows from Articles 5(3) and (4), as discussed below. Article 5(1) also does not specify when the Answer should be deemed to have been "filed," but the Secretariat would be likely to take the position, consistent with Article 3(3), that a document is "filed" when it is received by the Secretariat, although, as already discussed, Article 3(3) does not, by its terms, apply to submissions made by the parties.

[99] A different approach has been adopted in the AAA International Arbitration Rules, however, which provide (Article 3) that the respondent's statement of defense and counterclaim are to be submitted "[w]ithin 30 days after the commencement of the arbitration," which is the date of receipt of the notice of arbitration by the administrator.

[100] Until their most recent amendment on April 1, 1997, the AAA International Arbitration Rules provided for a 45-day period, but that period has now been shortened to 30 days.

of time – in fact, unrealistically so for many, or even most, international cases. Indeed, in some cases, it may take the whole 30 days, if not more, for the Respondent simply to locate, retain and brief counsel. In 1975, a provision was therefore added to the Rules permitting the Secretariat to extend the time limit in individual cases, which the Secretariat now does almost routinely (*see* the discussion of Article 5(2) *infra*).[101] Nonetheless, the ICC did not consider that it would be appropriate to alter the existing time period, given that one of the very objectives of the New Rules is to accelerate the arbitration process.

One minor difference, however, between Article 5(1) and Article 4 of the previous Rules is that it is now specified that the time period for the Answer begins to run as from the receipt of the Request "from the Secretariat." This clarification is intended to remove any uncertainty as to what has long been the Secretariat's practice. Indeed, occasionally the Claimant may send a copy of the Request directly to the Respondent before it is notified to the Respondent by the ICC. In such cases, it has sometimes been asked whether the "receipt" to which the Rules refer is intended to relate exclusively to receipt from the Secretariat or whether it might also include receipt from the Claimant directly. Article 5(1) now makes it clear that, although the Claimant is free to send the Request to the Respondent when submitting it to the ICC, the time available to the Respondent for answering it depends only on its date of receipt from the Secretariat.

Normally, the date of receipt will, as already discussed (*see* Article 4(5) *supra*), be evidenced by a document, either from the delivering postal service or courier, attesting that the Request was delivered on that date. As already noted with respect to Article 3(2), there is no requirement that delivery must be made to any particular authorized person. It is sufficient, for the purpose of the Rules, if the Request has been delivered to the Respondent's address. It is therefore immaterial whether the Request may, for example, subsequently have been lost in the Respondent's mail room or was routed to the wrong person in its organization, although these are circumstances, if they were to occur, that might be taken into consideration by the Secretariat in deciding upon an application for an extension of time.

Parties normally wish to comply with the deadline set forth in Article 5(1), as possibly extended pursuant to Article 5(2). However, there is no sanction under the Rules for a party's failure to do so.[102] Thus, if a party fails to submit its Answer within the period set forth in Article 5, it does not automatically lose the right to set out its defense subsequently.[103] On the contrary, until an Arbitral

---

[101] In fact, the Secretariat was in the habit of granting extensions prior to 1975, but it was only in 1975 that its authority to do so was first recognized in the Rules. *See* Eisemann, *"Le nouveau règlement d'arbitrage de la Chambre de Commerce Internationale," Droit et Pratique du Commerce International,* Vol. 1, No. 3 (1975), pp. 355, 356-57.

[102] *See, e.g.* , Eisemann, *supra,* note 101, p. 356 (*"Ce délai n'a toujours été qu'un délai d'ordre et non pas de forclusion."*) (Translation: "This period has never been more than an administrative deadline, and not a period of limitation.").

[103] This has repeatedly been confirmed in ICC arbitration Awards. *See, e.g.*, the extracts from the Awards in Cases Nos. 6039 (1992) and 6589 (1992), *ICC Ct. Bull.*, Vol. 8, No. 1 (1997), pp. 54, 63, *and* in Case No. 6192 (1992), *ICC Ct. Bull.*, Vol. 8, No. 2 (1997), p. 64.

Tribunal has been constituted and has drawn up its Terms of Reference (*see* the discussion of Article 18 *infra*), the Respondent is normally free to make such written submissions as it may wish. Absent an agreement of the parties, moreover, the Rules leave it to the Arbitral Tribunal to decide upon the appropriate procedures to be followed in the arbitration (*see* the discussion of Articles 15 and 20 *infra*), and arbitrators are normally very concerned to ensure that a Respondent has had a reasonable opportunity to present its defense. While a tribunal may, in establishing the procedures to be followed, take account of a Respondent's possible failure to use the opportunity that it had to submit an Answer in accordance with the Rules, it would nevertheless normally afford it a further opportunity to set out its defense, failing which the tribunal would be required to proceed with the arbitration (*see* the discussion of Article 6(3) *infra*).

A party that does not file its Answer within the period specified in Article 5(1) also runs the risk that, when deciding upon such matters as the constitution of the Arbitral Tribunal and the advance on costs, the Court will not have the benefit of the Respondent's view of the case. Although the Rules do not specify when the Court is to make these determinations, in the past the Secretariat has often awaited the expiration of the deadline for the submission of the Respondent's Answer before placing a case on the Court's agenda for the first time. Given the Court's wish to expedite the process, however, it is likely that, in the future, cases will more frequently be placed before the Court upon the expiration of the 30-day period set forth in Article 5(1), irrespective, moreover, of whether the Respondent has been granted an extension of time pursuant to Article 5(2). In addition, under Article 13 (as discussed below), the Secretariat is now required to transmit the file to the Arbitral Tribunal as soon as it has been constituted, provided that the required advances have been paid. Thus, delay in the submission of the Answer increases the likelihood that all that the Arbitral Tribunal will have in the file when it receives it from the Secretariat is a copy of the Claimant's Request.

Contents. No more than in the case of the Request do the Rules impose any rigid requirements regarding the form of the Respondent's Answer or the amount of detail to be provided with respect to the substance of the case therein. As the Respondent will normally have additional opportunities to elaborate upon, or add to, its defenses during the arbitration, how much it chooses to say in its Answer will generally depend upon the circumstances of the case, including, in particular, the content of the Request. It is important to remember, in this connection that, like the Request in the case of the Claimant, the Answer provides the Respondent with its first opportunity to make an impression on the Arbitral Tribunal.

Unlike some other arbitration rules, it is noteworthy that Article 5(1) does not explicitly require the Respondent to raise any objections that it may have to the jurisdiction of the Court and the arbitrators in its Answer.[104] As a practical

---

[104] *Compare*, for example, AAA International Arbitration Rules, Article 16(3); LCIA Rules, Article 23(2); UNCITRAL Rules, Article 21(3); WIPO Arbitration Rules, Article 36(c).

matter, it is usually in the Respondent's interest to do so at the earliest opportunity, particularly if it wishes to try to persuade the Court to refuse to accept the arbitration (as further discussed below in connection with Article 6(2)). However, there is no provision in the Rules that precludes the Respondent from raising a jurisdictional objection for the first time only after the arbitrators are in possession of the file or later during the proceedings,[105] although the later it does so, the greater is the risk that the objection in question will be found to have been waived, if it is waivable, or otherwise to be inadmissible.[106]

There are two additional matters upon which the Respondent should comment within the 30-day period of Article 5(1) or otherwise possibly lose its right to do so. The first is on the place of the arbitration, if this has not already been agreed, as, in the absence of an agreement, the Court will normally fix the place when the case is first presented to it by the Secretariat.[107] The other is on the number of arbitrators, the Claimant's related proposals and, if "required," any nomination of the Respondent (*see* Article 5(1)(d)). Indeed, as discussed in relation to Article 5(2), the Respondent's comments concerning the constitution of the Arbitral Tribunal and nomination, where "required," of an arbitrator must accompany any application for an extension of the time for the submission of the Answer.

[105] *See, e.g.,* the report of the Award in ICC Case No. 6140 (1989), *ASA Bull.*, No. 3 (1990), pp. 257-61. In another case, which came before a New York state court, it was argued that a Respondent party had waived its right to claim that it was not a proper party to an ICC arbitration by requesting an extension of time to file an Answer and consenting to the appointment of a sole arbitrator, without, however, also noting that it had an objection to its inclusion in the arbitration. The New York court rejected the argument, in the following terms:

> As can be seen, counsel was merely complying with the rules of the ICC when he consented to the number of arbitrators in his application for an extension of time. This Court will not interpret such rules, and petitioner's actions done in accordance with said rules, as being a procedural "catch 22" where petitioner, as a condition of obtaining an extension of time to respond, must waive his right to any say as to the number of arbitrators or by specifying the number of arbitrators, be deemed to have participated in the arbitration.

Jakubowski v. *Nora Beverages, Inc.,* Supreme Court of the State of New York, Index No. 112627/95 (October 11, 1995).

[106] In this respect, the Respondent must also be attentive to the possible requirements of any domestic arbitration laws that may be applicable to the arbitration. Thus, for example, under Article 186 of the Swiss Private International Law Act, any objection to jurisdiction must be raised "prior to any defense on the merits." For a discussion of when such an objection is required to be asserted in an ICC arbitration in Switzerland, *see* the report of the Award in ICC Case No. 6140, *supra,* note 105. *See also* UNCITRAL Model Law, Article 16(2).

[106] Article 5(1)(e) also invites the Respondent to comment on the applicable rules of law and the language of the arbitration. However, if the Respondent fails to do so in the Answer, it will have the opportunity to do so later before the Arbitral Tribunal. It nevertheless is useful for the Court to know the Respondent's views on these matters when constituting the Arbitral Tribunal.

Article 5(2)

> *The Secretariat may grant the Respondent an extension of the time for fil-*
> *ing the Answer, provided the application for such an extension contains*
> *the Respondent's comments concerning the number of arbitrators and*
> *their choice, and, where required by Articles 8, 9 and 10, the nomination*
> *of an arbitrator. If the Respondent fails so to do, the Court shall proceed*
> *in accordance with these Rules.*

As already noted, the Secretariat has, for many years, almost routinely granted extensions of time for the filing of the Answer. Article 5(2) does not substantively alter the related requirements, except that, in recognition of the past practice in this regard, Article 5(2) no longer provides, as its prior version did, that extensions may only be granted "in exceptional circumstances."

Article 5(2), like Article 4 of the former Rules, does not impose any limitations on the length of the extensions that the Secretariat may grant, nor do the Rules otherwise provide the Secretariat with specific guidance in this respect. The Secretariat is, thus, required to consider every application in the light of its particular circumstances. In the past, extensions of 30 days have been most common, although extensions of several months have been accorded in a few, truly exceptional circumstances (*e.g.*, where the Request for Arbitration fills dozens of boxes). For a time, it was the general policy of the Secretariat not to grant an extension of more than 30 days without the consent of the Claimant. Although such a rigid practice was later abandoned, the Secretariat nevertheless normally solicits the Claimant's comments on any request for an extension before making a decision, provided that it is possible to do so. Indeed, a common practical difficulty for the Secretariat is that extension requests are often made on the eve of the expiration of the 30-day deadline and require an almost immediate decision.

As already noted, the one condition that needs to be satisfied before the Secretariat can consider an extension request is that the Respondent must have commented on the number of arbitrators and their choice, including nominating an arbitrator, "where required."[108] The obvious purpose of this condition is to permit the Court to proceed with the constitution of the Arbitral Tribunal, notwithstanding the extension, so that the granting of an extension will not delay the arbitral proceedings.[109] In no circumstances may the Secretariat extend the

---

[108] Under Article 4 of the earlier Rules, the Respondent's obligation was to nominate an arbitrator "where appropriate." This arguably can be interpreted more broadly than the words "where required," although the actual reason for the change was simply, as in the case of Article 4(2)(e), to reinforce the notion that the nomination of an arbitrator is required in certain circumstances at this stage of the process.

[109] The potential for delay is, moreover, further reduced by the modification of the provision concerning the transmission of the file to the Arbitral Tribunal. As already noted above, under Article 13 of the New Rules, the file is to be transmitted to the Arbitral Tribunal upon its constitution, provided that all required advances (normally, the provisional advance fixed pursuant to Article 30(1)) have been paid, whereas under the former Rules (Article 10), it was arguably necessary to await the expiration of any extension of time granted for the Answer.

time limit for the Respondent to comment on the Arbitral Tribunal or to nominate an arbitrator if this is "required."

The difficulty, however, is that it may not always be clear whether the Respondent is "required" to nominate an arbitrator. This is because, as already discussed in relation to Article 4(2), the only provision that explicitly requires the Respondent to nominate an arbitrator in its Answer is Article 8(4), which makes this a requirement "[w]here the dispute is to be referred to three arbitrators." While, as already observed, this is clearly the case when the arbitration clause provides for three arbitrators, this will not otherwise be true until the parties have so agreed or the Court has so decided. Normally, if, in the absence of a specified number in the clause, the Claimant proposes three arbitrators and nominates an arbitrator in its Request, and the Respondent agrees with this proposal, then it can reasonably be argued that the Respondent is required to nominate an arbitrator as a condition to obtaining an extension. Although this has, from time to time, been the position of the Secretariat in recent years, it has not been followed consistently, and extensions have, thus, been granted on the theory that the Respondent's only immediate obligation in such circumstances is to comment on the number of arbitrators. Meanwhile, in those cases where the Claimant proposes three arbitrators without nominating an arbitrator in its Request, the Secretariat has not generally considered that the Respondent should be required to nominate an arbitrator in its Answer, even it agrees with the Claimant that three arbitrators should be appointed.[110]

Other difficult situations may also arise, such as, for example, where the Claimant proposes a non-"independent" arbitrator in its Request (*see* with respect to the requirement of independence, Article 7 *infra*) and the Respondent refuses to nominate an arbitrator until a new arbitrator is nominated by the Claimant, or where the Respondent contends that the Request is defective because the claims are not sufficiently described and that it should not be required to nominate an arbitrator, or possibly even comment on the number of arbitrators, until the Request has been rectified. The Rules do not contain ready-made solutions for all such situations, and it will therefore be necessary for the Secretariat, as in the past, to exercise its judgment, bearing in mind the "spirit" of the Rules, as mandated by Article 35 (*see infra*).

Article 5(3)

> *The Answer shall be supplied to the Secretariat in the number of copies specified by Article 3(1).*

---

[110] *See* Kreindler, *supra*, note 14, p. 59.

Article 5(4)

> *A copy of the Answer and the documents annexed thereto shall be communicated by the Secretariat to the Claimant.*

These two provisions are merely intended to make it clear, as it was not previously, that the Respondent submits the Answer to the Secretariat for notification to the Claimant. This does not preclude the Respondent from sending an additional copy of the Answer to the Respondent directly if it wishes to do so. However, the Secretariat nevertheless formally notifies a copy to the Respondent and retains the other copies for itself and the Arbitral Tribunal. Copies of the Answer are normally notified by the Secretariat to the Respondent upon receipt in accordance with the same procedures already described with respect to the Request (*see* the discussion of Article 4(1) *supra*).

Article 5(5)

> *Any counterclaim(s) made by the Respondent shall be filed with its Answer and shall provide:*
> a) *a description of the nature and circumstances of the dispute giving rise to the counterclaim(s); and*
> b) *a statement of the relief sought, including, to the extent possible, an indication of any amount(s) counterclaimed.*

Background. Although named as a Respondent in the Request for Arbitration, the Respondent has the right in the same arbitration proceedings to pursue its own claims against the Claimant, provided, of course, that the arbitration clause covering the Claimant's claims also extends to those of the Respondent (*see* the discussion of Article 6(2) *infra*).

Article 5 of the previous Rules provided in this regard that:

> If the Defendant wishes to make a counter-claim, he shall file the same with the Secretariat, at the same time as his Answer....

In now providing that "[a]ny counterclaims made by the Respondent shall be filed with its Answer" (and also indicating briefly what information the counterclaim is to contain), Article 5(5) is not significantly different. However, the new formulation of Article 5(5) was intended primarily to soften any possible implication arising from the former wording that a Respondent might subsequently be barred from introducing a counterclaim if it did not do so at the time of its Answer.

Indeed, on various occasions, former Article 5 has been construed by both parties and arbitrators as precluding the inclusion of counterclaims in the arbitration following the Respondent's Answer. However, this was not the intention of that provision, as has been widely recognized,[111] nor is such a view consistent with the general principle that the parties remain free to introduce new claims in the arbitration prior to the establishment of the Terms of Reference (*see* the discussion of Article 18 *infra*). Article 5(5) should therefore not be considered as in any way prohibiting the subsequent introduction of counterclaims. Indeed, under Article 19 of the New Rules (*see infra*), the Arbitral Tribunal may permit counterclaims to be introduced even after the establishment of the Terms of Reference, depending on the circumstances.

Of course, it is also the case that, under the ICC's system of costs (*see* Articles 30-31 *infra*), the introduction of counterclaims will cause the amount of the advance on costs for the arbitration to increase, and the Respondent must be prepared to bear all or a portion of that increase, failing which it may be prevented from pursuing its claims in the arbitration.

Claims against third parties and cross-claims. Although Article 5(5) does not expressly say so, it has been construed by the Court as entitling the Respondent to make counterclaims only against the Claimant and not against any party not named as a Claimant in the Request for Arbitration. Thus, unless the parties have otherwise agreed – or the Court's position changes – Respondents are not entitled to join new parties to the arbitration proceedings. Rather, it is the exclusive privilege of the Claimant to determine who are the parties to the arbitration.[112] Where there are multiple Respondents, a Respondent is also not entitled to make a cross-claim against another Respondent, unless all of the parties otherwise agree.

The Court's position is based on a strict reading of the Rules as well as the "insuperable problems"[113] that could otherwise arise in the administration of the arbitration. Indeed, while the Rules permit the conduct of arbitrations with more than two parties ("multi-party" arbitrations), they nevertheless have been drafted on the assumption that the parties can be divided into two camps: a Claimant camp and a Respondent camp. Thus, the Claimant camp is composed of those who have introduced the Request for Arbitration, and the Respondent camp includes those who have been named as Respondents in the Request. The balance of the Rules' provisions, whether concerning the exchange of submissions, the constitution of the Arbitral Tribunal or the payment of costs, have been drafted on the basis of this bipolar conception of the process. The joinder of a party after the Arbitral Tribunal has already been constituted, either in whole or in part, could also give rise to difficulties, particularly if the party whose joinder is

---

[111] *See, e.g.,* the extracts from the Awards in ICC Case Nos.6000 (1988), 6039 (1992), 7076 (1993) and 7237 (1993), *ICC Ct. Bull.*, Vol. 8, No. 1 (1997), pp. 67, 54, 66 and 65. *See also Fouchard Gaillard and Goldman*, p. 677.

[112] The Court's position is reflected in the "Final Report on Multi-Party Arbitrations," *see supra*, note 21, pp. 31-32, and has been generally explained in Bond, "The Experience of the ICC International Court of Arbitration," *Multi-party Arbitration* (ICC Publishing 1991), pp. 39, 41-43.

[113] *See* Bond, *supra,* note 112, p. 42.

sought would be deprived of the right to participate in the Arbitral Tribunal's constitution.[114]

Arguably, however, if the party whom the Respondent wishes to join is part of the same corporate group as the Claimant and is the subject of precisely the same counter-claims, there is not necessarily any reason why the bipolar configuration of the arbitration would be disturbed by its joinder, nor would there necessarily be a violation of any party's right to participate in the constitution of the Arbitral Tribunal. Nevertheless, until now, the Court has refused to permit the joinder of such a party without the Claimant's and such party's consent.

The parties are free to make their own special agreements to cater for multi-party disputes with triangular or other possible configurations. But failing that, a Respondent party wishing to join a third party to the proceedings or to file a cross-claim against a co-Respondent will be left with no alternative but to commence a new arbitration against such party, unless all of the parties concerned otherwise consent.[115]

The position of the Court has given rise to criticism. It has, for example, been argued that allowing the Claimant alone to choose the parties to the arbitration violates the Respondent's right to be treated equally.[116] However, until now, the Court's interpretation of its Rules has not been the subject of any conflicting jurisprudence, and it is, on the contrary, consistent with the only reported arbitral decision on this subject.[117]

Set-offs. Unlike certain other arbitration rules, Article 5 does not specifically refer to the possible assertion by the Respondent of set-offs. However, there is no obstacle to the Respondent doing so. The issue that most frequently tends to arise in this regard is whether a set-off, when asserted, should be treated as part of the Respondent's defense or as a counterclaim, particularly for the purpose of calculating the amount of the advance on costs for the arbitration (*see* the discussion of Article 30(5) *infra*). The answer to this may depend upon the nature of the set-off and its proper characterization under the applicable law.

---

[114] *See*, with respect to this, the discussion of Article 10 *infra*.

[115] This, in turn, raises the question of whether any such new arbitration might be joined with the arbitration already pending, pursuant to Article 4(6). Indeed, as Article 4(6) does not take into account the configuration of the parties in the arbitrations concerned as a condition of joinder, those conditions would theoretically be satisfied where, in one case, A is the Claimant and B and C are the Respondents while in the other B is the Claimant and A and C are the Respondents. However, it is unlikely that the Court would accept to join two such arbitrations, even if it theoretically has the power to do so under Article 4(6), if it considered that the joined case would not be capable of administration under the Rules.

[116] *See* Boisséson, *Le droit français de l'arbitrage interne et international* (GLN 1990), pp. 532-35; Leurent, "*La Jonction de Différents Contentieux et l'Arbitrage Multipartite,*" presented at a seminar in Paris of the Institute for International Research (October 21-22, 1992), unpublished, p. 20.

[117] *See* the extract from the Award in ICC Case No. 5625 (1989), *ICC Arbitral Awards 1986-1990*, p.484. *See also Fouchard Gaillard and Goldman*, pp. 677-78.

Article 5(6)

> *The Claimant shall file a Reply to any counterclaim within 30 days from the date of receipt of the counterclaim(s) communicated by the Secretariat. The Secretariat may grant the Claimant an extension of time for filing the Reply.*

Article 5(6), like its predecessor in the former Rules (Article 5(2)), formally recognizes the Claimant's right to respond to a counterclaim submitted with the Answer. It differs from its prior version principally insofar as it formally authorizes the Secretariat to extend the time limit for the Reply, as in the case of the Answer.[118]

Although formulated in seemingly mandatory terms – the Claimant "shall" file a Reply[119] – Article 5(6) is not, in fact, meant to preclude the submission of comments subsequently by the Claimant in respect of the Respondent's counterclaims. As already stated, both parties are free to make additional submissions prior to the establishment of the Terms of Reference, and, thereafter, they may do so as the parties themselves may agree or the Arbitral Tribunal otherwise considers appropriate. Of course, in deciding upon the appropriate procedures, the Arbitral Tribunal may take into account the opportunity that the Claimant had, under Article 5(6), to file a Reply and whether or not it did so.

Article 5(6) only provides for a Reply in the event of a counterclaim. But just as a Claimant's failure to submit a Reply in accordance with that provision does not necessarily prevent it from commenting subsequently on a counterclaim, that provision's failure to authorize a reply to the Respondent's defenses is not intended to deprive the Claimant of such a possibility. Rather, as already stated, the Claimant may make additional submissions prior to the Terms of Reference and thereafter as may be agreed by the parties or decided by the Arbitral Tribunal.

ARTICLE 6

Effect of the Arbitration Agreement

Although the title of this Article refers to the "effect" of the arbitration agreement, it is, in fact, principally concerned with the possible need to determine, first of all, whether any such agreement exists. Article 6, thus, establishes a foundation for the determination of the Court's and the Arbitral Tribunal's

---

[118] The prior Rules did not contain such a provision. But there did not appear to the Working Party to be any logical reason why the Claimant should not have the same possible right to an extension for the Reply as the Respondent in relation to the Answer.

[119] This is to be compared with Article 5(2) of the former Rules, which stated that "[i]t shall be open to the Claimant to file a Reply . . . ." It is also to be noted that the French version of Article 5(2) states that the Claimant "may" ("*peut*"), rather than "shall," file a Reply. The French version is, in this instance, more in keeping with the drafters' intention.

jurisdiction. In the event of a valid arbitration agreement, it further confirms the parties' agreement to be bound by the Rules in force upon the commencement of the arbitration and establishes the arbitrators' authority to proceed in the event of a party's default.

The provisions contained in Article 6 correspond to those previously set out in Articles 7 and 8 of the Rules. All of the provisions of those Articles have been retained, with certain modifications, except that former Article 7 has been integrated into what is now Article 6(2) and former Article 8(5), dealing with interim measures, has become the subject of a separate, expanded Article (Article 23). In general, none of the changes incorporated into Article 6 were made with the intention of altering the operation of the provisions in question. Rather, the object was, as appropriate, to bring them into closer alignment with the existing practices of the Court.

Article 6(1)

> *Where the parties have agreed to submit to arbitration under the Rules, they shall be deemed to have submitted ipso facto to the Rules in effect on the date of commencement of the arbitration proceedings unless they have agreed to submit to the Rules in effect on the date of their arbitration agreement.*

Article 8(1) of the previous Rules provided that an agreement to submit to arbitration "by the International Chamber of Commerce" should be deemed to be a submission to arbitration in accordance with the "present Rules." That provision was originally introduced into the Rules in 1955 and was retained, with only a slight modification, when new Rules were adopted in 1975.

The former provision served the relatively limited purpose of confirming that a reference in an arbitration clause to arbitration "by the ICC" should be construed as an agreement to arbitrate under the Rules of the ICC. This, it presumably was hoped, would prevent any possible argument that, in providing for arbitration by the ICC, the parties did not necessarily intend to arbitrate under the ICC Rules.[120] However, given that the only rules administered by the ICC, unlike some other institutions, are the ICC's own Rules, a party's agreement to arbitration "by the ICC" could not reasonably be interpreted as having any other meaning.[121]

---

[120] For a case where a party unsuccessfully made such an argument, *see Bucher-Guyer S.A. c/ Meiki Co. Ltd., Tribunal fédéral suisse* (March 17, 1976), *ICCA Yearbook* V (1980), p. 220.

[121] Thus, for example, while many institutions administer cases under the UNCITRAL Rules in addition to their own rules, the ICC has, until now, refused to do so. However, it accepts to act as an appointing authority for the purpose of the UNCITRAL Rules. *See* "ICC as Appointing Authority under the UNCITRAL Arbitration Rules," ICC Publication No. 409, as well as Article 3 of Appendix III ("Arbitration Costs and Fees") to the Rules and the ICC's recommended clause for this purpose (Appendix 1 *infra*).

The more difficult issue, and the one that the earlier Rules did not address, is which version of the Rules ought to apply when the Rules have been modified since the date of the parties' agreement. This is a matter as to which the mere reference to the "present" Rules, in the earlier version of this Article, did not provide any assistance. When the Rules were amended in 1988, the ICC took the position that the amended Rules would apply to all arbitrations commenced as from the date when the new Rules entered into effect unless, prior to then, the parties had agreed that the Rules previously in force would apply.[122] Although this was the most convenient position to take from an administrative point of view, it was not necessarily free from possible criticism. Indeed, it has been argued that, when agreeing to arbitration under the ICC Rules, the parties incorporate into their agreement the Rules in force at the time of their contract unless they expressly provide for the application of such Rules as may come into force at a later date.[123] The possibility that such arguments might be raised evidently was of concern to the Court in 1975, when much more substantial modifications of the Rules were adopted. At that time, the Court, thus, decided that, while the new Rules would apply in principle to all new arbitrations commenced after they entered into force, in the event that a party to an agreement made prior to such time expressly objected to their application, before the establishment of the Terms of Reference, the new Rules would not apply, given the "contractual basis" of arbitration.[124]

It can, of course, be argued that, insofar as the matter is one of contractual intent, it is not really for the arbitral institution to impose its own solution, as in the above cases, but rather for the Arbitral Tribunal or a court to construe the parties' agreement.[125] Indeed, the arbitral institution should not legitimately be entitled to compel the parties to arbitrate under rules to which they cannot legitimately be said to have agreed. But at the same time, whatever may have been the parties' intent when agreeing to arbitration, they should not be in a position either to compel an arbitral institution to continue administering a set of rules

---

[122] Letter from the Secretary General of the Court, dated November 20, 1987, to parties, counsel, arbitrators and entities and persons engaged in international commerce.

[123] *See, e.g., Craig Park and Paulsson*, §10.03, pp. 173-76. *But cf.* the decision of the Swiss Federal Tribunal in *Komplex* c/ *Voest-Alpine Stahl* (June 14, 1990), *ASA Bull.* (1994), p. 226, in which the Swiss court held, with respect to an ICC arbitration, that even though the arbitration clause had been entered into prior to 1988, the ICC Rules, as amended in 1988, were applicable to the arbitration. In addition, a series of English court decisions have established a "presumption that, where a clause requires arbitration according to the rules of a particular institution, this means the rules current when the arbitration is begun." *See* O'Conor, "Enforcement of Arbitration Awards: Arbitration Rules for the Time Being: *China Agribusiness* v. *Balli Trading*," *International Arbitration Law Review*, Vol. 1, No. 1 (1997), p. 42.

[124] Decision of the Court (unpublished), Doc. No. 410/2731 (October 16, 1975).

[125] *See*, in this regard the decisions of the New York courts in *Mobil Indonesia* v. *Asamera Oil (Indonesia) Ltd.*, as discussed in *Craig Park and Paulsson*, §10.03, pp. 175-76, and the extract from the Award in ICC Case No. 5622 (1992), *ICC Ct. Bull.*, Vol. 8, No. 1 (1997), p. 52. *See also* the decisions mentioned in note123 *supra*.

that have been replaced and that it is no longer prepared, or possibly even in a position, to continue administering. An arbitral institution, when issuing rules, does not necessarily warrant to the public that the rules will remain in effect indefinitely without ever being changed.[126]

Article 6(1) therefore seeks to strike a balance between the respective interests of the institution and the parties in relation to the arbitration rules that are to be applied when changes have been made. The principle, which is consistent with that to be found in the rules of other arbitral institutions,[127] is that the Rules in force on the date of commencement of the arbitration shall apply unless the parties have agreed that the Rules in effect on the date of their agreement should govern. It is not, however, open to the parties to provide that any other, earlier version of the Rules shall apply.

Insofar as Article 6(1) is deemed, by its terms, to be incorporated into the arbitration agreement of the parties, it should prevent any uncertainty, in relation to possible future Rules changes, regarding the version of the Rules to be applied. However, Article 6(1) can only operate prospectively, for an ICC arbitration agreement entered into prior to January 1, 1998 cannot, unless the parties otherwise provided, be deemed to incorporate a provision that did not exist at the time of the parties' agreement. Thus, notwithstanding Article 6(1), the Court, as in 1975 and 1988, will be required to decide what to do if the parties to an agreement entered into prior to 1998 disagree as to whether the New Rules are to be applied.[128]

---

[126] For a discussion of the arbitral institution's possible obligations in this regard, *see* Jarrosson, *supra*, note 46, pp. 384-87.

[127] *See, e.g.,* AAA International Arbitration Rules, Article 1; WIPO Arbitration Rules, Article 2.

[128] In this regard, it was reported at a meeting of the ICC Commission on October 28, 1997 that the Court established the following policy at its special working session in September 1997:

   – If the Claimant, when receiving the request for payment, states that there exists an agreement regarding the application of the old Rules, the case will initially be administered under the old Rules and the Secretary General will therefore not request the Claimant to pay the provisional advance.

   – If the Claimant pays the provisional advance but the Respondent states that there exists an agreement between the parties to submit the arbitration to the Rules in effect on the date of their arbitration agreement, the Secretary General will refrain from confirming the arbitrators.

In both cases the matter will be submitted to the Court. It is possible that the Court will come to a definitive determination of the Rules that are to be applied. It is, however, also possible that the matter will require the examination of further facts and that the Court will therefore leave the definitive determination to the Arbitral Tribunal, deciding only on the Rules which should apply until the determination by the Arbitral Tribunal is made. Remarks of R. Briner. The Court has indicated, meanwhile, that parties to an arbitration that commenced prior to January 1, 1998 are free to agree to the application of the New Rules.

Article 6(2)

> *If the Respondent does not file an Answer, as provided by Article 5, or if any party raises one or more pleas concerning the existence, validity or scope of the arbitration agreement, the Court may decide, without prejudice to the admissibility or merits of the plea or pleas, that the arbitration shall proceed if it is prima facie satisfied that an arbitration agreement under the Rules may exist. In such a case, any decision as to the jurisdiction of the Arbitral Tribunal shall be taken by the Arbitral Tribunal itself. If the Court is not so satisfied, the parties shall be notified that the arbitration cannot proceed. In such a case, any party retains the right to ask any court having jurisdiction whether or not there is a binding arbitration agreement.*

Background. Article 6(2) replaces Articles 7 and 8(3) of the former Rules. Like its predecessors, it is intended to apply where a Request for Arbitration is filed without any indication that the parties have agreed to submit their dispute to ICC arbitration or the jurisdiction of the ICC is otherwise contested. Although the general purpose of Article 6(2) does not differ from that of former Articles 7 and 8(3), it nevertheless incorporates certain changes, apart from consolidating those provisions, which are intended to make the new rule easier to comprehend and more consistent with the Court's practice. In addition, due to changes in the Court's Internal Rules (Appendix II to the Rules), Article 6(2) will be administered differently than were former Articles 7 and 8(3).

The provisions of Articles 7 and 8(3) now incorporated into Article 6(2) have existed in the Rules in substantially the same form since 1955. Under Article 7, the Court could refuse to permit an arbitration to proceed in the absence of a *"prima facie"* ICC arbitration agreement between the parties, while Article 8(3) permitted the Court to set the arbitration in motion if, notwithstanding the objection of a party, the Court was satisfied of the *"prima facie"* existence of such an agreement, but on condition that the Arbitral Tribunal would decide upon its own jurisdiction.

Prior to 1955, the Rules provided that, in the event of a disagreement between the parties as to "whether or not they are bound by an arbitration clause," this issue would be decided by the ICC Court itself.[129] The Court took it upon itself to decide the matter because it recognized that the arbitration process could be undermined if the parties were required to refer to and await the final decision of a court of law whenever the existence or validity of an ICC arbitration clause might be called into question, irrespective of the good or bad faith of such a contention, and it was not then considered that such a question could validly be submitted to an arbitrator. Rather, it was then the view that this "involves a decision which necessarily must be taken before the Arbitrator can

---

[129] This provision was added to the Rules in 1931.

commence to have any jurisdiction at all."[130] By 1955, however, the ICC had formed the view – which was innovative at the time – that the Arbitral Tribunal should have the power to determine the matter of its own jurisdiction, if contested, and the Rules adopted in that year, thus, for the first time incorporated that principle. It is a principle that has since gained widespread acceptance.[131]

Having determined that the arbitrators could themselves rule upon objections to their jurisdiction, the ICC was, thus, required to reconsider the provision in its earlier Rules that the ICC Court should decide whether the parties were bound by an ICC arbitration clause. The result was a new provision (Article 12 of the 1955 Rules, which became Article 7 of the 1975 and 1988 Rules) under which the Court would continue to play a role in this regard, although a much more limited one than before. Article 7, thus, provided that the Court would refuse an arbitration where:

– "there is no *prima facie*[132] agreement between the parties to arbitrate"; or
– "there is an agreement but it does not specify the International Chamber of Commerce"; and
– if the Defendant "refuses arbitration" or does not file an Answer within the period specified in the Rules.[133]

Given the power that the arbitrators have enjoyed under the Rules since 1955 to determine their own jurisdiction, the above provision was intended to be of

---

[130] Marx, "Commentary on the Revision of the Rules," *World Trade* (1931), pp. 301-03.

[131] The principle that the arbitrators have jurisdiction to determine their own jurisdiction ("competence-competence") has been accepted in international conventions (*see, e.g.,* Article 5(3) of the Geneva Convention of 1961 on International Commercial Arbitration and Article 41(1) of the Washington Convention of 1965 on the Settlement of Investment Disputes Between States and Nationals of Other States) as well as modern international arbitration legislation, such as, *e.g.,* Article 16 of the UNCITRAL Model Law, Article 1458 of the French New Code of Civil Procedure, Article 186 of the Swiss Private International Law Act and Section 30 of the English Arbitration Act 1996. For a general discussion of this principle, *see* Goldman, "The Complementary Roles of Judges and Arbitrators in Ensuring that International Commercial Arbitration is Effective," *60 Years of ICC Arbitration* (ICC Publishing 1984), p. 257; *see also, Fouchard Gaillard and Goldman,* pp. 409-30. Ultimately, the Arbitral Tribunal's determination will usually be the subject of judicial control once the tribunal has rendered its Award, although in some jurisdictions the power of the arbitrators to decide upon their own competence does not necessarily preclude the matter from being decided by the courts before the arbitrators have done so. *See, e.g.,* Section 32 of the English Arbitration Act 1996. *See also,* for a discussion of the approach to this issue in various jurisdictions, Park, "The Arbitrability *Dicta* in *First Options* v. *Kaplan*: What Sort of *Kompetenz-Kompetenz* Has Crossed the Atlantic?" *Arb. Int.,* Vol. 12, No. 2 (1996), p. 137.

[132] The words *"prima facie"* were introduced into the Rules in 1955 in what was then Article 13(3) and subsequently Article 8(3) as from 1975. They were, however, omitted – perhaps unintentionally – from Article 12 of the 1955 Rules (the predecessor of Article 7 of the 1975 Rules), an omission that was corrected in 1975.

[133] Although other arbitration rules do not contain a comparable provision, the institutions administering them may nevertheless make a similar review before accepting an arbitration.

limited effect. Indeed, if the ICC Court mistakenly refuses to set an arbitration in motion, and there are no courts to which the parties can reliably refer, a party might, as a consequence, be deprived of its only real chance of obtaining effective relief.

By its terms, Article 7 therefore only called upon the Court itself to make a determination relating to the "existence" of an ICC arbitration agreement, and this remains true of Article 6(2). Under Article 6(2), if pleas are made concerning the validity – as opposed to the existence – of such an agreement or its scope, or other possible objections are raised in respect of the commencement of an arbitration proceeding, founded, for example, on the contention that a particular claim is not arbitrable or that a condition precedent to the arbitration agreement has not been satisfied, the Court is to refer the matter to the arbitrators for decision. Indeed, in order to resolve such issues, it is normally necessary to examine and rule upon contested issues of fact or law, and the Court, as an administrative body, is not well-suited to doing so. As already discussed (*see* Article 1(1) *supra*), neither the parties nor their lawyers have the opportunity to appear in person before it, nor can any witnesses be heard. Rather, all decisions of the Court are made solely on the basis of the contractual documents and the parties' written submissions.

Of course, even the question of whether an ICC arbitration agreement exists between all of the parties to an arbitration may give rise to contested, and possibly complex, issues of fact or law. For this reason, the Court's only mandate under Article 7 (and Article 8.3) was to make a *"prima facie"* decision, which was, moreover, not intended to be definitive insofar as the parties preserved the right to submit the issue of the arbitration agreement's existence to the courts (or to the arbitrators, if the Court decided that the arbitration should proceed).[134] Depending on how it applied this *prima facie* test, the Court was nevertheless in a position to prevent an ICC arbitration from proceeding, at least until such time as a competent court might decide otherwise.[135]

How the *prima facie* test was to be applied, has, over the years, been the subject of shifting positions within the Court. Advocates of a strict approach have argued that the *prima facie* test requires a threshold showing of the actual existence of an agreement, while the proponents of greater liberality have urged that the Court should always allow an arbitration to proceed, unless it is evident that

---

[134] The French courts have recognized the administrative character of the ICC Court's decisions under Article 7. *See Ceskilovenska Obchodni Banka A.S. (Cekobanka) c/ Chambre de commerce internationale, Tribunal de grande instance de Paris* (October 8, 1986), *Rev. arb.* (1987), p. 367, and *R.E.D.E.C. et Pharaon c/ Uzinexport Import et Chambre de commerce internationale, Tribunal de grande instance de Paris* (July 13, 1988), *Rev. arb.* (1989), p. 97. *See also* Fouchard, *"Les institutions permanentes d'arbitrage devant le juge étatique,"* *Rev. arb.* (1987), p. 225.

[135] The ICC has, thus, been sued for applying former Article 7 (*see* the *Cekobanka* case, *supra,* note 134). It has, however, also been sued for its failure to apply Article 7 in certain cases (*see* the *R.E.D.E.C.* case *and* Fouchard, *supra*, note 134).

there is no ICC arbitration agreement between the parties. In recent years, it is the more liberal position that has most frequently prevailed within the Court. Indeed, the Court has normally preferred to allow contested issues of fact or law to be presented to an Arbitral Tribunal whenever there has appeared to be a reasonable possibility that an ICC arbitration agreement might be found to exist on the basis of a greater airing of the facts and the law than is possible before the Court.

The Court, thus, tended to apply Article 7 as if it provided that an arbitration should proceed where *prima facie* it appeared reasonably possible that an agreement might exist between the parties. This was not necessarily consistent, however, with the strict wording of Article 7, and it was therefore considered desirable to reconsider the articulation of the *prima facie* test during the preparation of the New Rules.

As regards the administration of Articles 7 and 8(3), the Court's Internal Rules (Article 12) formerly delegated to the Secretariat the task of making an initial *prima facie* determination, in the hope that this might reduce the number of matters that would eventually reach the Court. In practice, if the Secretariat considered that there was no *prima facie* arbitration agreement, it would send a letter to the Claimant (with a copy to the Defendant) notifying it of the application of Article 7. The Secretariat would, at the same time, inform the Claimant of its right to request a decision by the Court and fix a deadline for the submission of such a request. The Court would then normally be invited to decide on the matter at one of its monthly plenary sessions (although this was not mandated by either the Rules or the Court's Internal Rules).

The foregoing two-step process was intended to lessen the workload of the Court, but it rarely had this effect in practice. Indeed, it only infrequently occurred that both parties would accept the Secretariat's initial application of Article 7. Thus, the requirement that the Secretariat apply Article 7 before the Court itself made any decision in this regard usually only served to delay the Court's ultimate decision. Moreover, there was always a possibility that the Court would reverse the decision of the Secretariat, thus discrediting it in the eyes of the parties from the very outset of the arbitration. During the preparation of the New Rules, it was therefore considered desirable to reconsider this process.

Summary of changes. The principal changes incorporated into Article 6(2) may be summarized as follows:

– *Consolidation of former Articles 7 and 8(3).* The combination of former Articles 7 and 8(3) in a single provision brings together the two possible solutions to what is, in reality, a single issue for the Court, *i.e.*, whether to permit an arbitration to proceed where the existence or validity of the arbitration clause is contested by a party or where a party defaults.

– *Expansion of scope of former Article 8(3).* Unlike Article 8(3) of the former Rules, Article 6(2) expressly authorizes the Arbitral Tribunal to decide upon its own jurisdiction if a party raises a plea concerning the "scope" of the arbitration agreement. Although Article 8(3) was intended to confer broad power on the Arbitral Tribunal to decide upon its own jurisdiction, that Article only referred explicitly to the case where a party raised a plea concerning the "existence or validity" of the agreement to arbitrate.[136] In addition, Article 8(3), unlike Article 7, did not include the case where a party did not appear in the arbitration, and, thus, arguably did not authorize the Arbitral Tribunal to consider the matter of its jurisdiction in such a situation. Article 6(2), however, expressly authorizes the tribunal to do so.

– *Reformulation of the prima facie test.* Under Article 7, the arbitration was not to proceed where there was "no *prima facie* agreement between the parties to arbitrate." Article 8(3), in turn, permitted the arbitration to proceed where the Court was "satisfied of the *prima facie* existence of such an agreement." In the first case, the rule set forth an objective standard, while in the second it was more subjective, given the reference to the Court's "satisfaction." In both cases, however, there was arguably a need for the Court to find, if only on a *prima facie* basis, that an arbitration agreement actually existed, whereas, as already indicated, the Court would often set an arbitration in motion if it was merely satisfied that an arbitration agreement might exist. Article 6(2) therefore now states that the "Court may decide ... that the arbitration shall proceed if it is *prima facie* satisfied that an arbitration agreement under the Rules of Arbitration of the ICC may exist ... . If the Court is not so satisfied, the parties shall be notified that the arbitration cannot proceed." The reformulation of this provision, as discussed elsewhere, more closely reflects the Court's actual practice in recent years. The words *"prima facie"* have also been displaced in order to make it clear that it is the Court's determination that is of a *prima facie* nature and that it is not to be inferred from the Court's decision that it has concluded that there is, in fact, an agreement.[137]

– *Modification of the reference to the ICC.* Article 7 required that there be an agreement to arbitrate that "specif[ied] the International Chamber of Commerce." Article 6(2) now refers to "an arbitration agreement under the Rules." The reformulation is less ambiguous and more in keeping with the intent of the provision. Thus, for example, the Court would not normally set an arbitration in motion under the Rules if the ICC were "specified" as an appointing authority or if it were designated for the purpose of administering an arbitration

---

[136] A similar change was made to the AAA International Arbitration Rules (Article 15) in April 1997 "in order to make clear that the tribunal shall have the power to rule on any challenge to its jurisdiction." *See* "Commentary on the Proposed Revisions to the International Arbitration Rules of the American Arbitration Association" by the American Arbitration Association Task Force on the International Rules, *ADR Currents* (Winter 1996/1997), pp. 6, 8.

[137] This is, in fact, more consistent with the former French version of Article 7, which provided: *"Lorsque, prima facie, il n'existe entre les parties aucune Convention d'arbitrage ..."* (Translation: "When, *prima facie*, there does not exist between the parties an arbitration agreement...").

under other arbitration rules. The provision, as reworded, now makes it clearer that the ICC's only undertaking, under the Rules, is to administer arbitrations under those Rules. It may also be inferred from this language that the ICC is not obligated to administer arbitrations where the parties have agreed to alter the ICC Rules, except as provided for therein, and where it might, thus, be argued that the agreement is no longer an agreement "under the Rules."

– *Elimination of former Article 12 of the Court's Internal Rules.* As indicated above, Article 12 of the Court's Internal Rules provided that the Secretariat of the Court would make a preliminary determination regarding the application of Article 7. This provision has been eliminated from the new Internal Rules adopted by the Court in conjunction with the issuance of the New Rules. Thus, the Court will henceforth decide whether to allow an arbitration to proceed without the need for a preliminary determination by the Secretariat. However, Article 6(2) incorporates, albeit in slightly modified form, the provision – formerly in Article 12 of the Internal Rules – that the parties retain the right to request a competent court whether there is a binding arbitration agreement if the ICC Court decides that the arbitration cannot proceed. The drafters of the New Rules nevertheless did not see any need also to import into Article 6.2 from Article 12 the statement that the Court's decision is of an "administrative" nature, for, whatever the Court's decision, it is not intended to deprive either the courts or the arbitrators, as the case may be, of jurisdiction to consider whether the parties are bound by an ICC arbitration agreement.

Procedural considerations. Article 6(2) comes into play only if "the Respondent does not file an Answer" or a party "raises one or more pleas concerning the existence, validity or scope of the arbitration agreement." Thus, it does not preclude an arbitration from being set in motion if there is no prior ICC arbitration agreement, but the Respondent nevertheless submits an Answer without objecting to the commencement of an arbitration. As a Respondent may agree to submit to ICC arbitration, even in the absence of a prior agreement, the Secretariat of the Court therefore normally notifies the Request for Arbitration to the Respondent whether or not there appears to be an ICC arbitration agreement. In addition, in the event that, upon receipt of a Request for Arbitration, it does not appear to the Secretary General that there may be an ICC arbitration agreement, then he has been directed by the Court nevertheless to fix a provisional advance on costs pursuant to Article 30(1) (*see infra*) when the Request is notified to the Respondent.[138] If the Respondent contests the existence, validity or scope of the arbitration agreement or does not file an Answer, but the Claimant wishes the arbitration to proceed and pays the provisional advance, then the matter will be submitted to the Court for a decision.

---

[138] *See* Briner, *supra*, note 47, p. 8.

Under the former Rules, the question of whether the arbitration should be set in motion would normally be submitted to a Committee meeting of the Court rather than a plenary session. However, if issues of particular difficulty arose or the Committee members were not able to reach a unanimous decision, then the matter would be referred to a plenary session. In addition, as already noted, it was the Court's practice under the previous Rules to refer the required decision to a plenary session if the Secretariat had made a preliminary determination that Article 7 applied and a party contested that decision. In the future, it will be for the Court to determine whether, and in what circumstances, it wishes to refer such matters to the plenary session (although nothing in the Rules obliges it to).[139] There is also an issue as to whether the Secretary General of the Court ought to exercise his new power to confirm arbitrators (*see* Article 9(2)) in cases where the Court may be required to take a decision under Article 6(2).

Occasionally, a party may wish the Court to reconsider its decision, either to allow, or not to allow, an arbitration to proceed. There is nothing in the Rules that precludes the Court from reconsidering such a decision, although it has not generally been its practice to do so, except where there may be relevant new facts or other possibly exceptional circumstances. Thus, on at least one prior occasion, the Court reversed a decision that an arbitration should be allowed to proceed against a party where new facts were subsequently brought to its attention.[140] However, this was a rare case, and it cannot reasonably be presumed that the Court will generally be willing to reconsider its decisions under Article 6(2).

It may also occur that upon, or before, the submission of a Request for Arbitration, a party applies to a court for an order enjoining the parties from proceeding with the arbitration or otherwise declaring that there is no valid arbitration agreement between the parties. In some jurisdictions, such as France, the courts would not normally entertain such an application unless it were evident that there is no such agreement.[141] However, in others, the courts may accept to rule upon the matter, whether or not a Request for Arbitration is already pending before the ICC.[142] If such is the case, the ICC Court may find itself in the position of having to decide whether or not to take account of the proceedings before the courts.

The Court has not usually considered the pendency of parallel judicial proceedings to be an obstacle to the setting in motion of an arbitration proceeding

---

[139] *But see* with respect to this, *supra*, note 53.

[140] *See* the *R.E.D.E.C.* case, *supra*, note 134. In that case, the Defendant party in question was the President of two of the other Defendants and, in his corporate capacity, had signed a guarantee related to the subject of the arbitration. The Court reversed its original decision that the arbitration should be allowed to proceed against him personally after a lawsuit was brought against the ICC in respect of the same. It should not be assumed, however, that the filing of a lawsuit against the ICC will suffice to cause the Court to reconsider a decision. Thus, for example, it would not do so in the *Cekobanka* case, *supra*, note 134.

[141] *See infra,* note 155.

[142] *See* Park, *supra*, note 131, pp. 149-53.

if it is otherwise inclined to do so and the Court is not itself the subject of a rul-ing enjoining it from proceeding.[143] Never theless, it cannot be excluded that the Court might take account of a decision of a court at the place of the arbitration that there is no arbitration agreement between the parties and, thus, refuse to set an arbitration in motion in that place. It is to be noted, in this connection, that Article 6(2) does not oblige the Court to set an arbitration in motion if it is *"prima facie* satisfied" that an arbitration agreement may exist. All that Article 6(2) provides is that it "may" decide to do so. Depending on the circumstances, moreover, the Court's decision as to whether the arbitration should be set in motion could be influenced by parallel judicial proceedings at the domicile of one or more of the parties.

In one case, for example, the Court deferred any decision with respect to the setting in motion of an arbitration pending the resolution by the New York courts of a motion brought to stay arbitration proceedings against one of the Respondent parties named in a Request for Arbitration submitted to the ICC by a Canadian company. The Canadian Claimant initiated the arbitration proceed-ings against a New York corporation and its President on the basis of an arbitra-tion agreement contained in a sales contract between the Claimant and the New York company. The President, also a resident of New York, was named on the basis that he was the company's *alter ego*. Although the place of arbitration was not fixed in the arbitration agreement, the contract was governed by the laws of New York, and the parties advised the ICC that they wished the arbitration to be conducted in the United States (the Claimant in Washington, D.C. and the Respondents in New York). However, before the ICC Court decided upon the place of the arbitration proceedings and whether the arbitration should be allowed to proceed against the Respondent President, he applied for and obtained an order from the Supreme Court of the State of New York temporari-ly staying arbitration as to him personally pending a final decision on his appli-cation. Several months later, the New York court issued a judgment permanently staying the arbitration as to the President as it did not find that there was suffi-cient evidence to warrant the piercing of the "corporate veil" of the New York company.[144]

---

[143] The reason for the Court's position has been well-stated in *Craig Park and Paulsson,* §11.04, p. 197: "Any other rule would encourage the parties to deploy dilatory judicial pro-cedures, often in their own national courts, and to disregard their agreement to arbitrate." *See also*, with respect to this, Dimolitsa, "Issues Concerning the Existence, Validity and Effectiveness of the Arbitration Agreement," *ICC Ct. Bull.,* Vol. 7, No. 2 (1996), pp. 14, 20.

[144] *Jakubowski* v. *Nora Beverages, Inc., supra*, note 105. For a more general discussion of the willingness of U.S. courts to determine questions relating to the Arbitral Tribunal's jurisdiction in the face of an ICC arbitration clause, *see* Born, *International Commercial Arbitration in the United States* (Kluwer 1994), pp. 382-411. *See also Apollo Computer, Inc.* v. *Berg*, 886 F.2d 469 (1st Cir. 1989), which interprets former Articles 8(3) and 8(4) of the Rules as delegating to the arbitrator the power to decide disputes concerning the scope of the arbitration agreement.

Although the ICC was not a party to the proceedings in New York and was not itself bound by them, it nevertheless initially considered it appropriate to await the New York court's decision before setting the arbitration in motion because it was the parties' wish to conduct the arbitration in the United States, and the Claimant had submitted to and did not contest the jurisdiction of the New York court to rule on the matter before it. Ultimately, however, the ICC Court reversed its earlier decision and allowed the arbitration to proceed against both of the parties named by the Claimant, notwithstanding the decision of the New York court. The Court's ultimate attitude was, in fact, more consistent with its usual position in such circumstances.

The "prima facie" test. In practice, the ICC Court rarely refuses to set an arbitration in motion.[145] One of the principal reasons for this is that it is extremely unusual for a party to file a Request for Arbitration with the ICC in the absence of any evidence at all of an arbitration agreement. On the contrary, there will almost always be an arbitration clause. However, it may not be clear, for example, whether the parties agreed to ICC, or some other kind of, arbitration, or whether all of the parties named in the Request for Arbitration are bound by it. Thus, there will usually be related factual and legal issues dividing the parties as to which the Court may be reluctant to take a position. As already indicated, the Court tended to interpret very liberally the *"prima facie"* threshold formerly set forth in Article 7 and, thus, to allow arbitrations to proceed in cases of doubt. The modifications contained in Article 6(2) were made with this in mind.

Although the Court's jurisprudence is not static and is continually evolving, the following discussion of specific issues with which the Court has had to deal may nevertheless help to illuminate how Article 6(2) may be applied.[146]

– *Is There an Arbitration Agreement?*

Unlike many other arbitration rules, but like its predecessor provisions, Article 6(2) does not expressly require that the arbitration agreement between the parties be in writing.[147] Nor does Article 6(2) otherwise impose any requirements on the form that such an agreement must take. All that it requires is an agreement.

---

[145] In 1996, the ICC received 433 Requests for Arbitration, but Article 7 of the 1988 Rules was applied in fewer than ten cases.

[146] *See also*, with respect to the Court's practice in recent years, Dimolitsa, *supra*, note 143.

[147] A written agreement is nevertheless required under the New York Convention (Article II) and most national arbitration laws, including the UNCITRAL Model Law (Article 7(2)), although the laws of some countries may be less stringent and accept an oral or tacit agreement, as recognized in Article I(2)(a) of the Geneva Convention of 1961. Insofar as a written agreement is required, there may nevertheless be a question as to what constitutes such an agreement. *See, e.g., Craig Park and Paulsson,* §5.06, p. 75; Kaplan, "Is the Need for Writing as Expressed in the New York Convention and the Model Law Out of Step with Commercial Practice?" *Arb. Int.*, Vol. 12, No. 1 (1996), p. 27. In ICC arbitration, any difficulties in this regard may be remedied by the signature of the Terms of Reference (*see* Article 18 *infra*).

Nevertheless, the ICC Court can normally be expected to require at least some written evidence of the existence of an arbitration agreement before allowing an arbitration to proceed. The mere allegation that such an agreement exists will not ordinarily suffice. The written evidence that the Court may require, however, may fall short of a document bearing the signatures of the parties.

Thus, for example, the Court has accepted to set arbitrations in motion on the basis of arbitration clauses contained in standard conditions of contract where the parties disagreed as to whether the conditions in question had been accepted. The Court also allowed an arbitration to proceed where the only relevant document produced was a draft contract initialed by the parties and where it was alleged that the draft was, in fact, performed, although a final contract was never signed. In addition, agreements alleged to have arisen out of exchanges of letters, telexes or the like have on several occasions sufficed for the Court to allow arbitrations to go forward. Moreover, the Court has found *prima facie* evidence of an arbitration agreement where the copy of the agreement produced was alleged by the Defendant to be fraudulent. In all those instances, there were issues of fact or law that the Court considered should be ruled upon by the arbitrators.

In one case, however (*Cekobanka*),[148] which was submitted to the ICC in 1985, the Court applied then Article 7 where there was a disagreement between the parties as to whether an exchange of telexes had given rise to an agreement to arbitrate. There was no question that the Respondent, a Lebanese bank, had, in a series of telexes, offered to submit the dispute in question to ICC arbitration. The Claimant party, a Czech bank, had also, by telex, at least arguably accepted the offer. However, when it did so, the Lebanese bank replied that the offer was no longer outstanding, due to a change of circumstances, although it had never formally been withdrawn. When an ICC arbitration was nevertheless commenced against it, the Lebanese bank objected that there was no agreement between the parties.

The Court's refusal to allow the arbitration to proceed in the *Cekobanka* case, at least for the purpose of permitting an Arbitral Tribunal to decide whether there was an arbitration agreement between the parties, was strongly criticized by the Claimant party, who contended that, due to the political situation in Lebanon, it would not be able to pursue the matter before the Lebanese courts.[149] As the ICC Court would not reconsider its decision, the Claimant brought an action against the ICC before the Paris Court of First Instance (*Tribunal de grande instance*), in which it requested that the ICC be compelled to set the arbitration in motion. The Paris court decided, however, that the ICC had not committed any fault and that the ICC Rules had been respected. Its decision implicitly recognized, therefore, the considerable discretionary powers that the ICC Court enjoys in deciding whether to set an arbitration in motion.

---

[148] *See supra,* note 134.

[149] *See* Hautot, *"Les pouvoirs de la Cour d'arbitrage de la C.C.I. de décider ou non d'organiser l'arbitrage,"* *ASA Bull.* (1990), p. 12, note 1.

The position adopted by the ICC Court in the *Cekobanka* case was relatively strict, as compared to the Court's tendency in numerous cases since then to allow arbitration proceedings to go forward whenever there has appeared to be at least a reasonable possibility that an ICC arbitration agreement might be found to exist by a trier of fact. The Claimant in the *Cekobanka* case was armed with a legal opinion supporting its allegation that an ICC arbitration agreement had been created in addition to the exchange of telexes mentioned above. Given the evolution of the Court's jurisprudence in recent years with respect to former Article 7 and the reformulation of the *"prima facie"* test in Article 6(2), it is not unreasonable to assume that such a case would be decided differently today.[150]

The Court has generally had less difficulty with the argument that an arbitration agreement has ceased to exist by virtue of the expiration or termination of the agreement in which it is contained. Pursuant to what is now Article 6(4) of the Rules (*see infra*), which incorporates the principle of the arbitration agreement's "separability," an arbitrator does not cease to have jurisdiction by reason of a claim that the contract in which the arbitration agreement is contained is inexistent. The Court can, thus, normally be expected to allow an arbitration to proceed in such circumstances.

– Is the Arbitration Clause an ICC Clause?

As already indicated, Article 6(2) requires that there be an arbitration agreement "under the Rules." Its predecessor – Article 7 – required that the agreement "specify the ICC." It has been stated, with respect to former Article 7, that the ICC Court "will refuse to allow [the] arbitration to proceed unless there is an unambiguous reference to the ICC."[151] However, the Court has, on numerous occasions, permitted arbitrations to go forward where the arbitration clause not only did not refer unambiguously to the ICC, but arguably contained no mention of the ICC at all. Thus, for example, the Court has allowed arbitrations to proceed where the parties referred in their arbitration clause to:

- "the official Chamber of Commerce in Paris, France";
- "the Chamber of Commerce in Paris";
- "the Chamber of Commerce of Paris";
- "the Arbitration Commission of the Chamber of Commerce and Industry of Paris";
- "the Arbitration Court of the French Chamber of Commerce, Paris";
- "a Commission of Arbitration of French Chamber of Commerce, Paris";

---

[150] Indeed, several years after *Cekobanka*, the Court decided not to apply Article 7 in a case where the alleged arbitration agreement was claimed by the defendant party to be a mere offer letter that was never accepted. Although the circumstances were not identical, the Court's decision was more in keeping with its general tendency to allow disputed issues of fact to be decided by an Arbitral Tribunal.

[151] *Craig Park and Paulsson*, §2.03, p. 29; *see also id.*, §6.01, p. 106.

- "Arbitrage Court in Paris, France";
- "arbitration in Paris in the chamber of arbitration";
- "International Court of Arbitration as obtainable in Nigeria or in Sweden"; or
- "the Geneva Court of International Arbitration."

In allowing the arbitration to proceed in all of the above cases, the ICC Court applied a very broad brush to the requirement that the arbitration clause should specify the ICC.[152] Indeed, in each case the Court looked beyond the precise words used by the parties in order to determine whether it might have been their intention to refer to the ICC. Two factors, in particular, have weighed very heavily in the Court's approach to this question in the past. First, where the parties involved have been of different nationalities with no connection to the place specified in the arbitration clause, the Court has tended to assume that it must have been their wish to refer their disputes to an institution used primarily for international, as opposed to domestic, arbitration. Second, and more important, the Court has considered in each case whether there might be an arbitral institution, other than the ICC Court, to which the parties might have intended to refer. In the absence of another institution to which the clause could clearly be said to relate, the Court has tended to prefer to allow the question of the clause's proper construction, if this is disputed, to be referred to an Arbitral Tribunal rather than refuse the arbitration from the outset.

In this connection, the Court's approach has been comforted by the unique position that it has long occupied in Paris. Indeed, in Paris there is no other arbitration institution that calls itself a "Court" (nor is this the case, in fact, in many other places, although there are some other arbitral institutions that do, *e.g.*, the London Court of International Arbitration). Moreover, until very recently, no other "Chamber of Commerce" in Paris provided arbitration services, including, in particular, the Paris Chamber of Commerce and Industry – a distinct organization from the ICC, but with which the ICC is sometimes confused.[153]

Of course, in many of the above cases, the Court could have taken the alternative view that, in the absence of a clear reference to the ICC, the Court should

---

[152] *See also*, with respect to such cases, Benglia, "Inaccurate Reference to the ICC," *ICC Ct. Bull.*, Vol. 7, No. 2 (1996), p. 11.

[153] The possibility for confusion is particularly great in the French language as the ICC's French designation is CCI (*Chambre de Commerce Internationale*), which also can refer to a *Chambre de Commerce et d'Industrie* (Chamber of Commerce and Industry). In 1994, the Paris Chamber of Commerce and Industry established a "Center of Mediation and Arbitration" ("CMEA"), with its own set of arbitration rules. This may make it more difficult in the future to determine whether arbitration clauses referring to the Paris Chamber of Commerce should be referred to ICC arbitration, as in the past. It is to be noted, however, that the CMEA will only accept jurisdiction over disputes where at least one of the parties is French. For examples of cases where Arbitral Tribunals have construed references to the Paris Chamber of Commerce as designating the ICC, *see* the Awards in ICC Case No. 5103 (1988), *ICC Arbitral Awards 1986-1990*, p. 361, *and* ICC Case No. 6709 (1991), *ICC Arbitral Awards 1991-1995*, p. 435.

refuse to act and allow a competent court to decide whether an ICC, or other form of, arbitration should be organized. Particularly where the institution described in the arbitration clause does not exist, it might be argued that there is no basis upon which the Court can reasonably presume to assume jurisdiction, even on a preliminary basis.[154] However, the Court's position has unquestionably been influenced, in such cases, by a bias in favor of giving the greatest possible efficacy to the arbitration clause and, thus, allowing disputed issues relating to jurisdiction to be referred to arbitrators rather than the courts, at least in the first instance, except where it is evident that there was no intention to refer in the clause to the ICC. Such an approach has, moreover, been generally consistent with the attitude of the French courts.[155]

So too the Court has accepted arbitrations whenever the parties have provided for arbitration by the International Chamber of Commerce "of Geneva" or of other places such as Zurich or Stockholm where the ICC is not headquartered. There being no other organization in the world bearing such a name, both Arbitral Tribunals[156] and courts[157] have repeatedly construed such clauses as ICC clauses, the reference to the place being interpreted as the intended place of the arbitration.

There have, in addition, been a number of cases in which the Court has been required to decide whether to set an arbitration in motion where the relevant contract contained conflicting provisions regarding the settlement of disputes, *e.g.*, a provision for ICC arbitration in one clause and a reference to the juris-

---

[154] Thus, for example, it was decided in a case in Hong Kong that where the parties had referred in their arbitration clause to a non-existent institution (the "International Commercial Arbitration Association"), the matter was to be referred to *ad hoc* arbitration. *See Lucky-Goldstar International (H.K.) Limited* v. *Ng Moo Kee Engineering Ltd.*, Supreme Court of Hong Kong (May 5, 1993). *But cf. Circus Productions, Inc.* v. *Rosgoscirc* (S.D.N.Y. 1993), *ICCA Yearbook* XX (1995), p. 891, in which a United States District Court ordered the parties to arbitration before the American Arbitration Association in New York where they had mistakenly provided for a non-existent arbitral forum in their contract. (To the same effect, *see also HZI Research Center Inc.* v. *Sun Instruments Japan Co. Inc.* (S.D.N.Y. 1995), *Mealey's*, Vol. 10, No. 10 (October 1995), p. 11.) It may also be argued that, in such a case, the arbitration clause is inoperative or null. Thus, unlike in the previous two cases, a French court refused to refer the parties to arbitration where the arbitration clause designated a non-existent institution (the "International Court of Arbitration of The Hague") as the appointing authority for arbitrators (*Harper Robinson c/ Société Internationale de Maintenance et de Réalisation, Cour d'appel de Grenoble* (January 24, 1996), *Rev. arb.* (1997), p. 87).

[155] *See Société King Production c/ société Datel Production, Cour d'appel de Paris* (October 22, 1985), *Rev. arb.* (1986), p. 250; *Société Asland c/ société European Energy Corporation, Tribunal de grande instance de Paris* (December 13, 1988), *Rev. arb.* (1990), p. 521; *Société Deko c/ G. Dingler et société Meva, Cour d'appel de Paris* (March 24, 1994), *Rev. arb.* (1994), p. 515.

[156] *See, e.g.*, ICC Awards in Case Nos.2626 (1977), 3460 (1980), 4023 (1984), 4472 (1984), *ICC Arbitral Awards 1974-1985*, pp. 316, 425, 528, 524; ICC Award in Case No. 5294 (1988), *ICC Arbitral Awards 1986-1990*, p. 180; ICC Award in Case No. 5983 (1989), *ASA Bull.* (1993), p. 507.

[157] *See, e.g., Cour de justice de Genève* (judgment No. 320, November 8, 1979) (unpublished); *and* the decision of the Court of Appeal of Dresden (December 5, 1994), *ASA Bull.* (1995), p. 247.

diction of the courts in another. In the absence of any clear evidence of the parties' intent to the contrary, the Court has tended to accept such cases. In one particularly unusual matter, moreover, the Court accepted to set an arbitration in motion even though a provision for ICC arbitration in the general conditions of the contract had been expressly replaced by a different provision in the contract's particular conditions, the latter provision having been held to be invalid by a national court.

– *To Which Parties Does the Arbitration Agreement Apply?*

1. Non-signatories

Article 6(2) does not require that each of the parties to the arbitration must have signed the arbitration agreement, and it may be the case, by virtue of any one of a number of different legal theories (such as, *e.g.*, agency, assignment, *alter ego*, succession or the so-called "group of companies" theory[158]) that a non-signatory may be bound by an arbitration agreement. In such cases, however, it may not be apparent from the face of the agreement whether there is a legitimate basis for allowing the arbitration to proceed against the party in question, and the Court may be required to make what is a difficult and delicate decision as to whether the arbitration ought to be allowed to proceed against such party.

As a general rule, consistent with what has already been stated above, the Court has been inclined to allow arbitrations to proceed against parties who may not have signed, or who might not appear to be parties to, the arbitration agreement in question, provided that a plausible argument is made that they may nevertheless be bound by the same.[159] Obviously, a mere allegation to this effect will not suffice. The Court must be persuaded that there are serious issues of fact or law to be resolved. This may be the case, for example, where it is alleged that a party is bound by an arbitration agreement by virtue of its conduct or relationship with one of the signatory parties. Even if the argument advanced in support of the inclusion of a party in the arbitration may be a controversial one (as in the case of the "group of companies" theory, for example, *see* note 158 *supra*), the Court has not generally seen it as its role to evaluate the validity of its application in a particular case.

---

[158] *See Dow Chemical* v. *Isover-Saint Gobain*, ICC Case No. 4131 (1984), interim Award (September 23, 1982), *Rev. arb.* (1984), p. 137 *and ICCA Yearbook* IX (1984), p. 131; *see also* the extracts from ICC Awards on this subject, *ICC Ct. Bull.*, Vol. 2, No. 2 (November 1991), p. 20; the additional Awards cited by Derains in his Note on the Award in ICC Case No. 6519 (1991), *ICC Arbitral Awards 1991-1995*, p. 423; *Craig Park and Paulsson*, §5.09, p. 95; Sandrock, "Arbitration Agreements and Groups of Companies," *Etudes de Droit International en l'Honneur de Pierre Lalive* (Helbing & Lichtenhahn 1993), p. 625; *Fouchard Gaillard and Goldman*, p. 299; Fadlallah, "*Clauses d'arbitrage et groupes de sociétés,*" *Trav. Com. fr. DIP* (1985), p. 105.

[159] *See, e.g.*, the Note of Derains on ICC Award No. 6519 (1991), *supra*, note 158. *See also* Dimolitsa, *supra*, note 143, pp. 16-18.

This being said, under its former Chairman, the Court had a tendency to apply a relatively stricter standard, when deciding whether to an allow an arbitration to proceed in respect of physical persons or States not named as parties in the relevant arbitration agreement. It remains to be seen whether this will continue to be the tendency of the present Court, given, in particular, the reformulation of the *"prima facie"* test in Article 6(2).

(i)   Physical persons

Although the Court has often set arbitrations in motion against physical persons not named as parties in the contracts that were the subject of the arbitrations in question, it has generally been more hesitant to do so than in the case of corporate entities. In this regard, the *R.E.D.E.C.* case, in particular (*see* notes 134 *and* 135 *supra*), left its imprint on the jurisprudence of the Court.

The *R.E.D.E.C.* case concerned an ICC arbitration commenced in 1987 by Uzinexport Import, a Romanian company, against Attock Cement Company Ltd, of the Cayman Islands ("Attock"), and Attock Cement Pakistan Ltd ("Attock Pakistan") in connection with the construction of a cement plant in Pakistan. Although not a signatory of the construction contract with Uzinexport Import, which contained the relevant arbitration clause, R.E.D.E.C. was also named as a Defendant party for having, by a separate letter of guarantee, guaranteed the repayment by Attock of a credit provided by Uzinexport Import in connection with the project. R.E.D.E.C., a Saudi Arabian company, belonged to the same corporate group as Attock and Attock Pakistan. In addition to R.E.D.E.C., the Claimant named as a Defendant Mr. Pharaon, the Chairman of both Attock and R.E.D.E.C. In such capactiy, he had signed the R.E.D.E.C. guarantee, and it was alleged by Uzinexport Import that he was personally responsible therefore because of his alleged ownership and control of that company. Notwithstanding the objections of both R.E.D.E.C. and Mr. Pharaon that they were not parties to the arbitration agreement with Uzinexport Import, the Court decided to allow the arbitration to proceed against both of them under Article 8(3) of the then Rules. R.E.D.E.C. and Mr. Pharaon then instituted proceedings against the ICC before the Paris Court of First Instance in order to obtain an order suspending the arbitral proceedings against them.

Before the Court of First Instance rendered its decision, however, the ICC Court reconsidered its position and decided to exclude Mr. Pharaon from the arbitration, while maintaining R.E.D.E.C. in the proceedings. The Paris court ultimately refused to interfere with the decisions of the ICC Court, which was found to have acted in accordance with its powers under the ICC Rules.

As the ICC Court was not compelled by the Paris court to alter its decision with respect to Mr. Pharaon, and it cannot be said with any confidence that it would have been required to do so had it not acted on its own initiative, the Court, in reversing its decision, must have felt that the case for including Mr. Pharaon in the arbitration, solely on the basis that he had signed the R.E.D.E.C. guarantee in his capacity as Chairman and was alleged to be its *alter ego*, was extremely tenuous. The Court nevertheless felt that the arbitration should proceed in this instance against R.E.D.E.C. in view of the letter of guarantee that it had provided.[160]

Arguably, the different treatment of Mr. Pharaon and R.E.D.E.C. reflected a bias on the part of the Court resulting in the application of a stricter standard for individuals than for companies. This can possibly be explained by an understandable concern for the potentially greater prejudice that an individual, as compared to a company, may suffer if required to defend an arbitration, if only for the limited purpose of opposing the tribunal's jurisdiction. This being said, when an individual's control of a corporate entity is shown to be absolute (*e.g.*, by virtue of ownership of all, or nearly all, of its shares), the Court has generally been more inclined to allow an Arbitral Tribunal to decide whether there is a basis for treating such person as an *alter ego* rather than attempting itself to make any determination in this regard.

(ii)   States

As in the case of individuals, the ICC Court has, on several occasions in recent years, applied a stricter test in respect of claims asserted against a State that has not itself signed an arbitration agreement entered into by a related entity than in respect of a company in similar circumstances.

As a large number of ICC arbitrations have concerned contracts entered into by governmental or quasi-governmental entities,[161] parties have on many occasions sought to involve the State itself in such arbitrations, on the basis, for example, that the State approved or performed the contract in question or that it otherwise acquired the assets of the governmental entity that was formally a party thereto, acted as its *alter ego* or conducted itself in some other manner that might justify a finding that it had itself become liable for the actions of such entity. However, even where there has been a serious issue of possible State liability in such cases, the ICC Court has often been reluctant to allow the arbitration to proceed against the State itself (as opposed to a distinct State-owned entity) absent a relatively strong showing that the State was a party to the relevant contract. Indeed, for the Court, the State's normal immunity from jurisdic-

---

[160] But insofar as a guarantee is regarded as a separate and autonomous undertaking, as in the case of a typical bank guarantee, the arbitration agreement in the related contract is generally considered not to apply in the absence of evidence of a contrary intention. *See, e.g.,* Goutal, Note, *Bisutti c/ société financière Monsigny (Sefimo) et autre, Cour de cassation* (June 4, 1985), *Rev. arb.* (1987), p. 139; Leurent, "*Garanties bancaires et Arbitrage*," *Revue de Droit des Affaires Internationales* (1990), p. 414; Chambreuil, "*Arbitrage international et garanties bancaires*," *Rev. arb.* (1991), p. 33; Hanotiau, "*La pratique de l'Arbitrage International en Matière Bancaire*," *Les modes non-judiciares de règlement des conflits* (Bruylant 1995), p. 67; ICC Awards Nos. 3896 (1982) and 4392 (1983), *ICC Arbitral Awards 1974-1985*, pp. 481, 473; *cf.*, however, *Société Inex Film et société Interexport c/ société Universal Pictures, Cour d'appel de Paris* (March 16, 1978), *Rev. arb.* (1978), p. 501, *and Compania Espanola de Petroles S.A.* v. *Nereus Shipping S.A.*, 527 F. 2d 99 (2d Cir. 1975).

[161] *See* Jarvin, "*Participation à l'arbitrage C.C.I. des Etats et entreprises publiques*," *Rev. arb.* (1985), p. 585.

tion can be said to create a strong presumption against its inclusion in an arbitration in the absence of explicit consent thereto.

Difficult and complex issues may nevertheless arise.[162] Thus, for example, in the arbitration commenced in 1980 by Westland Helicopters United ("Westland") against the Arab Organization for Industrialization ("AOI") and the Arab British Helicopter Company ("ABH"), the Court permitted the arbitration to proceed, under Article 8.3 of the then Rules, not only against AOI and ABH but also the four States (Egypt, Qatar, Saudi Arabia and the United Arab Emirates) that had established AOI, notwithstanding the objection of Egypt that AOI was a distinct legal entity and that Egypt was not itself a party to any agreement with Westland.[163]

The *Westland* case arose out of a series of contracts concluded in 1978 between Westland and AOI for the creation of a joint company (ABH) that would have as its purpose the manufacture and sale of helicopters developed by Westland. In this connection, Westland also entered into a license agreement and a number of ancillary contracts with ABH. A Shareholders Agreement between Westland and AOI and all of the contracts with ABH contained clauses providing for the submission of disputes to ICC arbitration in Geneva. By a separate Memorandum of Understanding, the Higher Committee of AOI, which was composed of representatives of the four founding States, undertook to guarantee to the British government the performance of all obligations owed by AOI, or companies controlled by it, to Westland.

In 1979, following the conclusion of the "Camp David" accords and Egypt's recognition of Israel, the other three States represented in AOI announced the withdrawal of their investments from that entity and their intention to liquidate it. The Egyptian government, however, promulgated a law purporting to provide for AOI's continued existence as an Egyptian legal entity, its headquarters being in Cairo. Nevertheless, as AOI had in reality been liquidated, Westland filed a Request for Arbitration with the ICC for the damages incurred by it as a result.

In response to the Request, Egypt (unlike the three other States, who did not respond) objected that it was not a party to any of the agreements with Westland and argued that it should be excluded from the arbitration in accordance with Article 7 of the Rules. The ICC Court decided, however, that there was a suffi-

---

[162] *See, e.g.,* Böckstiegel, "The Legal Rules Applicable in International Commercial Arbitration Involving States or State-controlled Enterprises," *60 Years of ICC Arbitration* (ICC Publishing 1984), p. 117; *and* Böckstiegel, *Arbitration and State Enterprises* (Kluwer 1984). *See also* the papers submitted to the October 11, 1985 colloquium of the *Comité Français de l'Arbitrage* on the subject of *"Les Etats et l'arbitrage international,"* as reproduced in *Rev. arb.* (1985), p. 493; *and* Lew, ed., *Contemporary Problems in International Arbitration* (Martinus Nijhoff 1987), p. 241.

[163] The *Westland* case has been the subject of substantial commentary. *See, e.g.,* Leboulanger, *"Groupes d'Etat(s) et arbitrage,"* *Rev. arb.* (1989), p. 415; Cahier, "The Strengths and Weaknesses of International Arbitration Involving a State as a Party," Lew, ed., *Contemporary Problems in International Arbitration* (Martinus Nijhoff 1987), p. 241; *and* Lalive, "Arbitration with Foreign States or State-Controlled Entities: Some Practical Questions," in the same publication, p. 289.

cient basis for setting the arbitration in motion against Egypt (and the three other States) and that Egypt's jurisdictional objections should be ruled upon by an Arbitral Tribunal. The Egyptian government then requested the cantonal court of Geneva to annul the arbitral proceedings. But the Geneva court did not consider that it had any authority to grant such a request, and, in a judgment that was affirmed on appeal by the Swiss Supreme Court (*Tribunal fédéral*), the Geneva court rejected the application,[164] thus leaving the Arbitral Tribunal in a position to render a partial Award with respect to the matter of its jurisdiction. This it subsequently did in an interim arbitral Award that found that all four State parties were bound by the arbitration agreement between Westland and AOI and were therefore proper parties to the arbitration.[165] However, the tribunal's decision with respect to Egypt was ultimately annulled by the cantonal court of Geneva on the application of Egypt, the only one of the States to have filed a timely application for the same.[166]

In annulling the Arbitral Tribunal's decision that Egypt was a proper party to the arbitration, the Geneva court found that AOI was legally and financially independent from the four States that had created it, and it attached considerable importance to this. The Arbitral Tribunal had taken the position that, even if AOI had a distinct legal personality, which was not disputed, this did not necessarily exclude the possible responsibility of the States, which, in the view of the tribunal, should be presumed in the absence of any indication to the contrary in the documents creating AOI. Moreover, for the Arbitral Tribunal it followed from the imputation to the States of responsibility for the undertakings of AOI that the States must also be bound by the arbitration agreement that AOI had signed. The Geneva court disagreed. In its view, the possible existence of State responsibility could not be regarded as a substitute for a State's failure to agree to arbitration itself. It was, on the contrary, to be presumed, in the view of the court, that a sovereign State does not intend to waive its immunity from jurisdiction when it has not itself agreed to arbitrate, and such a presumption cannot be overcome simply by invoking an arbitration clause signed by a legally distinct entity, even if that entity is merely an instrumentality of the State. The decision of the Geneva court was subsequently upheld by the Swiss Supreme Court (*Tribunal fédéral suisse*).[167]

---

[164] *See République arabe d'Egypte c/ Westland Helicopters Ltd., Cour de justice de Genève* (November 26, 1982), *affirmed* by the *Tribunal fédéral suisse* (May 16, 1983).

[165] Extracts from the tribunal's Award of March 5, 1984 appear in *ICCA Yearbook* XI (1986), p. 127, *and Rev. arb.* (1989), p. 547.

[166] *République arabe d'Egypte, A.O.I., A.B.H. c/ Westland Helicopters Ltd., Cour de justice de Genève* (November 3, 1987), *Rev. arb.* (1989), p. 514.

[167] *See* judgment of July 19, 1988, *Rev. arb.* (1989), p. 525. Ultimately, the Arbitral Tribunal rendered an Award on June 28, 1993 in which the remaining State parties (Qatar, Saudi Arabia and the United Arab Emirates) were found subsidiarily liable for damages. Those States then sought to have the Award set aside by the Swiss courts, but in vain. The Swiss courts took the position that the States could no longer contest the arbitrators' finding of jurisdiction and that the Award was not otherwise contrary to Swiss public policy. *See Les Emirats Arabes Unis, le Royaume d'Arabie Saoudite, l'Etat du Qatar c/ Westland Helicopters Ltd., Tribunal fédéral suisse* (April 19, 1994), *ASA Bull.* (1994), p. 404.

The Swiss courts' decisions in the Westland case, coming on the heels of the French courts' annulment of another ICC arbitration Award against Egypt in the matter of *Southern Pacific Properties* v. *Arab Republic of Egypt and the Egyptian General Company for Tourism and Hotels* (the "Pyramids" case),[168] undoubtedly had a chilling effect, in the years that followed, on the ICC Court's willingness to allow arbitrations to proceed against States where they had not themselves signed an arbitration agreement.[169] In the wake of those decisions, the Court was generally more inclined than in prior years to apply Article 7 in respect of non-signatory States than non-signatory companies, for example. Whether or not it was right to do so, the Court nevertheless cannot legitimately be said to have erred in deciding to allow the arbitration to proceed against the State parties in the *Westland* case. Indeed, the mere fact that a distinguished panel of arbitrators subsequently arrived at the conclusion that the States were proper parties to the arbitration demonstrates that the issues raised were sufficiently serious to justify the Court's *prima facie* decision, even if the arbitrators' Award was partially annulled. Moreover, the subject of possible State liability for the undertakings of its instrumentalities remains a difficult and controversial subject, as to which the positions of the courts in different jurisdictions may vary, depending, in particular, on the facts of the case.[170] This is therefore likely to remain a delicate and difficult area for the Court in the years to come.

2. Multiple contracts

In requiring that there be "an arbitration agreement," Article 6(2), like former Articles 7 and 8(3), raises the question of whether all of the parties to the arbitration must be linked by a common arbitration agreement, or whether a single arbitration may be set in motion in respect of a series of separate, but possibly related, agreements. This is yet another difficult issue, with which the Court has had to grapple and as to which its jurisprudence has not always been consistent.

---

[168] *See* the Arbitral Tribunal's Award of March 11, 1983, *International Legal Materials,* No. 22 (1983), p. 752, *and* the judgment of July 12, 1984 of the Paris Court of Appeal annulling the Award, *Rev. arb.* (1986), p. 75, *and International Legal Materials,* No. 23 (1984), p. 1048, as affirmed by the Court of Cassation on January 6, 1987, *Rev. arb.* (1987), p. 469. In that case, the court annulled the finding of an ICC Arbitral Tribunal that Egypt was bound by the arbitration clause contained in a contract entered into by EGOTH, an independent Egyptian state authority, where the Egyptian Minister of Tourism had added his signature to the contract under the words "approved, agreed and ratified." As in the *Westland* case, the ICC Court had not applied Article 7 in respect of the Egyptian State, notwithstanding the latter's objection that it was not a party.

[169] Moreover, the ICC was sued by the Egyptian government in Cairo for its failure to apply Article 7 in the *Westland* case and was condemned by an Egyptian court of first instance to pay the government damages of U.S. $1,000,000, although the jurisdictional basis for the court's action was contested by the ICC. During subsequent appeal proceedings, the claim was withdrawn.

[170] *See* Böckstiegel, *Arbitration and State Enterprises, supra,* note 162, p. 34.

In recent years, the Court has often presumed that an agreement to arbitrate relates only to the contract in which it is contained, unless the parties have otherwise provided or there is sufficient evidence that they may have intended such agreement to extend to other related contracts.[171] However, the Court has not always followed such a strict approach. Thus, for example, in the *Westland* case, the Court permitted a single arbitration to proceed against both AOI and ABH in respect of their separate contracts with Westland and the different arbitration clauses contained therein, presumably because of the compatibility of the clauses and the close connections among all of the contracts concerned.

A similar approach was followed by the Court when three different French entities, Eurodif, Sofidif and Cogema, jointly introduced a Request for Arbitration in 1979 against the Iranian atomic energy organization (OEAI) and the Iranian organization for investment and economic and technical aid (OIAETI) in respect of a series of different contracts all relating to Iran's cooperation with France in a uranium enrichment project. There, notwithstanding the objections of OEAI and OIAETI, the Court permitted a single arbitration to go forward in respect of two different contracts that not only were each between different parties but that also contained different arbitration clauses.[172] The Award that was subsequently rendered, by an Arbitral Tribunal sitting in Paris, confirmed the tribunal's jurisdiction over all of the claims brought before it in respect of each of the contracts concerned in view of their complementarity and interdependence. However, the Award was annulled by the Paris Court of Appeal, and in a subsequent series of judgments, the French courts made clear their view that a single arbitration may be conducted in respect of different arbitration clauses only with the consent of all of the parties concerned.[173] Among other things, the courts held that, in the absence of any manifestation of an intention of the contracting parties to consolidate two arbitration clauses, such an intention cannot necessarily be said to arise merely from the complementarity and compatibility of the clauses in question.

---

[171] There may be circumstances in which an arbitration agreement may be considered to extend to contracts other than the one in which it is contained by virtue of the interdependence of the contracts concerned, *e.g.*, where they, in fact, form part of a single transaction. *See G.I.E. Acadi c/ société Thomson-Answare, Cour d'appel de Paris, Rev. arb.* (1988), p. 573; *SOABI v. Republic of Senegal,* ICSID Award (1988), *ICCA Yearbook* XVII (1992), p. 42; the extract from the Award in ICC Case No. 7184 (1994), *ICC Ct. Bull.,* Vol. 8, No. 2 (1997), p. 63; *see also Fouchard Gaillard and Goldman,* p. 317; Leboulanger, *supra,* note 95; Cohen, *"Arbitrage et Groupes de Contrats," Rev. arb.* (1997), p. 471.

[172] Each provided for ICC arbitration, but one provided for arbitration in Paris while the other did not specify the place of arbitration. Moreover, one of the Claimant parties was not a party to either contract, but was rather a party to a separate agreement providing for ICC arbitration in Geneva.

[173] *See OIAETI c/ Sofidif et OEAI, SERU, Eurodif et CEA, Cour d'appel de Paris* (December 19, 1986), *Rev. arb.* (1987), p. 359; *Société Sofidif et autres c/ OIEATI et autre, Cour de cassation* (March 8, 1988), Note Jarrosson, *Rev. arb.* (1989), p. 481; *OIAETI et Sofidif c/ COGEMA, SERU, Eurodif, CEA, Cour d'appel de Versailles* (March 7, 1990), *Rev. arb.* (1991), p. 326. *See also* Gaillard, *"L'affaire SOFIDIF ou les difficultés de l'arbitrage multipartite," Rev. arb.* (1987), p. 275.

Although the decisons of the French courts in the *Eurodif* case do not exclude a possible finding, in different circumstances, that the parties may have intended a single arbitration in respect of different arbitration agreements, it was not the Court's practice, for many years after *Eurodif*, to presume this to be the case. Thus, unless the Court's position evolves, it may refuse to allow a single arbitration to proceed in respect of different parties to different arbitration agreements if a party objects or there is not otherwise evidence of a common intention to conduct a consolidated arbitration.[174]

Insofar as the same parties have entered into more than one arbitration agreement in respect of different contracts, there may also be an issue as to whether they intended disputes relating to those different contracts to be consolidated in a single arbitration. Although the Court may, even in such circumstances, require separate arbitration requests to be filed, neither Article 6(2) nor any other provision of the Rules explicitly confers any such authority on the Court when deciding whether to set an arbitration in motion.[175] Indeed, provided that there is at least one arbitration agreement between all of the parties in question, it may be argued that it should normally be for the Arbitral Tribunal, and not the ICC, to decide whether all of the matters set forth in the Request for Arbitration fall within a single tribunal's jurisdiction.

The Arbitral Tribunal's determination of its own jurisdiction. If the Court has decided to set an arbitration in motion, then Article 6(2), like Article 8(3) of the former Rules, provides that "any decision as to the jurisdiction of the Arbitral Tribunal shall be taken by the Arbitral Tribunal itself." Ordinarily, in cases where a jurisdictional objection has been raised before the Court has determined that the arbitration should nevertheless proceed, the Court, in notifying its decision to the parties and the Arbitral Tribunal, specifically draws their attention to the relevant requirements of the Rules. The Court has, in the past, also subsequently verified that the question of the Arbitral Tribunal's jurisdiction is listed in the Terms of Reference as one of the issues to be determined in the arbitration. Although the inclusion in the Terms of Reference of such a list is no longer mandatory (*see* the discussion of Article 18 *infra*), the Court will presumably continue to verify, in appropriate cases, that the issue of jurisdiction has been included when such a list of issues is prepared.

There are a number of issues that may arise in connection with the Arbitral Tribunal's consideration of its own jurisdiction. Among these, first of all, is the question of whether the tribunal has the authority to examine the matter of its jurisdiction *sua sponte* in the absence of a jurisdictional objection of one of the parties. Under the former Rules, the drafting of Article 8(3) appeared to suggest that the Arbitral Tribunal was to decide upon its jurisdiction only where "one of the parties raise[d] one or more pleas concerning the existence or validity of

---

[174] *See* Hascher, *supra*, note 94.
[175] *See also*, in this connection, the discussion of Article 4(6) *supra*.

the agreement to arbitrate." Article 6(2), however, has been formulated in broader terms and arguably can be said to authorize, or even oblige, the Arbitral Tribunal to decide upon its jurisdiction in cases where the Respondent has not filed an Answer and there appears to the tribunal to be a possible issue as to its jurisdiction. That the Arbitral Tribunal should, on its own initiative, consider the matter of its own jurisdiction is, in fact, widely accepted in cases of default,[176] and the broader formulation of Article 6(2) therefore usefully clarifies the Arbitral Tribunal's authority to do so. Article 6(2) does not provide, however, that the Arbitral Tribunal shall otherwise decide upon its jurisdiction in the absence of a plea of one of the parties, and whether or not it may properly do so as a matter of law is not universally agreed, although there is strong support internationally for the proposition that it should do so if public policy would otherwise be violated.[177]

While Article 6(2) recognizes the Arbitral Tribunal's authority to decide upon its own jurisdiction, there are further, related issues that arise due to its failure to specify how and when the Arbitral Tribunal is to do so. Although it is common in international arbitrations for jurisdictional questions to be addressed as preliminary matters, the Rules do not oblige the Arbitral Tribunal to rule on a jurisdictional plea prior to considering the merits of the case and issuing a final Award.[178] Absent an agreement of the parties, the Arbitral Tribunal is therefore free to decide upon the question of its jurisdiction whenever it considers it appropriate.[179] From the perspective of the parties, an early decision on jurisdiction has the advantage of avoiding the possibly futile devotion of time to the merits for as long as there is a possibility that the arbitrators may find that they are without jurisdiction. This is the principal reason why jurisdictional issues are most frequently decided preliminarily. However, this may not always be approp-

---

[176] *See, e.g., Lalive Poudret and Reymond*, p. 384. *But compare*, for example, Article 21(1) of the UNCITRAL Rules, which only provides that the Arbitral Tribunal has the power "to rule on *objections* that it has no jurisdiction . . . ." (emphasis added).

[177] Thus, for example, it has been noted that, during the drafting of Article 16 of the UNCITRAL Model Law, the reference to the parties' "objections" contained in Article 21 of the UNCITRAL Rules was deliberately deleted in order to permit arbitrators to decide issues of jurisdiction on their initiative. However, the drafters of the Model Law nevertheless took the view that "with the exception of certain classes of jurisdictional objections – such as those going to arbitrability or public policy – the failure to raise a plea as to jurisdiction should operate as a waiver of the point." *Holtzmann and Neuhaus*, p. 479. *Compare, e.g.*, in relation to arbitration in Switzerland, Dutoit, Knoepfler, Lalive, Mercier, *Répertoire de droit international privé suisse* (Berne 1982), Vol. 1, p. 288 (an Arbitral Tribunal should always verify its own jurisdiction), and *Lalive Poudret and Reymond*, pp. 64-65 and 383-84 (to the contrary, except, insofar as international arbitration is concerned, where Swiss international public policy may be violated).

[178] *Compare* UNCITRAL Rules, Article 21(4) ("In general, the Arbitral Tribunal should rule on a plea concerning its jurisdiction as a preliminary question.").

[179] In an ICC arbitration, the Arbitral Tribunal may be obliged to decide upon its jurisdiction preliminarily if it has so provided in the Terms of Reference. *See, e.g.*, the decision of the French Court of Cassation in the *Eurodif* case (March 8, 1988), *supra*, note 173.

riate. In some cases, for example, the jurisdictional questions to be resolved may be so intertwined with issues of fact or law relating to the merits that they cannot properly be decided in advance. In others, the advantages of an early decision on jurisdiction may be outweighed by the delays that may occur, due to, for example, the time required for the preparation of an Award, its approval by the ICC Court (*see* Article 27 *infra*), and, if jurisdiction is accepted, the need for an additional round of pleadings and another hearing. A partial Award on jurisdiction may also be the subject of recourse before the courts.[180] Thus, whether jurisdictional issues should be decided in advance has to be considered in the context of each case.[181]

When the Arbitral Tribunal decides to consider the question of its jurisdiction as a preliminary matter, its decision, if jurisdiction is declined, should normally take the form of a final Award and, if jurisdiction is upheld, it should ordinarily be in the form of a partial Award. The Rules do not actually mandate this explicitly, however, and whether or not a decision on jurisdiction is considered to be an "Award" may vary, depending upon the law governing the arbitration.[182] In general, though, such decisions are normally considered to be final and subject to recourse before the national courts.[183] It would therefore seem to be in the spirit of the Rules (*see* Article 35 *infra*) that, however they may be characterized as a matter of national law, such decisions should ordinarily be issued in a form permitting their scrutiny and approval by the ICC Court.[184]

When issuing an Award confined to the question of its jurisdiction, the Arbitral Tribunal may, lastly, be required to deal with one or more applications for the Award of costs. Although the matter of costs is addressed in considerably more detail below (*see* Article 31), there are two questions, in particular,

---

[180] In most jurisdictions, however, an action against a partial Award on jurisdiction should not have the effect of suspending the arbitral proceedings. *See, e.g.*, UNCITRAL Model Law, Article 16(3).

[181] *See*, in this connection, the description of the experience of the Iran-U.S. Claims Tribunal in relation to the bifurcation of arbitral proceedings in Baker and Davis, *The UNCITRAL Arbitration Rules in Practice* (Kluwer 1992), pp. 106-07.

[182] As already discussed (*see* Article 2), there is no internationally-accepted definition of Award or consensus as to the types of preliminary decisions that must take the form of an Award. Thus, for example, in an international arbitration in Switzerland, an Arbitral Tribunal is to decide on its jurisdiction by means of a "preliminary decision" (although subject to judicial recourse) (Swiss Private International Law Act, Article 186), while in many other countries (such as France, for example, *see Fouchard Gaillard and Goldman*, pp. 748-53) such a decision would undoubtedly be regarded as an Award.

[183] *See, e.g.,* UNCITRAL Model Law, Article 16(3).

[184] This was also the conclusion of the ICC Commission's Working Party on Dissenting Opinions and Interim and Partial Awards. *See* "Final Report on Interim and Partial Awards," *ICC Ct. Bull.*, *supra*, note 62, p. 28. However, in a recent judgment, a French court has found that it is for the Arbitral Tribunal, rather than the ICC Court, to decide whether a particular decision constitutes an Award under the applicable law. *See Société Cubic Defense System* c/ *Chambre de commerce internationale*, *supra*, note 65.

relating to the Arbitral Tribunal's power to award costs that may arise in connection with a decision on jurisdiction. First, there is the question of whether it can make an Award of costs against the Claimant if it finds that there is not a valid arbitration agreement between the parties. Although the Arbitral Tribunal's authority to make such an Award has occasionally been questioned, there would ordinarily seem to be ample grounds to support a tribunal's assertion of such authority, given the parties' submission to the jurisdiction of the Arbitral Tribunal, at least for the purpose of deciding upon the matter of its jurisdiction and resolving related costs claims.[185] Second, where the tribunal decides that it does not have jurisdiction over one of multiple Respondent parties and, accordingly, that party is dismissed from the arbitration, while the arbitration continues against the others, there is a question concerning the Arbitral Tribunal's authority, concurrently with its decision on jurisdiction, to award costs to the departing party. Although it would appear normal for a departing party to be awarded its costs at such time, some of the arbitration costs – in particular, the fees and expenses of the arbitrators and the ICC – are not fixed until the conclusion of the arbitration. There would nevertheless not seem to be any impediment to a Claimant being ordered to indemnify a departing party for its "reasonable legal and other costs" (Article 31) and all or a portion of the amount contributed by it to the advance on costs for the arbitration.[186]

Article 6(3)

> *If any of the parties refuses or fails to take part in the arbitration or any stage thereof, the arbitration shall proceed notwithstanding such refusal or failure.*

This provision confirms the Arbitral Tribunal's authority to proceed with an arbitration in the event of a default of one of the parties. It is derived from a provision originally included in the Rules in 1927 concerning the refusal or failure of the "defendant" to "submit" to arbitration. However, over the years, its wording and potential scope have gradually been broadened. Thus, in 1955, the reference to the "defendant" was expanded to include either one of the parties, and in 1975, a party's refusal or failure to "submit" to arbitration became a refusal or failure "to take part in the arbitration" (Article 8(2) of the former Rules). With the New Rules, the refusal or failure in question has been further extended to include "any stage" of the arbitration.

The antecedents of Article 6(3) appear to have had as their original purpose the confirmation of the authority of both the Court and the Arbitral Tribunal to proceed with the arbitration solely on the basis of the parties' arbitration agree-

---

[185] *See* the discussion of Article 31(3) and note 776 *infra*.
[186] *See* the discussion of Article 31(2) *infra*.

ment. No further "submission" to arbitration was deemed to be necessary.[187] While Article 6(3) still serves this purpose, it further confirms the general authority of the Court and the Arbitral Tribunal to proceed notwithstanding a default of a party in respect of any aspect of the arbitration proceeding. Article 6(3) is complemented in this regard by a number of more specific provisions relating to the constitution of the Arbitral Tribunal (Articles 8 and 10), the Terms of Reference (Article 18) and hearings (Article 21).

Although not expressly stated in Article 6(3), it must be understood as assuming that all of the parties have received due notice of the arbitration and its various stages in accordance with the notice provisions contained in Article 3. However, neither Article 6(3) nor any other provision of the Rules establishes what may constitute due notice in a given case. The arbitrators are therefore required to exercise their judgment in this regard, bearing in mind that their Award may be vulnerable to attack if it can be established by the defaulting party that it was not given a reasonable opportunity to participate or to present its case. In general, the Court and ICC Arbitral Tribunals tend to take special care to ensure that parties are treated fairly in this regard.

Article 6(3) most commonly comes into play in relation to a defaulting Respondent, but, as already noted, it applies equally to all of the parties and, thus, theoretically permits an arbitration to proceed to an Award in the absence of a Claimant who, after commencing the arbitration, disappears or fails to prosecute its claim. In order for this to occur, however, either the Claimant would have had to pay its share of the advance on costs (*see* Article 30 *infra*) or any outstanding amounts would have to have been paid by the Respondent, which the latter will rarely be inclined to do unless it has counterclaims that it wishes to continue to pursue. In the event that the full amount of the advance on costs has already been paid, it may be open to the Arbitral Tribunal either to rule upon the Claimant's claims[188] or to dismiss them for failure of prosecution.[189]

---

[187] In fact, the laws of some countries, as is still true in a few (*see, e.g.,* Grigera Naón "Arbitration in Latin America," *Arb. Int.,* Vol. 5, No. 2 (1989), p. 137), did not recognize as binding an agreement for the arbitration of future disputes and required that the parties submit to arbitration once a dispute had arisen. This was one of the considerations that originally led to the development of the Terms of Reference (*see* Article 18 *infra*). Thus, the predecessors of Article 6(3) may, in the early years of ICC arbitration, have had more moral, than legal, force in some jurisdictions.

[188] *See,* for an example of such a case, Blessing, "The ICC Arbitral Procedure Under the New ICC Rules – What has Changed?" *ICC Ct. Bull.,* Vol. 8, No. 2 (1997), pp. 16, 18.

[189] *See,* in this regard, *Bremer Vulkan (FRG)* v. *South India Shipping Co.* [1981] 1 All E.R. 298 (English House of Lords).

Article 6(4)

> Unless otherwise agreed, the Arbitral Tribunal shall not cease to have
> jurisdiction by reason of any claim that the contract is null and void or
> allegation that it is non-existent provided that the Arbitral Tribunal
> upholds the validity of the arbitration agreement. The Arbitral Tribunal
> shall continue to have jurisdiction to determine the respective rights of
> the parties and to adjudicate their claims and pleas even though the con-
> tract itself may be non-existent or null and void.

Article 6(4) expresses the principle of the autonomy, or separability, of the arbitration agreement. Like the concept of "competence-competence," embodied in
Article 6(2), the notion that the arbitration agreement has an autonomous existence, distinct from the contract in which it may be contained, is one of the fundamental tenets of modern international arbitration law and practice.[190] The
essential function of this doctrine is to prevent the jurisdiction of an Arbitral
Tribunal from being frustrated by a mere allegation that the underlying contract
is null or invalid and, furthermore, to permit the Arbitral Tribunal to decide
whether this is the case and, if so, to decide upon the consequences.

The substance of the provision now set forth in Article 6(4) was originally
added to the Rules in 1955 together with the separate provision on the
arbitrator's "competence-competence." The separability provision was subsequently retained as Article 8(4) of the 1975 Rules and has not substantively been
changed in the New Rules. Given Article 6(4), the Court will ordinarily not
refrain from setting an arbitration in motion where it is alleged that the agreement containing an ICC arbitration clause is null and void or non-existent, subject, of course, to the requirements of Article 6(2). The separability doctrine has
come into play in a great many ICC arbitrations over the years concerning, for
example, claims of invalidity due to fraudulent inducement, bribery, other forms

---

[190] *See*, for a general treatment of the subject, Schwebel, *International Arbitration:
Three Salient Problems*, (Grotius Publications 1987), pp. 1-60. *See also* Sanders,
"*L'autonomie de la clause compromissoire*," *Hommage à Frédéric Eisemann, Liber
Americorum* (ICC Publishing 1978), p. 33; *Craig Park and Paulsson,* §5.04, pp. 65-72;
Fouchard Gaillard and Goldman, pp. 213-59. The principle of the arbitration clause's auton-
omy has been incorporated into the UNCITRAL Model Law (Article 16(1)) and other mod-
ern international arbitration laws (*e.g.*, Article 178 of the Swiss Private International Law
Act, Article 1053 of the Netherlands Arbitration Act 1986 and Section 7 of the English
Arbitration Act 1996) and has been confirmed by case law in a number of important jurisdictions, such as, for example, France (*Gosset c/ Carapelli, Cour de cassation, Dalloz* (1963),
p. 545), Germany (decision of the Federal Supreme Court (February 27, 1970), reported in
English translation in *Arb. Int.*, Vol. 6, No. 1 (1990), p. 79), Switzerland (*Tobler c/ Blaser*,
59 I 177 (1933)), England (*Harbour* v. *Kansa*, [1993] QB 701) and the United States (*Prima
Paint* v. *Flood & Conklin*, 388 U.S. 395 (1967)). However, it is not necessarily accepted
everywhere.

of corruption, or violations of public policy, and, thus, has given rise to a growing body of arbitral jurisprudence.[191]

As compared with many other arbitration rules and laws, the separability principle is formulated in Article 6(4) in very broad terms. Thus, Article 6(4) provides that the Arbitral Tribunal "shall continue to have jurisdiction to determine the rights of the parties ... even though the contract itself may be *non-existent* or null and void" (emphasis added). In contrast, neither the UNCITRAL Rules nor the UNCITRAL Model Law, for example, explicitly state what is to happen if the Arbitral Tribunal finds the contract to be non-existent; they only deal with the effects of a decision that the contract is null and void. Moreover, even in such case, they do not, unlike Article 6(4), affirm that the tribunal "shall continue to have jurisdiction," but state rather that, in the event of such a decision, the arbitration clause shall not *ipso jure* be regarded as invalid.

Although the principle of separability, as articulated in Article 6(4), is very broad, it should not be regarded as absolute. Thus, the affirmation in Article 6(4) that the tribunal "shall continue to have jurisdiction . . . even though the contract itself may be non-existent or null and void" does not mean that the tribunal might not separately find the arbitration agreement also to be either non-existent or null and void. Under the doctrine of separability, the mere fact that the main contract may be invalid does not suffice to invalidate the arbitration clause contained therein. But this does not preclude a possible showing of the invalidity of that clause as well if the relevant facts and circumstances specifically support such a finding. Thus, as a distinguished Arbitral Tribunal concluded a few years ago in an Award rendered in an ICC arbitration in Switzerland:

> There may be instances where a defect going to the root of an agreement between the parties affects both the main contract and the arbitration clause.[192]

The circumstances in which this might justifiably be found, however, would undoubtedly be rare. In the foregoing case, the tribunal speculated that a finding of the invalidity of the arbitration clause might be warranted in the event of a contract "obtained by threat." This might surely also be true if the contract containing the arbitration clause were shown to be a fraud, and that, in fact, there never was an arbitration agreement, or an agreement of any kind, between the parties.[193]

---

[191] *See, e.g.*, the Awards in ICC Case Nos. 2730 (1982), 2930 (1982), 3916 (1982) and 4555 (1985) in *ICC Arbitral Awards 1974-1985*, pp. 490, 118, 507, 536; *and* in Case Nos. 4145 (1983) and 4381 (1986), *ICC Arbitral Awards 1986-1990*, pp. 53, 263.

[192] ICC Case No. 6401 (1992), "Preliminary Award on Issues of Jurisdiction and Contract Validity," pp. 19-20 (unpublished). *See also*, to the same effect, *Lalive Poudret and Reymond*, p. 326, where it is stated with respect to Article 178(3) of the Swiss Private International Law Act (translation: "The real meaning of our provision is that the effect of the invalidity of the main contract must be examined separately when addressing the arbitration agreement").

[193] *See*, for a concurring view, *Craig Park and Paulsson*, §5.04, p. 69; *see also Fouchard Gaillard and Goldman*, p. 226.

It nevertheless should be remembered that, given the autonomous nature of the arbitration agreement, the law governing the question of its possible invalidity is not necessarily the same – although it may be – as the law that is applicable to the contract in which it is contained. Thus, for example, in France, the validity of an international arbitration agreement is deemed to be governed by a body of autonomous legal principles *(règles matérielles)* distinct from any domestic law.[194] In Switzerland, an international arbitration agreement is valid if it conforms to Swiss law, irrespective of the law governing the main contract.[195] In other countries, other principles may apply.[196]

Notwithstanding Article 6(4), there is nothing that either the ICC or the Arbitral Tribunal can do to prevent a party from instituting proceedings in a national court to enjoin an arbitration or possibly obtain other relief where it is its position that an arbitration agreement does not exist or is invalid owing to the non-existence or invalidity of the underlying contract. Whether or not a national court is likely to look favorably upon any such action will depend upon the extent to which the doctrine of separability is recognized in the law of that country. As in the case of other provisions of the Rules, Article 6(4) therefore does not preclude parallel court action that may be inconsistent with it, and parties should always take account of this when deciding upon the appropriate place of the arbitration.

[194] *See Fouchard Gaillard and Goldman*, p. 245; *see also*, for an explanation addressed to the non-French practitioner, Veeder, "Towards a Possible Solution: Limitation, Interest and Assignment in London and Paris," *ICCA Congress Series No. 7* (Kluwer 1996), pp. 268, 271.

[195] Swiss Private International Law Act, Article 178(3).

[196] *See Fouchard Gaillard and Goldman*, p. 235.

Chapter 4
The Arbitral Tribunal (Articles 7-12)

The series of Articles on the Arbitral Tribunal starting with Article 7 differ from the previous Rules in a number of important respects, not the least of which is the form of their presentation. In the previous Rules, all of the provisions concerning the Arbitral Tribunal were included in a single Article (Article 2) of extraordinary length and complexity. The difficulty of finding one's way through the thicket of untitled sub-sections constituting former Article 2 itself warranted a change that would make the relevant Rules easier to locate and apprehend.

This has been accomplished by substituting for the former provision six Articles, headed by a series of General Provisions (Article 7) reflecting, as the title suggests, principles of general application. The Articles that follow include a number of new provisions of varying significance, most notably the power of the Secretary General to confirm arbitrators (Article 9(2)) and special rules relating to multiple parties (Article 10) and truncated tribunals (Article 12(5)). In most other respects, however, Articles 7-12 are faithful to the provisions previously contained in Article 2, and there has not been any alteration of the basic principles relating to the constitution of the Arbitral Tribunal or its duties. As before, the parties are allowed considerable autonomy in connection with the establishment of the Arbitral Tribunal; they are free to agree on the number of arbitrators and to designate the arbitrators of their choice without regard to any roster or panel of approved arbitrators; arbitrators will also be appointed, as necessary, by the Court, usually with the assistance of the ICC's National Committees. In addition, it remains the case that all arbitrators not appointed by the Court must nevertheless be "confirmed" and that the Court has broad powers to replace arbitrators for lack of independence or otherwise.

ARTICLE 7
General Provisions

The general provisions set forth in Article 7 have, with only one exception (Article 7(5), which is new), been extracted from the former provisions of Article 2, without any substantial changes being made. Of those provisions, the first three relate to the arbitrator's obligation of "independence," as formerly set forth in Article 2(7). To these have been added a provision concerning the finality of the Court's decisions (as previously contained in Article 2(13)), an explicit reminder of the arbitrator's duty to act in accordance with the Rules (Article 7(5)) and a rule (formerly part of Article 2(1)) that expressly recognizes the parties' right to derogate from certain of the Rules' provisions concerning the Arbitral Tribunal.

Article 7(1)

> *Every arbitrator must be and remain independent of the parties involved in the arbitration.*

Background. Unlike in certain systems of domestic arbitration that distinguish between partisan party-appointed arbitrators and neutral sole or third arbitrators, it has long been the expectation in international arbitration in general, and ICC arbitration in particular, that none of the arbitrators, including those appointed by the parties, should be predisposed towards any of the parties and that, to the contrary, all of the arbitrators should be in a position to carry out their functions impartially and without bias.[197] The ICC Rules seek to achieve this by imposing the requirement in Article 7(1) that every arbitrator must be "independent," although Article 7(1) does not explain what is meant by "independence," nor does it, unlike the corresponding provision in many other arbitration rules and laws, explicitly set forth a requirement of impartiality.[198]

Because of the Rules' failure to explain what is meant by "independence," or to mention "impartiality" together with the reference to "independence," the nature of the requirement now set forth in Article 7(1) has been the subject of confusion and controversy.[199] It has from time to time been suggested, in particular, that the language contained in Article 7(1) ought to be amended to refer explicitly to impartiality.[200] However, as can be seen, the ICC did not take advan-

---

[197] *See, e.g.*, "Rules of Ethics for International Arbitrators" of the International Bar Association ("IBA"), *ICCA Yearbook* XII (1987), p. 199; *and*, for a general survey of relevant rules and practices, Smith, "Impartiality of the Party-appointed Arbitrator," *Arbitration*, Vol. 58, No. 1 (1992), p. 30. The reasonableness of the expectation that a party-appointed arbitrator can act impartially has been questioned, however. *See, e.g.*, Coulson, "An American Critique of the IBA's Ethics for International Arbitrators," *J. Arb. Int.*, Vol. 4, No. 2 (1987), p. 103; Rau, "Integrity in Private Judging," *South Texas Law Review*, Vol. 38, No. 2 (1997), p. 485.

[198] *See, e.g.*, UNCITRAL Rules, Articles 9 and 10; AAA International Arbitration Rules, Article 7; WIPO Arbitration Rules, Article 22; UNCITRAL Model Law, Article 12.

[199] Thus, it has been written that "the definition of 'independence' remains elusive." *Craig Park and Paulsson*, §13.03, p. 221. *See also* Kreindler, *supra*, note 14, p. 65.

[200] During the course of examining the proposed amendments to the Rules that ultimately were adopted and entered into effect in 1988, a long discussion is reported to have taken place within the ICC Commission as to whether the word "impartiality" should be introduced into the Rules. *See* the Summary Record of the meeting held on April 2, 1987, ICC Doc. No. 420/297. For an explanation of the ICC's failure to make the proposed change, *see* Bond, "The Experience of the ICC in the Confirmation/Appointment Stage of an Arbitration," *The Arbitral Process and the Independence of Arbitrators* (ICC Publishing 1991), pp. 9, 11.

tage of the Rules revision process to make such an amendment. Article 7(1), on the contrary, is formulated in the same manner as Article 2(7) of the former Rules and, thus, continues to refer only to "independence."

In fact, the language carried forward from Article 2(7) is of relatively recent vintage. It was only in 1975 that a provision was first added to the Rules explicitly imposing a requirement of "independence."[201] That provision (Article 2(4)) stated simply that, when a dispute was to be referred to three arbitrators, each party was to nominate an arbitrator "independent of the party nominating him." In 1980, the Court's new Internal Rules supplemented Article 2(4) by making the additional clarification that every arbitrator must be "independent" of "the parties involved in the arbitration," and this language was, in turn, imported into Article 2(7) in 1988.

When the requirement of independence was added to the Rules in 1975, the prominent French arbitration authority, Jean Robert, then the *Rapporteur* of the ICC Commission, commented that:

> The notion of independence is not explained, for the Court must be left free to judge. But its content goes without saying: no arbitrator who has, or has had, with either of the parties close relations liable to affect his freedom of judgment, often reflected in terms of economic interests, can be considered to be "independent" within the meaning of the Rules.[202]

The requirement of "independence" was therefore introduced into the Rules as a means to an end: attempting to ensure the arbitrator's "freedom of judgment," or, put another way, to avoid partiality and bias; and it was not intended that the concept be strictly circumscribed in order to permit the Court to consider, on a case by case basis, whether to regard the requirement as having been satisfied. Although the word "impartiality" was not itself used in the Rules, the prevention of partiality was clearly its primary object.

While the main purpose of Article 7(1) is to secure the appointment of impartial arbitrators, the drafters of the ICC Rules have preferred to express the relevant requirement in terms of independence because independence is a more objective notion.[203] Independence is generally a function of prior or existing relationships that can be catalogued and verified, while impartiality is a state of mind, which it may be impossible for anyone but the arbitrator to check or to know when the arbitrator is being appointed. It is therefore easier for the Court

---

[201] The requirement nevertheless pre-dated 1975 in practice. *See Craig Park and Paulsson,* §13.03, pp. 220-21.

[202] Report delivered at the Congress of the ICC in Madrid (June 17, 1975), ICC Doc. No. 420/179, p. 3. *See also*, to the same effect, Robert, *"Le Nouveau Règlement de Conciliation et d'Arbitrage de la Chambre de Commerce Internationale,"* Rev. arb. (1976), pp. 83, 84.

[203] *See* Hascher, "ICC Practice in Relation to the Appointment, Confirmation, Challenge and Replacement of Arbitrators," *ICC Ct. Bull.*, Vol. 6, No. 2 (1995), pp. 4, 5-6; Bond, *supra*, note 200, p. 11.

to determine, when confirming or appointing an arbitrator, whether that person is independent than to assess the extent of his or her impartiality.

Of course, the existence of a relationship between a prospective arbitrator and a party does not necessarily preclude that person from acting objectively and impartially in an arbitration.[204] But as an arbitrator's partiality or lack thereof will not, as just stated, usually be determinable at the outset of an arbitration, the ICC's independence requirement serves the broader goal of permitting the Court, from the outset, to exclude potential arbitrators whose impartiality may legitimately be doubted. In this manner, the Court seeks to ensure, to the extent reasonably possible, that a "trusting atmosphere" is preserved and that subsequent disruptions of the proceedings or challenges of the Award on the basis of an arbitrator's alleged bias are avoided.[205]

This having been said, the requirement of independence does not in and of itself guarantee an arbitrator's impartiality. Even an independent arbitrator may be biased. In the event that an arbitrator's partiality can be demonstrated, it, thus, remains open to a party either to object to that arbitrator's appointment or subsequently to seek the arbitrator's removal by means of the challenge procedure set forth in the Rules (*see* Article 11 *infra*). The absence of an express reference to impartiality in Article 7(1) should not be construed as meaning that an arbitrator's partiality is to be tolerated.[206] Moreover, apart from what the Rules may expressly provide, the law applicable to the arbitration may itself impose a requirement of impartiality.

Demonstrating partiality, however, can be difficult. In the first place, arbitrators may take pains to conceal any sympathies that they may have for a party in order not to lose credibility within the Arbitral Tribunal. It is, moreover, generally accepted that party-appointed arbitrators need not be completely "neutral" insofar as they may share the nationality of and also come from a similar "eco-

---

[204] In connection with the recent Arbitration Act 1996 in England, it has been observed that only "non-partial dependence" of an arbitrator should be a ground for the disqualification of an arbitrator, and, accordingly, the Act requires only that arbitrators be impartial, but not independent. *See, e.g.,* Veeder, "National Report – England," *ICCA Handbook on Commercial Arbitration,* Supp. 23 (Kluwer 1997), p. 27. Support for such a position can also be found in other jurisdictions (*see, e.g.,* Eisemann, *"La Double Sanction Prévue par la Convention de la B.I.R.D. en Cas de Collusion ou d'Ententes Similaires Entre un Arbitre et la Partie Qui l'a Désigné,"* Annuaire Français du Droit International* (1977), p. 436). While this may be a perfectly reasonable position for the law to take, it would nevertheless be almost impossible for an institution such as the ICC to distinguish between "partial" and "non-partial" dependence when deciding whether or not to confirm arbitrators.

[205] The importance of a "trusting atmosphere" was emphasized well before the requirement of independence was added to the Rules. *See* Eisemann, *"Déontologie de l'Arbitre Commercial International,"* Rev. arb.* (1969), pp. 217, 226. *See also* Hascher, *supra,* note 203, p. 11.

[206] *See* Bond, *supra,* note 200, p. 11, and Hascher, *supra,* note 203, p. 6. It is also to be noted in this connection that the Rules now expressly state (*see* Article 15(2)) that: "In all cases, the Arbitral Tribunal shall act fairly and *impartially* ... ." (Emphasis added.)

nomic, political and social *milieu*"[207] as the parties who have appointed them. Party-appointed arbitrators may also have made prior statements or expressed prior views on legal issues that may, at least in the abstract, be favorable to the position of one of the parties in the arbitration, without this necessarily being considered to be a disqualifying factor.[208] Parties therefore often expend considerable effort in seeking to identify an arbitrator whom they hope may be likely to be "sympathetic" to their position in an arbitration.[209] There may therefore be a fine line to tread between such possible "sympathies" and undue "partiality."[210]

Defining independence. It is sometimes said that impartiality concerns the relationship between the arbitrator and the subject-matter of the dispute, while independence relates to the relationship between the arbitrator and the parties.[211] There is, however, no internationally-accepted definition of "independence," and the word independence may sometimes also be used in a broader sense to refer to an arbitrator's independence of mind.[212] But ordinarily, as Jean Robert noted in 1975, the word is intended to signify the absence of "close relations" between an arbitrator and a party. More recently, Stephen Bond, a former Secretary General of the Court, described, as the essential feature of independence, the absence of a "close, substantial, recent and proven relationship" between a party and a prospective arbitrator.[213] How close is "close," how substantial is "substantial" and how recent is "recent," however, are all matters as to which there may be disagreement in the circumstances of a particular case. Thus, no matter how much more objective the notion of "independence" may be than that of "impartiality," "independence" nonetheless remains a vague con

---

[207] *See Craig Park and Paulsson,* §12.04, p. 212. *See also* Rau, *supra*, note 197, p. 507 ("[I]t is usually conceded that without violating in any way this theoretical obligation of independence, the arbitrator may quite acceptably share the nationality, or political or economic philosophy, or 'legal culture' of the party who has nominated him – and may therefore be supposed from the very beginning to be 'sympathetic' to that party's contentions ... ."). *But see* Hunter, "Ethics of the International Arbitrator," *Arbitration* (1987), pp. 219, 223 ("an impartial arbitrator will not allow this shared outlook to override his conscience and professional judgment").

[208] *See* Carter, "Living with the Party-Appointed Arbitrator; Judicial Confusion, Ethical Codes and Practical Advice," *Am. Rev. Int. Arb.*, Vol. 3 (1992), pp. 153, 168; Hunter, *supra*, note 207, p. 222.

[209] *See, e.g.*, Hunter, *supra,* note 207, p. 223 ("[W]hen I am representing a client in an arbitration, what I am really looking for in a party-nominated arbitrator is someone with the maximum predisposition towards my client, but with the minimum appearance of bias.").

[210] *See, e.g.*, Rau, *supra,* note 197, p. 508 ("Even in the best of circumstances an official rhetoric of 'independence' and tolerated latent 'sympathy' must exist in an uneasy tension ... .").

[211] *See* Hunter, *supra*, note 207, p. 222.

[212] For a discussion of an arbitrator's possible lack of "intellectual" independence, *see Craig Park and Paulsson*, §13.03, p. 221; *and* Bellet, Intervention in Minoli, *"Relations entre partie et arbitre,"* Rev. arb. (1970), pp. 221, 233.

[213] *See* Bond, *supra*, note 200, p. 13. For a general discussion of independence and impartiality, *see also Fouchard Gaillard and Goldman*, p. 580.

cept. In some cases, a person's lack of independence may be evident, *e.g.*, where the individual concerned is an employee of one of the parties. However, the issue of independence does not usually present itself in such stark terms. More commonly, it is a question of degree.

In the early years of arbitration (and still today in many quarters), it was generally considered that the degree of independence required should not necessarily rise to the same level as might be expected of a public judicial authority. Indeed, one of the often-cited advantages of arbitration is that arbitrators can be chosen who possess special, "hands-on" expertise in the area that is the subject of the arbitration. This often means that the most highly-qualified potential arbitrators will be individuals whose professional activities may inevitably have led them to have occasional, or possibly even regular, contacts or relationships with those involved in an arbitration in which they may be expected to act. Conversely, those without any such prior contacts or relationships may otherwise possess considerably less expertise. Thus, Frédéric Eisemann, then the Secretary General of the Court, wrote in 1971:

> We all know – it is often insisted upon excessively – that it is necessary for those arbitrators to be sufficiently 'impartial and independent'. For the Court, this does not mean that they must have no professional link or business relationship with the party in question; in particular, it is not a principle of the Court that their position be too strictly equivalent to that of a judge.[214]

As a practical matter, however, the Court has tended, in recent years, to construe the requirement of independence very broadly. An arbitrator's independence may therefore be questioned if there has been a relationship in the past, even if there is no longer a relationship at the time of the arbitration. Moreover, the relationship need not be a direct relationship. An arbitrator's independence may, thus, be called into question if someone with whom the arbitrator is closely asso-

---

[214] Eisemann, *"La Pratique Arbitrale de la Chambre de Commerce Internationale,"* *Rassegna dell'Arbitrato* (1971), pp. 177, 181 (translation from French). *See also*, more recently, Rau, *supra,* note 197, pp. 493-95 ("Occasional pronouncements on the 'law of arbitration' purport to identify the standards to which we hold arbitrators with those standards of impartiality demanded of public judicial officers. More often, however, it is blithely assumed that our expectations of arbitrators must be considerably more relaxed ... . Arbitrators [by comparison with judges] are more likely ... to be 'not apart from the marketplace' – are particularly likely, that is, when not sitting as arbitrators, to be actively engaged in professions whose members cross each other's paths daily – and this suggests that it may be unrealistic to insist on any degree of isolation that approaches the judicial ... [and] after all, arbitrators are likely to be valued at least in part precisely for the background and interests that they share with the parties themselves."). For an example of an arbitration in which this was the case, *see Société Drexel Burnham Lambert Limited et autres c/ société Philipp Brothers et autres, Tribunal de grande instance de Paris* (October 28, 1988), *Rev. arb.* (1990), p. 497.

ciated has a prior or existing relationship with one of the parties or when the relationship in question is with a party representative (*e.g.,* a party's counsel) rather than the party itself. The Court therefore requires all prospective arbitrators to disclose (*see* Article 7(2) *infra*):

> ... *inter alia,* whether there exists any past or present relationship, direct or indirect, with any of the parties, their counsel, whether financial, professional or of another kind ... [and that might be of such nature as to call into question the arbitrator's independence in the eyes of any of the parties].

The mere fact of such a relationship does not necessarily mean that the arbitrator does not possess the requisite independence. However, in cases of doubt, the Court has been more likely, particularly at the outset of an arbitration, to err on the side of disqualification.

In fact, the issue of an arbitrator's independence arises most frequently when the Court is examining whether to "confirm" or "appoint" an arbitrator (*see* Article 9(1) *infra*). The issue may also arise subsequently if an arbitrator is challenged by a party (*see* Article 11 *infra*), although the disclosure requirements contained in the Rules have had the inevitable effect of limiting the number of cases in which an arbitrator's independence is questioned during the arbitration proceedings. Arguably, the standard of independence applied by the Court should not differ, irrespective of when the issue arises. However, the Court has understandably tended to accord greater weight, at the beginning of an arbitration, to possible objections by a party to an arbitrator's appointment founded on reasonable doubts as to such person's independence. This is because of the importance, in the Court's view, of ensuring, to the extent reasonably possible, that the tribunal being constituted has the full confidence and trust of the parties. Indeed, this will normally be in the parties' interest in order to enhance the likelihood of voluntary compliance by the losing party with the arbitral Award eventually rendered. Where the necessary trust is absent at the very outset of an arbitration, this can be a harbinger of many possible difficulties to come, including possible recourse against the arbitrators' Award. This does not mean, however, that the ICC will refuse to confirm arbitrators whenever concerns are raised by a party that may, in fact, be frivolous or trivial. But the Court will always endeavor, to the extent possible, to avoid confirming an arbitrator where a party's objections have, at least, an appearance of reasonableness.

When questions arise with respect to an arbitrator's independence during the course of an arbitration, however, the position that the Court is likely to adopt is usually somewhat different, particularly if the arbitration is well advanced. The replacement of an arbitrator can, at that stage, be extremely disruptive. When an arbitrator is challenged during the course of an arbitration, it is therefore reasonable for the Court to weigh against the possible disadvantages of one party's loss of confidence in an arbitrator the disruptive effects of replacing him. As an arbitration advances, therefore, the Court has not normally accepted to replace an arbitrator unless it appears likely that he is not, in fact, independent. Thus, the mere fact that circumstances may arise that may call into question his independence "in the eyes of the parties" will not necessarily suffice to justify the acceptance of a challenge if the Court itself has no doubt as to the arbitrator's independence. On the contrary, acceptance of a challenge in such circumstances could work a considerable hardship on the non-challenging party if, as a result, the arbitration proceedings were severely disrupted.

There are so many different circumstances that the Court encounters with respect to the issue of independence that it is not possible to extract from its past decisions, and to summarize, any convenient set of principles.[215] Indeed, the Court itself deals with every case on its own merits. There are nevertheless a number of recurring situations that regularly test the limits of the Court's standard of independence. Among them are the following:

– *Relationships between a party and an arbitrator's law firm.* A large percentage of the arbitrators nominated to serve in ICC arbitrations are actively engaged in private law practice, often as partners of law firms. Although a regular and continuing relationship between a party and a lawyer would ordinarily suffice to cast doubt on the independence, as an arbitrator, of the lawyer concerned, the situations that arise are generally not so straightforward. Thus, for example, the lawyer in question may not personally have any relationship, or possibly even know, the party. The party may refer only small amounts of work to the lawyer's firm in specific fields unrelated to the subject of the arbitration. The law firm may not have performed any work for the party for several years. The law firm's only relationship may be with an affiliate of the party rather than the party itself. The relationship may be with a lawyer in a different office of the law firm in a different country.[216]

As law firms have grown in size and geographical spread in recent years, it has become increasingly common for lawyers to discover a prior or existing link of some kind with one or more of the parties to an arbitration. A typical case might be the Paris partner of a multinational law firm with hundreds of millions of dollars of worldwide revenues who learns that a partner in Hong Kong has recently advised, on a single matter for fees of U.S. $10,000, a sister company of the company wishing to nominate the Paris partner as an arbitrator. By any reasonable standard, this ought not to affect the independence of the Paris partner, but the Court might nevertheless expect such a relationship to be disclosed. If one of the parties objected to the appointment of such a person, the Court might decide, moreover, not to confirm the appointment.

Indeed, in recent years the Court has tended to accord considerable weight to the objections of parties, even where the relationship forming the basis for the objection might seem relatively insignificant in the eyes of the proposed arbitrator and the other party. However, the existence of any such relationships should not be viewed as disqualifying *per se*. Parties often do not object to the appoint-

---

[215] For a summary of the Court's recent practices, *see* Hascher, *supra*, note 203.

[216] For a discussion of this subject, *see Craig Park and Paulsson*, §13.05, pp. 230-31.

ment of arbitrators with marginal or indirect relationships with one of the parties to the arbitration.[217] But if there is an on-going or recent relationship between the law firm of a proposed arbitrator and a party to the arbitration or one of its affiliated companies, there is a risk that the proposed arbitrator will not be confirmed by the Court in the event of an objection by a party, even if the relationship is relatively minor.

Such an approach might be criticized as taking the principle of independence too far. In all such cases, however, the Court is ultimately required to assess the possibility that difficulties may occur subsequently, either during the arbitration or upon attempted enforcement of the Award, if the proposed arbitrator is confirmed. As it may be for a national court – in the context of an enforcement action, for example – to determine whether the Arbitral Tribunal was properly constituted, and the reasonableness of all national courts can regrettably not be assumed, the Court has generally sought to avoid any possible risk that an Award might be invalidated for an arbitrator's alleged lack of independence. This has caused the Court to proceed with a degree of caution that some might regard as excessive in certain cases. But, arguably, the Court's prudence may serve the interest of the party whose nominee has been refused confirmation, particularly if an alternative candidate is available who is beyond any possible reproach.

– *Relationships between an arbitrator and a party's counsel.* In 1989, the Court formally decided that all prospective arbitrators should be required to disclose not only past and present relationships with the parties themselves, but also with the parties' counsel. Although generally consistent with recommendations that had previously been formulated by other bodies, in particular, the International Bar Association[218] and the American Arbitration Association,[219] the Court's decision unleashed a storm of criticism, particularly in continental Europe.[220] Underlying that criticism was the concern that the community of international arbitration practitioners is so relatively small that the paths of many of the persons involved have inevitably crossed, either in past arbitrations, related professional organizations, or socially and that such previous contacts should not normally be regarded as calling into question a person's independence.[221]

---

[217] In 1990, the then Secretary General of the Court, Stephen Bond, reported that in over 95 per cent of the cases where facts or circumstances were disclosed by prospective arbitrators, the parties raised no objection to the confirmation of the person concerned. *See* Bond, "The ICC Arbitrator's Statement of Independence: A Response to Prof. Alain Hirsch," *ASA Bull.*, No. 3 (1990), pp. 226, 232.

[218] *See* Article 4(2) of the IBA "Rules of Ethics for International Arbitrators," *supra,* note 197.

[219] *See* "Code of Ethics for Arbitrators in Commercial Disputes," as jointly established by the American Arbitration Association and the American Bar Association, Canon II, *ICCA Yearbook* X (1985), p. 151.

[220] *See, e.g.,* Hirsch, "May Arbitrators Know the Lawyers of the Parties?" *ASA Bull.*, No. 1 (1990), p. 7; *and* the reply of the then Secretary General of the Court in Bond, *supra,* note 217.

[221] *See, e.g., Fouchard Gaillard and Goldman,* p. 584 (translation) ("Sometimes, the link that is denounced unites the arbitrator, not with a party, but with its counsel. His dependence will rarely be admitted ... .").

In fact, however, it has never been the Court's position that the ordinary professional or social relationships that lawyers or other professionals may have amongst one another should disqualify them from serving as arbitrators. Thus, for example, the fact that a person named as an arbitrator is known by the lawyer of the party appointing him, because they might both have been involved in a previous arbitration or are both members of one or more professional organizations, is not normally considered to be problematic, and, as a practical matter, such relationships are rarely disclosed. There may nevertheless be circumstances in which the relationship between a prospective arbitrator and the counsel of one of the parties is of such a nature as to call into question the independence of the arbitrator in the eyes of a party, and, indeed, the Court has occasionally refused to confirm arbitrators where a disclosed relationship has given rise to an objection.[222] Thus, for example, the proposed arbitrator's spouse may be a partner of the counsel of a party or the proposed arbitrator may be a recently retired partner of the law firm representing one of the parties. In cases such as those, where the links between arbitrator and counsel are closer than might be the case in the ordinary course of their professional activities, concerns about an arbitrator's independence may legitimately arise.

There are a number of other situations, however, where there may not necessarily be a consensus as to the impact of a possible relationship on an arbitrator's independence, but that may nevertheless raise varying degrees of concern for the Court. Thus, for example, a lawyer may propose as an arbitrator a person who is at the same time appearing as counsel or sitting as an arbitrator in another, unrelated arbitration in which the lawyer proposing him is an arbitrator. Arguably, a relationship of this kind should not normally affect the prospective arbitrator's independence, but it is nevertheless sometimes disclosed. It is much less common, however – indeed, it is very rare – for a prospective arbitrator to disclose a close social relationship with the counsel of a party, and yet, such close relationships are relatively common and could, if known, give rise to certain apprehensions. A taboo of silence nevertheless tends to surround them, and most arbitrators would strongly resist any suggestion that their independence could be affected by such a relationship.[223]

Similarly, in England, it is not unusual for barristers from the same "chambers" to appear as counsel and arbitrator in the same arbitration. In England, there is not generally considered to be anything troublesome about such a situation – a set of chambers is not a law firm, each member is an independent practitioner and, indeed, members of the same chambers regularly appear against one another in proceedings before the English courts.[224] Nevertheless, in the context

---

[222] *See* Hascher, *supra*, note 203, pp. 8-10.

[223] *See, e.g., Craig Park and Paulsson*, §13.03, p. 221 ("[T]ies of friendship may be disregarded as a matter of professional rigor.") (*citing* Bellet).

[224] *See* Kendall, "Barristers, Independance and Disclosure," *Arb. Int.*, Vol. 8, No. 3 (1992), p. 287; Report on the Arbitration Bill, dated February 1996, of the Departmental Advisory Committee on Arbitration Law (for England, Wales and Northern Ireland), pp. 26-27; *KFTCIC c/ Kori Estero, Cour d'appel de Paris* (June 28, 1991), Note Bellet, *Rev. arb.* (1992), p. 568.

of an international proceeding, a non-English party, in particular, may find it somewhat disconcerting that the counsel of the opposing party shares the same set of chambers as a member of the Arbitral Tribunal, that their offices may, in fact, be next door to each other and that they may have been close colleagues for years. Although an arbitrator in such a situation may consider himself to be independent and impartial, a certain uneasiness may nevertheless be created that the Court may not always be able to disregard in the event of an objection of one of the parties.[225] A similar uneasiness may also arise, moreover, when a counsel proposes as an arbitrator a lawyer from a law firm with which the counsel's firm has a special relationship, either because the two firms are part of one of the increasing number of law firm networks or alliances or the firms otherwise share offices or other facilities or regularly refer work to one another. Even though the existence of such a relationship is not necessarily incompatible with the requirement of independence, the Court has, in fact, refused to confirm an arbitrator in at least one such instance where an objection was raised by a party.[226]

– *Prior appointments as an arbitrator.* The case of the "repeat" arbitrator is yet a further example of a situation that has been the subject of occasional concern within the Court. Indeed, when a particular arbitrator accepts repeated appointments from the same party, the other party, if it is aware of this, may fear that the arbitrator has won the allegiance of the nominating party by taking its position in past arbitrations and that such a person's theoretical independence may be tainted by the wish to receive future appointments.[227] Although situations such as this are criticized from time to time, the Court has thus far been reluctant to presume that the independence of an arbitrator is necessarily eroded by such repeated appointments. Thus, the Court's General Counsel has recently written that "[t]he systematic nomination of the same arbitrator by a party does not necessarily affect the arbitrator's independence."[228] However, the Court nevertheless has ordinarily expected such prior appointments to be disclosed, and,

---

[225] In fact, in one recent case, where a barrister from the same chambers as the counsel of one of the parties was nominated as an arbitrator, the nomination was voluntarily withdrawn after the other party objected, and the Court was therefore not required to consider the matter.

[226] *See* Hascher, *supra,* note 203, p. 9. In the United States, moreover, the American Bar Association has taken the position, which has received judicial endorsement that when two firms become "affiliated" or "associated," and elect "to communicate that fact to the public and clients, there is no practical distinction between the relationship of affiliates under that arrangement and separate offices in a law firm," ABA Standing Committee on Ethics and Professional Responsibility, Formal Opinion (1984), pp. 84-351. *See also Mustang Enterprises, Inc.* v. *Plug-In Storage Systems, Inc.,* 874 F. Supp. 881 (N.D. Ill. 1995).

[227] *See* Hunter, *supra,* note 207, p. 222 ("An arbitrator who is in effect making a living from fees generated by repeated appointments from a particular party knows very well that he will not be appointed again if he concurs with the result which an aggrieved appointing party considers to be wrong.").

[228] *See* Hascher, *supra,* note 203, p. 7. *See also*, to the same effect, Reymond, *"Des connaissances personnelles de l'arbitre à son information privilégiée,"* Rev. arb. (1991), pp. 3, 12.

118   *A Guide to the New ICC Rules of Arbitration*

depending upon the particular circumstances, it cannot be excluded that the Court might refuse to confirm an arbitrator whose repeated, prior appointments call into question his or her independence in the eyes of a party.

A related, but different set of issues arises when a party nominates the same arbitrator in two or more arbitrations arising out of or connected with the same transaction or general subject matter. This may occur, for example, where multiple contracts relating to the same project give rise to separate arbitrations that the parties have not agreed to consolidate. In such cases, a party may nominate the same arbitrator in the hope that identical Arbitral Tribunals will be constituted in the related arbitrations so as to reduce the possibility of inconsistent results. Even where the tribunals are not likely to be identical (*e.g.,* where the other party is opposed to this), a party may feel that designating a common arbitrator will nevertheless serve the useful purpose of ensuring that one of the arbitrators, at least, is already generally familiar with the contract or project that is the subject of the arbitration. But herein lies the rub; for the other party may fear that the knowledge gained by the person in question from the other arbitration may make it difficult to consider, with complete impartiality, the issues in the parallel or subsequent arbitration for which he or she is also being nominated. This may be the case, particularly, when the arbitrator is required to decide similar or identical issues in one arbitration before an Award is to be rendered in the other.

There are a number of other, complex issues that may arise in this regard.[229] For example, when one party is not involved in the other, related arbitration but the other party is, both the other party and any common arbitrator would share knowledge arising from the other proceeding that would not necessarily be accessible to the party participating in only one of the proceedings. A party may therefore reasonably fear that it would be prejudiced as a result.[230] A claim of possible prejudice would seem harder to sustain, however, when the parties in the related proceedings are identical.

The Court considers all such cases in the light of their own circumstances and has not adopted any rigid practices concerning the acceptability of appointing the same arbitrator in related arbitrations.[231] However, in the event of an

---

[229] *See* Level, *supra,* note 91; Reymond, *supra,* note 228; Bedjaoui, *"Des fortes vérités de Cassandre aux modestes correctifs de Némésis (ou le souci communément partagé de voir la liberté fondamentale de choisir un arbitre n'être ni un danger ni en danger),"* Etudes de Droit International en l'Honneur de Pierre Lalive, (Helbing and Lichtenhahn 1993), p. 385; Bellet, Note on *Ben Nasser et autre c/ BNP et Crédit Lyonnais, Cour d'appel de Paris* (October 14, 1993), *Rev. arb.* (1994), pp. 380, 386.

[230] For an example of a recent ICC case in which no such prejudice was found to have occurred, notwithstanding the participation of an arbitrator in two related arbitration proceedings concerning a common construction project (one between the Contractor and the Owner and the other between the Contractor and the Subcontractor), in each case as the arbitrator nominated by the Contractor. *See Gouvernement de l'Etat du Qatar c/ Creighton Ltd, Cour d'appel de Paris* (12 January, 1996), *Rev. arb.* (1996), p. 428.

[231] *See* Gravel, *supra,* note 97, pp. 48-51.

objection by a party, it has refused to confirm the appointment of a common arbitrator for multiple, connected arbitrations raising identical issues and where the parties are not the same.

– *Civil servants.* States and governmental entities have often been parties in ICC arbitrations,[232] and occasionally they may nominate as arbitrators employees of the government or of an entity that is owned by the government. The ICC has, from time to time, been criticized for confirming such persons as arbitrators where an agency of the government is a party to the arbitration.[233] In fact, however, the Court would not normally confirm as an arbitrator, over the objection of a party, a person who is an employee of the agency that is a party to the arbitration or who has otherwise been involved with the matter in question. The more difficult issue that tends to arise is whether the Court should confirm as an arbitrator a person who is employed by a distinct governmental entity or who may have some other governmental connection, if one of the parties objects.

As in the case of the other matters discussed above, it is not possible to extract from the Court's past decisions, when such issues have arisen, any simple and immutable principles. To a certain degree, the Court's practices have, in the past, undeniably been affected, at least in part, by pragmatic considerations. In some countries, for example, it may be difficult, given the nature of the economic system, to identify a suitable arbitrator who does not have a governmental connection.[234] The Court has also been reluctant to brand as less than independent civil servants who are officially regarded as such in their own countries, *e.g.,* judges or independent legal counselors. The same has also generally been true in the case of university professors. The mere fact that the arbitrator proposed by a governmental party may have a governmental tie will therefore not necessarily suffice for the Court to refuse to confirm that person. The Court's position is likely to depend, in such cases, upon the precise nature of the prospective arbitrator's governmental connection.

– *Ex parte contacts immediately prior to appointment. Ex parte* communications between a party and a person whom it wishes to nominate as an arbitrator are, to a certain extent, inevitable. Indeed, a party will always be required to determine, at a minimum, whether an arbitrator is available to act and possesses the requisite independence. In addition, a party will normally wish to obtain information about a prospective arbitrator's qualifications and background. Communications between parties and prospective arbitrators for such limited

---

[232] *See, e.g., ICC Ct. Bull.,* Vol. 7, No. 1 (May 1996), p. 6 ("A state or public entity was a party to an arbitration in 14.1% of the requests submitted in 1995.").

[233] *See, e.g.,* Hunter, *supra,* note 207, p. 220.

[234] *See Redfern and Hunter,* p. 223; Bond, *supra,* note 200, p. 14; *Craig Park and Paulsson,* §13.03, pp. 222-23.

purposes are universally regarded as acceptable.[235] Parties may sometimes wish to know more than this, however. They may, for example, wish to probe the arbitrator's views with respect to issues that may arise in the arbitration or obtain the arbitrator's reaction to their description of the case. But once prospective arbitrators cross the line between a discussion of their background, qualifications and general views, on the one hand, and a discussion of the merits of the case, on the other, they place their independence in jeopardy.[236] Thus, on at least one occasion, the Court refused to confirm an arbitrator against whom an objection was made after he disclosed that he had engaged in extensive pre-appointment discussions of the case with the counsel of the party who had nominated him.[237]

Once arbitrators have been appointed, it is also not appropriate for them to engage in *ex parte* communications with the parties concerning the arbitration, although it is generally considered that communications for the limited purpose of discussing the selection of a third arbitrator are acceptable.[238] Parties may sometimes also expect that, for the duration of the arbitration, arbitrators will not otherwise have any *ex parte* contacts of any kind with a party. However, it is inevitable, in many cases, that arbitrators and counsel at least will cross paths, from time to time, during the course of an arbitration, whether it be in the context, for example, of a colloquium or other similar professional event or possibly another arbitration, and occasional contacts during an arbitration appear to be widely tolerated, provided that the arbitration is not discussed.[239] There have not, in any event, been any challenges of arbitrators before the ICC Court in recent years based on an arbitrator's occasional social contacts with a counsel during the course of an arbitration.

---

[235] *See, e.g.*, Article 5(1) of the IBA "Rules of Ethics for International Arbitrators," *supra,* note 197; WIPO Arbitration Rules, Article 21; AAA International Arbitration Rules, Article 7(2).

[236] Where this line should appropriately be drawn is not always evident, however. For a discussion of the relevant issues, *see* Carter, *supra,* note 208, p. 168; Lowenfeld, "The Party-Appointed Arbitrator in International Controversies: Some Reflections," *Texas International Law Journal,* Vol. 30, No. 1 (1995), pp. 59, 60-62.

[237] *See* Hascher, *supra,* note 203, pp. 7-8.

[238] *See, e.g.,* Article 5(2) of the IBA "Rules of Ethics for International Arbitrators," *supra*, note 197. *See also,* on the subject of such communications, *Craig Park and Paulsson*, §13.07, pp. 239-40.

[239] Article 5(5) of the IBA "Rules of Ethics for International Arbitrators," provides in this regard that: "No arbitrator should accept any gift or substantial hospitality, directly or indirectly from any party to the arbitration. Sole arbitrators and presiding arbitrators should be particularly meticulous in avoiding significant social or professional contacts with any party to the arbitration other than in the presence of the other parties." This probably represents as good a statement as any of the arbitrators' relevant duties, although co-arbitrators, like the presiding arbitrator, should also generally take care to minimize possible contacts with the parties or their counsel during an arbitration.

Article 7(2)

> *Before appointment or confirmation, a prospective arbitrator shall sign a*
> *statement of independence and disclose in writing to the Secretariat any*
> *facts or circumstances which might be of such a nature as to call into*
> *question the arbitrator's independence in the eyes of the parties. The*
> *Secretariat shall provide such information to the parties in writing and*
> *fix a time limit for any comments from them.*

The Statement of independence. In order to ensure compliance with the independence requirement of Article 7(1), Article 7(2) provides for the signature by
every prospective arbitrator of a statement of independence prior to the
arbitrator's appointment or confirmation.[240] Article 7(2) is identical to the corresponding provision previously contained in Article 2(7) of the former Rules,
except that the statement of independence is now explicitly mentioned and, as
discussed further below, the second sentence has been slightly altered. The statement of independence form that is currently in use invites arbitrators, consistent
with Article 7(2), to indicate whether they are independent and, if so, whether
there are any "facts or circumstances, past or present, that need to be disclosed
because they might be of such a nature as to call into question ... [their] independence in the eyes of any of the parties."

Both the Rules and the statement of independence form have been criticized
for expressing the arbitrators' disclosure requirement with reference to what
may be "in the eyes of the parties."[241] Indeed, the language of the ICC provision
differs in this respect from the more conventional formulation of the arbitrator's
corresponding obligation in other arbitration rules, *i.e.,* to disclose all circumstances "likely to give rise to justifiable doubts" as to the arbitrator's independence.[242] But the intention of Article 7(2) is really no different. Indeed, although
neither Article 7(2) nor the statement of independence form explicitly says so,
the facts and circumstances that need to be disclosed are those that might *reasonably* call into question the arbitrator's independence "in the eyes of the parties," and arbitrators are, thus, required to "stretch their minds"[243] so as to consider how particular facts and circumstances may be perceived by the parties.

---

[240] A copy of the form that arbitrators are required to sign appears at Appendix 5 *infra.*
The form, previously called "Statement of Independence," was revised as from October 1,
1995 in order to include a declaration that, in addition to being independent, the arbitrator
accepts to serve, is familiar with the requirements of the Rules and is "able and available to
serve as an arbitrator in accordance with all of the requirements of those Rules and accept[s]
to be remunerated in accordance therewith." The form is therefore now entitled "Arbitrator's
Declaration of Acceptance and Statement of Independence."

[241] *See, e.g.,* Kreindler, *supra,* note 14, p. 65, where it is asked how the prospective arbitrator is to know what is "in the eyes of the parties."

[242] *See, e.g.,* AAA International Arbitration Rules, Article 7(1); UNCITRAL Rules,
Article 9; WIPO Arbitration Rules, Article 22.

[243] *See* Bond, *supra,* note 200, p. 11.

The mere fact that an arbitrator may not himself consider that particular facts call into question his independence does not suffice to justify non-disclosure.[244]

Deciding whether and what to disclose is nevertheless a difficult and delicate exercise. No guidelines or rules have ever been articulated by the ICC in this respect, and the Court has strongly resisted doing so on the theory that any such guidelines would not only be inadequate, but possibly misleading as well, given the variety of circumstances that may be encountered. The statement of independence form, thus, admonishes prospective arbitrators that "[a]ny doubt should be resolved in favor of disclosure." As a practical matter, arbitrators adopt varying standards in deciding whether disclosure is necessary. Some may disclose contacts of an obviously trivial nature, while others may not feel it necessary to reveal relationships of significantly greater importance.[245]

It has never been the Court's practice to check or otherwise verify, in a systematic way, the accuracy or completeness of the information set forth in the statement of independence. Although the Secretariat may, from time to time, discuss with arbitrators whether certain information, of which it is aware, ought to be disclosed, the statement of independence ultimately remains the arbitrator's responsibility. Indeed, the Secretariat does not have the resources to investigate independently the relationships that an arbitrator may have with the parties or their counsel.[246] In the

---

[244] The drafters of what is now Article 7(2) took particular care to ensure that there could be no misunderstanding as to this. Indeed, when the Rules were amended in 1988, the prior text of the corresponding rule was modified in order to eliminate any reference to the arbitrator's "opinion" in this regard.

[245] An attempt to articulate an international standard for disclosure has been made by the IBA in its "Rules of Ethics for International Arbitrators," *see supra*, note 197 (Article 4). In addition to the matters that the ICC's statement of independence explicitly mentions as disclosable, the IBA Ethics recommend the disclosure of relationships with other members of the Arbitral Tribunal and "any person known to be likely to be an important witness in the arbitration." The ICC form has been criticized for failing to require expressly the disclosure of such matters. *See* R. Smit, *supra*, note 24, p. 66. However, when the statement of independence form is completed, it is unusual for a prospective arbitrator to be familiar with potential witnesses, although few would disagree that the existence of a relationship with a potential witness should be disclosed. Whether or not arbitrators should be required to disclose prior relationships with other arbitrators, however, is a subject as to which it is likely that there would be considerable disagreement.

[246] In this regard, the Secretariat might nevertheless be expected to be aware of relationships arising out of other ICC arbitration proceedings, whether past or present, *e.g.*, the prior nomination of a particular person as an arbitrator by the same party in other arbitrations. Although it has never been the practice of the Secretariat to investigate such matters thoroughly, it routinely retrieves from its computer data base a record of all cases in which every prospective arbitrator has been involved, either as counsel or as a party since the data base became operational in the early 1990s. It is therefore possible for the Secretariat to discuss with a prospective arbitrator the possible need for disclosure of any such matters, if they have been omitted. Occasionally, arbitrators may also be uncertain as to whether, or how, to disclose information that may be regarded as confidential. If it is not possible for an arbitrator to disclose a relationship without breaching a related obligation of confidentiality, then the arbitrator should not ordinarily accept the appointment. It is generally possible, however, for arbitrators to disclose relationships relating to other arbitration proceedings in such a manner as to avoid infringing any obligations of confidentiality that may be owed to the parties in respect of the same.

event that an arbitrator chooses not to disclose certain information that later comes to a party's attention, then the arbitrator runs the risk of being challenged (*see* Article 11 *infra*), and the non-disclosure of information that the Court considers should reasonably have been disclosed may, in and of itself, provide a basis for the replacement of an arbitrator, even if it would not, if originally disclosed, have justified the refusal to confirm an arbitrator.[247] It is, thus, for every arbitrator to assess this risk carefully, in the light of the circumstances of each case.

In order to ensure that arbitrators are in a position to consider fully the question of their independence, the parties generally need to provide all of the relevant information about themselves in their Request for Arbitration and Answer. Neither the arbitrators nor the ICC can otherwise necessarily be expected to realize, for example, that a particular party belongs to an unidentified corporate group. It may also occasionally occur that the dispute that is the subject of the arbitration is related to another dispute with which the prospective arbitrator may have some connection. An arbitrator will not necessarily be aware of this at the time of appointment, however, unless the dispute has been adequately described by the parties.

The parties' comments. In the event that facts or circumstances are disclosed by a prospective arbitrator, Article 7(2) stipulates that the Secretariat "shall provide such information to the parties in writing and fix a time limit for any comments from them." In fact, the practice of the Secretariat differs, depending on whether the prospective arbitrator has been nominated by a party for confirmation or has been proposed by a National Committee (*see* Article 9(3) *infra*) for appointment by the Court. In the former case, the Secretariat immediately sends a copy of the nominee's disclosures to the parties for comment. However, the Secretariat does not ordinarily do so if the information concerns an arbitrator proposed by a National Committee because the Court may not be inclined to accept the National Committee's proposal, and the Court also does not usually wish the parties to know the identity of the National Committee from which proposals have been sought before an appointment has been made.[248] In such cases, therefore, if a qualified statement of independence is received, the Secretariat will first refer the proposal to the Court. The Court then has the option of refus-ing to appoint the person concerned, without soliciting the parties' comments, or making the appointment, while affording the parties the

---

[247] *See* Hascher, *supra*, note 203, p. 15. *See also Craig Park and Paulsson,* §13.04, p. 225. In addition, the non-disclosure of information may jeopardize the enforcement of the Arbitral Award if the information in question is discovered following the completion of the arbitral proceedings. *See, e.g.,* Article 34(2) of the UNCITRAL Model Law. However, the mere fact of non-disclosure will not necessarily suffice to call the Award into question unless this fact, together with the relationships that were not disclosed, gives rise to a sufficient presumption of non-independence. *See, e.g., Gouvernement de l'Etat du Qatar c/ Creighton Ltd., supra,* note 230.

[248] This is principally in order to avoid possible interference by parties with the work of the National Committees. *See* the discussion of Article 9(3) *infra*.

opportunity to comment subsequently.[249] For this reason, Article 7(2), unlike Article 2(7) of the former Rules, no longer provides that the information in question is to be provided to the parties "upon receipt by the Secretariat."

When inviting the parties to comment on information disclosed in the statement of independence, the Secretariat is free to fix any time limit for comments that it considers to be appropriate. In fixing a time limit, the Secretariat does not generally grant the parties more than fifteen days so as not to delay unduly the constitution of the tribunal. Depending on the circumstances and the calendar of upcoming Court sessions, however, it may grant the parties less time than this. In most cases, the information disclosed by arbitrators does not give rise to an objection of any of the parties, and the arbitrator's appointment is then usually routinely confirmed (*see* Article 9 *infra*).[250] However, if an objection is made, the Court is required to decide, usually at a Committee session (*see* Article 1(4) *supra*), whether the appointment of the arbitrator in question should be confirmed.

Prior to the Court deciding on a possible objection to an arbitrator's appointment, there is no particular procedure that either the Court or the Secretariat is required to follow. A copy of the objection is always sent to all other parties, however, in order for them to be able to respond. But it has not always been the Secretariat's practice to invite comments from the arbitrator concerned, although the arbitrator may be informed of the objection either by the Secretariat or the party who made the nomination.

Traditionally, as already mentioned above (*see* Article 7(1)), the Court has accorded a great deal of weight to objections raised by parties prior to an arbitrator's confirmation. While an objection is not necessarily fatal to an arbitrator's possible confirmation, particularly if it is frivolous, it nevertheless often is.[251] As a consequence, the arbitrators appointed in ICC cases tend to be acceptable to all of the parties, and challenges, subsequent to an arbitrator's appointment, are rare (*see* Article 11 *infra*).[252] It is to be noted, however, that a party's failure to object to an arbitrator prior to that person's appointment does not preclude it from challenging the arbitrator later on the basis of the information disclosed in the arbitrator's statement of independence or other

---

[249] The Court's past practices in this regard have not always been consistent. During the last several years, the Court has occasionally appointed arbitrators, "subject to" the parties' comments or objections, the intention being that the appointment would not take effect, and have to be reconsidered by the Court, if either party objected within a specified period. In other, much rarer instances, however, the Court has appointed the arbitrator, leaving the parties with the opportunity to challenge the appointment in the event of an objection. For a description of yet a different approach followed in earlier years, *see* Bond, *supra,* note 200, pp. 10-11.

[250] *See supra,* note 217.

[251] Thus, Stephen Bond reported several years ago that in a sample studied by him, arbitrators were not confirmed by the Court in 72 per cent of the cases where questions were raised as to an arbitrator's independence. *See* Bond, *supra,* note 200, p. 12.

[252] *See* Hascher, *supra,* note 203, p. 11.

information of which it may have been aware prior to the arbitrator's appointment (*see* Article 11(2) *infra*).

Article 7(3)

> *An arbitrator shall immediately disclose in writing to the Secretariat and to the parties any facts or circumstances of a similar nature which may arise during the arbitration.*

Article 7(3) makes explicit the continuing nature of the arbitrator's disclosure obligation during the arbitration. It is essentially identical to the corresponding provision in Article 2(7) of the former Rules except that the former provision obligated the arbitrator to make disclosures until the "notification of the final Award," while Article 7(3) applies, more generally, "during the arbitration." The principal reason for the new language in Article 7(3) is that the Rules now contemplate the possible correction or interpretation of the final Award by the Arbitral Tribunal after its notification (*see* Article 29 *infra*). Thus, if the Arbitral Tribunal is requested to intervene at such a late stage, its members would be required to disclose any new facts or circumstances that might affect their independence.

In practice, arbitrators are, thus, required to be attentive to any new relationships that may arise with either the parties or their counsel, or possibly others (*e.g.*, witnesses), during the course of the arbitration. Such new relationships may arise without the arbitrator having any direct involvement, *e.g.*, as a result of a corporate reorganization or merger or a combination of law firms. Thus, for example, an arbitrator with no tie to either of the parties may suddenly develop a tie if a client of the arbitrator's law firm acquires one of the parties to the arbitration. There are many other similar situations that may arise, and, if the arbitration is well advanced when they do, they may have potentially disruptive consequences for the arbitration. It has, thus, been asked:

> [W]hether the fact that an improper relationship arises (through no fault of the arbitrator) in the course of and perhaps very late in the proceedings may be excused and become immaterial on account of the consideration that the advantage of gaining economy and time must take precedence over propriety or the semblance of propriety.[253]

This is an issue that the ICC Court has fortunately not frequently had to face, primarily because the parties themselves are ordinarily concerned with avoiding such disruption and, thus, if the arbitration is at an advanced stage, often raise no objection to the continued service of the affected arbitrator. However, this will not necessarily always be the case.

---

[253] *See* Wetter, "Ethical Guidelines," *Yearbook of the Arbitration Institute of the Stockholm Chamber of Commerce* (1993), pp. 99, 104.

There may also be instances – which happily are rare – where arbitrators knowingly put themselves into conflict with their obligations of independence under the Rules, *e.g.,* by joining a law firm of which one of the parties is a significant client. In such cases, an issue may arise as to the arbitrator's responsibility to the parties for the disruption that may occur, subject to Article 34 of the Rules (*see infra*). As discussed further below (*see* Article 12(4) *infra*), the Court could conceivably deprive resigning arbitrators of their fees in such circumstances.

Article 7(4)

> The decisions of the Court as to the appointment, confirmation, challenge or replacement of an arbitrator shall be final and the reasons for such decisions shall not be communicated.

Article 7(4) takes the place, in nearly identical terms, of Article 2(13) of the previous Rules. Article 2(13) was in turn added to the Rules in 1988 and was derived from several different provisions of the Internal Rules published by the Court in 1980. This is the only provision in the Rules that explicitly provides for the finality of the Court's decisions and prohibits the communication of the Court's reasons. The Court is, in fact, not otherwise required under the Rules to explain its decisions, nor is it under any obligation to reconsider decisions that it has previously made, but, in principle, it has the discretion to decide whether it wishes to do so. In respect of the types of decisions that are described in Article 7(4), however, the Court is deprived of any such discretion.

Finality of decisions. The statement in Article 7(4) that decisions of the Court "shall be final" is merely intended to signify that once the Court has made its decision, that decision shall not be the subject of further recourse before the Court. It is therefore final insofar as the Court is concerned. But this does not mean that a party is deprived of such judicial recourse as it may also enjoy as a matter of law.[254] The general purpose of this provision is to prevent parties from rearguing matters that have already been the subject of a Court decision, in the interest of expedition and also to avoid overcrowding the Court's already heavy agenda. In fact, it has long been the Court's usual practice, for these reasons, not to reconsider its decisions – not just those mentioned in Article 7(4) – in the absence of new facts that the Court was not previously in a position to consider (although it may nevertheless do so from time to time, in exceptional circumstances). Even in the case of Article 7(4), if new facts arise, the Court arguably should not be prevented from taking a new decision.

---

[254] Thus, for example, the UNCITRAL Model Law (Article 13(3)) permits a party to apply to a court to decide upon a challenge that has been rejected by an arbitral institution such as the ICC Court. In some other jurisdictions, however (*e.g.,* France and Switzerland), a party would not have any such right, although the arbitral Award might subsequently be challenged. *See, e.g., Fouchard Gaillard and Goldman*, p. 603.

Reasons for decisions. As already noted, there is nothing in the Rules requiring the Court to communicate the reasons for its decisions. Those decisions are, moreover, taken at confidential meetings that the parties are not permitted to attend (*see* Article 1(1) *supra*). However, Article 7(4) goes even further in expressly prohibiting the communication of the reasons for the Court's decisions in respect of the specific matters that are the subject of that Article. This is primarily to avoid causing possible embarrassment or offense to the arbitrators concerned and also to circumvent possible ensuing disputes with the parties concerning the Court's reasons, if they were to be provided, that might also make the Award, when issued, more vulnerable to attack.

Although broadly consistent with the practices of other arbitral institutions,[255] the Court's refusal to provide reasons for its decisions, in respect of challenges in particular, has from time to time been criticized. Indeed, a challenge of an arbitrator is a serious matter, and the Court's decision may, as one respected authority has noted, "have a very important effect on the rights of the parties."[256] The issue for the ICC and other institutions has, thus, been framed in the following terms:

> On the one hand, an arbitral institution has a legitimate interest in preserving the confidentiality of its internal administration, and in ensuring that challenges are disposed of expeditiously so as not to delay an award on the merits. On the other hand, a party which challenges in good faith might lose confidence in the arbitral process if there is no explanation whatsoever why its arguments were not persuasive.[257]

Be this as it may, the ICC was not convinced, when amending the Rules, that the practice reflected in Article 7(4) should be altered. In fact, the parties receive copies of their respective submissions to the Court in respect of all challenges. Article 11(3) of the Rules (*see infra*) now also requires, which was not previously the case, that they receive copies of the arbitrators' comments as well. Even if the Court does not provide reasons for its decisions, the parties are nevertheless therefore aware of the facts and issues that the Court has considered and remain free to avail themselves of such remedies before the courts as may be available, either during the arbitration or upon the issuance of the Award.

---

[255] *See, e.g.,* LCIA Rules, Article 3(9); WIPO Arbitration Rules, Article 29. *See also* Bond, "The Present Status of the International Court of Arbitration of the ICC: A Comment on an Appraisal," *Am. Rev. Int. Arb.,* Vol. 1, No. 1 (1990), pp. 108, 118-19.

[256] Hunter, "A View from the ICC Court of Arbitration," *International and ICC Arbitration* (King's College 1990), pp. 69, 76.

[257] Tupman, "Challenge and Disqualification of Arbitrators in International Commercial Arbitration," *International Comparative Law Quarterly,* Vol. 38 (1989), pp. 26, 49. *See also* Wetter, "The ICC in the Context of International Arbitration," *International and ICC Arbitration* (King's College 1990), pp. 40, 50-51.

Decisions of the Secretary General. While referring to decisions of the Court as to the confirmation of arbitrators, Article 7(4) makes no mention of the power now conferred on the Secretary General, under Article 9(2) (*see infra*), to confirm arbitrators. This therefore leaves open the question of whether a decision of the Secretary General to confirm an arbitrator should be regarded as final in the same manner as a decision of the Court. Although it will be for the Court to decide whether it wishes to reconsider decisions of the Secretary General, there would not, in principle, appear to be any obstacle in the Rules to the Court's doing so. As a practical matter, however, the Secretary General's decision-making authority under Article 9(2) is generally limited to cases where there is no disagreement between the parties as to the decision to be taken. There should therefore not ordinarily be any need for the reconsideration of the Secretary General's decisions.

Article 7(5)

> *By accepting to serve, every arbitrator undertakes to carry out his responsibilities in accordance with these Rules.*

This is a new provision, although it could not previously have been legitimately maintained that an arbitrator was not bound "to carry out his responsibilities" in accordance with the Rules.

While not entirely clear from the English version of this Article, its primary purpose is to create an express obligation on the part of the arbitrators to complete their mission when accepting to serve (subject to the provisions contained in Articles 11 and 12 concerning their replacement).[258] This is apparent from the French version of Article 7(5), which more accurately captures the drafters' intention by providing that (translation):

> By accepting to serve, the arbitrator undertakes to carry out his mission in accordance with these Rules until its completion.

Thus, an arbitrator cannot legitimately resign during the course of an arbitration without a valid reason. (*See* also in this regard Article 12(1) *infra.*)

Article 7(6)

> *Insofar as the parties have not provided otherwise, the Arbitral Tribunal shall be constituted in accordance with the provisions of Articles 8, 9 and 10.*

---

[258] Such an express obligation is also set forth in certain arbitration laws. *See, e.g.,* Article 1462 of the French New Code of Civil Procedure, upon which this provision has been modeled.

Article 7(6) is one of the few provisions of the Rules that expressly envisages possible derogations by the parties.[259] It has as its original source a provision that was first included in the Rules in 1955 and that, in the previous version of the Rules (Article 2(1)), was formulated in the following terms:

> Insofar as the parties shall not have provided otherwise, ... [the Court] appoints, or confirms the appointments of, arbitrators in accordance with the provisions of this Article.

Under Article 2(1), it was therefore possible for the parties to agree that arbitrators could be appointed in a manner other than that stipulated in the Rules.[260] The parties could, for example, dispense with the requirement of confirmation by the Court, designate an appointing authority other than the Court, or alter the relevant time limits. Depending on how it might be construed, moreover, the Article 2(1) proviso was potentially far broader than this and might be said to encompass the entirety of Article 2, which included provisions concerning the arbitrator's independence and procedures for the challenge of arbitrators and their replacement by the Court.[261] In 1990, the Court was required to consider whether to permit the constitution of a tribunal of four arbitrators, notwithstanding the provision in Article 2(2) of the then Rules (now Article 8(1)) for a tribunal of one or three arbitrators. The Court permitted the tribunal of four to be constituted on the basis of the Article 2(1) proviso. In other cases, however, the proviso has been construed more restrictively. Thus, for example, the Court has taken the position that the parties cannot agree to the appointment of two arbitrators and an "umpire" as this would be inconsistent not only with the provisions concerning the constitution of the Arbitral Tribunal but the scheme of the Rules in general.[262]

During the work on the New Rules, the Working Party concluded that the proviso should be retained. However, it was decided to limit it explicitly to the provisions concerning the constitution of the Arbitral Tribunal, as set forth in Articles 8, 9 and 10. The proviso therefore clearly does not extend to the provisions on the challenge and replacement of arbitrators, as contained in Articles 11 and 12, from which the parties are, in principle, not free to derogate. Nor does the proviso encompass any of the general provisions in Article 7, including

---

[259] The only other such provisions are Articles 6(1), 6(4), 23(1) and 32(1).

[260] The Court's obligation to respect any such derogation from the Rules in the parties' arbitration clause pursuant to former Article 2(1) has been affirmed by the French Court of Cassation. *See Sociétés E.T.P.M. et Ecofisa c/ société Gas del Estado, Cour de cassation* (December 4, 1990), *Rev. arb.* (1991), p. 81.

[261] *See* Kreindler, *supra*, note 14, p. 56 ("Needless to say, the extent of permissible derogation is unclear, and the issue requires clarification.").

[262] *See* the further discussion of this in respect of Article 8(1) and at note 272 *infra. See also* Bond, "The Constitution of the Arbitral Tribunal," *The New 1998 Arbitration Rules, ICC Ct. Bull.,* Special Supplement (1997), p. 22. *But cf.* Arnaldez, *"Réflexions sur l'autonomie et le caractère international du Règlement d'arbitrage de la CCI,"* *Clunet* (1993), pp. 857, 867.

notably the requirement (*see* Article 7(1) *supra*) that every arbitrator must be and remain independent of the parties.

With respect to the requirement of independence, in particular, there was not a consensus within the Working Party in favor of permitting the parties to waive that requirement. Although it has been asserted that in ICC arbitration the parties "may agree to waive the requirement of independence of the party-nominated arbitrators,"[263] there has not, in fact, been any general agreement as to this within the Court in recent years,[264] and whether or not the independence of an arbitrator can validly be waived also depends, moreover, upon the law applicable to the arbitration and the Award to be rendered. Indeed, in many jurisdictions, the requirement of arbitral independence (or impartiality) is mandatory, and the parties may therefore not agree to have a partial or non-independent arbitrator or otherwise waive that requirement.[265] This being said, the Rules nevertheless provide for the waiver by a party of its right to challenge an arbitrator for lack of independence (or otherwise) if such a challenge is not submitted within a specified period of time (*see* Article 11(2) *infra*). Moreover, it may be argued, on the basis of Article 33 (*see infra*), that a party that has not objected to an arbitrator during the arbitration cannot subsequently seek to have the Award set aside on the ground that the arbitrator was not independent or impartial if the facts and circumstances forming the basis for the attack on the Award were known during the arbitration.[266]

ARTICLE 8
Number of Arbitrators

The ICC Rules, like many other arbitration rules, provide for the appointment of either one or three arbitrators. In the event that the parties are unable to agree on

---

[263] *Craig Park and Paulsson,* §12.04, p. 211; §13.03, p. 223.

[264] Indeed, the Court has occasionally refused to confirm the appointment of party-nominated arbitrators whom the Court has not considered to be independent even though the parties had no objection to the person concerned. *See* Bond, *supra,* note 200, p. 14; Hascher, *supra,* note 203, p. 11.

[265] This may be considered to be the case, for example, under the UNCITRAL Model Law. *See Holtzmann and Neuhaus,* p. 409. This has also been stated to be the case under Swiss law. *See Lalive Poudret and Reymond,* pp. 343-44. Similarly, it is not open to the parties to an arbitration governed by the English Arbitration Act 1996 to agree upon the appointment of an arbitrator who is partial. *See* Veeder, *supra,* note 204, p. 27.

[266] For an example of a recent French (non-ICC) case where a party's application to have an Award set aside in such circumstances was rejected, *see Société Scintelle c/ Bourey, Cour d'appel de Versailles* (November 14, 1996), Note Hory, *Rev. arb.* (1997), p. 361. *See also* Cadiet, *"La renonciation à se prévaloir des irrégularités de la procédure arbitrale," Rev. arb.* (1996), p. 3. The Swiss courts have also found that a party's failure to object to an arbitrator's partiality may prevent the setting aside of an Award on that basis. *See Les Emirats Arabes Unis, le Royaume d'Arabie Saoudite, l'Etat du Qatar c/ Westland Helicopters Ltd., supra,* note 167. *But cf. Holtzmann and Neuhaus,* p. 408, regarding the position under the UNCITRAL Model Law.

the number, it is the Court that is authorized to decide the matter. If a sole arbitrator is to be designated, then the Court will make the appointment unless the parties have otherwise agreed, while in the case of three arbitrators, two are to be designated by the Claimant and Respondent, respectively, while the third is chosen by the Court or in accordance with any other agreement of the parties.[267]

These are the basic principles that have been incorporated in previous versions of the Rules, and they have not been altered in the New Rules. On the contrary, the four subparagraphs comprising Article 8 correspond, with only minor alterations, to Articles 2(2)-2(5) of the former Rules, although set forth in a slightly different order.

Article 8(1)

The dispute shall be decided by a sole arbitrator or by three arbitrators.

The designation of either one or three arbitrators is the ordinary rule in international arbitration, and Article 8(1) is consistent with many other arbitration rules in this regard.[268] As already noted, however (*see* Article 7(6) *supra*), Article 8(1) is not a mandatory rule, and the parties are therefore free to agree on another number of arbitrators. Indeed, unlike Article 8(1), the standard ICC arbitration clause published with the Rules (*see* Appendix 1 *infra*) provides for the settlement of disputes "by one or *more* arbitrators appointed in accordance with the said Rules" (emphasis added).

As a practical matter, however, parties rarely seek more than three arbitrators, and, over the course of the last decade, a greater number have been appointed in only one case. Occasionally, parties may consider appointing more than three arbitrators when there are multiple parties to the arbitration. But the perceived advantages of doing so are generally considered to be outweighed by the increased cost and potential for delay inherent in an expanded tribunal. In addition, the law governing the arbitration may limit the choices available to the parties. In some jurisdictions, for example, the law may preclude the constitution of an Arbitral Tribunal composed of an even number of arbitrators, given the possibility of a deadlock in such a case.[269] The Rules, however, do not themselves create an obstacle to the constitution of an even-numbered tribunal. Indeed, in the one case mentioned above with more than three arbitrators, the parties agreed upon a tribunal of four.[270]

---

[267] In the case of multi-party arbitrations, however, special rules apply. *See* Article 10 *infra*.

[268] *See, e.g.,* UNCITRAL Rules, Article 5; AAA International Arbitration Rules, Article 5; WIPO Arbitration Rules, Article 14(b).

[269] This is the case, for example, under Articles 1453-1454 of the French New Code of Civil Procedure, which generally apply, however, only to French domestic (and not international) arbitrations unless the parties otherwise agree.

[270] For a description of this case, *see* Gravel, *supra*, note 97, pp. 51-52.

The Court has nevertheless refused, as already mentioned (*see* Article 7(6) *supra*), to permit arbitrations to be conducted by two arbitrators, with an "umpire" to be appointed to render the Award if the two arbitrators initially appointed cannot agree. The "umpire" system is still commonly used in certain jurisdictions, and occasionally ICC arbitration clauses are drafted that incorporate it.[271] However, the Court has heretofore taken the position that such a system, particularly because it divides the arbitration into two separate stages, is incompatible with the Rules as a whole.[272]

Article 8(2)

> *Where the parties have not agreed upon the number of arbitrators, the Court shall appoint a sole arbitrator, save where it appears to the Court that the dispute is such as to warrant the appointment of three arbitrators. In such case, the Claimant shall nominate an arbitrator within a period of 15 days from the receipt of the notification of the decision of the Court, and the Respondent shall nominate an arbitrator within a period of 15 days from the receipt of the notification of the nomination made by the Claimant.*

As in earlier versions of the Rules (*see* Article 2(5) of the 1988 Rules), Article 8(2) provides that the number of arbitrators is to be determined by the Court in the absence of an agreement of the parties. It differs from the previous Rules, however, in expressly requiring the consecutive nomination of arbitrators by the parties if the Court decides that three arbitrators should be appointed.

The Court's decision on the number of arbitrators. Most of the time, the parties to ICC arbitrations agree on the number of arbitrators, either in their original arbitration agreement or after the arbitration commences. Thus, for the last several years, the parties have fairly consistently agreed on the number of arbitrators

---

[271] *See, e.g.,* Section 15 of the English Arbitration Act 1996. The February 1996 Report of the Departmental Advisory Committee on the then draft law noted the following in this regard, para. 94: "We should record that we considered whether the peculiarly English concept of an umpire should be swept away in favour of the more generally used chaired tribunal ... . In the end we decided not to recommend this, and to continue to provide default provisons for those who wanted to continue to use this form of Arbitral Tribunal."

[272] Thus, for example, neither the provisions concerning the Terms of Reference nor the fixing of the costs of the arbitration envisage what is, in effect, a two-tier procedure. It is not inconceivable, however, that appropriate adaptations of the Rules could be made by the parties to accommodate such a procedure if the Court were willing to accept it. *See* Arnaldez, *supra*, note 262, p. 867. Indeed, the appointment of an "umpire" was expressly envisaged in the Rules prior to 1955 (Article 12 of the 1933 and 1947 Rules). For an example of a case where the parties had provided for two arbitrators and an umpire, and a discussion of the consequences of the ICC's refusal to accept the arbitration, *see Sumitomo Heavy Industries* v. *Oil and Natural Gas Commission,* [1993] 1 Lloyd's Rep. 45.

in approximately 70 per cent of the cases administered by the ICC.[273] In approximately half of those cases, the parties agreed on the number in the arbitration clause and in the other half after the arbitration commenced. Approximately 30 per cent of the time, however, the parties have not been able to agree. Occasionally, this is because they genuinely cannot; in other cases, agreement may not be possible because of the refusal of a party to participate in the arbitration; and in still others, a party may simply wish to create difficulties for the other party (*e.g.,* a Respondent party who insists on the appointment of three arbitrators in a simple case merely to make the arbitration more expensive for the Claimant party, who considers a sole arbitrator to be sufficient).[274]

Unlike certain other arbitration rules that provide for the automatic designation of either one or, more commonly, three arbitrators in cases where the parties cannot agree,[275] the Rules confer upon the Court the important function of determining the number in such a situation.[276] This determination is ordinarily made by a Committee of the Court (*see* Article 1(4)) at one of its regular sessions after considering the circumstances of the arbitration, any relevant submissions of the parties and the recommendation of the Secretariat. The parties therefore have the benefit of an independent determination that is made with reference to such matters as the arbitration's size and complexity, the nature of

---

[273] *See* the statistics contained in Appendix 6 and in the *ICC Ct. Bull.,* Vol. 8, No. 1 (1997), p. 10; Vol. 7, No. 1 (1996), p. 8; Vol. 6, No. 1 (1995), p. 6.

[274] Sometimes, there may be a threshold issue as to whether the parties have, in fact, "agreed" on the number of arbitrators. This will not normally be cause for concern where the number is specified in the arbitration clause. However, it may happen that, during the exchange of communications between the parties and the Secretariat in relation to the number of arbitrators, after the commencement of the arbitration, a party will "agree" with the proposal of the other party on this subject, only to change its mind subsequently, before the meeting of the Court at which the matter is to be considered. When such cases have arisen in the past, the Court has considered the parties to be in disagreement. The Court has, thus, not generally treated the parties as irrevocably bound by views expressed in the correspondence exchanged by them with the Secretariat in respect of such matters. In an unpublished Award rendered in 1996 (ICC Case No. 8093 (1996)), an arbitrator was asked by a party to consider the regularity of his appointment as a sole arbitrator where one of the parties alleged, in similar circumstances, that the parties had "agreed" to three arbitrators. However, the arbitrator found that there had not been any such agreement.

[275] *See, e.g.,* UNCITRAL Rules, Article 5, and the Arbitration Rules of the Arbitration Institute of the Stockholm Chamber of Commerce, Article 5.

[276] The Court's decision is not ordinarily subject to any recourse. In at least one instance, however, a party sought to have an Award set aside by a Swiss court on the ground, *inter alia*, that the Court had improperly decided that a sole arbitrator, rather than three arbitrators, should be appointed. This contention was rejected, however, on the basis that: "The text of the Rules leaves to the Court of Arbitration an entire freedom of discretion." The Swiss court nevertheless held, however, that "the arbitral Award can be set aside because of the designation of a sole arbitrator only if it has been shown beyond any doubt that in a given case the importance of the dispute necessarily called for the presence of three arbitrators." *Bucher-Guyer S.A. c/ Meiki Co. Ltd., supra,* note 120, p. 223.

the issues presented, the number of parties and whether all of them are participating. Thus, unlike under some other rules, a party need not necessarily be forced to accept a number of arbitrators that may be inappropriate for a case simply because it has been unable to agree on the number with the other party.

Like its predecessor, Article 8(2) appears to establish a presumption in favor of the appointment of a sole arbitrator. According to that Article, a sole arbitrator is to be appointed "save where it appears to the Court that the dispute is such as to warrant the appointment of three arbitrators." In practice, however, the Court does not have a general bias in favor of appointing one arbitrator. Rather, its position has traditionally been influenced, to a considerable extent, by the size of the amount at stake in the arbitration. This is obviously because the number of arbitrators appointed will have a substantial impact on the cost of the arbitration for the parties. When three arbitrators, rather than one, are appointed, the fees and costs of the tribunal are multiplied by a factor of three. In addition, the time required to conduct the case is ordinarily prolonged, due to the need to coordinate the schedules of the three arbitrators and the need, in such case, for deliberations. In a small and simple case, therefore, there will rarely be any justification for the appointment of more than one arbitrator. Provided, however, that the sum in dispute is not so small as to make the appointment of more than one arbitrator uneconomical, the Court's ordinary preference is for three arbitrators.

Thus, in all but relatively small cases, the Court usually presumes, contrary to Article 8(2), that three arbitrators should be appointed. The Court's ordinary preference for three arbitrators is generally consistent with prevailing international practice, as reflected, for example, in the UNCITRAL Model Law. Under Article 10 of that law, as under the UNCITRAL Arbitration Rules (Article 5), three arbitrators are to be appointed whenever the parties are unable to agree on a number. There are several reasons why three arbitrators are generally preferred to a sole arbitrator in international cases, notwithstanding the greater cost and also the likelihood that the arbitration will require more time. First, where the parties are of different nationalities, they will each often wish to have on the tribunal an arbitrator who is of the same nationality and who is familiar with their law and customs. Indeed, one of the most commonly-perceived advantages of arbitration is the possibility that arbitration affords the parties to designate arbitrators. If only one arbitrator is to be appointed, the parties may not be able to agree on the arbitrator's identity, and more often than not that person will be designated, in the case of an ICC arbitration, by the Court. A sole arbitrator would normally also be of a neutral nationality (*see* Article 9(5) *infra*). In addition, the appointment of a sole arbitrator, rather than three, deprives the parties of the ability to constitute a tribunal with diverse and complementary skills, as may sometimes be appropriate. Finally, it entrusts decision-making responsibility to a single individual whose determinations of law and fact will, in most jurisdictions, not be subject to any recourse. Given the finality of the arbitration process, as compared, for example, with a trial before a court of first instance, parties may simply feel more comfortable knowing that their submissions are being reviewed by three heads rather than one.

In deciding whether an arbitration is nonetheless too small to warrant the appointment of three arbitrators, the Court has for many years applied the general rule of thumb that, if the amount in dispute does not exceed U.S. $1 million, a sole arbitrator should ordinarily be appointed. The Secretariat also actively encourages the parties to agree to a sole arbitrator in such cases, and, in fact, the percentage of ICC cases in which three arbitrators have been appointed, either by agreement of the parties or decision of the Court, has historically corresponded closely to the percentage of cases for which the amount in dispute has exceeded U.S. $1 million (*i.e.,* between 50 and 60 per cent).[276] The Court's U.S. $1 million rule of thumb has crept slightly upwards, however, in recent years. The Court may therefore now be more inclined than in previous years to appoint a sole arbitrator where the amount in dispute is slightly more than U.S. $1 million. But generally, where the amount in dispute is significantly more than that, it is more likely that the Court will appoint three arbitrators, unless the issues in dispute are obviously simple. It should nevertheless not be assumed that the foregoing rule is applied rigidly. Every case is considered by the Court on its own merits, and there are circumstances in which the size of the amount in dispute will not be the deciding factor.[278]

Time period for the nomination of arbitrators. In addition to providing for the Court's decision as to the number of arbitrators, Article 8(2) establishes a time limit for the nomination of arbitrators by the parties if the Court decides that three arbitrators are to be appointed. However, Article 8(2) differs in this respect from Article 2(5) of the previous Rules by providing that an arbitrator shall first be nominated by the Claimant (within a period of 15 days) and then by the Respondent (within a further period of 15 days). Article 2(5) provided instead that the parties would "each have 30 days within which to nominate an arbitrator."[279]

Although Article 2(5) did not specify whether the 30-day period referred to therein was to be applied to the parties consecutively or simultaneously, the Court's general practice was to invite the parties to nominate arbitrators during the same 30-day period in order to avoid further delay in the constitution of the Arbitral Tribunal. Such an approach was not consistent, however, with the expectation of many practitioners that the Respondent, as in the case of Article 8(4) discussed below, should not be required to nominate an arbitrator until the

---

[277] Thus, for example, in 1997, three arbitrators were appointed in 52 per cent of the cases submitted to the Court, while the amounts in dispute exceeded U.S. $1 million in 47.9 per cent of the cases set in motion in that year and were unquantified in 14.4 per cent of such cases. *See also ICC Ct. Bull.,* Vol. 8, No. 1 (1997), pp. 8, 10 for 1996.

[278] Thus, for example, where a dispute is principally concerned with the mere collection of a debt and no complex defenses have been raised, the Court would be likely to appoint a sole arbitrator, irrespective of the amount in dispute. The Court has also been relatively more inclined to direct the appointment of three arbitrators in cases involving States, even where ·
the amount in dispute may be relatively small.

[279] Prior to the amendment of the Rules in 1988, the corresponding period set forth in the Rules was 15 days, as it had been since 1955. It was then increased to 30 days in 1988.

Claimant has done so.[280] Although all of the members of the Working Party did not share this view, there was nevertheless strong support for the principle that the Claimant should be required to make its nomination before the Respondent does. This, it was felt, could be achieved, without delaying the Arbitral Tribunal's constitution, by reducing from 30 to 15 days the time accorded to the Claimant for this purpose and then allowing the Respondent no more than 15 more days to make its nomination.[281]

Under Article 8(2), the period allowed the Respondent for the nomination of an arbitrator is explicitly tied to, and dependent upon, the prior nomination of an arbitrator by the Claimant. Thus, until the Claimant does so, the Respondent is not required to act. The Respondent might therefore ultimately have more than 30 days from the notification of the Court's decision if the Claimant is late in nominating an arbitrator. Conversely, it might have less than 30 days from such time if the Claimant nominates an arbitrator in less than 15 days or if, for example, the Claimant already nominated an arbitrator before the Court's decision on the number (in which case, the Respondent would, in keeping with the spirit of Article 8(2), presumably be required to nominate its arbitrator within 15 days after receiving the notification of the Court's decision).

Article 8(2), no more than former Article 2(5), does not indicate what is to happen if the parties do not comply with the time periods set forth in that provision. It may therefore be asked whether a party forfeits its right to nominate an arbitrator if it does not do so within the period stated in Article 8(2). The Court has never taken such a strict position, however, with regard to other, similar provisions in the Rules.[282] It would therefore most likely be the Court's view that, upon the expiry of the time periods set forth in Article 8(2), the Court may appoint an arbitrator on behalf of the defaulting party (although Article 8(2), unlike Article 8(4), does not expressly say so), but that a late nomination would nevertheless be accepted if made before the Court's appointment of an arbitrator. Indeed, because it generally takes the Court a certain amount of time to appoint an arbitrator on behalf of a party, the Court has itself often accorded defaulting parties a last chance to nominate an arbitrator before appointing one in their place, the Court's view being that a party is more likely to cooperate subsequently if it has participated in the constitution of the tribunal.

Similarly, although Article 8(2) does not expressly provide for this, the Court could be expected to allow the parties time to agree jointly on a sole arbitrator in the event that the Court decides that only one arbitrator should be appointed.

---

[280] *See, e.g.*, Kreindler, *supra,* note 14, pp. 62-63 ("[Article 2(5)] ... should be interpreted to mean that, for the nomination of its own co-arbitrator, the Defendant is entitled to a period of thirty additional days *after* the Claimant has nominated its co-arbitrator ... .").

[281] The ultimate form of this provision was inspired by a similar provision in the WIPO Arbitration Rules (Article 17(c)), although, under the WIPO Rules, the time limit for the Respondent is not tied as explicitly as under Article 8(2) to the prior nomination of an arbitrator by the Claimant.

[282] *See* the discussion of Article 5(1) *supra.*

Article 8(3)

> *Where the parties have agreed that the dispute shall be settled by a sole arbitrator, they may, by agreement, nominate the sole arbitrator for confirmation. If the parties fail to nominate a sole arbitrator within 30 days from the date when the Claimant's Request for Arbitration has been received by the other party, or within such additional time as may be allowed by the Secretariat, the sole arbitrator shall be appointed by the Court.*

Article 8(3), like Article 2(3) of the previous Rules, is intended to afford the parties a large degree of autonomy in the designation of sole arbitrators. It, thus, provides that the parties may "jointly nominate a sole arbitrator for confirmation" where they "have agreed that the dispute shall be settled by a sole arbitrator." In principle, the parties may nominate whomever they choose, and they are not required to make their selection from a pre-approved roster or list; nor is there any restriction on either the nationality or qualifications of any such persons, provided only that they should normally be independent of the parties, in accordance with Article 7(1), as already discussed, and are available and able to conduct the arbitration in accordance with the Rules (*see* in this connection Article 9(1) *infra*).

Article 8(3) nevertheless does not permit the parties actually to "appoint" the arbitrator; they are only entitled, rather, to make a nomination, which is subject to "confirmation" by the Court or its Secretary General pursuant to Article 9. In practice, such confirmations have routinely been granted in the past, except possibly where, following an arbitrator's nomination, circumstances are disclosed that give rise to doubts as to the arbitrator's independence, and one of the parties then objects to the nomination. (As to the impact in the future on the Court's practices of questions relating to the arbitrator's availability and ability, *see* the discussion of Article 9(1) *infra*.) Until confirmed, an arbitrator is not considered by the Court to have been appointed.

Under Article 8(3), as was previously the case, the parties have 30 days from the date of receipt by the Respondent of the Request for Arbitration in which to make a joint nomination. In many cases, however, this may not be sufficient, particularly where the arbitration clause does not specify the number of arbitrators and the Respondent needs time to consider whether it prefers a tribunal of one arbitrator or three. Article 8(3) therefore now recognizes that the parties may be granted more time than the 30 days set forth therein. In fact, the Secretariat has, in the past, ordinarily allowed the parties additional time to attempt to agree on the identity of a sole arbitrator whenever they have jointly requested such an opportunity.

In practice, however, sole arbitrators are much more often chosen by the Court than by joint agreement of the parties. In 1996, for example, the parties jointly agreed on a sole arbitrator in fewer than 20 per cent of the cases in which a sole arbitrator was appointed during that year. In cases with three arbitrators, however, it is more common for the parties (or the co-arbitrators) to agree on the third arbitrator and, as a consequence, the Court's role in the constitution of the tribunal has gradually been diminishing in the ICC's larger and more complex cases. This may possibly be because of the assistance that the co-arbitrators are able to render in this regard in cases with three arbitrators. Where the parties attempt, without outside assistance, to come to an agreement, their mutual suspicions of each other's motives commonly make this difficult. Parties therefore occasionally request the Secretariat to furnish them with lists of names of potential arbitrators in order to facilitate their possible agreement. Although the Rules do not provide for this, the Secretariat has nevertheless commonly accommodated such requests, when made by the parties jointly, and this has often permitted the parties to reach agreements that might otherwise have eluded them.[283]

Article 8(4)

> *Where the dispute is to be referred to three arbitrators, each party shall nominate in the Request and the Answer, respectively, one arbitrator for confirmation by the Court. If a party fails to nominate an arbitrator, the appointment shall be made by the Court. The third arbitrator, who will act as chairman of the Arbitral Tribunal, shall be appointed by the Court, unless the parties have agreed upon another procedure for such appointment, in which case the nomination will be subject to confirmation pursuant to Article 9. Should such procedure not result in a nomination within in the time limit fixed by the parties or the Court, the third arbitrator shall be appointed by the Court.*

Article 8(4) expresses the normal rule that, when three arbitrators are to be appointed, the Claimant and Respondent shall each name an arbitrator and the third shall either be selected by agreement or by the arbitral institution. It is nearly identical to Article 2(4) of the previous Rules, subject to a few, minor modifications. It also needs to be read in conjunction with Article 10 (*see infra*), however, in the case of arbitrations with multiple parties.

Nomination of co-arbitrators. In ICC arbitration, as already noted, the parties do not appoint arbitrators; they nominate them for confirmation by the Court or its Secretary General.[284] Article 8(4), thus, begins by reiterating the requirement already set forth in Articles 4(3) and 5(1) (*see supra*) that the Claimant and

---

[283] Although not explicitly stated in Article 8(3), the parties are also free, pursuant to Article 7(6), to agree upon another procedure for the appointment of the sole arbitrator, including appointment by a person or entity other than the Court. *See also* in this regard, the discussion of the appointment of the chairman under Article 8(4) *infra*.

[284] The English (but not the French) version of Article 8(4) inadvertently refers only to confirmation "by the Court." However, the Secretary General may also now confirm co-arbitrators pursuant to Article 9(2), as discussed below.

Respondent are to nominate an arbitrator in their Request and Answer, respectively, where the dispute "is to be referred to three arbitrators."

Although seemingly straightforward, Article 8(4) does not expressly take account of the different situations that may, in fact, arise. Thus, for example, the Respondent may be required to nominate an arbitrator *before* filing its Answer if the time for filing it is extended pursuant to Article 5(2). In addition, the Claimant and Respondent should not necessarily be required to nominate arbitrators in their Request and Answer if they have not already agreed, prior to the arbitration, on the number of arbitrators. As already discussed (*see* Articles 4(3) and 5(2) *supra*), neither Article 8(4) nor any other rule indicates expressly when the parties are to make their nominations if the parties agree to three arbitrators after the arbitration has commenced. It may be argued that if the Claimant proposes three arbitrators in its Request and at the same time nominates an arbitrator, then the Respondent, within the period for the Answer set forth in Article 5(1), ought also to nominate an arbitrator if it agrees with the Claimant's proposal (*see* Article 5(2) *supra*). However, in the past, the Court has not insisted upon this and has instead normally fixed a deadline for the nomination of an arbitrator by the Respondent. If neither party nominated an arbitrator in the Request or Answer, then the Court would normally fix a deadline for the nomination of arbitrators by both parties. (This was usually a simultaneous deadline for both parties. However, given the new provision for consecutive nominations in Article 8(2), the Court, in order to be consistent, should probably also now fix consecutive deadlines when the parties have agreed to three arbitrators, but have not yet nominated anyone.)

As in the case of other arbitrators nominated by the parties, the Rules do not impose any express limitations on the qualifications of the persons whom the parties may nominate as co-arbitrators, provided that they are independent, as required by Article 7(1), and are available and able to conduct the arbitration in accordance with the Rules (*see* Article 9(1) *infra*); nor are they required to be chosen from any list or panel. Occasionally, parties solicit the Secretariat's advice or assistance in identifying arbitrators who might be nominated as co-arbitrators. However, the Secretariat has generally been reluctant to provide such assistance out of fear that its neutrality in administering the arbitration might otherwise appear to be affected. Names of potential arbitrators are generally available to parties, though, from the ICC's National Committees.

In the event that a party fails to nominate an arbitrator within the time indicated in Article 8(4), or within such other time as the Court may specify, Article 8(4), like Article 2(4) before it, provides that the appointment shall be made by the Court. In this connection, the Court is required to follow the procedure set forth in Article 9(6), and this can take a certain amount of time, depending upon the circumstances. If, in the interim, a party nominates an arbitrator, then the Court may nevertheless accept the nomination, even if it has technically been made out of time. Indeed, as already discussed, the Court has not generally considered that the relevant deadlines in the Rules prevent it from considering nominations made before the Court has itself acted. Moreover, there is nothing in the Rules, in any event, to preclude the Court from itself appointing an arbitrator nominated by a party. As already noted, it has generally been the Court's view that the arbitration process is best served if both parties have participated in the constitution of the Arbitral Tribunal.

Appointment of the chairman. Unless the parties "have agreed upon another procedure," Article 8(4) provides that the chairman of the Arbitral Tribunal shall be appointed by the Court. Under Article 2(4) of the previous Rules, the Court was to appoint the chairman unless the parties had provided that "the arbitrators nominated by them shall agree on the third arbitrator within a fixed time-limit," and they did so. However, in practice, the Court permitted the chairman to be selected in other ways as well. Thus, the chairman could be chosen by the parties directly or by another person or authority. From time to time, for example, the parties have provided for the designation of the chairman by the President of the ICC or the Chairman or Secretary General of the Court (as opposed to the Court itself). In certain other cases, the parties have provided that other arbitral institutions or judicial authorities should choose the chairman, and the Court has not objected to this.[285] The Court has nevertheless generally taken the position that the designation of a chairman by a person or entity other than the Court is subject to its confirmation.[286]

Article 8(4), thus, now explicitly recognizes the considerable freedom allowed the parties in respect of the chairman's designation, while at the same time making clear the need for the confirmation of any person not appointed by the Court itself (although Article 7(6) of the Rules appears to permit the parties to derogate even from the requirement of confirmation).[287] If, however, the parties wish the chairman to be designated by anyone other than the Court, including the co-arbitrators, they must expressly provide for this, unlike under certain other arbitration rules, according to which the parties or the co-arbitrators are required to attempt to agree upon a chairman before the arbitral institution intervenes.[288]

In the event that the parties agree that the chairman should be designated by someone other than the Court, then Article 8(4) nevertheless requires that the

---

[285] In the event that the appointing authority designated by the parties in their arbitration clause is either unwilling or unable to make the appointment, the Court will ordinarily make the appointment instead. *See infra*, note 289

[286] In a few, exceptional instances, apparently out of deference to the appointing authority designated by the parties (in one case, a Paris court), the Court has "taken note" of, rather than "confirmed," the appointment by such other authority.

[287] The Rules do not permit the parties to derogate, however, from the provisions concerning the challenge and replacement of arbitrators (Articles 11 and 12). Thus, even where a different appointing authority has been chosen by the parties, the Court retains the power to remove the arbitrators so appointed.

[288] *See, e.g.,* WIPO Arbitration Rules, Article 17. During the work on the New Rules, there were certain National Committees that would have preferred a rule that, like the WIPO Rules, would require the parties or co-arbitrators to try to agree on the chairman in all cases. This proposal was not accepted, however, because parties may sometimes prefer that the chairman be appointed in a different manner, and they can, in any event, try to agree on the chairman or direct the co-arbitrators to attempt to do so if they so wish.

alternative procedure agreed upon must "result in a nomination within the time limit fixed by the parties or the Court," failing which "the third arbitrator shall be appointed by the Court." Thus, if the parties provide that the chairman is to be designated by the co-arbitrators, but do not fix a time-limit within which they are required to do so, the Court can itself fix such a time-limit (which, when fixed by the Court, is typically 30 days), and can then proceed to appoint the chairman itself if the co-arbitrators have failed to appoint an arbitrator within the time-limit fixed and the parties do not jointly request that the time-limit be extended.[289]

In practice, the parties and, much more often, the co-arbitrators now agree upon the chairman in nearly half of the ICC's cases with three arbitrators.[290] Agreement on the chairman has become increasingly common because it removes the element of uncertainty that is inherent in leaving the choice to the ICC, both in relation to the chairman's nationality and identity.[291] No matter how well an arbitral institution such as the ICC may perform its task as an appointing authority, parties increasingly realize that there is no more important choice in connection with an arbitration than the choice of arbitrators, and, to the extent possible, this is therefore not a choice that should be allowed to escape the parties' control. If, however, the choice is left to the Court, then it proceeds in the manner set forth in Article 9 below.

ARTICLE 9

Appointment and Confirmation of the Arbitrators

The appointment and confirmation of arbitrators is one of the Court's most important functions. As opposed to the appointment of arbitrators, their confirmation is a distinctive feature of the ICC arbitration system. Indeed, while all arbitral institutions appoint arbitrators, as necessary, their rules do not general-

---

[289] For an example of an arbitral Award in which an Arbitral Tribunal found that it had been validly constituted in such circumstances, *see* the extract from the Partial Award in ICC Case No. 6209 (1990), *ICC Ct. Bull.*, Vol. 8, No. 1 (1997), p. 57. *See also* the Preliminary Award in Case No. 2321 (1974), *ICCA Yearbook* I (1976), p. 133 (where the appointment of a sole arbitrator by the Court was found to be valid, notwithstanding the parties' agreement that the arbitrator was to be appointed by another authority, as that other authority had refused to do so); *and Y. c/ X., Tribunal fédéral suisse* (April 16, 1984), ATF 110 Ia 59, *ASA Bull.* (1984), p. 226, *Rev. arb.* (1986), p. 596 (where the validity of the arbitrator's appointment in similar circumstances was upheld by a Swiss court).

[290] Thus, for example, out of 182 cases in 1997 in which the Court appointed or confirmed a chairman, 68 were agreed upon by the co-arbitrators and 21 were agreed upon by the parties, while 93 (approximately 50 per cent) were appointed by the Court directly. Seven years earlier, however, in 1990, approximately 70 per cent of the chairmen named were designated by the Court. *See* Bond, "The International Arbitrator: From the Perspective of the ICC International Court of Arbitration," *Northwestern Journal of International Law & Business,* Vol. 12, No. 1 (1991), pp. 1, 8-9. Since that time, the role of the Court has declined significantly.

[291] In this regard, it is widely accepted that when the parties provide for the selection of the chairman by the co-arbitrators, the latter may properly consult with the parties. *See, e.g.,* Article 5(2) of the IBA "Rules of Ethics for International Arbitrators," *supra,* note 197. *See also* Carter, *supra,* note 208, p. 168.

ly require that arbitrators designated by the parties, the co-arbitrators or others be confirmed.[292] How the Court is to carry out its related responsibilities, in respect of both the appointment and confirmation of arbitrators, is the subject of Article 9, which incorporates, with certain modifications, the provisions formerly contained in Article 2(6) of the previous Rules together with part of former Article 2(1) and an entirely new provision (Article 9(2)) on the confirmation of arbitrators by the Court's Secretary General.

Article 9(1)

> *In confirming or appointing arbitrators, the Court shall consider the prospective arbitrator's nationality, residence and other relationships with the countries of which the parties or other arbitrators are nationals and the prospective arbitrator's availability and ability to conduct the arbitration in accordance with these Rules. The same shall apply where the Secretary General confirms arbitrators pursuant to Article 9(2).*

Background. Article 9(1) lists a number of different criteria that the Court is to consider when confirming or appointing arbitrators. It is based on the last sentence of Article 2(1) of the former Rules, but has been expanded to include references to the arbitrator's (i) "availability" and (ii) "ability to conduct the arbitration in accordance with the [ ] Rules." The former provision otherwise already provided that, in confirming or appointing arbitrators, the Court was to have regard to the proposed arbitrator's "nationality, residence and other relationships with the countries of which the parties or other arbitrators are nationals." The Court is, of course, also required to consider the arbitrator's "independence." However, this is not mentioned in Article 9(1), given the separate provisions on this subject in Articles 7(1)-(3). Article 9(5) of the Rules further provides, as discussed below, that the sole arbitrator or the chairman of the Arbitral Tribunal shall be of a nationality other than those of the parties, unless neither of the parties objects to the appointment of a person having the nationality of one of them.

Although Article 9(1) applies to both the appointment and confirmation of arbitrators, the appointing and confirming functions are, in fact, very different. In appointing arbitrators, the Court is obviously free to have regard to whatever criteria it may consider important in the context of a particular case. These may include the criteria specifically listed in Article 9(1), but they are not necessarily exhaustive. Moreover, Article 9(1) does not impose any particular obligations on the Court, when appointing arbitrators, other than to "consider" the matters set forth therein.

---

[292] An exception, however, is the London Court of International Arbitration, whose Rules provide for the appointment of all arbitrators by the LCIA, whether or not nominated by a party or other person.

When confirming arbitrators, however, the Court is acting upon nominations made by others. In this regard, the precise nature and extent of the Court's obligations has never been clearly described in the Rules. It is, of course, obvious that the Court is not to confirm an arbitrator who does not satisfy the Rules' requirements of independence. But whether the Court has the discretion to refuse to confirm an arbitrator for other reasons, and, if so, whether there are any limits on the possible exercise of such discretion, has not previously been apparent from the Rules.

While the Court has, in practice, not generally wished to interfere with the selection of arbitrators by others, and has therefore normally confirmed arbitrators, subject to the requirement of independence being satisfied, Article 9(1) nevertheless now provides the Court with an express basis in the Rules for refusing to confirm arbitrators who might be regarded as unsuitable for other reasons. Indeed, the changes to former Article 2(1) make Article 9(1) a potentially powerful tool in this regard.

Article 2(1) of the Rules formerly provided that in "making or confirming" appointments:

> the Court shall have regard to the proposed arbitrator's nationality, residence and other relationships with the countries of which the parties or the other arbitrators are nationals.

But notwithstanding the reference in the above provision to "confirming" appointments, Article 2(1) does not, in fact, appear to have been intended to provide the Court with a basis for refusing to confirm arbitrators; nor does it appear to have been intended, in any way, to impede the selection of co-arbitrators, in particular. Rather, when introducing that provision into the Rules in 1975, its drafters appear to have been concerned with the need to ensure the objective "neutrality" of the sole arbitrator or chairman, who (unlike the co-arbitrators) may not generally be of the same nationality as any of the parties. In this regard, it was recognized in particular that ties other than nationality may occasionally be perceived as affecting an arbitrator's "neutrality," such as, for example, when a person is a long-standing resident of a country other than that of his nationality.[293] When the 1975 Rules were adopted, it was, thus, explained that the language being added was needed because:

> the arbitrator's nationality did not necessarily suffice to characterize him and thus ensure that his appointment should not be likely to be challenged by the parties or not fully acceptable to the other arbitrators."[294]

---

[293] *See*, *e.g.*, H. Smit, *supra*, note 45, p. 8 ("In determining whether their ties to a particular place are such that they might be feared to favor persons who live there, the proper criterion would appear to be the domicile rather than the nationality of the potential arbitrator.").

[294] Report of Jean Robert, *Rapporteur* of the ICC Commission, to the 25th Congress of the ICC, Madrid (June 17, 1975), *supra*, note 202.

The reference in Article 2(1) to the arbitrator's "residence and other relation ships," thus, appears to have been intended to complement the nationality requirement already contained in the Rules with respect to sole arbitrators and chairmen. Frédéric Eisemann, who had only recently retired as Secretary General of the Court, further observed that:

> [O]ne should not exaggerate the real significance of this rule, which is rather a reminder of the need, in making a judicious choice, to take account of imponderables of all kinds.[295]

In practice, as Frédéric Eisemann anticipated, Article 2(1) did not subsequently have a significant impact on the practices of the Court. Indeed, in appointing arbitrators, the Court was already in a position to take account of the criteria set forth in that Article. Moreover, in most cases, the Court has not generally considered an arbitrator's "neutrality" to be adversely affected by the arbitrator's place of residence or other possible relationships with the countries of any of the parties. Nationality has, on the contrary, tended to be the predominant criterion for the Court, consistent with Article 9(5) of the Rules.[296] As regards the confirmation of arbitrators, questions of "nationality, residence and other relationships" have not generally been a matter of concern to the Court, either in respect of co-arbitrators or even sole arbitrators or chairmen, when proposed by the parties jointly.

It is uncertain whether the new rule set forth in Article 9(1) will have a greater impact than its predecessor did. However, as reformulated, it more clearly applies to co-arbitrators, whom the Court can refuse to confirm if it is not satisfied as to their "availability and ability" to conduct the arbitration in accordance with the Rules. This is also consistent with the modification, in October 1995, of the arbitrator's statement of independence form (*see* Appendix 5), which now requires all prospective arbitrators to declare that they are "able and available to serve as an arbitrator in accordance with all of the requirements of" the Rules.

Both for the arbitrators and the Court, however, the evaluation of an arbitrator's "availability and ability" can be a delicate, and not necessarily uncontroversial, assessment to make, as discussed below.

The prospective arbitrator's availability. Notwithstanding the good sense of seeking to ensure an arbitrator's availability, this can be a problematic exercise. To begin with, the organization and conduct of an ICC arbitration is not entirely within the control of either the ICC or the arbitrators, but may depend to a large degree on the wishes and conduct of the parties. Indeed, as discussed

---

[295] *See* Eisemann, *supra*, note 101, p. 358 (translation).

[296] Thus, for example, in an arbitration in Paris between a French company and a non-French company, the Court would not normally hesitate to appoint as sole arbitrator or chairman a non-French arbitrator of a "neutral" nationality residing in France. Indeed, the selection of an arbitrator residing in France would be likely to be viewed positively as a means of limiting the costs of the arbitration for the parties.

below in connection with Article 15, the parties enjoy considerable freedom in establishing the procedures to be followed in the arbitration. Thus, for example, timetables for the exchange of pleadings and evidence and the conduct of hearings may be dictated by requirements of the parties of which the arbitrators may have no knowledge at the time of their appointment. Sometimes, moreover, the parties will wish to suspend the conduct of an arbitration pending, *e.g.*, settlement discussions or the resolution of related litigation.

It is therefore often the case, when arbitrators are nominated, that they cannot necessarily anticipate how precisely the arbitration is likely to evolve and whether or to what extent the conduct of the proceedings may or may not come into conflict with other professional commitments. Arbitrators may, moreover, have only a vague idea of the extent of the work that may be required when accepting their appointment. They may also not be able to anticipate the complexity of the issues that are likely to be raised or whether there may be counter-claims or preliminary issues to be resolved (*e.g.*, with respect to the Arbitral Tribunal's competence). Thus, a dispute that may initially appear to be straightforward may evolve into one that is, in reality, much more complex and time-consuming than may have been anticipated at the time of the arbitrators' appointment.

For all of these reasons, it may be difficult for any arbitrator, when accepting an appointment, to pledge to remain completely available to conduct the arbitration in accordance with the parties' wishes. As an ICC arbitrator once noted on this subject in a letter to the Secretariat:

[A]vailability clearly involves some commitment but cannot, I think, involve a commitment to arbitrate anywhere in the world for an unlimited period, *e.g.*, for six months in Murmansk.

Yet another prospective arbitrator put it this way:

I enclose duly completed copies of your forms accepting the nomination, but it must be subject to clarification on one point. Your covering letter indicates that the Secretariat stresses that the arbitral mission demands "complete availability until the closing of the matter." I am of course in practice: while I accept that if I am appointed I shall be available to *see* the Arbitration to its conclusion, that availability will be such as can be fitted in with other prior professional commitments. If complete availability is intended to mean that all other professional commitments are to be shelved, then I would not be in a position to accept the nomination. I trust the above is clear and look forward to hearing from you.

While expecting arbitrators to be available, the ICC has not, in fact, ever made it a condition of their engagement that they have no other professional commitments. Nor are ICC arbitrators expected to engage themselves unqualifiedly with respect to requirements that may be ill-defined or to a certain degree unforeseeable.[297] However, no one is ever obliged to act as an arbitrator, and it is therefore reasonable to expect that anyone who accepts to do so will be willing to give priority to that work so that it can be performed in accordance with the parties' reasonable expectations.[298] Indeed, it is those expectations that would appear to be paramount in this regard, and, prior to accepting an appointment, arbitrators should therefore always endeavor to determine what those expectations may be and to make an assessment of the work that is likely to be required, based on the information that is then available. Similarly, the parties should themselves endeavor to determine, prior to nominating or agreeing upon an arbitrator, whether that person is, in fact, sufficiently free of potentially conflicting commitments.

Possibly, the language added to Article 9(1) will, at least, serve as an added reminder of the need to do so.

The prospective arbitrator's ability. When considering whether to confirm arbitrators, the Court has not, in the past, generally attempted to assess their "ability to conduct the arbitration" in accordance with the Rules. Not only can this be an inherently hazardous exercise, but the Court, as already stated, has generally wished to allow the parties the widest possible freedom in selecting arbitrators. Moreover, the Court has the power under the Rules (*see* Article 12(2) *infra*) to replace arbitrators who are not fulfilling their functions satisfactorily during the course of the arbitration.

There may nevertheless be circumstances in which the Court, at the time of an arbitrator's nomination, may legitimately doubt the nominee's ability to fulfill his or her functions. The new language added to Article 9(1) therefore may prompt the Court, more often than in the past, to refuse to confirm an arbitrator in cases where, notwithstanding the prospective arbitrator's independence and availability, the appointment of such person might severely impede the proper conduct of the arbitration. Among the issues that arise from time to time, and as to which Article 9(1) may be invoked in the future, are the following:

Language. Parties generally expect that the arbitrators will have a sufficient mastery of the language of the arbitration. As has been noted:

---

[297] For an interesting discussion of the arbitrator's duties in respect of availability, *see K/S Norjarl A/S* v. *Hyundai Heavy Industries Co. Ltd.,* [1991] 3 All E.R. 211, in which, with respect to the scheduling of a hearing, Lord Justice Leggatt noted, p. 223:
> Arbitrators are under no absolute obligation to make particular dates available: their obligation is to sit on such dates as may reasonably be required of them having regard to all of the circumstances including the exigencies of their own practices.

In the event, however, that dates cannot be found to the satisfaction of the parties, then the judges in that case appeared to recognize the possible need for the arbitrators to withdraw.

[298] *See, e.g.,* Eisemann, *supra,* note 205, p. 222 ("*Il nous paraît donc normal d'exiger que l'acceptation de la mission engage l'arbitre à se consacrer en priorité à celle-ci.*") (translation: "It therefore appears normal to require that acceptance of the mission commits the arbitrator to give priority to the same.").

It is highly desirable (not to say essential) that an arbitrator has an adequate working knowledge of the language in which the arbitration is to take place. This is an obvious requirement, but one which is forgotten not only by parties but by appointing authorities as well. If an arbitrator is appointed who does not have a good knowledge of the language of the arbitration, it becomes necessary to engage an interpreter to translate the evidence of the witnesses and the arguments of the lawyers into a language which can be understood by the arbitrator concerned. Translating oral evidence accurately into another language is a very difficult task, particularly where a witness is being examined in minute detail on his evidence of fact or opinion. It also adds considerably to the expense of the arbitral proceedings; first, because of the interpreter's fees and, secondly, because of the extra time which is taken if everything of importance has to be translated from the working language of the arbitration into a language which the arbitrator himself can understand.[299]

Notwithstanding the foregoing, the Court has thus far been reluctant to establish any rigid practices in this respect. This is partly because the Rules themselves do not expressly set forth any linguistic requirements for the arbitrators; in addition, in some cases, the language of the arbitration may not yet be determined or may be in dispute when the tribunal is being constituted.

In at least one case under the former Rules, however, the Court refused to confirm an arbitrator nominated by a party (in replacement of an arbitrator who had resigned) because the nominee did not understand the language stated to be the language of the arbitration in the Terms of Reference and the other party objected to the nomination. Where, however, the language of the arbitration is a disputed issue, the Court has not generally required that all prospective arbitrators understand each of the languages in question. (It has normally endeavored to ensure, however, that the sole arbitrator or chairman appointed understands both languages so as not to prejudice the decision to be taken by the Arbitral Tribunal in this regard.) The Court has also not normally required that, when an arbitration is to be conducted in two languages, the arbitrators must all master both languages or that all arbitrators must otherwise be familiar with the language of the law applicable to the arbitration.[300] Moreover, even with respect to the chairman or sole arbitrator, in a particular case, it might sometimes be more important for the person appointed to possess other experience or skills rather than all of the linguistic abilities that might be relevant.

Thus, even in respect of a criterion as relatively straightforward as the language of the arbitration, determining the arbitrator's "ability" to conduct the arbitration is not necessarily easy or uncontroversial.

---

[299] *Redfern and Hunter*, pp. 215-16.

[300] In one case, however, a sole arbitrator appointed by the Court resigned after one of the parties objected that, although he mastered the language of the arbitration, he did not have adequate knowledge of Mandarin Chinese, Taiwanese law being applicable in the arbitration.

Legal qualifications. Consistent with other arbitration rules and most arbitration laws, the Rules do not require that an arbitrator have any legal training or experience.[301] In ICC arbitration cases, the parties nevertheless almost always nominate lawyers (or other legal professionals), and the ICC also ordinarily assumes, unless otherwise advised, that the parties expect it to do the same when appointing the sole or third arbitrator. As a former Secretary General of the Court has written:

> [I]n international commercial arbitrations, where awards must generally set out the reasoning of the Arbitral Tribunal; where the validity and enforceability of awards, if challenged, are decided upon by judges; and where questions of jurisdiction, applicable law and statutory interpretation must often (and increasingly) be decided upon by the Arbitral Tribunal, legal training is a minimum requirement and legal practice is preferable.[302]

In appointing arbitrators, the Court, thus, normally endeavors to ensure that the person appointed – while of a neutral nationality – has been trained in, or is otherwise familiar with, either the law likely to be applied in the arbitration, if this can be determined, or a similar legal system. The Court can also be expected to take into account in this regard the identity and skills of the other arbitrators, if any, and the ease with which the law in question can otherwise be apprehended through available publications and possible access to experts. Only very rarely have ICC arbitrators been opposed or challenged on the ground that they did not have appropriate legal qualifications, and such challenges as have been made have generally not prospered.

Thus, for example, in one case, the Respondent (a Swiss company) challenged the lawyer appointed by the Court as sole arbitrator in an arbitration to be conducted in India between that party and an Indian claimant. The arbitration clause provided that "German law shall apply" in the arbitration. Although the lawyer appointed had studied in Germany, understood German and had previously been involved in a number of litigation matters (outside Germany) in which German law was relevant, he was challenged on the basis that:

> [He] has no German law degree and is not an expert on German law himself. Even though he might have spent some time in Germany during his legal education long years ago he has never obtained sufficient knowl-

---

[301] The laws of some countries may, however, contain such a requirement. *See Redfern and Hunter*, p. 214.

[302] *See* Bond, *supra*, note 290, p. 5. *But compare* Mustill: "The assumption that a panel of three lawyers however expert and experienced in the law and in the handling of disputes, is invariably the right choice for every kind of dispute is not questioned as often as perhaps it ought to be." (*Cited in* Poudret, "Conclusions," *Arbitration and Expertise* (ICC Publishing 1994), p. 144.)

edge and experience as regards substantive German law, in particular the German law of trade as set out in the German Commercial Code and in other regulations which are very likely to be applicable and decisive in this case:

...

Furthermore, there is no possibility for Mr ... himself to gain the required depth of knowledge as regards the relevant substantive German law, in particular the German Commercial Code and certain regulations of the German Civil Code. This is because anyone who is to play a judging role in applying German law will (i) have to have the overview on all regulations which might be applicable to the case, which I expressly doubt Mr ... – other than a qualified German lawyer – will have, and (ii) will secondly have to understand not only the German law and regulations as they stand but – in order to obtain the admissible interpretation of such law – will have to be able to find and understand the German judgments published in accordance with specific regulations, the German commentaries published for example with reference to the German Commercial Code and all major German legal literature published in this connection. Since Mr ... as he himself admits, does not speak German, I, therefore, very much doubt, that he will be able to apply the German law correctly in all relevant respects. From all this follows that an expert on German law would have to be instructed by the court during the proceedings anyhow in order to support the arbitrator in avoiding to come to a wrongful decision, if Mr ... remained to be the appointed sole arbitrator in this case.

This would also not be fair towards the parties under a cost point of view because they would have to cover more expenses incurred in connection with the proceedings, although they had chosen to avoid incurring too much legal costs by deciding for a sole arbitrator.

The challenged arbitrator responded as follows:

It is true that I have no German law degree and am not myself an expert in German law. I have, however, over many years, had experience of handling cases governed by German law. This experience has involved discussing in detail rival contentions as to German law advanced by German lawyers acting for the parties and testing such contentions by evidence and cross-examination ... . I have participated in or chaired many hours of comparative seminars discussing and comparing German legal topics, mainly of a commercial nature.

...

I would expect to be able to judge fairly on the basis of the parties' respective evidence and arguments – just as a continentally – trained lawyer would do.

Had the Respondent been concerned to provide for a German-qualified arbitrator as well as for German applicable law, it could have so stipulated in the contract. Alternatively, it could have sought to influence the appointment by stipulating for an arbitrator to be chosen by the parties. Instead, it left the appointment of a suitable arbitrator to the ICC.

The Indian claimant, for its part, opposed the challenge, and it was ultimately rejected by the Court.

So too did the Court reject a challenge made against a Singaporean lawyer who had been appointed as sole arbitrator in a case between parties from Gibraltar and Sri Lanka and in which Sri Lankan law was to be applied. There, as in the former case, the Court considered, when appointing the arbitrator, that he would be capable of applying the law governing the arbitration even if he had no formal training in that law. The Court could not, in any event, have designated a Sri Lankan national to act as sole arbitrator unless both parties agreed (*see* Article 9(5) *infra*).

Although the challenges made in each of the above cases were rejected, they reflect the concern that parties may feel – particularly when a sole arbitrator is being appointed – if the person who will be deciding their case has no formal education or training in the law applicable to the arbitration. Situations such as this, which are not uncommon, demonstrate how relative a notion an arbitrator's "ability" can be in an international arbitration.

Expertise in the commercial or technical field that is the subject of the arbitration. It is a common expectation of parties that arbitrators will be familiar with the field (*e.g.,* maritime, construction, intellectual property) that is the subject of the arbitration. In appointing arbitrators, the Court therefore generally endeavors to identify a person knowledgeable in the relevant area, and all prospective ICC arbitrators are required to indicate their areas of expertise on a standard form of *curriculum vitae* that they are required to complete prior to appointment. However, there are no recent instances in which the Court has refused to confirm or removed an arbitrator for lacking sufficient commercial or technical expertise, and the Rules specifically contemplate, moreover, that an arbitrator may be assisted, to the extent appropriate, by an expert (*see* Article 20(4) *infra*).

Expertise in arbitration. It has been stated that:

> Probably the most important qualification for an international arbitrator is that he should be experienced in the law and practice of arbitration.[303]

This is a widespread view, particularly in regard to a sole arbitrator or chairman of an Arbitral Tribunal. It is, moreover, generally considered that any such arbitration experience should include experience of international arbitration accom-

---

[303] *Redfern and Hunter*, p. 217.

panied by both managerial ability and "international mindedness,"[304] for untold damage can be done to the international arbitration process when an arbitrator's attitude and approach to a case are unduly parochial or chauvinistic.

In selecting arbitrators, the Court, thus, generally seeks to identify persons with international arbitration experience. However, the Court does not regard this as either a rigid or absolute requirement. Nor will it refuse to confirm an arbitrator nominated by a party solely on the basis that that person has no prior arbitration experience. In those cases, however, where the tribunal is composed of three arbitrators and neither of the co-arbitrators has any significant experience of international arbitration – or ICC arbitration, in particular – the ICC will generally seek to ensure (when the choice is left to it) that the third arbitrator, at least, has sufficient experience to conduct the arbitration in a satisfactory manner.

Age, Physical and Material Resources. Lastly, matters such as age, health and an arbitrator's material resources may have an important impact on an arbitrator's ability to perform effectively and efficiently. Increasingly, moreover, the telecommunications facilities available to an international arbitrator will affect the arbitrator's ability to perform in accordance with the parties' (and the arbitral institution's) expectations. We have not yet reached the day when an arbitrator can be said to have a duty to possess a fax machine or an e-mail address. However, parties increasingly expect this. The Court, for its part, has not generally imposed any requirements in respect of such matters. Nor has it done so in regard to the arbitrator's age, although this may nevertheless be a legitimate consideration in certain cases.

It remains to be seen whether these or any of the other matters raised above will be invoked in connection with the application of Article 9(1).

Article 9(2)

> *The Secretary General may confirm as co-arbitrators, sole arbitrators and chairmen of Arbitral Tribunals persons nominated by the parties or pursuant to their particular agreements, provided that they have filed a statement of independence without qualification or a qualified statement of independence has not given rise to objections. Such confirmation shall be reported to the Court at its next session. If the Secretary General considers that a co-arbitrator, sole arbitrator or chairman of an Arbitral Tribunal should not be confirmed, the matter shall be submitted to the Court.*

Background. Prior to the New Rules, only the Court itself had the power to confirm arbitrators. Article 9(2), thus, for the first time confers limited authority on the Court's Secretary General in this connection.

---

[304] *See* Lalive, "On the Neutrality of the Arbitrator and the Place of Arbitration," *Swiss Essays on International Arbitration* (Schulthess 1984), pp. 23, 28.

Article 9(2) was added to the Rules in order to accelerate the time required for the constitution of the Arbitral Tribunal. In order for an arbitrator to be confirmed by the Court, it is necessary for the nomination to be brought before one of the Court's Committee sessions, which have for the last several years been held no more than three times a month (*see* Article 1(4) *supra*). The agenda and related documentation are, moreover, generally required to be submitted to the Committee members one week in advance of the Committee's meeting. Thus, in a typical case, it is likely to take at least a week, and more often longer, after the Secretariat is in possession of all relevant information, before an arbitrator can be confirmed by the Court. Delay in the confirmation of co-arbitrators usually also delays the time required for the appointment or confirmation of the chairman. By allowing the Secretary General to confirm arbitrators, the New Rules therefore permit time to be gained: the Secretariat is not required to await a session of the Court, and the Secretary General should be in a position to act immediately upon receipt of all of the information required to decide whether the arbitrator should be confirmed.

Extent of the Secretary General's authority. The Secretary General does not have the authority to refuse to confirm arbitrators. Under Article 9(2), he is only permitted to confirm them. As a consequence, he is authorized to exercise his power of confirmation only in cases where confirmation is usually little more than a formality, *i.e.,* where (i) the arbitrator has filed a statement of independence without qualification, or (ii) a qualified statement of independence has not given rise to any objections on the part of any of the parties. The idea is that the Secretary General may act where the confirmation of the arbitrator is not contested by anyone and where there is, thus, nothing to decide. Indeed, during the preparation of the New Rules, the ICC Commission was opposed to giving the Secretary General authority to decide whether arbitrators should be confirmed in cases where this might be the subject of a dispute between the parties. However, where there is no such dispute, it was generally agreed that the parties should not be required to await a meeting of the Court in order for an arbitrator formally to be confirmed.

Notwithstanding the general intention of the drafters, Article 9(2) nevertheless does not expressly take account of those situations where a prospective arbitrator's appointment may be contested for reasons unrelated to the question of the arbitrator's independence. Thus, for example, a party may object to the confirmation of an arbitrator who, although independent, does not understand the language of the arbitration or is otherwise considered to be unsuitable. As discussed above, the new text of Article 9(1) may provide parties with a broader basis than previously for contesting prospective arbitrators for reasons other than lack of independence, and, indeed, Article 9(1) explicitly directs the Secretary General to have regard to the matters set forth therein when confirming arbitrators pursuant to Article 9(2). But Article 9(2), as drafted, does not preclude the Secretary General from confirming arbitrators who may be the subject of an objection relating to one of the criteria listed in Article 9(1), provided that the other conditions of Article 9(2) are satisfied.

Given the general intention of Article 9(2), however, it can reasonably be expected that the Secretary General would not ordinarily confirm an arbitrator who is the subject of an objection, but would rather, as he is entitled to do, refer the matter to the Court. The Secretary General is not obliged to confirm arbitrators pursuant to Article 9(2). He is to exercise his discretion and would presumably do so in a manner consistent with the general objectives of that provision. The Secretary General might nevertheless confirm an arbitrator pursuant to Article 9(2) where an objection, unrelated to the question of the arbitrator's independence, is clearly frivolous.

This having been said, objections to ICC arbitrators for reasons unrelated to the question of their independence are rare, and relatively few nominations give rise to difficulties, in any event. Thus, it can reasonably be expected that, notwithstanding the limits on the Secretary General's authority, Article 9(2) will permit Arbitral Tribunals to be constituted more quickly than in the past in most cases without the need for any intervention on the part of the Court. Indeed, most ICC arbitrators are confirmed, rather than appointed directly by the Court. In 1997, for example, out of a total of 745 arbitrators appointed or confirmed, 481 (or two-thirds approximately) were confirmed following their nomination, primarily by the parties or co-arbitrators.[305] And of those who were confirmed, few, if any, gave rise to any objections on the part of any of the parties. Furthermore, during any given year, there are relatively few persons who cannot be confirmed.[306]

Even where there are no objections to an arbitrator, however, there are at least three special situations in which the Secretary General may not wish to confirm an arbitrator under Article 9(2). The first is where it is uncertain whether the New Rules, as opposed to the former Rules, are applicable. In any such case, the Secretary General could be expected to refer the matter of confirmation to the Court.[307] In addition, where a party has contested the existence of an ICC arbitration agreement or it is otherwise unclear whether the arbitration should be accepted (*e.g.,* because of a derogation from the Rules in the arbitration clause), the Secretary General may wish to leave the confirmation of arbitrators to the Court when considering whether to allow the arbitration to proceed. Lastly, in cases with multiple Respondent parties, the Secretary General will presumably not wish to confirm the arbitrator proposed by the Claimant unless the Respondents agree to nominate an arbitrator jointly (*see* Article 10 *infra*).[308]

---

[305] Of those arbitrators, 365 were co-arbitrators, 89 were chairmen and 27 were sole arbitrators.

[306] Thus, for example, while the Court appointed or confirmed approximately 3,400 arbitrators between the second half of 1988 and the end of 1994, it refused to confirm an arbitrator in only 40 cases approximately during that period. *See* Hascher, *supra*, note 203, pp. 6, 11.

[307] *See supra,* note 128.

[308] In addition, where the number of arbitrators is required to be decided by the Court under Article 8(2), the Court might at the same time choose to confirm any arbitrators that may have been nominated by the parties, even if such confirmation could otherwise be made by the Secretary General.

Confirmation procedure. Before arbitrators can be confirmed, they must submit to the Secretariat a completed statement of independence (*see* Article 7(2) *supra*) and form of *curriculum vitae*. Those forms are sent by the Secretariat directly to potential arbitrators for completion upon their nomination. Copies of the completed forms are ordinarily then sent by the Secretariat to the parties, although the Rules do not themselves require this, and this has not routinely been done in the past by all of the Secretariat's counsels, except where the arbitrator's statement of independence contains qualifications. It would nevertheless be reasonable to expect the Secretariat to transmit to the parties in all cases a copy of a prospective arbitrator's *curriculum vitae* and statement of independence, even if unqualified, prior to confirmation. The *curriculum vitae*, in particular, may contain information relevant to the suitability of the arbitrator's appointment.

Occasionally, in the past, in order to gain time, the Court has confirmed arbitrators "subject to receiving an unqualified statement of independence." The Court has usually done so, however, only where the arbitrator already advised the Secretariat orally of the arbitrator's independence, but was prevented for some reason from immediately returning the statement of independence form. In such case, the confirmation would not actually take effect unless and until such a statement were received, but there would not be any need to await a further meeting of the Court. Now that arbitrators are ordinarily to be confirmed by the Secretary General when the arbitrator's statement of independence is unqualified, and it will not be necessary to await a meeting of the Court in such case, there would no longer appear to be any justification for the confirmation of an arbitrator subject to the receipt of the arbitrator's statement.

In the event of a qualified statement of independence giving rise to a party's objection, the Secretariat will, as previously, be required to refer the matter to the next session of the Court at which the arbitrator's confirmation can be considered.

Consequences of non-confirmation. If the Court refuses to confirm an arbitrator, it normally invites the party (or other person or persons) responsible for the nomination to make a new proposal within a fixed period of time (typically 15 to 30 days), although the Court is not necessarily obligated to do so. Indeed, it might arguably take the alternative position that a party is required under the Rules to nominate an "independent" arbitrator, and that if it fails to do so, the Court may then appoint an arbitrator on its behalf.[309] The Court has generally been reluctant to adopt such an approach, however. In many of the cases where the Court has refused to confirm arbitrators, the arbitrator's independence or lack thereof could reasonably be the subject of disagreement. Depriving a party of its right to make a new nomination in such a case would therefore probably

---

[309] Unlike the ICC Rules, the LCIA Rules, in fact, contain an express provision (Article 11(1)) that authorizes the Court "not to follow the original nominating process" if a nominee is not suitable and is refused appointment.

be excessively harsh. Moreover, given the time required for the Court to make a default appointment, little time, if any, is ordinarily lost if a party is afforded the opportunity to nominate a new arbitrator. If, however, a party nominates a manifestly dependent arbitrator in apparent bad faith on one or more occasions, it is surely open to the Court to consider that an arbitrator has not been nominated in accordance with the Rules and, thus, to refuse to consider any further nominations and to appoint the arbitrator itself.

Article 9(3)

> *Where the Court is to appoint a sole arbitrator or the chairman of the Arbitral Tribunal, it shall make the appointment upon a proposal of a National Committee of the ICC that it considers to be appropriate. If the Court does not accept the proposal made, or if the National Committee fails to make the proposal requested within the time limit fixed by the Court, the Court may repeat its request or may request a proposal from another National Committee that it considers to be appropriate.*

Article 9(4)

> *Where the Court considers that the circumstances so demand, it may choose the sole arbitrator or the chairman of the Arbitral Tribunal from a country where there is no National Committee, provided that neither of the parties objects within the time limit fixed by the Court.*

Article 9(5)

> *The sole arbitrator or the chairman of the Arbitral Tribunal shall be of a nationality other than those of the parties. However, in suitable circumstances and provided that neither of the parties objects within the time limit fixed by the Court, the sole arbitrator or the chairman of the Arbitral Tribunal may be chosen from a country of which any of the parties is a national.*

The above three provisions, all previously included in Article 2(6) of the former Rules, set forth the principles applicable to the appointment by the Court of the sole arbitrator or chairman of the Arbitral Tribunal.[310] As under the previous Rules, they require the Court ordinarily to solicit proposals from ICC National Committees and leave it to the Court to determine the National Committee that

---

[310] Unlike Articles 9(3) and 9(4), however, Article 9(5) does not, in fact, say that it applies only to the appointment of arbitrators by the Court. It can therefore be argued that it sets forth a principle that is also required to be respected by co-arbitrators or others designated by the parties to appoint arbitrators, unless, of course, the parties otherwise agree, as they may pursuant to Article 7(6).

is appropriate. Only slight drafting changes have been made in the text of former Article 2(6).

The role of the National Committees. Ever since the first ICC Rules were issued in 1922, the National Committees have played a prominent role in the appointment of ICC arbitrators. The 1922 Rules, thus, stipulated:

> The Court of Arbitration shall request the National Committees to furnish it with the names of technically qualified arbitrators, as and when required, for appointment as arbitrators ... and from amongst them the ... [Court] shall proceed to appointment.

Successive versions of the Rules have made it equally clear that arbitrators appointed by the Court are to be proposed by National Committees, and this remains the ordinary rule today, as indicated in Article 9(3).[311]

The National Committees have assumed the role that they play in the appointment of arbitrators because they place at the disposal of the Court a far-flung, international network that is closely tied to the business and legal communities in the more than sixty countries in which they are present. (*See* the list of the ICC's National Committees at Appendix 3.) By virtue of being on the ground in so many places, the National Committees are in a far better position than the Court's Secretariat in Paris to identify locally-prominent professionals who may be qualified to act as arbitrators in ICC cases and, in particular, to assist the Court in expanding the pool of potential arbitrators beyond those who are already well-known internationally. As international arbitration becomes an increasingly global activity, the National Committees have a vital role to play in enabling the Court to fulfill its functions as a truly international institution. No other arbitral institution has a comparable international network of its own.

As the National Committees are autonomous organizations (*see* Chapter 1 *supra*), they are not all staffed and organized in the same manner for the purpose of proposing arbitrators to the Court. Some National Committees have permanent staff members who devote substantial time to identifying and meeting with potential arbitrators, while others do not. Some, such as the French and U.S. National Committees, have established arbitration committees or commissions composed of independent, local practitioners who assist the National Committees in performing their tasks. Many, if not most, have compiled informal rosters or lists of arbitrators whom they are prepared to propose. Still others have arrangements with local arbitration institutions (such as CEPANI in Belgium) to assist them in the performance of their tasks.

---

[311] By virtue of Article 7(6), however, parties are free to derogate from this rule if they so wish. In addition, if they designate either the Chairman or Secretary General of the Court or the President of the ICC as an appointing authority, as they occasionally do, the National Committees are not required to be solicited.

As a general rule, the National Committees in nearly all of the countries of Western Europe and North America, which have historically been heavily solicited by the Court for proposals, have formal structures in place for the proposal of arbitrators. In the United Kingdom, for example, the National Committee has, for many years, employed an arbitration consultant, who is responsible for making proposals of arbitrators to the Court under the general supervision of an arbitration panel composed of prominent outside lawyers. Some years ago, the then arbitration consultant, David Sarre, himself a retired company lawyer, described his functions in the following terms:

> [It] ... is the function of the Arbitration Consultant [to make the decision as to who should be nominated]. He is not, however, uncontrolled or unsupervised. For ... if someone who has not previously acted as an ICC arbitrator is to be nominated, at least two members of the Arbitration Panel are to be consulted ... [The Arbitration Panel] ... is, in effect, a committee which oversees the Arbitration Consultant in the discharge of its responsibilities. It is chaired by ... the other members being three Queen's Counsel and five solicitors. The Panel meets once a year when the Consultant makes a report, particularly on the nominations made in the course of the year. Preserving the confidentiality required in ICC arbitrations, the identity of parties is not disclosed even to members of the Panel. The information on which the Consultant based his choice of arbitrator is given, for example:
> - the nature of the dispute;
> - the amount involved;
> - the place of arbitration;
> - governing law (if known);
> - language of the arbitration;
> - (in the case of a tribunal of three) the co-arbitrators.
>
> At the meeting, discussion mainly centres on the criteria applied and the weight given to them in the making of each nomination. It is also understood that outside the meeting members discuss individuals with the Consultant in confidence, their qualities or lack of them. In this connection, the Consultant is also assisted in forming his opinions by confidential discussions with the Secretary-General and other colleagues in the Secretariat, and with practitioners who from time to time give feedback as to how arbitrators have fulfilled their function.[312]

In many other countries, similar structures are in place, and most National Committees, wherever they may be, take their responsibilities very seriously.

---

[312] Sarre, "ICC United Kingdom and Its Role in Arbitration," *International and ICC Arbitration* (King's College 1990), pp. 58, 59-60.

This is not to say, however, that all National Committees function perfectly. But notwithstanding occasional imperfections in the system, the ability of the Court to identify capable arbitrators in many parts of the world would be severely hampered without the National Committees' assistance.[313] Moreover, it is the Court, and not the National Committees, that actually appoints the arbitrators. Since they were amended in 1988, the Rules have explicitly recognized the Court's power to refuse to accept the proposal of a National Committee. As stated in Article 9(3), the Court can either request a National Committee to make a new proposal or it can request a proposal from another National Committee if it is dissatisfied with the proposal originally made. National Committees that do not perform their functions satisfactorily therefore risk losing the confidence of the Court and future invitations for proposals. As a consequence, they have every reason to try to identify arbitrators of the highest possible standing and to monitor their subsequent performance. The Court's Secretariat and the National Committees have long maintained an on-going dialogue for this purpose.

In addition to making clear the Court's power to refuse proposals of National Committees, the amendments to the Rules in 1988 included a provision (now Article 9(4)) for the first time permitting the Court to choose the sole arbitrator "from a country where there is no National Committee."[314] The obvious intention was to remove the barriers to appointment facing potential arbitrators in the many countries where there are no such Committees and, hence, to make more truly international the ICC's arbitrator selection process. However, the provision in question, like Article 9(4), was accompanied by the requirement that "neither of the parties objects within the time limit fixed by the Court." Thus, before appointing an arbitrator from another such country, the Secretariat is required to solicit the parties' views, a requirement that has tended to limit the appeal of

---

[313] *See*, for a further discussion of the National Committees' role, R. Smit, *supra*, note 24, pp. 61-63.

[314] The words "from a country" are generally understood by the Court to refer to the arbitrator's nationality, rather than his place of residence, which may be different. Although it does not actually say so, Article 9(4) is generally also assumed to mean that, in such cases, the Court need not request a proposal of such a person from a National Committee. This is because it is usually further assumed that a National Committee can only propose a person having the nationality of the National Committee. *See, e.g.,* Arnaldez and Jakandé, *"Les Amendements Apportés au Règlement d'Arbitrage de la Chambre de Commerce Internationale (C.C.I.),"* *Rev. arb.* (1988), pp. 67, 72 (translation: "The choice of the National Committee ... in fact determines the nationality of the arbitrator ... ."). However, this is not actually stated in the Rules, and there have been cases in which National Committees have proposed arbitrators residing and practicing law in the country of the National Committee without being citizens of that country. *See, e.g.,* Morera, "The Appointment of Arbitrators by the Court," *ICC Ct. Bull.*, Vol. 7, No. 2 (1996), pp. 32, 33. It might therefore have been possible to interpret Article 9(4), when read together with Article 9(3), as nevertheless requiring the Court to seek proposals from National Committees of persons from the other countries concerned. But this was not the intention when this provision was first adopted in 1988.

doing so because of the risk of a party objecting and time being lost in the process.[315]

In recent years, although the Court has made a concerted effort to select arbitrators from countries without National Committees whenever possible, this has nevertheless occurred relatively infrequently. Thus, for example, in 1995-1996, the Court appointed sole arbitrators and chairmen from such countries in only 16 out of the more than 400 cases in which such appointments were made.[316] The ICC has, in the meantime, been pursuing the broader goal of expanding the ICC's network of National Committees. Since the changes to the Rules in 1988, new National Committees have been established in Bangladesh, Chile, China, Hungary, Lithuania, Peru, and Syria.

The selection of the appropriate National Committee. Because of the role played by the National Committees in the arbitrator appointment process, the Court is required to make two decisions whenever it appoints a sole arbitrator or chairman. It must first decide upon an appropriate Committee and then decide whether to appoint an arbitrator proposed by that Committee. For many years, the Court's normal practice has been to make those two decisions separately. Thus, upon consideration of a proposal of the Secretariat, the Court decides at a first Committee meeting of the Court which National Committee to select. The Secretariat then solicits a proposal from that Committee, which, when received, is submitted to the Court for its consideration at a subsequent Committee meeting. As the Court normally only holds three Committee meetings in a typical month, the appointment of an arbitrator by the Court in this manner can easily take several weeks and sometimes even longer.[317]

During the preparation of the New Rules, the Working Party considered whether there might be a satisfactory way of accelerating this process. One possibility would have been to permit the selection of a National Committee to be made by the Secretariat, thus eliminating the need for two separate decisions of the Court. Although the Secretariat already makes recommendations to the Court

---

[315] The requirement of obtaining the parties' views has also nourished a debate within the Court as to the need to disclose the specific country from which the Court wishes to appoint an arbitrator when seeking the parties' consent. On the assumption that parties would generally wish to know this before giving the Court *carte blanche* to appoint an arbitrator from any one of the approximately 100 countries without a National Committee, the Secretariat has generally specified the country concerned when soliciting the parties' views. However, Article 9(4) arguably does not require this, and in some instances the Secretariat has not volunteered such information.

[316] The countries concerned were Benin (1), Czech Republic (2), Estonia (1), Ghana (1), Hungary (3) (before the establishment of a National Committee in 1996), Malaysia (4), Poland (1), Russia (1), Slovakia (1), and Slovenia (1).

[317] This has prompted the criticism that the use of National Committees unduly delays the constitution of the Arbitral Tribunal in ICC arbitration. *See, e.g.,* Parker School of Foreign Comparative Law, Columbia University, "ICC Rules Commentary," *World Arb. Rep.*, Vol. 3, (Supplement) (1992), pp. 3662, 3667.

in this regard, there was strong resistance within both the Working Party and the ICC Commission to giving it decision-making authority; it was felt, rather, that the ultimate decision should always be taken by the Court. The Working Party nevertheless considered that, when recommending a National Committee, the Secretariat should be allowed, if the Court so wishes, to lay before the Court at the same time that Committee's proposal of an arbitrator so that the two matters can be considered together. This explains the slight drafting change in the language of Article 9(3), which now provides that the Court's appointment shall be made "upon a proposal" of a National Committee, rather than, as under Article 2(6) of the former Rules, "after having requested" such a proposal, from which it might have been inferred that the Secretariat could not request a proposal from a National Committee until the Court had already selected one.

Be this as it may, it will be for the Court to decide how it wishes to proceed in this respect in the future. In the past, the Court has generally selected National Committees without any regard to the identity of the arbitrator whom the National Committee might propose, although it has, in a few instances, chosen Committees with a view to obtaining the proposal of a specific individual whom the Court wished to appoint. Such cases, however, have been the exception. Ordinarily, the Court's selection of a National Committee has been made, without having any specific persons in mind, on the more or less well-informed assumption that the National Committee in question would be in a position to propose an appropriate arbitrator. But sometimes the Court's decisions, particularly in the case of National Committees that have been solicited infrequently, represent little more than an act of faith in the National Committee's ability to identify a suitable arbitrator.[318]

In this regard, one of the criteria that inevitably affects the Court's decision-making is the distribution among the various National Committees of the Court's invitations for proposals. All of the ICC's National Committees are avid to receive as many opportunities as possible to propose arbitrators as this permits them to enhance their standing with the local legal community, which is equally desirous of receiving such appointments. Moreover, for the Court, distributing appointments among as many National Committees as possible is consistent with its goals of promoting the widest possible use of, and familiarity with, ICC arbitration and expanding the pool of experienced international arbitrators. The Court is, of course, always required to balance this objective against the need for the appointment in each case of an arbitrator who is truly suitable, and this is a difficult challenge. Thus, while the Court appointed arbitrators on the proposal of 35 different National Committees in 1997, the vast majority were still drawn from the National Committees of the handful of countries that have traditionally served as the principal venues for ICC arbitrations or otherwise as sources of

---

[318] Some National Committees regularly provide the Secretariat with updated lists of the arbitrators that they are in a position to propose. But most have either not wished to do so or select prospective arbitrators on a case-by-case basis without recourse to any such list.

international arbitration expertise. Indeed, more than half of the arbitrators appointed by the Court in 1997 were from five countries (Switzerland, France, the United Kingdom, Germany and Belgium, in that order).[319]

In selecting a National Committee, there a number of different factors that the Court ordinarily considers. The first is, of course, the nationality of the parties, given the requirement of Article 9(5), like Article 2(6) before, that the sole arbitrator or the chairman must ordinarily be of a different (or neutral) nationality.[320] According to Article 9(5), the Court may propose to appoint an arbitrator having the nationality of one of the parties "in suitable circumstances," but only if neither party objects,[321] and the Court, in fact, almost never proposes this except where the Secretariat has already received an informal indication from one or both of the parties that such a proposal would be welcomed.

Thus, the Court normally begins by excluding the National Committees barred by Article 9(5). This, of course, requires it, however, to determine each party's nationality, which is not necessarily as simple as it may sound. In the case of a physical person or a State, there ought not ordinarily to be any difficulty, although a party commencing an arbitration against an individual may not know the nationality of that person, which can be troublesome if the latter does not appear in the arbitration. In the case of a company, the Court has usually considered its nationality to be that of its place of incorporation. However, many companies in ICC arbitrations belong to larger corporate groups, which may be controlled by companies or individuals located in other jurisdictions. Thus, for example a "French" corporate entity may, in fact, be a wholly-owned subsidiary of a large U.S. corporation. This then raises the question of whether such an entity should be treated as French or American for the purpose of Article 9(5).

---

[319] In 1996, the top five were France, Switzerland, the United Kingdom, Canada and Belgium. Austria, Italy and the United States are also frequently solicited.

[320] Not all arbitration rules mandate the appointment of a sole arbitrator or chairman of a "neutral" nationality. Thus, for example, all that the UNCITRAL Rules provide in this respect is that (Article 6(4)): "In making the appointment, the appointing authority shall ... take into account ... the advisability of appointing an arbitrator of a nationality other than the nationalities of the parties." The AAA International Arbitration Rules also do not require the appointment of an arbitrator of a neutral nationality.

[321] This possibility was added to the Rules in 1975 in recognition of the need for flexibility in this regard. At the time, Jean Robert, then the *Rapporteur* of the ICC Commission, explained, that:

> There are indeed circumstances, which are left to the Court's discretion, where it would be advantageous to have the arbitrator chosen from one of the countries of which the parties are nationals – *e.g.* when both parties are nationals of the same country, or when both arbitrators proposed by the parties are themselves nationals of the same country and it would be advantageous that the arbitration take place in that country.

Report to the 25th Congress of the ICC, Madrid (June 17, 1975), *supra*, note 202. During the preparation of the New Rules, consideration was given to restricting Article 9(5) only to cases where the parties are not all of the same nationality. However, this proposal was not adopted, at least partly because the nationalities of the parties might not necessarily be the same as the entities controlling them.

The rules of at least one other arbitral institution, the London Court of International Arbitration ("LCIA"), provide in this regard that the nationality of the parties shall be understood to include "controlling shareholders or interests."[322] While the rationale for this provision can easily be understood, the ICC has never adopted such a rule. Indeed, it may not always be evident who the "controlling shareholders or interests" are or, even if known, what their nationalities may be, and, as already indicated, the Court does not systematically undertake to investigate this.[323] Moreover, where a party is controlled by shareholders having many different nationalities, the Court's ability to identify a suitable arbitrator might be unduly restricted.[324] Nevertheless, the Court can ordinarily be expected to take account of such controlling interests, to the extent known, and to apply informally a rule such as that of the LCIA, insofar as it seems appropriate.

Apart from the nationalities of the parties, the Court, consistent with Article 9(1), also usually considers the nationalities of the co-arbitrators in cases with three arbitrators. It therefore does not normally select a National Committee until the co-arbitrators have been confirmed. Although the Rules do not preclude the Court from appointing a chairman of the same nationality as one of the co-arbitrators, and in some cases the Court has, in fact, done so, the Court has usually wished to avoid creating a tribunal that may appear to favor one of the parties in this regard. Parties should therefore bear in mind that the nationality of the co-arbitrator whom they select is likely to have a bearing on the nationality of the chairman appointed by the Court. The only case in which the Court might usually be expected to consider appointing a chairman of the same nationality as a co-arbitrator is where both parties have appointed co-arbitrators of the same nationality, although the Secretariat will usually seek to ascertain the parties' wishes before the Court proceeds to do so. If one party objects, the Court would most likely appoint a chairman of a different nationality.[325] Parties may occasionally also contend that the chairman or sole arbitrator should not have the same nationality as a party's counsel, if the counsels are of different nationalities. But this is not a position that the Court has ordinarily countenanced.

In considering matters of nationality, the Court further attempts, insofar as it reasonably can, to take into account broader regional or geopolitical considerations. Thus, for example, during the last several years, the Court has avoided appointing American sole arbitrators or chairmen in cases with parties from

---

[322] *See* LCIA Rules, Article 6, which also includes the indication that "citizens of the European Union shall be treated as nationals of its different Member States."

[323] *See* the discussion of Article 7(2) *supra* and the arbitrator's statement of independence. Arguably, the identity of the controlling shareholders or interests needs to be known in order to ensure the independence of the arbitrators. However, the ICC has never required parties to disclose such information about themselves, which ultimately means that the other parties, and the arbitrators, may be required to carry out their own related investigations.

[324] *See also* on this subject, *Craig Park and Paulsson*, §13.05, p. 229.

[325] Certain Court members, however, have in the past expressed reservations about so-called "monochromatic" Arbitral Tribunals as a matter of principle. It is therefore important, if this is what the parties nevertheless desire, that they make the Secretariat aware of this.

Iran, Iraq or Libya, which have all been subject to U.S. government sanctions. In addition, in an arbitration between European and African parties, for instance, it might seek an arbitrator from another region. But whether or not this is appropriate in a particular case will depend upon a number of different factors, such as the place and language of the arbitration, the precise nature of the dispute, the identities of the co-arbitrators and the nature of their expertise. The Court has from time to time been criticized by lawyers from developing countries, in particular, for appointing sole arbitrators or chairmen from developed countries in a disproportionate number of cases involving parties from the developed and developing worlds; and while the statistics may bear this out, this is not the result of any particular Western bias on the part of the Court, but is rather a function of the circumstances of the cases concerned, including, for example, their venue and applicable law, both of which are usually chosen by the parties.

Indeed, among the other important factors that the Court typically takes into consideration are the language and law applicable to the arbitration, to the extent known, as well as the place of the arbitration. The place is important, primarily for reasons of cost. The Court does not normally consider it necessary to designate an arbitrator who resides at the place of the arbitration, except possibly in very small cases where it is important to achieve maximum cost efficiency. But it usually seeks an arbitrator who resides relatively near that place, *e.g.,* for an arbitration in Paris, an arbitrator residing in Western Europe, or for an arbitration in Hong Kong, an arbitrator residing in Southeast Asia.[326] Only where the sums at stake are so large that an arbitrator's place of residence should not matter does this cease to be an important factor. An arbitrator's proximity to the place of arbitration is, in any event, not sufficient to warrant the selection of a particular National Committee. Equally important are the language and law applicable to the arbitration. Thus, for example, if the contract underlying the dispute is in English and is governed by the law of a common law jurisdiction, the Court would ordinarily seek a proposal from the National Committee of a common law country. Conversely, if the contract were governed by the law of a civil law country, the Court could be expected to seek a proposal from a country with a similar legal system.

The appointment process. Once the Court has selected a National Committee, the Committee is contacted by the Secretariat. However, the Secretariat does not inform the parties of the Court's decision. They are informed only once an appointment has been made in order to prevent any possible interference with

---

[326] There nevertheless appears to be a misconception that the Court will ordinarily select the National Committee of the venue of the arbitration, provided that neither party is a national of that country. *See, e.g., Craig Park and Paulsson,* §12.03, pp. 207-08. In fact, the Court ordinarily considers all of the National Committees in the region that may be suitable, given the nature of the dispute and the nationality of the parties, as well as National Committees outside the region that are in a position to propose arbitrators who reside in the region. Thus, for example, the Canadian and U.S. National Committees may be invited to propose one of their nationals residing in Paris for an arbitration in Paris.

the appointment process, such as approaches by the parties to the National Committee directly. When contacting the National Committee, the Secretariat provides it with a written description of the dispute, including the identities of the parties, their counsel and the co-arbitrators. The language and law of the arbitration, if determined, are also specified as are the place of the arbitration, the amount of the dispute and any other special requirements of the arbitration. The National Committee is further reminded of the need to identify an arbitrator who is independent of the parties.

Article 9(3) indicates that the National Committee is required to "make the proposal requested within the time limit fixed by the Court." In fact, the Court rarely fixes such a time limit, but the National Committees are usually requested by the Secretariat to make their proposals within no more than 15 days. Increasingly, the Court has urged the Secretariat to seek more than one proposal, particularly in the largest, most delicate cases. But the submission of a sole proposal remains the norm. Depending on the National Committee, however, the proposal may be preceded by substantial informal consultation with the Secretariat with regard to possible candidates. Some National Committees, moreover, provide the Secretariat on a periodic basis with lists of approved arbitrators in order to facilitate this process. When making their proposals, the National Committees then provide the Secretariat with a copy of the prospective arbitrator's *curriculum vitae* and a completed statement of independence.

The documentation relating to the proposal is placed by the Secretariat before the Court at the next Committee meeting at which this is possible. In most cases, the proposal is accepted. However, the Court nevertheless refuses proposals from time to time, possibly because of a qualification in the arbitrator's statement of independence or because the candidate is otherwise considered to be unsuitable. The Court will then instruct the Secretariat to request a new proposal or designate a new National Committee. In considering the suitability of proposals, the Court tends to take into account the various matters discussed in connection with Article 9(1) above. Although the Court generally seeks candidates with unqualified statements of independence, it nevertheless does occasionally appoint arbitrators with qualifications that the Court considers to be trivial, subject possibly to the parties' objections (*see* Article 7(2) *supra*).

Article 9(6)

> *Where the Court is to appoint an arbitrator on behalf of a party which has failed to nominate one, it shall make the appointment upon a proposal of the National Committee of the country of which that party is a national. If the Court does not accept the proposal made, or if the National Committee fails to make the proposal requested within the time limit fixed by the Court, or if the country of which the said party is a national has no National Committee, the Court shall be at liberty to choose any person whom it regards as suitable. The Secretariat shall inform the National Committee, if one exists, of the country of which such person is a national.*

Article 9(6) describes the procedure to be followed when the Court is required to appoint an arbitrator on behalf of a party. It is nearly identical to the last paragraph of Article 2(6) of the former Rules and, like its predecessor, it requires the Court to seek a proposal from a National Committee when the party in question is a national of a country with such a committee. If the party is from another country, however (or if the National Committee does not make an acceptable proposal within the time fixed by the Court), the Court may appoint "any person whom it regards as suitable."

In practice, the Court is not required to make many default appointments. In 1996, for example, it was required to do so in only eleven cases. This may partly be because, as already discussed above, the Court has generally been willing to afford the parties every reasonable opportunity to make appointments themselves. One special situation that has given rise to difficulties in the past, however, is where the appointment is to be made by multiple parties and they are unable to agree on an arbitrator or otherwise fail to nominate one. Article 10 has been introduced into the Rules to deal with such situations and therefore needs to be read in conjunction with Article 9(6).

In soliciting proposals from National Committees under Article 9(6), the Court proceeds in essentially the same manner as in the case of Article 9(3). The only difference is that a decision of the Court is not required in order to choose the National Committee as the choice is mandated by the rule itself. In the event that there is no National Committee in the country of which the party is a national, the Court normally seeks to identify a suitable arbitrator who is a national of that country. However, if it is unable to do so, it may appoint an arbitrator of a different nationality, in which case it is required to inform the National Committee, if one exists, of the country of which such person is a national.[327] It is not required, however, to solicit a proposal from that committee.

ARTICLE 10

Multiple Parties

This is an entirely new provision that is intended to overcome the difficulties that may be encountered when arbitrators are to be appointed in an arbitration involving more than two (*i.e.,* "multiple") parties. Notwithstanding the title, it is important to note from the outset that Article 10 is not applicable to all cases involving multiple parties. It only applies if the tribunal is to be constituted of three arbitrators, and it is therefore of no relevance if only one arbitrator or a

---

[327] Under Article 2(6) of the former Rules, the Court was required to inform the National Committee before appointing the person in question. Under the new provision, however, this is no longer required, and the National Committee may be informed after the appointment has been made. National Committees have an interest in knowing about such appointments because they need to be able to take account of arbitrators' caseloads and experience when proposing arbitrators to the Court.

number of arbitrators other than three are to be appointed in a multi-party case.[328]

When three arbitrators are to be appointed, however, either by agreement of the parties or by decision of the Court pursuant to Article 8(2), the requirement that the Claimant and Respondent must each nominate a co-arbitrator can create a problem, particularly where the Respondent consists of multiple parties with differing interests, and they each assert an independent right to nominate an arbitrator. For many years, it was the Court's practice, in such cases, to require multiple Respondent parties (like multiple Claimant parties) to nominate an arbitrator jointly, failing which the Court would designate an arbitrator on their behalf.[329] Although the Court considered that this practice was consistent with the general scheme of the Rules and was implicit in the provisions relating to the constitution of the Arbitral Tribunal, the Court was nevertheless occasionally criticized for treating the parties unequally. The Court's critics argued in this regard that multiple Respondents should not be required to try to agree on an arbitrator if a sole Claimant party is free to nominate whomever it wishes.

It was in circumstances such as these that the French Court of Cassation issued its ruling in the *Dutco* case in 1992,[330] thus forcing the Court to reconsider its practices and leading ultimately to the provision that has become Article 10. Before discussing Article 10 further, it is therefore necessary to describe what occurred in *Dutco*.

The Dutco case. The *Dutco* case began as an ICC arbitration in Paris that Dutco, one of three parties to a consortium agreement, commenced against its other consortium partners, BKMI and Siemens. The consortium agreement related to the construction of a cement plant in Oman and contained the following arbitration provision:

> All disputes arising out of this Agreement, which cannot be settled amicably among the members, shall be finally settled in accordance with the rules of conciliation and arbitration of the International Chamber of Commerce by three arbitrators appointed in accordance with those rules. The seat of the Arbitration Court shall be Paris.

In initiating the arbitration, Dutco made separate and distinct claims against BKMI and Siemens for breaching the consortium agreement. As the arbitration clause provided for a tribunal of three arbitrators, Dutco nominated an arbitrator in its Request for Arbitration, in accordance with then Article 2(4) (now 8(4), of the Rules. BKMI and Siemens, however, contested the admissibility of the Request for Arbitration and argued that Dutco should be required to file two

---

[328] The parties may also derogate from Article 10 pursuant to Article 7(6).

[329] For a description of the Court's prior practice, *see* Bond, *supra,* note 112.

[330] *Sociétés BKMI et Siemens c/ société Dutco construction* (January 7, 1992), *supra,* note 16.

separate Requests for Arbitration, one against each of them, so as to permit BKMI and Siemens each to designate an arbitrator. But the Court disagreed and decided, consistent with its usual practice, that they should be required to nominate an arbitrator jointly, failing which an arbitrator would be appointed for them by the Court. BKMI and Siemens, thus, made a joint nomination "under protest," reserving all of their rights with respect to the regularity of the tribunal's constitution. Following the appointment of a third arbitrator by the Court, they then applied to the Arbitral Tribunal for an Award dismissing Dutco's action against them on the ground that the tribunal had been constituted in violation of the parties' arbitration agreement.

In an interim Award on this issue, the Arbitral Tribunal found that it had been properly constituted and that the arbitral proceedings could validly continue against both BKMI and Siemens. In so ruling, the Arbitral Tribunal considered, first of all, whether the arbitration clause contained in the consortium agreement reflected a common intention of the parties to participate in a single arbitration proceeding among all three of them. The tribunal concluded that this must have been their intention in view of the nature of the consortium agreement itself – which was likely to give rise to disputes in which all three parties would be interested – and the parties' failure to make any special provision for multi-party disputes in the arbitration clause, which only contained a general reference to the Rules. The Arbitral Tribunal then examined the circumstances of its constitution and concluded that then Article 2(4) of the Rules had been properly applied as, in the multi-party context, the word "party" should be taken to mean the Claimant or Claimants, on the one hand, or the Defendant or Defendants, on the other. The Arbitral Tribunal did not consider that such a construction of Article 2(4) conflicted with any rule of public policy or general principles of equality, as argued by BKMI and Siemens.[331]

BKMI and Siemens immediately applied to the Paris Court of Appeal to have the arbitrators' Award set aside on the grounds that (*see* Article 1502, subparagraphs 2 and 5 of the French New Code of Civil Procedure):

(i) the Arbitral Tribunal was irregularly constituted; and

(ii) recognition or enforcement of the Award was contrary to international public policy.

---

[331] It is to be noted, however, that in a parallel ICC arbitration proceeding arising under an identical ICC arbitration clause among three parties (two of whom were the same as in the *Dutco* case) with respect to a different construction project, the Arbitral Tribunal – contrary to the tribunal in *Dutco* – concluded that "no common intention of the parties allowing multi-party arbitration was established" and hence ruled that it had no jurisdiction to decide the claims filed against the two Defendants in a joint proceeding.

The Court of Appeal disagreed. In a judgment rendered on May 5, 1989, the court held that the tribunal had been properly constituted and that there had been no violation of public policy.[332] The court reasoned, *inter alia,* as follows (translation):

> Considering that the arbitration clause stipulated between the companies BKMI, Dutco and Siemens in the consortium agreement provides for the submission of disputes arising from that agreement to an Arbitral Tribunal composed of three members, designated in conformity with the ICC Rules;
> Considering that that agreement, integrated in the agreement linking the three companies in a consortium, expresses without ambiguity the common will of the parties to a single contract, to submit to an Arbitral Tribunal of three arbitrators "all disputes" resulting from their agreement, from which it must necessarily be deduced, in view of the multi-party nature of the contract itself – with the foreseeable possibility of disputes among the three partners – that the parties accepted the possibility that a single Arbitral Tribunal composed of three members could decide disputes among the three parties, with the arrangements that such a situation mandates with regard to the choice of arbitrators and the organization of the procedure.
> Considering, in this regard, that the reference to the rules of the ICC, which provide that "each party" nominates an arbitrator for confirmation by the Court of arbitration, must be understood in the circumstances to mean that the three parties to the agreement accepted, as it may be, that the two arbitrators to be nominated by each party – claimant and defendant – would be, one by the claimant or claimants, the other by the defendant or defendants.
> Considering that in the circumstances of the case, involving three parties to the same contract, this interpretation of the arbitration clause is the only one that permits it to be fully effective.

The court then went on to find that the arbitration proceedings, as set in motion by the ICC, did not otherwise conflict with any principle of international public policy or the fundamental rights of equality and defense of the parties. With respect to the issue of equality, in particular, the court concluded that the parties' rights could not be said to have been violated insofar as they freely agreed to the organization of a single arbitration proceeding in which all of the arbitrators were to be independent of the parties. In this connection, the court stated that (translation):

---

[332] *See* the report of the decision and the accompanying Note by Bellet, *Rev. arb.* (1989), p. 723. *See also* Seppala and Gogek, "Multi-party Arbitration under ICC Rules," *International Financial Law Review* (November 1989), p. 32.

[T]he independence [of the arbitrator] guarantees the strict equality of the parties in the conduct of the trial.[333]

As can be seen from the above extracts from the Paris court's decision, its conclusion flowed primarily from its construction of the parties' arbitration agreement. Having found that the arbitration clause was intended to cover disputes involving more than just two of the parties and that the clause provided for three arbitrators, the court considered that the parties must necessarily have anticipated that, in the event of a dispute involving all three of them, they would not each be able to designate an arbitrator.

The fundamental question subsequently put to the French Court of Cassation by BKMI and Siemens was whether the ruling of the Court of Appeal nevertheless consecrated a violation of their alleged right to equal treatment in the constitution of the Arbitral Tribunal. Without in any way questioning the Court of Appeal's construction of the parties' arbitration agreement, the Court of Cassation found that (i) the parties enjoyed a right of equality (which is not further elaborated upon in the judgment) in the constitution of the Arbitral Tribunal, and (ii) such right could not validly be waived in an arbitration agreement entered into before a dispute had arisen, a formulation that made irrelevant the Court of Appeal's findings with regard to the proper construction of the arbitration agreement itself.

As a practical matter, the Court of Cassation's decision had the effect of annulling the judgment of the Court of Appeal, but left the arbitral Award itself

---

[333] In so holding, the Paris Court of Appeal adopted a position consistent with an earlier decision of the Swiss courts in the *Westland* case, as discussed above (*see* Article 6(2) *supra*). In that case, the Claimant commenced an ICC arbitration against six Defendants, and the Court, in accordance with its normal practice, appointed an arbitrator on behalf of all of them as part of a three-member tribunal. The Egyptian government subsequently attacked the competence of the Arbitral Tribunal before the cantonal court of Geneva and argued, *inter alia*, that the tribunal should be recused on the ground that the Claimant had exercised a "preponderant influence" in its constitution. The court, in a decision that was affirmed on appeal by the Swiss Supreme Court (*Tribunal fédéral*), rejected the Egyptian objection to the tribunal's constitution. The Geneva court held (judgment of November 26, 1982, *supra*, note 164) (translation):

> In this case, the parties have submitted themselves to the Rules of the ICC and these have been applied, in particular, as has been seen, concerning the method of nomination of the arbitrators. One cannot claim that the application of such Rules gave to Westland a preponderant influence. The ICC system offers all guarantees and in any case more than others, since the parties only propose arbitrators, who are named by the Court of Arbitration of the ICC. The Arab Republic of Egypt is wrong when it claims that it has the right to be represented on the tribunal. The arbitrator, even if designated by one party is not the agent of that party, nor his representative.

In so ruling, the Geneva court, thus, lent its support to the approach adopted by the Court in constituting Arbitral Tribunals in such circumstances. It does not appear to have considered that either the Rules or any rule of public policy had been violated, or, in particular, that parties must be allowed to play an equal role in the constitution of the Arbitral Tribunal so long as the tribunal has been constituted in conformity with the parties' agreement and the neutrality and impartiality of the Arbitral Tribunal are guaranteed.

intact and remanded the matter for a rehearing before the Court of Appeal of Versailles. In the meantime, however, the parties settled their dispute amicably, leaving in their wake the ruling of the Court of Cassation and the public policy principle that it established.

Although a decision of the French courts relating to an ICC arbitration in France, and therefore not generally applicable to all ICC proceedings, the *Dutco* judgment nevertheless attracted considerable attention internationally and inevitably required the Court to reconsider its approach to the constitution of Arbitral Tribunals in multi-party cases.[334] In particular, the Court considered that it needed a means of constituting a three-member tribunal in multi-party cases that would not be vulnerable to attack on the ground that the parties were not being treated equally. Article 10 is, thus, intended to provide the Court with the necessary means, without, however, depriving it of the flexibility that it requires to deal with the many different circumstances that it may encounter or preventing the parties from making alternative arrangements, as they may consider appropriate.

Article 10(1)

> *Where there are multiple parties, whether as Claimant or as Respondent, and where the dispute is to be referred to three arbitrators, the multiple Claimants, jointly, and the multiple Respondents, jointly, shall nominate an arbitrator for confirmation pursuant to Article 9.*

Notwithstanding the *Dutco* jurisprudence, Article 10 begins by restating, in an adapted form referring to multiple parties, the general rule that the Claimant and the Respondent are each to nominate an arbitrator. While Article 10(1) does not itself indicate when such nominations are to be made, it can be assumed that the relevant rules of Articles 8(2) and 8(4) are to be followed for this purpose. The requirement that the nominations are to be made "jointly" is intended to ensure that all, and not just some, of the multiple parties concerned agree on the nomination.

Although formulated in imperative terms – the multiple Claimants and Respondents "shall" nominate an arbitrator – Article 10(1) is required to be read in conjunction with Article 10(2). Article 10(1), thus, sets out what is still intended to be the general rule. But, in appropriate cases, the parties' obligation to nominate an arbitrator may be altered by the operation of Article 10(2), which, as discussed below, has been specifically designed to overcome difficulties of the kind encountered in the *Dutco* case.

There are two basic reasons why the Rules retain, as a general principle, the requirement that multiple parties, whether as Claimant or Respondent, shall jointly nominate an arbitrator. The first is that the parties in ICC arbitrations ordinarily do not have any difficulty in doing so, and, indeed, this is normally

---

[334] *See* Schwartz, "Multi-Party Arbitration and the ICC: In the Wake of *Dutco*," *J. Arb. Int.*, Vol. 10, No. 3 (1993), p. 5; Gravel, *supra*, note 97, pp. 47-48.

the preferred course of multiple parties, particularly where the alternatives, as under Article 10(2), may seem less attractive. Only rarely has the Court, in fact, had to face the kind of problem that it encountered in the *Dutco* case. Secondly, the *Dutco* case arose in very special circumstances. The multiple Respondents were unaffiliated companies with different interests, and distinct claims were being made against each of them. In most ICC arbitrations where multiple parties are involved, however, the parties, whether on the Claimant or the Respondent side, are affiliated and their positions and interests are identical. As discussed below with regard to Article 10(2), it is doubtful that the rule set forth in that provision should be applied in such situations. There may be other situations as well in which Article 10(2) ought not to be utilized.

Article 10(1) does not state, however, what is to occur in cases where the multiple parties concerned fail to make a "joint" nomination and the Court decides not to apply Article 10(2). Presumably, it would be the Court's position, as under Article 9(6), that it would then be at liberty to appoint an arbitrator on behalf of those parties. In such cases in the past, the Court has followed the procedure laid down in that article for the appointment of arbitrators, except that, where the multiple parties are of different nationalities (a situation that Article 9(6) does not envisage), the Court has taken the view that it may appoint an arbitrator directly, without referring to a National Committee.[335]

Article 10(2)

> In the absence of such a joint nomination and where all parties are unable to agree to a method for the constitution of the Arbitral Tribunal, the Court may appoint each member of the Arbitral Tribunal and shall designate one of them to act as chairman. In such case, the Court shall be at liberty to choose any person it regards as suitable to act as arbitrator, applying Article 9 when it considers this appropriate.

The Court's power to appoint all of the arbitrators. Article 10(2) solves the *Dutco* problem by empowering the Court to appoint the entire Arbitral Tribunal where multiple Claimant or Respondent parties do not jointly nominate an arbitrator. In practice, this is normally only likely to occur in the case of Respondent parties as multiple Claimants will presumably be in agreement on such matters insofar as they have agreed to pursue their claims jointly. Under Article 10(2), if a Claimant nominates an arbitrator but multiple Respondents do not do so, the Court may refuse to confirm the arbitrator nominated by the Claimant and appoint an arbitrator on the Claimant's behalf as well as on the Respondents' behalf and also appoint a chairman. All of the parties are, thus, treated equally, and, in the name of equality, all are deprived of the right to nominate an arbitrator.

When initially proposed as a means of treating the parties equally, in conformity with the exigencies of *Dutco*, Article 10(2) was viewed by some as unac-

---

[335] *See* Bond, *supra*, note 112, p. 44.

ceptably undercutting the autonomy of the parties in respect of the Arbitral Tribunal's constitution. However, a broad consensus eventually emerged in favor of the approach adopted, and, indeed, other arbitral institutions have recently added similar provisions to their rules.[336] It is important to note, moreover, that Article 10(2) expressly recognizes the right of the parties to agree upon another method for the constitution of the Arbitral Tribunal in any such case, and this follows from Article 7(6) as well. Indeed, the Rules would even appear to permit the parties to agree on an "unequal" method of constituting the Arbitral Tribunal, contrary to *Dutco*.[337] If the parties have not agreed on any particular method of appointing arbitrators in such a case, however, a party contemplating the commencement of an arbitration against more than one party must consider whether it wishes to proceed in a single proceeding and possibly lose the right to nominate an arbitrator or to initiate separate proceedings in which its right to nominate an arbitrator would not be affected.

The discretion of the Court. Article 10(2) is not intended to apply automatically in all cases where multiple parties fail to make a joint nomination, but has been deliberately drafted so as to allow the Court to decide whether it should be applied in a particular case. In the circumstances covered by that provision, the Court "may" – but is not required to – appoint each member of the Arbitral Tribunal. Although some of those involved in drafting the Rules would have preferred the greater certainty of a mandatory rule, the majority believed that the Court should be allowed the discretion to decide whether its application is appropriate on a case-by-case basis.[338]

One of the reasons for this, as already noted, is that there are many cases with multiple parties that are not necessarily true multi-party arbitrations, *e.g.,* where multiple Respondents are under common control or otherwise have identical interests in the outcome of the arbitration. In such a case, the multiple entities concerned might more properly be seen as forming, in reality, a single Respondent party, and there would not seem to be any legitimate reason why they should not normally be expected to agree upon an arbitrator.[339] The same might also apply

---

[336] *See, e.g.,* AAA International Arbitration Rules, Article 6(5); LCIA Rules, Article 8(1); WIPO Arbitration Rules, Article 18. However, other rules, such as the UNCITRAL Rules, do not provide any special mechanism for the appointment of the Arbitral Tribunal in such circumstances.

[337] Such an agreement, if made prior to the arbitration, might give rise to difficulties in France, given the *Dutco* jurisprudence, but not necessarily elsewhere.

[338] In this regard, Article 10(2) differs from Article 6(5) of the AAA International Arbitration Rules, Article 8(1) of the LCIA Rules and Article 18 of the WIPO Arbitration Rules, all of which impose a mandatory solution, unless the parties otherwise agree.

[339] In this connection, one commentator has observed (translation):
[The *Dutco* ruling] ... was rendered in a particular situation: it is, however, necessary to ask oneself whether the solution would be the same in the case where the reality of the arbitration revealed an identity of the interests of the parties on the same side ...
Delvolvé, *"L'arbitrage multipartite en 1992,"* ASA Bull., No. 2 (1992), pp. 152, 193. *See also* "Final Report on Multi-party Arbitrations," *supra,* note 21, pp. 29-30.

where none of the multiple Respondents named in a Request for Arbitration appears in the arbitration proceeding, without objecting, however, to the principle of making a joint nomination. It is questionable whether it would be appropriate to deprive the Claimant of an opportunity to nominate an arbitrator in such a situation. There is also the more general issue of whether a rule derived from the decision of a court in only one jurisdiction (France) should necessarily be applied to arbitrations in all other jurisdictions. The drafters of the Rules concluded that the Court needs to be able to assess considerations such as these as they arise in practice.

Appointment of arbitrators. When the Court appoints arbitrators pursuant to Article 10(2), it is free "to choose any person it regards as suitable." It is therefore not required to solicit proposals from the ICC's National Committees, although it may do so if "it considers this appropriate." Article 10(2) also does not impose any particular constraints on the Court in respect of the arbitrators' nationalities. In selecting arbitrators, however, the Court can reasonably be expected to follow the general rule that the chairman shall be of a nationality other than those of the parties. The Court's normal inclination could ordinarily also be assumed to be to appoint co-arbitrators having the nationalities of the Claimants and Respondents, respectively. The most difficult issue that is likely to arise in this connection is what to do when multiple Claimants, on the one hand, or multiple Respondents, on the other, are of different nationalities. In the past, it was the Court's general preference, in such cases, to appoint a co-arbitrator of yet a different nationality so that none of the multiple parties concerned would appear to be favored. However, the Court would surely be attentive to any relevant submissions that the parties might have to make and also take full account of the circumstances of each particular case.

Another issue that the Court may have to face is whether to appoint as a co-arbitrator an arbitrator nominated by one of the parties. Ordinarily, the Court would probably not be inclined to do so as this would seem contrary to the very purpose of Article 10(2), which is intended to ensure that no party is unduly advantaged in the Arbitral Tribunal's constitution. However, if one or more, but less than all of a group of, multiple parties were to agree on a nomination, with the rest remaining silent, the Court might legitimately consider that it should confirm the nomination made as if it had been made on behalf of all of the parties jointly.

ARTICLE 11
Challenge of Arbitrators

Like other arbitration rules, the ICC Rules have long provided for the possible challenge of arbitrators by the parties. There is, thus, little that is new or innovative in Article 11. Rather, it imports into the New Rules the provisions on challenges previously contained in Articles 2(8) and 2(9), with only one significant modification, which concerns the circulation to the parties of the arbitrators' comments relating to the challenge (*see* Article 11(3)).

The powers that the Court enjoys under Article 11 can obviously have important consequences for the parties. A successful challenge, in particular, can severely disrupt the arbitration if it occurs at an advanced stage of the proceedings, and if, on the contrary, a challenge does not prosper, a party may be left with the conviction that it has little chance of obtaining a just Award. Notwithstanding their importance, the Court's relevant decisions, like the other decisions that it is required to take under the Rules, are of a purely administrative nature insofar as they only concern the organization and administration of the arbitration.[340] The Court's decisions therefore do not preclude whatever recourse the parties may enjoy in respect of the subject matter of the challenge under the laws of any competent jurisdiction, either against the decision itself or the arbitral Award ultimately rendered. The laws of different jurisdictions vary considerably in this regard and, thus, represent an important factor of which the parties ought always to take account when selecting a venue for an ICC arbitration proceeding.[341]

This having been said, challenges are a relatively rare occurrence in ICC arbitrations. According to a recent study of the Court's Secretariat, there are on average no more than a dozen challenges each year in respect of the more than one thousand arbitrators serving at any one time in the ICC's pending arbitrations.[342] This relatively small number has generally been attributed to the strictness with which the Court has applied the disclosure requirements of Article 7(2) prior to the arbitrators' appointment or confirmation.[343] Moreover, of the challenges that are made, only a small number actually succeed.[344] But the chal-

---

[340] This has repeatedly been confirmed by the French courts, which have refused to review the merits of the Court's decisions on challenges. *See, e.g., Société Opinter France c/ S.a.r.l. Dacomex, Cour de cassation* (October 7, 1987), *Rev. arb.* (1987), p. 479, and the earlier decision of the Paris Court of Appeal in that case (January 15, 1985), *Rev. arb.* (1986), p. 87; *Raffineries de pétrole d'Hohms et de Banias c/ Chambre de commerce internationale, Cour d'appel de Paris* (May 15, 1985), *Rev. arb.* (1985), p. 141. *See also*, more generally, Fouchard, *supra* , note 134.

[341] Thus, for example, Article 13(3) of the UNCITRAL Model Law provides that if a challenge is rejected by an arbitral institution such as the ICC Court, the challenging party may, within 30 days thereafter, request a court to decide on the matter. Under the English Arbitration Act 1996 (Section 24), the courts may also entertain an application for an arbitrator's replacement after a challenge has been rejected by the ICC Court. This would not be possible, however, in an international arbitration in either France or Switzerland. Indeed, Article 180 of the Swiss Private International Law Act of 1987 expressly excludes such recourse where the parties have agreed to arbitration rules including a challenge procedure. The parties are nevertheless free to attack the arbitral Award before the courts once it has been rendered. For a French case, *see, e.g., Paris Hotel Associates Ltd et autres c/ Hotel Gray d'Albion Cannes S.A. et autres, Cour d'appel de Paris* (June 1, 1995), *Rev. arb.* (1996), p. 528. An additional question that may arise in this connection is whether a party can also attack an arbitral Award for a reason that could have, but did not, serve as a basis for challenging an arbitrator during the arbitration. *See supra,* note 266, and Article 33 *infra.*

[342] *See* Hascher, *supra*, note 203, p. 11.

[343] *Id.*

[344] According to the Court's General Counsel, there were only ten successful challenges between July 1988 and the end of 1994. *Id.,* p. 12. *See also*, with respect to an earlier period, Bond, *supra,* note 200, p. 12.

lenge procedure set forth in Article 11 nevertheless serves as an essential tool in helping the Court to safeguard the integrity of the arbitral process.

Article 11(1)

> *A challenge of an arbitrator, whether for an alleged lack of independence or otherwise, shall be made by the submission to the Secretariat of a written statement specifying the facts and circumstances on which the challenge is based.*

Possible grounds for the challenge of an arbitrator. Unlike many other arbitration rules, Article 11(1) confers upon the parties[345] a broad right to challenge arbitrators, "whether for an alleged lack of independence *or otherwise*."[346] Thus, while many rules (as well as arbitration laws)[347] restrict the grounds for challenge to one or more specified circumstances – normally, an arbitrator's lack of independence or impartiality – the ICC Rules do not contain any such constraints and instead allow the Court unlimited discretion, in the case of a challenge, to remove an arbitrator for any reason that it may regard as appropriate.[348] Even though the Rules do not explicitly set forth a requirement of impartiality (*see* Article 7(1) *supra*), ICC arbitrators may therefore nevertheless be challenged for partiality as well as for failing to perform their functions properly or possibly other reasons. In this regard, moreover, the parties and the Court are required to have regard not only to the requirements of the Rules, but also to any mandatory provisions of law that may be applicable.[349]

In practice, challenges of ICC arbitrators have been made for a variety of different reasons, although they have most frequently concerned the independence or impartiality of the arbitrator concerned, including, in particular, the arbitrator's failure to disclose fully in the statement of independence possible relationships with the parties or their counsel (as discussed above in respect of Article 7(2)).[350]

---

[345] Although not stated in Article 11(1), only parties – and not other arbitrators – can challenge arbitrators. This is implicit, moreover, in Article 11(2).

[346] This is to be compared with Article 8 of the AAA International Arbitration Rules ("A party may challenge any arbitrator whenever circumstances exist that give rise to justifiable doubts as to the arbitrator's impartiality or independence.") and the similar provisions in Article 10 of the UNCITRAL Rules and Article 24 of the WIPO Arbitration Rules.

[347] *See, e.g.,* UNCITRAL Model Law, Article 12(2).

[348] The words "or otherwise" were, in fact, only added to the Rules in 1988. Prior to that time, the Rules did not specify the possible grounds for a challenge. As noted in *Craig Park and Paulsson*, §13.05, p. 227: "Historically, the grounds for challenge under the Rules have not been specified and the Court of Arbitration has inherent power to grant a challenge on any grounds it deems appropriate."

[349] *See, e.g.,* with respect to the requirement of impartiality, *supra*, note 206 and the accompanying text.

[350] For a description of the Court's most recent experience in this regard, *see* Hascher, *supra,* note 203. *See also* Aguilar-Alvarez, "The Challenge of Arbitrators," *Arb. Int.*, Vol. 6, No. 3 (1990), p. 203.

Indeed, challenges relating to an arbitrator's failure to disclose a relationship have tended to succeed more often than other challenges received by the Court and, in particular, where not only the undisclosed relationship, but the fact of non-disclosure itself, might reasonably be said to call into question the arbitrator's independence in the eyes of the parties. Challenges founded on an arbitrator's alleged misconduct of the arbitral proceedings have generally fared less well, however, notwithstanding the breadth of Article 11(1).[351] This is primarily because the Court has been reluctant to become involved in second-guessing procedural decisions of arbitrators made on the basis of their much more intimate appreciation of all of the relevant circumstances of a particular case, except possibly where the arbitrator's conduct is manifestly improper. Thus, for example, an arbitrator who failed to advance an arbitration with reasonable dispatch, in accordance with the Rules' requirements, could undoubtedly be challenged successfully on this basis.

Procedure for making a challenge. In order to challenge an arbitrator, a party is required to submit a written statement to the Secretariat explaining the basis for the challenge.[352] Copies of that statement should at the same time be sent to all of the other parties and the arbitrators in accordance with the requirements of Article 3(1). Although Article 11(1) does not lay down any further requirements in respect of the statement to be submitted, it is in the challenging party's interest to include as complete an explanation of its position as possible together with any supporting documentation. This is because the challenging party will not have the opportunity to make any oral submissions to the Court in respect of the challenge; nor will it necessarily be entitled to make any further written comments before the challenge is considered by the Court (*see* Article 11(3) *infra*). It should also be noted in this regard that the challenging party generally has the burden of substantiating the allegations that constitute the basis for the challenge. As the Court's General Counsel has recently noted:

> [I]f the party submitting the challenge can merely proffer vague assertions, unsupported by evidence that can be checked objectively, the Court will reject the challenge.[353]

---

[351] *See*, in this regard, Schwartz, "The Rights and Duties of ICC Arbitrators," *The Status of the Arbitrator* (ICC Publishing 1995), pp. 67, 87-88.

[352] Under the former Rules, the statement was required to be submitted to the Secretary General. However, in practice, the parties would nevertheless often write to the counsel responsible for the arbitration within the Secretariat. As the former rule was not being strictly applied, and there did not appear to be any reason why it needed to be maintained, it was decided to replace the former reference to the Secretary General with the current designation of the Secretariat. The same is also true in the case of Article 11(3) below.

[353] *See* Hascher, *supra,* note 203, p. 16.

Article 11(2)

> *For a challenge to be admissible, it must be sent by a party either within 30 days from receipt by that party of the notification of the appointment or confirmation of the arbitrator, or within 30 days from the date when the party making the challenge was informed of the facts and circumstances on which the challenge is based if such date is subsequent to the receipt of such notification.*

Article 11(2) corresponds to a provision that was introduced into Article 2(8) of the former Rules in 1988 in order "to combat the ... trend of putting forward grounds for challenge at the last minute by specifying a time-limit for challenging an arbitrator."[354] The relatively strict time-limit contained in Article 11(2) is therefore intended to reduce the number of challenges submitted for purely dilatory purposes at an advanced stage of the arbitration.

With respect to any facts or circumstances of which a party may become aware *after* the "receipt by that party of the notification of the appointment or confirmation" of the arbitrator in question, Article 11(2) allows a party a period of 30 days in which to make a challenge. However, in the case of facts and circumstances of which a party has knowledge *prior* to the notification of the arbitrator's appointment or confirmation, the 30-day time-limit only begins to run as from the date of receipt of such notification, which means that a party may, in effect, enjoy much more than 30 days as from the time when it became aware of the facts and circumstances in question. Thus, for example, if a prospective arbitrator discloses certain information in his statement of independence, but there is no objection to his confirmation, Article 11(2) nevertheless still permits a party to challenge the arbitrator thereafter on the basis of the information already disclosed by the arbitrator, provided that the challenge is made within 30 days of that party's receipt of the notification of the arbitrator's confirmation. As already noted (*see* Article 7(2) *supra*), a party's failure to object to the confirmation of an arbitrator does not deprive it of the right to challenge the arbitrator subsequently on the basis of information disclosed prior to the arbitrator's confirmation. Similarly, a party that may have objected unsuccessfully to an arbitrator's confirmation remains free thereafter to reformulate its objection as a challenge, provided that the time-limit of Article 11(2) is respected.

In view of the foregoing, whenever the Court receives a challenge, its first task is to verify whether the challenge is still timely. It may not always be possible for the Court to verify, however, the precise date upon which the party making the challenge "was informed of the facts and circumstances on which the challenge is based." Obviously, this will not normally be a problem if the facts were formally disclosed or otherwise arose out of a specific act or decision

---

[354] Letter, *supra*, note 7, p. 8.

of an arbitrator. But occasionally a party may claim to have discovered a particular fact – *e.g.,* an undisclosed relationship of the arbitrator – at an advanced stage of the arbitration, and neither the Court nor any of the arbitrators or other parties may be in a position to determine when the discovery was actually made, nor may the challenging party be able to prove that it did not, in fact, make the discovery earlier. In the face of such difficulties in the past, the Court has tended to accept the challenging party's word concerning the date upon which it was informed of the relevant facts unless it is evident that it could not have failed to be aware of them earlier.[355] There may also be circumstances in which the facts serving as the basis for the challenge are continuing, as, for example, in the case of an arbitrator's alleged delay in conducting the proceedings. In such cases, there would not necessarily be any one date as from which the time limit in Article 11(2) could necessarily be said to run.

Article 11(3)

> *The Court shall decide on the admissibility, and, at the same time, if necessary, on the merits of a challenge after the Secretariat has afforded an opportunity for the arbitrator concerned, the other party or parties and any other members of the Arbitral Tribunal, to comment in writing within a suitable period of time. Such comments shall be communicated to the parties and to the arbitrators.*

As under Article 2(9) of the former Rules, Article 11(3) provides that the Court shall decide upon challenges after affording an opportunity for all of the arbitrators and parties to submit any written comments that they may wish to make. Article 11(3) differs from the former provision, however, insofar as it specifies, in the interest of ensuring greater transparency, that such comments "shall be communicated to the parties and to the arbitrators." Unlike Article 2(9), Article 11(3) also makes it clear that the Secretariat's only obligation in respect of the parties is to solicit the comments of the "other" party or parties. In other words, the Secretariat is not required to provide the challenging party with an opportunity to make any further comments once it has submitted its challenge. This does not necessarily mean, however, that the challenging party ought necessarily to be precluded from doing so. However, the general intention is to avoid prolonged debates among the parties and the arbitrators concerning challenges so that the Court is in a position to act expeditiously.

Historically, the Court has always decided upon challenges at its monthly plenary sessions. This was formerly mandated by the Court's Internal Rules, as already noted, and the Court has decided to maintain this practice (*see* Article 1(4) *infra*). Its decisions are made, as in the case of all other decisions of the

---

[355] *See also*, with respect to this, *Craig Park and Paulsson,* §13.08, p. 242.

Court, solely on the basis of the written record before it; hence, the importance of the written submissions of the parties and the arbitrators.

As soon as a challenge is received by the Secretariat, the arbitrator being challenged, the other parties and any other members of the Arbitral Tribunal are invited by it to comment in writing, as required by Article 11(3). According to that provision, like Article 2(9) before it, the Secretariat is required to afford the persons concerned "a suitable period of time" within which to comment. Although the Rules do not themselves provide any guidance as to what may constitute a "suitable period of time," the Secretariat, in fixing a deadline for comments, has ordinarily been guided by the calendar of the Court and the need for relative expedition. A period of 15 days would, thus, typically be regarded as suitable, although the period granted might also be less, depending on the circumstances.

For many years, it was the Secretariat's practice not to circulate, either to the parties or the arbitrators, any of the comments received in respect of challenges. The parties and arbitrators could themselves circulate their comments, if they so wished, but they were not required by the Secretariat to do so. The comments were treated, rather, as being only for the benefit of the Court. Although not provided for in the Rules, the Secretariat's practice was guided by the Court's wish, in the interest of celerity, to avoid the submission of further comments in reply to the comments so submitted and was also motivated by the belief that the parties and arbitrators might, in such circumstances, be more willing to communicate frankly and fully with the Court with regard to the subject matter of the challenge.[356]

No matter how well-intentioned, however, the unwillingness of the Secretariat to circulate the comments received was commonly criticized as being unfair and potentially prejudicial to the challenging party, who would not be in a position to correct any misstatements that any such comments might contain. Arguably, moreover, the Secretariat's unwillingness to circulate the other parties' comments was contrary to the requirements of the Rules regarding the parties' communications, as now set forth in Article 3(1). When reviewing the Rules, the Working Party concluded that greater transparency was to be preferred to the Secretariat's prior practice, and under the New Rules therefore all of the comments received are to be communicated to the parties and the arbitrators.[357] It will be for the Secretariat to determine, in the circumstances of each case, whether to permit the parties to provide additional comments in response to the comments received.

---

[356] In practice, however, the members of the tribunal who are not the subject of the challenge have often been reluctant to comment, even in such circumstances. Moreover, this is why Article 11(3), like its predecessor, provides that the arbitrators are "afforded the opportunity," rather than "invited," to comment.

[357] *But see* Bond, *supra*, note 262, p. 24 ("I would predict that the ICC Court will have to develop internal procedures to avoid giving the parties comments by arbitrators that reveal the inner workings of the Arbitral Tribunal or the thinking of the tribunal on substantive issues before it.").

While the Court's decision with respect to a challenge is pending, the arbitrators may be required to determine whether to suspend their work. There is nothing in the Rules that requires them to do so, however, and ICC tribunals are not usually inclined to allow a challenge to delay the progress of an arbitration, particularly where they do not consider the challenge to have any merit. The Rules, unlike many other arbitration rules, also do not provide expressly for the possible voluntary withdrawal of an arbitrator in the event of a challenge.[358] ICC arbitrators are not precluded from doing so, however (subject to obtaining the Court's approval, as discussed further with respect to Article 12(1) *infra*), and occasionally they do choose to withdraw when they consider that this would be in the best interests of the arbitration, without necessarily acknowledging, however, that the challenge has any merit.

ARTICLE 12

Replacement of Arbitrators

Article 12 complements Article 11 by describing all of the situations, in addition to a successful challenge, in which an arbitrator may have to be replaced. These include the arbitrator's death or resignation, his revocation by all of the parties (which is expressly mentioned for the first time in the New Rules) and the inability or failure of the arbitrator to fulfill his functions in accordance with the Rules, in which event the Court may replace the arbitrator on its own initiative, even in the absence of a challenge. Article 12 also sets forth the procedures to be followed by the Court when replacing an arbitrator *sua sponte* and provides, more generally, for the reconstitution of the Arbitral Tribunal, as appropriate, as well as describing the impact of the arbitrator's removal and replacement on the conduct of the proceedings.

Originally the subject of a single paragraph, the provisions concerning the arbitrator's replacement were greatly expanded in 1988 in order to (i) require explicitly the Court's acceptance of an arbitrator's resignation, (ii) specify more clearly the circumstances in which the Court may, on its own initiative, replace an arbitrator, and (iii) describe the procedure to be followed in replacing arbitrators and the consequences of the same for the conduct of the proceedings (Articles 2(10)-(12) of the prior Rules). Those expanded provisions have all been retained, with minor adjustments, as subparagraphs of Article 12. However, Article 12 also includes two important innovations. The first, which appears in Article 12(4), allows the Court to decide whether or not to follow "the original nominating process" when an arbitrator is being replaced, and the second, which is more controversial, permits the Court to decide, in limited circumstances, that an arbitrator who has died or been removed need not be replaced (*see* Article 12(5)).

---

[358] *See, e.g.,* AAA International Arbitration Rules, Article 8(3); UNCITRAL Rules, Article 11(3); WIPO Arbitration Rules, Article 28.

Article 12(1)

> *An arbitrator shall be replaced upon his death, upon the acceptance by the Court of the arbitrator's resignation, upon acceptance by the Court of a challenge or upon the request of all of the parties.*

The substance of Article 12(1) is identical to that of Article 2(10) of the former Rules, except for the addition of the "request of all of the parties" (revocation) as a case of replacement. Article 12(1) is required to be read together with Article 12(2), which describes the additional power of the Court to replace arbitrators who are prevented from, or who are not, fulfilling their functions. Of the circumstances listed in Article 12(1), only the revocation of the arbitrator by the parties and the arbitrator's resignation call for any particular comment.

Revocation. One party alone cannot require an arbitrator to be replaced. The only way in which a party can by itself cause the replacement of an arbitrator is by a successful challenge. It is an entirely different matter, however, when all of the parties wish a particular arbitrator to be replaced. Insofar as the arbitrator's jurisdiction is founded on the agreement of the parties, it is only logical that, where all of the parties agree, they should be able to require the arbitrator's removal. Possibly because this would seem to be such an obvious point, many arbitration rules (including the former versions of the ICC Rules) do not explicitly provide for the arbitrator's revocation by the parties' agreement. However, the parties are widely recognized to have a legitimate right to revoke arbitrators by agreement,[359] and it was considered desirable that this be made clear in the Rules so that there would not be any doubt in this respect in ICC arbitrations in the future.

Resignation. The resignation of an arbitrator can severely disrupt an arbitration, particularly if it occurs at a late stage of the proceedings. In order to prevent abusive resignations, for possibly partisan reasons, the ICC, thus, added to its Rules in 1988 the express requirement, now found in Article 12(1), that the resignation of an arbitrator must be accepted by the Court.[360] Until the resignation has been accepted, it is not considered to have any effect.[361] In so providing, the Rules differ from some other arbitration rules *(e.g.,* the UNCITRAL Rules) and laws *(see, e.g.,* the UNCITRAL Model Law) that do not expressly restrict the

---

[359] *See, e.g.,* UNCITRAL Model Law, Article 15.

[360] *See,* in this connection, Bond, comments in *ICCA Congress Series No. 5* (Kluwer 1991), p. 284. When an arbitrator seeks to resign for purely partisan reasons, it can, of course, be argued that the arbitral process would be best served by his replacement. In such case, however, the Court would be more likely to refuse to accept an abusive resignation and, instead, to replace that person under Article 12(2) of the Rules if there were grounds for doing so.

[361] *See* Arnaldez and Jakandé, *supra,* note 314, p. 81.

arbitrator's right to resign.[362] Moreover, the requirement of Article 12(1) has been reinforced by the addition to the Rules of Article 7(5) (*see infra*).

The Rules nevertheless do not themselves expressly set out the circumstances in which an arbitrator may or may not legitimately resign, and this is therefore a matter as to which the Court is required to exercise its discretion. In the past, resignations were normally considered by the Court at its Committee, rather than plenary, sessions. However, the Court now appears to have decided that it should be for the plenary session to consider whether to accept resignations under the New Rules.[363] Fortunately, the Court has not been called upon to do so very often in recent years, and it is also very rare that an arbitrator seeks to resign simply to subvert or delay the arbitral process.

Most often, an arbitrator's resignation in an ICC case is the result of illness. Occasionally, however, it may be motivated by a change in professional activity that makes continued performance as an arbitrator impossible, *e.g.*, appointment to a judgeship or governmental position. There have also been instances in which arbitrators have submitted resignations after joining new law firms or companies and, as a result, have been prevented from continuing to act. The Court has ordinarily accepted such resignations, which suggests that, in the Court's view, acceptance of an arbitration should not necessarily prevent an arbitrator subsequently, during the course of an arbitration, from making a professional change conflicting with the continued performance of his or her mission. Arguably, however, it would be inappropriate for an arbitrator to accept an appointment if the professional change in question could reasonably have been anticipated at the time of acceptance. Moreover, the resigning arbitrator may not have a reasonable claim for full (if any) remuneration in such circumstances.

The Court has also accepted the resignation of arbitrators where, following their appointment, the parties agreed to suspend the arbitration for a prolonged

---

[362] Some arbitration laws restrict the right of an arbitrator to resign. *See* Gaillard, "Laws and Court Decisions in Civil Law Countries [Topic 8]," *ICCA Congress Series No. 5* (Kluwer 1991), pp. 274-75. Although during the discussions that preceded the completion of the UNCITRAL Model Law, it was also proposed to include a provision that would prohibit an arbitrator from resigning for "capricious reasons," it was ultimately concluded that:

> [I]t is impractical to require just cause for the resignation (or to attempt to list all possible causes justifying resignation) since an unwilling arbitrator could not, in fact, be forced to perform his functions.

Holtzmann and Neuhaus, pp. 464-65, 473. It was, however, further noted that the Model Law "does not deal with the legal responsibility of an arbitrator or other issues pertaining to the contractual party-arbitrator relationship." It was therefore suggested that an arbitrator's right to resign might be restricted by agreement between the parties and the arbitrator. *See also* Veeder, "Laws and Court Decisions in Common Law Countries and the UNCITRAL Model Law," *ICCA Congress Series No. 5* (Kluwer 1991), pp. 277-78. Apart from the issue of whether arbitrators can be compelled to perform their functions, the desirability of forcing them to do so has been questioned. *See* Mustill and Boyd, *The Law and Practice of Commercial Arbitration in England* (Butterworths, 2d ed. 1989), p. 231 ("Nothing would be less conducive to the proper administration of justice than the conduct of a reference by a recalcitrant arbitrator.").

[363] *See supra*, note 52 and accompanying text.

period of time. Indeed, arbitrators should not reasonably be expected to continue to remain "on hold" indefinitely while an arbitration is in abeyance or otherwise continue to serve where circumstances outside of their own control arise, subsequent to their appointment, that could not reasonably have been expected prior to that time.[364]

In addition, there have been rare situations in which ICC arbitrators have resigned due to threatening or abusive conduct of a party (or its counsel), and the Court has accepted such resignations. Although the Court would not usually consider it appropriate for an arbitrator to resign simply because a party requests the arbitrator to do so – as already stated, a party does not have the right under the Rules unilaterally to revoke an arbitrator (including an arbitrator whom it may originally have designated) – when extreme conduct of a party makes it unreasonably difficult or unpleasant for an arbitrator to continue to serve, the Court may be willing to accept a tender of resignation. Thus, for example, the Court accepted the resignation of a party-appointed arbitrator in circumstances where he appeared to fear for his physical safety in the event that he continued to serve.

In another exceptional case, the Court accepted the resignation of an entire Arbitral Tribunal following repeated harassment by the Claimant's counsel of the members of the Arbitral Tribunal and, in particular, the arbitrator appointed by the Claimant itself, including requests for that arbitrator's resignation and replacement, verbal abuse, and other conduct that, in the opinion of the tribunal, made it impossible for it to continue to conduct the arbitration "in the conditions of serenity necessary for the discussion" of the issues in the arbitration. It is to be emphasized, however, that the circumstances of that case were extreme, both the arbitrators and the Court considered the conduct of the Claimant's counsel to be unjustified, and the ability of the arbitrators to continue to conduct the proceedings in a proper manner had been severely compromised.[365]

An issue that arises more frequently is whether an arbitrator should resign when challenged by a party. Although the Court has accepted the resignations of arbitrators in such circumstances, prior to the challenge being examined by the Court, there is nevertheless a question as to whether arbitrators have a duty to the parties not to resign if they consider the challenge to be unfounded and made solely for dilatory purposes. It would certainly be legitimate for an arbitrator to take the position that, in the event of a challenge, where one of the parties opposes it and the arbitrator does not consider the challenge to be meritorious, it is for the Court to decide the matter in accordance with Article 11(3) of the Rules and

---

[364] The same might be said to apply where the parties subsequently agree upon procedures for the conduct of the arbitration that the arbitrators do not feel that they are competent to administer or possibly agree upon a change of the place of arbitration specified in the arbitration clause. *See* in this regard Mustill and Boyd, *supra,* note 362, p. 282.

[365] Although counsel appearing before a court can usually be sanctioned by the judge for improper behavior, there is relatively little that an Arbitral Tribunal can do to curb repeated discourteous or otherwise improper conduct by counsel, as the arbitrators found in this case.

that, in the circumstances, it would be inappropriate for an arbitrator to prejudge the matter by resigning.[366] Sometimes, however, an arbitrator may consider that, whatever the actual merits of the challenge, it would be in the best interests of the arbitration and of both parties ultimately for the arbitrator to be replaced, in order to permit the arbitration to proceed in a better climate of confidence and trust and to minimize the likelihood of recourse against the arbitral Award when it is rendered. The decision of whether to stay or to go in such circumstances inevitably involves the consideration of a number of different factors that may be particular to the case in question. The Court has therefore generally respected the decisions made by arbitrators in such cases. Moreover, there appears to be a relatively broad international consensus (as reflected, for example, in Articles 13-14 of the UNCITRAL Model Law) that an arbitrator may legitimately choose to withdraw if challenged, even if the challenge is not considered to be founded, and withdrawal in such case need not constitute an admission of the validity of the challenge.[367]

Article 12(2)

> *An arbitrator shall also be replaced on the Court's own initiative when it decides that he is prevented de jure or de facto from fulfilling his functions, or that he is not fulfilling his functions in accordance with the Rules or within the prescribed time limits.*

Article 12(2) provides the Court with broad power to remove arbitrators who are either unable or failing to perform their functions in accordance with the Rules. It is identical to the corresponding provision formerly contained in Article 2(11) of the Rules, except for the addition of the phrase "on the Court's own initiative." Those words have been added in order to emphasize that it is the Court, and not the parties, that initiates the replacement of arbitrators pursuant to this provision. If a party wishes to have an arbitrator replaced for the reasons set forth in Article 12(2), it can challenge the arbitrator under Article 11, and it must do so within the time limit specified in that Article. Article 12(2), which contains no comparable time limit, is intended only to provide the Court with a tool of its own that it can choose to use if there has not been a challenge.[368] It is not intended to pro-

---

[366] Such a position would, moreover, be consistent with the rule to be found in the Code of Ethics for Arbitrators in Commercial Disputes prepared by the American Arbitration and Bar Associations, *supra*, note 219. According to Canon II.E of that Code, the arbitrator, if challenged for partiality or bias by one of the parties, should allow the relevant challenge procedures in the governing arbitration rules to be followed. *See also* H. Smit, "Managing an International Arbitration: An Arbitrator's View," *Am. Rev. Int. Arb.*, Vol. 5 (1994), pp. 129, 135.

[367] *See, e.g.*, UNCITRAL Model Law, Article 14(2); UNCITRAL Rules, Article 11(3).

[368] There have nevertheless been a few, exceptional cases, in which the Court has replaced arbitrators on the basis of former Article 2(11) while simultaneously rejecting a related challenge made by a party. In those cases where this has occurred, the Court preferred to reject the challenge, but nevertheless replace the arbitrator in question because, while prevented from fulfilling his functions, the arbitrator was nevertheless not considered to have acted in a culpable manner.

vide the parties with an additional means of, in effect, challenging arbitrators after the time limit for challenges has expired.[369]

Notwithstanding the breadth of this provision, it has only infrequently been used to replace arbitrators. Thus, for example, according to the Secretariat's statistics, only five arbitrators were replaced under former Article 2(11) between July 1988 and the end of 1994.[370] In one of those cases, the chairman of the tribunal and a co-arbitrator were both replaced after a venomous conflict between the two of them regarding the conduct of the arbitration made it impossible for them, in the Court's view, to continue to conduct the proceedings in a proper manner. In another case, the chairman was replaced for, among other things, failing to attend to the arbitration for extended periods of time, thus delaying considerably the progress of the proceedings.[371] In yet a further case, the chairman and a co- arbitrator were replaced (the other co-arbitrator having already resigned) on the basis of the Court's determination that they were prevented *de facto* from continuing as arbitrators where a partial Award that they had rendered was annulled and a new Award was required to be made in the same proceedings on the same subject matter. In the circumstances of that case, the Court considered that the arbitrators could no longer perform their duties with the necessary degree of impartiality.

In all of the above cases, the circumstances were either unusual or extreme. The Court has, thus far, been reluctant, however, to replace arbitrators in the much larger number of cases, of which there are unhappily still too many, in which arbitrators have failed to proceed with the degree of expedition that the parties might reasonably have expected at the outset of the arbitration or where possibly questionable procedural decisions may have been made. One reason why greater use has not been made of the Court's relevant powers is that the replacement of an arbitrator can itself be even more disruptive of the process than the problem that it is intended to resolve. Thus, for example, the replacement of a plodding arbitrator, at an advanced stage of an arbitration, may ultimately cause even more delay than would be suffered if the arbitrator in question were allowed to continue with, and complete, the arbitration. For this reason, the parties themselves are often opposed to the replacement of arbitrators by the Court.

Article 12(3)

> *When, on the basis of information that has come to its attention, the Court considers applying Article 12(2), it shall decide on the matter after the*

---

[369] *See also* Bond, *supra*, note 262, p. 25.

[370] *See* Hascher, *supra*, note 203, p. 17.

[371] In that case, the arbitrator objected that the Court had extended the relevant time periods under the Rules. However, those extensions did not excuse the arbitrator's delay in the view of the Court or preclude the Court from replacing the arbitrator on the basis that he was not fulfilling his functions "within the prescribed time limits" to which the Rules refer.

> arbitrator concerned, the parties and any other members of the Arbitral
> Tribunal have had an opportunity to comment in writing within a suitable
> period of time. Such comments shall be communicated to the parties and
> to the arbitrators.

The procedure laid down in Article 12(3) is based on Article 2(10) of the former Rules and is almost identical to the procedure that applies in the event of a challenge (*see* Article 11(3)). As in the case of Article 11(3), the parties and the arbitrators are all afforded an opportunity to comment in writing, and the comments received are also now to be circulated to all of them. The decision of whether to replace an arbitrator is then required to be taken by the Court at one of its plenary sessions.[372] Like the Court's decisions in respect of challenges, the Court's related decisions are of an administrative character and are not themselves subject to any recourse in the absence of a mandatory legal provision to the contrary.[373]

The Article 12(3) procedure nevertheless differs from Article 11(3) insofar as the former is required to be initiated by the Court and not, as in the latter case, by a party. Thus, before the Court actually decides whether to replace an arbitrator, a determination has to be made whether "information that has come to its attention" merits the solicitation of the parties' and arbitrators' comments and the submission of the matter to the Court for a decision. In the past, this determination has ordinarily been made at a meeting of the Committee of the Court on the basis of information provided to it by the Secretariat.[374] Indeed, as it is the Secretariat, rather than the Court itself, that is responsible for the day-to-day administration of all arbitrations, any information that might reasonably serve as the basis for an arbitrator's replacement would ordinarily first come to the attention of the Secretariat and, unless it were then passed on to the Court (or a party or arbitrator otherwise were to write directly to a member of the Court), the Court would not necessarily be aware of the need to consider an arbitrator's

---

[372] *See* Briner, *supra* , note 47, p. 9. Formerly, the Court's Internal Rules (Article 11) reserved to the plenary only decisions concerning "allegations that an arbitrator is not fulfilling his functions" and did not expressly require the plenary to decide whether an arbitrator was "prevented" from doing so. Thus, for example, the Court's Committee, rather than the plenary, could arguably decide upon the replacement of an arbitrator whose physical condition indisputably prevented the continuing performance of his functions. It remains to be seen whether the Court will, in fact, require such matters to be referred to the plenary session in the future.

[373] Thus, for example, the Paris court of first instance (*Tribunal de grande instance*) recently dismissed a lawsuit filed against the ICC for failing, among other things, to replace an arbitrator pursuant to Article 2(11) of the former Rules. *See Société Cubic Defense System c/ Chambre de commerce internationale, supra*, note 65. *But cf. Holtzmann and Neuhaus*, pp. 440-41, concerning the question of whether the decision of an arbitral institution to replace an arbitrator pursuant to a provision such as Article 12(2) would be insulated from judicial recourse under Article 14 of the UNCITRAL Model Law. *See also*, in this connection, Schwartz, "The ICC Arbitration Rules and the UNCITRAL Model Law," *Arb. Int.,* Vol. 9, No. 3 (1993), pp. 231, 235-37.

[374] This is not mandated by the Rules, however, and it is for the Court to decide upon the relevant procedure to be followed.

replacement. The proper application of Article 12(3), thus, often depends in the first instance on the Secretariat's assiduity in bringing information to the Court's attention.

This should not generally be a problem in respect of those matters that are regularly required to be placed by the Secretariat on the Court's agenda, such as the review of Terms of Reference, the scrutiny of arbitrators' Awards or the possible need to extend the related deadlines in the Rules. Thus, for example, if the Court observes that a deadline is repeatedly required to be extended, it can, and often does, itself consider whether an arbitrator should be replaced as a result. However, other procedural problems that may arise during the course of the arbitration would not normally come to the Court's attention unless raised by the Secretariat. In this connection, parties (and sometimes arbitrators as well)[375] may occasionally approach the Secretariat in order to bring information to its attention that may, in their view, warrant an arbitrator's replacement. Although parties may even formally apply, from time to time, for an arbitrator's replacement on the basis of the provision now contained in Article 12(2), they do not actually have any standing, as already noted, to require the Court to initiate such a proceeding, and the Secretariat is therefore not obliged to act upon any such application. As already noted above, a party can oblige the Court to decide whether to replace an arbitrator only by filing a challenge pursuant to Article 11(1). But parties are sometimes reluctant to challenge arbitrators out of fear of antagonizing them if the challenge is unsuccessful, and that is why they sometimes seek instead to cause the Court to take the initiative under what is now Article 12(2).[376]

In the event that the Secretariat has information that may possibly warrant consideration by the Court, it is then for the Court to decide whether to launch a replacement proceeding. As already stated, this determination has ordinarily been made in the past at meetings of the Court's Committee. The Committee may, at such time, decide that the matter should not be pursued any further, in which case it would never come before the plenary session for a decision. If, however, the Committee were to decide that the information before it justified bringing the matter before the plenary session, it would then direct the Secretariat to provide the parties and the arbitrators with an opportunity to comment on the "information" possibly justifying the replacement of the arbitrator concerned. This obvi-

---

[375] It is unusual for arbitrators to complain to the Secretariat about a fellow arbitrator. But there is nothing that precludes them from doing so discreetly. Indeed, this is to be preferred to raising the matter with the parties. *See*, in this connection, Schwartz, *supra*, note 351, pp. 84-85.

[376] In such cases, parties often approach the Secretariat on an informal basis in the expectation that the Secretariat will not inform the other parties or arbitrators, precisely because, fearing the possible adverse reaction of the arbitrator concerned, they do not wish it to be known that they have complained about his conduct. The Secretariat has generally been willing to respect the wish of parties for confidentiality in such circumstances (*see* with respect to this, the discussion of Article 3(1) *supra*), although all parties and arbitrators will subsequently be provided with an opportunity to comment on any information received by the Secretariat if a replacement proceeding is initiated by the Court.

ously requires the Secretariat to describe the information in question with a sufficient degree of precision to permit meaningful comment by the parties and the arbitrators. The procedure followed and the time accorded the parties and arbitrators for their comments is the same as in the case of Article 11(3).

Article 12(4)

> *When an arbitrator is to be replaced, the Court has discretion to decide whether or not to follow the original nominating process. Once reconstituted, and after having invited the parties to comment, the Arbitral Tribunal shall determine if and to what extent prior proceedings shall be repeated before the reconstituted Arbitral Tribunal.*

Part of this Article is new and part is essentially identical to the corresponding provision in the previous Rules. The first sentence concerns the procedure to be followed by the Court when appointing or confirming a new arbitrator to take the place of the arbitrator being replaced (whatever may be the reason for the replacement). It modifies the rule previously set forth with respect to this in Article 2(12) of the former Rules. The second sentence, meanwhile, describes what is to happen once the tribunal has been reconstituted. In this regard, there has been no substantive change from former Article 2(12).

Appointment of a new arbitrator. In the event of the replacement of an arbitrator, Article 2(12) of the Rules formerly provided that "the procedure indicated in the preceding paragraphs 3, 4, 5 and 6 (corresponding, respectively, to paragraphs 8(3), 8(4), 8(2) and 9(3)-9(6) of the New Rules) shall be followed." In other words, the procedure to be used was to be the same as the one originally applied for the arbitrator being replaced. If the arbitrator in question had been appointed by the Court directly, then the Court was also to appoint the new arbitrator. But if the arbitrator being replaced had been nominated by a party, then the party concerned was to be given the opportunity to nominate a new arbitrator.[377]

---

[377] By including a reference to former Article 2(5), which corresponds to Article 8(2) of the New Rules, the former provision also appears to have authorized the Court, when replacing an arbitrator, to revisit any decision that it may previously have been required to make as to the number of arbitrators in the absence of an agreement between the parties on this subject. *See*, in this regard, Arnaldez and Jakandé, *supra,* note 314, p. 83, where it is noted that the reference to Article 2(5) was specifically added to Article 2(12) as one of the amendments to the Rules in 1988. Thus, for example, in the event of the replacement of a sole arbitrator, the Court could decide that the tribunal should thereafter be comprised of three arbitrators and cause three arbitrators to be appointed. It is doubtful, however, that it could reduce the number of arbitrators from three to one on the basis of that provision unless all three arbitrators were removed. It is unclear whether Article 12(4), as now drafted, would permit the Court, to change the number of arbitrators as Article 2(12) expressly did, although there is not any reason why the Court should necessarily be precluded from reconsidering an earlier decision on this subject in appropriate circumstances.

Although this is likely to continue to be the Court's usual practice, Article 12(4) now gives the Court the discretion, in appropriate circumstances, not to follow the procedure that was originally used. Article 12(4) does not affirmatively state what alternative procedure would be used in such case. However, the intention is to allow the appointment to be made by the Court. Thus, the Court could refuse to permit a party to nominate a new arbitrator in replacement of the arbitrator originally nominated by it and instead appoint a new arbitrator directly.

The new language contained in Article 12(4) was inspired by a similar, although broader, provision in the arbitration rules of the London Court of International Arbitration. Article 11(1) (formerly Article 3(5)) of those rules provides that:

> In the event that the LCIA Court determines that any nominee is not suit-able or independent or impartial or if an appointed arbitrator is to be replaced for any reason, the LCIA Court shall have a complete discretion to decide whether or not to follow the original nominating process.

The LCIA rule may, thus, be applied not only in the case of a replacement, but also when the Arbitral Tribunal is originally being constituted in order to prevent the repeated nomination of unsuitable arbitrators, possibly in bad faith solely to delay the tribunal's constitution. The ICC Rules do not contain an explicit provision to this effect, but, as already noted (*see* Article 9(2)), the Court could arguably treat the nomination of a manifestly unsuitable arbitrator as equivalent to a failure to nominate an arbitrator in accordance with the Rules.

In the case of an arbitrator's replacement, the new provision contained in Article 12(4) does not give any indication of the circumstances in which the Court might choose not to follow the original nominating process, primarily because the drafters considered that this should be for the Court to decide on a case-by-case basis.[378] However, the Court can reasonably be expected to use its new power only exceptionally, in cases of abuse, *e.g.*, where the arbitrator being replaced has acted in a partisan fashion in collusion with the party that nominated him or was otherwise known by the nominating party to be unsuitable at the time of his nomination.[379] The Court would also presumably seek to verify,

---

[378] The ICC's approach is to be compared with that of WIPO, however, which, in adopting a similar rule (WIPO Arbitration Rules, Article 33(b)) specified that the Center could deprive a party of a right to appoint a new arbitrator if the arbitrator originally appointed by it "has either been successfully challenged on grounds which were known or should have been known to that party at the time of appointment, or has been released from appointment as an arbitrator ... [because the arbitrator has become *de jure* or *de facto* unable to fulfill, or fails to fulfill, the duties of an arbitrator]."

[379] In the United States, where there is case law on the question of whether a court should exercise its power to appoint an arbitrator in replacement of a party-appointed arbitrator who has failed to act or resigned, it has been held that such power would not be exercised unless it appeared that the resignation creating the vacancy was part of a pattern to delay or obstruct the arbitration. *See Linwood* v. *Sherry,* 171 N.Y.S.2d 941 (1958); *and Bluhm* v. *Pereira,* 75 N.Y.S.2d 170 (1948).

before preventing a party from nominating a new arbitrator, that this would not conflict with any mandatory provisions of applicable law or otherwise give rise to a possibly legitimate claim of unequal treatment in the constitution of the Arbitral Tribunal, as in the *Dutco* case discussed above (*see* Article 10).[380]

Whether or not the Court's new power under Article 12(4) is actually used, however, it provides the Court with a potentially powerful means of dissuading improper behavior that might warrant an arbitrator's removal, either pursuant to a challenge or at the initiative of the Court. It should also discourage partisan arbitrators from resigning in bad faith in order to try to delay or disrupt the arbitration proceedings. Indeed, if any such arbitrator were required to be replaced, the party that originally nominated that person would no longer be assured of a right to nominate a new arbitrator. The mere threat of this should in itself suffice to curb abusive conduct in many cases.

Effect on prior proceedings. In the event that an arbitrator is required to be replaced, it becomes necessary to determine whether and, if so, to what extent any part of the arbitration needs to be repeated. Article 12(4), like Article 2(12) before it, thus provides that it shall be for the Arbitral Tribunal to decide, after having invited the parties' comments, whether any "prior proceedings" shall be repeated.

In providing for the possible repetition of prior "proceedings," Article 12(4) differs from, and is arguably broader in scope, than other rules that simply provide for the possible repetition of prior "hearings."[381] The question may therefore arise as to what "proceedings" may properly be repeated and whether, in particular, it is appropriate for a reconstituted tribunal to prepare new Terms of Reference or to reopen matters that may already have been the subject of interim or partial Awards. When the language that is now contained in Article 12(4) was originally added to the Rules in 1988, it appears to have been the drafters' intention that the word "proceedings" should be construed as broadly as pos-

---

[380] The arbitration laws in many jurisdictions, as under Article 15 of the UNCITRAL Model Law, provide that substitute arbitrators are to be appointed according to the rules that were applicable to the appointment of the arbitrator being replaced. However, they also generally permit the parties to agree otherwise. *See, e.g.,* Article 1030(1) of the Netherlands Arbitration Act of 1986 and Article 179 of the Swiss Private International Law Act. Although this is not expressly stated in Article 15 of the Model Law, it has nevertheless been construed as permitting the parties to agree on a procedure for appointing replacement arbitrators that is different from the original procedure. *See Holtzmann and Neuhaus*, pp. 465-66. The English Arbitration Act 1996 (Section 27(1)) also expressly recognizes the party's right of autonomy in this regard.

[381] *See, e.g.,* AAA International Arbitration Rules, Article 11(2); UNCITRAL Rules, Article 14; WIPO Arbitration Rules, Article 34. In addition, the UNCITRAL Rules distinguish between the replacement of a sole arbitrator or chairman, in which case any previous hearings must be repeated, and the replacement of a co-arbitrator, in which case the Arbitral Tribunal is required to decide whether this is necessary.

sible, subject only to the possibly varying requirements of national law.[382] Thus, the "acceptance of the Terms of Reference," in particular, was listed among the matters to be considered by the reconstituted tribunal in the brief, explanatory letter submitted by the then Chairman of the Court to the Chairman of the ICC Commission together with the proposed amendments to the Rules.[383]

As a practical matter, there will rarely be any need for new Terms of Reference to be prepared when an arbitrator is replaced. The Rules do not require this, and, indeed, it would be normal to expect that, in accepting to serve, a new arbitrator at the same time accepts to carry on the mission of the arbitrator being replaced, as reflected in any existing Terms of Reference. There would also not seem to be any legitimate basis upon which a newly-constituted Arbitral Tribunal could choose, without the parties' agreement, to reopen proceedings that had already been the subject of a partial Award regarded as final under the law applicable to the arbitration proceedings, although prior decisions of a purely interlocutory or interim nature could conceivably be revisited, if necessary.[384] The issue that the reconstituted tribunal will most commonly be required to address therefore will be whether to repeat any oral proceedings conducted prior to the appointment of the new arbitrator, *e.g.,* for the examination of witnesses or oral argument.

It has been written in this regard that:

[An Arbitral Tribunal] may not, by refusing to repeat any part of the hearing, deprive a party of the opportunity adequately to present its case to the whole tribunal that is to render the award. As a practical matter, a tribunal would be well advised to repeat any hearing at the request of the new arbitrator or any party. This will greatly minimize the danger of attack on the award for failure to have afforded this opportunity.[385]

---

[382] *See* Arnaldez and Jakandé, *supra*, note 314, p. 84. In fact, however, many national arbitration laws do not indicate to what extent prior proceedings are required to be repeated in such circumstances. The UNCITRAL Model Law is silent on this subject as are many other laws. The English Arbitration Act 1996 (Section 27) expressly provides, however, in the manner of the ICC Rules, that the Arbitral Tribunal shall determine whether "the previous proceedings shall stand" unless the parties otherwise agree. The Netherlands Arbitration Act of 1986 (Article 1030), unlike most laws, provides that, unless otherwise agreed, the arbitral proceedings shall continue from the stage they had reached.

[383] Letter, dated September 8, 1996, from Michel Gaudet to the Chairman of the Commission, *supra*, note 7. It also appears to have been the Secretariat's position at the time that a reconstituted Arbitral Tribunal could legitimately consider whether to draft new Terms of Reference.

[384] In this regard, there may be a legitimate concern as to whether decisions made prior to the replacement of an arbitrator who has been successfully challenged for bias, for example, should be considered to be tainted and, in the case of partial Awards, subject to being set aside. Insofar as any Awards previously made are final, however, the tribunal, as reconstituted, would have no authority to revisit them unless this were permitted by the law applicable to the proceedings. For an interesting discussion of the relevant issues and the reconstituted tribunal's powers in this regard, *see* the final Award in ICC Case No. 6476 (1994), *ICC Ct. Bull.,* Vol. 8, No. 1 (1997), p. 59.

[385] *See* H. Smit, *supra,* note 45, pp. 11-12.

However, given the additional cost and inconvenience, which may be substantial, of repeating prior oral proceedings in international arbitrations, arbitrators are more often than not disinclined to do so, particularly where a written record has been made of the proceedings previously held. Of course, there may be circumstances in which the arbitrators' Award is likely to turn on something that could properly be assessed only at a hearing, *e.g.*, the credibility of a key witness, in which case a new arbitrator could reasonably be expected to request an additional hearing. But such cases tend to be the exception rather than the rule.[386]

Other consequences of an arbitrator's replacement. Apart from the question of whether prior proceedings should be repeated, other issues may arise upon an arbitrator's replacement with which Article 12(4) does not specifically deal. Among these, first of all, is the question of whether the arbitrator being replaced is entitled to any remuneration.

As discussed further below with regard to the determination of the arbitrator's fees (*see* Article 31), the Court enjoys broad discretion in this regard and is therefore in a position to take account of all of the circumstances surrounding an arbitrator's replacement and, in particular, whether the arbitrator concerned was required to be replaced for misconduct or for unavoidable reasons, such as illness or death. Generally, the Court has tended to reduce, or may even deny, fees in the case of arbitrators considered to be responsible, through misbehavior, for their replacement. This is broadly consistent with the approach followed internationally. Indeed, in both civil and common law systems, the "first sanction available" for an arbitrator's misconduct is the reduction or forfeiture of the arbitrator's fees.[387] Moreover, even where an arbitrator is required to be replaced for reasons outside his control, the Court may nevertheless consider it appropriate, in fixing his fees, to take account of the extent of any work that may be required to be repeated so that the new arbitrator is properly remunerated without the parties having to bear the entire burden of paying for the same work twice.

Because of the delay and disruption that an arbitrator's replacement may cause, there may also be an issue as to his personal liability for any damage suffered by the parties as a result. In this regard, Article 34 of the Rules (*see infra*) now provides that the arbitrators shall not "be liable to any person for any act or omission in connection with the arbitration." But whether, notwithstanding this provision, an arbitrator might be found liable for damage caused by misconduct

[386] *See also*, in this connection, the experience of the Iran-U.S. Claims Tribunal, as recounted in Baker and Davis, *supra,* note 181, pp. 70-71. There, the authors report that, when judges were replaced, new hearings were rare: "[A]t the time of Judge Virally's death, some eleven cases in which he participated were still pending, but only two of these cases were reheard. In most cases the new Chairman ... was satisfied that he could adequately proceed on the basis of written record, assisted by Judge Virally's notes and drafts and the recollection of Judge Virally's legal assistants who remained at the Tribunal."

[387] *See* Holtzmann, "Introductory Note," *ICCA Congress Series No. 5* (Kluwer 1991), p. 292.

in the circumstances of a particular case will depend on the law that is applicable.[388]

Article 12(5)

> *Subsequent to the closing of the proceedings, instead of replacing an arbitrator who has died or been removed by the Court pursuant to Articles 12(1) and 12(2), the Court may decide, when it considers it appropriate, that the remaining arbitrators shall continue the arbitration. In making such determination, the Court shall take into account the views of the remaining arbitrators and of the parties and such other matters that it considers appropriate in the circumstances.*

Article 12(5) permits the Court to decide not to replace an arbitrator when a vacancy is created within an Arbitral Tribunal in any of the circumstances listed in Articles 12(1) and 12(2) (which are intended to cover all of the cases in which an arbitrator would ordinarily be required to be replaced). Article 12(5) therefore creates an exception to the requirement of replacement set forth in those other two Articles. It also, unlike Article 12(2) itself (which only provides for an arbitrator's "replacement"), authorizes the Court to remove an arbitrator pursuant to that Article, but not to replace him. Evidently, Article 12(5) is capable of being applied only where the Arbitral Tribunal is composed of more than one arbitrator, although this is not explicitly stated.[389]

This is an entirely new provision, which was added to the New Rules primarily in response to the widely-perceived need for an institution such as the ICC to have an additional arrow in its quiver in combatting obstructionist tactics on the part of partisan arbitrators or otherwise in preventing delay when an arbitration has nearly been completed.

An Arbitral Tribunal from which a member has withdrawn or disappeared, for whatever reason, is often referred to, in international arbitration parlance, as a "truncated" tribunal.[390] Although a very old problem, particularly in internation-

---

[388] *See* Holtzmann, *supra,* note 387, pp. 292-94, and the reports of Gaillard, Veeder and Szasz referred to therein. *See also*, with respect to the arbitrator's statutory immunity under the English Arbitration Act 1996, Veeder, *supra,* note 204, p. 32 ("The statutory immunity does not protect an arbitrator from liability incurred by reason of his resigning as an arbitrator.").

[389] Similar provisions in other arbitration rules (*see* AAA International Arbitration Rules, Article 11(1); LCIA Rules, Article 12(1); WIPO Arbitration Rules, Article 35) are all expressly stated to be applicable in the case of a three-person tribunal. However, such provisions do not take account of the possible need for their application where the tribunal may have more than three arbitrators.

[390] The subject of the truncated tribunal and its authority, primarily in the context of public international arbitration, has been extensively reviewed in Schwebel, *supra,* note 190. Judge Schwebel more recently revisited the subject in relation to international commercial arbitration in the fourth Goff Lecture delivered in Hong Kong in 1994, as reproduced in Schwebel, "The Validity of an Arbitral Award Rendered by a Truncated Tribunal," *ICC Ct. Bull.,* Vol. 6, No. 2 (November 1995), p. 19. *See also* on this subject, Solhchi, "The Validity of Truncated Tribunal Proceedings and Awards," *Arb. Int.,* Vol. 9, No. 3 (1993), p. 303; *ICCA Congress Series No. 5* (Kluwer 1991), pp. 242-267.

al public arbitrations, the subject of "truncated" tribunals has received renewed attention in recent years, due principally to a small number of celebrated cases in which party-appointed arbitrators have either formally resigned or simply refused, at a late stage, to continue to participate in arbitration proceedings for apparently partisan reasons.[391] But there are other situations that occasionally arise as well through no fault of either the parties or the arbitrators. Thus, for example, an arbitrator may die after the Arbitral Tribunal has completed its deliberations, but before it has actually issued its Award. In cases such as this, an issue may also arise as to whether the arbitrator in question needs to be replaced.[392]

Other arbitration institutions (notably, the American Arbitration Association, the London Court of International Arbitration, the Permanent Court of Arbitration in The Hague, and the World Intellectual Property Organization) have all adopted provisions concerning "truncated" tribunals in recent years, and it was therefore inevitable that the ICC would examine the desirability of doing so as well when amending its Rules. Although the inclusion of such a provision in the Rules was not entirely free of controversy – primarily because of concerns that were expressed about the validity of a tribunal composed of an even number of members in certain jurisdictions – Article 12(5) was nevertheless considered to provide the Court with a useful tool that would, of course, have to be used cautiously, taking into account the circumstances of each case.

The provision that was finally adopted is, however, a relatively modest one, as compared to those of other institutions.

First of all, it applies only "subsequent to the closing of the proceedings" (as described in Article 22 *infra*) and therefore cannot be invoked before all hearings in the arbitration have, in principle, been completed and all written submissions and evidence produced. Unlike the corresponding provisions in the AAA,

---

[391] One of those cases was an ICC arbitration in Zurich (*Ivan Milutinovic PIM* c/ *Deutsche Babcock AG, Tribunal fédéral* (April 30, 1991)), as described by Judge Schwebel in his article in *ICC Ct. Bull., supra,* note 390, pp. 22-29. In that case, one of the co-arbitrators purported to resign following the examination of witnesses at the second of two oral hearings held prior to the issuance of a Partial Award. (The Court did not accept the resignation, although the Rules applicable to the arbitration, unlike the present Rules, did not explicitly require it to do so.) Despite being invited to attend a meeting with the other arbitrators for the purpose of deliberating on the Partial Award, the co-arbitrator in question refused to do so, and the remaining two arbitrators proceeded to issue an Award, which was approved by the Court. Ultimately, however, that Award was set aside by the Swiss courts. The Swiss Federal Tribunal held, in particular, that, unless the parties agreed otherwise, the arbitral Award was required to be made with the participation in the deliberations of all three arbitrators. If one arbitrator refused to participate, then the proper remedy would have been for him to be replaced and not for the remaining arbitrators to render an Award. For a similar decision in a recent French (non-ICC) case, *see Agence Transcongolaise des Communications-Chemin de Fer Congo* c/ *La Compagnie Minière de l'Ogoove-Comelog, S.A., Cour d'appel de Paris* (July 1, 1997) (unpublished).

[392] In a recent ICC case, the Court, in fact, approved an Award issued by the two arbitrators remaining after the death of a co-arbitrator as it had been established that the Award had been approved by the co-arbitrator prior to his death, although he had not had an opportunity to sign it.

LCIA, Permanent Court of Arbitration and WIPO rules, which are applicable at any time during the arbitration, Article 12(5) allows the Court to authorize the completion of an arbitration by a "truncated tribunal" only when all that remains to be done is for the Arbitral Tribunal to make its Award.[393] Article 12(5) is, thus, solely concerned with the withdrawal or disappearance of an arbitrator once the tribunal is ready to begin, or has already commenced, its deliberations.[394]

Article 12(5) also differs from the other rules mentioned above in that it applies only where a vacancy has actually been created within the Arbitral Tribunal. The other rules authorize the "remaining" arbitrators to continue with the arbitration where an arbitrator "fails to participate" in the arbitration, but where the arbitrator concerned has neither died or resigned nor been removed and is, thus, formally still in place. The ICC provision, however, does not authorize the remaining arbitrators to act in the absence of another arbitrator unless that person is no longer an arbitrator. It therefore avoids possible difficulties in determining whether an arbitrator is "failing" to participate, whether such failure is unjustified and, if so, whether it is possible for such a person subsequently to recommence participating. Under the ICC Rules, an arbitrator who is truly failing to participate and who, as a consequence, can be said not to be fulfilling his functions as an arbitrator should, in principle, be removed by the Court pursuant to Article 12(2).[395] This will then prevent any possible uncertainty as to that person's continuing entitlement to participate in the arbitration, and the remaining arbitrators can complete the arbitration without having to be concerned about the possible future attitudes or behavior of that person. This is not possible under the other rules, however, as they do not provide for the removal of an arbitrator without his replacement, and appear, on the contrary, to require a choice to be made between removing an arbitratrator, on the one hand, and not removing him, but proceeding without him, on the other. Under Article 12(5), the choice is different. Either an arbitrator is to be removed and replaced or simply removed without a replacement.

---

[393] The other rules all expressly provide that one of the factors to be considered in determining whether the remaining arbitrators should proceed in the absence of another is the "stage of the arbitration." However, the right of the arbitrators to continue is not dependent upon the stage that has been reached.

[394] Had it existed at the time, Article 12(5) would therefore not have applied in the *Ivan Milutinovic* case described in *supra*, note 391, as the arbitrators had only reached the stage of deliberating on a Partial Award.

[395] An arbitrator's failure to participate has to be distinguished, however, from an arbitrator's refusal to agree to or sign the Award. *See,* with respect to the latter, Article 25 *infra*. Moreover, it would not necessarily follow from an arbitrator's refusal to attend a meeting for the purpose of deliberating, that he is refusing to participate if, for example, he has communicated his views to his co-arbitrators in some other manner. However, if an arbitrator simply disappears or otherwise refuses to deliberate in any manner with the other arbitrators, then it may be appropriate for the arbitrator to be removed by the Court for failing to perform his duties.

In the case of the ICC, moreover, the relevant choice is to be made by the Court, while the other institutions mentioned above have all left the decision to the remaining arbitrators. The ICC considered, however, that it was more consistent with the Court's role in the administration of the arbitration and, in particular, its responsibility in deciding whether an arbitrator should be removed in the first place for the Court also to decide whether an arbitrator who has been removed should be replaced. In connection with that decision, Article 12(5) requires the Court to take account of the views of the parties and the arbitrators and "such other matters that it considers appropriate in the circumstances." These are likely to include, in particular, any considerations that may bear on the validity and enforceability of the Award to be rendered, consistent with the general rule contained in Article 35 (*see infra*).

Chapter 5
The Arbitral Proceedings (Articles 13-23)

ARTICLE 13
Transmission of the File to the Arbitral Tribunal

*The Secretariat shall transmit the file to the Arbitral Tribunal as soon as
it has been constituted, provided the advance on costs requested by the
Secretariat at this stage have been paid.*

Background. This Article corresponds to Article 10 of the previous Rules,
although the text of the earlier rule has been completely reworked. Former
Article 10 provided for the transmission of the file to the Arbitral Tribunal as
soon as the Respondent's Answer to the Request for Arbitration had been
received or, at the latest, upon expiration of the time limit fixed for the filing of
the Answer. Since the Answer was supposed to be filed within thirty days of the
Respondent's receipt of the Request for Arbitration (subject to possible extensions by the Secretariat), users were under the impression that the file was transmitted to the Arbitral Tribunal within thirty days. Unfortunately, for a variety of
reasons, this was not possible.

First, the transmission of the file under Article 10 was subject to the provi-
sions of Article 9, which indicated that the Secretariat could make the file's
transmission conditional upon payment of the advance on costs fixed by the
Court.[396] In practice, however, the Secretariat would not transmit the file to the
Arbitral Tribunal unless fifty per cent of the advance on costs had been paid.
Since the advance on costs was fixed by the Court after receipt of the
Respondent's Answer, the file could not be transmitted to the Arbitral Tribunal
within the time limit contemplated by Article 10.

Second, the Court would not normally begin constituting the Arbitral
Tribunal until the thirty-day time limit for filing the Answer had expired. Indeed,
the Respondent was not then (nor is it now) required to comment on either the

---

[396] For a discussion of the advance on costs, *see* Article 30 *infra*.

number or the choice of arbitrators until the expiration of that time (*see* Article 5(1) *supra*). Thus, even if the initial fifty per cent advance on costs were waived by the Secretariat (a theoretical possibility under Article 9(3)), it would still have been impossible to transmit the file within the thirty days contemplated by Article 10 since there would not yet have been a tribunal to which the file could be transmitted.

Article 13 has simplified the rule regarding transmission of the file by eliminating any reference to time limits. Instead, it simply sets out the two conditions that must be met before transmission can take place: first, the Arbitral Tribunal must have been constituted; and second, the advance on costs requested by the Secretariat must have been paid.[397] As soon as these two conditions are fulfilled, the file will be transmitted.

These modifications should eliminate the misimpression that the transmission of the file occurs thirty days after the filing of the Request for Arbitration. This does not mean, however, that transmission will occur later under the New Rules than it did under the previous Rules. To the contrary, in the great majority of cases, it should occur sooner. However, this is due not so much to Article 13, which is neutral timewise, but to the introduction of new provisions intended to accelerate the constitution of the Arbitral Tribunal (*see* Article 9(2) *supra*) and the establishment of a provisional advance on costs (*see* Article 30(1) *infra*).

Advance on costs. As discussed below, Article 30(1) provides that, as soon as the Request for Arbitration has been received, the Secretary General may ask the Claimant to pay a "provisional advance in an amount sufficient to cover the costs of arbitration until the Terms of Reference have been drawn up." This provisional advance may, at the Secretary General's discretion, be fixed before an Answer has been filed or, indeed, before the original thirty-day deadline for filing an Answer has expired. It is, as stated, payable only by the Claimant. The provisional advance was introduced into the Rules principally in order to permit the rapid transmission of the file to the Arbitral Tribunal. Indeed, a Claimant wishing the file to be transmitted to the Arbitral Tribunal rapidly has only to pay it before the tribunal is constituted.

Article 13 nevertheless does not refer specifically to the "provisional advance." Rather, it makes the transmission of the file conditional on the payment of "the advance on costs requested by the Secretariat at this stage." This is because the Working Party anticipated that there might be circumstances in which the Secretary General does not fix a provisional advance,[398] or in which, prior to the constitution of the Arbitral Tribunal, the Court fixes the advance on

---

[397] These requirements are nevertheless to be contrasted with the provisions of other arbitration rules. *See, e.g.*, WIPO Arbitration Rules, Article 37, which provides for the transmission of the file to each of the arbitrators as they are appointed rather than to all of the arbitrators at once, as under Article 13.

[398] Under Article 30(1), as discussed *infra,* the Secretary General "may," but is not required to, fix a provisional advance.

costs provided for in Article 30(2) (*see infra*) and it is considered appropriate, prior to the transmission of the file, to request the payment of some of that amount. Thus, although in the usual case the "advance on costs" to which Article 13 refers is intended to be the "provisional advance," Article 13 nevertheless leaves room for the Secretariat to require the payment of other or additional amounts in special circumstances, if appropriate.[399]

Transmission of the file. It is not until the file is transmitted to it that the Arbitral Tribunal normally sees the submissions already made by the parties in the arbitration, including, in particular, the Request for Arbitration and the Answer.[400] Together with the parties' submissions, the Secretariat transmits to the Arbitral Tribunal the following information:

- A report on the financial status of the case accompanied by a request that the Tribunal inform the Secretariat of any change in the amount in dispute;
- A reminder that the first task of the Tribunal is to establish the Terms of Reference in accordance with Article 18 of the Rules;
- A reminder of the need to respect the time limits laid down by the Rules and that extensions are to be granted by the Court at its discretion or pursuant to the Arbitral Tribunal's reasoned requests;
- A note detailing the procedures for reimbursement of the arbitrators' expenses (*see* Appendix 4(c) *infra*) and payment of their fees;
- A note on making arrangements for hearings; and
- A note indicating that the advance on costs fixed by the Court to cover the arbitrators' fees and expenses does not include value added taxes that may be payable in respect of the arbitrators' fees (*see* Appendix III to the Rules, Article 2(9) and Article 31 *infra*).[401]

When the file has been transmitted, the parties are informed of the event, invited to correspond directly with the Arbitral Tribunal and instructed to copy the Secretariat on all such direct communications (*see* Article 3(1) *supra*).

---

[399] For a discussion of possible special cases, *see* Article 30(1) *infra*.

[400] In cases with three arbitrators, however, the co-arbitrators may be furnished with copies of the Request and possibly the Answer earlier to assist them in selecting a third arbitrator if the parties have agreed that they should attempt jointly to designate that person *(see* Article 8(4) *infra).*

[401] The note that has been used for the last several years provides that, in the event an arbitrator is required to pay such taxes, the arbitrator may seek to recover the same from the parties by invoicing them directly for the amount of tax due. In such case, the parties shall pay this amount directly to the arbitrator, in addition to the advance on costs paid to the ICC.

ARTICLE 14
Place of the Arbitration

One of the most important choices to be made prior to or at the outset of any arbitration is the determination of its place (in effect, its legal seat). As already indicated (*see* Chapter 1 *supra*), an ICC arbitration may take place anywhere in the world. The parties are free to agree on the place, either in their arbitration clause or subsequently. But if they do not, it will be fixed by the Court.[402]

In selecting the place of the arbitration, both the parties and the Court have far more choice today than they once did.[403] Twenty years ago, largely due to the prevalence of unfavorable local laws on international arbitration, the number of countries in which an international arbitration could be safely situated was considerably smaller. Today, however, that number has increased significantly as a result of a worldwide trend towards modernization and liberalization of arbitration laws.[404] Nevertheless, the choice of a *situs* for an international arbitration remains a decision that must be made with care.

There are, first of all, a number of legal factors that need to be weighed in this connection. For example, the local law regarding recourse against arbitral Awards must be considered, as well as any mandatory local rules that, if violated, could cause an Award to be set aside. The extent to which local courts may be likely either to assist or interfere with the arbitration process should also be assessed. Perhaps most importantly, it must be determined whether the country under consideration is a party to any international conventions on the recognition and enforcement of arbitral Awards (*e.g.,* the New York Convention) that are also adhered to by the country or countries in which execution of the Award may be sought. Finally, political factors such as the independence of the judiciary, freedom of access to the country and the risk of political unrest may also need to be evaluated. By taking such considerations into account when choosing the place of arbitration, parties can avoid potential pitfalls.

Article 14 takes the place of Article 12 of the former Rules. Although the first of its three subparagraphs is nearly identical to former Article 12, the sec-

---

[402] From time to time, the parties also agree that the place shall be chosen by the Arbitral Tribunal. Although this is not provided for in the Rules, the Court has nevertheless accepted this.

[403] The vast majority of ICC arbitrations are nevertheless still situated in Western Europe. As can be seen from the statistics set forth in Appendix 6 *infra*, this was the case with respect to approximately 80 per cent of the ICC arbitrations set in motion in 1997, with France and Switzerland being the chosen venues in 50 per cent of the ICC's new cases during that year. Those places were followed in popularity by the United Kingdom, the United States and Austria.

[404] *See, e.g.,* Craig, "Some Trends and Developments in the Laws and Practice of International Commercial Arbitration," *Texas International Law Journal*, Vol. 30, No. 1 (1995), p. 1. This trend has been greatly encouraged by the promulgation of the UNCITRAL Model Law. *See* Sanders, "Unity and Diversity in the Adoption of the Model Law," *Arb. Int.,* Vol. 11, No. 1 (1995), p. 1.

ond two, which are new, introduce into the Rules a distinction between the formal place of the arbitration, which is the subject of Article 14(1), and the places, according to Articles 14(2) and 14(3), where meetings and hearings can be held, irrespective of the formal place. Indeed, as the place of the arbitration may be distant geographically from the parties, their counsel, the arbitrators or the site of the events in dispute, it is not uncommon in international arbitrations for meetings to be held occasionally at locations other than the place of the arbitration for reasons of convenience.

Article 14 (1)

> The place of the arbitration shall be fixed by the Court, unless agreed upon by the parties.

As noted above, this provision essentially reproduces the text of former Article 12. The only difference is that the phrase "place of arbitration" has been changed to "place of *the* arbitration." This is not merely a stylistic change. The intent was to stress that while the choice of a *situs* creates a link between the arbitration and a specific place, this does not mean that all arbitration activities must be performed there. Another approach to creating this emphasis that the Working Group considered was to substitute the word "seat" (*"siège"* in French) for the word "place." Indeed, *"siège"* was the term used in the French version of the prior Rules. However, because the word "place" has come to be used widely internationally (*e.g.,* in the New York Convention and in contemporary international arbitral legislation such as the UNCITRAL Model Law (Article 20)), it was decided that "place" should be retained.[405]

Party Agreement. Under Article 14(1), as was previously the case under Article 12, the Court has no role to play where the parties have agreed on the place of the arbitration. Thus, the Court's overall involvement in the selection of places tends to be limited. Indeed, in over 85 per cent of the cases submitted to ICC arbitration, the parties agree on this issue.[406] As recommended in the notes to the ICC's standard arbitration clause (*see* Appendix 1 *infra*), parties often set out the place of the arbitration in their contract. It is not unusual, however, for them to agree on this point after the commencement of the arbitration proceedings.

Although there is in principle nothing for the Court itself to do under the Rules where the parties have agreed on the place of the arbitration, the Court long

---

[405] As a consequence, moreover, the French version of the Rules has been revised to conform to the English version. In contrast, the new LCIA Rules, which entered into effect on January 1, 1998, now use the word "seat" in order to be consistent with the use of that term in Section 3 of the English Arbitration Act 1996.

[406] Verbist, "The Practice of the ICC International Court of Arbitration with Regard to the Fixing of the Place of Arbitration," *Arb. Int.,* Vol. 12, No. 3 (1996) p. 347. Party agreement as to the place of arbitration exceeded 85 per cent in 1997. *See* Appendix 6.

ago developed the practice of "confirming" the place agreed upon by the parties.[407] Such "confirmations" have in the past been made at the Court's Committee sessions (*see* Article 1(4) *supra*). However, it is unclear what purpose, if any, this really serves or whether there are any circumstances in which the Court might legitimately refuse to confirm the place agreed upon by the parties.

The Court has, in any event, taken the position that it is without authority to change the place of the arbitration once it has been agreed upon.[408] Although the Working Party seriously considered expanding the Court's authority to change the place of the arbitration in exceptional cases,[409] in the end, no modifications were made. The Court's practice of "confirming" the parties' agreement may nevertheless convey the misimpression that the Court has the power to refuse to confirm an agreed place and to require that it be changed.

It is to be noted, however, that the Court normally avoids "confirming" a place of arbitration, as discussed below, in cases where it is unclear whether the parties have, in fact, agreed upon the place of the arbitration or, if so, what their agreement actually is.

Court's criteria for fixing the place. Where the parties have not agreed on the place of the arbitration, it is fixed by the Court. This decision is usually made at one of the Court's Committee meetings upon consideration of any comments provided by the parties[410] and the recommendations of the Secretariat.[411] The list of criteria the Court weighs in making its decision is extensive.

– *Local Laws and Conventions.* Of paramount importance is whether the country being considered as a potential site is a signatory to the New York Convention or any other multilateral or bilateral conventions on the recognition and enforcement of arbitral awards. This is key in that most often the enforcement of an award will be sought in a country other than that designated as the place of arbitration. The Court also evaluates the local law regarding international arbitration. The factors considered under this heading include, *inter alia:* the likely degree of intervention in the arbitral process by local courts; the nature and extent of possible judicial recourse against the Award; whether limitations exist as to the

---

[407] Why the Court originally developed this practice is unclear. Indeed, under the 1955 Rules, which were applicable at the time, no such "confirmation" by the Court was required. Article 18 of the 1955 Rules merely provided that "the proceedings before the arbitrator shall take place in the country determined by the Court of Arbitration, unless the parties shall have agreed in advance upon the place of arbitration."

[408] *See* Verbist, *supra*, note 406, pp. 348-49.

[409] *E.g.,* where a state of war at the place of arbitration makes it impossible to conduct an arbitration, or unbeknownst to the parties when they reached their agreement, any Award rendered would likely be contrary to public policy or otherwise unenforceable under the local laws.

[410] Under Articles 4(3) and 5(1) of the New Rules, the parties are to include comments regarding the place of arbitration in the Request for Arbitration and Answer. The Court also may invite such comments on its own initiative. *See* Verbist, *supra*, note 406, p. 349.

[411] *See* Verbist, *supra*, note 406, p. 349.

arbitrability of some matters; whether arbitration agreements, awards or other documents are subject to formal requirements; and the degree of freedom accorded the parties or the Arbitral Tribunal to choose the applicable substantive or procedural law.[412]

– *Neutrality.* The Court strives to ensure that if, as is usually the case, the parties are of different nationalities, they will perceive the place selected as being neutral.[413] This means that, in most cases, the Court will not situate the arbitration in either of the parties' country of origin. In weighing this factor, the Court may, depending on the circumstances, consider not only the country of origin of each party, but also that of any parent company or group to which the party might belong and of which the Court is aware.[414] Likewise, if one of the parties has proposed a place to which the other has objected, the Court usually tries to identify another suitable venue, provided that there are reasonable alternatives.[415]

– *Convenience.* The convenience of any potential site is another important factor considered by the Court. Generally, the Court will attempt to identify a site that is equally convenient (or inconvenient) for all parties. This does not mean, however, that the site chosen will necessarily be equidistant from the parties. For example, in the unlikely event that the parties' counsel and the arbitrators were all located in the same city, the Court might strongly favor this city as the place of arbitration, all else being equal. Similarly, where agreement has been reached as to the constitution of the Arbitral Tribunal, the Court may consider locating the arbitration at or near the sole arbitrator or chairman's place of business, especially in cases where the amount in dispute is relatively small and the desire to contain costs is thus correspondingly high.[416]

– *Other Considerations.* Other factors may, in certain cases, also influence the Court's determination. Where the arbitration clause specifies the applicable law, this may weigh against certain sites and in favor of others. Where the parties have agreed on a language for the arbitration, this may also make certain locations more appropriate than others, particularly where the Court wishes to select a sole arbitrator or chairman residing at the place of the arbitration. The Court also weighs a host of practical considerations, such as:

---

412 *See* Jarvin, "The Place of Arbitration: A Review of the ICC Court's Guiding Principles and Practices when Fixing the Place of Arbitration," *ICC Ct. Bull.,* Vol. 7, No. 2 (1996), p. 55.

413 But Article 14(1) does not require the Court to fix the place in a neutral country.

414 *See* Verbist, *supra,* note 406, p. 352. *But see* as to this, *supra,* note 323.

415 For this reason, a party may want to consider the possible reaction of the other party before proposing a particular venue in its comments on this subject pursuant to Articles 4 and 5 *(see supra).*

416 *See* Verbist, *supra,* note 406, p. 354.

- Costs (in terms of both time and money) of traveling to the potential site. As mentioned, these considerations become all the more important where the amount in dispute is relatively small;
- Adequacy of a potential site's communications, transportation and other infrastructures;
- Availability of support services, such as accommodations, meeting rooms and secretarial assistance;
- Customs issues such as the relative ease with which different participants may be able to obtain visas; and
- The security of a potential site, *e.g.,* whether there is civil unrest.

Cases where it is unclear whether the parties have agreed on a place. Sometimes, it may not be clear whether the parties have agreed on a place of arbitration or otherwise what they may have agreed on this subject. Thus, for example, cases have arisen where the contract was concluded in two originals, each in a different language, only one of which specified the place of arbitration, or where the original contract specified one place, but an amendment to the contract specified another. In other cases, the parties may have agreed to arbitrate certain types of disputes in one place and other types of disputes in another, and it may be unclear which category the arbitration falls in. In cases such as these, the Court has normally left it up to the Arbitral Tribunal to construe the parties' agreement and, accordingly, to determine the agreed place.[417] In contrast, where the parties stipulate that the arbitration shall occur either in place "A" or in place "B" but cannot further agree as between these two options once a dispute has arisen, the Court's practice has been to choose one of the two places and fix it as the place of the arbitration.[418]

A much more frequent case, however, is where the arbitration clause provides that any dispute will be resolved under the "Rules of the International Chamber of Commerce in Paris." The issue in such cases is whether the reference to Paris is meant to indicate the place of arbitration or merely the location of the ICC's headquarters. In such cases, the Secretariat normally asks the parties what the reference to Paris was intended to mean. Unless all of the parties concerned indicate that it was not their intention to designate Paris as the place of the arbitration, the Court normally "decides" that Paris shall be the place of the arbitration (as opposed to "confirming" or "fixing" Paris). This is intended to avoid any possible attempt by a party subsequently to have the Award annulled on the ground that the parties' choice of the place of arbitration was not respected. By "deciding" that Paris shall be the place of the arbitration, the Court does not take any position as to whether or not there was, in fact, an agreement between the parties. If there was, then the Court's decision is consistent

---

[417] *Id.* Jarvin, *supra,* note 412, p. 57. In some such cases, the Court has fixed a neutral – usually a third – site provisionally. In others, it has done nothing.

[418] *See* Verbist, *supra,* note 406, p. 349; *see* Jarvin, *supra,* note 412, p. 57.

with that agreement. If not, the Court has the authority under Article 14(1), in any event, to fix Paris as the place.

In perhaps an excess of caution, the Court follows the same policy where the clause refers to the "ICC *of* Paris." Meanwhile, inaccurate descriptions of the institution such as the "ICC Geneva," "ICC Zurich" or "ICC Stockholm" will normally be interpreted as indicating the intended place of arbitration (*see also*, with respect to such clauses, Article 6(2) *supra*). In all such cases, it is the Secretariat's practice to inform the parties of its policy before requesting the Court to consider the matter, thus providing the parties with an opportunity to agree on another venue if they wish.[419]

Changing the place of arbitration. One final issue is whether, once it has been established, the place of the arbitration may be changed. Such cases are rare, but not without precedent. Clearly, the parties are free to modify their agreement as to the place at any time prior to the constitution of the Arbitral Tribunal and even thereafter (notwithstanding its "confirmation" by the Court), with the Arbitral Tribunal's concurrence. If, however, the parties seek to change the place of the arbitration after the arbitrators' appointment, but over their objection, the arbitrators may have a legitimate ground for resignation (with compensation for any work done prior to that time), particularly if they accepted their appointment on the assumption that the arbitration would be in a certain place.[420] Moreover, if the parties wish to change the place after it has already been included in the Terms of Reference (*see* Article 18 *infra*), there is at least a theoretical issue as to whether they would be entitled to do so without the arbitrators' consent.[421]

On at least one occasion, it was the Court that decided, at an early stage, to change the place of the arbitration that it had itself fixed after discovering that an Award rendered at such place would not be recognized in the country where enforcement was likely to be sought.[422] It is uncertain, however, whether the Court would permit the parties, by agreement, to change a place fixed by the Court, although it is difficult to see why the Court should prevent this if the arbitrators (if already appointed) have no objection.

Article 14(2)

> *The Arbitral Tribunal may, after consultation with the parties, conduct hearings and meetings at any location it considers appropriate unless otherwise agreed by the parties.*

[419] *See* Verbist, *supra,* note 406, p. 352.

[420] This will not always be the case, however. Indeed, in some cases, the place of the arbitration will not yet have been determined at the time of an arbitrator's appointment.

[421] The issue is largely theoretical, however, because it is difficult to imagine the parties trying to impose on the Arbitral Tribunal a place that they could not accept. In such a case, if the parties both felt strongly enough, the parties would have the option either of revoking the arbitrators (*see* Article 12(2) *supra*) or commencing a new arbitration.

[422] *See* Jarvin, *supra*, note 412, p. 58.

Background. This is a new provision. However, it closely resembles similar provisons in other arbitration rules,[423] and, in fact, it has a very old precedent in the first arbitration rules adopted by the ICC in 1922. The 1922 Rules gave the arbitrators the right "where the law permits[,] to take evidence in countries other than that in which the arbitration takes place."[424]

This precursor to Article 14(2) addressed the most common example of a situation in which it might be necessary to conduct a portion of the arbitral proceedings at a location other than the place of the arbitration. Since the place of arbitration is often fixed by the parties or by the Court at a neutral location, with which neither of the parties is connected, it may sometimes be more economical for the Arbitral Tribunal to hear certain witnesses where they reside (depending on their number and location) instead of summoning them to the place of the arbitration. Moreover, one of the parties may request the Arbitral Tribunal to inspect goods, equipment, or other physical evidence at the place of performance of the contract, although this place may be different from the place of the arbitration. Perhaps because it was assumed that the fixing of the place of the arbitration should not limit the arbitrators in the performance of such duties, the express authorization given in the 1922 Rules was not repeated in later versions of the ICC Rules.

Experience has shown, however, that it may sometimes be convenient to conduct arbitral activities other than the taking of evidence at a place different from the place of the arbitration. Thus, for example, if an Arbitral Tribunal sitting in Geneva were required to conduct a site inspection and hear witnesses resident in Indonesia, then it might also be cost-effective to take advantage of the presence of all the participants by coupling the Arbitral Tribunal's evidence-gathering with a meeting devoted to hearing oral arguments on the related issues, even though the place of the arbitration may be Geneva.

The New Rules take account of such realities while protecting the parties against possible abuses. Thus, unlike some other rules,[425] Article 14(2) requires the Arbitral Tribunal to consult with the parties before deciding to conduct a hearing or meeting at a location other than the place of the arbitration. Usually, a proposal concerning the venue of a meeting and its agenda will, thus, be made either by the Arbitral Tribunal or one of the parties, a discussion will take place on that proposal, and, after being fully informed of the parties' views, the Arbitral Tribunal will make its decision. This obliges the arbitrators to explain to the parties why they consider their decision appropriate and this, in turn, should generally suffice to discourage the most blatant abuses. It is difficult to imagine, for example, an Arbitral Tribunal explaining to the parties that it

---

[423] *See, e.g.,* AAA International Arbitration Rules, Article 13(2); LCIA Rules, Article 16(2); UNCITRAL Rules, Article 16; WIPO Arbitration Rules, Article 39. *See also* UNCITRAL Model Law, Article 20.

[424] 1922 Rules of the Court of Arbitration of the International Chamber of Commerce, Article XVI/XXXVII.

[425] *Cf.* AAA International Arbitration Rules, Article 13(3); LCIA Rules, Article 16(2); UNCITRAL Rules, Article 16.

intends to fix a hearing in Barbados, although the place of the arbitration is Stockholm, simply because its members prefer the weather in the Caribbean. Perhaps even more important than discouraging abuse, however, the obligation to consult the parties before deciding to hold a hearing or a meeting at a location other than the place of the arbitration should prompt discussions between the parties and the Arbitral Tribunal as to the usefulness of such a decision.

Unlike other rules, Article 14(2) also provides that the parties may oust or limit the arbitrators' authority to fix hearings and meetings at places other than the place of the arbitration.[426] However, it is probably not advisable for the parties to exclude this possibility entirely unless they are confident that the flexibility that Article 14(2) permits would not be of any utility in the circumstances of a particular case.[427] Alternatively, they might agree to limited restrictions on the holding of specific meetings or hearings at venues other than the place of the arbitration.

"Hearings" versus "Meetings." Although Article 14(2) refers to both "hearings" and "meetings," the Working Party did not intend there to be any significant distinction between those terms. Both were included because in certain common law jurisdictions, the notion of a hearing applies only to meetings where witnesses are heard, whereas in other jurisdictions it applies to any meeting where the Arbitral Tribunal and the parties are present. The intent, therefore, was to obviate any discussion as to the nature of the proposed meeting. If the parties are to participate in that meeting, Article 14(2) applies. As a result, Article 14(2) also covers meetings for the inspection of goods, equipment or property that may be the subject of the arbitration but are not situated at the place of the arbitration.

Article 14(3)

> *The Arbitral Tribunal may deliberate at any location it considers appropriate.*

In contrast to Article 14(2), which permits the parties to limit the Arbitral Tribunal's freedom to hold "hearings" or "meetings" wherever it may choose, Article 14(3) allows it to hold its "deliberations" at any location it considers appropriate, without consulting the parties and regardless of any objections they might have. Indeed, in practice the parties are rarely informed either of the location or the organization of the arbitrators' deliberations, thus diminishing the possibility of any party interference.

---

[426] *See* the rules referred to in note 423 *supra*. The ICC rule, however, is similar to the corresponding provision in the UNCITRAL Model Law (Article 20(2)).

[427] But this cannot necessarily be foreseen. Thus, for example, in one case, an arbitrator was prevented, for health reasons, from traveling to the place of the arbitration for a hearing, and he had no alternative but to suggest that the hearing be held at his place of residence. Had the parties excluded this possibility, and made it a requirement that all hearings must be held at the place of the arbitration, this could have seriously disrupted the arbitration.

In practice, ICC arbitrators often decide to deliberate at a location other than the place of the arbitration. For example, if all members of the tribunal reside in the same city and that city is not the place of the arbitration, it would unnecessarily increase the costs of the arbitration if they were obliged to hold deliberations at the arbitration's seat. Likewise, if the chairman of the tribunal resides at the place of the arbitration but the two co-arbitrators both reside in another city, it may be more economical to hold deliberations in that other city. Finally, if the three arbitrators all live in different cities, which is commonly the case, holding deliberations in any of them may make no difference economically. On the other hand, scheduling considerations could favor one location over another. For example, if scheduling conflicts prevent one of the arbitrators from traveling during a certain period, it may be more efficient to deliberate in the city of that arbitrator, even if it is not the place of the arbitration.

It should also be noted that the New Rules do not oblige the arbitrators to meet physically for their deliberations. Indeed, they sometimes do not, depending on the complexity of the case and on their personal inclinations. Thus, for example, deliberations can take place by correspondence. In simple cases, the chairman of the Arbitral Tribunal may prepare a draft Award on which the co-arbitrators are then invited to comment in writing. In less simple cases, the members of the Arbitral Tribunal may meet initially to agree on the substance of the Award and then continue their deliberations on matters of detail by correspondence.

The validity of deliberations by correspondence has nevertheless been questioned in the past in certain jurisdictions. While accepted by the French Court of Cassation in 1981 and by the Swiss Federal Tribunal in 1985,[428] Italian courts continue to be reluctant to approve this practice and will not uphold an Award unless the arbitrators have met in *conferenza personale*.[429] Although some form of deliberation by correspondence now seems to be accepted nearly everywhere, ICC arbitrators should verify that this is in fact the case at the place of the arbitration.

It is, in any event, to be noted that, wherever the Arbitral Tribunal may deliberate, the Award is deemed to be made at the place of the arbitration (*see* Article 25(3) *infra*).

ARTICLE 15
Rules Governing the Proceedings

Thirty years ago, arbitrators commonly looked to the law of the place of the arbitration to answer procedural questions that might arise during the arbitration. Thus, prior to 1975, the Rules provided that where the Rules were silent and the parties had not chosen a "law of procedure," the arbitrator was to look to "the law

---

[428] *Industria Motora Rakovica* c/ *Lynx Machinery Ltd, Cour de cassation* (28 January, 1981), Note Fouchard, *Rev. arb.* (1982) p. 425; *Arrêt Sefri, Tribunal fédéral suisse* (23 October, 1985), ATF 111 Ia, 336.

[429] *See* Article 837 of the Italian Code of Civil Procedure, adopted in 1994, which nevertheless permits deliberations by *"teleconferenza"* (video conference).

of the country in which the arbitrator holds the proceedings."[430] In 1975, however, in what has been described as a "revolutionary innovation,"[431] the Rules were revised in order to separate the arbitration, to the extent possible, from local procedural law. Thus, under Article 11 of the Rules adopted in that year, the arbitrators were authorized to decide procedural issues, at their discretion, without reference to any national law or comprehensive body of procedural rules.[432] This fundamental principle continues to characterize Article 15, which, but for one addition (*see* Article 15(2) *infra*), does not differ substantively from its predecessor.

Article 15(1)

> *The proceedings before the Arbitral Tribunal shall be governed by these Rules, and, where these Rules are silent, any rules which the parties or, failing them, the Arbitral Tribunal may settle on, whether or not reference is thereby made to the rules of procedure of a national law to be applied to the arbitration.*

Article 15(1) reproduces, with minor alterations, the text of former Article 11. Like Article 11, it allows the parties and the arbitrators the greatest possible freedom in structuring the proceedings before the Arbitral Tribunal, subject only to the Rules themselves and any provisions of law that may apply mandatorily. In this regard, it establishes the following hierarchy among the governing rules: first, the Rules themselves; second, where no provisions of the Rules apply, any rules that the parties may agree upon; and third, any rules the arbitrators may settle.

The requirements of the Rules. As a practical matter, the Rules themselves provide little more than a framework for the conduct of the proceedings. As discussed further below, their requirements are few, apart from the basic guarantees generally associated with a fair and impartial proceeding, such as the right to a hearing (*see* Article 20 *infra*) and to a "reasonable opportunity" to present one's case (*see* Article 15(2) *infra*). The Rules otherwise confer broad powers on the Arbitral Tribunal to establish the facts "by all appropriate means" (*see* Article 20 *infra*) and afford the parties the opportunity to agree upon the language of, and rules of law applicable to, the arbitration, failing which these matters shall be decided by the Arbitral Tribunal (*see* Articles 16 and 17 *infra*). In each individual case, therefore, it will fall to the parties and the arbitrators to determine most of the procedural rules that may be appropriate.

---

[430] Article 16 of the 1955 Rules.

[431] *See* Eisemann, "The Court of Arbitration: Outline of its Changes from Inception to the Present Day," *60 Years of ICC Arbitration* (ICC Publishing 1984), pp. 391 at 398.

[432] *See* Hascher, "The Law Governing Procedure: Express or Implied Choice by the Parties – Contractual Practice," *ICCA Congress Series No. 7* (Kluwer 1996), p. 322; Goldman, "*La volonté des parties et le rôle de l'arbitre dans l'arbitrage international,*" *Rev. arb.* (1981), p. 469. Of the procedural rules that might apply, it is necessary to distinguish between procedural rules developed for court proceedings and for arbitration, if any.

Agreements of the parties. As indicated, Article 15 gives priority to any agreements on procedure that the parties may reach, failing which it is for the arbitrators to fix the rules to be followed.[433] The deference shown by Article 15 to the wishes of the parties is consistent with the consensual nature of the arbitration process. Indeed, the arbitrators' authority is initially derived from the parties' agreement, and the parties can agree to replace the arbitrators at any time (*see* Article 12(1) *supra*). This does not mean, however, that the parties' autonomy is unlimited. It is limited, first of all, by the express requirements of the Rules themselves pursuant to Article 15 and also by any mandatory rules of law that may apply.[434] In addition, as a practical matter, the parties are required to take into consideration the needs and wishes of the Arbitral Tribunal, for the arbitrators must obviously feel comfortable with whatever procedures the parties may wish them to administer and feel confident that they will be in a position to carry out their functions properly, failing which they may legitimately wish to resign.[435]

---

[433] For a discussion of such agreements by parties in ICC arbitrations, *see* Hascher, *supra*, note 432.

[434] In this regard, it may be asked whether the parties can legitimately derogate from the hierarchy established by Article 15 or from any of the Rules to which that Article refers. This is a question as to which there is no clear answer since, as discussed elsewhere in this book, it is for the Court to decide whether it considers particular derogations to be acceptable, except in the few cases where they are permitted by the Rules expressly. However, the Court has, in the past, not objected to Terms of Reference that effectively altered the hierarchy of Article 15 by providing that, in the silence of the Rules, all rules of procedure would be fixed by the arbitrators at their discretion (without reference to any rights of the parties in this regard). Apart from this, there may be room for disagreement as to whether the Rules are "silent" as to a particular matter.

[435] *See, e.g.,* Mustill and Boyd, *supra*, note 362, p. 282:
If the parties have agreed upon a procedure before or at the time when the arbitrator is appointed, he is bound to follow it ... . Failure to comply with the agreement of the parties is misconduct, which may invalidate the award.
An agreement on procedure made by the parties after the arbitrator has agreed to act is on a rather different footing. Here, it cannot be said that compliance with the agreement is a condition of his appointment, and if the parties were to insist on a procedure which he found objectionable, he would be within his rights in declining to act. As a matter of prudence, as well as courtesy, the parties should seek the arbitrator's approval of the agreed procedure. The arbitrator may, and indeed should, make his views known if the parties propose a way of conducting the reference which he considers may lead to confusion, delay or expense.
Nevertheless, if the parties decline to take his advice, he should yield. He is, after all, no more than the agreed instrument of the parties. If there is a conflict between the parties, an arbitrator who tries to please them both is likely to fall into error. But if they are in agreement, he should in the end do what they wish, for it is their money, and not his, which is being spent on the reference.
See also, in this connection, Mayer, "*Le Pouvoir des Arbitres de Régler la Procédure, Une Analyse Comparative des Systèmes de Civil Law et de Common Law,*" *Rev. arb.* (1995), p. 163; Jarrosson, Note, *Société Sofidif et autres* c/ *OIAETI et autre, Cour de cassation* (March 8, 1988), *Rev. arb.* (1989), pp. 481, 482; *and* Jarrosson, Note, *Société Sermi* c/ *société Buzzichelli Holding, Cour d'appel de Paris* (April 24, 1992), *Rev. arb.* (1992), p. 601, where it is argued that the Arbitral Tribunal possesses inherent powers concerning the organization of the arbitral proceedings that cannot be ousted by the parties' agreement.

In practice, therefore, the rules established for any given arbitration are usually, and should be, the result of a process of give and take between the parties and the arbitrators. In the event, as often happens, that the parties themselves have no common view of the manner in which the arbitration ought to proceed, then, under Article 15, it will be for the Arbitral Tribunal to exercise its discretion in this regard.

Determination of rules by the Arbitral Tribunal. In exercising its discretion in respect of procedural matters, the Arbitral Tribunal, as Article 15(1) makes clear, is not required to apply the procedural rules of any national law,[436] and, indeed, this is not normally appropriate.[437] Not only are such rules often designed for judicial, rather than arbitral, proceedings,[438] but they also may not be suited to the needs of an international dispute, where the parties may have very different conceptions of the appropriate means of pleading and proving their cases. Thus, as discussed further below (*see* Article 20 *infra*), international arbitrators have increasingly sought to develop procedures that borrow from the different legal traditions of the parties to the arbitration, to the extent appropriate. In so doing, of course, they are bound to respect fundamental notions of due process, as is now emphasized, moreover, by Article 15(2) of the Rules (*see infra*).

Usually, ICC arbitrators undertake to address the procedural framework for the proceedings when the Terms of Reference are being drawn up (*see* Article 18 *infra*). At that time, they will normally discuss with the parties such matters as the number and dates of future exchanges of memorials, the production of documents, and the possible need for witnesses or experts. If the Terms of Reference are signed by correspondence, the discussion regarding the organization of the proceedings usually takes place by telephone conference call. The

---

[436] Article 11 of the previous Rules permitted the exclusion of any "municipal" procedural law. The word "municipal" has, however, been replaced in Article 15 by "national" in the rules because many users of ICC arbitration were confused by the reference to "municipal."

[437] This was, in fact, recognized in ICC arbitration well before the entry into force of the 1975 Rules. *See*, for example, the Award in ICC Case No. 1512 (1971), *ICCA Yearbook* I (1976), p. 128 ("the arbitrators have a wide discretion in matters of procedure"). This trend was confirmed after the entry into force of the 1975 Rules by such Awards as the one made in a 1978 arbitration, where the Arbitral Tribunal stated that: "[I]n the silence [of the Rules] the Arbitral Tribunal will apply the Rules which it considers appropriate" (ICC Case No. 2879 (1978), *ICC Arbitral Awards 1974-1985*, p. 332). This is also the approach most commonly taken by modern arbitration rules (*see* LCIA Rules, Article 14; UNCITRAL Rules, Article 15(1); Rules of the National and International Chamber of Commerce of Milan, Article 15(1); and AAA International Arbitration Rules, Article 16(1) and by contemporary national laws on arbitration (*see, inter alia,* Article 1494 of the French New Code of Civil Procedure; Article 1036 of the Netherlands Arbitration Act 1986; Article 15 of the Portuguese Law of 1986; Article 182(2) of the Swiss Private International Law Act; Article 25 of the Egyptian Law of 1994; Article 816 of the Italian Code of Civil Procedure; Section 34 of the English Arbitration Act 1996; and Article 19(2) of the UNCITRAL Model Law.

[438] Although there may exist separate procedural rules for arbitration, these rarely contain much detail.

arbitrators solicit the parties' views and very often seek to obtain their agreement as to the general structure of the proceedings. Any such procedural agreements can then be included in the Terms of Reference, although as discussed further below (*see* Article 18), such matters are more appropriately set forth in one or more procedural orders of the Arbitral Tribunal.[439] The parties' agreement is, of course, not required for the issuance of a procedural order, and the Arbitral Tribunal is, thus, free to adapt its directions subsequently, as necessary. Thus, for example, the organization of evidentiary proceedings is frequently the object of a further procedural order following the exchange of memorials. In complicated cases, a meeting with the parties may be necessary before such a procedural order is issued so that the Arbitral Tribunal can ascertain the parties' wishes prior to making its decision, in the absence of an agreement between the parties.

Mandatory procedural rules. While Article 15(1) permits the Arbitral Tribunal to disregard the "rules of procedure of a national law," ICC arbitrators, like all arbitrators, must nevertheless be attentive to the mandatory procedural laws of the place of the arbitration, as the breach of such a law may, in most countries, serve as a basis for setting an Award aside.[440] It is for this reason, moreover, that, when scrutinizing draft Awards in accordance with Article 27 of the Rules (*see infra*), the Court "considers, to the extent practicable, the requirements of mandatory law at the place of arbitration."[441] Moreover, ICC arbitrators may take into account the mandatory procedural rules of a country where enforcement of their Award is likely to be sought,[442] irrespective of the possible grounds for setting it aside at the place of the arbitration (*see*, in this connection, Article 35 *infra*).[443] Addressing this potentially broad array of mandatory rules is not necessarily as cumbersome an exercise as it may at first appear, however, given the increasing harmonization of arbitration laws internationally.

---

[439] *See*, for a collection of such orders, Hascher, *Collection of ICC Procedural Decisions in ICC Arbitration 1993-1996* (Kluwer 1997).

[440] *See* Hascher, *supra*, note 432, p. 330. This is not universally true, however. Thus, for example, Article 1717(h) of the Belgian Judicial Code excludes the setting aside of an Arbitral Award made in Belgium when there is no Belgian party or interest in the case. *See also* Article 192 of the Swiss Private International Law Act, which authorizes parties without a domicile in Switzerland to exclude any recourse against arbitral Awards made there.

[441] Appendix II to the Rules, Article 6.

[442] *See* the Award in ICC Case No. 2879 (1978), *supra*, note 437, p. 346, and accompanying Note by Derains.

[443] It is to be noted, however, that while the Arbitral Tribunal may give due regard to the mandatory procedural rules of countries where enforcement might be sought, if known, it does not necessarily have an obligation to do so, provided that it is conducting the proceedings in accordance with generally accepted international standards and the mandatory rules of the place of arbitration.

Article 15(2)

> *In all cases, the Arbitral Tribunal shall act fairly and impartially and ensure that each party has a reasonable opportunity to present its case.*

This provision is new to the ICC Rules, although it expresses a principle that is at the heart of universally-accepted concepts of "due process," "natural justice" and the like. Similar provisions may also be found in other arbitration rules[444] and in many national arbitration laws.[445] At first glance, Article 15(2) may, thus, appear to state the obvious. Indeed, it is difficult to imagine parties agreeing to arbitrate if they do not have faith in the fairness and impartiality of the process. However, the language of Article 15(2) was nevertheless carefully and deliberately chosen.

Thus, for example, unlike Article 15(1) of the UNCITRAL Rules or Article 18 of the UNCITRAL Model Law, Article 15(2) provides that the parties are to be treated "fairly," rather than "with equality." This is because, in some cases, treating the parties in precisely the same manner may lead to unfair results, at least if "equality" is viewed in the abstract. A case may be imagined, for example, where party A refuses to make a payment apparently due under a contract with party B on the ground that it was discharged of its obligation by a letter from a representative of party B. Party B alleges that the letter was obtained through bribery. If there is *prima facie* evidence that party B's allegation might be true, fairness could require the arbitrator to treat the parties "unequally" by, for example, giving party B more time to gather its evidence, since proving bribery is more time consuming than presenting a letter of discharge.[446] Depending on how equal treatment is defined, the results may, thus, be more or less unfair.

Article 15(2) also differs from some other rules (and the UNCITRAL Model Law) in providing that each party shall have a "reasonable," as opposed to a "full," opportunity to present its case.[447] Indeed, what is a "full" opportunity may be the subject of endless debate and may not necessarily comport with what is either reasonable or necessary. Under Article 15(2), it is therefore intended that the Arbitral Tribunal shall have the discretion to decide when it has heard enough and whether it would be unreasonable to permit the continued exchange of either memorials or evidence that may no longer be of any use to the arbitrators. As discussed further below, this is also consistent with the Rules' other provisions relating to the conduct of the proceedings.[448]

---

[444] *See, e.g.,* UNCITRAL Rules, Article 15(1); AAA International Arbitration Rules, Article 16(1); LCIA Rules, Article 14(1).

[445] *See, e.g.,* UNCITRAL Model Law, Article 18, which provides: "The parties shall be treated with equality and each party shall be given a full opportunity of presenting its case."

[446] Of course, the notion of fairness should not be pushed too far. An arbitrator should not lend assistance to a party, for example, on the rationale that it was not adequately advised by its lawyer or because the merits of its case attract more sympathy than those of the other side.

[447] *See, e.g.,* UNCITRAL Rules, Article 15(1).

[448] *See, e.g.,* Article 22 ("When it is satisfied that the parties have had a reasonable opportunity to present their cases, the Arbitral Tribunal shall declare the proceedings closed.").

One final observation that should be made about Article 15(2) concerns the requirement that the Arbitral Tribunal act "impartially." As already discussed with respect to the matter of arbitrator independence (*see* Article 7(1) *supra*), the Rules do not expressly require a showing, during the appointment process, of an arbitrator's "impartiality," primarily because of the difficulty of objectively assessing an arbitrator's state of mind at that time. Article 15(2), thus, serves to emphasize that the impartiality of the arbitrator is nevertheless a fundamental requirement in ICC arbitration.

ARTICLE 16

Language of the Arbitration

In the absence of an agreement by the parties, the Arbitral Tribunal shall determine the language or languages of the arbitration, due regard being given to all relevant circumstances, including the language of the contract.

The provision in the earlier Rules regarding the language of the arbitration was contained in a sub-paragraph of former Article 15. The authors of the New Rules, however, felt that this issue was important enough to justify a separate Article.[449]

The governing principle of Article 16 is that the parties may choose whatever language or languages they wish to be used in the arbitration. Indeed, unlike Article 15(3) of the former Rules, this is now explicitly stated in Article 16. The introductory provisions to the ICC's standard arbitration clause (*see* Appendix 1 *infra*) also suggest to the parties that "it may be desirable for them to stipulate in the arbitration clause itself" the language of the arbitration. This is advice that parties would do well to heed. By agreeing to the language in the arbitration clause, many of the uncertainties that accompany the commencement of an arbitration can be avoided (*see* Article 4(3) *supra*). It is extremely helpful to know in advance what the language of the arbitration will be when choosing counsel or a party-appointed arbitrator, drafting a Request for Arbitration or an Answer, or assessing whether the arbitration is or is not likely to involve significant translation costs. Knowing the language of the arbitration also greatly assists the Court in appointing or confirming arbitrators.

Party agreement. When the parties agree, the language chosen often is the same as that of the contract in which the arbitration clause is contained.[450] If the contract has been concluded in more than one language, one of these is usually chosen.

---

[449] On this subject generally, *see* Lazareff, "The Language of Institutional Arbitration," *ICC Ct. Bull.* Vol. 8, No. 1 (1997), p. 18.

[450] But this is not necessarily the case. Thus, for example, it has been advocated that the language of the arbitration should be the same as that of the law selected to govern the contract. *See* Breitenstein, *"La langue de l'arbitrage : Une langue abstraite ?" ASA Bull.* (1995), p. 18. But this may not be a very practical approach, depending upon the language of the law concerned.

Sometimes it is stipulated that the arbitration should be conducted in more than one language, a possibility that Article 16 expressly envisages by referring to the "language or languages" of the arbitration. This is not, however, to be encouraged in most cases. The use of multiple languages may significantly increase costs by necessitating the use of translators for documents and possibly for hearings. The appointment of skilled, experienced, independent and neutral arbitrators can also be complicated because it may be difficult, or even impossible, to find arbitrators with such qualifications who at the same time have command of the multiple languages selected. Moreover, if two or more languages are used, the Terms of Reference, orders and Awards may have to be drafted in the languages specified, with the attendant risk of inconsistent texts.

Nevertheless, *after* a dispute arises, several languages may be used in the same arbitration if this is suited to the circumstances of the case and does not create difficulties for the participants. Where multiple languages are used, however, it is important to designate one language as the principal language of the arbitration for the drafting of the Terms of Reference, orders and Awards. For example, the Terms of Reference in one recent arbitration provided:

> The language of the proceedings will be English. However, French will be allowed as an optional language, bearing in mind that English will remain the main language of the proceedings and that any Procedural Order and any award will be made in that language.
> Documents will be submitted in English and those for which the original language is not English will be submitted in original with a free translation into English.

Even if only one language is chosen as the language of the arbitration, however, multiple language issues can arise with respect to evidentiary submissions. For example, if documentary evidence is written in a language other than that of the arbitration, it may need to be translated. Normally, a free translation will be sufficient. If a party objects, however, a sworn translation might be required. With regard to oral evidence, simultaneous or consecutive translations performed either by a participant (subject to verification by one of the arbitrators) or a sworn translator may be used.

Absence of agreement. Where the parties are unable to agree, the Arbitral Tribunal must determine the language of the arbitration. The Tribunal's decision in this regard usually coincides with the drafting of the Terms of Reference. If there is significant disagreement as to which language should be used, however, a decision might need to be made sooner. Indeed, a decision may be necessary simply to know which language to use in drafting the Terms of Reference. The language of the arbitration thus, is often the subject of the Arbitral Tribunal's first procedural order.[451]

---

[451] *Cf.* UNCITRAL Rules, Article 17, which indicates that the Arbitral Tribunal should determine the language or languages of the arbitration as soon as it is constituted.

The Arbitral Tribunal's authority under Article 16 to determine the language or languages of the arbitration is unchanged from Article 15(3) of the previous Rules. However, the former Rules instructed the Arbitral Tribunal, in arriving at this determination, to give due regard "in particular" to the language of the contract. This was already a somewhat looser approach than that taken by some other arbitration rules, which, in essence, provide that, where the parties have not otherwise agreed, the language of the arbitration shall be that of the contract.[452] In the New Rules, however, the significance of the language of the contract has been de-emphasized. Under Article 16, the Arbitral Tribunal is to give due regard to all relevant circumstances, "including," rather than "in particular," the language of the contract.

As the only circumstance expressly mentioned in Article 16 is the language of the contract, it is obviously intended to remain an important factor for the Arbitral Tribunal to consider when making its decision.[453] However, the Working Party was of the view that other circumstances may be equally, if not more, important in certain cases, and that arbitrators should therefore not be dissuaded from taking account of them, if appropriate. Thus, for example, where both the arbitrators and the lawyers for each side are either French or fluent in French, this may weigh in favor of using French as the language of the arbitration, even if the contract is in English. The case for doing so might be even stronger if witnesses would be required to testify in French, if relevant documentation were in French and French law applied. Moreover, there have been cases where, in such circumstances, one of the lawyers insisted on English, on the ground that the contract was in English, solely in order to disadvantage the other lawyer, whose English was poor. Article 16 is, thus, intended to discourage this sort of abuse.[454]

Finally, it should be noted that the language chosen as the language of the arbitration does not bind the Court and its Secretariat. As already indicated, the working languages of the Court are French and English, and it is under no obligation to use any other languages. The Secretariat and its counsel are nevertheless fluent in numerous languages and presently also administer cases in both German and Spanish in addition to using other languages, as required, from time to time (*see* Article 1(5) *supra*).

---

[452] Subject to modification by the Arbitral Tribunal if warranted by the circumstances. *See, e.g.*, AAA International Arbitration Rules, Article 14; LCIA Rules, Article 17; WIPO Arbitration Rules, Article 40(a).

[453] In contrast, Article 17 of the UNCITRAL Rules does not mention any specific element to be considered by the arbitrators.

[454] For an example of a case where an ICC arbitrator selected a language other than the language of the contract, partly in order to avoid advantaging one of the parties, *see* the decision of the Court of Appeal of Cologne (December 16, 1992), *ICCA Yearbook* XXI (1996), p. 535.

ARTICLE 17
Applicable Rules of Law

It is only since 1975 that the Rules have contained an express provision on the law applicable to the merits of the dispute.[455] While the provision adopted at the time (former Article 13(3)) was in line with then prevailing notions concerning the choice and application of the proper substantive law, over the years it came to be viewed as out-of-step with modern trends or, at least, insufficiently flexible. Article 17 is therefore intended to bring the Rules into line with developments in international arbitration practice and comparable provisions in other international arbitration rules.[456] It has been described as a "landmark," although nevertheless not "revolutionary."[457]

Article 17(1)

> *The parties shall be free to agree upon the rules of law to be applied by the Arbitral Tribunal to the merits of the dispute. In the absence of any such agreement, the Arbitral Tribunal shall apply the rules of law which it determines to be appropriate.*

Background. Like Article 13(3) before it, Article 17(1) is founded on the principle that the parties are "free to agree" upon the law applicable to the merits of the dispute. In the event that they fail to do so, it is then for the Arbitral Tribunal to decide what law ought to be applied. In the vast majority of ICC arbitrations, the choice of an applicable law does not give rise to any difficulty because it has been the subject of an agreement between the parties, usually in their contract.[458]

Article 17(1) contains two important changes from the text of the former provision on this subject. First, it replaces the prior reference to "law" with a reference to "rules of law." Not only are the parties free to agree on the application of "rules of law," but the Arbitral Tribunal is also expressly authorized to decide to apply appropriate "rules of law" in the event that the parties have not otherwise agreed. Second, in making such a decision, the Arbitral Tribunal is no longer required to choose the applicable law (or "rules of law") by reference to an

---

[455] All that was expressly stated in the 1955 Rules in this respect was that (Article 19(3)) the arbitrator did not have the power to act as *"amiable compositeur"* unless the parties so agreed.

[456] *See, e.g.,* AAA International Arbitration Rules, Article 28(1); LCIA Rules, Article 22(3); WIPO Arbitration Rules, Article 59.

[457] *See* Blessing, *supra,* note 188, p. 23.

[458] *See ICC Ct. Bull.,* Vol. 8, No. 1 (1997), p. 10 ("The governing substantive law applicable to the merits of the arbitration was mentioned in contractual provisions in 87% of cases [in 1996] (as compared to 81.7% in 1995).").

appropriate rule of conflict, as was previously the case. Instead, it may simply apply directly the rules of law that it determines to be appropriate.[459]

Rules of law. "Rules of law" is an obviously broad expression that, over the course of the last two decades, has increasingly crept its way into the international arbitration lexicon. The phrase can be found in the UNCITRAL Model Law (Article 28) (although not in the earlier UNCITRAL Rules) and in the most recent versions of the international arbitration rules of the AAA, LCIA and WIPO.

During the promulgation of the choice of law provision in the UNCITRAL Model Law, the proposed introduction of the phrase "rules of law" was a source of controversy.[460] The expression was criticized as an ambiguous one that might lead to uncertainty and other difficulties. Ultimately, the provison that emerged was a compromise that permitted the parties to agree to the application of "rules of law," but, in the event of their failure to agree, restricted the Arbitral Tribunal's choice to "the law determined by the conflict of laws rules which it considers applicable." For the drafters of the UNCITRAL Model Law, the expression "rules of law," moreover, was interpreted relatively narrowly as embracing:

> the national law of any State ... the national laws of different States ... (that is *dépeçage*) ... a given national law but ... [excluding] the provisons on a specific topic ... rules embodied in a convention or similar legal text elaborated on the international level, even if not yet in force ...

but not "general legal principles" or "law developed in "arbitration awards.""[461] As regards the latter, it appears to have been feared that the related rules were not sufficiently ascertainable.[462]

In the years since the Model Law's promulgation, however, the phrase "rules of law" has tended to be construed more broadly and has also gained more widespread acceptance.[463] It is, thus, now often described as including "legal rules pertaining to notions of a transnational law, *lex mercatoria* or general principles of law ... or the 1994 UNIDROIT Principles."[464] Of these, the so-called *lex mercatoria* (or literally, law of the merchant) is perhaps the most widely known,

---

[459] For a general discussion of the substantive law applicable in international arbitration, *see* Grigera Naón, *Choice of Law Problems in International Commercial Arbitration* (J.C.B. Mohr 1992); Gaillard, ed., *Transnational Rules in International Arbitration*, (ICC Publishing 1993); *Redfern and Hunter*, pp. 95 *et seq.*; *Fouchard Gaillard and Goldman*, p. 793; "The Law Applicable in International Arbitration," *ICCA Congress Series No. 7* (Kluwer 1996), p. 197.

[460] *See Holtzmann and Neuhaus*, pp. 766-68.

[461] *Id.*, p. 768.

[462] *Id.*

[463] This is not universally so, however. *See, e.g.,* Section 46 of the English Arbitration Act 1996, which is formulated in a manner similar to the former Rules.

[464] *See* Blessing, "Regulations in Arbitration Rules on Choice of Law," *ICCA Congress Series No. 7* (Kluwer 1996), p. 391; *see also* Blessing, *supra*, note 188, p. 24 and the works cited in note 459 *supra*. The UNIDROIT Principles are contained in *Principles of International Commercial Contracts*, International Institute for the Unification of Private Law (UNIDROIT) (Rome 1994).

given the extraordinary degree of attention and controversy that it has attracted over the years.[465] Indeed, the *lex mercatoria* and, more generally, references to anational and transnational rules have been criticized as ill-defined, uncertain, elusive and even "mythical."[466] The most vocal criticism has tended to come from the common law world, while support for the application of such principles has traditionally been strongest in continental Europe, where they were already being promoted more than three decades ago. In much of the developing world, meanwhile, such concepts still tend to be viewed with suspicion.

Nothwithstanding the controversy generated by references to transnational legal rules or the *lex mercatoria*, the actual application of such rules in ICC arbitration remains relatively uncommon. When contracting, it is most often to a single national law that the parties refer,[467] and this also remains the approach of most ICC arbitrators. However, in certain circumstances, recourse to such rules has appeared legitimate and appropriate to ICC arbitrators, and Awards have, thus, been made on this basis and also survived subsequent judicial challenge.[468]

---

[465] The term "*lex mercatoria*" has been described in a number of different ways and is increasingly used interchangeably with the expressions "general principles of international commercial law" or "transnational" rules of law. But, at its origin, it was more specifically concerned with a set of rules arising out of, and adapted to, international commerce. It has, thus, also sometimes been confused with the distinct concept of "trade usages" (*see* Article 17(2) *infra*) and with the exercise of powers of "*amiable composition*" (*see* Article 17(3) *infra*). But an arbitrator applying the *lex mercatoria* or transnational rules of law rather than State-created rules is nevertheless still deciding on the basis of law. *See Société Compania Valenciana de Cementos Portland c/ société Primary Coal Inc.*, *Cour de cassation* (October 22, 1991), Note Lagarde, *Rev. arb.* (1992), p. 457; Note Goldman, *Clunet* (1992), p. 177. *See* generally on this subject the works cited in note 459 *supra* and Goldman, "*La lex mercatoria dans les contrats et l'arbitrage international: réalité et perspectives*," *Clunet* (1979), p. 475; Paulsson, "*La lex mercatoria dans l'arbitrage CCI*," *Rev. arb.* (1990), p. 55; Lowenfeld, "*Lex mercatoria*: An Arbitrator's View," *Arb. Int.*, Vol. 6 (1990), p. 133; Mustill, "The New *Lex Mercatoria*, Twenty Five Years Later," *Liber Amicorum for Lord Wilberforce*, reprinted in *Arb. Int.*, Vol. 4 (1988), p. 86, 149; Gaillard, "Thirty Years of *Lex Mercatoria*: Towards the Discriminating Application of Transnational Rules," *ICCA Congress Series No. 7* (Kluwer 1996), p. 570.

[466] *See, e.g.,* Delaume, "The Proper Law of State Contracts and the *Lex Mercatoria*: A Reappraisal," *ICSID Review – Foreign Investment Law Journal*, No. 3 (1988), p. 79.

[467] There are different approaches that are nevertheless sometimes adopted in respect of national laws, such as the so-called "*tronc commun*" approach. See Rubino-Sammartano, "The Channel Tunnel and the *Tronc Commun* Doctrine," *J. Arb. Int.,* Vol. 10, No. 3 (1993), p. 59. In addition, references to the UNIDROIT Principles (*see* note 464 *supra*) are becoming more common, although still rare.

[468] *See Norsolor S.A. v. Pabalk Ticaret Sirketi* (March 18, 1982), *ICCA Yearbook IX* (1984), p. 159 (Austrian Supreme Court) and the judgments relating to the Award's enforcement in France, *Rev. arb.* (1983), p. 465; *see also Deutsche Schactbau-und Tiefbohrgesellschaft v. Ras Al Khaimah National Oil Co. and Shell International Petroleum Co. Ltd.*, [1987] 2 Lloyd's Rep. 246:

> By choosing to arbitrate under the rules of the ICC ... the parties have left the proper law to be decided by the arbitrators and have not in terms confirmed the choice to national systems of law. I can see no basis for concluding that the arbitrators' choice of proper law, a common denominator of principles underlying the laws of the various notions governing contractual relations is outwith the scope of the choice which the parties left to the arbitrators.

The possible appeal of such transnational principles has been explained in the following terms in a recent ICC Award:

> Application of international standards offers many advantages. They apply uniformly and are not dependent on the peculiarities of any particular national law. They take due account of the needs of international intercourse and permit cross-fertilization between systems that may be unduly wedded to conceptual distinctions and those that look for a pragmatic and fair resolution in the individual case.[469]

In cases where it appears appropriate to refer to such rules, Article 17(1), thus, now explicitly gives the parties and the arbitrators the right to do so.

Party agreement. The freedom of the parties to choose the law to be applied to the merits of the dispute is widely accepted.[470] As noted by one ICC Arbitral Tribunal:

> The principle of autonomy – widely recognized – allows the parties to choose any law to rule their contract, even if not obviously related to it.[471]

Thus, the Arbitral Tribunal does not ordinarily have to assess whether the parties' choice as regards the applicable law is well-founded or has any particular connection with the subject matter of the dispute. It has only to respect it.[472] Under the New Rules, the parties' freedom, as discussed above, also now expli-

---

[469] ICC Case No. 8385 (1995), Note Derains, *Clunet* (1997), p. 1061.

[470] Most of the time, this choice is expressed in the contract, often in the arbitration clause itself. However, parties should exercise care in this regard because they will wish to ensure that their choice of a governing law does not apply only in the case of an arbitration. It should also be noted that the choice of a law governing the contract is not necessarily the same as the choice of a law governing the "merits of the dispute," as under Article 17(1). Indeed, "the merits of the dispute" may extend to issues that are not governed by the contract as such. For recommendations in this regard, *see* Derains, "Choice of the Law Applicable to the Contract and International Arbitration," *ICC Ct. Bull.,* Vol. 6, No. 1 (1996), p. 10.

[471] ICC Case No. 4145 (1983), *see* note 191 *supra.*

[472] In the event that the Arbitral Tribunal fails to apply the law chosen by the parties, there may be a risk, at least in some jurisdictions, that the Award will be set aside. Indeed, this recently occurred in a non-ICC arbitration in Egypt upon an Egyptian court's finding that the Arbitral Tribunal had failed to apply the law agreed by the parties, as required by Egyptian law (an adapted version of the UNCITRAL Model Law). *See In the Matter of the Arbitration of Certain Controversies between Chromalloy Aeroservices and the Arab Republic of Egypt,* 939 F. Supp. 907 (D.D.C. 1996). However, this would not necessarily be the case in other jurisdictions. *See* on this subject Kühn, "Express and Implied Choice of the Substantive Law in the Practice of International Arbitration," *ICCA Congress Series No. 7* (Kluwer 1996), pp. 380, 388-89.

citly extends to "rules of law" (although this was already generally considered to be permissible under the previous Rules).[473]

The freedom that the parties enjoy to choose the law governing the merits of their dispute is nevertheless not unlimited. A considerable body of commentary and case law has, thus, emerged with respect to the possible application to a dispute of mandatory public laws (*e.g.,* antitrust or securities laws) irrespective of the choice of law made by the parties.[474] Moreover, depending upon how the parties have articulated their choice, it may not be exhaustive. Thus, for example, the choice of a law intended to govern the contract will not necessarily extend to claims of an extra-contractual nature arising in connection therewith and that nevertheless fall within the scope of the parties' arbitration clause, *e.g.,* claims arising in tort (although in many such cases, arbitrators have applied the *lex contractus* where the tortious acts were commited during performance of the contract).[475]

Absence of agreement. Under former Article 13(3), where the parties had not agreed upon the applicable law, the Arbitral Tribunal was to apply the law designated by "the rule of conflict" it deemed appropriate. Under Article 17, this requirement has now been abandoned, and ICC arbitrators are therefore free to choose directly (by "*voie directe*") the appropriate applicable law without reference to any choice of law rule. The abandonment of the former requirement is consistent with recent trends in international arbitration that are now widely accepted.[476] It is also the culmination of a gradual evolution in international thinking on this subject.

---

[473] It is now recognized in many countries that the parties may make their contract subject to anational rules. This is the stance taken by, *inter alia*, Article 1496 of the French New Code of Civil Procedure, Article 187(1) of the Swiss Private International Law Act, Article 28 of the UNCITRAL Model Law (as noted *supra*), Article 813 of the Lebanese New Code of Civil Procedure, Article 458bis(14) of the Algerian Legislative Decree of August 23, 1983, and Article 73(1) of the Tunisian Law of August 26, 1993. Such a right also was expressly recognized in 1992 by the work of the International Law Association's Cairo Conference. *See* Gaillard, ed., *supra,* note 459.

[474] *See, e.g.,* Lazareff, "Mandatory Extraterritorial Application of National Law Rules," *ICCA Congress Series No. 7* (Kluwer 1996), p. 538; Hochstrasser, "Choice of Law and Foreign Mandatory Rules in International Arbitration," *J. Arb. Int.*, Vol. 11, No. 1 (1994), p. 57; Derains, "Public Policy and the Law Applicable to the Dispute in International Arbitration," *ICCA Congress Series No. 3* (Kluwer 1987), p. 227; Mayer, "Mandatory Rules of Law in International Arbitration," *Arb. Int.*, Vol. 2, No. 4 (1986), p. 274.

[475] *See* Reymond, "*Conflits de lois en matière de responsabilité délictuelle devant l'arbitre international,*" *Travaux du Comité Français de Droit International Privé, 1988-1989*, p. 97.

[476] *See, e.g.,* AAA International Arbitration Rules, Article 28(1); LCIA Rules, Article 23(a); WIPO Arbitration Rules, Article 59. *See also* Article 1496 of the French New Code of Civil Procedure. *But cf.* UNCITRAL Model Law, Article 28, which requires the application of an "applicable" rule of conflict, and Section 46 of the English Arbitration Act 1996.

Thus, it was the prevailing view forty years ago that, in the absence of party agreement, the arbitrators should determine the applicable substantive law by applying the choice of law system of the place of arbitration.[477] But this view was not universally shared, and, indeed, some commentators were already contending at the time that the international arbitrator "is not bound to apply the rules of conflict of one country rather than the rules of another ... ."[478] Thus, within a few years, the prevailing view had shifted, and, in 1961, when the European Convention on International Commercial Arbitration (the "Geneva Convention") was adopted, it provided (Article VII(1)):

> The parties shall be free to determine, by agreement, the law to be applied by the arbitrators to the substance of the dispute. Failing any indication by the parties as to the applicable law, the arbitrators shall apply the proper law under the rule of conflict that the arbitrators deem applicable ... .

By the early-1970s, this more modern approach had become firmly established in ICC practice.[479] Thus, when a provision on the applicable substantive law (Article 13(3)) was first added to the Rules in 1975, it tracked almost *verbatim* the language of the Geneva Convention. Article 13(3) provided:

> The parties shall be free to determine the law to be applied by the arbitrator to the merits of the dispute. In the absence of any indication by the parties as to the applicable law, the arbitrator shall apply the law designated as the proper law by the rule of conflict which he deems appropriate.

ICC practice continued to develop, however, and soon arbitrators began to view the phrase "the rule of conflict" as designating individual conflict rules as opposed to a *system* of conflict rules. An award rendered in 1982, for example, stated that:

> The Arbitral Tribunal has a broad power of appreciation in the choice of the applicable law, a discretionary power, and, if it is free to refer to all systems of conflict of law to which it has access, it is in no way obliged to give preference to one of the systems over another.[480]

---

[477] *See, e.g.,* the resolution adopted by the Institute of International Law in Amsterdam in 1957 (*Annuaire de l'Institut du droit international*, Vol. II (1957), p. 484). *See also* Mann, "Lex Facit Arbitrum," *Liber Amicorum Martin Domke* (1967), p. 157, *and reprinted in Arb. Int.*, Vol. 2, No. 3 (1986), p. 241.

[478] *See* Batiffol, "L'arbitrage et les conflits de lois," *Rev. arb.* (1957), p. 111.

[479] *See* the Award in ICC Case No. 1512 (1971), *supra*, note 437 ("[T]he international arbitrator has no *lex fori*, from which he can borrow rules of conflict of laws.").

[480] *See* the Award in ICC Case No. 2730 (1982), *supra*, note 191.

Indeed, by the late-1970s, arbitrators were regularly employing a variety of methods for choosing the appropriate substantive law where this had not been agreed to by the parties, including: (i) application of the place of arbitration's conflict of law system; (ii) the cumulative application of the conflict systems of the different States that might be in some way connected to the dispute or the arbitration; (iii) the use of general principles of private international law; and (iv) the so-called *"voie directe"* rule.[481]

Questions were nevertheless sometimes raised as to whether all of these diverse approaches were consistent with the text of Article 13(3). In particular, doubts were occasionally expressed as to whether an arbitrator could validly decide to apply anational rules under Article 13(3) insofar as any "rule of conflict" that might be used would inevitably point only to a national law.[482] It was, thus, considered appropriate by the authors of the New Rules to adapt the provision on the choice of the applicable law to the realities of ICC arbitration practice, both in respect of the manner in which the applicable law is determined and the possible application by the arbitrators, like the parties, of "rules of law."

Notwithstanding the alteration of the former text, an Arbitral Tribunal nevertheless remains free to apply a rule of conflict if it considers this appropriate, whether that rule originates in a national legal system, an international convention or general principles of international private law. Indeed, the arbitrators may devise their own rule of conflict. However, whatever method is employed, the arbitrators must provide a reasoned explanation for their choice in accordance with the legitimate expectations of the parties.[483]

Indeed, decisions regarding the law to be applied to the merits often take the form of a partial Award. In some cases, the arbitrators may prefer to issue such decisions in the form of an order since the parties will want to know the tribunal's determination as quickly as possible, and an order can be delivered more quickly than an Award. Any such orders, however, would be required to be

---

[481] *See generally*, Lalive, *"Les règles de conflit de lois appliquées au fond du litige par l'arbitre international siégeant en Suisse,"* Rev. arb. (1976), p. 155; *Craig, Park and Paulsson*, §§8.04, 17.02; Derains, *"Attente légitime des parties et droit applicable au fond en matière d'arbitrage commercial international,"* Travaux du Comité Français du Droit International Privé, 1984-1985, p. 81.

[482] *See, e.g.,* comments of A. Baum *in* Gaillard, ed., *supra*, note 459, p. 52 ("It can be argued that a choice of law rule cannot lead to the application of transnational rules but only to the rules of the legal system which is the most closely connected with the situation.")

[483] For examples of the decisions of ICC arbitrators on this subject, *see* the extracts of Awards in *ICC Ct. Bull.*, Vol. 1, No. 2 (1990), p. 22.

incorporated subsequently into an Award setting forth the reasons for the Arbitral Tribunal's decision.[484]

Article 17(2)

> *In all cases, the Arbitral Tribunal shall take account of the provisions of the contract and the relevant trade usages.*

This provision, which is virtually unchanged from its predecessor, Article 13(5), addresses a concern that is often paramount in the minds of users of the ICC Rules. Parties frequently turn to arbitration out of a fear that were they to submit their diputes to a judicial forum, the structure of their relationship and the realities of the environment in which they conduct their business would become submerged under waves of obscure legal technicalities.[485] Article 17(2) serves to assure parties that "[i]n all cases," whatever legal rules may apply to their dispute, the Arbitral Tribunal will not lose sight of either the terms of their contract or the business practices of their trade.

In this respect, Article 17(2) does not differ from most other arbitration rules. However, it is to be noted that, insofar as the contract is concerned, Article 17(2) merely obliges the Arbitral Tribunal "to take account of its provisions," and, unlike some other rules, does not explicitly require the tribunal to render its decision "in accordance" therewith.[486] One reason for this is that the Arbitral Tribunal cannot reasonably be expected to decide "in accordance" with the provisions of the contract if they are not valid under the applicable rules of law.[487]

---

[484] *See* "Final Report on Interim and Partial Awards," *supra*, note 62, p. 28:
Pre-judicial questions, including decisions relating to jurisdiction, and decisions on the applicable law, may be treated together for the purposes of this discussion as falling within the category of decisions which, in theory, may be the subject of an award but are not required to be so by legal principles. In general, however, since such decisions are intended to be final, and can normally be challenged before national courts, it seems desirable that they should be reasoned and drawn up in the form of an award. The attention of the Working Party has been drawn to the present policy of the Court of Arbitration that, regardless of any agreement of the parties, decisions on jurisdiction and the applicable law should be made in the form of an award to be scrutinised pursuant to Article 21 of the Rules, whenever they are made.

[485] *See Craig Park and Paulsson,* §17.03 ("Businessmen frequently feel that courts do not understand the realities of trade and commerce. Arbitrators, whose mission is derived entirely from the parties' contract should, and generally do, give precedence to the rules the parties established for the relationship, *i.e.* the terms of their contract.").

[486] *Cf.* AAA International Arbitration Rules, Article 28(2)); UNCITRAL Rules, Article 33(3). *See also* UNCITRAL Model Law, Article 28(4)).

[487] *See* Award in ICC Case No. 2119 (1978), *ICC Arbitral Awards 1974-1985*, annotated by Derains, where the arbitrators held that a clause indicating that a contract should be "performed and interpreted in accordance with French law" meant that "the contractual provisions were directly applicable, insofar as they did not run counter to the mandatory provisions of French law." In addition, when acting as an *amiable compositeur* pursuant to Article 17(3) *infra*, the Arbitral Tribunal may, to a certain extent, legitimately depart from the terms of the contract, while nevertheless continuing to take them into account.

Indeed, if a contract has to be performed "in accordance with" a given law but contains stipulations that are contrary to that particular law's public policy, it cannot be performed as stipulated.

Meanwhile, the relevant "trade usages" to which Article 17(2) refers should not be confused, as they sometimes are, with the distinct concept of *lex mercatoria*. Because both *lex mercatoria* and trade usages are to a certain extent each related to customary business practices, the frontier between the two is not always clearly perceived.[488] But the term "*lex mercatoria*," as already discussed (*see* note 465 *supra*), is ordinarily intended to refer to legal rules arising out of international commerce. Trade usage, on the other hand, normally constitutes part of the parties' agreement (unless excluded). That is, parties expect that the contracts they conclude, unless specifically agreed otherwise, will be performed in accordance with the usual practices observed in their area of business. Thus, unlike *lex mercatoria*, trade usage is internal, not external to the parties' agreement:

> Usages may be deemed incorporated into the contract as a matter of specific intent (for instance, if reference is made in the contract to Incoterms, or contracting regulations), or by implication (a custom is not referred to but is deemed by the arbitrators to have been within the contemplation of the parties).[489]

Trade usages may be broadly grouped into two categories. First are those usages that arise out of the parties' own course of dealing. Second are those practices known to and regularly observed by contracting parties in the particular area of trade. This distinction is reflected, for example, in Article 1(8), "Usages and Practices," of the UNIDROIT Principles of International Contracts, as follows:

(1) The parties are bound by any usage to which they have agreed and by any practices which they have established between themselves.
(2) The parties are bound by a usage that is widely known to and regularly observed in international trade by parties in the particular trade

---

[488] *See, e.g.* Award in ICC Case No. 3380 (1980) (Lalive, Chairman), *ICCA Yearbook* VII (1982), pp. 116, 119 ("It is not excluded that [general principles of law] are, partly, the same as the "trade usages ... ."). *See also Fouchard Gaillard and Goldman*, pp. 856-58.

[489] *Craig, Park and Paulsson*, §17.03, p. 295. Whether or not one accepts as a theoretical matter that trade usage may be regarded as an express or implied contractual term, as a practical matter, it is commonly taken into account by international arbitrators. *See, e.g.,* Aksen, "The Law Applicable in International Arbitration: Relevance of Reference to Trade Usages," *ICCA Congress Series No. 7* (Kluwer 1996), pp. 471-72 ("In fact, while it is difficult to quantify with certainty, my recollection is that trade usage helps determine the result as much as the applicable law clause does.").

concerned except where the application of such usage would be unreasonable.[490]

Article 17(3)

> *The Arbitral Tribunal shall assume the powers of an amiable compositeur or decide ex aequo et bono only if the parties have agreed to give it such powers.*

A provision concerning the possible exercise by the Arbitral Tribunal of the powers of an *"amiable compositeur"* has been included in the Rules ever since the first ICC Rules were published in 1922. What is new in Article 17(3) is the addition of the term *"ex aequo et bono."* In adding the latter expression to the Rules, the ICC was motivated by the same considerations that have caused both phrases to be included in other rules and laws,[491] *i.e.,* some legal systems use one term and some use the other, while considerable uncertainty surrounds their precise meaning and the possible differences, if any, between the two.[492]

Historically, both terms are products of the civil law and have to do with an arbitrator deciding a case on the basis of fairness and equitable considerations. The related issues that typically arise are whether and, if so, to what extent, an arbitrator who is so authorized can disregard either the provisions of law that would otherwise apply or the terms of the parties' contract. Moreover, there may also be a question as to the enforceability of the arbitrators' Award in jurisdictions that may not recognize an arbitrator's authority to derogate from the law.[493]

---

[490] *See also*, the United Nations Convention on Contracts for the International Sale of Goods, Article 9, which similarly provides: "(1) The parties are bound by any usage to which they have agreed and by any practices which they have established between themselves; (2) The parties are considered, unless otherwise agreed, to have impliedly made applicable to their contract or its formation a usage of which the parties knew or ought to have known and which in international trade is widely known to, and regularly observed by, parties to contracts of the type involved in the particular trade concerned."

[491] *See, e.g.,* UNCITRAL Model Law, Article 28(3) ("The arbitral tribunal shall decide *ex aequo et bono* or as *amiable compositeur* only if the parties have expressly authorized it to do so."); UNCITRAL Rules, Article 33(2) ("The arbitral tribunal shall decide as *amiable compositeur* or *ex aequo et bono* only if the parties have expressly authorised the tribunal to do so and if the law applicable to the arbitral procedure permits such arbitration."); AAA International Arbitration Rules, Article 28(3); WIPO Arbitration Rules, Article 59(a).

[492] *See, e.g.,* in this connection, *Fouchard Gaillard and Goldman*, p. 847; *Craig Park and Paulsson*, Chapter 18, p. 308; Loquin, *L'amiable composition en droit comparé et international* (Librairies Techniques 1980); Christie, "Amiable Composition in French and English Law," *Arbitration*, Vol. 58, No. 4 (1992), p. 259; Briner, "Special Considerations which May Affect the Procedure (Interim Measures, *Amiable Composition*, Adaptation of Contracts, Agreed Settlement)," *ICCA Congress Series No. 7* (Kluwer 1996), p. 362; Kerr, "'Equity' Arbitration in England," *Am. Rev. Int. Arb.,* Vol. 2, No. 4 (1991), pp. 377, 383-86.

[493] This was, until recently, a subject of concern in England, in particular. *See* Kerr, *supra*, note 492. However, Section 46 of the English Arbitration Act 1996 now expressly authorizes an Arbitral Tribunal to decide a dispute in accordance with considerations other than the law.

At its most basic, the term *"amiable compositeur"* refers to an arbitrator's power to depart from the strict application of a legal rule, if necessary, in order to reach a fairer resolution of a dispute. In determining whether a strict rule of law should or should not be adapted, *amiable compositeurs* seem to follow two general approaches.[494] First, the result that would arise from strict application of legal rules can be compared against such general principles as the presumption that parties normally intend their dealings to result in a *quid pro quo*, that the risks of their bargain will be borne equally and that both parties will perform in good faith.[495] Second, the *amiable compositeur* may "seek a business solution which creates or recreates a peaceable or even friendly climate between the parties ... and [thereby weakens] the juridical character of the dispute in favour of its technical, psychological and commercial aspects."[496]

In French law, where the institution of the *amiable compositeur* originated, the power of such a person to disregard the law appears very broad. Indeed, it is generally admitted that an *amiable compositeur* can disregard any laws from which a party would be free to derogate, *i.e.,* all those other than mandatory rules of law. Moreover, an *amiable compositeur* in France may also depart, to some extent, from the strict application of the contract, without, however, being able to modify the basic terms of the parties' bargain.[497] Whether or not, however, an arbitrator acting as an *amiable compositeur* or deciding *ex aequo et bono* would be considered to have precisely the same degree of freedom to depart from either the law or the terms of the contract in all jurisdictions is not entirely certain. But it is increasingly doubted that there is any meaningful difference between the two concepts.[498]

As in the case of the former Rules, the New Rules strictly limit the authority of an Arbitral Tribunal to decide *ex aequo et bono* or as an *amiable compositeur*. Under Article 17(3), it may assume such authority "only if the parties have agreed" to grant it this power. Moreover, where such authority has been conferred, Article 18(1)(g) provides that it must be specified in the Terms of Reference, thus alerting the Court. In addition, irrespective of whether such authority has been conferred on an Arbitral Tribunal, it is still required to prepare a reasoned Award pursuant to Article 25(2) of the Rules and to submit it to the Court for scrutiny and approval pursuant to Article 27 (*see infra*).

---

[494] *See generally* Loquin, *supra*, note 492.

[495] *See Craig Park and Paulsson,* §8.05, p. 138.

[496] *See* Christie, *supra*, note 492, p. 264. For an example of an ICC arbitrator's interpretation of his powers as an *amiable compositeur*, see Award in ICC Case No. 3755 (1988), *ICC Ct. Bull.*, Vol. 1, No. 2 (1990), p. 25.

[497] *See, e.g., Fouchard Gaillard and Goldman*, pp. 852-53. But pursuant to Article 18(2) of the Rules, an ICC arbitrator must "in all cases" nevertheless "take account of the provisions of the contract."

[498] *See Fouchard Gaillard and Goldman*, p. 849; *see also* Derains, commenting on ICC Case No. 6503 (1990), *ICC Arbitral Awards 1991-1995*, p. 613.

ARTICLE 18
Terms of Reference; Procedural Timetable

The Terms of Reference are one of the most distinctive features of ICC arbitration. No document of this type is required to be drawn up under the rules of any of the other major international arbitration institutions, although it has become increasingly common in non-ICC arbitrations for a document resembling the Terms of Reference to be prepared.[499]

Background. The Terms of Reference have their origin in a requirement of the first ICC Rules published in 1922 (Article XXXIV), according to which the Secretary of the Court was to draw up a "form of submission" describing, among other things, the names of the parties and arbitrators, the place and subject of the arbitration and the claims of the parties. The "form of submission" was then to be sent to the parties concerned for signature. If one of the parties refused to sign, the Court could direct the arbitration to proceed in default. The ICC's objective was apparently two-fold: first, to lend to the arbitration from the outset the formal *imprimatur* of the Court; and second, to obtain a signed form of submission (*compromis*) that would be recognized as binding in jurisdictions, of which there were still many, that did not recognize the validity of an agreement to arbitrate future disputes.[500] During the Court's first three decades, there were few changes in the Rules' requirements relating to the "form of submission." Then, in 1955, as part of the major reform of the ICC Rules that occurred in that year, the "form of submission" was eliminated, and in its place emerged the "Terms of Reference," to be drawn up by the arbitrator (rather than the Court).

The Terms of Reference that were introduced into the 1955 Rules were very similar to the Terms of Reference contained in the Rules when they were next revised in 1975 and to the document that is now required to be drawn up under Article 18. Unlike today, however, the Terms of Reference were then always required to be approved by the Court, and no deadline was specified for their preparation, provided, only, that they be drawn up "[b]efore beginning the hearing of a case" (1955 Rules, Article 19). In 1975, the requirement of Court

---

[499] The Terms of Reference have been the subject of considerable comment. *See* "Practical Guide" prepared by a Working Group of the ICC Commission (S. Lazareff, Chairman), *ICC Ct. Bull.*, Vol. 3, No. 1 (1992), p. 24; *see also* Schäfer, "Terms of Reference in the Past and at Present," *ICC Ct. Bull.* Vol. 3, No. 1 (May 1992), p. 8; Arnaldez *"L'acte déterminant la mission de l'arbitre,"* Etudes offertes à Pierre Bellet (Litec 1991), p. 1; Reiner, "Terms of Reference: the Function of the International Court of Arbitration and Application of Article 16 by the Arbitrators," *ICC Ct. Bull.*, Vol. 7, No. 2 (1996), p. 59; Schneider, "The Terms of Reference," *The New 1998 ICC Rules of Arbitration, ICC Ct. Bull.,* Special Supplement (1997), p. 26; *Craig Park and Paulsson*, Chapter 15, p. 251.

[500] *See* Schäfer, *supra*, note 499, p. 9.

approval was removed, except where one of the parties would not sign them, and a two-month deadline was introduced for their communication to the Court.[501]

The changes made in 1975 were intended to simplify and accelerate the procedures associated with the Terms of Reference, which were then the subject of considerable criticism, the principal one being that they were a source of undue delay without any countervailing benefits. Indeed, during the discussion of the 1975 Rules revisions within the ICC Commission, the retention of the Terms of Reference was approved by only a slight majority.[502] Although such criticisms persisted for years after the adoption of the 1975 Rules,[503] increasing numbers of practitioners have come to appreciate them as a useful device in the context of international arbitration proceedings. Thus, in contrast to the controversy surrounding them in 1975, the Terms of Reference were the subject of widespread support during the preparation of the New Rules. Indeed, all of the ICC's National Committees but one favored their retention. The greater source of controversy concerned the Working Party's proposal (as discussed *infra*), that the Arbitral Tribunal be given the option of deciding whether to include in the Terms of Reference a list of the issues to be determined, which the then Rules required in all cases.

The support that the Terms of Reference currently enjoy can be attributed, in large measure, to the order that they are capable of bringing to an international proceeding at an early stage of the process. It is no longer necessary, in most jurisdictions, for parties to enter into a submission agreement after a dispute has arisen.[504] The Terms of Reference therefore no longer have any legal function in

---

[501] It was also in 1975 that it was for the first time specified that the Terms of Reference were to be drawn up in the light of the parties' "most recent submissions," an addition that was specifically made, as discussed further below, in order to indicate that parties were free to make additional claims and submissions up until that time. *See* Eisemann, *supra*, note 101, p. 360.

[502] Typical of the criticisms at the time was the following observation: "[T]he rules could very well do without that provision. In quite a few cases the omission of that provision would save all participants in the process considerable effort and time without draw-backs for the finding of justice." Böckstiegel, "The New Arbitration Rules of the International Chamber of Commerce," *International Economic Order: Essays in Honor of F.A. Mann* (Verlag C.H. Beck 1977), pp. 575, 586.

[503] *See, e.g.,* Wetter, *supra*, note 13, p. 101 (Terms of Reference described as an "antiquated relic").

[504] But this is not universally true. *See* GrigeraNaón, *supra*, note 187. In those places where a submission agreement may be required, the Terms of Reference may therefore still serve the useful purpose of ensuring that there is one. In addition, where the original arbitration agreement has been lost or where there may otherwise be doubts concerning the existence or validity of an arbitration agreement, the unconditional signature of the Terms of Reference by all parties may be regarded as a new agreement to arbitrate. *See Zanzi Fruitgrowing Equipment SpA c/ Semena I Possadatchen Material, Cour d'appel de Paris* (February 25, 1993) (unpublished); *Société Kis France c/ Société A.B.S., Cour d'appel de Paris* (March 19, 1987), *Rev. arb.* (1987), p. 498. *See also American Construction Machinery Equipment Corporation Ltd.* v. *Mechanised Construction of Pakistan Ltd,* 659 F. Supp. 426 (S.D.N.Y. 1987). *But cf.* the judgment of the Court of Appeal of Cologne, Germany (December 16, 1992), *supra,* note 454 (court refused to treat Terms of Reference signed by only one of the parties as an arbitration agreement). *See also Craig Park and Paulsson,* §15.05, pp. 261-68; *Fouchard Gaillard and Goldman,* pp. 687-89.

most cases. But by setting forth the particulars of the dispute and, above all, the claims of the parties within the framework of a simple document:

> [The Terms of Reference] permit[] the arbitral tribunal to establish a rational structure and organization for the future path of the entire arbitration.[505]

The Terms of Reference are also widely perceived as having the following advantages, *inter alia*:[506]

– Providing the parties and the arbitrators with an opportunity to identify and possibly agree on procedural and other matters, such as the applicable law, the language of the arbitration and the timetable for the arbitration.
– Affording the parties and arbitrators the further possibility of identifying the substantive issues that will be required to be addressed in the arbitration.
– Obliging the parties to ensure that all of their claims and counterclaims have been raised (subject, however, to the provisions of Article 19, as discussed *infra*).
– Delimiting the precise scope of the Arbitral Tribunal's mandate in order to help ensure that the Award ultimately rendered is neither *ultra* nor *infra petita*.

Indeed, in relation to the last of the foregoing matters, the Terms of Reference have long served as a useful aid to the Court, in checking whether all of the parties' claims and counterclaims (but no others) have been decided, when it scrutinizes the arbitrators' draft Award pursuant to Article 27 (*see infra*). Without the Terms of Reference, this would be a more arduous exercise, given the large quantities of often inconsistent pleadings and notes supplied by the parties.[507]

Changes. Article 18, thus, makes few changes from the provisions concerning the Terms of Reference that were formerly set forth in Article 13 of the prior Rules. The principal change is that the Arbitral Tribunal has been given the option, if "inappropriate," of omitting the list of issues that was previously required to be included in all cases. In addition, Article 18 no longer requires, as did Article 13(2), that the Court set a time-limit for the execution of the Terms of Reference by a party that has refused to sign them. Nor is the entry into effect of the Terms of Reference any longer dependent upon full payment of the advance on costs fixed by the Court for the arbitration (*see* Article 30 *infra*), as was formerly the case under Article 9(4). All of these changes are intended to

---

[505] *See* Bond, *supra*, note 255, p. 116. The importance of addressing at an early stage the many issues that may arise in connection with the preparation of Terms of Reference has recently led UNCITRAL to issue its "Notes on Organizing Arbitral Proceedings" (1996).

[506] *See* "Practical Guide," *supra*, note 499, p. 27.

[507] But as discussed below, the Terms of Reference cannot be relied upon exclusively in this regard.

ensure that the Terms of Reference do not impede the progress of the arbitration. Similarly, in order to encourage the expeditious conduct of the case, a new provision has been added (Article 18(4)) that requires the Arbitral Tribunal to establish a "provisional timetable" when drawing up the Terms of Reference.

Article 18(1)

> *As soon as it has received the file from the Secretariat, the Arbitral Tribunal shall draw up, on the basis of documents or in the presence of the parties and in the light of their most recent submissions, a document defining its Terms of Reference. This document shall include the following particulars:*
> *a) the full names and descriptions of the parties;*
> *b) the addresses of the parties to which notifications and communications arising in the course of the arbitration may be made;*
> *c) a summary of the parties' respective claims and of the relief sought by each party, with an indication to the extent possible of the amounts claimed or counterclaimed;*
> *d) unless the Arbitral Tribunal considers it inappropriate, a list of issues to be determined;*
> *e) the full names, descriptions and addresses of the arbitrators;*
> *f) the place of the arbitration; and*
> *g) particulars of the applicable procedural rules and, if such is the case, reference to the power conferred upon the Arbitral Tribunal to act as amiable compositeur or to decide ex aequo et bono.*

Contents of the Terms of Reference. Apart from the names and addresses of the parties and arbitrators and the place of the arbitration, Article 18(1), like Article 13(1) of the prior Rules, provides for the inclusion in the Terms of Reference of three broad categories of information: (i) a summary of the parties' respective claims; (ii) a list of issues; and (iii) particulars of applicable procedural rules. Unlike under Article 13(1), however, the list of issues may now be excluded if "inappropriate." In addition, there is no longer any provision for the inclusion of "such other particulars as may be required to make the arbitral award enforceable at law, or may be regarded as helpful by the Court or the arbitrator." As a practical matter, this provision was generally disregarded, and it did not appear to the drafters of the New Rules that it needed to be maintained. The preparation of the Terms of Reference nevertheless provides both the parties and the Arbitral Tribunal with an appropriate opportunity to review, and take account of, any mandatory provisions of law that may be applicable to the arbitration. Furthermore, although not required, it is common for arbitrators to set out in the Terms of Reference the relevant arbitration clause. This is generally regarded as useful by the Court when reviewing the Terms of Reference, particularly if they are required to be approved pursuant to Article 18(3), and subsequently when scrutinizing the arbitrators' Award.[508]

(i) *Summary of Parties' Claims*

The summary of the claims required by Article 18(1) lies at the heart of the Terms of Reference. It is normally expected to include, in addition to the claims, a summary of the parties' related arguments.[509] The summary is relevant, not only for the purpose of verifying subsequently that the arbitrators have decided all of the claims referred to them, but also because it circumscribes the parties' right to introduce "new" claims or counterclaims thereafter under Article 19 of the Rules, as discussed below.[510] In this connection, one of the most delicate issues in ICC arbitration has long been how to determine whether or not a claim made after the Terms of Reference is a "new" claim and, if so, whether it falls "outside the limits" of the Terms of Reference according to Article 19.[511] Indeed, there appear to be many different conceptions internationally as to what constitutes a "claim" and, more particularly, of what is a "new claim."[512] Parties and arbitrators need to be attentive to these issues when the Terms of Reference are being prepared and also to take account of how the "claims" may evolve during the course of the arbitration. However, the description of the claims in the Terms

---

[508] The Rules only contemplate a single set of Terms of Reference for an ICC arbitration. However, in one unusual case several years ago, where one of the parties contested the tribunal's jurisdiction, the Court permitted partial Terms of Reference to be prepared with respect to the jurisdictional phase of the arbitration on the understanding that they would be followed by additional Terms of Reference for the remainder of the arbitration if the Arbitral Tribunal upheld its jurisdiction. *See also Craig Park and Paulsson*, §15.02, p. 256 ("Where jurisdiction is seriously contested, two Terms of Reference may be conceivable: one to determine the jurisdictional questions and another concerning the merits of the dispute to be drafted subsequently if jurisdiction is found to exist."). As stated, however, the Rules do not provide explicit authority for such an approach and it is uncertain whether the Court would necessarily accept this, notwithstanding the foregoing precedent.

[509] *See* "Practical Guide," *supra,* note 499, pp. 34-35.

[510] Parties may sometimes seek to have included in the summary of their claims a reservation of their right to introduce new claims subsequently. However, any such reservation, if unilateral and unlimited, would be likely to be considered by the Court as contrary to Article 19. Reservations made with the agreement of all parties and subject to specified conditions have been permitted, however. *See, e.g.,* the Award in ICC Case No. 7314 (1995), *ICC Ct. Bull.,* Vol. 8, No. 2 (1997), p. 72; *and* "Practical Guide," *supra,* note 499, p. 70.

[511] *See,* with respect to this issue in particular, Reiner, *supra,* note 499, p. 65.

[512] Part of the difficulty stems from the different terminology used in different legal systems for "claims" or elements of "claims." This is, in fact, illustrated by the French version of the Rules, where Article 18 requires a summary of the parties' *"prétentions"* while Article 19 restricts the introduction of new claims to new *"demandes."* *See also* Perret, *"Les Conclusions et les Chefs de Demande dans l'Arbitrage International,"* ASA Bull. (1996), No. 1, p. 7; *and* Perret, *"Les conclusions et leur cause juridique au regard de la règle, ne eat judex ultra petita partium,"* Etudes de Droit International en l'honneur de Pierre Lalive (Helbing & Lichtenhahn 1993), p. 594.

of Reference should not normally foreclose the making of new allegations or arguments or the introduction of new evidence in the arbitration.[513]

In addition, the erroneous omission from the Terms of Reference of a claim or counterclaim contained in the parties' previous submissions ought not to preclude its inclusion in the subsequent proceedings. The purpose of the Terms of Reference is to describe the parties' claims, but not in any way to replace or supersede them. For the same reason, the signature by a party of the Terms of Reference does not, in any way, constitute an acceptance of any of the claims or defenses being asserted by the other party in the arbitration. Rather, it is no more than an acknowledgment that the parties' respective claims have been properly described.

Fearing a possible omission from the Terms of Reference, or otherwise because they do not wish to make the effort to work their way through the claims, arbitrators may occasionally propose that the summary of the claims consist of a simple reference to the earlier submissions of the parties. However, this is not generally regarded as acceptable by the Court and, indeed, would defeat one of the very purposes of the Terms of Reference, which is to impose a certain discipline on the arbitrators in organizing the proceedings at an early stage.

Unlike former Article 13(1), Article 18(1) requires that the summary of claims be accompanied by a description of the "relief sought" and "to the extent possible" an indication of "the amounts claimed or counterclaimed." The latter requirement relates to the Court's need to know the amount of the "sum in dispute" when fixing the advance on costs in accordance with the scales appended to the Rules (*see* Article 30 *infra*).[514] Under the New Rules, the advance on costs can ordinarily be expected to be fixed or reviewed by the Court when the Terms of Reference are received by it from the Arbitral Tribunal.

(ii) *List of Issues*

The list of "issues" to be determined is not to be confused with the description of the parties' claims. The reference to "issues" in Article 18(1), as in Article 13(1), is intended to identify:

> the questions of fact and substantive or procedural law which at the time of drafting appear to be relevant to the adjudication of the parties' claims.[515]

The list of "issues" is not required to be comprehensive, nor is it intended to preclude the consideration of other "issues" that may arise in the course of the arbi-

---

[513] *See, e.g.,* "Practical Guide," *supra,* note 499, p. 34 and the discussion of Article 19 *infra*.

[514] However, in order to avoid any risk that an increase in the amount of the claim might subsequently be said to fall outside the limits of the Terms of Reference, parties should normally reserve their right to increase that amount.

[515] *See* "Practical Guide," *supra,* note 499, p. 35.

tration. It is, of course, commonly the case that the "issues" in an arbitration will evolve as the case progresses. Thus, unlike in the case of the claims, the arbitrators' mandate and their authority to consider additional issues should not be restricted by the description of the issues in the Terms of Reference.[516] The inclusion in the Rules of a requirement that the issues be listed therefore derives, not from any wish to limit the confines of the arbitration, but rather from the desire to promote efficiency through early identification of the questions requiring resolution and possibly also to assist the parties and the arbitrators in understanding the claims being made.

This being said, listing the issues at the time of the Terms of Reference may not always be easy or even helpful, particularly in those cases where the parties have not provided sufficient details of their respective claims and defenses. In such cases, it may simply be too early for the Arbitral Tribunal to prepare a meaningful list of issues. Occasionally, moreover, the identification of issues, and the related degree of specificity, may become a battleground between the parties, with each of them maneuvering to obtain a list that it considers is as favorable as possible to its position in the case. This, in turn, may lead to delay in the completion of the Terms of Reference or possibly even result in the refusal by one of the parties to sign them. In the face of such difficulties, some ICC arbitrators, thus, have developed the practice of simply describing the issues as those arising from the claims and counterclaims of the parties.[517] While such a practice was most probably not within the contemplation of the ICC when the requirement that the issues be described was originally included in the Rules, it has nevertheless been grudgingly tolerated by the Court whenever the Terms of Reference are signed by all of the parties.

In the circumstances, it was decided, when the New Rules were adopted, to make the list of issues an optional requirement. Thus, Article 18(1), unlike Article 13(1), provides that it may be omitted if considered by the Arbitral Tribunal to be "inappropriate." In addition, the word "list" was substituted for the term "definition," which was used in the prior Rules. The earlier requirement that the Terms of Reference "define" (rather than "list") the issues may have conveyed the impression to some that the description of the issues is intended to be definitive.

---

[516] This has been confirmed, moreover, by a decision of the French Court of Cassation on March 6, 1996 in which it was held that the arbitrators' mandate is a function of the parties' claims and not the definition of issues in the Terms of Reference (*Société Farhat Trading Company c/ société Daewoo, Cour de cassation*, Note Arnaldez, *Rev. arb.* (1997), p. 69,. *But cf., Steel Authority of India, Ltd.* v. *Hind Metals, Inc.*, [1984] 1 Lloyd's Rep. 405 (ordered that an ICC Award be remitted to the Arbitral Tribunal, *inter alia*, because it had not fully adjudicated on the issues set forth in the Terms of Reference).

[517] This formulation of the issues came to be known within the Court as the "Goldman formula," after the eminent French law professor and arbitrator, Berthold Goldman, who was one of its proponents. *See* Schneider, *supra*, note 499, pp. 28-29.

It will therefore now be for the Arbitral Tribunal to decide on a case-by-case basis whether or not it is "inappropriate" to list the issues to be determined. Article 18(1) creates a presumption that they normally should be. Indeed, it was deliberately drafted in such a manner as to make the omission of such a list the exception rather than the rule.[518] However, the matter has been left entirely to the Arbitral Tribunal's discretion, and it may reasonably determine that such a list should be omitted where, for example, its preparation would otherwise give rise to undue delay or other complications or where such a list cannot meaningfully be prepared. Certain issues should nevertheless probably always be listed, such as, for example, the question of the Arbitral Tribunal's jurisdiction, whenever this is required to be decided pursuant to Article 6(2), or disputes as to the applicable law or possibly other matters upon which the parties have been unable to agree during the preparation of the Terms of Reference.

(iii) *Procedural Rules*

As already discussed (*see* Article 15 *supra*), the proceedings before the Arbitral Tribunal are to be governed, in the first instance, by the provisions of the Rules and, where they are silent, by such additional rules as the parties may agree or, failing such agreement, by such rules as the arbitrators may determine, subject only to any provisions of law that may mandatorily apply.

In practice, detailed provisions concerning the procedural rules to be applied in the arbitration are often not included in the Terms of Reference, and, indeed, arbitrators are generally discouraged by the Court from including too much procedural detail in that document. Rather, arbitrators are generally advised to set out details of procedure in separate procedural orders as and when appropriate in order to retain as much flexibility as possible during the course of the proceedings.[519] This is especially important in the case of timetables, which it may otherwise be difficult to alter subsequently without the agreement of all of the parties once they have been incorporated in Terms of Reference that all the parties have signed. Moreover, as procedural issues may often be contentious, an attempt to resolve them in the Terms of Reference may unduly delay the completion of that document.

There are nevertheless certain procedural matters that it may be useful to resolve, if uncertain, in the Terms of Reference. One of them is the language of the arbitration, if not already decided, given the obvious cost and inconvenience to all concerned if this issue is allowed to linger. In addition, it is common for the Arbitral Tribunal to specify in the Terms of Reference how any procedural

---

[518] *See* Schneider, *supra,* note 499, p. 28, where it is noted that the text of the rule approved by the ICC Commission originally provided that a list of issues would be included only if this was considered appropriate by the Arbitral Tribunal. However, when the Rules were ultimately adopted by the ICC Council, the presumption was reversed.

[519] *See, e.g.,* Hascher, *supra,* note 439, p. 24. *See also* "Practical Guide," *supra,* note 499, pp. 36-37.

decisions are to be taken, *e.g.,* whether the chairman of a tribunal of three arbitrators should have the power to decide certain matters on his own, if this is desired.[520]

Preparation of the Terms of Reference. Article 18(1) provides that the Arbitral Tribunal shall draw up the Terms of Reference "[a]s soon as it has received the file from the Secretariat." This is a change from Article 13(1), which provided instead that the Terms of Reference were to be prepared by the arbitrators "[b]efore proceeding with the preparation of the case." The new wording, in line with many of the other Rules changes, emphasizes the need for the Arbitral Tribunal to proceed with expedition. But at the same time, it eliminates certain of the ambiguities inherent in the previous language concerning the powers of the Arbitral Tribunal prior to the Terms of Reference's preparation. Indeed, because of the way in which Article 13(1) was worded, arbitrators and parties were often uncertain whether and, if so, to what extent, the tribunal had the power, before the Terms of Reference were drawn up, to make orders or give directions (other than for the purpose of establishing the Terms of Reference), such as, for example, ordering interim or conservatory measures (*see* Article 23 *infra*) or determining the language of the proceedings (*see* Article 16 *supra*). Although the Terms of Reference are intended to provide a framework for the arbitration and are, thus, to be completed before the arbitrators embark upon the substantive phase of the arbitration, the arbitrators should nevertheless have the power, as from the time when they receive the file pursuant to Article 13 and until the Terms of Reference have been completed, to take such actions as may be necessary in connection with the proceedings, subject to the general principles set forth in Article 35 (*see infra*). That they are not precluded from doing so should now be clearer from Article 18(1).

Article 18(1) is otherwise identical to its predecessor in providing that the Terms of Reference are to be drawn up "on the basis of documents or in the presence of the parties and in the light of their most recent submissions." The reference to the parties' "most recent submissions" is sufficiently broad (and, indeed, was intentionally drafted in that way)[521] to permit the inclusion in the Terms of Reference of claims or counterclaims submitted subsequent to the exchange of the Request for Arbitration and the Answer. While it is, thus, generally considered that the parties are free to make new claims up until the Terms of Reference have been drafted, there is nevertheless an issue as to whether parties should be permitted to make last-minute submissions, *e.g.,* at the meeting being held for the purpose of signing the Terms of Reference, if this would delay their completion and, as a result, the arbitration. In practice, because of the restrictions in the Rules on the introduction of new claims thereafter (*see* Article 19 *infra*), ICC

---

[520] *See,* in this connection, Reymond, *"Le président du tribunal arbitral,"* Etudes offertes à Pierre Bellet (Litec 1991), p. 467.
[521] *See* Eisemann, *supra,* note 101.

tribunals have tended to be indulgent in this regard, but some tribunals have taken the position, reportedly in "exceptional circumstances," that such submissions could and should be excluded if made too late.[522] As a practical matter, problems of this kind can normally be avoided by the Arbitral Tribunal if it fixes a deadline for the submission of any further claims sufficiently in advance of the Terms of Reference's finalization.

In preparing the Terms of Reference, meanwhile, the arbitrators have the option of proceeding either on "the basis of documents" or "in the presence of the parties." In practice, these two possibilities are most often combined. Thus, draft Terms of Reference are prepared in the light of the documents submitted by the parties and are circulated to them by the Arbitral Tribunal for comments. This draft is then amended to take account of the comments received and a meeting is organized during which the Terms of Reference are normally signed. It is at this meeting that procedural details not included in the Terms of Reference are also often discussed with the parties.

Although not required by Article 18(1), it is usually desirable to hold a meeting for the purpose of finalizing the Terms of Reference. Apart from the opportunity that this gives the parties to meet the arbitrators and opposing counsel, possibly for the first time, the mere fixing of a date for such a meeting enhances the likelihood that the Terms of Reference will, in fact, be completed by that time. Even if there may be differences among the parties and arbitrators concerning the draft Terms of Reference prior to the meeting, arbitrators generally come to such meetings with the firm intention of obtaining a signed document before the day is done. However, when the Terms of Reference are drawn up and signed by correspondence exclusively, the process of completing them, particularly if there are disagreements between the parties, may be considerably prolonged. There may nevertheless be cases where the size of the dispute is not large enough to justify the cost of a meeting if either the arbitrators or the parties would be required to travel. Moreover, when it is difficult for the arbitrators and the parties to find a mutually convenient date for such a meeting by the time when the Terms of Reference are ready, or nearly ready, for signature, it may be appropriate simply to proceed by correspondence, with the assistance, as is increasingly common, of a telephone conference call.[523]

In the event that the Arbitral Tribunal and the parties choose to hold a meeting, it will normally be at the place of the arbitration, although this is not required (*see* Article 14(2) *supra*). The Terms of Reference should, in any event, be deemed to be made at the place of the arbitration, even if the related meeting is held elsewhere. They should also always bear one or more dates as, unless the Terms of Reference are required to be approved pursuant to Article 18(3), the time limit for the final Award starts to run "from the date of the last signature

---

[522] *See* "Practical Guide," *supra,* note 499, p. 31.
[523] For a discussion of other relevant considerations, *see* "Practical Guide," *supra,* note 499, pp. 29-30.

by the Arbitral Tribunal or of the parties" of that document (*see* Article 24(1) *infra*). The Terms of Reference are also normally to be drafted in the language (or languages) of the arbitration.[524]

Lastly, it should always be remembered that the Terms of Reference, although signed by the parties, are intended to be the arbitrators' document. Parties are not precluded from proposing drafts or draft language, and this can often assist the Arbitral Tribunal in arriving at a document that is acceptable to the parties, particularly, in relation to the summaries of their respective claims. But one of the intended advantages of the Terms of Reference is that, when summarizing the claims, the arbitrators are required:

> to read and understand the parties' submissions and to concentrate their minds upon the issues in dispute.[525]

Effects of the Terms of Reference. The Terms of Reference are not intended to replace the parties' arbitration agreement. But because they bear the signatures of all of the arbitrators and the parties (unless one of the parties refuses to sign them), they may nevertheless produce a number of effects. Thus, as already noted (*see* note 504 *supra*), they may, in certain circumstances, be regarded as a form of submission agreement (*compromis*) in those jurisdictions where one is required, or otherwise as an agreement to arbitrate where there may be doubts as to the existence or validity of such an agreement between the parties. Parties contesting the jurisdiction of the Arbitral Tribunal may therefore be reluctant to sign the Terms of Reference for fear of waiving their objections in this regard. It has, however, been accepted that a party does not waive its position on jurisdiction and agree to arbitration if it signs the Terms of Reference subject to an express reservation as to the same.[526]

Apart from possibly reflecting the parties' submission to the jurisdiction of the arbitrators, the Terms of Reference may be regarded as a binding agreement between the parties as to the various procedural matters set forth therein.[527] Some courts have, in fact, taken the position that, in the event of a conflict between the Terms of Reference and the Rules, it is the Terms of Reference that "control."[528]

---

[524] Documents in more than one language, while permitted, are nevertheless discouraged. *See* "Practical Guide," *supra,* note 499, p. 38.

[525] *See* Harman, "Getting the best from ICC arbitration," *ICC and International Arbitration* (King's College 1990), pp. 147, 152.

[526] *See, e.g., Craig Park and Paulsson,* §15.05, p. 261; *République arabe d'Egypte* c/ *Southern Pacific Properties Ltd. et Southern Pacific Properties (Middle East), supra,* note 168.

[527] *See Craig Park and Paulsson,* §15.05, p. 268.

[528] *See LaPine Technology Corporation* v. *Kyocera Corporation,* 130 F.3d 884 (9th Cir. 1997) *Mealey's*, Vol. 12, No. 12 (1997), p. 3. *See also Krupp Industrietechnik GmbH* c/ *Etibank Gene Murdulugu, Cour d'appel de Paris* (September 30, 1993) (unpublished). The Court could normally be expected, however, to prevent such conflicts in respect of matters as to which it does not consider that the parties are free to derogate. *See* Reiner, *supra,* note 499, pp. 61-62; *and* the discussion of Article 18(2) *infra*.

With respect to the arbitrators, the Terms of Reference should be regarded as equally binding. Indeed, the French Court of Cassation has specifically held that an international Award made in France may be set aside for the Arbitral Tribunal's failure to respect its mission if the tribunal has disregarded obligations resulting from "express and precise clauses of the Terms of Reference."[529]

Changes. While the Terms of Reference are intended, at the beginning of the arbitration, to provide a snapshot of the proceedings and to record the agreement of the parties and the arbitrators with respect to various matters, there has never been any requirement in the Rules that they be amended during the course of the arbitration to reflect changes in the matters described or agreed therein (except, under the former Rules, in the case of new claims, as discussed further *infra*).[530] Thus, for example, nothing is said in the Rules about the possible need to amend the Terms of Reference if, during the arbitration, a party's name or address changes, if it is merged into another entity or its counsel changes, and in practice, the Court has never insisted upon such amendments being made. Nor do the Rules require the Terms of Reference to be changed to reflect the replacement of an arbitrator or their signature, in such case, by the new arbitrator. The Court, for its part, has also not required this. In one case, however, where an entire Arbitral Tribunal was replaced following the annulment of a partial Award and the effective recommencement of the proceedings, new Terms of Reference were prepared at the initiative of the arbitrators and parties (*see also,* in this connection, the discussion of Article 12(4) *supra*).

Insofar as the parties' claims are concerned, the former Rules required the execution by the parties of a "rider" in the case of new claims falling outside the "limits fixed by the Terms of Reference" (former Rules, Article 16). However, no change was required to be made in the Terms of Reference in the event that claims described therein were withdrawn or otherwise abandoned.[531] Under the New Rules, as discussed below (*see* Article 19), even the requirement of a rider has been eliminated in the event that new claims are admitted in the proceedings. Although the elimination of this requirement has attracted criticism,[532] the

---

[529] *See Sociétés Sofidif et autres* c/ *OIEATI et autre, supra,* note 435, and the report of the prior decision of the Paris Court of Appeal, *id.* In this regard, it is also to be remembered that, under Article V(1)(d) of the New York Convention, the enforcement of an Award may be refused if the "arbitral procedure was not in accordance with the agreement of the parties."

[530] *See also* Reiner, *supra,* note 499, pp. 61-62.

[531] In this connection, it is generally assumed that nothing should prevent a party from withdrawing a claim included in the Terms of Reference. *See, e.g.,* Schweizer, Note on the judgment of the Swiss Federal Tribunal (April 19, 1994), *Westland Helicopters Limited* c/ *The Arab British Helicopter Company, ASA Bull.* No. 2 (1995), pp. 191, 195. However, in at least one ICC case, a party successfully argued before the Arbitral Tribunal that once a claim had been included in the Terms of Reference it could not be withdrawn without the other party's consent, failing which the Arbitral Tribunal was obliged to rule upon it.

[532] *See* Arnaldez, *supra*, note 499, p. 75.

Terms of Reference have, in fact, never been required to reflect faithfully the evolution of the arbitration. In regard to the parties' claims, the scope of the Arbitral Tribunal's mandate flows, as already indicated, from the claims that have been properly placed before the arbitrators in accordance with the parties' agreements and the Rules and not from the description of those claims in the Terms of Reference.

While the preparation of the Terms of Reference, thus, represents a useful exercise at the outset of the arbitration, if they are not kept current there should not be any adverse consequences for the parties.[533]

Article 18(2)

> *The Terms of Reference shall be signed by the parties and the Arbitral Tribunal. Within two months of the date on which the file has been transmitted to it, the Arbitral Tribunal shall transmit to the Court the Terms of Reference signed by it and by the parties. The Court may extend this time limit pursuant to a reasoned request from the Arbitral Tribunal or on its own initiative if it decides it is necessary to do so.*

Signature of the Terms of Reference. As in the case of the former Rules (Article 13(2)), Article 18(2) provides that the Terms of Reference "shall be signed by the parties and the Arbitral Tribunal." Although the Rules provide for the possible "approval" of the Terms of Reference by the Court if a party refuses to sign them (*see* Article 18(3) *infra*), arbitrators generally endeavor to obtain the signatures of all of the parties in the interest of maintaining an atmosphere of cooperation and trust and avoiding subsequent efforts to obstruct the proceedings.

Given the nature of the information that is required to be set forth in the Terms of Reference, most of which is purely descriptive, there should not normally be any legitimate obstacle to their signature by all of the parties, and, in practice, there are few cases (other than where a party is not participating in the proceedings) in which a party refuses to do so. The two most frequent sources of difficulty in obtaining the parties' agreement have typically been the list of "issues to be determined" and "particulars of the applicable procedural rules." However, in the event of disagreements with regard to the former, the Arbitral Tribunal has the option, as already discussed, of simply eliminating such a list. As regards the procedural rules, the usual solution to any disagreement is to provide separately for such matters in procedural orders or otherwise, as appropriate, to list them as issues to be decided. Indeed, in general, any matters that appear to be contentious

---

[533] In view of the foregoing, however, the Court cannot rely exclusively on the description of the claims in the Terms of Reference when seeking to verify, during its scrutiny of the arbitrators' Award pursuant to Article 27, whether it is *infra* or *ultra petita*. Indeed, it is required in each such case to check what changes may have occurred since the Terms of Reference. For the same reason, the Terms of Reference cannot be relied upon by the arbitrators either as a comprehensive check list in all cases.

should normally either be deleted or described as disputed issues, to the extent possible.[534]

Occasionally, a Respondent party may also be reluctant to sign the Terms of Reference because it does not recognize the arbitrators' jurisdiction, and it does not wish to take the risk that its signature of the same, even subject to an express reservation, might in any way prejudice its position. It is, however, now widely recognized, as already noted, that the signature of the Terms of Reference, if properly qualified, should not have this effect.

Article 18(2) does not impose any requirements concerning the persons who are to sign the Terms of Reference on behalf of the parties. Although not explicitly stated in the Rules, the Terms of Reference may be signed by any person having the authority to do so, including a party's counsel, as is often the case. Although the Rules do not explicitly require the persons signing the Terms of Reference to provide the Arbitral Tribunal and other parties with evidence of their authority to do so (such as a power of attorney), the Arbitral Tribunal may legitimately request the production of such evidence, where appropriate.[535] In this connection, it should be borne in mind that in many jurisdictions special authority is required to enable an attorney validly to enter into an arbitration agreement on a client's behalf. Thus, insofar as the Terms of Reference may in any way alter the original agreement to arbitrate or otherwise confer jurisdiction on the Arbitral Tribunal, a special power of attorney may be required by any attorney signing that document.[536] A prudent arbitrator should, thus, normally request the production of counsels' powers of attorney if it is intended that they sign the Terms of Reference. Alternatively, if such a power is not provided when the Terms of Reference are signed, it may be submitted afterwards.

Transmission of the Terms of Reference to the Court. As under the previous Rules, Article 18(2) requires the Arbitral Tribunal to transmit a signed copy of the Terms of Reference to the Court within two months of the date on which the file was transmitted to it by the Secretariat (*see* Article 13 *supra*). Neither Article 18(2) nor any other provision of the Rules indicates, however, what the Court is then to do with them.

It was once the case, as already noted, that upon receipt, the Terms of Reference were required to be reviewed and approved by the Court. But the requirement of Court approval was eliminated in the 1975 version of the Rules when the Terms of Reference are signed by all of the parties. This change was made as a concession to those who argued that the requirement of Court approv-

---

[534] For suggestions concerning what Arbitral Tribunals should do when parties are not cooperative, *see* "Practical Guide," *supra,* note 499, pp. 30-31.

[535] *See* "Practical Guide," *supra*, note 499, p. 32.

[536] *See,* for an example of a case where difficulties were encountered in this regard, *Boisson et autres* c/ *société Totem Holding et autres, Cour d'appel de Paris* (October 19, 1995), *Rev. arb.* (1996), p. 82.

al was an unnecessary source of delay.[537] In the years following the 1975 reform of the Rules, the Court nevertheless developed the practice of reviewing the Terms of Reference in order to "take note" of them. The Court's primary purpose in doing so was to satisfy itself that the Terms of Reference were prepared in conformity with the requirements of the Rules and did not contain any derogations from the Rules that the Court could not accept. In rare cases where the Terms of Reference were found to conflict with the Rules, the Court, thus, refused to "take note" of them and returned them to the Arbitral Tribunal with the request that they be appropriately amended.[538]

None of the changes in the New Rules bear any relation to the Court's practices in this regard. However, independently of the Rules changes, the Court has been reconsidering the manner in which the Terms of Reference ought to be scrutinized.[539] As noted elsewhere, moreover, the Rules formerly provided that the Terms of Reference would not "become operative" (former Article 9(4)) until full payment of the advance on costs. In contrast, Article 18(3) now provides that the "arbitration shall proceed" when the Terms of Reference are signed. Thus, the Court will need to let the parties and arbitrators know rapidly if it does not consider the document signed by them and the parties to constitute Terms of Reference within the meaning of Article 18.

Extensions of the deadline for the Terms of Reference. Article 18(2) carries forward into the New Rules the power that the Court enjoyed under the former Rules to extend the two-month time limit for the Terms of Reference on the "reasoned request" of the Arbitral Tribunal or on the Court's "own initiative." The Court has no obligation under this provision to extend the time limit in question. However, it has normally considered that it cannot reasonably do otherwise if the Terms of Reference are not likely to be received within the time required and the parties wish to keep the arbitration alive. In rare instances where the parties have lost interest in the proceedings or otherwise disappeared, the Court has allowed the time limit to lapse.[540]

Because of the Court's fear of a deadline possibly expiring inadvertently, it has put in place a formal procedure intended to prevent this from occurring. The Secretariat has, thus, for many years been required at the first Committee meeting of each month to report to the Committee on every case in which the dead-

---

[537] *See* Eisemann, *supra*, note 101, p. 360.

[538] For a discussion of the Court's practices in this regard, *see* Reiner, *supra,* note 499, pp. 61-62.

[539] For many years, Terms of Reference have been scrutinized by the Court's Committee (*see* Article 1(4) *supra*). However, the Court is now reportedly considering removing the Terms of Reference from the agenda of the Committee while nevertheless continuing to review them, as necessary. The Court would, at the same time, no longer formally "take note" of the Terms of Reference.

[540] For a discussion of the Court's practices, *see* Bruna, "Control of Time-Limits by the International Court of Arbitration," *ICC Ct. Bull.,* Vol. 7, No. 2 (1996), p. 72.

line will be expiring prior to the first Committee of the following month. Generally, the Court's practice has been to extend the deadlines for all of the cases concerned by an additional two months, primarily as a precautionary measure. Depending on the circumstances, the Secretariat is at the same time invited to press the Arbitral Tribunal to complete its task more rapidly.

The advantage of this process is that it permits the Court to monitor on a regular basis all cases that are not progressing as rapidly as required under the Rules and to identify possible difficulties as to which the Secretariat may be able to provide assistance. But at the same time, it has tended to routinize the granting of extensions and conveyed the impression that the deadline set forth in Article 18(2) may be rolled over indefinitely. Increasingly, in recent years, the Court has, thus, attempted to develop a more customized approach to the granting of extensions, although this also increases the risk of an administrative oversight. Of course, this risk can be reduced if an Arbitral Tribunal requiring an extension takes the initiative of requesting one (which not all do).

Because of the Court's general practice of granting standard extensions, the Secretariat many years ago stopped notifying the Court's decisions to the parties unless requested to do so by the Arbitral Tribunal. The Secretariat apparently was concerned that the Court's practice would not be understood. However, there would not appear to be any legitimate reason why the parties should not regularly be informed of the Court's relevant decisions.[541]

As a practical matter, extensions of the deadline for the Terms of Reference have in the past been required to be granted in many, if not most, cases. But there is nothing inevitable about this, and, hopefully, the added flexibility of Article 18(1) will help to accelerate the process in appropriate cases.

---

[541] In one instance, a party sought to have an ICC Award set aside on the ground that it had not been informed of a decision of the Court to extend a deadline (in that case, the deadline for the arbitrators' Award). But the application was rejected, the only relevant consideration, in the court's view, being whether the deadline had, in fact, been extended. *Société Casco Nobel France* c/ *Sico inc. et Kansa, Cour d'appel de Paris* (November 13, 1992), *Rev. arb.* (1993), p. 632. Similarly, in a judgment rendered by the Federal Constitutional Court of Germany on December 10, 1990, the court upheld a ruling of the Federal Supreme Court (3rd Civil Chamber, April 18, 1988) in which it was held that the failure of the ICC Court to provide a party to an ICC arbitration with an opportunity to comment prior to a decision of the Court concerning the extension of the deadline for the Award did not violate German public policy. *See Internationales Wirtschaftsrecht*, RIW 1988 Heft 8, p. 642. The French courts, meanwhile, have on several occasions confirmed the administrative character of the Court's relevant decisions and will not review their appropriateness. *See Société Appareils Dragon* c/ *société Construimport, Cour d'appel de Paris* (January 22, 1982), *Rev. arb.* (1982), p. 91; *and Société Appareils Dragon* c/ *Empresa central de abastecimientos y vantas de equipos, Cour d'appel de Paris* (June 8, 1983), *Rev. arb.* (1987), p. 309.

Article 18(3)

> *If any of the parties refuses to take part in the drawing up of the Terms of Reference or to sign the same, they shall be submitted to the Court for approval. When the Terms of Reference are signed in accordance with Article 18(2) or approved by the Court, the arbitration shall proceed.*

Refusal to sign the Terms of Reference. Article 18(3), like Article 13(2) of the previous Rules, is intended to prevent a party from blocking the progress of the arbitration by refusing to sign the Terms of Reference. Thus, if a party refuses to sign that document, it may be "approved" by the Court, and the arbitration shall proceed.[542]

It is to be noted that the Court has no power under Article 18(3) to approve the Terms of Reference if an arbitrator refuses to sign them. In the event that an arbitrator is unwilling to sign the Terms of Reference and a solution cannot be found, then either he or the other arbitrators are not properly performing their functions and should be replaced (*see* Article 12(2) *supra*). Indeed, for the reasons already discussed, there should not be any legitimate obstacle to preparing Terms of Reference that all of the arbitrators would be willing to sign. Thus, the Court is empowered to approve the Terms of Reference only when it is a party that refuses to sign them.

In this connection, Article 18(3) refers to the refusal of "any" of the parties, unlike its French version and Article 13(2) of the former Rules, which provide that the Court may act if "one" of the parties does not sign. In fact, the drafters' intention falls somewhere between "any" and "one." The Court would clearly not approve Terms of Reference unless signed by at least one of the parties. However, in cases with multiple parties (*e.g.,* multiple Respondents), the refusal to sign of more than one party on the same side ought not to preclude the Court from approving the Terms of Reference. Usually, as might be assumed, it is the Respondent that refuses to sign. Article 18(3) nevertheless also empowers the Court to approve the Terms of Reference if it is the Claimant that does not wish to do so.

Article 18(3) applies, by its terms, only to a "refusal," rather than the "failure," of a party to sign the Terms of Reference or to participate in their drawing up.[543] In a case where a party is not participating in the proceedings, it will nevertheless generally be presumed that this is because it refuses to do so. But

---

[542] A party's refusal to sign the Terms of Reference does not prevent it, however, from participating in the arbitration thereafter.

[543] Article 13(2) of the former Rules further specified that the case had to be one of those mentioned in either Article 8(2) or 8(3) of the former Rules, *i.e.,* where one of the parties refuses or fails to take part in the arbitration (Article 8(2)) or raises one or more pleas concerning the existence or validity of the agreement to arbitrate (Article 8(3)). However, as there may be other cases where a party refuses to sign the Terms of Reference, this qualification was eliminated from Article 18(3).

because Article 18(3) applies only to "refusals" (and not mere "failures"), an Arbitral Tribunal should normally endeavor to ensure that a non-participating party has had a reasonable opportunity to sign the Terms of Reference before they are submitted to the Court for approval. Indeed, in at least one instance, the Court would not approve Terms of Reference where the Court believed that the Respondent had "failed," but not "refused," to sign them because of a state of civil war in its country.[544]

Meanwhile, in cases where the Terms of Reference are signed by a party, but subject to a qualification, this is normally treated by the Court in the same way as a refusal to sign. For the Court, the signatures of the parties should be unconditional.

Approval by the Court. The Court's approval of the Terms of Reference is not meant to signify approval of all of the matters described therein, but is only intended to permit the arbitration to proceed.[445] In deciding whether to approve the Terms of Reference, the Court's primary consideration therefore is whether the Terms of Reference have been prepared in accordance with the requirements of the Rules. The Court is also particularly concerned to ensure that no provisions have been included in the Terms of Reference that would ordinarily require the defaulting party's agreement, such as, for example a statement recognizing the validity of the Arbitral Tribunal's constitution, the rules of law to be applied to the merits of the dispute, if not already agreed, or the authority of the Arbitral Tribunal to act as an *amiable compositeur.* If Terms of Reference containing such provisions are submitted to the Court for approval, the Arbitral Tribunal will be invited to prepare a new text for submission to the parties before approval by the Court.[546]

Upon approval of the Terms of Reference by the Court (as when they have been signed by all concerned), Article 18(3) provides that the arbitration shall proceed. In addition, according to Article 24(1), the time limit within which the Arbitral Tribunal must render its final Award begins to run on the date of notification of such approval to the tribunal by the Secretariat. Article 13(2) of the Rules previously provided that, upon the approval of the Terms of Reference, the Court was to fix a time limit for their signature by the defaulting party and that the arbitration could proceed only upon the expiration of that time limit. But this requirement did not appear to serve any practical purpose, while nevertheless delaying the arbitration. It was therefore excluded from the New Rules in the expectation that this would further accelerate the process.

---

[544] *See* Reiner, *supra,* note 499, p. 62. *But cf.* Article 6(3), which provides that the arbitration shall proceed if any of the parties "refuses or fails to take part." If Article 18(3) is to be applied consistently with Article 6(3), the word "refusal" is required to be construed broadly.

[545] *Guide to ICC Arbitration* (ICC Publishing 1994), p. 40.

[546] For further details concerning the Court's practices, *see* Reiner, *supra,* note 499, pp. 62-63.

Article 18(4)

> *When drawing up the Terms of Reference, or as soon as possible thereafter, the Arbitral Tribunal, after having consulted the parties, shall establish in a separate document a provisional timetable that it intends to follow for the conduct of the arbitration and shall communicate it to the Court and the parties. Any subsequent modifications of the provisional timetable shall be communicated to the Court and the parties.*

This is a new provision that was added to the Rules in order to encourage the acceleration of the arbitration process. By requiring the Arbitral Tribunal to establish a provisional timetable in conjunction with the drawing up of the Terms of Reference, the Rules oblige both the arbitrators and parties to look beyond the immediate next steps in the arbitration and to focus as concretely as possible on the needs of the proceeding as a whole. Although in many cases it may be difficult, at the Terms of Reference stage, to anticipate every step that may be required to be taken in the arbitration – for example, the Arbitral Tribunal may not yet know whether witnesses will have to be heard, whether and what type of discovery might have to be ordered or whether the appointment of a technical expert will be necessary – the preparation of a provisional timetable nevertheless constitutes a useful discipline that should encourage the parties and arbitrators to decide upon the relevant procedural requirements of the case as soon as possible, and, in the process, the Arbitral Tribunal should be in a better position to control the pace of the proceedings.[547]

In preparing the timetable, the Arbitral Tribunal should be attentive to the requirement of Article 24 that the final Award be rendered within six months. This is, of course, not a rigid requirement as the time limit may be extended, if necessary, and many arbitrations cannot reasonably and fairly be conducted in such a compressed period of time. Indeed, the parties themselves will often require more time for the exchange of their submissions and evidence than a six-month timetable would allow. Thus, subject to the Court's powers of control (as discussed further *infra*), the provisional timetable is not required to fit within the six-month period provided for in Article 24(1). But it should nevertheless provide for as much expedition as the arbitration can reasonably bear, taking account of the parties' expectations. If the parties, with whom the Arbitral Tribunal must consult when preparing the timetable, wish to proceed with more or less speed, then the Arbitral Tribunal can take account of this from the outset.

As Article 18(4) makes clear, the timetable provided for therein is merely "provisional" and may be modified, as necessary, during the course of the arbitration. In making any such modifications, the Arbitral Tribunal should consult with the parties, as when preparing the timetable originally. Neither the original

---

[547] Although not stated expressly, it was intended by the drafters that, insofar as possible, the provisional timetable should cover the entire arbitration up until the final hearing.

timetable nor any subsequent modifications are required to take any particular form, except that they must be set forth in a document, which could simply be a letter, other than the Terms of Reference themselves. This is reasonable in that the timetable is provisional and must remain flexible and subject to amendments. Such modifications would be more difficult if the timetable were part of the Terms of Reference, a document that is normally signed by the parties and, thus, cannot be modified without their agreement.

The provisional timetable as well as its amendments must be communicated not only to the parties, but also to the Court. This will assist the Court in monitoring the Arbitral Tribunal's compliance with the six-month time limit for the Award contained in Article 24 and the possible need for extensions. Under Article 24, it is the Court that decides whether extensions are necessary, and it is therefore theoretically possible for it, upon receiving a provisional timetable that provides for a longer period of time, to inform the Arbitral Tribunal and the parties that the timetable is not acceptable and must be compressed. Indeed, the Court is not bound under the Rules to respect the timetable produced pursuant to Article 18(4), and it also has the power, under Article 12(2) (*see supra*), to replace arbitrators who, in the Court's view, are unwilling or unable to conduct the arbitration in accordance with the Rules' requirements and, in particular, the "prescribed time limits."

As a practical matter, however, the Court is unlikely to exert any pressure on the Arbitral Tribunal to alter its timetable if it is satisfactory to the parties or otherwise appears reasonable in the circumstances, and, in such cases, the necessary extensions of time should therefore be forthcoming. But the powers that the Court enjoys under Articles 12 and 24 nevertheless help to ensure that the Arbitral Tribunal will not impose upon the parties an unduly protracted timetable that is incompatible with the parties' reasonable expectations under the Rules.[548]

ARTICLE 19
New Claims

After the Terms of Reference have been signed or approved by the Court, no party shall make new claims or counterclaims which fall outside the limits of the Terms of Reference unless it has been authorised to do so by the Arbitral Tribunal, which shall consider the nature of such new claims or counterclaims, the stage of the arbitration and other relevant circumstances.

Background. Article 19 replaces Article 16 of the previous Rules, a provision that was not a model of clarity and that raised numerous difficulties.[549] According to Article 16, new claims or counterclaims were admissible after the adoption of the

---

[548] Article 18 does not require that the provisional timetable be approved by the Court. But, as in the case of the Terms of Reference, the Court has the power to ensure compliance with the Rules' relevant requirements.

[549] *See Fouchard Gaillard and Goldman*, p. 685.

Terms of Reference only if they remained "within the limits fixed by" that document or were specified in a "rider" thereto signed by the parties and communicated to the Court. As a consequence, unless a new claim fell within the limits fixed by the Terms of Reference, a party could prevent the introduction into the arbitration of new claims by the opposing party simply by refusing to sign a "rider," no matter how reasonable the inclusion in the arbitration of the new claims in question might be. Moreover, as Article 16 did not provide for the possible approval of a "rider" by the Court, as in the case of the Terms of Reference (*see* Article 18(3) *supra*), the admission of new claims was effectively barred under that provision in any case where the opposing party was not participating in the arbitration.

The rigidity of Article 16 and the harshness of its consequences, particularly in default cases, gave rise to considerable criticism.[550] Although there is broad support for the proposition that, in order to avoid disruption and delay, there ought to be a moment in any arbitration proceeding when new claims should no longer be allowed, not all cases are the same, and in certain circumstances the admission of a new claim may not only be reasonable and legitimate but preferable to the alternative, *i.e.,* the commencement of a new arbitration. Thus, for example, after the adoption of the Terms of Reference, new facts relating to the subject matter of the arbitration may be discovered that provide a basis for a new claim that is nevertheless closely related to those already before the Arbitral Tribunal. Depending on the stage reached in the arbitration, the introduction of such a claim may be perfectly reasonable. But Article 16, unlike other arbitration rules, left the fate of such a claim in the hands of the opposing party. In contrast, other rules allow the arbitrators to decide whether to permit the introduction of new claims, depending upon the circumstances.[551]

Article 19, thus, eliminates the requirement of a "rider" in the case of new claims falling outside the limits of the Terms of Reference and authorizes the Arbitral Tribunal to admit such claims, depending upon the "nature of such new claims or counterclaims, the stage of the arbitration and other relevant circumstances."

Admission of new claims. While permitting greater flexibility than Article 16 of the previous Rules, Article 19 nevertheless sets forth the general principle that "no party shall make new claims or counterclaims which fall outside the limits of the Terms of Reference." Thus, as under former Article 16, it is still intended that all of the parties' claims will normally be raised before the establishment of the Terms of Reference (or that they will otherwise fall within the limits of that document). This has the advantage of forcing the parties to focus their attention on possible additional claims prior to that time and helps to ensure that the arbitration process will not subsequently be disrupted by the need to consider new matters.

---

[550] *See* Reports of Capper and Perrot presented at a Colloquium of the ICC Institute of International Business Law and Practice (Paris, March 6, 1995), on the subject of *"Les conclusions et les chefs de demande dans l'arbitrage international"* (unpublished).

[551] *See* UNCITRAL Rules, Article 20; AAA International Arbitration Rules, Article 4; LCIA Rules, Article 22; WIPO Arbitration Rules, Article 44.

To the foregoing general principle, however, Article 19 introduces an exception by conferring authority on the Arbitral Tribunal to allow the introduction of new claims after the establishment of the Terms of Reference that fall outside the limits of that document. Thus, the scope of the Arbitral Tribunal's jurisdiction is no longer limited, as under the former Rules, by the Terms of Reference (and any "rider" thereto), but is dependent only upon the parties' arbitration agreement[552] and on how the tribunal chooses to exercise the broad discretion that it possesses under Article 19. In this connection, all "relevant circumstances" may be considered, although particular emphasis is placed by Article 19 on the "nature of the new claims or counterclaims" and the "stage of the arbitration." Thus, for example, while an Arbitral Tribunal may be reluctant to admit a new claim if this would require it to reopen the evidentiary portion of the proceedings, it might nevertheless be inclined to accept the introduction of a claim based on the same facts as the claims already at issue in the arbitration, provided that this would not unduly interfere with the efficiency of the proceedings.[553]

In addition, although not stated explicitly in Article 19, it arises by implication from that provision that, as under Article 16 of the former Rules, the parties are free to introduce new claims without the authorization of the Arbitral Tribunal if they remain within the limits fixed by the Terms of Reference. However, the parties' freedom in this regard is not absolute. Indeed, in contrast to the earlier Rules, the New Rules expressly provide (*see* Article 22 *infra*) that the Arbitral Tribunal "shall declare the proceedings closed" once it is satisfied that the parties have had "a reasonable opportunity to present their cases." Thereafter, no further submission may be made, even for the purpose of filing a new claim that arguably falls within the limits of the Terms of Reference, without the authorization of the Arbitral Tribunal. Presumably, most Arbitral Tribunals would normally be unlikely to grant such eleventh-hour authorizations for the purpose of allowing a new claim to be heard. Moreover, a party's right to make new submissions is also necessarily subject to the procedural timetable fixed by the Arbitral Tribunal for the proceedings.

Nevertheless, because of the different treatment reserved under Article 19, as under Article 16 of the former Rules, to claims falling inside or outside "the limits fixed by the Terms of Reference," the Arbitral Tribunal will be required to make a determination in this regard whenever a party wishes to introduce a new claim in the arbitration. Over the years, this is a matter as to which ICC Arbitral Tribunals have adopted widely varying approaches, depending on the circumstances, the meaning given to the word "claim" and the arbitrators' different conceptions of what falls "within the limits of" the Terms of Reference. Thus, for example, cer-

---

[552] In this connection, it goes without saying that, although not expressly stipulated in Article 19, the Arbitral Tribunal cannot validly admit in the arbitration claims falling outside the parties' arbitration agreement.

[553] Obviously, when a new claim is admitted, the Respondent party must have the opportunity to respond to it in accordance with the requirements of Article 15(2) *(see supra)*.

tain arbitrators have construed very expansively the Terms of Reference's scope so as to include any new claim based on the same facts or, if based on different facts, for the same relief, or otherwise "linked" directly or indirectly to the claims already before the Arbitral Tribunal.554 Other tribunals, meanwhile, have taken a more restrictive approach and have, thus, treated as new claims outside the limits of the Terms of Reference claims based on the same facts, but on different legal grounds, or claims for the same relief, but based on different facts.555

The question of whether an increase in the amount of a claim should be considered as a new claim falling outside the limits of the Terms of Reference has also been much debated (although such increases are generally allowed).556 There is clearly no difficulty, however, when the Terms of Reference expressly reserve the possibility of a new quantification of the claim or when the claim is not quantified.557 On the other hand, some arbitrators have treated as an inadmissible new claim a change in the currency in which the relief at issue has been requested.558 The possible treatment of set-off claims, meanwhile, has also given rise to different approaches, depending on whether they are regarded as defenses or, in the manner of Article 30(5) (*see infra*), as comparable to counterclaims.559

Generally, a request for interim or conservatory relief (*see* Article 23 *infra*) should not be affected by Article 19.560 Nor should Article 19 preclude the articulation of new factual or legal arguments in support of the claims already submitted in the arbitration.561

---

554 *See, e.g.,* Awards in ICC Case No. 4462 (1985), *ICCA Yearbook* XVI (1991), p. 54; *and* ICC Case No. 6618 (1991), *ICC Ct. Bull.,* Vol. 8, No. 2 (1997), p. 70; as well as the cases cited in Reiner, *supra,* note 499, pp. 68-69. *See also* Perret, *supra,* note 512; Arnaldez, *supra,* note 499, p. 29; *and* "Practical Guide," *supra,* note 499, p. 40.

555 *See, e.g.,* Award in ICC Case No. 6309 (1991), *ICC Arbitral Awards 1991-1995,* p. 401; *and* Reiner, *supra,* note 499, p. 66.

556 *See* Reiner, *supra,* note 499, p. 66; *and Craig Park and Paulsson,* §15.02, p. 255. For a contrary view, *see Fouchard Gaillard and Goldman,* p. 686.

557 *See, e.g.,* Award in ICC Case No. 5514 (1990), *ICC Arbitral Awards 1991-1995,* p. 459.

558 *See* Reiner, *supra,* note 499, p. 67, and the cases cited therein.

559 *Id.*

560 *See* Award in ICC Case No. 4126 (1984), *ICC Arbitral Awards 1974-1985,* p. 516; *and* Reiner, *supra,* note 499, p. 66.

561 *See* the cases cited in Reiner, *supra,* note 499, pp. 65-66. In fact, the Arbitral Tribunal may itself sometimes invite a party to present a new argument. The Award in ICC Case No. 6286 (1990), *ICC Arbitral Awards 1991-1995,* p. 256, provides a good example of such a request by an Arbitral Tribunal. In that case, the Claimant, which had been excluded from a consortium, alleged that its exclusion was wrongful and claimed damages, although the agreement's default provision denied damages to a validly excluded member of the consortium. The Arbitral Tribunal, applying Swiss law, thus, ruled that: "Claimant has been validly excluded from the Consortium, but [the Arbitral Tribunal] finds that the [default provision] of the agreement is void insofar as it excludes any indemnification. It will be up to the Claimant to redefine its conclusions in this respect, in accordance with Article 16 of the ICC Rules. The Arbitral Tribunal finds that such conclusions would be covered by the Terms of Reference." However, when taking such an approach, the Arbitral Tribunal must avoid helping one of the parties in a manner that might breach its duty to conduct the proceedings impartially (*see* Article 15(2) *supra*).

This having been said, under Article 19, the distinction between what falls inside or outside the "limits" of the Terms of Reference is less important than before. Although arbitrators will, as already noted, still be required to make some determination in this respect, at the end of the day they will still have the authority to admit new claims into the proceedings if they consider this to be justified. However, if it is the Arbitral Tribunal's view that new claims may fall outside of the limits fixed in the Terms of Reference and should not otherwise be allowed, it should normally ensure that the parties are informed of this as soon as possible after the parties have had an opportunity to comment on the matter.

ARTICLE 20

Establishing the Facts of the Case

As already discussed, Article 15 sets forth the general principle that, except where they are silent, the provisions of the Rules are to govern the proceedings before the Arbitral Tribunal. A number of those provisions – those relating to the actual conduct of the case from the Terms of Reference until the proceedings are closed – are concentrated in Articles 20 and 21, which replace the provisions formerly contained in Articles 14 and 15.

As can be gleaned from a quick perusal of Articles 20 and 21, they are not intended to provide a detailed code of procedure for the arbitration. On the contrary, because of the Rules' universal vocation, the parties and arbitrators are allowed the greatest possible flexibility in organizing the proceedings. Articles 20 and 21, like their predecessors, therefore, provide the parties and arbitrators with only a general procedural framework and, thus, leave it to the participants to fill in the details in a manner that is most suitable to the exigencies of each case, taking into account the legal traditions and expectations of the persons concerned. Although the generality of these provisions has from time to time been criticized as providing too little guidance and predictability, there was a broad consensus during the preparation of the New Rules that the flexibility inherent in former Articles 14 and 15 should be retained.[562]

---

[562] Because of the relatively sparse detail contained in most international arbitration rules relating to matters of procedure, a great deal of attention has been given to this subject in the literature relating to international arbitration. Among the many helpful works on this subject are the following: *Taking of Evidence in International Arbitral Proceedings*, (ICC Publishing 1990), which reproduces the contributions to a colloquium in Paris of the ICC Institute for International Business Law and Practice; Hascher, *supra*, note 439; "Planning Efficient Arbitration Proceedings," *ICCA Congress series No. 7* (Kluwer 1996); *and* "The Standards and Burden of Proof in International Arbitration," *Arb. Int.,* Vol. 10, No. 3 (1994), p. 317. *See also* Hunter, "Modern Trends in the Presentation of Evidence in International Commercial Arbitration," *Am. Rev. Int. Arb.*, Vol. 3, Nos.1-4 (1992), p. 204; *Redfern and Hunter*, p. 318; *Fouchard Gaillard and Goldman*, p. 703. In addition, in 1983, the International Bar Association adopted "Supplementary Rules Governing the Presentation and Reception of Evidence in International Commercial Arbitration," *see ICCA Yearbook* X (1985), p. 145 ("IBA Supplementary Rules on Evidence").

Article 20 therefore does not differ substantially from the corresponding Article in the previous Rules. But certain provisions have been clarified, and two provisions (Articles 20(5) and 20(7)) have been added.[563]

Article 20(1)

> *The Arbitral Tribunal shall proceed within as short a time as possible to establish the facts of the case by all appropriate means.*

The above language, which is identical to the first sentence of former Article 14(1), was added to the Rules in 1975. Together with Article 15, Article 20(1) serves as the required point of departure whenever decisions need to be taken with respect to matters of arbitral procedure that are not the subject of express provisions in the Rules.

The first and most important thing to be noted about Article 20(1) is the freedom that it accords the Arbitral Tribunal to proceed "by all appropriate means." This language was deliberately chosen by its drafters in order to avoid imposing the procedural practices of any particular legal system on the participants in ICC arbitrations. As was explained at the time:

> ICC arbitrators come from all parts of the world. Some are used to the oral and adversarial system of the Common Law countries. Others are more accustomed to the written and inquisitorial system as practiced on the European continent. The fundamental differences between the two systems explain, indeed justify, the concision of the provisions relating to the conduct of the proceedings.[564]

The discretion enjoyed by the Arbitral Tribunal under Article 20(1) is therefore extremely broad, subject only to (i) the Rules' other provisions, (ii) where the Rules are silent, any relevant agreements of the parties pursuant to Article 15 and (iii) mandatory requirements of law. Among the matters left to be settled by "appropriate means" are such questions as the nature and sequence of the parties' further written submissions, the rules that should govern the production

---

[563] For an extensive study of the application of former Articles 14 and 15, *see* Blessing, "The Procedure before the Arbitral Tribunal," *ICC Ct. Bull.*, Vol. 3, No. 2 (1992), p. 18. *See also Craig Park and Paulsson,* Chapter 23, p. 373; *and*, with respect to new Articles 20 and 21, Jarvin, "Aspects of the Arbitral Proceedings," *The New 1998 ICC Rules of Arbitration, ICC Ct. Bull.,* Special Supplement (1997), p. 38.

[564] Translation from Eisemann, " *supra*, note 101, pp. 362-63. *See also* Robert, *supra*, note 202.

of evidence, including its admissibility, materiality and weight,[565] and the calling and examination of witnesses.

Because Article 20(1) obliges the Arbitral Tribunal (as opposed to the parties) to "establish the facts of the case," it is nevertheless sometimes said that the Rules "follow the continental civil-law [*i.e.,* inquisitorial] approach" to fact-finding.[566] However, as just stated, it was never intended by the drafters that the Rules should have built-in procedural bias. Quite to the contrary, they are intended for universal use, and many ICC arbitrations have been conducted over the years by common law lawyers in the manner to which they are accustomed. Article 20(1) and the provisions that follow nevertheless do assume that the Arbitral Tribunal will play a more active role in managing and conducting the proceedings than might once have been the custom in common law jurisdictions. But even in those jurisdictions, arbitrators are being urged to become more involved in directing the proceedings, in the interest, among other things, of increased efficiency.[567] Moreover, as international arbitration activity has expanded in the years since 1975, there has been an increasing convergence in the procedures used by international arbitrators from different legal traditions. This is exemplified by initiatives such as that of the International Bar Association in drawing up rules of evidence for use in international arbitration proceedings (*see* note 562 *supra*).[568]

In addition to requiring the Arbitral Tribunal to adopt "appropriate procedures," Article 20(1) obliges it to proceed "within as short a time as possible." Speed, therefore, is of the essence. But efficiency should not be confused with brutality. The means at the Arbitral Tribunal's disposal cease to be "appropriate" if they breach basic principles of due process. Article 15(2), as already discussed, usefully reminds Arbitral Tribunals that "in all cases" they must act "fairly and impartially" and "ensure that each party has a reasonable opportunity to present its case." The general rule set out in Article 35 ("the Arbitral

---

[565] Many other arbitration rules confer specific authority on the arbitrators to decide upon the admissibility, relevance, materiality and weight of evidence (*see e.g.,* UNCITRAL Rules, Article 25; AAA International Arbitration Rules, Article 20(6), which further specify, however, that the tribunal "shall take into account applicable principles of legal privilege"). Although the ICC Rules do not contain an explicit provision on the admissibility and weight of evidence, authority to decide upon such matters is usually considered to be inherent in the arbitrators' powers under Articles 15 and 20. It is to be noted, however, that in some jurisdictions these are considered to be matters of substantive law rather than procedure.

[566] *See, e.g., Craig Park and Paulsson,* §23.01, p. 374; Jarvin, *supra,* note 563, p. 38.

[567] Thus, for example, the AAA International Arbitration Rules, Article 16(3) now explicitly authorize the tribunal to "direct" the order of proof and to exclude evidence, among other things. *See also* Holtzmann, "Streamlining Arbitral Proceedings: Some Techniques of the Iran-United States Claims Tribunal," *Arb. Int.,* Vol. 11, No. 1 (1995), p. 39, *and* Marriott, "England's New Arbitration Law," *ICC Ct. Bull.,* Vol. 8, No. 1 (1997), p. 28, where it is noted that the new English law "has been hailed as permitting arbitrators to adopt an inquisitorial rather than an adversarial approach."

[568] *See also* Blessing, *supra,* note 563, p. 30; Reymond, "Civil Law and Common Law Procedures: Which is the more Inquisitorial? A Civil Lawyer's Response," *Arb. Int.,* Vol. 5, No. 4 (1989), p. 357; Paulsson, "Overview of Methods of Presenting Evidence in Different Legal Systems," *ICCA Congress Series No. 7* (Kluwer 1996), p. 112; Hunter, *supra,* note 567.

Tribunal shall act in the spirit of these Rules") provides further protection for the parties in this regard. As one experienced arbitrator has noted:

> [W]ithin the hierarchy of procedural maxims, the maxim of a speedy conduct of the arbitral proceedings is clearly *less* important than the overriding maxim to see to it that the parties have sufficient and adequate opportunities to be heard ... .[569]

Article 20(2)

> *After studying the written submissions of the parties and all documents relied upon, the Arbitral Tribunal shall hear the parties together in person if any of them so requests or, failing such a request, it may of its own motion decide to hear them.*

Article 20(2) is identical to the second sentence of Article 14(1) of the former Rules. Its main purpose is to provide the parties with a right to a hearing if "any of them so requests," a right that is further confirmed by Article 20(6) (*see infra*). Failing a request by the parties, Article 20(2) also empowers the Arbitral Tribunal to convene a hearing on its own initiative. However, in either case, the parties must be given the opportunity to be heard "together." In principle, *ex parte* hearings are not permitted, except when a party "although duly summoned, fails to appear without valid excuse" (*see* Article 21(2) *infra*).[570]

While providing generally that the Arbitral Tribunal shall "hear" the parties, Article 20(2) does not indicate the precise nature or extent of the parties' rights in this regard. Indeed, unlike some other arbitration rules,[571] Article 20(2) does not guarantee the parties a right to a hearing for the purpose of presenting oral evidence (*see* with respect to this Article 20(3) *infra*). It accords a right of hearing to the "parties," but not necessarily witnesses or other persons whom the parties may wish to have heard. Nor does it require that the parties be heard with respect to procedural or interlocutory issues. The implication, rather, is that the parties are entitled to a hearing on the merits. But it is for the Arbitral Tribunal to determine in each case what is reasonably necessary in order for it to decide upon the matters at issue, consistent with the parties' right to a fair, but relatively expeditious, procedure. Thus, the parties' right to a hearing is not unlimited.

Hearings are nevertheless a normal occurrence in the lives of nearly all ICC arbitrations (except possibly in very small cases), and they are ordinarily held both with respect to important interlocutory matters and in order to address the

---

[569] *See* Blessing, *supra,* note 563, p. 31.

[570] *But see* Grossen, "Comments and Conclusions," *Conservatory and Provisional Measures in International Arbitration* (ICC Publishing 1993), pp. 115-16, where it is argued that *ex parte* hearings should be permitted in connection with applications for interim and conservatory measures. For a contrary view, *see* Bernardini, "The Powers of the Arbitrator," in the same publication at p. 21.

[571] *See, e.g.,* UNCITRAL Rules, Article 15; WIPO Arbitration Rules, Article 53.

merits through the examination of witnesses and oral submissions. But the associated expense, particularly when some or all of the arbitrators, parties, their counsel, possible experts and witnesses are required to travel to the place of the hearing, often provides an incentive to all concerned to limit their frequency and duration and to commit as much to writing as possible. Moreover, with so many participants involved, it may often be difficult for the arbitrators and the parties to schedule a hearing if large blocks of time are required. Considerations such as these have increasingly led Arbitral Tribunals, including those schooled in the common law, to combat excessive orality. Moreover, multiple hearings with respect to the same matters or additional hearings concerning collateral or supplemental issues that can be dealt with satisfactorily in writing are likely to be refused.

Article 20(1) therefore does not require the Arbitral Tribunal to accede to every request that a party may make for a hearing. Indeed, there may come a time in an arbitration when an Arbitral Tribunal, no matter how sympathetic to the parties' wish to be heard, is justified in taking the position, in respect of hearings as well as other matters, that "enough is enough."[572] This is illustrated by the following extract from an ICC Award, in which the Arbitral Tribunal noted, in explaining its refusal to grant a Claimant an additional hearing on the merits:

> Having regard to the general circumstances of the case, including the delay that has already taken place and the greater delay and expense that would be involved in granting the claimant's application, we decided in our discretion to refuse it.[573]

Article 20(3)

> *The Arbitral Tribunal may decide to hear witnesses, experts appointed by the parties or any other person, in the presence of the parties, or in their absence provided they have been duly summoned.*

Like the last paragraph of Article 14(1) of the former Rules, Article 20(3) empowers the Arbitral Tribunal to hear any other person in the presence of the parties (or in their absence, provided that they have been duly summoned). The only difference is that Article 20(3) now specifies that the persons concerned include "witnesses" and "experts appointed by the parties." Although this was already implicit in Article 14(1), it was nevertheless felt that it would be useful to make it clear, in the case of experts in particular, that the existence of a separate provision concerning their appointment by the Arbitral Tribunal (*see* Article 20(5) *infra*) does not preclude their appointment by the parties.

In addition to witnesses and experts appointed by the parties, however, Article 20(3), like its predecessor, still provides generally for the possible hear-

---

[572] *See Craig Park and Paulsson,* §24.04, p. 392.
[573] *See* Award in ICC Case No. 4975 (1988), *ICC Arbitral Awards 1986-1990*, p. 165.

ing of "any other person." This broad reference is particularly useful because some of the persons whom the parties and arbitrators may wish to hear may not be regarded either as "experts" or as "witnesses" in some jurisdictions. Thus, for example, in many civil law jurisdictions, a party representative or employee is not considered to be a "witness."[574] The reference to "any other person" in Article 20(3), thus, precludes sterile discussions as to the precise legal capacity of a particular person. Indeed, whether or not a person can properly be described as a "witness" in an international arbitration has little practical significance. It is the Arbitral Tribunal's duty to evaluate the weight, significance and credibility of oral statements (from whatever source) on the basis of its own judgment and expertise, having due regard to all of the circumstances.[575]

Unlike in the case of the parties under Article 20(2), the Arbitral Tribunal is not necessarily required to hear the persons mentioned in Article 20(3), even if this is requested by a party. The tribunal "may," but has no obligation to, do so, subject, however, to a party's entitlement to the "reasonable opportunity to present its case" as guaranteed by Article 15(2) (*see supra*) or otherwise by law. Indeed, that an ICC Arbitral Tribunal may, depending on the circumstances, refuse to hear witnesses without denying a party due process has been confirmed by courts in both France[576] and England, where the High Court (Kerr, J.) held, in connection with an application for refusing the enforcement of an ICC Award made in Geneva, that the ICC arbitrator had not breached natural justice in refusing to hear oral testimony because such testimony was "completely unnecessary" in the circumstances of that case.[577] In the United States as well, it has been held (although outside the specific context of ICC arbitration) that "arbitrators, like courts, may waive the probative value of testimony against the risk of wasting time, prolonging hearings and confusing issues."[578] This being said, Arbitral Tribunals normally hear witnesses in ICC arbitrations, and any tribunal that refuses to do so or that otherwise seeks to restrict the presentation of oral testimony must have strong reasons for its position. It otherwise runs the risk of the Award being set aside.

Entirely apart from their right to exclude witnesses or other persons under Article 20(3), arbitrators may also decide to hear them on their own initiative.

---

[574] For instance, in French procedural law, such a person is a "*sachant,*" rather than a witness, and, at least in theory, his evidence has less weight. Indeed, an ICC Award was annulled by a French court in one instance in part because the court, unlike the ICC Arbitral Tribunal, was not prepared to accord any particular weight to testimony of the Claimant party's representatives concerning the existence of an arbitration agreement with both of the Respondent parties. See *République arabe d'Egypte c/ Southern Pacific Properties Limited et Southern Pacific Properties (Middle East), supra,* note 168.

[575] *See* Blessing, *supra,* note 563, p. 41.

[576] *Société Soubaigne c/ société Limmareds Akogar, Cour d'appel de Paris* (March 15, 1984), *Rev. arb.* (1985), p. 285; *Honeywell Bull S.A. c/ Computacion Bull de Venezuela CA, Cour d'appel de Paris* (June 21, 1990), *Rev. arb.* (1991), p. 96.

[577] *Dalmia Dairy Industries Ltd.* v. *National Bank of Pakistan* [1978] 2 Lloyd's Rep. 223, 269.

[578] *Iron Ore Company of Canada* v. *Argonaut Shipping, Inc.,* U.S. District Court, S.D.N.Y. (September 9, 1985), *ICCA Yearbook* XII (1987), p. 173. *See also* Hoellering, "Dispositive Motions in Arbitration," *ADR Currents* (Summer 1996), p. 8, and the cases cited therein.

Arbitrators nevertheless do not generally have the power to compel the appearance of persons who do not wish to be heard, although either they or a party may be entitled to solicit the aid of a court in obtaining testimony in certain jurisdictions.[579]

In order to save hearing time, as discussed further below (*see* Article 21(3) *infra*), it has become commonplace in ICC arbitrations for parties to present the direct testimony of witnesses either wholly or partly by means of written witnesses statements.[580] But if this is done, the witnesses are nevertheless generally required to be made available at the hearing for questioning. In addition, the manner in which such witness statements are prepared has occasionally raised troublesome issues, given that lawyers from some jurisdictions may not consider that they can legitimately assist in their elaboration, while there is no obstacle to doing so for others.[581] How witnesses and other persons are otherwise to be "heard" is further addressed below (*see* Article 21(3) *infra*).

Article 20(4)

> *The Arbitral Tribunal, after having consulted the parties, may appoint one or more experts, define their terms of reference and receive their reports. At the request of a party, the parties shall be given the opportunity to question at a hearing any such expert appointed by the Tribunal.*

Background. Article 20(4) replaces Article 14(2) of the former Rules. Like its predecessor, it reaffirms the specific power of the Arbitral Tribunal to appoint "experts" but it adds the requirements that it must (i) first consult the parties and (ii) give them an opportunity to question the expert at a hearing.

The ICC Rules have long provided for the possible appointment of experts by the Arbitral Tribunal to report on matters relevant to the matters in dispute and as to which independent expertise is necessary. The Rules do not place any restrictions on the kinds of experts that the Arbitral Tribunal may appoint, and, thus, permit the appointment of technical, financial and even legal experts if this

---

[579] *See, e.g.,* UNCITRAL Model Law (Article 27) *and* Article 184(2) of the Swiss Private International Law Act, on the basis of which a court in Geneva, at the request of an ICC Arbitral Tribunal ordered the appearance of witnesses domiciled in Switzerland and abroad. *ASA Bull.* (1994), pp. 307, 310, 314 and 316. In addition, in at least one unreported case, a federal court in the United States ordered the deposition of a third-party witness at the request of one of the parties to an ICC arbitration, with the consent of the Arbitral Tribunal, pursuant to 28 U.S.C. §1782(a). The question of whether that statute is applicable to international arbitration proceedings has not yet been finally settled, however. *See, e.g., In re: Application of Technostroyexport,* 853 F. Supp. 695 (S.D.N.Y. 1994); *and In the Matter of the Application of Medway Power Ltd.* (S.D.N.Y.1997), *Mealey's,* Vol. 12, No. 12 (1997), p. 8; *In re: The Application of National Broadcasting Co., Inc. and NBC Europe, Inc.* (S.D.N.Y. 1998), 1998 U.S. Dist. LEXIS 385.

[580] *See, e.g.,* the IBA Supplementary Rules on Evidence, *supra,* note 562.

[581] *See* in this regard Paulsson, "Standards of Conduct for Counsel in International Arbitration," *Am. Rev. Int. Arb.,* Vol. 3, Nos.1-4 (1992), p. 214.

is deemed necessary.[582] The use of tribunal-appointed experts derives from a practice common in civil law jurisdictions, where such experts are routinely appointed by the courts in order to report on disputed factual matters, usually of a technical nature. The expert may have a variety of different missions, ranging from the mere observation of facts to determining the cause of damages that may be the subject of the dispute. The report of the expert is of probative value only and is not intended to bind the court that may ultimately adjudicate the dispute between the parties, although, as a practical matter, such reports are usually accorded a great deal of weight, given the independence and neutrality of the preparer.

Although an ordinary feature of litigation in civil law courts, the use of experts in international arbitration might, at first, seem surprising. One of the often-repeated advantages of arbitration, after all, is the opportunity that it affords the parties to select arbitrators with special expertise in the field that is the subject of the dispute. The arbitrators therefore might normally already be expected to be experts.[583] Moreover, the appointment of an expert, in addition to the arbitrators, can add considerably to the cost of the proceedings and leave the parties with the impression that they are required to conduct an additional proceeding – an expertise – within the arbitration to which they had originally agreed. But things are not always so simple. Some international disputes can be very complex and, thus, raise a variety of legal, technical and financial or other issues for which a diversity of skills may be required in order to achieve their satisfactory resolution. In some such situations, an Arbitral Tribunal may, thus, feel the need to obtain the assistance of an expert with skills that are complementary to those of the tribunal's members. The possible appointment of an expert by an Arbitral Tribunal has, thus, become a standard feature of arbitration rules in addition to those of the ICC and is also expressly envisaged by arbitra-

---

[582] It is sometimes asked whether the Arbitral Tribunal may appoint an expert to report on a problem of law. Some Arbitral Tribunals have answered in the affirmative under Article 14(2) of the former Rules (*see* the Order in Case No. 6848 (1992), Note Hascher, *Clunet* (1992), p. 1047), and nothing in Article 20(4) expressly precludes this. Indeed, until 1975, the Rules (Article 20 of the 1955 Rules) expressly provided for the possible appointment of a legal expert. It appears to have been envisaged that such an expert might be appointed to assist a technically competent, but not legally, qualified arbitrator. *See* Eisemann, *supra*, note 205, p. 221. The appointment of legal experts in ICC arbitrations is extremely rare, however. Indeed, experts are generally considered to be required to report on matters of fact. Although in many national courts, establishing the requirements of a "foreign" law may be treated as a factual matter, the notion of a "foreign" law is meaningless in an international arbitration, which cannot be considered to have any particular forum for this purpose. Similarly, international arbitrators are generally appointed in the expectation that they are capable of apprehending and deciding upon the legal issues raised. Only in very exceptional cases, therefore, should the appointment of a legal expert be contemplated. For an example of a case in which the appointment of an expert was refused, *see* note 585 *infra*.

[583] *See, e.g.,* Poudret, *supra*, note 302, p. 143 ("Is not one of the main arguments in favor of arbitration that specialists well informed about the issues involved are used, thus obviating the need to consult experts?").

tion laws in many countries.[584] This being said, the practice of appointing such experts in ICC arbitration is still much more prevalent among civil law lawyers than their common law counterparts, who are more accustomed to weighing expert evidence presented by each of the parties.

Apart from empowering the Arbitral Tribunal to appoint experts, Article 20(4) has little to say about their precise role, if appointed, and a number of complex issues may arise in this connection as to which Article 20(4) provides no guidance. A tribunal-appointed expert nevertheless should not be regarded as an additional arbitrator. Any such expert should therefore not participate in the tribunal's deliberations, nor ordinarily meet with the tribunal outside the presence of the parties. The expert also should not be used to discharge either party of any obligation that it may have to prove its case,[585] although the extent of a party's related burden may be perceived differently in various legal systems.[586]

The appointment of experts. Article 20(4) now expressly requires the Arbitral Tribunal to consult with the parties before appointing an expert. Such consultation should normally concern not only the question of whether an expert should be appointed, but the precise nature of the expert's mission ("terms of reference") as well as his identity and cost. The requirement of consultation assumes that it is either the Arbitral Tribunal itself or one of the parties that is proposing the appointment of an expert. But there may also be circumstances in which the parties jointly request such an appointment. Although Article 20(4) does not itself require the Arbitral Tribunal to do so in such case, it could ordinarily be expected to give effect to the parties' joint wishes in this respect.

Similarly, although Article 20(4) might arguably be said to give the Arbitral Tribunal the right to appoint an expert even if none of the parties desires this, there is not any way in which the Arbitral Tribunal can, as a practical matter, impose an expert on the parties against all of their wishes, as the expert is required to be paid by the parties.[587] Thus, the Arbitral Tribunal will be in a position to appoint an expert only if at least one of the parties is prepared to fund the related cost.

---

[584] *See, e.g.,* AAA International Arbitration Rules, Article 22; LCIA Rules, Article 21; UNCITRAL Rules, Article 27; WIPO Arbitration Rules, Article 55; UNCITRAL Model Law, Article 26.

[585] *See* for instance, the explanation given by the Chairman of an Arbitral Tribunal in refusing to appoint an expert in ICC Case No. 6465, Note Hascher, *Clunet* (1994), p. 1088.

[586] For a general discussion of the issues arising in connection with the appointment of experts, *see Arbitration and Expertise, supra,* note 583.

[587] See Appendix III to the Rules, Article 1(11), which provides: "Before any expertise ordered by the Arbitral Tribunal can be commenced, the parties, or one of them, shall pay an advance on costs fixed by the Arbitral Tribunal sufficient to cover the expected fees and expenses of the expert as determined by the Arbitral Tribunal. The Arbitral Tribunal shall be responsible for ensuring the payment by the parties of such fees and expenses." The advance in question is, thus, distinct from the advance on costs otherwise fixed by the Court (*see* Article 30 *infra*).

Identifying a suitable expert can be a difficult matter. Either an individual or a firm may be appointed, but in either case must be independent, even though this is not stated explicitly in the Rules. And finding an expert who has no links or prior relationships with any of the parties can be problematic, particularly in highly sophisticated fields where there may only be a handful of firms and individuals possessing the required level of expertise. The problem of finding a suitable expert may be further complicated if the expert is required to be someone who has not previously expressed views that cast doubt on his neutrality. In identifying suitable experts, Arbitral Tribunals may, thus, wish to solicit the assistance of the ICC International Centre for Expertise, which was established in 1976 for the purpose, *inter alia*, of proposing independent experts for international disputes and which has since gained considerable experience in this respect.[588]

Arbitral Tribunals should nevertheless always think twice before appointing an expert, as this is often costly and will ordinarily prolong the duration of the arbitration. Indeed, it is not uncommon in the authors' experience for an expertise procedure to take as much as a year, and sometimes even longer, to complete.

The conduct of the expertise procedure. Former Article 14(2) did not describe the procedures to be followed in the event that an expert is appointed. Article 20(4), thus, now specifies that the parties shall be given the opportunity to question any such expert at a hearing at "the request of a party." This is, in fact, consistent with what was the usual practice in ICC arbitrations, even before there was such an express requirement, and the corresponding provisions on this subject in other arbitration rules. Indeed, a dialogue between the parties or their own experts and the expert appointed by the Arbitral Tribunal is normally essential in order to assess the value of the latter's findings.

Article 20(4), in comparison with other arbitration rules, nevertheless still leaves much unsaid about the procedures to be followed in relation to the expert's work.[589] Thus, for example, it is not expressly stated whether or to what extent the expert is entitled to request the production of documents by either of the parties for his inspection, whether the other parties shall also have the right to obtain such documents or whether the parties are entitled to be present when the expert is carrying out any required inspection of documents, goods or facilities. Nor does Article 20(4) even explicitly say that the parties are entitled to receive a copy of the expert's report. Although the parties should nevertheless normally be entitled to receive copies of whatever information the Arbitral Tribunal or the expert may rely upon, and should have a reasonable opportunity to comment thereon, consistent with Article 15(2) (*see supra*), these and other similar matters should usually be covered by the expert's terms of reference,

---

[588] *See* Charrin, "The ICC International Centre for Expertise – Realities and Prospects," *ICC Ct. Bull.*, Vol. 6, No. 2 (1995), p. 33. *See also* the Rules of the Centre at Appendix 9 *infra*.
[589] *Cf., e.g.,* UNCITRAL Rules, Article 27.

as established by the Arbitral Tribunal. In addition, the Arbitral Tribunal will be required to ensure that the cost of the expert is controlled and that the parties are fully informed of the costs being incurred as the expertise progresses.

Article 20(5)

> *At any time during the proceedings, the Arbitral Tribunal may summon any party to provide additional evidence.*

This provision is new. It for the first time makes explicit in the Rules the power that the Arbitral Tribunal was already generally considered to have to order the production of evidence by a party.[590] The arbitrators' powers under Article 20(5) can be exercised either *sua sponte* or on the request of a party, as in the case of witnesses under Article 20(3). Unlike Article 20(3), however, Article 20(5) does not confer any authority on the Arbitral Tribunal in respect of third parties.

Most frequently, Article 20(5) can be expected to be invoked in connection with requests by the parties for the discovery of documents. Unlike in common law court proceedings, a party has no right to the discovery of documents in an ICC arbitration proceeding. But such discovery is not excluded either, as is now clear from Article 20(5). It is, thus, left to the Arbitral Tribunal to decide on a case-by-case basis how much, if any, discovery should be allowed, taking account of the specific circumstances of each case, absent a contrary agreement of the parties.

As a rule, discovery in ICC arbitration, as in international arbitration generally, tends to be less extensive than in proceedings before the courts in common law jurisdictions such as the United States. Thus, it is often repeated that there is no place in international arbitration for the so-called "fishing expedition." Indeed, in arbitration the possible desire of a party for discovery normally has to be weighed against the parties' usual expectation that arbitration will be more efficient and expeditious than the typical court proceeding.[591] Moreover, in international arbitration, in particular, many of the participants are from jurisdictions where discovery procedures are not used and, as a consequence, they may not have anticipated such a possibility when agreeing to arbitration. Such discovery as there is in international arbitration therefore tends to be limited to documents, or categories of documents, that can be identified with reasonable specificity and that can be shown to be relevant to the issues dividing the par-

---

[590] *See e.g.,* Order in ICC Case No. 5542 (1993), Note Hascher, *supra*, note 439, p. 62; *Société Nu Swift Plc c/ société White Knight et autres, Cour d'appel de Paris* (January 21, 1997), Note Derains, *Rev. arb.* (1997), p. 429; *Craig Park and Paulsson*, §26.01, p. 409; *Fouchard Gaillard and Goldman*, p. 704.

[591] *See, e.g.,* Rau and Sherman, "Tradition and Innovation in International Arbitration Procedure," *Texas International Law Journal*, Vol. 30, No. 1 (1995), p. 102 ("In the United States, where broad discovery is available in the courts, arbitration has been promoted on the basis of avoiding the expense, delay and invasion of privacy that discovery entails.").

ties in the arbitration.[592] The Arbitral Tribunal can also be expected to have due regard for the legitimate expectations of the parties, given their respective backgrounds and those of the counsel representing them.

In the event that an Arbitral Tribunal orders the production of documents, but a party refuses to comply, there is usually little that the arbitrators can do to force compliance. They are nevertheless free to draw any negative inferences that may flow from a party's refusal to produce the documents requested,[593] and, indeed, it is for this reason that non-compliance with the Arbitral Tribunal's orders is rare. Moreover, in some jurisdictions, it may be possible for the Arbitral Tribunal or a party to seek the assistance of a court in such event.[594]

Article 20(6)

> *The Arbitral Tribunal may decide the case solely on documents submitted by the parties unless any of the parties requests a hearing.*

Article 20(6) replaces Article 14(3) of the former Rules, which also authorized the Arbitral Tribunal to decide solely on documents. However, Article 14(3) permitted this only if the parties requested or agreed that the Arbitral Tribunal should do so, which was arguably inconsistent with Article 14(1) (*see* Article 20(2) *infra*).[595] Article 20(6) now eliminates the need for a request or agreement of the parties in order for the Arbitral Tribunal to proceed on the basis of the documents only, and instead, in conformity with Article 20(2), allows the

---

[592] *See, e.g.,* in this connection, Rogers, "Improving Procedures for Discovery and Documentary Evidence," *ICCA Congress Series No. 7* (Kluwer 1996), pp. 131, 138; IBA Supplementary Rules on Evidence, Article 4(4), *supra*, note 562 (party may request document only if "document is identified with reasonable particularity"); Blessing, *supra*, note 563, p. 34 (in an ICC arbitration, documents may be requested only if "clearly identified"); Baker and Davis, *supra*, note 181, p. 113 (The Iran-United States Claims "Tribunal was generally reluctant to order production of documents if the requesting party could not describe the desired documents specifically, or if the requesting party did not satisfy the Tribunal that it had taken all possible steps to locate the document itself.").

[593] Needless to say, this is done prudently, after warning the recalcitrant party of the risks of refusing to comply with the order. For example, in the Award in ICC Case No. 8694 (1996), the Arbitral Tribunal formally cautioned the parties that "the conscious failure of a party to produce documents relevant to the issues in the arbitration might result in the tribunal drawing an inference adverse to that party." *See* Note Derains, *Clunet* (1997), p. 1056.

[594] *See, e.g.,* the statutes referred to in note 579 *supra*. *See also* Brower, "Discovery and Production of Evidence in the United States: Theory and Practice," *and* Sutton, "Discovery and Production of Evidence: the U.S. and England Distinguished," both in *Taking of Evidence in International Arbitral Proceedings* (ICC Publishing 1990).

[595] The reference to an "agreement" of the parties was apparently intended to include a tacit agreement, *i.e.*, where the parties do not object to a proposal from the arbitrators. *See* Robert, *supra*, note 202, p. 87.

Arbitral Tribunal to do so unless a hearing is requested.[596] In cases where one of the parties is not participating, this should remove any doubt as to the Arbitral Tribunal's authority to decide the arbitration on the basis of the documents without the defaulting party's explicit consent.

In simple cases, proceeding without a hearing can save time and money.[597] However, before deciding to make an Award solely on the basis of the documents, the Arbitral Tribunal should satisfy itself, by soliciting the parties' views in advance, that none of them wishes a hearing. Documents-only ICC arbitrations are, in fact, relatively rare.

Article 20(7)

> *The Arbitral Tribunal may take measures for protecting trade secrets and confidential information.*

Although, as already noted (*see* Chapter 1 *supra*), it is widely assumed that the arbitration process is confidential, the Rules have never contained any provisions expressly obligating either the parties or the arbitrators to protect the confidentiality of the arbitration. The only explicit provisions on this subject (other than Article 20(7)) are contained in the Court's Internal Rules (Appendix II to the Rules, Article 1), and they only concern the confidential character of the work of the Court itself.[598] In this regard, the Rules do not differ from most other arbitration rules. However, within the last few years, certain institutions have adopted express confidentiality provisions,[599] and the desirability of doing so has been the subject of considerable discussion. It was therefore inevitable that the ICC would be required to consider what, if anything, ought to be added to the Rules on this topic. Ultimately, Article 20(7) is what emerged.

As can be seen, Article 20(7) falls short of actually providing that the arbitration proceedings are confidential. During the preparation of the Rules, the Working Party encountered a great deal of difficulty in formulating a general confidentiality provision acceptable to all because of the many legitimate exceptions that may arise.[600] For instance, in the framework of discussions

---

[596] In so providing, Article 20(6) is, thus, now identical to the corresponding provision in the 1955 Rules, which was changed in 1975.

[597] *See* the Award in ICC Case No. 6670 (1992), Note Arnaldez, *ICC Arbitral Awards 1991-1995*, p. 447. *See also InterCarbon Bermuda, Ltd.* v. *Caltex Trading and Transport Corporation*, U.S. District Court, S.D.N.Y. (January 12, 1993), *ICCA Yearbook* XIX (1994), p. 802.

[598] The Rules nevertheless also protect the privacy of the proceedings by barring "persons not involved" from attending hearings without the approval of the Arbitral Tribunal and the parties (Article 21(3) *infra*) and prohibiting the delivery of the Award by the Secretariat to anyone other than the parties (Article 28(2) *infra*).

[599] *See* AAA International Arbitration Rules, Article 34; LCIA Rules, Article 30; WIPO Arbitration Rules, Articles 52 and 73-76.

[600] *See* Paulsson and Rawding, *supra*, note 17, p. 48.

relating to a proposed merger, a party may need to disclose information regarding an arbitration. In such or other cases, information may also be required to be disclosed to bankers, insurers, regulatory authorities, shareholders, other business partners of various kinds and possibly others, depending on the specific circumstances. There is broad support for the view that the privacy of arbitration proceedings should be respected, and, thus, that the persons involved should not be allowed to make public the subject matter of an arbitration without a legitimate reason (*e.g.*, through campaigns in the press). But in view of the many different circumstances that may arise, the Working Party considered it preferable to leave issues of confidentiality to be addressed on a case-by-case basis by the arbitrators and the parties.

Article 20(7) was initially inspired by a more elaborate provision in the WIPO Arbitration Rules (Article 52) concerning the disclosure of trade secrets and other confidential information. The WIPO provision, however, does not concern the confidentiality of the arbitration as such; there are separate provisions in the WIPO Rules on that subject (Articles 73-76). It is intended, rather, to protect the confidentiality of information *before* it is produced or disclosed in an arbitration. Thus, for example, a party may be reluctant to allow the other party, who may be a competitor, to have unrestricted access to certain proprietary, confidential or other secret information concerning its business, although it may be required to produce such information in order to support its position in the arbitration. Article 52 of the WIPO Rules, thus, confers on the arbitrators the power to issue a protective order similar to the one that might be issued by a court in conjunction with the production or discovery of documents.[601] Under Article 20(7), it is now made clear that an ICC Arbitral Tribunal has the same power. Thus, for example, the Arbitral Tribunal can order discovery, but forbid the use of the documents produced in a context other than the arbitration.[602]

The reference in Article 20(7) to "confidential information" (which is not defined) is nevertheless sufficiently broad that an order of the Arbitral Tribunal could also extend to documents produced for the purpose of the arbitration itself, such as pleadings, witness statements and the Award, or other information relating to the arbitration or even its existence, to the extent appropriate. Thus, for example, if one party provides information to the press about the arbitration,

---

[601] The WIPO provision also contains an innovative, although controversial, mechanism under which a so-called "confidentiality adviser" can report on specific issues arising from confidential information communicated to him, but not disclosed to the Arbitral Tribunal or other parties.

[602] It is less clear, however, whether documents can be submitted to the Arbitral Tribunal only, without being communicated to the other side. Indeed, the failure of a party to provide documents upon which it relies to the other party may be regarded as a breach of the latter's right to due process and expose the Award to possible annulment. *See* Blessing, "Arbitrability of Intellectual Property Disputes," *Arb. Intl.*, Vol. 12, No. 2 (1996), p. 191; *Fouchard Gaillard and Goldman*, p. 708.

the Arbitral Tribunal might, on the basis of Article 20(7), be requested to order it to stop doing so. Even if the arbitrators would not ordinarily have the means of forcing compliance with such an order, it might be capable of judicial enforcement in certain jurisdictions or otherwise serve as the basis of a claim for damages, if breached. Moreover, a party may be reluctant to disregard such an order, in any event. The moral authority of an Arbitral Tribunal's order should not be underestimated.

Independent of the Arbitral Tribunal's intervention, of course, the parties are free to negotiate a confidentiality agreement for a particular arbitration or to include a clause on this subject in their arbitration agreement. One issue to which the parties should be attentive, however, is how the agreement, if breached, is to be enforced. Although the parties can confer specific authority on the Arbitral Tribunal in this respect, or otherwise seek to rely on Article 20(7) during the course of the arbitration, this is not likely to be adequate, given the continuing risk of a violation after the arbitration has been completed and the arbitrators are *functus officio*. Thus, in order to ensure continuing protection, it will usually be necessary to provide for appropriate recourse.

ARTICLE 21
Hearings

Article 21 contains the provisions relating to the conduct of hearings that were formerly set forth in Article 15. No substantive alterations have been made to the previous text, except that former Article 15(3) concerning the language of the arbitration has been deleted and made the subject of a separate provision (Article 16 *supra*). Like Article 20, Article 21 merely lays down a few broad principles without, however, seeking to regulate every detail relating to a hearing's organization.

Article 21(1)

> *When a hearing is to be held, the Arbitral Tribunal, giving reasonable notice, shall summon the parties to appear before it on the day and at the place fixed by it.*

As indicated in the above provision, it is the Arbitral Tribunal that fixes the day and place of the hearing. It is, however, required to give the parties "reasonable notice," and the Arbitral Tribunal's freedom to determine the place is also limited by the requirements of Article 14 (*see supra*). What constitutes "reasonable" notice is not stated in Article 21(1),[603] and this will, thus, depend on the circumstances of each case.

---

[603] In this respect, it does not differ from most other arbitration rules, many of which, however, like the UNCITRAL Rules, provide for "adequate" notice. The AAA International Arbitration Rules contain the added requirement that the tribunal shall give the parties at least 30 days advance notice of the initial oral hearing.

As a practical matter, and notwithstanding the formality of the language used in Article 21(1) – *i.e.,* the Arbitral Tribunal "shall summon the parties" – hearing dates in international arbitrations are generally determined with the agreement of the parties and the arbitrators, after consideration of the dates available to all concerned. As it is often difficult to find convenient dates on short notice, experienced arbitrators will normally explore the different possibilities with the parties and the other members of the tribunal at the earliest possible opportunity, and block dates, if only tentatively, sometimes as early as the first meeting with the parties with regard to the Terms of Reference. In the event of difficulties, it is, of course, the Arbitral Tribunal that has the last word, and it may, thus, impose a date. But this is normally necessary only when one party is unreasonably seeking to delay or obstruct the process.

Subject to Article 14, the Arbitral Tribunal may, as stated, also determine the location that it considers to be appropriate. If the arbitration is in Paris, the facilities of the ICC headquarters may be used. However, the ICC has few available hearing rooms and arrangements must, thus, be made well in advance. Outside Paris, ICC National Committees may also be in a position to make facilities available or to provide assistance (*see* Appendix 3 *infra*). In addition, the Court has made arrangements with a certain number of other arbitral institutions (including the Hong Kong International Arbitration Centre and the Japan Commercial Arbitration Association) to enable their premises to be used for ICC arbitrations. But most commonly, hearings are held in hotel meeting rooms, other conference or meeting facilities, such as, in Paris, the *Maison de l'Avocat*, or the offices of one of the arbitrators (or possibly a party's counsel). In this regard, the Arbitral Tribunal needs to be sensitive, however, to possible "psychological" issues and the preference of many parties to meet on "neutral" ground. Thus, the office of a co-arbitrator or a party's counsel should not ordinarily be used without the agreement of all of the parties. The arbitrators' chief considerations should otherwise be that the parties enjoy sufficient space and comfortable working conditions and that appropriate arrangements can be made, if desired, for tape recording, the parties' audiovisual requirements, secretarial assistance and the like. In addition, parties will normally wish to have their own meeting rooms so that they can confer, as necessary, during breaks in the hearing.

Article 21(2)

> *If any of the parties, although duly summoned, fails to appear without valid excuse, the Arbitral Tribunal shall have the power to proceed with the hearing.*

This provision, like Article 15(2) of the former Rules, confirms the right of the Arbitral Tribunal to proceed with a hearing in the absence of one of the parties. It, thus, supplements the general rule on this subject in Article 6(3) and the provision on default concerning the Terms of Reference in Article 18(3). Article

21(2) differs from its predecessor, however, in that it is no longer stated that, in the absence of a party, the proceedings "shall be deemed to have been conducted in the presence of all parties."

In contrast to Article 6(3), which authorizes the Arbitral Tribunal to proceed in the event that a party "refuses" or "fails" to take part (and Article 18(3), which permits the Terms of Reference to be approved in the case of a "refusal"), Article 21(2) explicitly conditions the Arbitral Tribunal's right to proceed on the absence of a "valid excuse" in the event that a party does not appear. Although the Rules do not provide any guidance as to what may constitute a "valid excuse," the purpose of this provision is comparable to that of other arbitration rules, which require "sufficient" or "good cause" to be shown in order to prevent a hearing from proceeding.[604] As under those other rules, it is left to the Arbitral Tribunal to decide, in the circumstances of each case, what constitutes a sufficiently good reason for postponing a hearing.[605] Given their wish to ensure that the parties have a reasonable opportunity to be heard, arbitrators are often inclined to be relatively indulgent in this regard, except where it appears that a party's behavior is deliberately dilatory or obstructionist.

Although nowhere stated in the Rules, a party's failure to appear at a hearing, or more generally to participate in the arbitration, is not normally deemed to constitute an admission of the other party's claims or allegations. In other words, it is not generally acceptable for an Arbitral Tribunal to issue a default Award in such circumstances. Rather, the Claimant is still required to prove its claims. This is a widely-accepted principle of international arbitration, as reflected, for example, in Article 45 of the Washington (ICSID) Convention of 1965 and Article 25(b) of the UNCITRAL Model Law. But it may nevertheless be permissible to draw negative inferences from a party's failure to appear.[606]

Article 21(3)

> *The Arbitral Tribunal shall be in full charge of the hearings, at which all the parties shall be entitled to be present. Save with the approval of the Arbitral Tribunal and the parties, persons not involved in the proceedings shall not be admitted.*

Article 21(3) corresponds to Article 15(4) of the former Rules. As stated, it confers broad authority on the Arbitral Tribunal to conduct the hearings in the manner it considers appropriate. However, the Arbitral Tribunal should normally

---

[604] *See, e.g.,* AAA International Arbitration Rules, Article 23; UNCITRAL Rules, Article 28; WIPO Arbitration Rules, Article 56. *See also* UNCITRAL Model Law, Article 25.

[605] In at least one case, however, the Court refused to approve a draft Award submitted for scrutiny pursuant to Article 27 where it appeared that the arbitrator had conducted a hearing in the absence of a party that could not have appeared due to the fighting in Bosnia-Herzegovina.

[606] *See Holtzmann and Neuhaus,* pp. 700-01; *Fouchard Gaillard and Goldman,* p. 687.

consult with the parties in order to be able to take into account their requirements and expectations, which may vary considerably, depending upon the jurisdictions in which their lawyers are accustomed to practicing.

Thus, for example, it will be important to clarify from the outset what the general purpose and structure of any hearing should be. Although this may seem evident to the Arbitral Tribunal, it may not be to the parties. Indeed, common law
lawyers often assume that the main purpose of a hearing is to hear witnesses and
present opening and closing statements, while civil law lawyers are generally
unaccustomed to having oral arguments and witness evidence presented at the
same hearing. They also do not normally expect an opening statement and may
request that a special hearing for oral argument be established after the hearing
devoted to witness evidence. Either approach is acceptable, provided that a choice
is made in advance by the Arbitral Tribunal, in consultation with the parties.

Unpredictability should also be avoided concerning the taking of witness
evidence. In this respect too national traditions vary considerably. Thus, civil
law lawyers may expect the Arbitral Tribunal to start the questioning, while
common law lawyers are used to direct and cross-examination performed by
counsel. In international arbitration, these differences tend to be less acute
because of the willingness of arbitrators to borrow from both traditions, as
exemplified, for example, by the IBA Supplementary Rules on Evidence.[607]

Insofar as pleading is concerned, it is the Claimant who has the last word in
some common law countries. But on the continent of Europe, it is generally the
Respondent who speaks last, and this is also the trend in international arbitration.
Whichever it is to be, however, the parties should be informed in advance. In addition, the Arbitral Tribunal and counsel must also ordinarily discuss how much
time each party anticipates it will require for argument and the presentation of
evidence. Each party should have a sufficient opportunity, consistent with Article
15(2) (*see supra*), to present its case, and the Arbitral Tribunal must therefore
ensure that the party that begins first does not deprive the other party of the time
that it may reasonably require.[608] Whether the delivery to the tribunal of pleading
notes is to be permitted is also a question requiring clarification in advance. Thus,
for example, French lawyers are accustomed to presenting the Arbitral Tribunal at
the hearing with a file containing both the text of their oral presentation and the
documents to which they have referred ("*cote de plaidoiries*"). Such a file can be
a useful instrument for an Arbitral Tribunal's deliberations. However, if the arbitrators expect or agree to receive it, they must inform the parties in advance and

---

[607] *See* note 562 *supra.*

[608] In this regard, it has also been suggested that the Arbitral Tribunal should avoid inter-
rupting counsel too often during oral argument. *See* Boisséson, *supra,* note 116, p. 795.
Although some questioning or commentary by the Arbitral Tribunal may help counsel to
focus on the relevant issues, too many interruptions may turn oral argument into a conversa-
tion between the tribunal and counsel, with the consequence of throwing counsel off balance
and creating confusion.

require that each arbitrator and party be given a copy. Similar issues arise with respect to the possible preparation of transcripts, either by tape recording or court reporters, as is common in some jurisdictions.

The above catalogue of issues is by no means exhaustive. However, it serves to emphasize the need for careful advance planning in order to eliminate, or at least reduce, the risk of surprise. Provided that the parties' requirements and expectations are reasonable, the Arbitral Tribunal can normally be expected to accommodate them, subject, however, to what has already been said above about the power that the Arbitral Tribunal enjoys to limit the proceedings to what it reasonably believes to be necessary for the proper resolution of the matters before it. In this regard, the Arbitral Tribunal and one or more of the parties may have divergent views. Indeed, this is not infrequently the case in an international arbitration. It will therefore be for the Arbitral Tribunal to establish balanced rules, which take into account, to the extent reasonably possible, the needs of each party. For reasons such as these, no two ICC arbitrations are necessarily alike.

Finally, it is to be noted that Article 21(3) protects the privacy of all hearings by providing that no person who is not involved in the proceedings can be admitted without the agreement of the Arbitral Tribunal and the parties. It is therefore customary, at the beginning of the hearing, for all those present to identify themselves. Although there is rarely any dispute as to who should be considered to be "involved in the proceedings," disagreements may nevertheless occasionally arise. Thus, for example, in one instance a party sought to challenge an ICC Award, albeit unsuccessfully, on the ground that, *inter alia,* the Arbitral Tribunal's administrative secretary should not have been allowed to attend a hearing.[609] A more frequent issue, however, is whether witnesses should be allowed to be present, in particular, during the testimony of other witnesses. Although the Rules do not, unlike some other arbitration rules,[610] expressly confer any specific powers on the Arbitral Tribunal in this regard, there can be little doubt that the tribunal should be able to require the retirement of witnesses, if appropriate.

Article 21(4)

> *The parties may appear in person or through duly authorised representatives. In addition, they may be assisted by advisers.*

This provision replaces Article 15(5) of the former Rules. It is the same, except that the words "authorised representatives" are now used in place of "accredited agents," a term borrowed from the lexicon of inter-governmental diplomacy and somewhat enigmatic in the field of international arbitration. The "authorised representatives" of a party should not be confused with its advisers. An attorney

---

[609] *See Honeywell Bull S.A.* c/ *Computacion Bull de Venezuela CA, supra,* note 576, p. 96.
[610] *See, e.g.,* AAA International Arbitration Rules, Article 20(4); UNCITRAL Rules, Article 25(4).

may have both capacities, but this will not necessarily be the case. As an adviser, he or she does not need a power of attorney. As a representative, *i.e.,* if the party itself is not present, a lawyer may need such a power. This depends on the relevant Bar rules or law that may be applicable.[611]

There is no requirement under the Rules that a party be represented by a lawyer, although this is almost always the case. Nor do the laws of most countries or local rules regulating the practice of law impose any related requirements. There nevertheless have been rare problems in the past in this regard, although not in the principal international arbitration venues.[612]

ARTICLE 22
Closing of the Proceedings

Article 22 is a new rule inspired by comparable provisions in a number of other arbitration rules.[613] Its primary purpose is to prevent proceedings from dragging on indefinitely once each of the parties has had a reasonable opportunity to present its case. Moreover, in order to encourage the Arbitral Tribunal to conclude its deliberations expeditiously, Article 22, unlike other such provisions, requires it to inform the Secretariat of the approximate time that it will require in order to complete a draft of its Award for scrutiny by the Court pursuant to Article 27 (*see infra*).

Article 22(1)

> When it is satisfied that the parties have had a reasonable opportunity to present their cases, the Arbitral Tribunal shall declare the proceedings closed. Thereafter, no further submission or argument may be made, or evidence produced, unless requested or authorized by the Arbitral Tribunal.

Under Article 15(2), the Arbitral Tribunal must, as already noted, "ensure that each party has a reasonable opportunity to present its case." It is therefore incumbent upon it, prior to declaring the proceedings closed, to ensure that neither party wishes to make any additional submissions. If either party expresses such a wish, the Arbitral Tribunal will then be required to assess whether such a request is reasonable. Thus, for example, the Arbitral Tribunal may consider it reasonable to allow the parties to make written post-hearing submissions summarizing their respective final positions, while refusing to accept new documentary evidence that might require it to reopen the proceedings. It is up to the

---

[611] *See,* for an example of such a provision, Article 1038 of the Netherlands Arbitration Act 1986.

[612] *See* Rivkin, "Restrictions on Foreign Counsel in International Arbitration," *ICCA Yearbook* XVI (1991), p. 402. Such restrictions have recently been removed in China, *"Nouvelles de l'Arbitrage à l'Etranger: Chine,"ASA Bull.* (1995), p. 32, 50.

[613] *See, e.g.,* AAA International Arbitration Rules, Article 24; UNCITRAL Rules, Article 29; WIPO Arbitration Rules, Article 57.

Arbitral Tribunal to decide but, as in the other cases already discussed above, the parties should not be taken by surprise.

After the proceedings have been closed, no further submissions of any kind may be made unless requested or authorized by the Arbitral Tribunal. In some cases, the Arbitral Tribunal may take the initiative of reopening the proceedings because, during the course of its deliberations, it may find that it is lacking information on a certain issue, or an issue may appear to be important to the Arbitral Tribunal that neither party has addressed. In order for the Arbitral Tribunal to reopen the proceedings at the request of a party, however, there would ordinarily have to be a very strong showing that the submission could not have been made sooner and that it is highly relevant.

Parties should not, by reading Article 21(1) *a contrario,* presume that, until the proceedings have been declared closed, any submission can be made at any time. Arbitral Tribunals have the authority to require compliance with their procedural directions.[614]

Article 22(2)

> *When the Arbitral Tribunal has declared the proceedings closed, it shall indicate to the Secretariat an approximate date by which the draft Award will be submitted to the Court for approval pursuant to Article 27. Any postponement of that date shall be communicated to the Secretariat by the Arbitral Tribunal.*

Once the proceedings have been closed, the parties are obviously anxious to receive an Award as soon as possible. While the Rules fix a time limit for the issuance of the final Award (*see* Article 24(2)), that limit may be extended, as discussed further below, and almost always has to be, in some cases repeatedly. Although this is not necessarily attributable to lack of diligence on the part of the arbitrators, there are nevertheless cases in which deliberations are delayed because insufficient attention has been given to planning them or because no precise target date has been fixed for the completion of the arbitrators' work. Article 22(2) is, thus, intended to force the Arbitral Tribunal to fix a target for itself. It is not a binding target, and it need only be "approximate." Moreover, it is not required to be communicated to the parties. But it is hoped that this requirement will encourage greater expedition and alert the Court to possible problems in this connection as early as possible.

This being said, the time required for deliberations depends very much on the characteristics of each case, the completeness and clarity of the parties' presentations of their respective positions and the attitudes and availability of the members of the Arbitral Tribunal as deliberations progress. Disagreements among the arbitrators, in particular, can sometimes consume far more time than

---

[614] *See Fouchard Gaillard and Goldman*, p. 711.

might initially have been imagined, and whatever the Arbitral Tribunal may have first forecast, therefore, may be subject to change.

ARTICLE 23
Conservatory and Interim Measures

Article 23 cures an important ambiguity in the former Rules by explicitly authorizing the Arbitral Tribunal to order interim or conservatory relief. As the Rules previously provided (Article 8(5)), it also permits the parties to seek such relief from a "competent judicial authority" in certain circumstances without infringing the agreement to arbitrate.

The availability of effective interim or conservatory relief in conjunction with potential or pending arbitration proceedings is obviously vital to the arbitral process. Indeed, in some cases, an arbitration may be an exercise in futility if interim relief cannot be obtained rapidly, *e.g.*, to secure assets or to enjoin certain conduct. Thus, the ICC Rules have long recognized the right of the parties to apply to the courts for interim or conservatory relief. Permitting applications to the courts for such relief before an Arbitral Tribunal has been constituted and is in a position to act is justified by the need to assist and ensure the efficacy of the arbitral process.[615] Even thereafter, the interim relief that a party may require (*e.g.*, the attachment of assets) may not otherwise be available. All of the principal international arbitration rules therefore allow the parties to seek judicial recourse for this limited purpose.[616]

Most such rules also explicitly authorize the arbitrators to make orders for interim or conservatory relief, although this has been a more controversial subject in some jurisdictions, particularly in years past. Indeed, until the entry into force of the Swiss Private International Law Act in 1989, the power to order conservatory measures in connection with arbitrations in Switzerland, an important venue for ICC arbitrations, was reserved exclusively to the courts, and this is still the case in some places today.[617]

---

[615] The legitimacy of this has been recognized, moreover, by the courts in most jurisdictions, although there is an aberrational line of United States cases in which it has been held that under Article II(3) of the New York Convention, courts are precluded from granting pre-Award attachments because the intent of the New York Convention is that there be no significant judicial intervention until after an arbitration Award is made. *McCreary Tire & Rubber Co. v. CEAT*, 501 F.2d 1032 (3d Cir. 1974); *Cooper v. Ateliers de la Motobecane S.A.*, 456 N.Y.S.2d 728 (1982). *But see* (to the contrary) *Carolina Power & Light Co. v. Uranex*, 451 F. Supp. 1044 (N.D. Cal. 1977); *Rogers, Burgun, Shahine & Deschler, Inc. v. Dongson Constr. Co.*, 598 F. Supp. 754 (S.D.N.Y. 1984); *Matrenord, S.A. v. Zokor International Ltd.*, *slip. op.* No. 84-1639 (E.D. Ill. Dec. 19, 1984).

[616] *See e.g.*, AAA International Arbitration Rules, Article 21; LCIA Rules, Article 25; UNCITRAL Rules, Article 26; WIPO Arbitration Rules, Article 46.

[617] *See* Blessing, note 188, *supra*, p. 31 ("In Europe, for instance, Austria, Italy, Greece and some Scandinavian countries reserve th[e] authority [to grant interim measures] to State courts. The reserved prerogatives of State courts cannot normally be departed from by agreement of the parties, for instance by agreeing to submit disputes to the ICC Rules").

The ICC Rules in effect thirty years ago therefore did not refer to or otherwise acknowledge any possible authority of the Arbitral Tribunal to issue interim or conservatory measures. Instead, they merely authorized the parties to apply to the courts "in cases of urgency, whether prior to or during the proceedings" (1955 Rules, Article 13(5)). By 1975, however, the power of the arbitrators to order such relief was more widely accepted, and it was therefore proposed to add to the Rules a specific provision permitting this. But rather than saying so explicitly, the new rule that emerged (Article 8(5)) merely referred to "the relevant powers reserved to the arbitrator," thus, implying that the arbitrator may have such powers. The implication was reinforced, however, by the addition, at the same time, of a new restriction on the right of the parties to refer to the courts following the transmission of the file to the Arbitral Tribunal. Thereafter, a party would be allowed to apply to the courts for such relief only in "exceptional circumstances." While not setting forth the arbitrators' powers explicitly, Article 8(5) nevertheless created a unique bias (not present in most other arbitration rules) against recourse to the courts once the arbitrators are in possession of the file. It was thereafter generally considered that, in the absence of a contractual or legal impediment, ICC arbitrators could, thus, issue orders for interim or conservatory relief.[618]

The failure of the Rules to say this expressly, however, continued to nourish doubts as to the extent of the powers "reserved to the arbitrator" under the ICC Rules. Indeed, a particularly vivid illustration of this was provided by the judgment of the English House of Lords in 1994 in the related cases of *Coppée-Lavalin S.A./N.V.* v. *Ken-Ren Chemicals and Fertilizers Ltd ("Ken-Ren")* and *Voest-Alpine Aktiengesellschaft* v. *Ken-Ren*.[619] In those cases, the House of Lords found that, under the then applicable law of England – which has since been modified by the Arbitration Act 1996 – the English courts would be justified, in the circumstances, in exercising their discretion to order the provision of security for costs by the Claimant party in two ICC arbitrations being conducted in London. Among the factors that appear to have had a bearing on the House of Lords' judgment was its uncertainty as to the power of ICC arbitrators to make such an order under the ICC Rules.[620]

In the light of such uncertainties and other related considerations, as mentioned below, the ICC undertook to revisit Article 8(5) when preparing the New Rules.

---

[618] For a detailed analysis of former Article 8(5), *see* Schwartz, "The Practices and Experience of the ICC Court," *Conservatory and Provisional Measures in International Arbitration* (ICC Publishing 1993), p. 45.

[619] [1994] 2 Lloyd's Rep. 109.

[620] On the subject of the *Ken-Ren* cases generally, *see* Sarre, "Security for Costs in ICC arbitration in England – The *Ken-Ren* Cases," *International Commercial Arbitration in Europe, ICC Ct. Bull.,* Special Supplement (1994), p. 58. Under the English Arbitration Act 1996, parties may now seek security for costs only from the arbitrators.

Article 23(1)

> *Unless the parties have otherwise agreed, as soon as the file has been transmitted to it, the Arbitral Tribunal may, at the request of a party, order any interim or conservatory measures it deems appropriate. The Arbitral Tribunal may make the granting of any such measure subject to appropriate security being furnished by the requesting party. Any such measures shall take the form of an order, giving reasons, or of an Award, as the Arbitral Tribunal considers appropriate.*

The inclusion in the Rules of Article 23(1) now makes it clear that the Arbitral Tribunal has the power to "order any interim or conservatory measures it deems appropriate." The expression "interim or conservatory measures" has not been defined, thus permitting the Arbitral Tribunal to construe those words as broadly as may be appropriate in each case.[621] Moreover, unlike the UNCITRAL Rules (Article 26) and the UNCITRAL Model Law (Article 17), Article 23(1) does not require that the measures concern "the subject-matter of the dispute." Thus, provided that there is a sufficient connection with the arbitration, the Arbitral Tribunal's authority may extend to other matters of an interim or conservatory nature. Although not specifically mentioned, the drafters, thus, considered the wording of Article 23(1) to be broad enough to embrace applications for security for costs.[622]

Article 23(1) also now helpfully clarifies the Arbitral Tribunal's power to order interim or conservatory measures "as soon as the file has been transmitted" to it by the Secretariat. The tribunal is therefore not required to wait until the Terms of Reference have been drawn up, as was sometimes thought in the past. But no mechanism, outside the courts, is provided for the granting of interim relief until

---

[621] The variety of conservatory and interim measures encountered in connection with international arbitration proceedings is enormous and extends far beyond the mere conservation or disposal of goods to injunctions of all kinds, the preservation of evidence, the protection of trade secrets, orders for provisional payment, the appointment of experts to report upon factual matters, the posting of guarantees and the like. *See generally*, Bond, "The Nature of Conservatory and Provisional Measures," *Conservatory and Provisional Measures in International Arbitration* (ICC Publishing 1993), p. 8; *and* Bernardini, "The Powers of the Arbitrator," in the same publication, p. 21.

[622] Notwithstanding the experience of the *Ken-Ren* cases, those drafting the New Rules were reluctant to mention security for costs expressly because they did not wish to encourage the proliferation of such applications, which, apart from being rare, are generally disfavored in ICC arbitrations. *See, e.g.,* the Award in ICC Case No. 7047 (1994), *ASA Bull.* (1995), p. 31. *See also* Sandrock, "The *Cautio Judicatum Solvi* in International Arbitration Proceedings," paper presented at the ASA Conference in Zurich (January 31, 1997) on "Costs and their Allocation." On the basis of Article 23(1), it should also be possible for an Arbitral Tribunal to order a party to pay its share of the advance on costs for the arbitration. *See* Article 30 *infra*.

the tribunal is in possession of the file.[623] In this regard, the ICC published rules, separate from its arbitration rules, for a pre-arbitral referee procedure in 1990.[624] The rules provide for the designation of a "referee" empowered to make various interim orders. During the preparation of the New Rules, it was proposed to incorporate the pre-arbitral referee rules into the arbitration rules. However, there was little support for this proposal, primarily because of the general perception that the pre-arbitral rules have not generated a following. They shall therefore remain in force alongside, but distinct from, the rules of arbitration.

The ICC was reluctant to specify in Article 23(1) what form orders of interim or conservatory relief ought to take. Article 23(1), thus, leaves it up to the arbitrators to determine whether such a decision should take the form of an order, with reasons, or an Award, a matter that will often depend upon the nature of the measure and the laws of the place of the arbitration or the country where the measure is to be carried out. In some jurisdictions, an interim order of an arbitrator, even if stated to be an Award, may not be enforceable as such, and this may, as a consequence, limit the effectiveness of such an order.[625] Indeed, neither the UNCITRAL Model Law nor the New York Convention defines the term "Award," adding to the uncertainties in this regard. In the specific context of ICC arbitration, however, whether a decision of an arbitrator is styled as an Award or an order may effect its need for prior scrutiny by the Court pursuant to Article 27 of the Rules (*see infra*).[626] Partly for this reason, a Working Party of the ICC Commission recommended some years ago that interim measures should generally be issued as orders, rather than Awards, except possibly where an Award is desired in the hope that it will enhance the possible enforcement of the arbitrators' decision.[627]

---

[623] Prior to 1955, however, the Rules contained a provision authorizing the President of the Court of Arbitration to appoint an expert to order conservatory and other measures before the arbitrator "entered upon his duties." *See* Schwartz, *supra*, note 618, p. 46. Why the ICC decided to eliminate that provision in 1955 is unclear. However, according to Frédéric Eisemann, the then Secretary General of the Court, it gave rise to "problems." Eisemann, *supra*, note 431, p. 395.

[624] The ICC's Pre-Arbitral Referee Rules are reprinted in Appendix 10 *infra*. For a commentary on those rules, *see* Hausmaninger, "The ICC Rules for a Pre-Arbitral Referee Procedure: A Step Towards Solving the Problem of Provisional Relief in International Commercial Arbitration?" *ICSID Rev. – For. Inv. L. Jour.*, Vol. 7 (1992), p. 82; *see also* Derains, "*Expertise Technique et Référé Arbitral*," *Rev. arb.* (1982), p. 239.

[625] *See* Pryles, "Interlocutory Orders and Convention Awards: The Case of *Resort Condominiums* v. *Bolwell*," *Arb. Int.* Vol. 10, No. 4 (1994), p. 385.

[626] In this connection, the French courts have held that it is the Arbitral Tribunal, rather than the ICC Court, that should decide whether a particular decision is required to take the form of an order or an Award. *See* note 65 *supra*.

[627] *See* Final Report on Interim and Partial Awards, *supra*, note 62, p. 29:
Interim measures of protection are, by definition, not intended to be final and irreversible. Moreover, such decisions are generally not accompanied by detailed reasons. Scrutiny by the Court of Arbitration cannot therefore make any meaningful contribution. Moreover, as great speed is normally of the essence in a request for an interim measure of protection, scrutiny would sometimes render the remedy ineffective ... . If it is made in the form of an award, then it must of course be scrutinized under Article [27] of the Rules – otherwise, the validity of the order might be called into question.

Although arbitrators cannot otherwise compel compliance with their decisions, parties are nevertheless generally reluctant to disregard them.

In appropriate circumstances, the arbitrators may also condition the granting of interim relief on "appropriate security being given" by the requesting party. This is a power for which other arbitration rules also expressly provide.

Although not expressly stated, the arbitrators' powers are subject to possible mandatory provisions of law to the contrary in certain jurisdictions. In addition, Article 23(1) is one of the few provisions in the Rules from which the parties are expressly allowed to derogate.

Article 23(2)

> *Before the file is transmitted to the Arbitral Tribunal, and in appropriate circumstances even thereafter, the parties may apply to any competent judicial authority for interim or conservatory measures. The application of a party to a judicial authority for such measures or for the implementation of any such measures ordered by an Arbitral Tribunal shall not be deemed to be an infringement or a waiver of the arbitration agreement and shall not affect the relevant powers reserved to the Arbitral Tribunal. Any such application and any measures taken by the judicial authority must be notified without delay to the Secretariat. The Secretariat shall inform the Arbitral Tribunal thereof.*

Article 23(2) addresses the two instances in which a party may seek a court's assistance in obtaining conservatory or interim relief. The first, as already noted, is where the file has not yet been transmitted to the Arbitral Tribunal. The second is where the Arbitral Tribunal is already in possession of the file, but the circumstances nevertheless make recourse to a court "appropriate."

The reference in Article 23(2) to "appropriate circumstances" replaces the requirement of "exceptional circumstances" in former Article 8(5).[628] While the new language is seemingly less restrictive, it is not intended to alter the presumption that, once the Arbitral Tribunal is in possession of the file, requests for interim or conservatory relief are normally to be addressed to it. This should not be the case, however, where the Arbitral Tribunal is without authority to grant the relief required or is not otherwise in a position to do so. What the change from "exceptional" to "appropriate" recognizes is that the circumstances in which a party may not be able to obtain suitable relief from an Arbitral Tribunal are not necessarily "exceptional."

---

[628] For a discussion of the meaning of "exceptional" under Article 8(5), *see* Schwartz, *supra*, note 618, p. 54-56.

Nevertheless, a party must take care that an action initiated before the courts does not constitute a waiver or infringement of the agreement to arbitrate.[629] Whether or not it may depends upon whether the action in question should properly be regarded as an "interim or conservatory" measure under Article 23(2) and, if the Arbitral Tribunal is already in possession of the file, whether it is "appropriate" to refer to the courts. Once the Arbitral Tribunal has been seized, except possibly in cases of extreme urgency or where it is clear that the Arbitral Tribunal could not grant the relief required, the prudent course would therefore probably be to seek the Arbitral Tribunal's intervention first. Indeed, Article 23(2), unlike former Article 8(5), expressly provides in this connection for the possible application by a party to a court for the "implementation" of any measures ordered by the Arbitral Tribunal. This, of course, does not mean that a court would necessarily accept to provide the assistance required. Whether it would do so depends, not upon the language of Article 23(2), but upon the law of the place where such relief is sought.

The foregoing is equally true in respect of any interim or conservatory measures that a party may seek to obtain. Before granting any such relief, a court must be satisfied that it is, in fact, competent to do so[630] and that the measure is truly of an "interim or conservatory" nature. Different kinds of relief may, thus, be available in different jurisdictions. In France, for example, before the Arbitral Tribunal has been constituted a "*juge des référés*"[631] may intervene and grant "any measures that are not seriously disputed or that are justified by a dispute that has arisen."[632] This procedure is available "whenever certain factors connecting the dispute with France are satisfied, such as if one of the parties has French nationality, if the place of performance is in France, or if France is the place where the damage which is the cause of the dispute took place."[633]

---

[629] *See* ICC Case No. 5650 (1989), *ICC Arbitral Awards 1991-1995*, p. 34, (Arbitral Tribunal determined that a party waived its right to arbitrate not only because it asked the Court to appoint an expert, but also because it requested that the other party be condemned to pay damages); *see also* ICC Case No. 2444 (1976), *ICC Arbitral Awards 1974-1985*, p. 285; *and* ICC Case No. 4156 (1983), p. 515.

[630] For an example of a case where a court considered whether it should order interim relief in connection with an ICC arbitration in another jurisdiction, *see Channel Tunnel Group Limited* v. *Balfour Beatty Construction Limited*, [1993] A.C. 334 (English House of Lords).

[631] *See* Article 849 of the French New Code of Civil Procedure. A *juge des référés* is either the president of the commercial court or the president of the general jurisdiction trial court, the *Tribunal de grande instance*. Hauteclocque, "French Judicial Expertise Procedure and International Arbitration," *J. Arb. Int.,* Vol. 4, No. 2 (1987), pp. 77-78

[632] *See* Hauteclocque, *supra,* note 631, p. 78; *see generally, Fouchard Gaillard and Goldman,* p. 741; and Boisséson, *supra,* note 116, p. 761.

[633] *See* Hauteclocque, *supra,* note 631, p. 78.

The *"référé"* procedure is commonly used to obtain the appointment of an expert to assess, for example, the cause of a construction defect. Although this "expert is not to act as a substitute for those who will later have the task of deciding the case, but simply to provide clarification and detail on points linked to the actual or potential subject matter of the dispute,"[634] in some instances his factual findings may, as a practical matter, have a crucial impact on the outcome of a dispute.[635]

An example of an expert appointed to assess such fundamental factual issues under the *"référé"* procedure is the recently decided *Eurodisney* case.[636] Disney had contracted with *Impresa Pizzarotti* to construct a portion of its Eurodisney theme-park in France. When difficulties arose between the parties, Disney commenced an arbitration under the contract's ICC arbitration clause. However, after the arbitrators had been nominated, but before the Terms of Reference were transmitted to the tribunal, *Impresa Pizzarotti* obtained an order from a *juge des référés* appointing an expert to assess various facts regarding the project. The expert's mission broadly required him "to describe the work completed as of the date of the contract's termination and assess the extent of that work in light of the contractual stipulations, to state whether the work is in conformity with the initial forecasts and, if it is not, [to describe] how and to what degree ... ."[637] Although Disney complained that this mission went far beyond the limited role such experts are supposed to play under the *"référé"* procedure and was neither truly interim nor conservatory, the appointment and the expert's mission were upheld by France's highest court.[638]

In the wake of the Eurodisney case, it might be asked whether it is possible to limit contractually a party's right of recourse to the courts for interim relief under Article 23(2). Unlike Article 23(1), Article 23(2) does not provide for pos-

---

[634] *Id.*

[635] *Id.*, at p. 97:

As previously stated, the only task assigned to the judicial expert is that of giving an opinion on a technical problem. He must not in any way make a ruling on the liability (in the legal sense of the term) of any of the parties. However, very often the technical aspects of a case influence or even totally determine its legal aspects. Consequently, the findings in the expert's report are crucial. For example, if an expert has to determine the cause of a plane crash occurring on landing, his findings are bound to have an effect on the legal liabilities.

[636] *Société Eurodisney c/ société Impresa Pizzarotti, Cour de cassation* (11 October, 1995), *Rev. arb.* (1996), pp. 191-233.

[637] *Id.*, at 229.

[638] Another controversial use of this procedure in ICC arbitration is where a party convinces a *juge des référés* that its claim is not "seriously contestable" and, on this basis, obtains an order for provisional payment of all or part of the claim. *See* Goldman, *"Arbitrage Commercial International," Juriscl. dr. intl.*, fasc.586-5-1, No. 104; Boisséson, *supra*, note 116, p. 761; Gaudemet-Tallon, Note, *Société Balenciaga c/ société Allierti et Giovanozzi, Cour de cassation* (November 28, 1989) and *Société Horeva c/ société Sitas*, (March 6, 1990), *Cour de cassation, Rev. arb.* (1990), p. 637. *See also* the Award in ICC Case No. 2444 (1976), *supra*, note 629.

sible derogations by the parties, although it is difficult to see why such a derogation should give rise to a problem, provided that it is otherwise valid.[639]

As under the previous Rules, Article 23(2) provides that when conservatory or interim measures are requested from a judicial authority, the application must be notified to the Secretariat of the Court, which will then inform the Arbitral Tribunal. The same notification must be made concerning the measures themselves, should they be granted. However, while this notification is required by the New Rules, if it is not made, this has no effect on the legitimacy of the conservatory or interim measures requested from the state court or the right of the defaulting party to arbitrate.

[639] Such a derogation would appear to be valid in France. *See* Hory, *"Mesures d'instruction in futurum et arbitrage,"* Rev. arb. (1996), pp. 191, 198 ("the power of the state judge to order conservatory measures ... can be set aside only by an express agreement of the parties or by an implicit agreement resulting from the adoption of arbitration rules which include such a renunciation") (quoting *Société Atlantic Triton c/ République populaire de Guinée et société guinéenne de pêche (Soguipêche), Cour de cassation* (November 18, 1996), *Clunet* (1987), p. 125. Regarding the exclusion of judicial interim relief by party agreement under United States law, *see* Mills, "State International Arbitration Statutes and the U.S. Arbitration Act: Unifying the Availability of Interim Relief," *Fordham International Law Journal*, Vol. 13 (1989-90), p. 604; *but see Anaconda* v. *American Sugar Refining Co.*, 322 U.S. 42 (1944) (holding that parties could not exclude court jurisdiction to grant seizure of a vessel).

Chapter 6
Awards (Articles 24-29)

The issuance by the Arbitral Tribunal of an Award is the culmination of the arbitral process. Articles 24 to 29 bring together in one section of the New Rules all of the relevant provisions on this subject that were formerly contained in Articles 17 to 19 and 21 to 25. The New Rules do not significantly alter the previous provisions concerning the Award. Indeed, the Rules' two most distinctive features in this regard have been retained, *i.e.,* the imposition of a six-month time limit on the Arbitral Tribunal for the issuance of the final Award and the scrutiny of all draft Awards by the Court (*see* Articles 24 and 27 *infra*). The Rules' prior provisions have been supplemented, however, by a new Article (Article 29) on the correction and interpretation of the Award, which brings the Rules into line with modern international arbitration practice.

ARTICLE 24
Time Limit for the Award

Unlike most other international arbitration rules, the ICC Rules have always fixed a time limit for the issuance of the Arbitral Tribunal's final Award.[640] Although extendible by the Court, the time limit emphasizes the need for expedition, and, indeed, the Arbitral Tribunal's failure to complete the arbitration in a timely manner can serve as a basis for the replacement of one or more of its members pursuant to Article 12(2) (*see supra*). Article 24 reproduces, with only slight alterations, the provisions on this subject that were contained in Article 18 of the former Rules. Neither the length of the time limit (six months) nor its extendibility have changed. However, the time limit is no longer dependent upon the payment of the advance on costs, as was previously the case. In addition, former Article 18(3), which concerned the Court's possible refusal to grant an extension, has been deleted.

---

[640] Thus, for example, no such time limit is included in the AAA, LCIA or UNCITRAL Rules. *But cf.* WIPO arbitration Rules, Article 63.

Article 24(1)

> *The time limit within which the Arbitral Tribunal must render its final Award is six months. Such time limit shall start to run from the date of the last signature by the Arbitral Tribunal or of the parties of the Terms of Reference, or, in the case of application of Article 18(3), the date of the notification to the Arbitral Tribunal by the Secretariat of the approval of the Terms of Reference by the Court.*

Like its predecessor, Article 24(1) obliges the Arbitral Tribunal to "render" its final Award within six months, subject to possible extensions under Article 24(2).[641] The six months in question begin to run immediately upon the signature of the Terms of Reference (or, in the case of their approval by the Court, the notification of such approval by the Secretariat), and the Award is not considered to have been "rendered" until it has been scrutinized and approved by the Court pursuant to Article 27 (*see infra*), and signed by the Arbitral Tribunal.[642] Thus, in order to comply with the requirement of Article 24(1), it is not sufficient for the Arbitral Tribunal to submit a draft of the Award to the Court within the period stipulated in that Article.[643]

The six-month period laid down by Article 24(1) was introduced into the Rules in 1975. Prior to that time, the final Award was required to be rendered within sixty days. But by 1975, this was no longer considered to be realistic. The same might possibly be said today about the requirement that the Award be rendered within six months. Indeed, there are few ICC Awards that are ever rendered within such a relatively short period of time, and satisfaction of the six-month time limit, thus, tends to be the exception rather than the rule. During the preparation of the New Rules, the Working Party therefore considered extending the time limit to nine or possibly even twelve months. Alternatively, it was

---

[641] The parties may agree to shorten this time limit, however. *See* Article 32 *infra*.

[642] Under the former rule, the time limit did not begin to run until the Terms of Reference, in addition to being signed, had become "operative" through the payment of the advance on costs. However, as this requirement has been eliminated (*see* Article 30 *infra*), the period specified in Article 24(1) does not depend in any way on the status of the advance on costs. Moreover, Article 24(1) does not otherwise make any provision for its possible suspension in any circumstances. Although it might be possible to argue that the time limit ought to be suspended if, for example, the Arbitral Tribunal is directed by the Secretariat to suspend its work pursuant to Article 30(4) (*see infra*) or pending the replacement of an arbitrator, it would be complicated, as a practical matter, for the Secretariat and the Court to keep track of possible suspensions. The Court has therefore not generally taken account of such events in monitoring compliance with the time limit and has instead merely extended the time limit, as necessary. *See* Article 24(2) *infra*.

[643] *See also* on this point, *Société Ripolin Georget Freitag* c/ *société Henry Clarks & Sons, Cour de cassation* (April 27, 1981), Note Bernard, *Rev. arb.* (1983), p. 105.

proposed that the time limit be eliminated and that the Rules provide instead for the issuance of the Award "without undue delay" (as is implicitly required by most other arbitration rules).

Ultimately, however, it was decided to retain the six-month time limit. Although it was recognized that such a deadline may be difficult to satisfy in complex cases, the Working Party nevertheless considered that such a period remains a reasonable goal. Given that one of the main objectives of the New Rules is to accelerate the ICC arbitration process, most of the Working Party's members were reluctant to relax the requirements of the former Rules in this respect. Moreover, it was hoped that Article 24(1) would serve as a guidepost to the Arbitral Tribunal when preparing its provisional timetable for the arbitration pursuant to Article 18(4) (*see supra*).

Article 24(2)

> *The Court may extend this time limit pursuant to a reasoned request from the Arbitral Tribunal or on its own initiative if it decides it is necessary to do so.*

This provision is substantially the same as the corresponding Article in the former Rules. As in the case of the Terms of Reference (*see* Article 18(2) *supra*), the Court, thus, continues to have the power to extend the time limit for the Award, either on its own initiative or pursuant to a "reasoned request" from the Arbitral Tribunal. Such extensions are also granted by the Court, as necessary, in the same manner as for the Terms of Reference. Thus, the Secretariat reports to the first Committee meeting of the Court each month on every case in which the deadline will be expiring during the following month, and it has been the Court's usual practice to extend the deadline in question by an additional three months (as opposed to two months in the case of the Terms of Reference) for as many times as may be necessary.

In recent years, the Court has nevertheless increasingly sought to take a more customized approach towards the extension of the time limit for the Award, and its ability to do so should be enhanced by (i) the Arbitral Tribunal's obligation under the New Rules (Article 18(4)) to produce and amend, as necessary, a provisional time table and (ii) the requirement (*see* Article 22(2)) that, when closing the proceedings, the Arbitral Tribunal shall indicate to the Secretariat an approximate date by which the draft Award will be submitted to the Court for approval pursuant to Article 27. As in the case of the Terms of Reference, the Court is nevertheless not required to give any reasons for its decision to extend the time limit. Nor is it required to solicit the parties' prior comments or even to inform them of its decision.[644]

---

[644] *See* note 541 *supra*. *See also* the Award in ICC Case No. 2730 (1982), *supra*, note 191, concerning the relationship between the time limit in the ICC Rules, the time limit of the law of the place of arbitration and the concept of *"péremption d'instance."*

Although the Court has been criticized for routinely extending the time limit for the Award, it usually has no reasonable alternative if the time limit is about to expire without an Award being rendered. The former Rules (Article 18(3)) further provided in this connection that, when no extension is granted, the Court shall, after replacing the arbitrators, "determine the manner in which the dispute is to be resolved." However, the meaning of this provision was obscure, and it was never invoked. It has therefore now been deleted. Indeed, even where the Court decides to replace one or more of the arbitrators, it nevertheless also extends the time limit for the Award as a precaution. The only cases in which the time limit is not extended are those in which neither party has expressed an interest in the continuation of the proceedings. In such circumstances, the time limit may be allowed to lapse.

ARTICLE 25

Making of the Award

Article 25 combines in one Article the provisions concerning the Award that were formerly contained in Articles 19 and 22 and also introduces the explicit requirement (Article 25(2)) that the Award shall state the reasons upon which it is based. Unlike Article 24, which only concerns the final Award, Article 25 applies to all Awards of the Tribunal, whether interim, partial or otherwise (*see* Article 2 *supra*). However, no more than Article 2 does Article 25 specify which decisions of the Arbitral Tribunal are required to take the form of an Award. As already discussed in connection with Article 2, it is therefore necessary for the Arbitral Tribunal to consider, whenever making a decision, whether it needs to be included in an Award or may satisfactorily be issued in the form of an order.

Article 25(1)

> *When the Arbitral Tribunal is composed of more than one arbitrator, an Award is given by a majority decision. If there be no majority, the Award shall be made by the chairman of the Arbitral Tribunal alone.*

Like Article 19 of the previous Rules, Article 25(1) permits Awards to be made by a majority decision or, in the absence of a majority, by the chairman alone. The drafting of this provision has been slightly altered, however, to reflect its possible application whenever there is "more than one arbitrator" and not just where, as stated in former Article 19, "three arbitrators have been appointed." (Although not expressly stated in Article 25(1), it may reasonably be construed as applying as well to orders of the Arbitral Tribunal.)

The power of the chairman of the Arbitral Tribunal to decide alone, in the absence of a majority, has been an important characteristic of the ICC Rules since 1955.[645] The Rules differ in this respect from the UNCITRAL Rules (Article

---

[645] This has been regarded as such a fundamental provision of the ICC Rules that the Court has, in the past, refused to accept derogations from it.

31(1)) and certain others, which require a majority in all circumstances. The latter approach has the disadvantage, however, of requiring the chairman to obtain the agreement of at least one of the co-arbitrators, which can force compromises that may be neither legitimate nor reasonable.[646] In contrast, the ICC approach permits the chairman to maintain a completely independent position and discourages partisan conduct on the part of the co-arbitrators, who know that the chairman is not required to agree with either of them in order to issue an Award. This serves, in and of itself, to promote the integrity of decision-making under the ICC Rules.

This having been said, when more than one arbitrator has been appointed, most ICC Awards are unanimous. Only a few are made by a majority, and Awards of the chairman alone are extremely rare.[647]

While providing for the possible making of an Award by less than all of the Arbitral Tribunal's members, Article 25(1) nevertheless does not explicitly lay down any requirements regarding the Award's signature. The Arbitral Tribunal is therefore required to be attentive to any relevant provisions of law that might mandatorily apply at the place of the arbitration in this regard. In the event that an arbitrator refuses to sign the Award, the Award should usually indicate that the arbitrator in question was given the opportunity to sign, but refused to do so, and the reason for such refusal.[648]

Neither Article 25(1) nor any other provision of the Rules refers to the possible issuance by an arbitrator of a dissenting opinion. In this respect, the Rules do not differ from most other arbitration rules or laws. Indeed, the use of dissenting opinions has not generally been encouraged in international arbitration, and concerns have, from time to time, been expressed in certain jurisdictions (particularly, in civil law countries) about their possible impact on the enforceability of the Award if they violate the secrecy of the Arbitral Tribunal's deliberations.[649]

---

[646] Thus, for example, in a case of contractual liability, the arbitrator appointed by the Claimant may consider that the Claimant is entitled to damages amounting to U.S. $2,000,000, while the arbitrator appointed by the Respondent believes that the latter has no liability. If the chairman concludes that the Claimant is entitled to U.S. $1,000,000, he can impose his views under Article 25(1). If a majority decision were required, however, he would need to work out a compromise with one of the co-arbitrators. For a discussion of the experience of the Iran-U.S. Claims Tribunal in this regard, *see* Böckstiegel, "Experience as an Arbitrator Using the UNCITRAL Arbitration Rules," *Etudes de Droit International en l'Honneur de Pierre Lalive* (Helbing & Lichtenhahn 1993), p. 423.

[647] Thus, for example, in 1996, only one Award was rendered by the chairman alone out of the 217 Awards submitted to the Court for scrutiny during that year. *See* Hascher, "Scrutiny of Draft Awards by the Court: 1996 Overview," *ICC Ct. Bull.,* Vol. 8, No. 1 (1997), p. 17. *See also,* as an example of one such Award, the Award in ICC Case No. 3881 (1984), Note Jarvin, *ICC Arbitral Awards 1986-1990*, p. 257.

[648] *See, e.g.,* AAA International Arbitration Rules, Article 26(1); LCIA Rules, Article 26(4); UNCITRAL Rules, Article 32(4); WIPO Arbitration Rules, Article 62(d).

[649] For a discussion of the considerations relating to the use of dissenting opinions in international arbitration, *see* "Final Report on Dissenting and Separate Opinions" of the ICC Commission Working Party on this subject (M. Hunter, Chairman), *ICC Ct. Bull.,* Vol. 2, No. 1 (1990), p. 32.

The Rules nevertheless do not themselves preclude the communication to the parties of dissenting opinions, and such opinions are issued together with a small fraction of ICC Awards every year.[650] However, a dissenting opinion is not considered by the Court to form part of the Award and, thus, while read by the Court, is neither formally scrutinized nor approved by it pursuant to Article 27 (*see infra*). Moreover, the Court long ago adopted the practice of communicating dissenting opinions to the parties only if the non-dissenting arbitrators have no objection[651] and if there does not otherwise appear to be any legal impediment to doing so.[652]

Article 25(2)

> *The Award shall state the reasons upon which it is based.*

This is a new provision that comports with modern international arbitration practice[653] as well as the usual practice in ICC arbitration. Indeed, under the previous Rules, the Court systematically required Awards to be reasoned, and this was widely assumed to be inherent in the provision for the scrutiny and approval of Award by the Court.[654] The only instances, which were exceptional, in which the Court did not require reasons were cases where the parties had agreed that they did not want any to be given, and this was permitted by the law at the place of the arbitration.[655] It will now be for the Court to determine whether derogations from Article 25(2) should be permitted in such circumstances.

Apart from being required by the law in most jurisdictions today, the reasons set forth in the Award should demonstrate that the Arbitral Tribunal has given full consideration to the parties' respective submissions. Indeed, the tribunal's reasoning may, in certain cases, enhance the likelihood that the parties will vol-

---

[650] In 1996, 19 Awards were accompanied by dissenting opinions. *See* Hascher *supra,* note 647. *See also* the case mentioned in note 647 *supra,* in which there were two dissenting opinions.

[651] The Court's practice in this regard has been found to be valid by the Swiss courts. *See Elektroprivreda c/ G.E.C. Alsthom S.A., Tribunal fédéral suisse* (May 25, 1992), *ASA Bull.* (1992), p. 381.

[652] This was formerly stated in Article 17 of the Court's previous Internal Rules to be one of the matters checked by the Court when scrutinizing draft Awards. Although the Internal Rules (Article 6) no longer refer expressly to dissenting opinions, consideration of their admissibility would nevertheless fall within the Court's examination of the mandatory legal requirements at the place of the arbitration.

[653] *See, e.g.,* AAA International Arbitration Rules, Article 27(2); LCIA Rules, Article 26(1); UNCITRAL Rules, Article 32(3); WIPO Arbitration Rules, Article 62(c); UNCITRAL Model Law, Article 31(2).

[654] *See, e.g., Société Swiss Oil c/ République du Gabon et société Petrogab, Cour d'appel de Paris* (June 16, 1988), Note Jarrosson, *Rev. arb.* (1989), p. 309.

[655] Article 31(2) of the UNCITRAL Model Law is an example of a provision that permits the parties to agree that reasons shall not be given. Reasons are also not required, under that law, in the case of a consent Award.

untarily abide by the arbitrators' decision,[656] and the sufficiency and coherence of the tribunal's reasons are therefore important considerations when the Award is being scrutinized by the Court pursuant to Article 27.

Article 25(3)

> *The Award shall be deemed to be made at the place of the arbitration and on the date stated therein.*

Article 25(3) corresponds to Article 22 of the former Rules, but is now more precise. Thus, instead of providing, as did Article 22, that the Award is deemed to be made at the place of the "arbitration proceedings," Article 25(3) states that it is deemed to be made at the place of the "arbitration." This is because the proceedings may, pursuant to Article 14(2), be held at a place other than that of the arbitration. Similarly, Article 25(3) now also deems the Award to be made "on the date stated therein" and not on the date "when it is signed." Indeed, when there are three arbitrators, the Award may be signed on three different dates.[657] Article 25(3) therefore now permits the Arbitral Tribunal to specify an appropriate date, although it follows from Article 27 that the date of the Award cannot precede its approval by the Court.

The presumption that the Award is made at the place of the arbitration obviates any need for the arbitrators to meet at that place in order to sign it. Indeed, arbitrators rarely meet solely for the purpose of signing an Award, which is more frequently circulated among them for signature or, in the case of sole arbitrators, signed where they reside. Without such a deeming provision in the Rules, there might, thus, be a risk that the Award would be found to be made at a place other than that of the arbitration.[658]

ARTICLE 26
Award by Consent

> *If the parties reach a settlement after the file has been transmitted to the Arbitral Tribunal in accordance with Article 13, the settlement shall be recorded in the form of an Award made by consent of the parties if so requested by the parties and if the Arbitral Tribunal agrees to do so.*

---

[656] *See* Fontaine, "Drafting the Award: A Perspective From A Civil Law Jurist," *ICC Ct. Bull.*, Vol. 5, No. 1 (1994), p. 30; Lloyd, "Writing Awards: A Common Lawyer's Perspective," *ICC Ct. Bull.*, Vol. 5, No. 1 (1994), p. 38.

[657] For an example of a case where the consequences of this under former Article 22 were considered, *see Société Eiffage c/ société Butec, Cour d'appel de Paris* (June 17, 1997), Note Bureau, *Rev. arb.* (1997), p. 583. Although not stated in the Rules, the provisions of Article 25(3) should apply to orders of the Arbitral Tribunal as well as Awards.

[658] *See, e.g.,* the decision of the English House of Lords in *Hiscox v. Outhwaite* [1991] 3 WLR 297, *ICCA Yearbook* XVII (1992), p. 599.

Article 26 is the only provision in the Rules that deals expressly with the possible settlement of the arbitration after the file has been transmitted to the Arbitral Tribunal. It is identical to Article 17 of the former Rules, except that it requires an Award by consent to be issued only if (i) this is requested by the parties and (ii) the Arbitral Tribunal agrees to do so.

Unlike Article 26, Article 17 appeared to require the issuance of a consent Award whenever an arbitration settled following the file's transmission to the arbitrators. However, the Court does not actually insist upon this and has always allowed the parties, as an alternative, simply to withdraw their claims and request the administrative closure of the file, following which the Court fixes the ICC administrative expenses and the arbitrators' fees and expenses (*see* Article 31 *infra*). Awards by consent are therefore to be issued only when requested by the parties. This is now made clear in Article 26.

Article 26 adds the additional requirement, however, that the Arbitral Tribunal must also agree to make an Award by consent. It is in this respect similar to certain other rules, which also allow the Arbitral Tribunal to exercise its discretion in this regard.[659] Although it might be asked why the parties should not be permitted to oblige the Arbitral Tribunal to render a consent Award, the Working Party considered that circumstances may arise in which this should not be required. Thus, for example, an Arbitral Tribunal may legitimately be reluctant to formalize as an Award an agreement that is contrary to relevant mandatory laws or that is otherwise fraudulent or illegal. Although the Arbitral Tribunal should normally seek to accommodate the parties if they wish to obtain a consent Award, there are surely reasonable limitations on its possible obligations in this connection.

Meanwhile, as the parties are not required to obtain a consent Award as a condition to terminating the arbitration following a settlement, they need to consider in each case whether there is any advantage in doing so. The conventional reason for seeking such an Award is to make the terms of the settlement subject to enforcement in the same manner as any other Award, *e.g.,* in accordance with the New York Convention. Although it has occasionally been questioned whether an Award by consent constitutes a genuine Award for this purpose,[660] there nevertheless appears to be a broad consensus, consistent with the ICC Rules, most other arbitration rules and the UNCITRAL Model Law (Article 31(2)), that it is.[661]

Similarly, although not expressly stated in Article 26, an Award by consent has generally been considered by the Court to be governed by all of the other provisions of the Rules relating to Awards (Articles 24 to 29). Thus, for exam-

---

[659] *See, e.g.,* AAA International Arbitration Rules, Article 29(1); LCIA Rules, Article 26(8). *But cf.* UNCITRAL Rules, Article 34(1); WIPO Arbitration Rules, Article 65(b), which do not allow the arbitrators any such discretion. Permitting the arbitrators discretion in these circumstances has been questioned. *See* H. Smit, *supra,* note 45, pp. 27-28.

[660] *See Fouchard Gaillard and Goldman,* p. 758; Boisséson, *supra,* note 116, p. 808.

[661] *See also* van den Berg, *The New York Arbitration Convention of 1958* (Kluwer 1981), p. 50.

ple, the Court requires consent Awards, like other Awards, to be submitted in draft form to the Court for scrutiny and approval (*see* Article 27 *infra*), although such Awards are not usually required to be submitted to the Court's plenary session. It might nevertheless be asked whether, and if so, to what extent, a consent Award is also required to state the "reasons upon which it is based" pursuant to Article 25(2). Most other arbitration rules expressly exempt consent Awards from any such requirement. However, the simple statement that an Award is based on a settlement would appear to be an adequate reason for the Award within the meaning of Article 25(2). The arbitrators should not otherwise be required to state the considerations on which the settlement is based.

Ordinarily, a consent Award will bring the arbitration to an end and therefore needs to set out the costs of the arbitration in accordance with Article 31(3) of the Rules (*see infra*). However, a consent Award may also reflect a partial settlement of a dispute, thus permitting the arbitration to continue in respect of the remaining issues.[662]

Article 27

> *Before signing any Award, the Arbitral Tribunal shall submit it in draft form to the Court. The Court may lay down modifications as to the form of the Award and, without affecting the Arbitral Tribunal's liberty of decision, may also draw its attention to points of substance. No award shall be rendered by the Arbitral Tribunal until it has been approved by the Court as to its form.*

The scrutiny and approval of draft Awards by the Court is a fundamental feature of ICC arbitration and one that distinguishes it from all of the other major international arbitration rules. When the Working Party was charged with responsibility for the preparation of the New Rules, the preservation of the scrutiny process was, thus, an express part of its mandate. Accordingly, Article 27 does not substantively alter the provisions on this subject that were formerly contained in Article 21 of the previous Rules.[663]

The purpose of scrutiny. The scrutiny of draft Awards by the Court serves a dual purpose. As stated in Article 27, the first is to identify possible defects of

---

[662] *See, e.g.,* the Award in ICC Case No. 4761 (1984), Note Jarvin, *ICC Arbitral Awards 1986-1990*, p. 298.

[663] There are nevertheless two small differences between Article 27 and Article 21 of the former Rules. While Article 21 referred to "partial or definitive" Awards, Article 27 contains no such reference. This is because the word "Award" has now been defined in Article 2. The other difference is that Article 27 provides that no Award shall be "rendered" until it has been approved by the Court, while Article 21 stated that no Award shall be "signed" before approval. This is intended to clarify that the Award is not made until it has been approved. When it is physically signed, however, is not relevant.

"form," while the second is to draw the arbitrators' attention to points of "substance." Although Article 27 does not itself explain the difference between "form" and "substance," the distinction between the two is crucial as the Court can require the Arbitral Tribunal to incorporate into its Award modifications of form, while the Arbitral Tribunal is free to disregard any matters that the Court may draw to its attention in respect of the Award's substance.[664] Indeed, the Court only approves the Award "as to its form" and not its substance. The latter is the Arbitral Tribunal's sole responsibility.

Notwithstanding the importance of the distinction between form and substance, the difference between the two is not always obvious. When in doubt, the Court has, thus, tended to construe the former more narrowly in order to avoid any possible complaint that it has improperly interfered with the Arbitral Tribunal's liberty of decision. Defects of form nevertheless typically include typographical or computational errors, the absence of elements that may be required to be included in the Award under the law of the place of the arbitration, the absence of reasons or the Award's failure to respect the Arbitral Tribunal's mandate, *i.e.,* where it is *infra* or *ultra petita.*[665] The Court verifies such matters in order to enhance the likelihood that the Award will be capable of enforcement and that it does not contain defects that might cause it to be set aside.

Apart from such matters, the Court may call the arbitrators' attention to substantive aspects of their Award that the Court may find confusing, insufficiently reasoned, inconsistent or contrary to provisions of applicable law. The Court's concern, in making such comments, is to assist the arbitrators in producing an Award that will be of the highest possible quality and that the parties will be more likely to accept and carry out voluntarily as a consequence. Although the Court cannot force the arbitrators to take account of its comments with respect to substance, arbitrators usually do, at least to some extent.

The Court presently scrutinizes slightly more than 200 Awards per year. Of that number, nearly 30 per cent are returned to the arbitrators with comments as to either their form or their substance.[666]

---

[664] In the event that an arbitrator refuses to incorporate into an Award a modification of form mandated by the Court, he could theoretically be replaced under Article 2(12) *supra.* However, there is little precedent for this. *See* Eisemann, *supra,* note 101, p. 364.

[665] In this regard, Article 17 of the Court's Internal Rules formerly provided that, when scrutinizing draft Awards, the Court "pays particular attention to the respect of the formal requirements laid down by the law applicable to the proceedings and, where relevant, by the mandatory rules of the place of arbitration, notably with regard to the reasons for awards, their signature and the admissibility of dissenting opinions." This provision has been replaced, however, by Article 6 of the new Internal Rules (Appendix II to the Rules), which simply states that the Court "considers, to the extent practicable, the requirements of mandatory law at the place of arbitration." The qualification "to the extent practicable" has been added in order to indicate that the Court's efforts are "neither infinite nor unlimited." *See* Grigera Naón, *supra,* note 47, p. 44.

[666] *See* Hascher *supra* note 647, p. 17, where it is noted that out of 217 Awards scrutinized in 1996, 26 could not be approved when first submitted to the Court and 34 more were approved subject to modifications as to form.

Scrutiny procedures. All draft Awards are first communicated by the Arbitral Tribunal to the counsel in charge of the file at the Secretariat.[667] The counsel will then ordinarily review the Award and may take the initiative of calling obvious errors to the Arbitral Tribunal's attention or raising matters that may reasonably be anticipated to give rise to questions before the Court. A copy of the draft will also be given to the Secretary General and Deputy Secretary General/General Counsel of the Court for review at that stage. The counsel in charge of the file will then discuss with the Secretary General and the General Counsel whether the Award should be submitted for scrutiny to the Court's monthly plenary session ("A" Awards) or to one of the Court's thrice-monthly Committees ("B" Awards) (*see* Article 1(4) *supra*).[668] This decision will normally depend upon the number and nature of the Awards to be scrutinized during the period in question. Normally, the submission of Awards to the Plenary Session is reserved for those presenting particular difficulties (*e.g.,* where there is a dissenting opinion) or where there is some other element of complexity or the amounts at issue are particularly large.[669]

In the case of so-called "A" Awards, a member of the Court is usually requested to prepare a written report setting forth the reporter's recommendations concerning the approval or modification of the draft. A copy of the report is then placed before the plenary session of the Court for oral discussion together with the draft Award, any previous Awards rendered in the arbitration, the Terms of Reference, and a report from the Secretariat describing the relevant facts and the arbitral procedure. Copies of the foregoing documents are generally sent to the persons intending to attend the plenary session at least one week in advance. Following the Court's oral discussions, a decision is formulated that sets forth the Court's position and that is then communicated by the Secretariat to the Arbitral Tribunal, but not the parties, who are not informed of the Court's deliberations.

All other Awards ("B" Awards) are submitted for review to a Committee of the Court. In the event that all of the members of the Committee unanimously agree that the Award can be approved or otherwise needs to be modified, then it

---

[667] The drafts are usually unsigned and undated. However, it is good practice for them to bear the initials of all of the arbitrators, thus, establishing that it has been approved by all of them. In addition, arbitrators occasionally communicate executed signature pages to the Secretariat in order to expedite the subsequent notification of the Award to the parties if it is approved. Although such a practice was arguably inconsistent with former Article 22, it should be permissible under Article 25(3).

[668] For a description of the scrutiny process, *see also* McGovern, "Scrutiny of the Award by the Court," *ICC Ct. Bull.,* Vol. 5, No. 1 (1994), p. 46.

[669] It was formerly the case, under Article 11 of the Court's previous Internal Rules, that all Awards were required to be submitted to the plenary session. However, the Court long ago developed the practice of limiting the discussion at the plenary to only some Awards and reviewing the others in depth at a Committee, following which the Committee would recommend approval or non-approval to the plenary. As the acceptance of the Committee's recommendations was ordinarily a formality, the Court has now conferred authority on the Committee to approve Awards itself if its members arrive at a unanimous decision in this respect. *See* Article 1(4) *supra*.

is no longer required to be submitted subsequently to a plenary session, as once was the case (*see* note 669 *supra*). However, submission of the draft to a plenary session is necessary if the Committee does not make a unanimous decision. The Committee's new authority to approve Awards should significantly accelerate the scrutiny process in many cases.[670]

In view of the above procedures, it is generally necessary for the Secretariat to receive the Arbitral Tribunal's draft Award well in advance of the Committee or plenary session to which it will be submitted. Moreover, additional time must be allowed if the draft is in a language other than English or French (the Court's two working languages) as the Secretariat will ordinarily need to have it translated in such case prior to submission to the Court (although the Secretariat will nevertheless usually seek to have the original text reviewed by a Court member fluent in the language concerned).

In the event that the draft Award is not approved by the Court, a new draft must be resubmitted for scrutiny in accordance with the above process after any required modifications of form have been made and points of substance have been considered by the Arbitral Tribunal. When only minor modifications of form are required, the draft may be approved, subject to such modifications being made, in which case the revised Award, when received by the Secretariat, does not need to be resubmitted to the Court, unless, as occasionally occurs, it contains additional modifications (other than of a purely clerical nature) that were not previously seen or requested by the Court. The Secretariat is therefore required to review all revised drafts in order to ensure that they have been modified in accordance with the Court's directions.

As should be apparent from the above, the scrutiny of Awards by the Court is a labor-intensive process involving many persons within both the Court and its Secretariat. Although the Court's scrutiny may delay the finalization and notification of Awards, it can at the same time avoid the much longer delays that might result if an Award were set aside due to a defect that would not otherwise have been noticed. Moreover, in many cases, the general quality of the Awards is positively affected.

Validity of scrutiny. The validity of the Court's scrutiny of draft Awards has been challenged in the past. It has, for example, been argued that, in scrutinizing Awards, the Court unduly interferes with the arbitrators' liberty of decision, violates the secrecy of their deliberations and deprives the parties of due process as they are not included in the exchanges between the Court and the Arbitral Tribunal with respect to draft Awards.[671] But with the exception of the Supreme

---

[670] *See also* Article 1(3) *supra* concerning the power of the Chairman to approve Awards in cases of urgency.

[671] These criticisms were developed, in particular, in Kassis, *supra*, note 95. *See also* Schlosser, *Das Recht der internationalen privaten Schiedgeritchtsbarkeit* (1975), p. 480. *But see,* for a refutation of Kassis, Paulsson, "Vicarious Hypochondria and Institutional Arbitration," *Yearbook of the Arbitration Institute of the Stockholm Chamber of Commerce* (1990), p. 96.

Court of Turkey in 1976[672] and a Syrian administrative court in 1988,[673] those national courts that have been asked to consider such arguments have rejected them unequivocally.[674] Moreover, not only the legitimacy but the desirability of the scrutiny process is today widely recognized.

ARTICLE 28
Notification, Deposit and Enforceability of the Award

Article 28 deals with the formalities following the making of the Award and the Award's effects. It regroups, with only slight modifications, the provisions on these subjects that were formerly contained in Articles 23, 24 and 25 of the prior Rules.

Article 28(1)

> *Once an Award has been made, the Secretariat shall notify to the parties the text signed by the Arbitral Tribunal, provided always that the costs of the arbitration have been fully paid to the ICC by the parties or by one of them.*

As in the case of many other institutional arbitration rules, Article 28(1) provides for the notification of the Award to the parties by the Secretariat (rather than the arbitrators). The notification is made to the parties or their representatives, subject to the requirements of Article 3(2), and is, thus, normally dispatched to the parties either by registered mail or special courier, depending on the destination. However, the parties may also make arrangements for the simultaneous collection of the Award at the ICC's headquarters in Paris when all of them, or their representatives, are able to be present. The Secretariat will not otherwise deliver the Award to one party before the others.

Article 28(1) conditions the notification of the Award on prior payment of the "costs of the arbitration" to the ICC. The costs concerned are the ICC administrative expenses and the arbitrators' fees and expenses (*see* Articles 30-31

---

[672] The *Keban* judgment (March 10, 1976), excerpted in English in *Arbitration,* Vol. 46, No. 4 (1980), p. 241. However, this judgment is no longer considered to be good authority in Turkey. *See* Tekinay, "Turkey's Adhesion to the Geneva and New York Conventions," *ICC Ct. Bull.,* Vol. 3, No. 1 (1992), p. 14.

[673] *See* Schwartz, "Arbitration Awards – Challenge and Enforcement," *Globalization and Harmonization of Basic Notions in International Arbitration,* (IFCAI 1996), pp. 141, 148. This decision was subsequently overturned by the Syrian Council of State (judgment 271/1 of December 26, 1994).

[674] *See, e.g., Syrian Petroleum Company* c/ *GTM-Entrepose S.A., Tribunal fédéral suisse,* (July 16, 1990); *see also*, with respect to the administrative nature of the Court's decisions, Note by Metzger accompanying the *Appareils Dragon* cases cited *supra*, note 541. See *also Fouchard Gaillard and Goldman*, p. 766, note 84.

infra).[675] As a practical matter, the Court is not ordinarily required to invoke this provision as it has been its practice not to scrutinize the draft Award under Article 27 if any portion of the advance on costs is still outstanding. Moreover, the Court will not ordinarily fix the administrative expenses and arbitrators' fees and expenses in an amount exceeding the amount of the advance, although it is not otherwise precluded from doing so (*see* Article 31(1) *infra*).

Article 28(2)

> Additional copies certified true by the Secretary General shall be made available on request and at any time to the parties, but to no one else.

Pursuant to Article 28(1), the Secretariat will notify to each party only one original-signed copy of the Award. The parties may need additional copies, however, particularly if they are required to commence proceedings for the Award's enforcement, or possibly for other purposes. The Secretariat will therefore provide the parties (or their authorized representatives) with additional copies of the Award "certified true by the Secretary General."[676]

The Secretary General's certification of copies of the Award is intended, in particular, to facilitate the enforcement of the Award in accordance with the New York Convention, which requires (Article IV(1)) the production of the "duly authenticated original award or a duly certified copy thereof." Whether or not the Secretary General's certification of a copy of the Award is adequate for this purpose will ordinarily depend, however, on the law of the country where enforcement is sought.[677] If additional formalities are required in connection with the Secretary General's certification, the Secretariat is usually willing to provide the assistance required.

In prohibiting the delivery by the Secretariat of copies of the Award to anyone other than the parties, Article 28(2) complements the provisions in the Court's Internal Rules (Appendix II to the Rules, Article 1) on the confidentiality of the Court's work. However, neither Article 28(2) nor the Internal Rules have been construed as preventing the publication by the Court of "sanitized" extracts of Awards or their publication by others with the Court's permission.[678]

---

[675] Article 28(1) therefore does not take account of sums that the Arbitral Tribunal may be required to recover from the parties directly, such as amounts payable to tribunal-appointed experts (*see* Article 1(11) of Appendix III to the Rules) or VAT (*see* Article 2(9) of Appendix III).

[676] Pursuant to Article 5 of the Court's Internal Rules (Appendix II to the Rules), the certification in question may also be made by the Court's Deputy Secretary General/General Counsel in the Secretary General's absence.

[677] *See* van den Berg, "Consolidated Commentary," *supra*, note 72, pp. 474-75.

[678] A "sanitized" extract is one from which the names of the parties or any other factual elements permitting their identification have been removed. Such extracts are published in every issue of the Court's *Bulletin*, each year in the last issue of *Clunet* since 1974 and in the *ICCA Yearbook*.

Although the Court does not normally solicit the parties' permission before publishing such extracts, it has for many years refrained from any such publication if it is instructed by either of the parties not to do so.

Article 28(3)

> *By virtue of the notification made in accordance with Paragraph 1 of this Article, the parties waive any other form of notification or deposit on the part of the Arbitral Tribunal.*

Article 28(3), like Article 23(3) of the former Rules, provides for the waiver by the parties of any form of notification or deposit of the Award by the Arbitral Tribunal, but this is effective only insofar as any such requirements are waivable. The Arbitral Tribunal and the parties must therefore be attentive to any mandatory legal requirements that may apply notwithstanding Article 28(3). Thus, for example, the Spanish Supreme Court set aside an ICC Award that was rendered in Madrid without being notarized in accordance with the then applicable Spanish law on arbitration.[679] However, such or similar requirements are rare in countries with modern international arbitration legislation, and Spanish law has, in fact, been amended in this regard.[680]

In many countries, it may nevertheless be necessary for the Award to be deposited with a judicial authority before any recourse can be exercised against it in the courts. Indeed, this is the case in the Netherlands, a common venue for ICC arbitrations.[681] Moreover, even where the deposit of the Award is not required, its notification by the ICC pursuant to Article 28(1) may not constitute a valid notification for the purpose of setting in motion statutes of limitation relating to possible judicial actions in respect of the Award.[682]

---

[679] *See ABC c/ C. Española, SA, Tribunal Supremo* (March 28, 1994), Note Mantilla Serrano, *Rev. arb.* (1994), p. 749.

[680] Such notarization is no longer required, in the case of international arbitration, under the Spanish arbitration law of December 5, 1988.

[681] *See* Article 1058 *et seq.* of the Netherlands Arbitration Act 1986.

[682] Thus, for example, the period during which a party may commence an action for the setting aside of an international arbitration Award in France under Article 1504 of the French New Code of Civil Procedure does not begin to run until a party has been formally notified of the *exequatur* of the Award in France. *See, e.g., N.V. Lernout et Hauspie Speechproducts c/ société Compumedia SL, Cour d'appel de Paris* (March 22, 1996), *Rev. arb.* (1997), p. 83.

Article 28(4)

> An original of each Award made in accordance with the present Rules
> shall be deposited with the Secretariat.

The Secretariat permanently maintains in its archives original copies of all ICC Awards. As indicated in Article 1(6) of the Court's Internal Rules (Appendix II to the Rules), it also retains copies of the Terms of Reference, all decisions of the Court and all correspondence between the Secretariat and the arbitrators and parties relating to the arbitration. However, all other documents submitted by the parties or the arbitrators during the arbitration are either returned to them upon request or destroyed following the notification of the final Award (*see* Internal Rules, Article 1(7)).

Article 28(5)

> The Arbitral Tribunal and the Secretariat shall assist the parties in com-
> plying with whatever further formalities may be necessary.

Article 28(5) is identical to Article 25(2) of the former Rules, but because of its generality and the manner in which the Rules have been reorganized, it may be easily misunderstood.

Former Article 25(2) appeared in an Article entitled "Deposit of award" and was intended to oblige the arbitrators and the Secretariat to assist the parties in complying only with those "further formalities" that might be necessary for the "deposit" of the Award, but not any others. Indeed, during the drafting of the 1975 Rules, it was originally proposed to include an additional provision obliging the arbitrators and the Secretariat to assist the parties in complying with formalities relating to the enforcement of the Award, but that provision was deleted because it was considered "dangerous."[683]

During the preparation of the New Rules, it was not intended to expand the scope of former Article 25(2) (now Article 28(5)), and therefore the "further formalities" to which this provision refers should be understood as relating only to the deposit of the Award. The Secretariat has nevertheless itself provided the parties with additional assistance relating to enforcement proceedings in appropriate cases, but such assistance has never been mandated by the Rules. Thus, for example, the Secretariat frequently provides the parties with certified copies of documents relating to the arbitration in addition to the Award. It also provides written certification of relevant events in the arbitration. However, it has generally been reluctant to provide assistance of a partisan nature, particularly where enforcement of the Award is contested in the courts.

---

[683] *See* Summary Record of Meeting of the ICC Commission on October 8, 1974, ICC Doc. No. 420/169, p. 6.

Article 28(6)

> *Every Award shall be binding on the parties. By submitting the dispute to arbitration under these Rules, the parties undertake to carry out any Award without delay and shall be deemed to have waived their right to any form of recourse insofar as such waiver can validly be made.*

Article 28(6) corresponds to Article 24 of the former Rules. It is in all relevant respects the same as the previous provision, except that, instead of providing that the Award shall be "final," as did Article 24, Article 28(6) states that it shall be "binding."

There were two principal reasons for this change. The first is that not all Awards are necessarily "final." Indeed, Article 2, which is new (*see supra*), now expressly includes Awards of an "interim" nature within the definition of "Award." But "interim" Awards should nevertheless be regarded as "binding." Furthermore, there is generally no need for an Award to be "final" in order to be enforceable, provided that it is "binding." Indeed, one of the major contributions of the New York Convention to modern arbitration practice was to eliminate finality as a condition for the enforcement of Awards, as was previously the case under the Geneva Convention of 1927, and to require only that the Award be binding."[684]

If understood to mean non-appealability, finality is, in any event, still ensured to the same extent as before by the second sentence of Article 28(6), which provides, as did its predecessor, that "the parties undertake to carry out any Award without delay and shall be deemed to have waived their right to any form of recourse insofar as such waiver can validly be made." This sets forth the general obligation of the parties to comply with Awards promptly and voluntarily, a requirement that has encouraged their spontaneous performance and also enhanced their enforceability.[685] Moreover, "recourse" against the Award is waived to the extent that it possibly can be.[686] This should have the effect of preventing appeals against the Arbitral Tribunal's findings of fact or law in jurisdictions where such appeals may still be permitted.[687] However, many, if not most, jurisdictions nevertheless will not give effect to a waiver of all recourse, *e.g.,* in

---

[684] *See* Article V(1)(e) of the New York Convention and the discussion of that provision in van den Berg, *supra* note 72, p. 494.

[685] *See Gotaverken* v. *GNMIC,* Swedish Supreme Court (August 13, 1979), described in *Craig Park and Paulsson*, §22.03, p. 365.

[686] Article 24 of the previous Rules provided for the waiver of any form of "appeal." The word "recourse" has been substituted in the New Rules for "appeal," however, in order to cover all of the different forms of judicial action that may be initiated in different jurisdictions against an Award, whether for review, remission, setting aside or annulment.

[687] This is the case, for example, under Section 69 of the English Arbitration Act 1996, with respect to questions of English law. The language contained in Article 28(6) of the Rules has been found by the English courts to validly exclude such appeals under the previous English law, and this should continue to be the case under the new law. *See Arab African Energy Corporation Ltd* v. *Olieprodukten Nederland BV,* [1983] 2 Lloyd's Rep. 419; *Marine Contracters, Inc.* v. *Shell Petroleum Development Co. of Nigeria Ltd.,* [1984] 2 Lloyd's Rep. 77.

respect of possible violations of due process, international public policy or the competence of the Arbitral Tribunal.[688]

In some cases, parties have derogated from the requirements of Article 28(6) by providing in their arbitration agreement for rights of recourse beyond those that cannot validly be waived.[689] It will be for the Court to determine whether such derogations should be permitted in the future.

ARTICLE 29

Correction and Interpretation of the Award

This is a new Article that has been inspired by similar provisions in other international arbitration rules and modern international arbitration laws. Indeed, all of the major international arbitration rules today provide that the Arbitral Tribunal, although otherwise *functus officio,* may correct clerical, typographical or computational errors in an Award after it has been rendered, and many also provide for the possible interpretation of any ambiguities contained therein.[690]

The previous Rules did not contain any provisions on the correction or interpretation of Awards, and, indeed, it was commonly assumed that the scrutiny of draft Awards by the Court should make this unnecessary. However, no system is perfect, and, in very rare cases, the Court was faced with applications for the correction of Awards, some of which were plainly meritorious, as well as an occasional request for an Award's interpretation. In the absence of an express rule on this subject, the Court allowed itself to be guided by the general rule now contained in Article 35 ("the Court and the Arbitral Tribunal shall act in the spirit of these Rules and shall make every effort to make sure that the Award is

---

[688] Thus, for example, parties are not permitted to exclude the possible grounds for the setting aside of an international arbitration Award under the provisions of the French New Code of Civil Procedure. Nor is this generally regarded to be permissible under the UNCITRAL Model Law, although it is silent on this subject. *See* Sanders *supra,* note 404, p. 23. In the United States, the U.S. Court of Appeals for the Sixth Circuit has also held that the waiver of recourse contained in Article 24 of the former Rules does not preclude a party from asserting the defenses to the enforcement of awards that are available under the New York Convention. *See M. & C. Corp.* v. *Erwin Behr GmbH & Co., KG,* 87 F.3d 844 (6th Cir. 1996). Article 192 of the Swiss Private International Law Act and Article 78(6) of the Tunisian Arbitration Code of 1993, however, permit non-residents to exclude all possible recourse against an Award rendered locally. But the Swiss provision has been construed as requiring a specific exclusion agreement to this effect, which the relevant provision in the ICC Rules is not considered to satisfy. *See Clear Star Limited c/ Centrala Morska Importoura-Eksportova "Centromor" et Centromor SA, Tribunal fédéral suisse* (April 9, 1991), Note Tschanz, *Rev. arb.* (1991), p. 709. In Belgium, meanwhile, all recourse against a Belgian award is automatically excluded under the arbitration law of 1985 if neither party is Belgian.

[689] *See LaPine Technology Corporation* v. *Kyocera Corporation, supra,* note 528.

[690] *See, e.g.,* AAA International Arbitration Rules, Article 30; UNCITRAL Arbitration Rules, Articles 35 and 36. The LCIA Rules, Article 27 and WIPO Arbitration Rules, Article 66, provide for possible corrections, but not interpretation. Unlike the ICC Rules, however, all of the foregoing provide for possible "additional" Awards when the Arbitral Tribunal has failed to decide upon a claim referred to it.

enforceable at law") and by the procedural rules applicable to the arbitration. On this basis, it permitted a number of Awards to be corrected.[691]

During the preparation of the New Rules, there was a broad consensus that the *lacuna* in the Rules on this subject should be filled. Although the addition of a provision on the correction of Awards was universally favored, allowing for an Award's possible interpretation was more controversial.[692] Ultimately, however, a provision was included on both topics. There was little support, on the other hand, for the inclusion of a provision on the possible issuance of additional Awards when the Tribunal fails to decide on a claim. Although such a provision is a standard feature of most other rules, it has, thus, been omitted from the New Rules.[693]

Article 29(1)

> *On its own initiative, the Arbitral Tribunal may correct a clerical, computational or typographical error, or any errors of similar nature contained in an Award, provided such correction is submitted for approval to the Court within 30 days of the date of such Award.*

Article 29(1) permits an Arbitral Tribunal, on its "own initiative," to correct a "clerical, computational or typographical error, or any errors of similar nature" contained in an Award after it has been made. Similar provisions are contained in other arbitration rules, which, like Article 29(1), also impose time limits in order to prevent continuing uncertainty with respect to the finality of the Award.[694] Unlike other rules, however, Article 29(1) requires the correction to be submitted to the Court for approval pursuant to Article 27, as in the case of the original Award itself.[695]

---

[691] *See, e.g.,* the Award in ICC Case No. 6653 (1993), Note Arnaldez, *Collection of ICC Arbitral Awards 1991-1995*, p. 525. *See also* Kühn, "Rectification and Interpretation of Arbitral Awards," *ICC Ct. Bull.,* Vol. 7, No. 2 (1996), p. 78.

[692] The more controversial nature of interpretation explains the absence of any provision on this subject in either the LCIA or WIPO Arbitration Rules. In addition, under the UNCITRAL Model Law (Article 33), interpretation is permitted only if the parties so agree, unlike in the case of a correction. On this subject, *see* Knutson, "The Interpretation of Final Awards: When is a Final Award not Final?" *J. Arb. Int.,* Vol. 11, No. 2 (1994), p. 99; Gunter, "*L'Interprétation de la Sentence : examen de quelques questions à la lumière d'un cas réel,*" *ASA Bull.* (1996), p. 574.

[693] *See* note 690, *supra.* The only reason expressed for excluding such a provision from the ICC Rules was that the scrutiny process under Article 27 makes such a provision unnecessary.

[694] *See, e.g.,* LCIA Rules, Article 27(2); UNCITRAL Rules, Article 36(1); WIPO Arbitration Rules, Article 66(b).

[695] Article 29(1) provides that the correction must be "submitted for approval to the Court within 30 days of the date of such Award." The intention is that the Arbitral Tribunal should submit its correction to the Secretariat within that period. It is then for the Secretariat to refer it to the Court as soon as possible thereafter.

Whether or not an error is of the nature covered by Article 29 may not always be obvious, and in different jurisdictions there may be disparate views on this subject. Ultimately, however, it is for the Arbitral Tribunal to determine whether an error falls within the scope of Article 29(1) (or Article 29(2) *infra*).[696] In the event that the members of an Arbitral Tribunal disagree with respect to the possible need for a correction, it should be possible for either the majority or the chairman, acting alone, to make the decision, in view of Article 29(3) below, even if the Award being corrected was issued by the arbitrators unanimously.

Article 29(2)

> *Any application of a party for the correction of an error of the kind referred to in Article 29(1), or for the interpretation of an Award, must be made to the Secretariat within 30 days of the receipt of the Award by such party, in a number of copies as stated in Article 3(1). After transmittal of the application to the Arbitral Tribunal, it shall grant the other party a short time limit, normally not exceeding 30 days, from the receipt of the application by that party to submit any comments thereon. If the Arbitral Tribunal decides to correct or interpret the Award, it shall submit its decision in draft form to the Court not later than 30 days following the expiration of the time limit for the receipt of any comments from the other party or within such other period as the Court may decide.*

Article 29(2) deals with possible requests by a party for the correction or the interpretation of an Award. Like Article 29(1), it establishes a 30-day time limit for the application in question, except that the period commences, in the case of Article 29(2), on the date of receipt of the Award by the party making the application and not on the date of the Award, as under Article 29(1). The time limit for the initial application is then followed by further, but flexible, time limits for the comments of the other party and the decision of the Arbitral Tribunal. As in the case of Article 29(1), any decision of the Arbitral Tribunal to correct or interpret the Award must be submitted to the Court for its approval.

During the preparation of the New Rules, concerns were expressed by some concerning the desirability of the time limits in question. With respect to the matter of interpretation, in particular, it was argued that possible ambiguities might not be noticed until much later during the enforcement stage. Ultimately, however, the drafters of the Rules concluded that the need for finality justified the imposition of the time limits in question, which are similar to those contained in other rules.

---

[696] For a discussion of the jurisprudence of the Iran-U.S. Claims Tribunal in this regard, *see* Baker and Davis, *supra*, note 181, p. 194.

Article 29(2) does not otherwise make any distinction between applications for the correction or the interpretation of an Award. Nor does it attempt to define what is meant by "interpretation." During the drafting of the comparable provision in the UNCITRAL Rules, "interpretation" was intended to refer to "clarification" of the dispositive part of the Award, *i.e.,* the arbitrators could be requested to clarify "the purport of the award and the resultant obligations and rights of the parties," but not to revisit or elaborate upon the reasons for the Award.[697]

This being said, requests for interpretation are rare in international arbitration practice, and such requests are even more rarely assented to. Thus, for example, through 1996, the Iran-U.S. Claims Tribunal had never granted a request for the interpretation of an Award, notwithstanding its power to do so under Article 35 of its rules (which are based on the UNCITRAL Rules).[698] As one commentator has observed, such requests are commonly "not-so-subtle requests" that the Award be reconsidered on the merits.[699] The authors are aware of only one case in which an ICC Arbitral Tribunal granted a request for the interpretation of an Award under the former Rules.

Apart from determining whether such requests should be expressly permitted under the Rules, the Working Party considered whether the Arbitral Tribunal should be entitled to receive additional compensation for fees and expenses in connection with a request for correction or interpretation. If the need for an Award's correction or interpretation is attributable to the Arbitral Tribunal's own negligence, there would not appear to be any legitimate reason why it should receive additional compensation for repairing the damage done. The Working Party therefore did not recommend the inclusion of any specific provision on this subject in the New Rules. However, the Court has nevertheless provided in Article 2(7) of Appendix III to the Rules (Arbitration Costs and Fees) that the Court may fix an advance to cover additional fees and expenses of the Arbitral Tribunal (but not the ICC itself) in appropriate cases under Article 29(2).

Article 29(3)

> *The decision to correct or interpret the Award shall take the form of an addendum and shall constitute part of the Award. The provisions of Articles 25, 27 and 28 shall apply mutatis mutandis.*

During the preparation of the New Rules, the Working Party considered whether a decision to correct or interpret an Award should be regarded as a new Award or as part of the original Award. In deciding that it should be the latter, the Working Party adopted the approach already followed in other arbitration

---

[697] *See* Baker and Davis, *supra*, note 181, p. 192.

[698] *See* Aldrich, *The Jurisprudence of the Iran-United States Claims Tribunal* (Clarendon Press 1996), p. 453.

[699] *See* Baker and Davis, *supra*, note 181, p. 194.

rules.[700] It also logically follows that the decision should be subject to all of the provisions in the Rules that applied to the original Award, including scrutiny pursuant to Article 27. Moreover, as already noted, by virtue of the application of Article 25(1), a decision to correct or interpret an Award is not required to be unanimous, even if the original Award was made by all of the arbitrators.

[700] *See* LCIA Rules, Article 27(1); UNCITRAL Rules, Article 35(2); WIPO Arbitration Rules, Article 66(a). It has been asked whether the period available for contesting an Award ought to be suspended, as a result, until the period for possible corrections or interpretations has expired. Another question that has been raised is what is to happen if one party has already commenced proceedings to set aside an Award before its correction or interpretation. *See* Gunter, *supra,* note 692, p. 583. The Paris Court of Appeal has recently decided in this regard that such an action does not affect any subsequent request for the correction or interpretation of the Award, but that if the Award is set aside, the decision of correction or interpretation is necessarily set aside as well. *See Billot* c/ *société TFN, Cour d'appel de Paris* (February 24, 1995), Note Derains, *Rev. arb.* (1996), p. 141.

Chapter 7
Costs (Articles 30-31)

Apart from the ultimate outcome and the time that may be required for the conduct of an arbitration, there is usually no aspect of the arbitration process that is of greater concern to the parties than its cost. Articles 30 and 31 set forth the provisions relating to the costs of the ICC and the arbitrators that were formerly contained in Articles 9 and 20 of the Rules as well as Articles 14-16 of the Internal Rules. Article 30 provides for the payment of such costs in advance, in several stages, while Article 31 is concerned with their final determination. Article 31 also requires the Arbitral Tribunal to decide how such costs should be borne by the parties together with "the fees and expenses of any experts appointed by the Arbitral Tribunal and the reasonable legal and other costs incurred by the parties for the arbitration."

Articles 30 and 31 differ from the corresponding provisions of the former Rules in a number of respects, the most important change being the inclusion in Article 30 of a "provisional advance" on costs to be fixed by the Secretary General of the Court upon the receipt of the Request for Arbitration. In addition, various modifications have been made in Appendix III to the Rules ("Arbitration Costs and Fees") and the accompanying Scales of Administrative Expenses and of Arbitrator's Fees ("Cost Scales"), with which Articles 30 and 31 must be read. Appendix III was required to be adapted in order to take account of the changes incorporated in Articles 30 and 31. In addition, practices that previously were the subject of separate Secretariat memoranda are now described in the Appendix to ensure greater transparency. Meanwhile, the sums set forth in the Cost Scales have been increased, as from January 1, 1998. The increases in question apply to all arbitrations commenced since that date, irrespective of the version of the Rules that governs the arbitration.

Notwithstanding the foregoing changes, the basic scheme of the Rules in respect of costs has not been altered.[701] Both the ICC's administrative expenses

---

[701] For a discussion of the ICC cost system prior to the New Rules, *see* Bühler, "Costs in ICC Arbitration: A Practitioner's View," *Am. Rev. Int. Arb.*, Vol.3 (1992), p.116; *and* Schwartz, "The Costs of ICC Arbitration," *ICC Ct. Bull.*, Vol.4, No.1 (1993), p.8.

and the arbitrators' fees are to be fixed exclusively by the Court,[702] and, in doing so, the Court is to apply the Cost Scales, except possibly in exceptional circumstances. Indeed, the Cost Scales are at the heart of the ICC's system of costs.[703]

In the case of both the ICC's administrative expenses and the arbitrators' fees, the scales, which are sharply regressive, have been established with reference to successive slices of the "sum in dispute."[704] The ICC's administrative expenses are fixed solely on the basis of that sum up to a maximum amount (which presently cannot "normally" exceed U.S. $75,800), subject to the power of the Court to derogate from the scale in "exceptional circumstances" (Appendix III, Article 2(5)).[705] In the case of the arbitrators' fees, however, each bracket of the scale contains both a "minimum" and a "maximum" fee, separated by a very wide band, thus leaving the Court with considerable discretion in each case.[706] In addition, the Court may derogate from the scale in "exceptional circumstances" (*see* Article 31(2) *infra*). However, such derogations are intended to be rare, and parties and arbitrators should therefore normally assume that the fee to be fixed will fall within the scale and, in the typical case, somewhere near the average between the "minimum" and the "maximum." In exercising its discretion in this regard, the Court is required to take into consideration "the diligence of the arbitrator, the time spent, the rapidity of the proceedings and the complexity of the dispute" (Appendix III, Article 2(2)).[707]

---

[702] This principle, insofar as it relates to the arbitrators' fees and expenses, is now the subject of an express provision in Appendix III, which states (Article 2(4)): "The arbitrator's fees and expenses shall be fixed exclusively by the Court as required by the Rules. Separate fee arrangements between the parties and the arbitrator are contrary to the Rules."

[703] *But see* in this connection *Craig Park and Paulsson*, §21.02, p.352 ("If, with the agreement of the arbitrators, the parties themselves propose to the Court a fee arrangement different from . . . the ICC Scale, the Court tends to adopt the agreed scheme. But it retains absolute discretion to do so, and as a formal matter will nevertheless establish the fees itself. The ICC does not encourage such arrangements and few are in fact made."). Indeed, whether the Court would accept such an arrangement in a particular case is highly uncertain.

[704] In order to apply the Cost Scales, it is necessary to multiply each successive slice of the sum in dispute by the corresponding percentages in the scales. To facilitate the calculation of the relevant sums, Appendix III, thus, includes an additional table immediately following the scales in question.

[705] Under the previous version of Appendix III, any such derogations from the scale were "in no event" to exceed the ceiling set forth in the scale (then U.S. $65,500) (former Appendix III, Article 2(c)). Article 2(5) of Appendix III now provides, however, that, in the event of a derogation, the administrative expenses shall "normally" not exceed the maximum amount of the scale.

[706] Thus, for example, for an amount in dispute of U.S. $1,000,000, the applicable fee ranges from a "minimum" of U.S. $11,250 to a maximum of U.S. $53,500. These sums, like all other amounts in the scale, are for one arbitrator. According to Article 2(3) of Appendix III, when a case is submitted to more than one arbitrator, the Court shall have the right to increase the total fees "up to a maximum which shall normally not exceed three times the fees of one arbitrator." The Court could presumably take the position that it should fix a higher amount if there were more than three arbitrators.

[707] Of these considerations, only the reference to the "diligence of the arbitrator" is new as compared to the criteria that were previously described. They were formerly to be found, however, in Article 18 of the Court's Internal Rules (Appendix II) rather than in Appendix III.

In fixing arbitrators' fees in accordance with a published fee scale based on the "sum in dispute," the ICC differs from a number of the other leading international arbitration institutions (such as, *e.g.,* the American Arbitration Association, the London Court of International Arbitration and the Arbitration Institute of the Stockholm Chamber of Commerce).[708] Although a fee scale is not a perfect instrument and earlier versions of the scales were subject to criticism,[709] it nevertheless presents a number of advantages. In particular, it provides both the parties and the arbitrators with a general idea, from the very outset of the arbitration, of the normal limitations (minimum and maximum) on the arbitrators' remuneration. It also provides a financial framework for the arbitration that is broadly compatible with the amount at stake, and the parties are on notice that, if they unduly inflate the amount of their claims, the amount of the arbitrators' fees may increase as a consequence. The system, thus, discourages the submission of frivolous claims and counterclaims in addition to creating an incentive for efficiency.[710] The ICC has yet to be persuaded that there is any inherently superior system.[711]

Against this background, the specific provisions of Articles 30 and 31 are now considered.

[708] In the case of such institutions, arbitrators' fees are generally fixed on the basis of an hourly or daily billing rate negotiated or fixed by the institution or the arbitrators. In *ad hoc* cases, meanwhile, the arbitrators normally enjoy considerable discretion in determining how they wish to be remunerated, subject to the parties' consent.

[709] *See, e.g.,* Wetter, *supra,* note 13, p.103; *and* Werner, "Remuneration of Arbitrators by the International Chamber of Commerce," *J. Arb. Int.,* Vol.5, No.3 (1988), p.135. Such criticisms are, however, to be compared with Robine, "What Companies Expect of International Commercial Arbitration," *J. Arb. Int.,* Vol.9, No.2 (1992), pp.31, 43 ("Parties are [ ] concerned with predicting costs. Scales such as those of the ICC meet this concern.").

[710] *See Craig Park and Paulsson,* §21.03, p.356 ("In average cases, it should always be kept in mind that the ICC system creates an incentive for efficiency; not being paid at a daily rate, ICC arbitrators have no 'private' reason to prolong the case.").

[711] In 1988, the Court constituted an *ad hoc* working group of its members to study its practices in respect of arbitrators' fees. The working group was composed of Court members from ten different countries, both developed and developing, so as to ensure the broadest possible exchange of opinions and experiences in respect of arbitrator remuneration around the world. In addition, the working group solicited opinions regarding the ICC's arbitrator fee system from 362 parties and 319 arbitrators from 89 different countries (in proportion to the participation in ICC arbitration of parties and arbitrators from such countries). After an extensive review, lasting nearly two years, the working group came to the conclusion that there was no legitimate basis for a dramatic overhaul of the ICC's basic system of arbitrator remuneration. The working group found that:

> The system as it presently stands continues to attract arbitrators of different nationalities who are either specialists in arbitration or had such diverse backgrounds as practicing lawyers, judges, professors and others ... [and] parties are generally satisfied with the present system.

It was noted, however, that the scale of arbitrators' fees, which, at the time, dated from March 1980, should nevertheless be reviewed "due to inflationary increases affecting arbitrators' costs ... hourly fees and overhead." The fees payable to arbitrators under the scale were, thus, increased in 1993 and again in 1998.

Article 30
Advance to Cover the Costs of the Arbitration

Article 30 replaces the series of provisions that were previously contained in Article 9 of the former Rules and Articles 14-16 of the Court's Internal Rules, while effecting a number of important modifications relating principally to the creation of a new provisional advance (Article 30(1)) and the interplay between the payment of advances and the progress of the arbitration proceedings. Article 30 also must be read in conjunction with Article 1 of Appendix III.

Article 30(1)

> *After receipt of the Request, the Secretary General may request the Claimant to pay a provisional advance in an amount intended to cover the costs of arbitration until the Terms of Reference have been drawn up.*

Background. The provisional advance to be fixed pursuant to Article 30(1) is one of the innovations of the New Rules. As already discussed in connection with Article 13 above, it has been introduced primarily in order to accelerate the transmission of the file to the Arbitral Tribunal. Under the previous Rules, only the Court itself could fix advances on costs, and the Secretariat was authorized to "make the transmission of the file to the arbitrator conditional upon the payment by the parties or one of them of the whole or part" of such advance (former Rules, Article 9(3)). Prior to 1986, the Secretariat's usual practice was to require the payment of the whole of the advance before submitting the file to the arbitrators. However, as from 1986, this practice was altered so that, in addition to the advance payment accompanying the Request for Arbitration (*see* Article 4(4) *supra*), the advance would be paid in two staggered installments: half prior to the submission of the file to the arbitrators and half upon the establishment of the arbitrators' Terms of Reference.

The foregoing system had the disadvantage of cumulating a number of different possible sources of delay. First, the Court had to fix an advance, which it would not normally do, at the earliest, until after the expiration of the initial 30-day period for the submission of the Respondent's Answer. The Claimant and Respondent parties would then each be invited to pay 50 per cent (*see* Article 30(3) *infra*) of the first half of the advance. If the Respondent failed to pay its share, the Claimant would then be invited to substitute for it. Months could go by before the first half of the advance was paid.[712] Under the New Rules, the Secretary General, thus, has the power to fix a "provisional" advance immediately upon receipt of the Request, (in addition to the payment required to accompany the Request under Article 1(1) of Appendix III), and that advance is payable solely by the Claimant, following which the file should normally be submitted to

---

[712] *See Craig Park and Paulsson,* §14.04, p.249.

the Arbitral Tribunal, if constituted.[713] The possible additional burden on the Claimant resulting from the requirement that it pay the totality of the provisional advance is off-set, to at least some extent (*see* the discussion *infra*), by the fact that it is intended to cover the costs of the arbitration only "until the Terms of Reference have been drawn up" and not all of the costs of the arbitration, as in the case of the advance that is subsequently to be fixed by the Court (*see* Article 30(2)).

The provisional advance, thus, does not eliminate the need for the Court, as soon as practicable, to itself fix an advance on costs, as under the former Rules. Moreover, the fixing of a provisional advance by the Secretary General is not mandatory. Although it is to be expected that such an advance will be fixed in most cases, there may be situations (as discussed further below) in which this might not be considered to be appropriate.

Calculation of the provisional advance. Article 30(1) does not explain how the provisional advance is to be calculated. It is, thus, for the Court to lay down appropriate guidelines for the Secretary General in this regard. For the time being, the only such guidelines that have been published are set forth in Article 1(2) of Appendix III, which provides as follows:

> The provisional advance on costs fixed by the Secretary General according to Article 30(1) of the Rules shall normally not exceed the amount obtained by adding together the administrative expenses, the minimum of the fees (as set out in the scale hereinafter) based upon the amount of the claim and the expected reimbursable expenses of the Arbitral Tribunal incurred with respect to the drafting of the Terms of Reference. If such amount is not quantified, the provisional advance shall be fixed at the discretion of the Secretary General. Payment by the Claimant shall be credited to its share of the advance on costs fixed by the Court.

As can be seen from the above, the Secretary General enjoys considerable discretion in fixing the amount of the provisional advance. Article 1(2) merely establishes the amount that "normally" shall not be exceeded, while leaving it to the Secretary General to determine what is appropriate in each case. The Secretary General's calculation of the provisional advance is to be based, however, solely on the amount of the Claimant's claim and, unlike the advance to be fixed by the Court subsequently, is not to take account of any counterclaims of the Respondent.[714] This is intended to permit the Secretary General to fix the prov-

---

[713] As noted in connection with Article 13 *supra*, the Rules do not expressly provide that the file shall be transmitted to the Arbitral Tribunal upon the payment of the provisional advance. However, this should normally be the case whenever a provisional advance is fixed.

[714] For further details concerning the calculation of the amount of the claim, *see* the related discussion in connection with Article 30(2) *infra*. In the event that the amount of the claim has not been quantified, the provisional advance is fixed at the Secretary General's discretion. Appendix III, Article 1(2).

sional advance as quickly as possible following the receipt of the Request for Arbitration without awaiting the expiration of the time period set forth in the Rules for the submission of the Respondent's Answer.[715] Moreover, as the provisional advance is payable by the Claimant alone, it would not be reasonable to include the Respondent's possible claims in the calculation of that amount. As a result, however, no advance payments are required to be made by the Respondent, even if it has counterclaims, until after the Court has fixed an advance on costs. The Respondent will therefore normally enjoy a "free ride" in the arbitration until the establishment of the Terms of Reference.

In order to ensure that the Court has sufficient funds on hand to cover the costs of the arbitration until that time, Article 1(2) permits the Secretary General to require the payment, by way of the provisional advance, of an amount corresponding to the ICC's administrative expenses and the minimum fees payable to the Arbitral Tribunal in respect of the claim, as set out in the Cost Scales, together with an estimate of the Arbitral Tribunal's reimbursable expenses "incurred with respect to the drafting of the Terms of Reference." For many years prior to the amendment of the Rules, the Court's general practice was to fix the ICC's administrative expenses at an amount corresponding roughly to 50 per cent of the amount payable under the applicable scale in the event of the withdrawal of the arbitration upon the establishment of the Terms of Reference. In addition, the arbitrators normally would be entitled to receive an advance on their fees at that stage corresponding to at least half of the minimum amount set forth in the arbitrator fee scale. Those sums would be calculated, however, on the basis of the aggregate amount in dispute, including all claims and counterclaims. As the provisional advance is to be calculated solely on the basis of the Claimant's claims, an issue, thus, arises as to whether the Court will continue in the future to determine the ICC's administrative expenses and the arbitrators' fees on the basis of the aggregate amount in dispute in the event that an arbitration is withdrawn at or before the time when the Terms of Reference are completed. Presumably, in order to allow the Court as much discretion as possible in this regard, the Secretary General may be inclined to fix the amount of the provisional advance at or around the amount of the maximum figure "normally" permitted under Article 1(2) of Appendix III.

In fixing the provisional advance, the Secretary General may also be required to make a preliminary assessment of the likely number of arbitrators in the event that the number has not been fixed in the parties' arbitration agreement or otherwise previously agreed. Indeed, the assumptions that the Secretary General may make in this regard could reasonably be expected to have a substantial impact on the amount of the provisional advance as the Arbitral Tribunal's fees

---

[715] *But cf.* Bühler, "Correction and Interpretation of Awards and Advances on Costs," *The New 1998 ICC Rules of Arbitration," ICC Ct. Bull.,* Special Supplement (1997), pp.53, 56 ("The Secretary General is required to make his decision following receipt of the Answer from the Respondent."). As stated above, however, there is no requirement that the Secretary General await the Respondent's Answer.

and expenses would vary by a factor of one to three. Although the Secretary General has indicated that, in such instances, he "may fix the provisional advance based on the circumstances of the case,"[716] unless he solicits the Respondent parties' views on the number of arbitrators before fixing the provisional advance, he would be making his determination before knowing whether the parties agree on the number (except, of course, where it has already been set forth in the arbitration clause). It may therefore be appropriate for the Secretary General to permit the Respondent parties to express their views on the number of arbitrators before he fixes the provisional advance. If he does not do so, however, the question may arise as to whether the provisional advance should be adjusted if, after it has been fixed, the parties agree on a number of arbitrators different from the number assumed by the Secretary General when fixing it initially. Questions such as this will be required to be addressed by the Secretary General as they arise in practice.[717]

Similarly, when fixing the provisional advance, the Secretary General may not yet know the place of the arbitration or the places of residence of the arbitrators. However, the possible need for the arbitrators to travel will inevitably affect the level of their reimbursable expenses and, thus, bear on the costs that are intended to be secured by the provisional advance.

In view of considerations such as the foregoing, the provisional advance cannot reasonably be expected to function as a precise instrument in all cases, and the Court may, thus, be expected to fix an advance under Article 30(2) (*see infra*) as soon as it has all of the information permitting it to do so on a reasonable basis. In such cases, the Secretariat may then consider it appropriate to call upon the parties to make additional payments, even prior to the establishment of the Terms of Reference, in order to ensure that adequate funds are on hand to remunerate the arbitrators properly and to cover the ICC's administrative expenses for the work carried out up until such time in the event that the arbitration is withdrawn.[718]

Special cases. As already noted, Article 30(1) does not require the Secretary General to fix a provisional advance, and there may therefore be circumstances in which he does not consider it appropriate to do so. Among these there is, first of all, the situation where it is uncertain whether the New Rules or the previous

---

[716] *See* Grigera Naón, *supra*, note 47, p.47.

[717] One commentator on the New Rules has stated that the Secretary General is expected to make his decision on the provisional advance "once it is known whether one or three arbitrators will be appointed" (*see* Bühler, *supra*, note 715). However, Article 30(1) does not expressly require this, and the Secretary General has suggested that the provisional advance might be fixed earlier. *See* Grigera Naón, *supra*, note 47, p.46.

[718] Indeed, even though, according to Article 30(1), the provisional advance is "intended to cover the costs of arbitration until the Terms of Reference have been drawn up," this should not be construed so restrictively as to prevent the Secretariat from requiring the payment of additional sums if the provisional advance originally fixed is subsequently considered to be indadequate.

Rules are applicable. In such cases, the Court has decided that the Claimant will not be requested to pay a provisional advance if it is the Claimant's position that the parties have agreed on the application of the former Rules.[719]

There may also be situations in which the Secretary General is uncertain as to whether the arbitration should be allowed to proceed, such as, for example, where the parties have amended the Rules in their arbitration clause.[720]

In still other cases, the payment of more than a provisional advance may be considered to be appropriate for the transmission of the file to the Arbitral Tribunal. Thus, for example, the Secretariat has in the past generally required the payment of the full amount of the advance on costs fixed by the Court prior to transmitting the file to the Arbitral Tribunal in "fast-track" cases. This has been in order to avoid possible delay or disruption subsequently. Notwithstanding the introduction of the provisional advance, the Secretariat may, thus, consider it appropriate to continue to require the payment of a greater amount in such cases before transmitting the file to the Arbitral Tribunal.

Article 30(2)

> *As soon as practicable, the Court shall fix the advance on costs in an amount likely to cover the fees and expenses of the arbitrators and the ICC administrative costs for the claims and counterclaims which have been referred to it by the parties. This amount may be subject to readjustment at any time during the arbitration. Where, apart from the claims, counterclaims are submitted, the Court may fix separate advances on costs for the claims and the counterclaims.*

Background. Article 30(2) replaces the corresponding provision formerly contained in Article 9(1) of the Rules and establishes the general authority of the Court to fix advances on costs for the arbitration. Like the previous provision, it lays down as the normal rule the fixing of a single advance on costs intended to cover both the claims and counterclaims, if any. At the same time, however, it provides, as did its predecessor, for the possibility of separate advances on costs where there are both claims and counterclaims. But, unlike former Article 9(1), Article 30(2) also expressly provides that the advances fixed by the Court "may be subject to readjustment at any time during the arbitration." This has, in fact, always been the case in order to permit the Court to have adequate funds available to remunerate the arbitrators properly at the conclusion of the arbitration, when the fees are actually fixed (*see* Article 31 *infra*). As parties have occasionally claimed to be surprised by the readjustment of advances during the course of the arbitration, the drafters of the Rules considered that it would be helpful to

[719] *See supra,* note 128.
[720] As regards cases where the Secretary General is uncertain about the existence of an arbitration agreement, *see* the discussion of Article 6(2) *supra*.

draw the provisional nature of all such advances to the parties' attention by including an express provision to this effect in Article 30(2).

Like Article 30(1), Article 30(2) also has to be read together with the corresponding provisions in Appendix III to the Rules, including, in particular, Articles 1(4), 1(7) and 1(10), all of which are discussed, as necessary, below.

The advance on costs to be fixed by the Court pursuant to Article 30(2) is required to be distinguished from the separate security, generally referred to as "security for costs," that a party may occasionally wish to obtain from another party – usually the Claimant – for its costs in the arbitration (other than those fixed by the Court). The ICC Rules do not expressly provide for any such separate security, although, as already discussed, parties may apply to the Arbitral Tribunal for the same under Article 23.[721]

Time of fixing the advance. Article 30(2) provides that the Court shall fix the advance on costs "[a]s soon as practicable." The previous Rules did not say anything at all about when the advance was to be fixed. But as a practical matter, the advance was normally fixed as soon as the Secretariat considered that sufficient information was available to permit the Court to do so. There is no reason why the Court's previous practices in this regard need to change significantly under the New Rules.

The advance on costs is normally fixed by the Court at one of its Committee sessions. In the past, the advance has normally been fixed when the arbitration is presented by the Secretariat to the Court as a "New Case" (*see* Article 1(5) *supra*). This would normally occur as soon as possible after the expiration of the initial period fixed in the Rules for the submission of the Respondent's Answer, by which time the Secretariat would be aware of the parties' positions concerning the number of arbitrators and the place of the arbitration. In cases where the Respondent obtained an extension of time for filing its Answer, however, the Secretariat might choose, although it was not required to do so, to wait until it received the Answer before submitting a New Case to the Court so that the Court would know whether there were any counterclaims before fixing the advance on costs.

Under the New Rules, given the provisional advance to be fixed initially by the Secretary General, it can reasonably be expected that the Court will normally be invited by the Secretariat to fix the advance on costs after the Respondent has filed its Answer together with its counterclaims, if any.[722] In exceptional

---

[721] ICC arbitrators have ordered parties to provide security for costs, although such cases are rare. *See*, in this connection, Schwartz, *supra*, note 701, p.20. In general, ICC arbitrators have been reluctant to order security for costs. In certain jurisdictions (England and Singapore), however, parties have applied for, and obtained, such orders from the courts at the place of arbitration, although this should no longer be possible in England under the Arbitration Act 1996.

[722] *See* Grigera Naón, *supra,* note 47, p.46 (the Court shall fix the global advance "as soon as practicable, *i.e.,* when there are sufficient elements available to evaluate the amount in dispute because, for example, the amount of the counterclaims is known ... .").

cases, however, the Court may consider it appropriate to do so earlier, *e.g.,* where an exceptionally long extension of time has been granted to the Respondent for its Answer or where the Court otherwise considers the amount of the provisional advance to be insufficient to cover the estimated costs of the arbitration until the establishment of the Terms of Reference. Whenever the advance on costs is fixed, though, the payment of that sum ought not normally to be required prior to the submission of the file to the Arbitral Tribunal, as already discussed (*see* Article 13). It will subsequently be for the Secretariat to ensure that adequate funds are available to cover the anticipated costs of the arbitration (*see* the discussion of Article 30(4) *infra*).

Calculating the advance. As under the previous Rules, the advance on costs is intended to cover the fees and expenses of the arbitrators and the ICC administrative costs for the claims and counterclaims referred to arbitration.[723] There is nothing in either the New Rules or Appendix III that ought to change the manner in which the advance on costs is fixed in the future.

As a practical matter, the advance is normally fixed on the basis of the Cost Scales and an estimate of the expenses of the Arbitral Tribunal, taking into account, among other things, the place of the arbitration, the arbitrators' likely travel costs, if any, and the hearing time that may be required (the latter being a particularly significant source of out-of-pocket expense in an international arbitration). The Cost Scales have, as already mentioned, been prepared with reference to the "sum in dispute" in the arbitration. This amount is considered by the Court to be the aggregate amount of all claims and counterclaims submitted in the arbitration.[724] Although this may sound straightforward, there are nevertheless a number of issues that arise in connection with the scales' application.

First, it is to be noted that the Cost Scales are expressed in U.S. dollars. Thus, if the claims and counterclaims are stated in a currency other than U.S. dollars, they are required to be converted into dollars for the purpose of applying the scales. In this regard, the Court's usual practice is to apply the exchange rate prevailing on the date of receipt of the Request for Arbitration, and to apply that rate for the duration of the arbitration without regard to subsequent exchange rate variations (except possibly in exceptional circumstances).[725]

---

[723] These are the only costs covered by the advance. Thus, excluded from the advance are the costs of experts who may be appointed by the Arbitral Tribunal pursuant to Article 20(4) of the Rules. Under Article 1(11) of Appendix III to the Rules, the Arbitral Tribunal is to fix a separate advance to cover the expected fees and expenses of any such expert in the event that an expert is to be appointed.

[724] The respective amounts of the claims and counterclaims are, thus, simply added together, even if they are essentially concerned with the same issues, except possibly where claims for the same sum are advanced in the alternative.

[725] From time to time, the ICC has considered whether to maintain the practice of using the U.S. dollar as a universal currency for the payment of ICC arbitration fees. However, until now it has considered that the advantages outweigh any possible disadvantages.

Apart from the matter of the exchange rate to be applied to the claims, there may be a question as to the amounts that should properly be included in their calculation. Thus, for example, the parties' principal claims are often accompanied by claims for arbitration costs (*see* Article 31(3) *infra*) and for interest. It has not generally been the Court's practice, however, to treat claims for costs as part of the "sum in dispute" when applying the Cost Scales, nor are claims for interest generally included, except possibly when interest is the principal subject of the claim or otherwise represents a substantial part of the amount at stake in the arbitration.[726]

In the event, meanwhile, that the relief claimed is not of a monetary nature or is not quantified, the Court is entitled to fix the arbitrators' fees and the ICC's administrative expenses "at its discretion" (Appendix III, Articles 2(1) and 2(5)).

As a practical matter, when the claims are not quantified, the Court's general practice for the last several years has been to fix the advance on costs initially at U.S. $50,000 in cases with a sole arbitrator and U.S. $100,000 in cases with three arbitrators unless it appears from the information contained in the parties' submissions that this would clearly be inappropriate.[727] Thus, for example, where the claims are not quantified but it appears to the Court that the stakes of the arbitration are nevertheless substantial and the issues complex, it may fix an initial advance in excess of U.S. $100,000 in cases with three arbitrators. Conversely, it may fix a lower advance if the case appears, on its face, to be relatively simple. Indeed, the Court has made a greater effort in recent years to adapt the amount of the advance in unquantified cases to the particular circumstances of each case.

Even when the claims are quantified, however, the Cost Scales do not automatically provide a figure for the corresponding advance to be fixed by the Court. This is because, for each bracket of the scale of arbitrators' fees, there is, as already noted, a minimum and a maximum figure. When fixing the arbitrators' fees at the conclusion of the arbitration between the minimum and the maximum, the Court is expected to take account of a number of factors, including the complexity of the case and the arbitrators' performance (*see* Article 31(1) *infra*). But

---

[726] The Court has, in fact, never had a rigid policy in respect of interest. For many years, the Court would include interest as part of the sum in dispute, if quantified, but not if unquantified. This practice was later discontinued, however, and interest was generally not taken into account, particularly interest accruing during the course of the arbitration as it was not considered appropriate for either the ICC or the arbitrators to have a financial interest in the prolongation of the arbitration. Other arbitral institutions have dealt with the question of interest in different ways. An interesting example is the Zurich Chamber of Commerce, which does not count interest in calculating the amount in dispute except when the interest claims exceed the amount of the principal sum, in which case they replace the latter in calculating the value in dispute.

[727] The above figures correspond roughly to the amount of the advance on costs that would be fixed under the Cost Scales in force prior to January 1, 1998 for an amount in dispute of slightly less than U.S. $1,000,000. But as the Cost Scales have now been increased, it is possible that the foregoing figures will also be increased.

these factors cannot usually be assessed by the Court when fixing the advance on costs. It has, thus, been the Court's general practice, when fixing the advance, to use the average figures for arbitrators' fees set forth in the scale. As the arbitration evolves, it is necessary for the Secretariat to reconsider on a regular basis whether the amount of the advance continues to be suitable, given, in particular, the amount of work required to be performed by the arbitrators, their diligence and other relevant circumstances.

Readjustment of the advance. As the advance on costs is initially fixed by the Court at a time when it cannot actually assess all of the factors that are required to be taken into account subsequently in determining the arbitrators' fees, and the arbitrators' out-of-pocket disbursements for the arbitration can also not yet be known, the advance is necessarily of a provisional nature. Moreover, it may also be necessary to adjust the amount of the advance if the sum in dispute fluctuates during the course of the arbitration. Article 30(2), as already mentioned, thus, provides that the advance may be subject to readjustment at any time during the arbitration, as does Article 1(10) of Appendix III, which further specifies that such readjustments may be made:

> in particular, to take into account fluctuations in the amount in dispute, changes in the amount of the estimated expenses of the arbitrator, or the evolving difficulty or complexity of the arbitration proceeding.

In principle, any such readjustments may have the effect of either increasing or decreasing the amount of the advance. However, except where the amount in dispute is reduced at an early stage of the arbitration, it is relatively unusual for the amount of the advance to be decreased. While increases in the amounts of the claims will ordinarily lead to increases in the amount of the advance at any time during the arbitration, decreases that occur after the Terms of Reference have been established are not necessarily considered to justify a reduction, except possibly where they also have the effect of reducing significantly the work required of the arbitrators. Moreover, the Court has rarely been inclined in the past to reduce an arbitrator's remuneration below the average figure used for the purpose of determining the advance, except possibly in exceptional cases, while it has readily increased advances in order to take account of the amount of work that the arbitrators have been required to perform as well as greater than anticipated levels of out-of-pocket expenditures.[728]

This having been said, the Court has traditionally been very reluctant to increase the advance significantly at a late stage of the arbitration. Indeed, it generally wishes to avoid surprising the parties, to the extent possible, once the

---

[728] As already noted with respect to the new provisions of the Rules on the correction and interpretation of Awards (Article 29), the Court may also now fix an additional advance to cover the fees and costs related to an application in this connection (*see* Appendix III, Article 2(7)).

proceedings are near their end. Parties often argue, in this regard, that they proceeded with the arbitration, rather than settling or withdrawing it, on the assumption that it would cost them a certain amount to do so. They therefore normally consider it to be the Court's duty to effect any readjustments that may be required sooner rather than later. It is, thus, incumbent upon both the Secretariat and the arbitrators, regularly during the arbitration, to satisfy themselves that the level of the advance is adequate, given the on-going and anticipated work and expenses of the Arbitral Tribunal. Some arbitrators are vigilant in promptly reporting such information to the Secretariat, while others are much less so and wait until the arbitration is nearly complete before advising the Secretariat that they consider the advance to be inadequate to remunerate them for all of the work that they have done. In the latter case, however, it will often already be too late, in the Court's view, to request the parties to advance additional funds. (Thus, for example, the Court has not generally been willing in the past to increase the amount of the advance when a draft of the final Award is already available for scrutiny by the Court.)

Usually, before the Court is invited by the Secretariat to reconsider the amount of the advance, the Secretariat advises the parties that the matter is going to be submitted to the Court for its consideration, thus affording them an opportunity to comment. From time to time, a party may object to the readjustment of the advance, and the Court may, thus, have to make a determination regarding the arbitrators' possible entitlement to greater than average remuneration in circumstances where the views of the parties and the arbitrators are radically different. Steering a reasonable course between the sometimes conflicting views of the parties and arbitrators in this respect is one of the Court's most difficult, yet important, tasks.

Separate advances. Although, as already noted, Article 30(2) provides initially for a single advance on costs covering all of the claims and counterclaims referred to arbitration, like Article 9(1) of the former Rules, it nevertheless also permits the Court to fix separate advances on costs when counterclaims are submitted in addition to the principal claims.

Notwithstanding its power to fix separate advances on costs, it is not the Court's practice to do so on its own initiative in the absence of a request of one of the parties. The Court will also not normally fix separate advances on costs unless it is satisfied that the parties are unwilling to pay the single, global advance that it is the Court's practice to fix first. Indeed, it is the Court's usual practice to fix a single, global advance initially because it is hoped that each party will pay half, in accordance with Article 30(3), as discussed below. In the event that a party refuses to do so, however, the provision for separate advances in Article 30(2) ensures that the other party is not required to advance any portion of the costs relating to the claims being made against it.

When fixing separate advances on costs, the Court applies the Cost Scales separately to the claims and counterclaims, respectively. Because of the regressive nature of the scales, the aggregate amount of separate advances will, thus, always be greater – often substantially so – than the amount of a single advance fixed for both the claims and counterclaims if the advances are calculated on a like basis.[729] For this reason, it will rarely be financially advantageous for a party to request the Court to fix separate advances on costs unless there is such a substantial difference between the amounts of the claims and counterclaims that the amount of the separate advance is likely to be less than half of the global advance for the claims and counterclaims together or where one of the parties is otherwise unwilling to pay its share of the advance on costs fixed initially for all of the claims.

Article 30(3)

> *The advance on costs fixed by the Court shall be payable in equal shares by the Claimant and the Respondent. Any provisional advance paid on the basis of Article 30(1) will be considered as a partial payment thereof. However, any party shall be free to pay the whole of the advance on costs in respect of the principal claim or the counterclaim should the other party fail to pay its share. When the Court has set separate advances on costs in accordance with Article 30(2), each of the parties shall pay the advance on costs corresponding to its claims.*

Background. Article 30(3) sets forth the general rule, previously contained in Article 9(2), that the advance on costs is payable in equal shares by the parties.[730] Thus, even when a Respondent party does not have any claims, it is expected, unlike in the case of the provisional advance, to contribute to the advance on costs to the same extent as the Claimant. The parties' respective obligations in this regard are not intended, however, to prejudice the Arbitral Tribunal's ultimate determination in its Award of the manner in which the costs of the arbitration are to be borne by the parties (*see* Article 31(3) *infra*). Thus, at the end of the day,

---

[729] Thus, for example, the advance on costs for a sum in dispute of U.S. $2,000,000 would be likely to be in the vicinity of U.S. $170,000 (applying the Cost Scales for three arbitrators and adding an allowance for out-of-pocket expenses), while two separate advances for claims and counterclaims of U.S. $1,000,000 each would be approximately U.S. $115,000-$120,000 (or U.S. $230,000-$240,000 in the aggregate). It has long been the Secretariat's practice to calculate separate advances in this manner so that adequate funds are available in the event that either the claims or counterclaims are subsequently withdrawn. However, if no claims are withdrawn, the amount of the arbitrators' fees and the ICC's administrative costs will be calculated at the conclusion of the arbitration on the basis of the aggregate sum in dispute, and consequently part of the advance will often be returned to the parties at that time.

[730] In this regard, as stated in Article 30(3), any provisional advance paid by the Claimant pursuant to Article 30(1) is credited to its share of the advance. In addition, the Claimant is to receive credit for the payment accompanying its Request for Arbitration (Appendix III, Article 1(1)). Article 2(8) of Appendix III further provides that one-half of the administrative expenses paid for an attempted ICC conciliation shall be credited to the administrative expenses of the arbitration.

one of the parties may be found to be entitled to be reimbursed by the other for the sums that it may have been required to advance for the arbitration pursuant to Article 30(3).

The parties are nevertheless considered, under Article 30(3), to have an obligation, during the course of the arbitration, to share equally in the payment of the advance fixed by the Court, as it may be readjusted from time to time, except when separate advances are fixed for the claims and counterclaims, in which case each of the parties shall pay the advance on costs corresponding to its claims. In requiring that the parties share equally in the payment of the advance, the Rules resemble those of most other arbitral institutions, although, under some arbitration rules, the manner in which advances should be shared is left to the discretion of the institution on a case-by-case basis.[731]

In the case of the ICC Rules, the requirement that the advance be paid in equal shares is, as just stated, intended to give rise to an obligation on the part of each of the parties. Indeed, Article 30(3) provides that the advance "shall be payable" by each of them, respectively.[732] As discussed further below, the Rules nevertheless do not expressly contain any sanction (other than the possible deemed withdrawal of a claim) for the non-payment by a party of its share of the advance on costs and merely provide, in this connection, that the other party may itself pay the whole of the advance on costs.[733] Where the Respondent party has asserted counterclaims, but refuses to pay its share of the advance, it is also open to the Claimant, in such circumstances, to request that separate advances be fixed, as already noted.

[731] *See, e.g.,* LCIA Rules, Article 24.

[732] Arguably, under Article 9(2) of the previous Rules, the parties' obligation to share also extended to any separate advances that the Court might fix. However, the Court's Internal Rules (Article 14) provided that, in such case, the Secretariat "requests each of the parties to pay the amount corresponding to its claims." This reflected the pragmatic concern that, when separate advances on costs are fixed, the parties could not normally be expected to contribute to the advance for the other party's claims. The Secretariat's practice in this regard, as formerly set forth in the Internal Rules, has, thus, now been imported into Article 30(3), which at the same time, moreover, eliminates any obligation of the parties to share in the payment of separate advances. While the new provision of Article 30(3) follows logically from the Court's longstanding practice, it nevertheless arguably permits a Respondent party to avoid its obligation to share in the advance corresponding to a Claimant's claim simply by filing a small counterclaim, if separate advances are then fixed. However, notwithstanding the terms of Article 30(3), it is difficult to see why a counterclaimant in such circumstances should have any less of an obligation to contribute to the advance fixed for the Claimant's claim than a Respondent with no counterclaims.

[733] Somewhat misleadingly, however, Article 30(3) provides that "any party shall be free to pay the whole of the advance on costs *in respect of the principal claim or the counterclaim* should the other party fail to pay its share." (Emphasis added.) The reference to "the principal claim or counterclaim" is anomalous, given the requirement, in the following sentence, that each of the parties shall pay the advance on costs corresponding to its claims in the event that the Court sets separate advances on costs for the claims and counterclaims, respectively. Thus, in the absence of separate advances, it is, in fact, the whole of the single, global advance in respect of the principal claim *and* any counterclaims that must be paid.

This having been said, most Respondent parties in ICC arbitrations contribute, as required, to the advance on costs fixed by the Court. While there are, of course, many parties that do not, and the Court is not itself in a position to compel parties to pay the amounts required to be paid pursuant to Article 30(3), the great majority wish to be perceived, in the eyes of the arbitrators, as "good citizens" who respect their contractual commitments. This wish is itself normally sufficient to motivate parties to comply with their obligations under Article 30(3), to the extent that they are able to do so.[734]

Means of payment. The parties are generally required to pay their respective shares of the advance on costs, or separate advances, in cash. However, many years ago, in order to ease the burden of payment, the ICC began accepting bank guarantees in lieu of cash in certain circumstances. The ICC's practices in this regard were previously the subject of various Notes issued by the Secretariat, the principal terms of which have now been reproduced in Articles 1(5), 1(6), 1(8) and 1(9) of Appendix III.

Bank guarantees may be used in two different situations. The first, and most common, is where one of the parties fails to pay its half share of the advance on costs. Provided that it has itself paid its full share of the advance, the other party may, in such event, post a bank guarantee, instead of paying cash, to cover the unpaid portion of the advance owed by the defaulting party (Appendix III, Article 1(6)). In addition, in the event that separate advances are required to be fixed (usually as result of a default) and the amount of the separate advance to be paid by a party exceeds that party's one-half share of the global advance previously fixed in respect of the same claims, then a bank guarantee may be posted in order to cover any such excess (Appendix III, Article 1(8)). The intention, in the latter case, is to ensure that a party is not required to advance any more cash than it otherwise would be required to do simply by virtue of the fixing of separate advances, which is usually necessitated by a party's refusal to pay its share of the advance.

In addition to the case of default, the ICC has long accepted bank guarantees in lieu of cash to cover parts of very large advances. Article 1(5) of Appendix III, thus, stipulates that a party may post a bank guarantee for any amount in excess of "an amount fixed from time to time by the Court." Prior to the entry

---

[734] It has nevertheless been suggested that there may be circumstances in which a Respondent may have "valid reasons for not participating in the payment of the advance on costs." *See* Bühler, *supra,* note 701, p.148 ("There are two cases where a respondent may be inclined not to follow the 'rules of the game': (i) when it challenges the jurisdiction of the Arbitral Tribunal; (ii) when it has no prospect of recovering its costs from the claimant, either because the latter has filed for bankruptcy, or receivership, or is otherwise in a financial position which makes reimbursement of the costs incurred by the respondent from the outset unlikely, if not impossible."). In the former case, however, a party may be able to recover its advance from the Claimant if its jurisdictional challenge succeeds. In the latter, the Respondent has the option of requesting the tribunal to order the Claimant to provide security for the Respondent's costs. *See* Article 23 *supra.*

into force of the New Rules, the Secretariat's practice was to accept bank guarantees for any part of a party's share of the advance in excess of U.S. $300,000 "to the extent that the circumstances of the case so allow."[735] The parties' right to post a guarantee in such circumstances was expressed in conditional terms because more than U.S. $300,000 in cash might be required in some proceedings to cover expenses and advances to the arbitrators. Thus, the Secretariat could not undertake to accept bank guarantees in all cases for all of a party's share of the advance in excess of U.S. $300,000. The Court has yet to determine what its precise policy will be under the New Rules in this regard.[736]

In the event that a party wishes to post a bank guarantee, it must be with a bank and in a form that is acceptable to the ICC (*see* Appendix III, Article 1(9)). At the conclusion of the arbitration, after the fees and expenses of the arbitrators and the ICC's administrative costs have been fixed by the Court, the Secretariat will normally give the party that posted the guarantee the option of substituting cash for the part of the guarantee that would otherwise be required to be called to cover the amounts due to the arbitrators and the ICC.

Consequences of non-payment by Respondent. In the event that a Respondent party fails to pay its share of the advance and the Claimant nevertheless wishes to proceed with the arbitration, the Rules do not, as already stated, leave the Claimant with any alternative other than to pay the whole of the advance itself (using a bank guarantee, if desired, as just discussed) or, if the Respondent has filed counterclaims, to request the fixing of separate advances. Although the Secretariat has taken the position, in the past, that "it is not an accepted practice in ICC arbitrations for a party to refuse to pay all or a part of its share of the advance on costs and to leave it to the other party to pay for the defaulting party,"[373] the Respondent is nevertheless not precluded, in such circumstances, from continuing to participate in the proceedings, at least for the purpose of defending itself.[738] A non-paying Respondent can be prevented, however, from pursuing any counterclaims it may have if a separate advance for its counterclaims has been fixed and that advance has not been paid.

Given the absence of any express sanction in the Rules for a Respondent's failure to pay its share of the advance (except in respect of the prosecution of counterclaims), Claimant parties have occasionally sought to obtain interim relief from arbitrators and courts in such circumstances. Thus, for example, the

---

[735] Note from the Secretariat of the International Court of Arbitration to All Parties for Information Concerning the Application of the Schedule of Conciliation and Arbitration Costs (January 1, 1993), reprinted in *ICC Ct. Bull.*, Vol.4, No.1 (May 1993), p.26.

[736] *See* Grigera Naón, *supra*, note 47, p.48.

[737] *See supra*, note 735.

[738] In this respect, the Rules do not differ from those of other institutions, although it has been argued that non-paying parties should be prevented from participating in arbitration proceedings. *See* H. Smit, *supra*, note 45, pp.31-32.

Claimant in a recent arbitration applied to the Arbitral Tribunal for an interim order directing the Respondent to pay its share of the advance on costs on the ground that the Respondent's failure to do so constituted a breach of the parties' arbitration agreement and had prejudiced the Claimant by requiring it to pay the Respondent's share of the advance. Although the Arbitral Tribunal found that it had the authority to make the order requested by the Claimant and that the Respondent was, in fact, obligated under the ICC Rules to pay its share of the advance, it nevertheless decided, in an unpublished Award, not to order the Respondent to do so because the Claimant had not established any irreparable harm.[739] The Arbitral Tribunal noted, in particular, that the Claimant might ultimately be determined to be responsible for all of the costs of the arbitration, and was not, in the meantime, unable to pay the Respondent's share of the advance. Had it been impossible for the Claimant to pay the Respondent's share, however, an order granting the Claimant's request might arguably have been justified in the opinion of the tribunal.

Although there have not yet been any instances in which, to the authors' knowledge, an ICC Arbitral Tribunal has ordered a Respondent party to pay its share of the advance on costs, there has been at least one case in which a court has accepted to do so. In that case, on the application of a Claimant (the receiver of a bankrupt German company), the Superior Court of New Jersey ordered the Respondent parties (two U.S. companies and an individual domiciled in the United States) to pay to the ICC within fourteen days the sum of U.S. $4,000, corresponding to the Respondents' share of the advance on costs fixed by Court.[740] Although the Claimant's application was unopposed and the Superior Court's Order does not indicate the reasons for its decision, it appears entirely consistent with the provisions of the Rules.

Alternatively, it may be argued that a party that fails to pay its share of the advance on costs repudiates, or renounces, the arbitration agreement, thus entitling the other party to pursue its claims against the defaulting party in court.

---

[739] For a discussion of certain aspects of this Award, *see* Mitrovic, "Advance to Cover Costs of Arbitration," *ICC Ct. Bull.*, Vol.7, No.2 (1996), pp.88, 89.

[740] *Ulrich Schubert* v. *H.O. Engineering, Inc., et al.*, Order of the Superior Court of New Jersey, Middlesex County, Docket No.L-4310-90 (March 4, 1994).

Although there is judicial support for such a position,[741] this may neverthelesss not be of much comfort to a Claimant party preferring arbitration. Where a Claimant chooses to continue with the arbitration and to pay the Respondent's share of the advance on costs, it, in any event, retains the possibility of claiming reimbursement of the sums that it has been required to advance, possibly with interest, in the arbitration proceedings.

Inability of Claimant to pay. Occasionally, it is the Claimant party that is unable to pay its share of the advance on costs. From time to time, the Court is, thus, requested by Claimants pleading indigence to accord them special treatment by, for example, fixing the advance on costs at a lower level than it normally would based on the Cost Schedules. As a general matter, no matter how much the Court may sympathize with such requests, it has not considered it appropriate to try to take account of the parties' financial circumstances in fixing the amount of the advance on costs. This is because, first of all, the Secretariat is not usually in a position to verify the parties' assertions in this regard and, secondly, the Court needs to be in a position to remunerate the arbitrators adequately and to cover the ICC's own costs, irrespective of the parties' circumstances. A party initiating ICC arbitration proceedings should therefore not assume that it will be able to proceed with the arbitration if it does not have the resources necessary to cover the advance on costs that will normally be payable to the ICC for the claim in question.

In the event that a party does not have sufficient financial resources to proceed with an ICC arbitration, the question may then arise as to whether it can, as an alternative, validly commence proceedings before the courts on the ground, *e.g.*, that the arbitration clause is "incapable of being performed" (New

---

[741] *See, e.g.,* in Germany, the decision of the Federal Supreme Court (March 7, 1985), NJW (1985), pp.1903-04. *See also Société TRH Graphics c/ société Offset Aubin, Cour de cassation* (November 19, 1991), *Rev. arb.* (1992), p.462 (which concerned an ICC arbitration in France), and Mitrovic, *supra,* note 739, p.89, describing a decision of the Committee of the Court in which it approved a request for the postponement of a payment pending a decision of an English court as to whether a Respondent's failure to pay its share of the advance constituted a waiver of the arbitration agreement. Unlike the ICC and most other arbitration rules, Article 55 of the International Arbitration Rules of the Zurich Chamber of Commerce specifically provides in this regard that: "If a party fails to pay the advance ordered, the other party may choose to advance the arbitration costs or renounce the arbitration. If it renounces, the parties are no longer bound to the arbitration agreement with respect to the particular dispute." *But cf.* Wetter and Priem, "Costs and Their Allocation in International Commercial Arbitration," *Am. Rev. Int. Arb.*, Vol.2 (1991), pp.249, 318 ("It is believed that such a rule would not be recognized as legally valid in most jurisdictions outside Switzerland."). Relying on *Lalive Poudret and Reymond*, p.359, Wetter and Priem also question the validity of the rule even in Switzerland. *See also* Gaillard, "Laws and Court Decisions in Civil Law Countries [Topic 2]," *ICCA Congress Series,* No.5 (Kluwer 1991), pp.104, 105 ("[A]ll disputes between the parties, including those concerning the eventual termination of the arbitration agreement for non-performance, should be settled by the arbitrators.").

York Convention, Article II(3)). However, this is a question as to which there is not any authority of which the authors are aware.[742]

Interest. The sums paid by the parties pursuant to Article 30(3) are intended, as already indicated, to cover the fees and expenses of the arbitrators and the administrative costs of the ICC. Although certain amounts are disbursed by the ICC to the arbitrators during the course of the arbitration (*see* the discussion of the ICC's policies in this regard in connection with Article 31(1) below), the bulk of the arbitrators' fees are paid to them only at the conclusion of the arbitration. The ICC may therefore hold some of the funds advanced by the parties for a relatively long period of time before disbursing them to the arbitrators or, if appropriate, returning them to the parties.

The practice of the Court does not differ from that of most other arbitral institutions in this regard. While a few institutions have undertaken in recent years to credit interest to the parties on the sums advanced by them,[743] the ICC has never done so, and this has occasionally been a source of criticism.[744] However, without the interest earned from sums held by the ICC during the arbitration, the ICC would inevitably be required to increase the amount of its administrative charges by an equivalent amount to make up for the resulting loss of revenue.[745]

Article 30(4)

> *When a request for an advance on costs has not been complied with, and after consultation with the Arbitral Tribunal, the Secretary General may direct the Arbitral Tribunal to suspend its work and set a time limit, which must be not less than 15 days, on the expiry of which the relevant claims, or counterclaims, shall be considered as withdrawn. Should the party in question wish to object to this measure it must make a request within the aforementioned period for the matter to be decided by the Court. Such party shall not be prevented on the ground of such withdrawal from reintroducing the same claims or counterclaims at a later date in another proceeding.*

[742] Parties have alternatively sought to press their claims in court on the ground that the amount of the advance fixed by the Court was so high as to be prohibitive and unconscionable, but not successfully to the authors' knowledge. *See*, however, in connection with a non-ICC case, the decision of a New York state appellate court (*Matter of Arbitration between Teleserve Systems, Inc. and MCI Telecommunications Corp.*, 659 N.Y.S.2d 659, (1997)) in which the court held that a filing fee of U.S. $204,000 (U.S. $4,000 plus 5 per cent of the amount claimed) was unreasonable, unjust, unconscionable and therefore unenforceable.

[743] *See, e.g.,* the Schedule of Costs of the LCIA, which provides: "Monies deposited with the LCIA are placed in a special deposit account and the interest accruing remains with the account and is credited to the amount deposited by the parties." *See also* Article 13 of the Arbitration Rules of the Arbitration Institute of the Stockholm Chamber of Commerce.

[744] *See, e.g.,* Wetter and Priem, *supra,* note 741, p.317.

[745] *See Craig Park and Paulsson,* §3.03, pp.41-42.

Background. This is a new sub-paragraph that imports into the Rules a provision formerly contained in the Court's Internal Rules (Article 15) on the deemed withdrawal of claims and that also formalizes the Secretariat's practice of directing the Arbitral Tribunal, as necessary, to suspend its work when a request for an advance on costs has not been complied with. At the same time, it replaces Article 9(4) of the previous Rules, which provided that the Terms of Reference would "only become operative" and that the arbitrator was "only [to] proceed in respect of those claims for which the advance on costs has been duly paid."

Former Article 9(4) was frequently a source of confusion as well as being a potential source of delay. Indeed, upon the establishment of the Terms of Reference, the Secretariat would usually call for the payment of the outstanding amount of the advance on costs, and, pending the payment of that amount, the Terms of Reference were not deemed to be effective. Although this should not necessarily have prevented the parties from continuing to exchange pleadings or the arbitrators from making procedural directions, neither this nor the precise consequences of Article 9(4) were entirely clear; nor was it clear whether the Arbitral Tribunal could legitimately proceed with the arbitration in the event of the readjustment of the advance, pending the payment of the additional amounts required to be advanced in such case.

Under Article 30(4), the entry into force of the Terms of Reference no longer depends upon the payment of the advance on costs, and more flexibility is permitted, in general, with respect to the conduct of the proceedings, pending the full payment of that amount. Thus, for example, a Respondent's delay in paying its share of the advance need not necessarily delay the progress of the arbitration, provided that sufficient funds are otherwise on hand to cover the arbitrators' fees and expenses and the ICC's administrative costs for the work being performed. The new rule means, however, that the Secretariat will be required to monitor carefully the financial status of every arbitration that is allowed to proceed without the full amount of the advance on costs having been paid and to use prudently the powers conferred upon it by Article 30(4) in this connection.

Suspension of the Arbitral Tribunal's work. As soon as the advance on costs has been fixed by the Court, the Secretariat invites the parties to pay their respective shares. The Rules do not lay down any particular requirements in this regard, and it is therefore for the Secretariat to fix whatever deadline it may consider appropriate for the payments in question. The initial deadline fixed by the Secretariat for the payment of the advance may vary, but is typically 30 days. The failure by a party to respect that deadline will not itself have any adverse consequences, however. It is only after such an initial request for the payment of the advance has not been complied with that the Secretariat may consider directing the Arbitral Tribunal to suspend its work pursuant to Article 30(4).

Ordinarily, there ought not to be any need for the Secretary General to direct the Arbitral Tribunal to suspend its work prior to the establishment of the Terms of Reference. Indeed, the provisional advance required to be paid prior to the transmission of the file to the Arbitral Tribunal is intended to cover the estimated costs of the arbitration up until that time. There may nevertheless be circumstances in which the payment of at least part of the advance subsequently fixed by the Court is required to cover the cost of establishing the Terms of Reference. The possible suspension of the Arbitral Tribunal's work prior to that time under Article 30(4) therefore cannot be excluded in such a case.

Most frequently, however, the possible need for the suspension of the Arbitral Tribunal's work will arise only if the advance on costs has not been paid once the Terms of Reference have been prepared. As from that time, the Secretariat will be required to verify that sufficient funds are available to cover any work that the arbitrators may be required to perform. In this regard, the Court has decided that, in general, after the preparation of the Terms of Reference, the Arbitral Tribunal shall "proceed only with respect to those claims or counterclaims in regard to which the whole of the advance on costs has been paid" (Appendix III, Article 1(3)). However, this is not intended to be a rigid rule. Thus, for example, the Arbitral Tribunal may be allowed to proceed if less than the whole of the advance has been paid, but sufficient funds are available to cover work that may be required, *e.g.*, upon the payment by the Claimant of its share of the advance, but pending the payment by the Respondent of its share. Moreover, if the advance is increased by the Court during the arbitration, the whole of the advance may be unpaid for a certain period, but this ought not to disrupt the conduct of the arbitration, provided that, and for as long as, sufficient funds are available for the work that the arbitrators are required to perform. Article 30(4) therefore permits more flexibility than former Article 9(4). However, whenever the amount of the advance on costs is increased, the Secretariat will be required to verify that the amounts paid by the parties are adequate to cover the cost of the proceedings if they are allowed to continue, particularly if the increase occurs on the eve of a hearing.[746]

Under Article 30(4), only the Secretary General of the Court can direct the Arbitral Tribunal to suspend its work. The Arbitral Tribunal therefore does not have the right to do so on its own initiative.[747] However, any such suspension

---

[746] It is also to be remembered that Article 28(1) of the Rules provides that the Award shall not be notified to the parties unless "the costs of the arbitration have been fully paid to the ICC." In practice, therefore, the Court will not generally scrutinize the arbitrators' draft Award pursuant to Article 27 unless the amount of the advance on costs has been paid. In some jurisdictions, the law expressly enjoins arbitrators from withholding their Award pending the payment of their fees and expenses (*e.g.*, Section 23 of the Swedish Arbitration Act), but it has been argued that, even in such jurisdictions, institutions should be permitted to withhold Awards pending payment if such a power is incorporated in the arbitration rules to which the parties have agreed. *See* Wetter and Priem, *supra*, note 741, p.325. *See also*, in this connection, Section 56 of the English Arbitration Act 1996.

[747] *See* Grigera Naón, *supra*, note 47, p.45. It is to be noted, however, that the French version of the Rules provides that the Secretariat (rather than the Secretary General) is so empowered.

must, as stated in Article 30(4), be preceded by consultation between the Secretary General and the Arbitral Tribunal. Pursuant to Article 30(4), the Secretary General may direct the Arbitral Tribunal to suspend its work in respect of the claims or counterclaims separately. It is, thus, theoretically possible for the arbitration to proceed in respect of the one, but not the other, although it would surely not be desirable for any such suspension to be prolonged, given not only the disruption, but the uncertainties that might result as a consequence. Article 30(4), thus, contemplates that, in directing the Arbitral Tribunal to suspend its work, the Secretary General may set a time limit for compliance with a request for an advance on costs, on the expiry of which the relevant claims or counterclaims shall be considered as withdrawn.[748] As discussed below, however, a party may require the Secretary General's direction to be reviewed, and possibly rescinded or altered, by the Court.

The deemed withdrawal of claims. Pursuant to Article 30(4), as under Article 15 of the Court's previous Internal Rules, the claims or counterclaims of either party may be deemed to be withdrawn if a request for an advance on costs has not been satisfied within a time limit fixed by the Secretary General. This provision enables the Secretariat, in effect, to terminate the arbitration in respect of either or both of the parties' claims if the corresponding advance on costs has not been paid by a stipulated date. As under former Article 15 of the Internal Rules, any such deemed withdrawal is not intended to prevent the subsequent reintroduction of the same claims or counterclaims. However, as Article 30(4), unlike the previous provision, now makes clear, any such claims may only be reintroduced in a different proceeding.[749] Thus, once a claim has been deemed to be withdrawn, it may not be resubmitted in the same arbitration, although the parties could presumably agree otherwise.

Under Article 30(4), the time limit for payment is required to be fixed by the Secretary General and may not be less than 15 days. It previously could not be less than 30 days under former Article 15, but has been shortened in order to reduce the potential for related delay of the arbitration. As a practical matter, however, the Secretary General can reasonably be expected to take into account the particular circumstances of each case when fixing a time limit, such as, for example, the possible need for governmental exchange control approval of the payment in question. In the past, it was the practice of the Secretariat to grant

---

[748] It is not entirely clear from Article 30(4) whether the Secretary General is required to set such a time limit whenever it directs the Arbitral Tribunal to suspend its work. However, it can reasonably be assumed that it would normally be appropriate for the Secretary General to do so, in any event.

[749] A party's right to reintroduce a claim may be affected, however, by provisions of national law concerning, for example, the possible renunciation of the arbitration agreement or the expiration of a relevant statute of limitations. *See, e.g., Société TRH Graphics c/ société Offset Aubin,* Note Hascher, *supra,* note 741, p.464. *See also* Bühler, *supra,* note 701, p.149.

the party in question more time rather than less in most cases (*e.g.*, as much as 60 days) in order to avoid any suggestion that the period allowed for payment was not reasonable. The Secretary General retains considerable discretion in this regard, although the time limits fixed by him pursuant to this provision are subject to the control of the Court, as under former Article 15.

Article 30(4) provides in this connection that should "the party in question" wish to object to the time limit fixed by the Secretary General, it may request that "the matter" be "decided by the Court," provided, however, that any such request is made within the period fixed by the Secretary General. In other words, if the Secretary General fixes a 15-day period for payment, and a party objects to this, it must request a decision of the Court within the 15 days fixed for payment, failing which the claim is deemed withdrawn and the Court no longer has any authority to reconsider the Secretary General's determination. By providing expressly only for the possible objection of "the party in question," Article 30(4) also appears to limit the right of requesting a Court decision to the party or parties required to make the payment that is the subject of the relevant time limit. Thus, Article 30(4) does not expressly foresee that the Claimant, for example, might object to the length of a time limit fixed for the payment by the Respondent of the separate advance for its counterclaim. However, former Article 15 did not limit the parties' right of objection to "the party in question," and it is doubtful that any such restriction was actually intended when the New Rules were adopted. Presumably, therefore, the Court would not refuse to consider an objection raised by any party.

When a party objects to a time limit fixed by the Secretary General, this should, in keeping with the Secretariat's past practice, have the effect of suspending the running of the time limit as from the day upon which the objection is received by the Secretary General. The Court then has the power either to alter or rescind the time limit fixed by the Secretary General or to refuse to reconsider it. In the latter case, it was nevertheless the Court's usual practice in the past to allow at least as much additional time for the payment of the advance in question as still remained when the objection was received by the Secretariat, even if the objection was rejected. Thus, parties could effectively obtain more time for payment simply by objecting to the time limit fixed by the Secretariat. This will presumably continue to be the case under the New Rules. In practice, however, the Court has not frequently altered the time limits fixed by the Secretariat.

In order to avoid a claim's deemed withdrawal pursuant to Article 30(4), a party must ensure that payment of the amount in question has been received by the ICC prior to the expiration of the relevant deadline. It ordinarily does not suffice for payment instructions to have been given. In the case of a bank transfer, the funds must, thus, have been credited to the ICC's account. The Secretariat must otherwise have received a check for the amount due.

In the event that the Claimant's claims are deemed to be withdrawn under Article 30(4), and the Respondent does not have any counterclaims, this normally brings the arbitration to an end. A Respondent may nevertheless wish to obtain an Award from the Arbitral Tribunal for its costs in such circumstances. In principle, there is nothing in the Rules that precludes this. However, the Court would be required to fix a new advance on costs to cover the cost of continuing with the arbitration for this limited purpose. If the claims deemed to be withdrawn are counterclaims of the Respondent, then the arbitration will thereafter proceed in respect of the Claimant's claims only, and, accordingly, the Respondent should have an obligation to share in the advance on costs fixed by the Court in respect of those claims. Thus, any sums that the Respondent may previously have advanced separately in respect of the counterclaims ought to be applied against its share of the advance for the claims remaining in the arbitration.

Article 30(5)

> *If one of the parties claims a right to a set-off with regard to either claims or counterclaims, such set-off shall be taken into account in determining the advance to cover the costs of arbitration in the same way as a separate claim insofar as it may require the Arbitral Tribunal to consider additional matters.*

The rule set forth in this Article is virtually identical to a provision that was previously contained in the Court's Internal Rules (Article 16). It is intended to permit the Court to include the amount of a "set-off" claim in the amount in dispute for the purpose of calculating the ICC's administrative costs and the arbitrators' fees in accordance with the Cost Scales.

The Rules do not define what constitutes a "set-off" claim as opposed to a counterclaim, and, indeed, the precise definition of such a claim may differ in different legal systems.[750] For this reason, the decisive factor for the Court in determining whether to include the amount of a set-off in the amount in dispute is whether it "may require the Arbitral Tribunal to consider additional matters," *i.e.,* matters in addition to those raised by the claims and counterclaims themselves and the other defenses thereto. In assessing whether this is the case, the Secretariat normally consults with the arbitrators. But it is rare for a set-off not to be found to require the consideration of additional matters.[751]

Insofar as the amount of a set-off is taken into account for the purpose of calculating the advance on costs, then it also may be the subject of a separate

---

[750] It has, in fact, been argued that a set-off is in reality a defense and not a claim and that, as a defense, it ought not to be treated as a claim at all. *See, e.g.*, Karrer, "Arbitration Saves! Costs: Poker and Hide-and-Seek," *J. Arb. Int.*, Vol.3, No.1 (1986), pp.35, 41-42.

[751] One commentator has, thus, suggested that "it would be more appropriate to reverse the exception . . . since normally it requires arbitrators to examine additional questions of fact or law." *See* Bühler, *supra*, note 701, p.123.

advance, like a counterclaim, under Article 30(2). Even though the Rules do not expressly provide for this, the Court has, in fact, fixed separate advances for set-off claims on a few occasions.

ARTICLE 31

Decision as to the Costs of the Arbitration

Article 31 sets forth, with a few alterations, the provisions formerly contained in Article 20 of the Rules. While Article 30 is concerned with the fixing of the advance on costs, Article 31 provides for the final determination by the Court of the ICC's administrative expenses and the arbitrators' fees and expenses as well as for decisions on costs by the arbitrators. Like Article 30, Article 31 must be read together with Appendix III to the Rules, in particular Article 2.

Article 31(1)

> The costs of the arbitration shall include the fees and expenses of the arbitrators and the ICC administrative costs fixed by the Court, in accordance with the scale in force at the time of the commencement of the arbitral proceedings, as well as the fees and expenses of any experts appointed by the Arbitral Tribunal and the reasonable legal and other costs incurred by the parties for the arbitration.

Background. Article 31(1), like former Article 20(2), serves the general purpose of defining the "costs of the arbitration" that are to be the subject of a decision on costs pursuant to either sub-paragraph (2) or (3) of Article 31. These include the following items, as already mentioned: (i) the arbitrators' fees and expenses; (ii) the ICC administrative costs; (iii) the fees and expenses of any experts appointed by the Arbitral Tribunal; and (iv) the reasonable legal and other costs incurred by the parties for the arbitration. While very similar to the corresponding provision in the previous Rules, Article 31(1) nevertheless includes a number of changes, made principally to clarify the text, as described below.

Arbitrators' fees. The arbitrators' fees are, as already noted, to be fixed by the Court in accordance with the arbitrator fee scale, subject only to the possibility of a derogation under Article 31(2). In this regard, Article 31(1), unlike former Article 20(2), now makes it clear that the applicable fee scale is the "scale in force at the time of the commencement of the arbitral proceedings." This is not only consistent with the Court's long-standing practice, but with the ICC's need to ensure appropriate compensation for persons appointed as ICC arbitrators. Indeed, although it has occasionally been contended by parties that the fee scale in force on the date of the arbitration agreement ought to apply, this could prevent the arbitrators from being adequately compensated, particularly if the agreement was entered into many years before the commencement of the arbitration.[752] The new text of Article 31(1) ought to eliminate any possible uncertainty in this respect. Moreover, it follows from that provision that the scale in force at the time of commencement of the arbitral proceedings is to apply irrespective of the version of the Rules that may be applicable.

As already noted, the fee scale sets forth the minimum and maximum fees that are payable to each arbitrator for the sum in dispute. In the case of a tribunal composed of three arbitrators, the Court normally fixes separately the fees of the Chairman and the co-arbitrators. Although nowhere written in either the Rules or Appendix III, it has been the Court's general practice for many years to award forty percent of the arbitrators' total fees to the Chairman and thirty percent to each of the co-arbitrators in recognition of the Chairman's greater burden of work in the usual case, unless the arbitrators agree otherwise. The Court has not, in the past, been willing to alter this allocation on its own initiative, even where it may appear that one or more of the co-arbitrators may have actually borne a heavier burden than usual.

It is also to be noted that the fee scale is not intended to cover any of the arbitrators' out-of-pocket disbursements for the arbitration, which are separately reimbursed (*see infra*). Nor does it include any possible value-added tax ("VAT") or "other taxes or charges or imposts applicable to the arbitrator's fees" (*see* Appendix III, Article 2(9)). It has long been the ICC's practice to leave the matter of the recovery from the parties of any such taxes or charges to the arbitrators, while nevertheless admonishing the parties that they are expected to pay them. This is now explicitly stated in Article 2(9) of Appendix III. Whether VAT, in particular, is applicable to the arbitrators' fees (and, if so, how and when it should be collected from the parties) is nevertheless a complex question that has not yet given rise to uniform practices on the part of ICC arbitrators residing in jurisdictions (primarily in the European Union) where such taxes may be due.[753] However, this is a matter that is presently the subject of increased attention in the wake of a controversial decision of the European Court of Justice affecting an ICC arbitrator residing in Germany.[754]

---

[752] *See*, in this regard, O'Conor, *supra*, note 123, p.44, commenting on the rejection by an English court (in an unreported decision on January 20, 1997) of the contention of a party to a CIETAC arbitration agreement that it was prejudiced by the increase in the applicable scale of arbitration fees between the date of the arbitration agreement and the commencement of the arbitration. States O'Conor: "It is easy to see why changes in rules which affect the institution itself (and the arbitrators appointed by it) must be permitted to change over time."

[753] For a discussion of some of the related issues, *see* Le Gall, "The Fiscal Status of the Arbitrator," *The Status of the Arbitrator* (ICC Publishing 1995), p.100; Le Gall, *"Le Statut Fiscal de l'Arbitre International en Europe,"* L'Internationalité dans les Institutions et le Droit - Etudes Offertes à Alain Plantey (Pédone 1995), p.331; *see also* Bühler, *supra*, note 701, pp.129-30.

[754] *Bernd von Hoffman and Finanzamt Trier*, European Court of Justice, Sixth Chamber (September 16, 1997), as reported in *Mealey's*, Vol.12, No.10 (1997), H-1.

Apart from providing that the arbitrators' fees are fixed by the Court, neither Article 31(1) nor Appendix III states when the Court is required to do so. In practice, the fees of the arbitrators are fixed by the Court upon the conclusion of the arbitration, either immediately following the approval of the arbitrators' draft Award pursuant to Article 27 or, if the arbitration is withdrawn without an Award being rendered, following such withdrawal. In addition, the Court may fix the fees of arbitrators earlier in the event of their replacement.

When the arbitrators' draft Award is approved at a plenary session of the Court, the arbitrators' fees are fixed at the same time. In most other cases, the fees are fixed by the Committee of the Court. In either case, however, the Court has before it a recommendation of the Secretariat based on the sum in dispute and an evaluation of the various criteria listed in Article 2(2) of Appendix III, *i.e.,* "the diligence of the arbitrator, the time spent, the rapidity of the proceedings, and the complexity of the dispute." In this connection, the Secretariat will usually ask the arbitrators to communicate to it the number of hours that they have devoted to the arbitration. Although the arbitrators are not intended to be compensated on an hourly basis, in cases where the Arbitral Tribunal has been required to devote substantial time to a matter, and the amount of time spent appears reasonable to the Secretariat and the Court, this will often cause the Court to fix the fees above the average figure derived from the arbitrator fee scale, provided, however, that the advance on costs has previously been fixed at a sufficiently high level. In order to ensure that the Court has adequate funds to award greater than average fees in such cases, the arbitrators should therefore keep the Secretariat regularly informed, while the arbitration is in progress, of the time that they are being required to spend on the arbitration so that adjustments can be made, as necessary, to the advance on costs. Once the draft Award has been submitted to the Court, however, the Court is usually extremely reluctant, as already noted, to increase the amount of the advance. It is most often in those cases where the arbitrators do not regularly keep the Secretariat advised of the amount of time that they are spending on the arbitration that they risk being dissatisfied with the level of their remuneration.

Apart from the amount of time that the arbitrators may be required to devote to an arbitration, their diligence in advancing the proceedings is probably the single most important factor that is likely to affect the Court's decision on fees. Although the rapidity of the proceedings obviously depends on a number of different factors, some of which are beyond the arbitrators' control, arbitrators are normally rewarded by the Court when they are perceived as performing their functions with expedition and efficiency. Conversely, an arbitrator's remuneration may suffer for lack of diligence. In such cases, or possibly for other reasons, the Court may decide to fix the fees at a level that is lower than the corresponding amount of the advance on costs and, thus, be required to reimburse part of the advance to the parties. The parties should expect that, in reimbursing any outstanding sums to the parties, the ICC will usually do so in a manner consistent with the parties' payment obligations under the Rules.[755] Moreover, in the absence of joint instructions from the parties, the ICC will not normally take account of any decisions concerning the sharing of costs that may be contained in the arbitral Award (*see* Article 31(3) *infra*) as the ICC does not consider it appropriate to involve itself in the Award's actual execution.

The reimbursement of part of the advance to the parties will also often be necessary when an arbitration is withdrawn or is the subject of a consent Award prior to a final Award being rendered. In such case, Article 2(6) of Appendix III now provides that:

> If an arbitration terminates before the rendering of a final award, the Court shall fix the costs of the arbitration at its discretion, taking into account the stage attained by the arbitral proceedings and other relevant circumstances.

With regard to the arbitrators' fees, the Court takes account of the same factors that it is required to consider when an arbitration has been completed. In addition, it may consider the role, if any, that the arbitrators may have played in helping the parties to settle their dispute. The arbitrators' fees will, however, normally be less than for a completed case.

Neither the Rules nor Appendix III expressly deal, meanwhile, with the arbitrators' possible entitlement to fees in the event that they are required to be replaced, *e.g.,* in the case of a resignation, death or a successful challenge. In such cases, arbitrators are not necessarily considered to be entitled to any fees, particularly if they are themselves to blame for their replacement. But the Court's decision will depend upon all of the circumstances, the stage reached in the arbitration and the possible need for work to be repeated. Moreover, even in those cases where the arbitrator being replaced is not in any way at fault, the fees awarded by the Court may not compensate the arbitrator for all of the work carried out if some of it has to be repeated. Indeed, the Court has not in the past

---

[755] Thus, for example, if the total advance fixed is U.S. $10,000 and party A has paid U.S. $7,500, of which U.S. $2,500 has been paid in substitution for party B, who has paid only U.S. $2,500, and U.S. $2,500 remains to be reimbursed to the parties, the whole amount will be reimbursed to party A. If, however, separate advances of U.S. $7,500 and U.S. $2,500 had been fixed for party A and party B, respectively, and they had each paid the full amount of such advances, then 75 per cent of any outstanding balance would be reimbursed to party A and 25 per cent to party B.

considered, as a general rule, that the parties should be required to pay twice for the same work to be carried out by an arbitrator.[756]

Considerations of this kind have guided the Court's practices in according advances to arbitrators during the course of the arbitration. Although the bulk of the arbitrators' fees are normally payable only upon the conclusion of the arbitration, following the notification of the Award (or, in the absence of an Award, following the arbitration's withdrawal), the Court nevertheless advances fees to arbitrators prior to that time, but normally only when requested and upon the completion of "concrete," non-repeatable steps in the arbitration.[757] Indeed, the Court is normally concerned to avoid advancing to arbitrators any more than it might be appropriate to award if, for any reason, they were suddenly required to be replaced. This policy is also intended to provide arbitrators with an incentive to render their Awards as rapidly as practicable.

The ICC's general unwillingness to make advance payments to arbitrators for uncompleted work in progress has occasionally been subject to criticism on the ground that arbitrators are required, as a consequence, to bear "the entire burden of financing remuneration for ongoing work."[758] However, the ICC's critics on this subject generally overlook the institution's reasonable wish to protect the

---

[756] This is consistent with the view expressed with respect to this question in Mustill and Boyd, *supra,* note 362, p.244, in which the following is stated:

> Sometimes an arbitrator's participation in a reference may terminate prematurely on grounds for which he is responsible, although not morally to blame. For example, he may die, or become incapable of acting, or resign with the consent of the parties. In such a case the question may arise whether he is entitled to payment for the work which he has done. The arbitrator could argue that if, as we have suggested, there is a right to payment in cases where the reference stops short as the result of an act by the parties, this must entail that the remuneration is regarded as a reward for work done, not for benefit conferred; and if this is so then the position must be the same whatever the reason for the curtailment of the reference. The arbitrator has, so it would be argued, a vested right to remuneration which is not lost if his participation in the reference comes to an end. We doubt whether the logic can be carried through in this way. Somebody has to suffer in this situation, and the distribution of the loss is a matter of policy. We suggest that it should fall on the arbitrator, on the ground that the loss of the fee due to reasons concerned with himself is a risk which the arbitrator can reasonably be taken to have assumed, when he agreed to take on the reference.

[757] Thus, the first such advance is normally made upon the completion of the Terms of Reference, if requested. For a discussion of the Court's practices in this regard, *see* Byrne, "Payment of Advances on Fees to Arbitrators in ICC Proceedings," *ICC Ct. Bull.,* Vol.7, No.2 (1996), p.84.

[758] *See* Wetter and Priem, *supra*, note 741 (where it is, however, erroneously stated that the ICC follows the policy of paying fees only after the end of the proceedings; as noted above, advances are, in fact, accorded to ICC arbitrators during the course of the proceedings, generally as concrete steps are completed). *See also*, in this connection, Werner, *supra*, note 709, p.136.

parties to the arbitration against the risk that an arbitrator may have to be replaced before the arbitration has been completed and his work redone.[759]

Lastly, arbitrators need to bear in mind that they are not generally considered by the Court to be entitled to a fee unless and until the file has been transmitted to them under Article 13 of the Rules. Indeed, the ICC will not be in a position to remunerate the arbitrators, in any event, until the payment of the advance that is a condition for the file's transmission. Ordinarily, this should not pose a problem. However, in those cases where co-arbitrators are requested by the parties to appoint the Chairman of the Arbitral Tribunal, they may devote time and money to the arbitration with no guarantee of remuneration if the arbitration is withdrawn before any amount is paid to the ICC by the parties in respect of the arbitrators' fees and expenses.

Arbitrators' expenses. While referring separately to the arbitrators' "fees" and "expenses," Article 31(1) does not otherwise undertake to define the latter nor explain how they are to be determined. It has nevertheless long been the Court's practice to recognize a distinct category of reimbursable "expenses" of arbitrators in addition to their fees. Contrary to what is suggested by Article 31(1), however, such expenses are not actually "fixed" by the Court, nor are they the subject of a scale. Rather, they are reimbursed to the arbitrators by the Secretariat, upon the arbitrators' application as and when they are incurred, on the basis of the Secretariat's determination of their reasonableness. They are, however, paid out of the advance on costs fixed by the Court for the tribunal's estimated fees and expenses, and the level of the amounts reimbursed to the arbitrators as expenses will, thus, necessarily affect the amount that is available to be fixed by the Court as fees. In deciding whether to adjust the advance from time to time during the course of the arbitration and when fixing the fees of the arbitrators, the Court is therefore inevitably required to review the amounts charged by the arbitrators as expenses. In this manner, the total sum payable to the arbitrators, whether as fees or expenses, is effectively determined by the Court.

Once the Court has fixed the arbitrators' fees, the Secretariat communicates this information, together with the amount of the expenses, to the arbitrators for inclusion in their Award in accordance with Article 31(3) or, if there is no Award, otherwise notifies the amounts in question to the arbitrators and the parties. The Secretariat does not ordinarily provide the arbitrators and the parties with a detailed breakdown of the expenses incurred by the arbitrators. But it should be in a position to do so if this is requested.

---

[759] Indeed, Mustill and Boyd have commented (*supra*, note 362, p.245, note 13): "But if ... [the arbitrator] has in fact already [been] paid on account, at the time of the termination, we cannot see the Court straining to find a way in which the parties can recover what has been paid—for by consenting to remuneration on this basis, they can be regarded as having taken on themselves the risk of premature termination."

Guidelines concerning the reimbursement of the arbitrators' expenses are published from time to time by the Secretariat.[760] The items covered concern such matters as expenses for transportation, meals and lodging (which may be reimbursed either on a *per diem* basis or upon the presentation of relevant invoices or receipts scrutinized, prior to payment, by the Secretariat) as well as expenses relating to the rental of meeting rooms, clerical assistance, and the use of telephones and faxes for tribunal business. The Secretariat's guidelines are nevertheless not comprehensive, and questions may, from time to time, arise as to either the reasonableness of certain expenses or the propriety of even treating them as expenses (rather than as, *e.g.,* overheads covered by the arbitrator's fees). Indeed, the overheads borne by ICC arbitrators, and the resources available to them, in connection with the conduct of their other professional activities, if any, may vary dramatically. Thus, for example, a retired law professor accepting occasional arbitral appointments and operating out of his residence (with virtually no overheads) may be required to engage a secretary when acting as an arbitrator. He may then seek to be reimbursed for the related cost as an expense. In contrast, however, it does not occur to many law firm partners with permanent secretarial support to apply to the Secretariat for the reimbursement of similar costs, when acting as arbitrators, even though a substantial portion of their fees may be absorbed by such and related items of overhead expense. Whether and to what extent such expenses, in either case, ought to be reimbursable or deemed to be covered by the arbitrators' fees is an issue as to which the Secretariat has not necessarily acted consistently over the years.[761]

It should be noted, however, that in the Secretariat's separate Note of October 1, 1995 concerning the appointment by Arbitral Tribunals of administrative secretaries,[762] it is stated that:

> [T]he scale of arbitrators' fees set forth in Appendix III to the ICC Rules is intended to cover the Arbitral Tribunal's normal cost of carrying out the administrative tasks associated with the performance of the Arbitral Tribunal's work, with the exception of out-of-pocket disbursements (*e.g.,* for telephone, telefax, postage, special courier, photocopying and travel).

For this reason, the Note states that the remuneration of an administrative secretary (apart from the secretary's reasonable out-of-pocket disbursements) should

---

[760] The most recent such guidelines are contained in the "Revised Notice to Arbitrators: Personal and Arbitral Tribunal Expenses" (1993), as reproduced in Appendix 4(c).

[761] *But see* Bühler, *supra,* note 701, p.133 ("The ICC Court will normally not accept separate charges for word processing, secretarial overtime, books, subscriptions to specialized journals, conferences or seminars, office supplies, or storage charges, unless there are specific reasons to burden the parties with such expenses, and provided special arrangements are made with the ICC Court in time.").

[762] *See* the copy reproduced at Appendix 4(b).

normally be covered by the arbitrators' fees rather than reimbursed separately as an expense.[763]

This has induced certain ICC arbitrators to obtain the parties' agreement to the treatment of such remuneration as a tribunal expense,[764] although, if they do, the Court is nevertheless still free to take account of this when fixing the arbitrators' fees. In the end, as already noted, the Court is the master of the arbitrators' total compensation, irrespective of how it may be characterized.

ICC administrative costs. Like the fees of the arbitrators, the ICC administrative costs are fixed by the Court in accordance with the scale in force at the time of commencement of the arbitral proceedings. Unlike in the case of the arbitrator's fees, however, the applicable scale does not, as already noted, allow for the exercise of any discretion, except where the sum in dispute is not stated. Otherwise, the amount of the administrative costs is ordinarily the product of a simple arithmetic calculation. According to Article 2(5) of Appendix III, the Court nevertheless "may fix the administrative expenses at a lower or higher figure than that which would result from the application of such scale" in "exceptional" circumstances, "provided that such expenses shall normally not exceed the maximum amount of the scale." But this is a power that has rarely been used.

The ICC administrative costs cover not only the services rendered by the Court, but all disbursements of the Court in connection with a particular case (*e.g.,* for postage, international courier services, telephone, telefaxes, or photocopies).[765] Moreover, no matter how complicated the administration of the case may become, the administrative charge will generally remain unchanged so long as the amount in contention does not vary.[766] The ICC's scale, thus, has the virtue of permitting the parties to assess in advance the likely amount of the ICC's administrative charge, unlike some other systems under which the amount of such charges may fluctuate quite considerably.[767]

---

[763] When issued, this Note attracted certain criticism. *See* Lalive, *"Inquiétantes Dérives de l'Arbitrage CCI,"* *ASA Bull.,* No.4 (1995), p.634; Schwartz, "Reply," *ASA Bull.,* No.1 (1996), p.32.

[764] While stating that the arbitrator's fees and expenses shall be fixed "exclusively" by the Court, Article 2(4) of Appendix III only expressly bars separate "fee" arrangements between the parties and the arbitrators and not separate arrangements on costs. Such separate arrangements nevertheless run counter to the general principle that in ICC arbitration the parties should not be placed in the awkward position of having to negotiate matters pertaining to costs with the Arbitral Tribunal directly.

[765] In contrast, certain other arbitral institutions invoice the parties separately for some or all such costs in addition to the amounts payable for their administrative fees.

[766] However, under Article 2(5) of Appendix III, the Court may require the payment of additional sums as a condition to holding an arbitration in abeyance at the request of the parties or of one of them with the acquiescence of the other. In those rare cases where an abeyance fee has been charged, it has generally been a modest amount.

[767] This would be the case, for example, under the fee scale of the American Arbitration Association and the Schedule of Costs of the London Court of International Arbitration.

In the event that an arbitration is withdrawn prior to a final Award, the amount of the administrative charge, like the arbitrators' fees, will normally be reduced based on an assessment of the stage reached in the arbitration and the work carried out by the Court. As the administrative work of the Court and its Secretariat is usually heavy in the early stages of the arbitration, the Court's general practice in the past has been to assess at least 25 per cent of the administrative charge in cases where an Arbitral Tribunal has been constituted and 50 per cent where the Terms of Reference have been established. However, the only amount that the parties are required to pay to the ICC prior to the constitution of the Arbitral Tribunal is the sum that is to accompany the Request for Arbitration (presently U.S. $2,500).

The ICC's administrative costs have the reputation of being high in comparison with those of other arbitral institutions. But the functions of the Court and its Secretariat are also unique.

Expenses of experts. The reference in Article 31(1) to the expenses of experts has been modified, as compared with former Article 20(2), in order to make it clear that the experts in question are experts "appointed by the Arbitral Tribunal" pursuant to Article 20(4). The costs of any such experts are determined by the arbitrators, rather than the Court, and, as already indicated, are required to be the subject of a separate advance on costs fixed by the Arbitral Tribunal (Appendix III, Article 1(11)). By referring specifically only to tribunal-appointed experts, Article 31(1) does not mean to exclude the cost of experts retained by the parties from the costs of the arbitration. Such expenses may be included in the parties' costs, as discussed below.

Parties' costs. In addition to the items described above, the "costs of the arbitration" are stated in Article 31(1) to include "the reasonable legal and other costs incurred by the parties for the arbitration." This formulation of the parties' costs differs from the one previously contained in Article 20(2) of the former Rules, which defined those costs as "the normal legal costs incurred by the parties." That language was not consistent, however, with the corresponding text in the French version of the Rules, which was arguably broader.[768] The use of the word "normal" was also the subject of confusion. Article 31(1) therefore now refers to the parties' "reasonable" costs. It also expands the category of allowable costs to "legal and other costs incurred by the parties for the arbitration" so as to permit the arbitrators the greatest possible discretion in this regard.[769] Indeed, as the

---

[768] The French version of the Rules formerly defined the parties' costs as: "*les frais normaux exposés par les parties pour leur défense*" (translation: "the normal costs incurred by the parties for their defense"). There was, thus, no specific mention of purely "legal" costs.

[769] The prior reference to legal costs only in the prior English version of the Rules was construed by some as excluding from the costs of the arbitration executive time and disbursements, including those of in-house counsel, and general administrative costs. *See, e.g.,* Wetter and Priem, *supra,* note 741, pp.315-16.

Rules do not contain a definition of such costs, the manner in which the relevant language of Article 31(1) should be construed is left to the appreciation of the arbitrators in each case.[770]

Typically, the "legal and other costs" that form part of the costs of the arbitration include such items as the fees and expenses of legal counsel, the costs of experts, consultants and witnesses, other costs associated with the production of documents or attendance at hearings and the costs of interpreters and translators. There are other items, however, as to which arbitrators may have conflicting views, such as, for example, the allowability of costs associated with ancillary judicial proceedings (which most arbitrators would probably exclude)[771] or the cost of the time of the parties' personnel, including, in particular, in-house legal staff (which appears to be increasingly accepted, at least in respect of in-house counsel, to the extent that the cost can be satisfactorily substantiated).[772] There also does not appear to be any consensus as to the allowability of claims for pre-judgment interest on a party's costs.[773]

A further issue that may arise is whether the costs claimed are, in fact, the costs of a party to the arbitration if they have been borne by another person, such as, for example, an insurer or other indemnifier not itself a party to the arbitration. In the only reported instance in which an ICC Arbitral Tribunal considered this question, it concluded that such costs were properly recoverable in the arbitration.[774]

Article 31(2)

> *The Court may fix the fees of the arbitrators at a figure higher or lower than that which would result from the application of the relevant scale should this be deemed necessary due to the exceptional circumstances of the case. Decisions on costs other than those fixed by the Court may be taken by the Arbitral Tribunal at any time during the proceedings.*

---

[770] The broad definition of costs in Article 31(1) is to be contrasted with the more restrictive language contained in some other arbitration rules (*e.g.,* UNCITRAL Rules, Article 38).

[771] *See,* in this regard, Bühler, *supra,* note 701, p.91; *and* the Awards in ICC Case No. 5896 (1992), *ICC Ct. Bull.,* Vol.4, No.1 (1993), p.37, and ICC Case No. 6268 (1990), *ICCA Yearbook* XVI (1991), p.119. But according to the arbitrators, in the circumstances of the latter case, the costs concerned might have been recoverable as damages for the breach of the arbitration agreement insofar as the judicial proceedings in question were commenced by the other party in violation of that agreement.

[772] *See, e.g.,* the Awards in ICC Case Nos. 6345 (1991), 6564 (1993), 6670 (1992) and 6959 (1992), *ICC Ct. Bull.,* Vol.4, No.1 (1993), p.44-48; *but cf.* the Award in ICC Case No. 6293 (1990), *ICC Ct. Bull.,* Vol.4, No.1 (1993), p.43.

[773] Compare, for example, Wetter and Priem, *supra,* note 741, pp.326-27 (approving) with the Award in ICC Case No. 5896 (1992) *supra,* note 771 (rejecting). In the authors' experience, pre-judgment interest is rarely, if ever, allowed by ICC arbitrators with respect to a party's costs.

[774] *See* the Award in ICC Case No. 7006 (1992), *ICC Ct. Bull.,* Vol.4, No.1 (1993), p.49. *See also,* for a concurring view, *Compagnie de Bauxites de Guinée* v. *Hammermills, Inc.,* U.S. District Court for the District of Columbia, C.A. No.90-0169 (May 29, 1992).

There are two parts to this provision, the first of which is essentially identical to the corresponding provision in the former Rules and the second of which is new. Like Article 20(3) of the previous Rules, Article 31(2) authorizes the Court to derogate from the arbitrator fee scale in "exceptional circumstances." The second sentence of Article 31(2), however, has no equivalent in the former Rules.

Derogations from the arbitrator fee scale. The Rules do not themselves indicate what circumstances may properly be regarded as "exceptional." This is, thus, left to the Court to decide on a case-by-case basis. In practice, however, the Court is extremely reluctant to derogate from the fee scale as one of the advantages of a scale is that it permits the parties, from the outset, to evaluate their possible exposure in respect of the arbitrators' fees. Nevertheless, the Court may consider it appropriate to derogate from the scale if the arbitrators would otherwise be grossly under-compensated, given, in particular, the time that they may have been required to devote to the arbitration, or if, on the contrary, they would receive an excessive windfall.

This being said, there have been few, if any, cases in which the Court has fixed the fees of the arbitrators below the minimum figure set forth in the scale. But cases in which the Court considers it appropriate to increase the fees above the maximum are more common. Those cases are almost always cases in which the arbitrators have been required to devote exceptional amounts of time to the arbitration, although the Court nevertheless does not pay arbitrators on an hourly or daily basis. Its objective, rather, is to accord the arbitrators reasonable compensation in light of all of the circumstances, including the amounts at issue, the time spent by the arbitrators and the conduct of the parties.

In order to be able to award the arbitrators fees in excess of the maximum figure in the scale, the Court is usually required to increase the amount of the advance beforehand. Before the Court does so, the Secretariat usually informs the parties that the Court anticipates that it may be appropriate to derogate from the scale in the circumstances of the case. The parties are therefore made aware of the possibility of a derogation and have an opportunity to comment thereon before paying the additional sums required to be advanced for this purpose.

Decisions on costs. As set forth in Article 31(3), the general rule in ICC arbitration is that the costs of the arbitration are fixed in the final Award, unless the arbitration is terminated earlier. It is also the final Award that contains the arbitrators' decision on the allocation of those costs between the parties. The costs are not generally fixed and allocated until the final Award because the Court is not in a position to fix the fees of the arbitrators and the ICC administrative costs earlier on the basis of the Cost Scales. Moreover, in deciding how the costs of the arbitration ought to be allocated, the arbitrators normally wish to be able to take account of the arbitration's ultimate outcome.

There may nevertheless be circumstances in which it is appropriate for the arbitrators to decide upon the allocation of costs prior to the final Award. Occasionally, for example, the arbitrators may wish to include a decision on costs in a partial Award resolving certain of the issues in the arbitration. The arbitrators may also decide in a partial Award that they have no jurisdiction over one of the parties to the arbitration and that, accordingly, the party in question should recover its costs from the party that improperly included it in the proceedings. (With respect to the possible entitlement of a party to costs notwithstanding the Arbitral Tribunal's finding that it is without jurisdiction, *see* the discussion of Article 31(3) *infra*.) The second sentence of Article 31(2) has therefore been added to the Rules in order to provide the arbitrators with explicit authority in this regard.

The arbitrators' powers under Article 31(2) do not extend, however, to the costs fixed by the Court, given that those costs are not fixed until the end of the arbitration. In the event that the arbitrators decide to exclude a party from the arbitration, there would nevertheless not appear to be any reason why they could not, prior to the conclusion of the arbitration, order another party to indemnify the party being excluded for the portion of the advance on costs that it may have paid to the ICC for the arbitration, as well as for its "reasonable legal and other costs" incurred for the arbitration.

Article 31(3)

> *The final Award shall fix the costs of the arbitration and decide which of the parties shall bear them or in what proportion they shall be borne by the parties.*

Background. Article 31(3) imposes an obligation on the Arbitral Tribunal to set forth the costs of the arbitration in the final Award and, at the same time, to decide upon their allocation. It is essentially identical to the corresponding provision (Article 20(1)) in the former Rules, except that the Award is now stated to be the "final" Award (as was already the case in the French version of Article 20(1)), and, unlike former Article 20(1), Article 31(3) no longer states that the Award shall fix the costs "in addition to dealing with the merits of the case."

That the Award must be the "final" Award follows, as already noted, from the Court's practice of fixing the arbitrators' fees and the ICC administrative costs upon the completion of the arbitration. The reference to "the merits of the case," meanwhile, has been eliminated because it was occasionally argued, on the basis of that language, that, failing a decision on the merits, the arbitrators had no power to make an Award on costs, such as, for example, when a decision that there is not a valid arbitration agreement has the effect of bringing the arbitration to an end without an Award on the merits.[775] ICC arbitrators have nevertheless found that, notwithstanding their lack of jurisdiction to decide the merits of the dispute in such circumstances, they may award costs to a party that has reques-

---

[775] *See* the Award in ICC Case No. 5896 (1992) *supra*, note 773.

ted them to do so in conjunction with an application for the dismissal of the other party's claim on jurisdictional grounds.[776] Although the arbitrators' power to do so is not explicitly stated in Article 31(3), the elimination of the reference to the "merits" will hopefully make it clearer than before that their power to award costs is not limited to cases that proceed to an Award on the substance of the dispute.[777]

Fixing of costs. While Article 31(3) states that the final Award "shall fix" the costs of the arbitration, the only costs that are actually "fixed" by the arbitrators are, as already noted, the fees and expenses of tribunal-appointed experts and the costs of the parties.[778] Moreover, it is not actually necessary for the arbitrators to fix the costs of a party (notwithstanding the use of the word "shall") except to the extent that they are to be borne by another party. (Thus, if it is the arbitrators' decision that each of the parties shall bear its own costs, there is not anything that they need to fix in this regard.) The fees and expenses of the arbitrators and the ICC administrative costs, meanwhile, are independently determined by the Court in the manner described above (*see* Article 31(1)) and are then communicated by the Secretariat to the arbitrators for inclusion in their Award following the approval of the draft submitted to the Court pursuant to Article 27.[779]

Insofar as the costs of the arbitration are a subject of the Award, the arbitrators' related decisions could be affected in the event that the Award were subsequently set aside. However, as the fees and expenses of the arbitrators and the ICC are the subject of a distinct decision of the Court, the arbitrators' and the ICC's entitlement to the same pursuant to that decision do not necessarily depend upon the fate of the Award.[780]

---

[776] *Id.* Indeed, in ICC arbitration, the existence of an agreement conferring such authority on the Arbitral Tribunal should normally be found in the Terms of Reference. *See* "Final Report on Interim and Partial Awards," *supra*, note 62, p.28. *See also*, in this connection, Wetter and Priem, *supra*, note 741, p.326 ("In practice, at the time of formation of a tribunal faced with fundamental objections to its own jurisdiction, a special agreement may and ought to be made to cover this contingency in so far as the fees and costs of the tribunal are concerned.").

[777] Thus, it should also be possible for the arbitrators to make an Award on costs upon the request of a party following the withdrawal of the other party's claims.

[778] In place of the word "fix," the French version of the Rules uses the more general word *"liquide,"* from which it can be understood that the final Award finally deals with the costs.

[779] In contrast, the amount of any legal or other costs of the parties that the arbitrators intend to award is normally set forth in the draft submitted to the Court for scrutiny under Article 27. In one case, however, where the arbitrator inserted the amount of the legal costs being awarded after the draft Award had been approved by the Court (and the amount was therefore not subject to scrutiny), it was found by a U.S. court called upon to set aside the Award for this reason, *inter alia*, that this was not contrary to the Rules. *Compagnie des Bauxites de Guinée* v. *Hammermills, Inc.*, *supra*, note 774.

[780] But *see* Mustill and Boyd, *supra*, note 362, pp.245-46, where it is suggested that the arbitrators' entitlement to a fee may be forfeited if their Award is annulled. In a recent French, non-ICC Case, an arbitrator was ordered to reimburse its fees to a party where two Awards were annulled because of the arbitrator's failure to disclose his relationship with the other party. *See Société Raoul Duval c/ V., Tribunal de grande instance de Paris* (May 12, 1993), *Cour d'appel de Paris* (December 6, 1994), *Rev arb.* (1996), p.411.

Allocation of costs. As the arbitrators are required to decide in what proportion the costs of the arbitration are to be borne by the parties, they should normally accord the parties an opportunity to submit whatever comments they may have in this regard. Moreover, the arbitrators should do so even if neither of the parties has formally made a claim for costs during the arbitration, given the need for the arbitrators to deal with the matter of costs in their Award.[781]

Increasingly, claims for the reimbursement of costs constitute a substantial part of the relief requested in ICC arbitrations; yet the attitudes and practices of both arbitrators and parties vary considerably in this connection, given the many different approaches to the matter of costs in different jurisdictions.[782] Thus, some parties do not even think of claiming costs, others make only cursory submissions, and still others submit detailed pleadings accompanied by supporting documentation. The approaches of ICC arbitrators are just as diverse.[783] While many Awards contain just a few lines on this question, in some cases the matter of costs may itself be the subject of a separate, final Award after the merits have been dealt with in an earlier (in such case) partial Award.[784]

Under Article 31(1), the arbitrators have complete discretion to allocate the costs as they see fit. Unlike some other arbitration rules (such as, for example, the UNCITRAL Rules, Article 40, or those of the Arbitration Institute of the Stockholm Chamber of Commerce, Article 29), the Rules do not provide for the bearing of the costs "in principle" by the unsuccessful party. Nor is the arbitrators' discretion necessarily limited by any related legal requirements.[785] Not surprisingly, however, the treatment of costs by arbitrators is often influenced by their national backgrounds. In this regard, there are three different approaches that appear to be most commonly followed. One is to order that all of the costs be borne by one of the parties (*i.e.,* the losing party). It is, thus, for example, the usual rule in England that the successful litigant is entitled to an Award of costs (*i.e.,* the costs follow the event). Another approach, prevalent in Germany, Switzerland and Austria, in particular, is the allocation of the costs in proportion

---

[781] How much of an opportunity the parties should have is a matter that will depend on the circumstances of each case. For an interesting decision on this subject, *see Compagnie de Bauxites de Guinée* v. *Hammermills, Inc., supra,* note 774.

[782] *See,* in this regard, Bühler, *supra,* note 701; Wetter and Priem, *supra,* note 741; *and* Nurick, "Costs in International Arbitration, *"7 ICSID Review - Foreign Investment Law Journal* (1992), p.57.

[783] *See* the extracts from the ICC Arbitral Awards reproduced in the *ICC Ct. Bull.*, Vol.4, No.1 (1993), p.31.

[784] This is, in fact, relatively uncommon in ICC arbitration, but has the advantage in appropriate cases of permitting the parties to make their submissions on the basis of the arbitrators' decisions as to the merits. *See,* for support of such an approach, Wetter and Priem, *supra,* note 741, p.334. In most cases, the parties are required to make their submissions, however, before the merits have been decided.

[785] Thus, for example, in the case of *Brega Oil Marketing Company* v. *Techint Compagnia et Tecnica Internazionale SpA*, the cantonal court of Vaud, Switzerland (February 17, 1993), found that an ICC Arbitral Tribunal in an arbitration in Lausanne was not required to apply Swiss law in allocating the costs between the parties.

to the outcome of the case *(e.g.,* 75/25 or 60/40), taking into account the relative success of the claims and defenses. Yet a further possibility is to require that the costs be shared equally by the parties or that they bear their own costs. Arbitral tribunals may also consider that administrative costs and arbitrators' fees and expenses, on the one hand, should be treated differently from legal and other possible expenses, on the other.

In 1991, the ICC Court's Secretariat undertook the study of the final Awards rendered in ICC arbitrations between March 1989 and September 1991 in order to assess the manner in which arbitrators have dealt with the allocation of arbitration costs in ICC cases.[786] In summary, the Secretariat's findings were as follows:

(i)   In those cases where the Claimant won all or most of what it claimed (as in 48 of the Awards surveyed), the arbitrators most commonly (in 39 cases) ordered the Respondent to bear all or most (usually in proportion to the success of the claim) of the arbitrators' fees and expenses and the ICC administrative costs, although the arbitrators occasionally split the costs between the parties in such circumstances.[787] In one such case, for example, the Arbitral Tribunal observed that, although the Claimant was entirely successful in the arbitration, each party had contributed equally to the emergence of the dispute. In another case, the tribunal required the Claimant to contribute to part of the arbitration costs, even though "nearly 100 per cent successful," because the claim was submitted "relatively late."

(ii)   In such cases *(i.e.,* where the Claimant was a decisive winner), the arbitrators also often, although much less frequently (in 24 cases out of 48), ordered the Respondent to pay all or part of the Claimant's "normal" (now "reasonable") legal costs, thus demonstrating that arbitrators will not necessarily treat in the same manner the costs of the arbitration proper and the legal costs of the parties. Thus, for example, in one of the cases reviewed, the Arbitral Tribunal (composed of two Swiss lawyers and one American) awarded the Claimant 80 per cent of the amount claimed by it in the arbitration and, accordingly, ordered the Respondent to bear 80 per cent of the arbitration costs. With respect to the Claimant's legal costs, however, the tribunal held that each party should bear its own on the basis that:

> [The] dispute raised difficult issues of law ... all of which justified a full-scale litigation.

---

[786] The study, which has not been published, was carried out by two interns of the Court, Christopher Boyd and Angelika Dölker.

[787] For the sake of convenience, the ICC administrative costs and the arbitrators' fees and expenses will hereafter be referred to as the "arbitration costs" as distinguished from the parties' legal and other costs.

When awarding "normal" (now "reasonable") legal costs, moreover, tribunals have adopted a variety of approaches, sometimes awarding all of the costs claimed and in others effecting reductions, often in relation to the proportion of the claim that has succeeded.[788]

(iii) In those cases (9) where the Claimant was awarded approximately half of the amount claimed or the Claimant and Respondent won approximately equal amounts, the arbitrators most frequently (in 7 cases) ordered that the arbitration costs be shared equally and (in 8 cases) that the parties bear their own legal costs. In one case, however, it was held by a British sole arbitrator that, where the Claimant was awarded 56 per cent of the value of its claim, the Respondent should pay all of the arbitration costs and reimburse to the Claimant approximately 50 per cent of its legal expenses on the apparent basis that such was the amount "reasonably incurred." In another case, where a party had succeeded with respect to 60 per cent of its claim, the Respondent was ordered to bear 60 per cent of the arbitration costs, but the Claimant was not awarded any of its legal costs.

(iv) Out of 36 Awards in which the Claimant obtained substantially less than half of the amount claimed or less than the amount awarded to the Respondent, the arbitrators most frequently either split the arbitration costs equally (in 13 cases) or had the Claimant pay them all (12 cases). In every one of the latter cases, however, the arbitrators either dismissed the Claimant's claims entirely or found themselves incompetent to conduct the arbitration. In some cases, where the claim failed entirely, the arbitrators nevertheless decided that the arbitration costs should be shared rather than borne entirely by the Claimant (in one case because the Respondent had "not been sufficiently forthcoming with the information necessary to find the truth" and had failed to comply with two of the tribunal's orders regarding the production of evidence, and in another because the

---

[788] In an extract from an arbitral Award published in Wetter and Priem, *supra,* note 741, p.292, it is stated, with respect to the expenses and lawyers' fees of the winning party, that the amount awarded, in international arbitration, is, "as a rule, substantially less than the actual expenses of the winning party." However, no such "rule" emerged from the ICC's study. It is nevertheless often the case that "normal" ("reasonable") legal costs are found to be lower than actual legal costs. Usually, the former constitute the arbitrator's estimate of the expenditures reasonably necessary to present the case or the fees prescribed by the applicable fee schedule in countries such as Germany, Switzerland, and Austria. (*See,* for example, the German ZPO Anhang II). Where there are no fixed fee schedules, the determination of which legal costs are "normal" ("reasonable") is left to the arbitrator's discretion. One Australian arbitrator explained his method as follows:

> The approach that I take to both "normal legal fees" and "fees and expenses of any experts" is not fettered by the constraints of the law regarding taxed costs. I assess what I regard as properly classifiable as normal, taking into account a broad range of considerations including local practice, local level of fees and the fairness and justice of the level of costs that should be borne by the unsuccessful Respondent.

"dispute stemmed from a difficult problem of interpretation of the agreement and no party can be blamed for having decided to submit it to the decision of the Arbitral Tribunal.") In those cases where the Claimant was awarded a relatively low percentage of the amounts claimed, the arbitration costs were usually ordered to be shared equally or on a proportional basis (relative to the degree of success of the claims), although in the particular circumstances of two cases the arbitrators felt that as the principal claims were well-founded, the bulk of the arbitration costs should be borne by the Respondents.

(v)   Finally, the parties were most frequently (in 24 cases) ordered to bear their own legal expenses in the 36 Awards just mentioned. Three Awards allocated normal legal costs proportionately to the outcome of the case. In five cases (in every one of which the claim was either dismissed or withdrawn), the Claimant was ordered to pay all of the Respondent's normal legal costs and in two others a substantial proportion. In one case, where the Claimant was awarded only a small percentage of its claim, the Claimant was ordered to pay two-thirds of the Respondent's normal legal costs, while the latter was ordered to pay one-third of the Claimant's.

From the above, it can be seen that arbitrators have adopted a variety of approaches in allocating costs in ICC arbitrations, often depending on their own national biases, the substantive outcome of the arbitration and also the behavior of the parties, *e.g.,* in some cases allowing for honest differences of opinion over difficult issues and in others penalizing bad faith or uncooperative behavior. Whatever the ultimate decision, however, the arbitrators have normally been expected by the Court to provide reasons for their decisions, and this is an obligation that has now been reinforced by the inclusion in the Rules of Article 25(2).

Chapter 8
Miscellaneous (Articles 32-35)

ARTICLE 32
Modified Time Limits

This is an entirely new provision. It is also one of the few provisions in the Rules (see also Articles 6(1), 6(4), 7(6) and 23(1)) that expressly authorizes the parties to derogate from them (although it is to be noted that the permitted derogation is only stated to include the shortening, and not the extension, of the time limits set forth in the Rules).[789]

Article 32 serves two related, but different purposes, as reflected in the two sub-paragraphs of which it is composed. The first is to make it clear that the parties may provide for expedited, or "fast-track," arbitration proceedings, while the second is to permit the Court to "save" fast-track proceedings that it may not be possible to complete within the stipulated time periods, notwithstanding the parties' and arbitrators' best efforts.

Even before the New Rules, the Court accepted to administer arbitrations with shortened time limits. In one particularly impressive example of such a case, two complex arbitrations were consolidated and a final Award rendered within eighty days of the submission of the first of the two Requests for Arbitration in question.[790] The consolidated cases concerned the redetermination of the price of a commodity product. The arbitration was conducted by a tribunal of three arbitrators, the Terms of Reference were prepared, signed and transmitted to the Court within eight days of the arbitrators' receipt of the file, and the Award was rendered within ten days thereafter following expedited written submissions of the parties,

---

[789] This being said, it is difficult to imagine that the Court would refuse the parties the right to agree to longer deadlines than those set forth in the Rules if this is what they desire. Indeed, parties and arbitrators commonly agree to timetables during ICC arbitrations that have the effect of requiring the deadlines in the Rules to be extended by the Court.

[790] *See* the series of articles on this case in *ICC Ct. Bull.,* Vol.3, No.2 (1992), p.4. *See also* the extract from the Award in Case No. 7385/7402, *ICC Ct. Bull.,* Vol.8, No.1 (1997), p.56.

a one-day oral hearing in New York and scrutiny and approval of the Award by the Court, with the Chairman of the Court using his power to take "urgent decisions" on the Court's behalf under Article 1(3) of the Rules.[791]

Although an exceptional case conducted with much greater expedition than would be appropriate for most disputes, this experience and other "fast-track" arbitrations thereafter generated a great deal of interest internationally[792] and inevitably led the Working Party to consider whether special adaptations (or additions) should be made to the Rules to accommodate those wishing to organize future "fast-track" proceedings thereunder. Indeed, other arbitral institutions have recently issued special rules for expedited proceedings.[793] As already noted, however (*see* Chapter 1 *supra*), this was an option that was ultimately rejected by the Working Party.

There were several reasons for the Working Party's reluctance to attempt to fashion special "fast-track" procedures. First of all, there was a broad consensus, based on the experience of the ICC and others, that every dispute is different and that there is not likely to be any single set of rules or procedures that can satisfy the "fast-track" requirements of all arbitrations where the parties may desire an expedited procedure. In this connection, special concerns were voiced, in particular, about the need to ensure in all cases that the parties' desire for expedition is really suited to the circumstances of the case in question, taking into account considerations of fairness and due process as well as the Court's supervisory responsibilities under the Rules. It was also noted that, unlike most other arbitration rules, the ICC Rules, in fact, already impose a stringent (six-month) deadline on the Arbitral Tribunal for the issuance of its Award (*see* Article 24 *supra*), and priority therefore ought to be given to making more effective the deadlines already contained in the Rules rather than creating additional procedures. This was, moreover, not considered to be necessary, given the freedom that the parties already have to fashion expedited procedures if desired.

What finally emerged, therefore, was Article 32, principally as a reminder to the parties of the "fast-track" possibilities inherent in the process.

---

[791] *See* Davis, *supra,* note 49.

[792] *See, e.g.,* Amoussou-Guenou *et al.,* "International Fast-Track Commercial Arbitration," *Comparative Law Yearbook of International Arbitration,* Special Issue (Graham & Trotman/Martinus Nijhoff 1994), p.357; Rovine, "Fast-Track Arbitration: A Step Away from Judicialization of International Arbitration," *The Judicialization of International Arbitration* (Transnational Publishers 1994), p. 45; Mustill, "Comments on Fast-Track Arbitration," *J. Int. Arb.,* Vol.11, No. 4 (1994), p. 121; Davis *et al.,* "When Doctrines Meet – Fast Track Arbitration and the ICC Experience," *J. Arb. Int.,* Vol.10, No.4 (1993), p.69; Downie, "Fast-Track International Commercial Arbitration: Proposed Institutional Rules," *Am. Rev. Int. Arb.,* Vol.2, No.4 (1991), p.473.

[793] *See, e.g.,* the Rules for Expedited Arbitrations of the Arbitration Institute of the Stockholm Chamber of Commerce; WIPO Expedited Arbitration Rules; Section G of the Chamber of Commerce and Industry of Geneva Arbitration Rules.

Article 32(1)

> *The parties may agree to shorten the various time limits set out in these Rules. Any such agreement entered into subsequent to the constitution of an Arbitral Tribunal shall become effective only upon the approval of the Arbitral Tribunal.*

Article 32(1) provides the parties with the broadest possible power to shorten any of the deadlines contained in the Rules, including, *inter alia*, the thirty days granted the Respondent to file an Answer (Article 5(1)), the two months within which the Terms of Reference must be established (Article 18(2)), and the six months accorded the Arbitral Tribunal for rendering its Award (Article 24(1)).[794] The only limitation imposed on the parties' freedom in this regard is the requirement that the arbitrators' approval be obtained if the parties agree to shorten any such time limits after the Arbitral Tribunal's constitution. This is a reasonable restriction as the arbitrators will inevitably be affected by the parties' agreement. When the parties have already provided for expedited procedures prior to the Arbitral Tribunal's constitution, the arbitrators are free to take account of this when deciding whether or not to accept their appointment.

Notwithstanding the freedom accorded the parties under Article 32(1), it is important for them to consider carefully the reasonableness and fairness of any expedited deadlines that they may wish to establish. Parties can all too easily underestimate the time that may be required in order to ensure that each party has an adequate opportunity to present its case consistent with the due process to which the parties are universally considered to be entitled. In addition, it is often overlooked by parties, when shortening deadlines, that there are a number of things that can occur during an arbitration to disrupt it and frustrate the best-laid plans. Thus, for example, an arbitrator may be required to be replaced, a party may go bankrupt, or a party's counsel or a principal witness may fall ill. In the case of ICC arbitration, moreover, there is the need for the Court to fulfill its own responsibilities, such as scrutinizing and approving the arbitrators' Award before it is rendered. While the Rules contain a deadline for the making of the Award, which the parties may shorten, they do not impose any specific deadlines on the completion by the Court of its own tasks. In this regard, the Court has never accepted that it should be bound, in performing its own responsibilities, by expedited deadlines to which the parties (and possibly the arbitrators) may agree, which partly serves to explain the addition to the Rules of Article 32(2).

---

[794] It is important to note that Article 32(2) only applies to time limits contained in the Rules. The parties are not given the power to oblige the Court, for example, to perform its functions (*e.g.,* appoint arbitrators) within specified time periods as the Rules do not contain any corresponding deadlines.

Article 32(2)

> *The Court, on its own initiative, may extend any time limit which has been modified pursuant to Article 32(1) if it decides that it is necessary to do so in order that the Arbitral Tribunal or the Court may fulfil their responsibilities in accordance with these Rules.*

The power granted to the Court under the above provision was considered by the Working Party to be a necessary corollary to Article 32(1). Circumstances may arise, as just indicated, where, notwithstanding the best intentions and efforts of everyone concerned, it is simply not possible to comply with the shortened time limits to which the parties may originally have agreed. Of course, it is always possible for the parties themselves to agree to extend any such deadlines. But if they do not, Article 32(2) provides the Court with an opportunity to keep the arbitration alive (without, however, obliging it to do so).

The Court's powers under Article 32(2) are identical to the powers that the Court otherwise possesses under Articles 18(2) and 24(2) to extend the time periods for the Terms of Reference and the arbitrators' Award.[795] As the latter have come to be extended almost routinely by the Court, it might be feared that the mere existence of a power of extension would suffice to undermine the "fast-track" nature of the arbitration.[796] However, in the ICC's experience to date, both arbitrators and parties have tended to take seriously the expedited deadlines to which the parties may have agreed. Insofar as the Court is concerned, moreover, it needs to be in a position to ensure that it can perform its functions properly under the Rules. Thus, for example, whatever deadlines the parties may have agreed upon for the issuance of the Award, the Court must have sufficient time to scrutinize it and should not feel under any undue pressure to approve it if it is considered that the Award should be returned to the arbitrators for correction.

There nevertheless remains the question of whether the Court would accept to administer an arbitration if the parties, without regard to Article 32(2), provided for a non-extendable time period in their ICC arbitration clause. Under the previous Rules, which did not contain a provision comparable to Article 32, the Court accepted cases (including the "fast-track" case described above) where the arbitration clause arguably precluded extensions by the Court of the period

---

[795] Article 32 (2) is broader, however, as it extends to any other time limit that the parties may have modified, such as, for example, the time for filing the Answer or nominating or challenging an arbitrator. But it is difficult to see how the extension of most such other time limits would be necessary to permit the Arbitral Tribunal or the Court to fulfil their responsibilities.

[796] *See, e.g.,* Tschanz, "The Chamber of Commerce and Industry of Geneva's Arbitration Rules and their Expedited Procedure," *J. Arb. Int.,* Vol. 10, No. 4 (1993), p. 51, 56 ("[I]f the arbitration institution is specifically given the power to extend the time-limit of an expedited arbitration, then there is a high likelihood that it will give extensions as a matter of routine and it will even do so in cases where the extensions could have been avoided had the parties been under a clearly non-extendable deadline from the start.").

set forth in the clause without the parties' agreement.[797] The Court nevertheless found itself in the uncomfortable position, in such cases, of exposing itself to criticism if the arbitration could not be completed within the contractually agreed period. It would therefore not be unreasonable to expect the Court in the future to insist upon acceptance by the parties of Article 32(2) as a condition to administering "fast-track" arbitrations under the Rules.

ARTICLE 33
Waiver

A party which proceeds with the arbitration without raising its objection to a failure to comply with any provision of these Rules, or of any other rules applicable to the proceedings, any direction given by the Arbitral Tribunal, or any requirement under the arbitration agreement relating to the constitution of the Arbitral Tribunal, or to the conduct of the proceedings, shall be deemed to have waived its right to object.

Article 33 imports into the Rules for the first time a provision on waiver that is similar to that to be found in other arbitration rules[798] as well as in certain arbitral legislation (*see, e.g.,* the UNCITRAL Model Law, Article 4).[799] It expresses the widely-accepted principle (known variously, *e.g.,* as waiver, estoppel, *venire contra factum proprium*) that a party should not be permitted to complain long after the fact of irregularities as to which it did not raise any objection when it originally could have. As stated by a U.S. federal court:

> [A party cannot] wait in ambush and then render wasteful years of effort at an expenditure of millions of dollars. A party cannot remain silent, raising no objection during the arbitration proceedings, and when an award adverse to him has been handed down, complain of the situation of which he had knowledge from the first.[800]

As reflected in the foregoing passage, waiver provisions such as Article 33 are normally founded on the assumption that the party concerned had knowledge, without objecting, of a failure to comply with a requirement relevant to the arbitration (*see, e.g.,* UNCITRAL Rules, Article 30). Article 33 does not actually

---

[797] In fact, the Court took the precaution of obtaining the parties' agreement to such an extension in the case described above. *See* Davis, *supra,* note 49, p.7.

[798] *See, e.g.,* AAA International Arbitration Rules, Article 25; LCIA Rules, Article 32(1); UNCITRAL Rules, Article 30; WIPO Arbitration Rules, Article 58.

[799] *See also* Section 73 of the English Arbitration Act 1996. For a discussion of relevant French law, *see* Cadiet, *supra,* note 266, p.3; *and,* for an example of a U.S. case, *ISEC* v. *Bridas* (S.D.N.Y. 1990), *ICCA Yearbook* XVII (1992), p.639, *and* Note, Derains, *Rev. arb.* (1994), p.739.

[800] *Hunt* v. *Mobile Corporation,* 583 F. Supp. 1092 (S.D.N.Y. 1984).

state, however, that a party can only be deemed to have waived its right to object to a matter of which it previously had knowledge. It may therefore be argued that, in certain circumstances at least, a party's knowledge of a failure to comply can legitimately be presumed under Article 33 and need not be affirmatively established.[801] But insofar as Article 33 is intended to prevent objections from being raised late in bad faith, knowledge of the irregularity in question ought ordinarily to be an essential condition for the application of that provision. Indeed, it was not the intention of the drafters to preclude parties from raising objections with respect to matters of which they could not have been aware.

When such objections are required to be raised, however, is less clearly stated in Article 33 than in other rules, which generally provide that objections must be recorded "promptly" (*see, e.g.,* UNCITRAL Rules, Article 30). In contrast, Article 33 is merely stated to be applicable when a party "proceeds with the arbitration without raising an objection."[802] This language should suffice to preclude an objection from being raised for the first time in a proceeding subsequently initiated before a court for the purpose of attacking the arbitrators' Award, but it is less clear whether and, if so, when a failure to object should be treated as a waiver by the arbitrators during the arbitration itself. It would nevertheless seem to be within the spirit of Article 33 for an Arbitral Tribunal, on the basis of that provision, to deny untimely objections of a party that it should have been in a position to raise earlier.

Indeed, Article 33 has otherwise been drafted in very broad terms in order to encompass any irregularity in the proceedings, regardless of whether it is the Court, its Secretariat, the Arbitral Tribunal or one of the parties that is responsible.[803] Unlike most other such rules, it also extends to "any other rules applicable to the proceedings," which may include, for example, legal requirements supplementing the Rules and any relevant agreements between the parties. Thus, this provision should strengthen the binding force of ICC arbitral Awards by reducing the possibility of any recourse against them, within the spirit of Article 28(6).

Parties nevertheless need to bear in mind that Article 33 can produce its effects in subsequent judicial proceedings only to the extent that the matters deemed to be waived thereunder are, in fact, waivable. There should not normally be any obstacle to the waiver of provisions contained in arbitration rules or agreements insofar as they are creatures of the party's consent. But the same is

---

[801] This would, in fact, be consistent with the position under French law, which appears to have influenced the manner in which Article 33 has been drafted, as compared to the equivalent provisions in other rules. *See,* in this regard, Hory, *supra,* note 266.

[802] There is, moreover, no requirement that the objection be made in writing.

[803] Article 33 also ought to apply irrespective of whether the party concerned believes that there would be any utility in raising an objection with the arbitrators. *See* in this regard, the comment of Derains on *Société Nu Swift PLC* c/ *société White Knight et autres, supra,* note 590.

not necessarily considered to be true in all jurisdictions with respect to legal rules of mandatory application.[804]

ARTICLE 34
Exclusion of Liability

Neither the arbitrators, nor the Court and its members, nor the ICC and its employees, nor the ICC National Committees shall be liable to any person for any act or omission in connection with the arbitration.

Because of the increasingly litigious environment in which both international arbitrators and institutions function, arbitral institutions have been required in recent years to give greater attention to the possible need to protect themselves and arbitrators from possible claims arising in connection with the performance of their functions.[805] Although in many jurisdictions both arbitrators and institutions are recognized, in view of their quasi-judicial functions, to enjoy varying degrees of immunity from suit,[806] a growing number of arbitral institutions have nevertheless considered it desirable to add provisions to their rules expressly excluding their own and the arbitrators' liability in connection with their arbitral functions.[807] Article 34, thus, represents the ICC's attempt to provide arbitrators operating under its auspices (and itself) with the greatest possible protection against lawsuits, which have increasingly come to be seen as a potential source of disruption and harassment in connection with the arbitral process.

Although a new provision in the Rules, Article 34 is nevertheless not without precedent in rules issued by the ICC. Indeed, a comparable provision (Article 6(8)) was included in the ICC Rules for a Pre-Arbitral Referee Procedure that entered into force in 1990 (*see* Appendix 10 *infra*), except that that provision, unlike Article 34, carved out an exception for "conscious and deliberate wrongdoing." Similar exceptions are contained in the corresponding provisions of other arbitration rules. In contrast, Article 34 excludes all liability of the arbitrators and all participants in the Court's activities for any act or omission, without exception.

---

[804] Thus, for example, Article 4 of the UNCITRAL Model Law may be read to preclude the waiver of mandatory provisions under that law, which include, for example, the requirement implicit in Article 12(2) that arbitrators be impartial and independent. *See Holtzmann and Neuhaus,* pp.408-10; *cf.,* Hory, *supra,* note 266, where French law is distinguished; *and* Cadiet, *supra,* note 266.

[805] *See, e.g.,* Redfern, "The Immunity of Arbitrators," *The Status of the Arbitrator* (ICC Publishing 1995), p.121.

[806] *See,* in this regard, "Final Report on the Status of the Arbitrator" of the ICC Commission Working Party on this subject (P. Fouchard, Chairman), *ICC Ct. Bull.,* Vol.7, No.1 (1996), p.27.

[807] *See* AAA International Arbitration Rules, Article 35; WIPO Arbitration Rules, Article 77; LCIA Rules, Article 31. *See also* Sections 29 and 74 of the English Arbitration Act 1996.

In adopting such a broad exclusion, the ICC recognized that it would not be likely to be effective in all jurisdictions. Indeed, while the New Rules were under discussion, the ICC Commission adopted a report on the status of the arbitrator in which it was observed that:

> In most national laws, total exclusion of liability by such a contractual approach would be ineffective if the arbitrator was accused of certain particularly serious faults (deliberate or inexcusable wrongful acts or omissions). Indeed, they state that clauses restricting or excluding liability may not be invoked as a defence to such wrongful acts or omissions. Yet, in the national laws which do not allow the arbitrator absolute immunity, the only wrongful acts or omissions for which the arbitrator is liable to incur liability are acts of this kind.[808]

It nevertheless became apparent during the discussion of successive drafts of Article 34 within the Commission that the most appropriate formulation of possible exceptions to the immunity of the arbitrator and arbitral institution may differ, depending upon the jurisdiction concerned. It was therefore concluded that Article 34 should be expressed in the widest possible terms so that it could be applied as broadly as the applicable law might allow. It will therefore ultimately be a matter for local jurisdictions to decide whether and to what extent Article 34 should be given effect. In this regard, courts will also be required to consider how broadly to construe the application of Article 34 to acts or omissions "in connection with" the arbitration.

As a practical matter, the authors are not aware of any cases in recent years in which ICC arbitrators have been successfully sued for damages. Any such suits could normally be expected to be brought either at the place of arbitration or the domicile of the arbitrator concerned, with the possible application of the laws of either of those jurisdictions. In the case of the ICC, suits have occasionally been lodged against it in Paris, but without success. Some years ago, however, an Egyptian court purported to assert jurisdiction over the ICC, notwithstanding the ICC's objection, and ordered it to pay damages of U.S. $1,000,000 to the Egyptian State for allowing an arbitration to proceed against it.[809] While appeals in the case were still pending, the claim was withdrawn.

---

[808] *See supra,* note 806, p.27.
[809] The arbitration was the *Westland* case discussed in connection with Article 6(2). *See supra,* notes 166-68.

Article 35
General Rule

In all matters not expressly provided for in these Rules, the Court and the Arbitral Tribunal shall act in the spirit of these Rules and shall make every effort to make sure that the Award is enforceable at law.

Article 35 corresponds to Article 26 of the previous Rules. It has existed in its present form in the Rules, with only slight alterations, since 1955 and is generally intended to guide both the Court and the arbitrators when a question or issue may arise in the conduct of the arbitration that is "not expressly provided for" in the Rules. As the Rules are not intended to be a comprehensive code for the conduct of an arbitration, Article 35 serves the useful purpose of providing the Court and arbitrators with both general guidance and authority to act, as appropriate, in respect of matters with which the Rules do not deal explicitly.

Thus, for example, prior to the New Rules (Article 10), Article 26 was invoked by the Court in order to justify its practices in relation to the constitution of the arbitral tribunal in multi-party cases, a subject that the Rules did not expressly cover.[810] Similarly, in the absence of a provision in the former Rules on the correction or interpretation of Awards (now Article 29), the Court relied upon Article 26 in authorizing an Arbitral Tribunal to consider an application for the interpretation of an Award.[811] In each such case, the Court came to the conclusion that, in the absence of an express provision in the Rules, the positions adopted by it were those that were most in keeping with the general scheme of the Rules (their "spirit") and the ultimate enforceability of the Award.

Because of its reference to the enforceability of the Award, which is, of course, the *raison d'être* of the arbitration process, Article 35 is widely misunderstood as imposing a related obligation on both the Court and the Arbitral Tribunal, in all circumstances. Thus, for example, it is frequently asserted, without further qualification, that this provision "obliges the tribunal to use every effort to make sure that the award is enforceable at law."[812] Similarly, based on a broad construction of that provision, Arbitral Tribunals have often felt obliged, when rendering their Awards, to consider the enforceability of their decisions not only at the place of the arbitration but at other possible places of execution.[813]

---

[810] *See* Bond, *supra,* note 112, p.44. *But cf.* Darling and Ramsay, "Powers and Jurisdiction of the Arbitral Tribunal," *International and ICC Arbitration* (King's College 1990), pp.104-08 ("It is suggested that the purpose of . . . [Article 26] is not to permit new *ad hoc* rules to be made upon a major provision such as multi-party arbitration but to permit the Court or the arbitrator to interpret the Rules in the spirit rather than the letter of the Rules. In other words, it is there to assist in the construction of the existing Rules.")

[811] *See* ICC Case No. 6653, Note Arnaldez, *supra,* note 691, p. 528.

[812] *See Craig Park and Paulsson,* §17.04, p.303.

[813] *See, e.g.,* the Award in ICC Case No.6697, *Société Casa c/ société Cambior, Rev. arb.* (1992), p.135 (Arbitral Tribunal held that it was precluded by then Article 26 from rendering an Award that would not be enforceable at the domicile of one of the parties, where execution would be sought).

While both the Court and arbitrators should always be concerned about the efficacy of the arbitral process and, thus, endeavor to ensure that the Award is in conformity with the mandatory requirements of law at the place of the arbitration, Article 35 is, as already stated, intended to serve the much more limited purpose of guiding the Court's and arbitrators' actions in relation to the arbitration procedure whenever there may be a *lacuna* in the Rules. It is not intended, however, to have any influence on the Arbitral Tribunal's resolution of substantive issues in the arbitration. Nor does it require the Arbitral Tribunal to ensure that the Award would be subject to execution in any particular country, provided that it has been rendered in accordance with the formal requirements of the place where made. Indeed, an international arbitrator will not necessarily be in a position to know, in any event, where execution of an award is likely to be sought. Thus, as one tribunal held in relation to then Article 26, when its jurisdiction was challenged on the basis that its Award would not be enforceable in the country of the Respondent party:

> [T]his requirement of Article 26 is not relevant to the question of jurisdiction. It is obvious that if a Tribunal would decline to exercise jurisdiction on the basis of the possible difficulties of a future enforcement in a given country, then there would be no award at all, susceptible of being enforced in other jurisdictions.
>
> In this case there may be difficulties, perhaps not insuperable, in the enforcement of this tribunal awards [*sic*], in some national jurisdictions.
>
> But if the tribunal finds, as it does, that it has jurisdiction, it cannot fail to exercise it. Otherwise, it would be concurring in a failure to exercise jurisdiction and could even be accused of a denial of justice.[814]

The substantive decisions of ICC Arbitral Tribunals are, thus, required to be made on the basis of the requirements of the Rules, the parties' relevant agreements, the rules of law applicable thereto and the mandatory requirements of the place of arbitration. Article 35, however, does not impose any additional obligations on the Arbitral Tribunal in this regard.

---

[814] ICC Case No. 4695 (1984), *ICC Arbitral Awards 1986-1990*, p.33. *See also Craig Park and Paulsson*, §11.03, pp.193-94.

Appendices

STANDARD ICC ARBITRATION CLAUSE

The New Rules are accompanied by the following recommended arbitration clause:

> All disputes arising out of or in connection with the present contract shall be finally settled under the Rules of Arbitration of the International Chamber of Commerce by one or more arbitrators appointed in accordance with the said Rules.

The above clause differs slightly from the standard clause published together with the previous version of the Rules. The principal difference is the elimination from the new clause of any reference to the ICC Rules of Conciliation. The Rules of Conciliation have been deleted on the recommendation of a Working Group of the ICC Commission on International Arbitration, which rendered a report on the standard clause in 1991. The Working Group noted that the reference to the Rules of Conciliation was confusing and risked casting doubt on the binding nature of the agreement to arbitrate.

In accordance with the Working Group's recommendation, the first line of the clause has also been amended to read: "All disputes arising out of or in connection with the present contract ... ." The previous text referred only to "disputes arising in connection with" the contract, which was not entirely consistent with the French version of the clause.[815]

Although succinct, the above clause has a number of important attributes that are essential for an effective arbitration clause. The first is that it makes arbitra-

---

[815] At the same time, the French version has been altered so that it is now entirely consistent with the English language clause.

tion mandatory by specifying that disputes "shall" be settled in accordance with the clause. It is also broadly worded in order to embrace "all disputes arising out of or in connection with" the contract, which will confer the widest possible jurisdiction on the Arbitral Tribunal. Other phrases (such as references to disputes "arising under" the contract) may be construed more narrowly and preclude the arbitration of matters that the parties might otherwise have wished to be arbitrated (for example, a claim for fraud in the inducement).[816] In addition, the clause clearly designates the arbitration rules to be applied, in this case, those of the International Chamber of Commerce.

The ICC regularly sees much longer and more complex arbitration clauses, but they may be less effective than the standard ICC clause simply because they give rise to difficulties of interpretation of one kind or another.[817] That, in turn, may prolong – or even thwart – the arbitration process.

While the recommended ICC clause is adequate as a basic clause, the ICC Rules brochure reminds parties that:

> [I]t may be desirable for them to stipulate in the arbitration clause itself the law governing the contract, the number of arbitrators and the place and language of the arbitration. The parties' free choice of the law governing the contract and of the place and language of the arbitration is not limited by the ICC Rules of Arbitration.

In addition, as noted in the Rules brochure, the laws of certain countries may impose special requirements regarding the specific contents of the arbitration clause. Thus, for example, under the law of the People's Republic of China, an arbitration clause must identify the institution that is charged with the administration of the arbitration. There has recently been litigation in the Chinese courts regarding the adequacy of the ICC standard clause in this regard as it refers expressly only to the Rules of Arbitration of the ICC, but does not explicitly state that the arbitration is also to be administered by the ICC. Although the ICC Rules provide for administration by the ICC Court – and, thus, the ICC has never considered it necessary to add an explicit reference to the Court in the standard clause – this may nevertheless be advisable when the arbitration concerns a Chinese party. Because there may be other, similar requirements hidden in the arbitration laws of various countries, it will therefore always be advisable for a party to review the arbitration laws that may be relevant before finalizing an arbitration clause.[818]

---

[816] There has been substantial jurisprudence with respect to such matters in the United States in particular. *See, e.g.,* Bond, "How to Draft an Arbitration Clause (Revisited)," *ICC Ct. Bull.,* Vol.1, No.2 (1990), p.14.

[817] *See* Bond, *supra,* note 816. *See also* Davis, "Pathological Clauses: Frédéric Eisemann's still Vital Criteria," *Arb. Int.,* Vol.7, No.4 (1991), p.365.

[818] Thus, it has been said that when execution of an arbitration Award may be sought in the United States, it is advisable to include in the arbitration clause a stipulation that judgment may be entered upon an Award in a court of competent jurisdiction. *See* Bond, *supra,* note 816.

Similarly, when adding language to, or varying a standard arbitration clause such as that of the ICC, it is essential to ensure that the language being added does not conflict with the arbitration rules being selected. In the case of the ICC, as discussed elsewhere in this book, the Court may refuse to accept an arbitration where the arbitration clause either seeks to vary the ICC Rules (for example, by eliminating the Terms of Reference, or the requirement of scrutiny by the ICC Court of the arbitrator's Award) or includes provisions that may otherwise be considered by the Court to be incompatible with the Rules. It is therefore important to take care before adding to, or embroidering upon, the recommended ICC clause.

Having said this, there are, as previously noted, a number of matters that it may be desirable to add to the recommended ICC clause, as follows:

Language of the arbitration (*see* Article 16 *supra*). As already discussed, the language of the arbitration is an extremely important consideration that may have significant practical consequences for the parties. Indeed, this will not only affect the possible need for translation and interpretation (which can be very costly), but may also restrict the parties' choice of arbitrators and counsel. Surprisingly often, however, the arbitration clauses seen by the ICC do not make any provision for the language of the arbitration, and occasionally this may lead to difficulties.

It is to be remembered in this connection that Article 16 of the Rules does not mandate the use of the language of the contract as the language of the arbitration. In ICC arbitration, therefore, an express stipulation regarding the language should usually be included in the arbitration clause if the parties wish to eliminate any uncertainty as to this important question.

Place of the arbitration (*see* Article 14 *supra*). The three well-known rules of real estate – "location, location, location" – apply with at least equal force in international arbitration. Indeed, the place of the arbitration will determine the extent to which state courts may, or may not, interfere with the arbitration process and the extent of the recourse available against an arbitral Award. Thus, in some jurisdictions (*e.g.*, Belgium) there may be no recourse whatever against certain categories of Awards, while in others (*e.g.*, Pakistan) the courts may have broad powers to review the conduct of the arbitration and the arbitrators' determinations. In yet others (*e.g.*, China), there may be uncertainty as to the validity of an arbitration Award rendered there (other than under the auspices of a statutorily recognized organization). Thus, the choice of a place requires a careful review of the legislation that would apply to the arbitration if held in that place.

In the absence of very special circumstances (as when the other party is situated in a country that is not a party to the New York Convention, or other relevant treaty, or when it might otherwise be difficult to enforce the arbitration Award), the place of the arbitration should always be a neutral, "arbitration-friendly" venue. However, if it is likely to be difficult to obtain agreement on such a venue when the contract is being negotiated, it is preferable not to make any provision in the arbitration clause on this subject and to leave the choice of a place to the

ICC Court, in accordance with Article 14 of the Rules. Indeed, one of the advantages of ICC arbitration is that the Court can make this decision, if required; and the Court will normally situate the arbitration in a suitable neutral venue.

In considering the place of the arbitration, it is important to bear in mind that the selection of a venue does not necessarily preclude hearings or other meetings of the arbitrators and the parties from occurring elsewhere (*see* Article 14(2) *supra*).

Composition of the Arbitral Tribunal (*see* Articles 7-12 *supra*). The recommended ICC arbitration clause does not specify the number of arbitrators to be appointed, nor does it lay down any requirements regarding their qualifications. Although parties may sometimes wish to provide for such matters when drafting the arbitration clause, there can also be disadvantages in doing so.

The number of arbitrators will affect the cost of the arbitration and probably also its duration. It is common in international arbitrations for the tribunal to be composed of three arbitrators so that the Claimant and Respondent can each designate an arbitrator. However, this may not make financial sense if the amount at issue does not justify the cost. If, when drafting the arbitration clause, the parties cannot anticipate the magnitude of the disputes that may subsequently arise, it may be hazardous to fix the number of arbitrators at that time. The parties will still have the opportunity, when a dispute arises, to attempt to agree on a number, and, if they are unable to do so, the Court will decide the matter, as already noted (*see* Article 8(2) *supra*).

With respect to the arbitrators' qualifications, neither the Rules nor the laws of most countries set forth any particular requirements, and the parties may therefore wish to specify their wishes in the arbitration clause (although this is relatively rare in ICC practice). The parties must be careful if they choose to do so, however, that they do not establish conditions that will so narrow the pool of potential arbitrators as to make the constitution of a tribunal excessively difficult.

Applicable rules of law (*see* Article 17 *supra*). Except to the extent that the parties agree that the arbitrators should assume the powers of an *amiable compositeur* or decide *ex aequo et bono*, the Award, as already discussed, is to be rendered in accordance with the rules of law designated by the parties as applicable to the merits of dispute, failing which the arbitrators shall apply the rules of law that they determine to be appropriate. It will therefore clearly be desirable for the parties, whenever reasonably possible, to specify the rules of law that they wish to govern the substantive issues in the arbitration, either in the arbitration clause or elsewhere in the contract.

In this regard, it is important to distinguish between the applicable substantive law from the law applicable to the arbitral proceedings. The parties are not required, under the Rules, to specify an applicable procedural law and should not normally do so, in which case only such provisions as otherwise apply mandatorily normally – at the place of the arbitration – would be applicable.

Multi-party arbitration. As discussed elsewhere in this book, if the arbitration is intended to include more than two parties, it may be appropriate to take account of this in the arbitration clause. (*See* the discussion of Article 10 of the Rules above and the report of the ICC Working Party on this subject.)

Expedited arbitration. As the ICC does not have special rules for expedited (or "fast-track") proceedings, parties are required to make appropriate provisions in their arbitation clause. However, they must take care that any such provisions are really workable and otherwise compatible with the Rules.

OTHER STANDARD ICC CLAUSES

Standard clause for appointments under the UNCITRAL Rules. The ICC recommends that parties wishing the ICC to act as an appointing authority under the UNCITRAL Arbitration Rules use the following clause:

> Any dispute, controversy or claim arising out of or relating to this contract, or the breach, termination or invalidity thereof, shall be settled by arbitration in accordance with the UNCITRAL Arbitration Rules as at present in force. The appointing authority shall be the International Chamber of Commerce (ICC) acting in accordance with the Rules adopted by the ICC for this purpose.

The ICC presently charges U.S. $2,500 for such appointments (*see* ICC Rules, Appendix III, Article 3).

Standard clause for an ICC Pre-arbitral Referee Procedure. The ICC recommends that all parties wishing to make reference to the ICC Rules for a Pre-arbitral Referee Procedure use the following clause in their contracts:

> Any party to this contract shall have the right to have recourse to and shall be bound by the Pre-arbitral Referee Procedure of the International Chamber of Commerce in accordance with its Rules.

Parties are reminded that if they wish to have recourse to ICC arbitration as well as to the ICC Pre-arbitral Referee Procedure, a specific reference to both procedures should be stipulated. For that purpose the following clause is recommended:

> Any party to this contract shall have the right to have recourse to and shall be bound by the Pre-arbitral Referee Procedure of the International Chamber of Commerce in accordance with its Rules. All disputes arising in connection with the present contract shall be finally settled under the Rules of Conciliation and Arbitration of the International Chamber of

Commerce by one or more arbitrators appointed in accordance with the said Rules.[819]

Model expertise clause. The clause recommended by the ICC's International Centre for Expertise is as follows:

> The parties to this agreement agree to have recourse, if the need arises, to the International Centre for Expertise of the International Chamber of Commerce in accordance with the ICC's Rules for Expertise.

Since expertise and arbitral proceedings are distinct, the ICC recommends parties to separate technical and legal disputes in contracts by inserting the model clause for expertise, in addition to the arbitration clause. Failure to do so, however, does not prevent the possible use by ICC arbitrators of the services of the International Centre for Expertise if they need to appoint technically-qualified experts. Parties wishing to make reference to ICC arbitration are reminded that they should also include the standard ICC arbitration clause in their contracts.

---

[819]   This provision is now required to be amended to conform to the new standard arbitration clause.

Appendix 2

Bola Ajibola (Nigeria)

Gunnar Nerdrum (Norway)

M.A.K. Afridi (Pakistan) *Alternate Member: Mahomed J. Jaffer*

Jorge Avendaño V. (Peru)

Antonio Pires de Lima (Portugal) *Alternate Member: Joâo Luís Pinheiro Lopes dos Reis*

Hasan E. Al-Mulla (Saudi Arabia) *Alternate Member: Saleh B. Al Tayar*

Jean Gabriel Benglia (Senegal)

K.S. Chung (Singapore)

Mervyn King (South Africa)

Juan Antonio Cremades (Spain)

C. Chakradaran (Sri Lanka)

Hans Bagner (Sweden)

Pierre Neiger (Switzerland)

Faez Anjak (Syria)

Salah Mejri (Tunisia)

Mahmut Birsel (Turkey)

David St. John Sutton (United Kingdom)

Stephen R. Bond (United States)

Héctor Gros Espiell (Uraguay)

James Otis Rodner (Venezuela)

Dobrosav Mitrovic (Yugoslavia)

Appendix 3

ICC National Committees and Groups
As from January 1, 1998

Argentina
Chair: Ernesto E. Grether
Secretary General: Herberto Hugo
  Karplus
Offices: c/o Camara Argentina de
  Comercio
  Avenida Leandro N. Alem 36
  1003 – Buenos Aires
Tel: (54-1) 331 8051 / 343 9423
Fax: (54-1) 331 8055
E-mail: ececao@overnet.com.ar

Australia
Chair: Christopher Cullen
Secretary General: Howard Grant
Offices: PO Box E 118, Kingston
  Australia ACT 2604
Tel: (61-2) 62 95 19 61
Fax: (61-2) 62 95 01 74

Austria
Chair: Leopold Maderthaner
Executive Director: Maximilian
  Burger-Scheidlin
Offices: Wiedner Hauptstrasse 63
  (Schaum)
  A-1045 Wien
Tel: (43-1) 50105 3701
Fax: (43-1) 50206 3703
E-mail: iccal@aw.wk.or.at

Bangladesh
Chair: Mahbubur Rahman
Secretary General: Abul Quasem
Offices: Dhaka Chamber Building
  (Ground floor)
  65-66, Motijheel Commercial
  Area
  GPO Box 3861 – Dhaka 1000
Tel: (880-2) 955 7478
Fax: (880-2) 955 7429
E-mail: iccb@citechco.net

Belgium
Chair: Eugène van Dyck
Secretary General: Guy Keutgen
Offices: c/o FEB, 8 rue des Sols
  B 1000 Brussels
Tel: (32-2) 515 08 35
Fax: (32-2) 515 08 75
E-mail: cci@vbo.feb.be

Brazil
Chair: Theophilo de Azeredo Santos
Secretary General: Sylvio Piza
  Pedroza
Offices: Avenida General Justo 304-
  7°, Andar
  20021-130 Rio de Janeiro – R.J.
Tel: (55-21) 240 70 70 / 297 00 11
Fax: (55-21) 240 69 20

Burkina Faso
Chair: El Hadj Oumarou Kanazoé
Secretary General: Salif Lamoussa
  Kaboré
Offices: c/o Chambre de Commerce,
  d'Industrie et d'Artisanat du
  Burkina Faso
  Boîte Postale 502 –
  Ouagadougou 01
Tel: (226) 30 61 14/15 or 31 12 66/67
Fax: (226) 30 61 16

Cameroon
(Under reorganization)

Canada
(Canadian Council for International
  Business)
Chair: Robert T.E. Gillespie
President and CEO: Bob Keyes
Offices: Delta Office Tower, Suite 501
  350 Sparks Street
  Ottawa, Ontario K1R 7SB
Tel: (1-613) 230 54 62
Fax: (1-613) 230 70 87
E-mail: bfisher@ccib.org

Chile
Chair: Mario Agliati
Executive Secretary: Christian
  Novlon Boisier
Offices: Cámara Naciónal de
  Comercio de Chile
  Merced, 230 – Santiago
Tel: (56-2) 365 40 00
Fax: (56-2) 365 40 01

China
Chair: Yu Xiaosong
Secretary General: Liu Fugui
Offices: c/o China Chamber of
  International Commerce
  (CCOIC)
  1, Fu Xing Men Wai Street
  Beijing 100860
Tel: (86-10) 6801 3344 / 6802 3554
Fax: (86-10) 6802 3554
Website: www.icc-china.com
Email: hfli@public.east.cn.net

Colombia
Chair: Guillermo Fernández de Soto
Secretary General: Christine Ternent
Offices: c/o Cámara de Comercio de
  Bogotá
  Carrerá 9, N°16-21
  PO Box 29824
  Santafé de Bogota
Tel: (57-1) 284 82 68 / 281 91 64
Fax: (57-1) 284 77 35 / 284 29 66
E-mail: guillerf@ccb.org.co
  christt@ccb.org.co

Cyprus
Chair: Christodoulos Mavroudis
Secretary General: Panayiotis
  Loizides
Offices: c/o Cyprus Chamber of
  Commerce and Industry
  (Chamber Building)
  38, Girvas Dighenis avenue
  3, Deligiorgis Street
  PO Box 1455 – Nicosia CY 1509
Tel: (357-2) 44 95 00 / 46 23 12
Fax: (357-2) 44 90 48 / 45 86 30

Denmark
Chair: Erik B. Rasmussen
Secretary General: Lars Krobaek
Offices: Börsen
    DK 1217 Köbenhawn K.
Tel: (45-33) 95 05 00
Fax: (45-33) 15 22 66
E-mail:
    handelskammeret@commerce.dk

Ecuador
Chair: Juan Falconi Puig
Executive Director: Maritza Reynoso
    de Wright
Offices: Avenida Olmedo 414 y
    Boyaca, Piso 1
    Casilla PO Box 09 01
    7515 Guayaquil
Tel: (593-4) 32 59 64 / 32 59 66
Fax: (593-4) 32 59 66

Egypt
Chair: Mohamed Farid Khamis
Secretary General: Yehia El Gamal
Offices: c/o Federation of Egyptian
    Chambers of Commerce
    4 Midan El Falaki (Bab El
    Louk)
    Cairo
Tel: (20-2) 355 11 64 / 354 29 43
Fax: (20-2) 355 79 40

Finland
Chair: Pertti Voutilainen
Secretary General: Timo Vuori
Offices: World Trade Center Helsinki
    Aleksanterinkatu, 17 – PO Box
    1000
    FIN 00100 Helsinki
Tel: (358-9) 669 459 / 6969 6638
Fax: (358-9) 6969 6647
E-mail: timo.vuorl@wtc.fi

France
Chair: François de Laage de Meux
Conseiller du Président, déléguée dans
    les fonctions de Secrétaire
    Général: M-C Psiménos de
    Metz-Noblat
Offices: 9, Boulevard Malesherbes
    75008 Paris
Tel: (33-1) 42 65 12 66
Fax: (33-1) 49 24 06 39

Germany
(ICC Deutschland)
Chair: Ludger W. Staby
Secretary General: Angelika Pohlenz
Offices: Mittelstrasse 12-14, D – 506
    72 Köln
    Postfach 10 08 26, D – 50448
    Köln
Tel: (49-221) 257 55 71
Fax: (49-221) 257 55 93
E-mail: icc@icc-deutschland.de

Greece
Chair: Emmanuel Niades
Secretary General: Byron Katsaros
Offices: 27 Kaningos Street – Athens
    10682
Tel: (30-1) 38 10 879
Fax: (30-1) 38 31 189
E-mail: iccgr@eexi.gr

Hungary
Chair: Lajos Tolnay
Secretary General: Marta Szili
Offices: Kossuth Lajos tér, 6-8
    H 1055 Budapest
Tel: (36-1) 153 3178
Fax: (36-1) 153 34 96
Website: www.icc.co.hu
E-mail: icchun@mail.matav.hun

Iceland
Chair: Olafur B. Thors
Secretary General: Vilhjalmur
    Eglisson
Offices: House of Commerce,
    Kringlan 7
    IS 103 Reykjavik
Tel: (354) 588 6666
Fax: (354) 568 6564
E-mail: mottaka@chamber.is

India
Chair: Chirayu R. Amin
Secretary General: Amit Mitra
Offices: Federation House, Tansen
    Marg.
    New Dehli 110 001
Tel: (91-11) 373 8760 70 / 373 9229
Fax: (91-11) 332 0714 / 372 1504
E-mail: iccindia@del2.vsnl.net.in

Indonesia
Chair: Aburizal Bakrie
Secretary General: I. Sucipto Umar
Offices: c/o P.T. Tirtames Comexindo
    BRI II Building, 26th Floor
    JL. Jend. Sudirman 44-46
    Jakarta 10210
Tel: (62-21) 5707434 / 5713415
Fax: (62-21) 5719008 / 5719009

Iran
(Islamic Republic of)
Chair: Ali Naghi Seyed Khamoushi
Secretary General: Mohammed
    Mehdi Behkish
Offices: 254, Taleghani Avenue
    Teheran 15814
Tel: (98-21) 838 127
Fax: (98-21) 838 330

Ireland
Chair: Desmond Miller
Director: Tom Cox
Offices: 22 Merrion Square – Dublin 2
Tel: (353-1) 661 2888
Fax: (353-1) 661 2811
E-mail: chambers@lol.le

Israel
Chair: Moshe Sanbar
Secretary General: Itzhak Y. Kashiv
Offices: 84, Hahashmonaim Street
    PO Box 20027 – Tel Aviv 61200
Tel: (972-3) 563 10 48 / 10 49
Fax: (972-3) 562 32 74

Italy
Chair: Carlo Callieri
Managing Director: Mauro Ferrante
Offices: Via XX Settembre N°5
    IT 00187 Roma
Tel: (39-6) 48 82 438 / 48 82 575
Fax: (39-6) 48 82 677
E-mail: icc.cci.italia@flashnet.it

Ivory Coast
(Under reorganization)

Japan
Chair: Reijiro Hattori
Secretary General: Masaki Goka
Offices: Suite 311, Tosho Bldg. 3-2-2
    Marunouchi Chiyoda-ku –
    Tokyo 100
Tel: (81-3) 3213 8585
Fax: (81-3) 3213 8589

Jordan
Chair: Mohammed Asfour
Secretary General: Amin Husseini
Offices: PO Box 7029 – Amman 111
  18
Tel: (962-6) 66 54 92 / 67 44 95
Fax: (962-6) 68 59 97
Website: www.fjcc.com
E-mail: fjcc@ncts.com.jo

Korea
Chair: Park Yong Sung
Secretary General: Lee Boo-Hong
Offices: 45, Namdaemun-ro 4-ga,
  Chung-gu
  (CPO Box 25) – Seoul
Tel: (82-2) 316 3536/8
Fax: (82-2) 757 94 75
Website: www.kcci.or.kr
E-mail: 07978@www.kcci.or.kr
  lotus@www.kcci.or.kr

Kuwait
Chair: Abdulrazzak Al-Khaled
Secretary General: Majed Jamaluddin
Offices: Ali Al-Salem Street, KCCI
  Building
  PO Box 775 Safat – Kuwait
  13008
Tel: (965) 241 7285 / 241 6391
Fax: (965) 240 4110 / 243 3858
E-mail: kuwait1@ncc.moc.kw

Lebanon
Chair: Adnan Kassar
Secretary General: Louis G. Hobeika
Offices: Georges Haimari Street
  Elias Abdel-Nour Bldg.
  Achrafieh-Sassine
  PO Box 11 – 1801 Beirut
Tel: (961-1) 200 437/438
Fax: (961-1) 321 220
E-mail: iccleb@sodetel.net.lb

Lithuania
Chair: Mindaugas Cerniauskas
Executive Director: Algimantas
  Akstinas
Offices: c/o Association International
  Chamber of Commerce –
  Lithuania
  18, V. Kudirkos Street – 2600
  Vilnius
Tel: (370-2) 222 630
Fax: (370-2) 222 621

Luxembourg
Chair: Paul Meyers
Secretary General: Paul Hippert
Offices: 7, Rue Alcide de Gasperi
  L – 2981 Luxembourg
Tel: (352) 42 39 39 303
Fax: (352) 43 83 26
E-mail: direction@cc.lu
  paul.hipper@ci.edu.lu

Madagascar
(Under reorganization)

Mexico
Chair: Guillermo Cadena Acévedo
Secretary General: Sergio Soto Priante
Offices: Edificio WTC, Oficina N°20
  nivel 14
  Av. de las Naciones N°. 1
  Colonia Nápoles
  03810 México, D.F.
Tel: (52-5) 488 26 78 / 488 26 79
Fax: (52-5) 488 26 80
E-mail: camecic@albec.com.mx

Morocco
Chair: Abderrahman Tazi
Assistant: Khalid Belkhoutout
Offices: 201, Boulevard de Bordeaux
  Appartement 505 (5e étage)
  20 000 – Casablanca
Tel: (212-2) 22 51 11 / 47 39 03
Fax: (212-2) 47 39 34

Netherlands
Chair: Herman A. van Karnebeek
Secretary General: Harald Scholtz
Offices: Bezuidenhoutseweg 12
  PO Box 95309
  2509-Av. Den Haag
Tel: (31-70) 383 66 46
Fax: (31-70) 381 95 63
Website:
  www.ourworld.compuserve.com/
  homepages/harald-scholtz
E-mail: h.scholtz@icc.nl

Nigeria
(Under reorganization)

Norway
Chair: Hans Ole Bjøntegård
Secretary General: Ole-Christian
  Solheim
Offices: Drammensvn 30 –
  PO Box 2483
  Solli – 0202 Oslo
Tel: (47-22) 54 17 00
Fax: (47-22) 56 17 00

Pakistan
(Under reorganization)

Peru
Chair: Samuel Gleiser-Katz
Secretary General: Angela Gainza
  Morgante
Offices: Avenida Gregorio Escobedo
  396
  Oficina 301 – Lima 11
Tel: (51-1) 463 4263 / 460 2252 /
  261 7985
Fax: (51-1) 463 9629
E-mail: cci-peru@camaralima.org.pe

Portugal
Chair: Joao Mendes de Almeida
Assistant: Manuela Silva
Offices: Rua Portas de Santo Antao 89
  1194 Lisboa Codex
Tel: (351-1) 346 33 04
Fax: (351-1) 322 40 52

Saudi Arabia
Chair: Khalil A. Kurdi
Secretary General: Usamah M.M.
  Al-Kurdi
Offices: c/o Council of Saudi
  Chambers of Commerce and
  Industry
  PO Box 16683 – Riyadh 11474
Tel: (966-1) 405 32 00/148
Fax: (966-1) 402 47 47

Senegal
(Under reorganization)

Singapore
Chair: Kwek Leng-Joo
Secretary General: Abdul Aziz
  Mahmood
Offices: Chamber of Commerce
  Building
  47, Hill Street, N°03-01 Chinese
  Singapore 179365
Tel: (65) 338 97 61
Fax: (65) 339 56 30
Website:
  www.asiaconnect.com/sicc/home
E-mail: singlcc@asianconnect.com

South Africa
Chair: T. N. R. Main
Secretary General: R.W.K. Parsons
Offices: 3rd Floor, JCC Hosue
    Cnr Empire and Owl Streets
    Milpark
    PO Box 91267, Auckland Park
    Johannesburg 2006
Tel: (27-11) 482 25 24
Fax: (27-11) 726 13 44
E-mail: sacob@cis.co.za

Spain
Chair: Guillermo de la Dehesa
    Romero
Secretary General: Luis Solá
    Vilardell
Offices: Avinguda Diagonal, 452 454
    08006 Barcelona
Tel: (34-3) 416 93 00
Fax: (34-3) 416 93 01
E-mail: iccspain@cambrabcn.es

Sri Lanka
Chair: M.J.C. Amarasuriya
Chief Executive Officer:
    Premachandra A. Pathirana
Offices: 1st Floor, CNAPT Centre
    51, Sir Marcus Fernando
    Mawatha
    PO Box 1733 – Colombo 7
Tel: (94-1) 69 12 90 / (94) 075 33 33 92
Fax: (94-1) 69 12 90

Sweden
Chair: Björn Svedberg
Secretary General: Tell Hermanson
Offices: Västra Trädgardsgatan 9
    PO Box 16050 – S 103 21
    Stockholm
Tel: (46-8) 440 89 20
Fax: (46-8) 411 31 15
E-mail: icc@iccsweden.se

Switzerland
Chair: Gaudenz I. Staehelin
Secretary General: Florent Roduit
Offices: CC/ICC Chambre de
    Commerce Internationale –
    Internationale Handelskammer
    c/o Vorort
    Hegibachstrasse, 47
    Case Postale 1072
    CH 8032 Zurich
Tel: (41-1) 389 93 50
Fax: (41-1) 389 93 51
E-mail: icc@vorort.ch

Syria
Chair: Abdul Rahman Attar
Secretary General: Rateb Al-Shallah
Offices: Federation of Syrian
    Chambers of Commerce
    Moosa Bin Nusair Street
    PO Box 2908 – Damascus
Tel: (963-11) 333 59 20 / 333 40 41
Fax: (963-11) 333 59 20

Togo
Chair: Alexis Lamseh Looky
Secretary General: Michel Kwame
    Meyisso
Offices: c/o Chambre de Commerce,
    d'Agriculture et d'Industrie de
    Togo
    Angle av. de la Présidence et
    av. Georges Pompidou
    B.P. 360 – Lomé
Tel: (228) 21 20 65 / 21 70 65
Fax: (228) 21 47 30

Tunisia
Chair: Hédi Djilani
Secretary General: Moncef Kooli
Offices: 1, rue des Entrepreneurs –
    1000 Tunis
Tel: (216-1) 341 607 / 242 810
Fax: (216-1) 332 968

Turkey
Chair: E. Fuat Miras
Executive Director: Demet Ariyak
Offices: Atatürk Bulvari N°149
    06640 Bakanliklar – Ankara
Tel: (90-312) 417 87 33
Fax: (90-312) 417 14 83
E-mail: icc-tr@info.tobb.org.tr

United Kingdom
Chair: Patrick J. Gillam
Director: Richard C.I. Bate
Offices: 14/15, Belgrave Square
    London SW1X 8PS
Tel: (44-171) 823 2811
Fax: (44-171) 235 5447
E-mail:
    106142.2273@compuserve.com

United States
(US Council for International
    Business-USCIB)
Chair: Richard D. McCormick
President: Abraham Katz
Offices: 1212 Avenue of the
    Americas
    New York, NY 10036
Tel: (1-212) 354 4480
Fax: (1-212) 575 0327
Website: www.uscib.org
E-mail: info@uscib.org

Uruguay
Chair: Ambrosio Bertolotti
Secretary General: Gustavo Vilaró
    Sanguinetti
Offices: c/o Cámara Nacional de
    Comercio
    Rincón 454, 2° piso
    Casillo de Correo 1000 –
    Montevideo
Tel: (598-2) 916 12 77
Fax: (598-2) 916 12 43
E-mail: canadece@adlnet.com.vy

Venezuela
(Under reorganization)

Yugoslavia
(Fed. Republic)
Chair: Mihailo Milojevic
Secretary General: Petar Stankovic
Offices: Knez Milhajlova, 10 –
    11000 Beograd
Tel: (381-11) 633 144 / 184 144
Fax: (381-11) 3248 754 / 3225 903

*Chinese Taipai Business Council of
    the ICC*
Chair: Jeffrey L.S. Koo
Secretary General: Shin-Yuan Lai
Offices: 13th Floor; 390 Fu Hsing
    South Road
    Section 1, Taipai 10640 – Taiwan
Tel: (886-2) 707 01 11
Fax: (886-2) 701 76 01
E-mail: cnaic@mail.tpe.wownet.net

Appendix 4(a)

ICC Court Secretariat

November 1997

Amended ICC Rules of Arbitration in Force
As from 1 January 1998

To: 1) All parties, counsel and arbitrators involved in ICC arbitration proceedings
2) Entities and persons engaged in international commerce

This letter will inform you of limited but significant amendments to the ICC
Rules of Arbitration and its Appendixes, which will enter into force on *1
January 1998*. The amended ICC Rules of Arbitration are hereafter referred to
as the "1998 Rules". The Appendixes thereof are hearafter collectively designated as "New Appendixes" and individually as "New Appendix".

The New Appendixes in part reflect the innovations introduced by the 1998 Rules
and also incorporate certain rules based on the practices of the International
Court of Arbitration for the International Chamber of Commerce (the "Court")
or of its Secretariat ("the Secretariat") or the latter's notes issued to users and
arbitrators. However, certain provisions previously found in Appendixes to the
old rules have now become part of the 1998 Rules.

To reflect properly the separation and independence of the ICC arbitration
system and ICC conciliation, New Appendix III to the 1998 Rules no longer
covers cost or fee issues concerning ICC conciliation. The ICC Conciliation
Rules – which have not been modified – now have a separate Appendix dealing
with ICC Conciliation fees and costs. Also, the standard ICC arbitration clause
has been modified to refer exclusively to ICC arbitration, as follows:

> "All disputes arising out of or in connection with the present contract
> shall be finally settled under the Rules of Arbitration of the International
> Chamber of Commerce by one or more arbitrators appointed in accor-
> dance with the said Rules".

The amendments do not alter the basic system of ICC arbitration, with its unique
features specifically designed to meet the needs of business arbitration, but rather are aimed at further increasing the efficiency and effectiveness of ICC arbitration by, *inter alia*:

1. Reducing delays by

(i)   vesting the Secretary General with the power to transmit the file to the
Arbitral Tribunal, as soon as it has been constituted, once the claimant has paid an

advance on costs which shall be fixed by the Secretary General on the basis of the amount of the claimant's claim in order to cover fees, expenses of the arbitrators and the fees for administration of the arbitration by the Court until the Terms of Reference have been drawn up (arts. 13, 30(1), 1998 Rules; art. 1(2) of New Appendix III). Under old rules, the transmission of the file to the Arbitral Tribunal was only possible after the Court had fixed a global advance for costs calculated on all the claims and counterclaims involved in the arbitration, the defendant party had been given the opportunity to pay for its share of such costs and, had he failed to do so, the claimant had paid for both such share and his. Under the 1998 Rules, the Court shall fix as soon as practicable such global advance (art. 30(2)); however the transmission of the file to the Arbitral Tribunal will not depend on such payment when the Secretary General has fixed a provisional advance under article 30(1) of the 1998 Rules and such advance has been paid;

(ii)   authorizing the Secretary General to confirm party-nominated arbitrators, sole arbitrators or chairmen of arbitral tribunals having filed an unqualified statement of independence or, if qualified, if the qualifications have not raised objections to such arbitrator's confirmation (art. 9(2), 1998 Rules). In such cases, it is no longer necessary to have the Court decide on such confirmation;

(iii)   detaching the effectiveness of the Terms of Reference from the payment of the global advance on costs. However, the Secretary General, having consulted with the Arbitral Tribunal, may set a time limit of not less than 15 days for the payment of any pending portion of the global cost advance, during which the Arbitral Tribunal will be requested by the Secretary General to suspend work in respect of the relevant claims or counterclaims, which shall be considered as withdrawn if such payment is not timely made (art. 30(4), 1998 Rules; art. 1(3), New Appendix III); and

(iv)   facilitating fast-track arbitrations by expressly permitting the parties to shorten procedural delays under the 1998 Rules in order to expedite arbitral proceedings. However, the Court may extend such delays when their shortening by the parties would hamper the proper handling of the reference by the Arbitral Tribunal or the Court (art. 32, 1998 Rules).

2.   Enhancing the flexibility and transparency of the ICC arbitration system by

(i)   authorizing the Arbitral Tribunal not to list in the Terms of Reference the issues to be determined if the listing of such issues is considered inappropriate (art. 18(1) (d), 1998 Rules);

(ii)   eliminating the requirement that Terms of Reference not having been signed by a party but approved by the Court become effective only after the expiration of a delay for such party to sign the Terms of Reference;

(iii) vesting the Arbitral Tribunal with the power to admit new claims or counterclaims not included in the Terms of Reference even if objected to by a party. It is no longer required to incorporate new claims or counterclaims admitted after the Terms of Reference into a rider to be communicated to the Court (art. 19, 1998 Rules); and

(iv) when an arbitrator is challenged, providing that comments from such arbitrator, the other arbitral panel members and the parties on the challenge shall be communicated to all arbitrators and parties involved in the arbitration in order to permit maximum transparency of challenge proceedings (art. 11(3), 1998 Rules). A similar principle applies when an arbitrator is replaced by the Court (art. 12(3) 1998 Rules).

3. Filling gaps existing in the old rules by

(i) incorporating a provision (art. 10, 1998 Rules) dealing with the constitution of Arbitral Tribunals in multiple-party arbitration scenarios, which may arise in case of arbitrations with more than two parties;

(ii) permitting to overcome deadlock situations in which an arbitrator has died or been removed by vesting the Court with the power, once the arbitral proceedings have been declared as closed by the Arbitral Tribunal, to authorize the remaining arbitrators to continue deliberations and make the award (art. 12(5), 1998 Rules);

(iii) incorporating a new provision (art. 29, 1998 Rules) whereby the Arbitral Tribunal, at its own initiative or at the request of a party, may correct any clerical or mathematical errors contained in the award. Under this same provision, at the request of a party, an Arbitral Tribunal may also interpret its award; and

(iv) introducing a provision excluding the liability of arbitrators, the Court, the ICC and its employees and of ICC National Committees for any act or omission in connection with an arbitration (art. 34, 1998 Rules).

4. Furthering the organization of arbitral proceedings by the arbitrators and the parties in order to expedite the conduct of ICC arbitrations in compliance with the requirement set forth in article 15(2), 1998 Rules, that the Arbitral Tribunal "... act fairly and impartially and ensure that each party has a reasonable opportunity to present its case" by

(i) providing that the Arbitral Tribunal shall, after having consulted with the parties, establish a provisional timetable that it intends to follow in the conduct of the arbitration, which shall be communicated to the Court and the parties (art. 18(4), 1998 Rules); and

(ii)   providing that after being satisfied that the parties have had a reasonable opportunity to present their case, the Arbitral Tribunal shall declare the proceedings closed and shall indicate to the Secretariat the approximate date by which the draft award shall be submitted to the Court for scrutiny. After such declaration, the parties may not make any further submissions, produce any evidence or advance any argument unless requested or authorized by the Arbitral Tribunal (art. 22, 1998 Rules).

The above only highlights the major, but not all, modifications introduced by the 1998 Rules and should not be considered as an exhaustive description of the said Rules.

The 1998 Rules will govern ICC arbitrations which commence on or after 1 January 1998. Before such date, parties may also agree to have the 1998 Rules govern ICC arbitrations they intend to initiate prior thereto. After such date, but not later than on the date of the respective terms of reference, the parties may agree that ICC arbitrations commenced before 1 January 1998 shall be governed by the 1998 Rules. The parties may also agree to submit to the ICC Rules of arbitration in effect on the date of their arbitration agreement (art. 6(1), 1998 Rules). The new fee scales incorporated into New Appendix III and the advance payment of US$ 2500 corresponding to administrative fees to be made together with the filing of the arbitration request shall be effective as of 1 January 1998 in respect of all arbitrations commenced on or after such date and irrespective of the version of the ICC Rules applying to the arbitration (arts. 1(1), 4(1), New Appendix III).

International arbitration has become the preferred method of resolving international commercial disputes. With over 9500 cases submitted to it since its establishment in 1923, and hundreds of new cases submitted every year, the ICC International Court of Arbitration has a privileged position to observe developments in international arbitration.

As an expression of continuous efforts to improve ICC arbitration, the 1998 Rules provide international business actors with an arbitration system fully able to meet their needs, even as these needs change in the face of relentless evolution in both international commerce and international arbitration. This is perhaps one of the reasons accounting for substantial voluntary compliance with ICC awards and their enforcement by national courts despite the opposition of recalcitrant parties.

Enclosed herewith is a publication containing the ICC Conciliation Rules and the 1998 Rules of Arbitration in English/French.

Should you have any questions or comments regarding the meaning or application of the amended Rules or other points relating to ICC Arbitration, please do not hesitate to contact the Secretariat of the Court.

The publication containing the ICC Conciliation Rules and the 1998 Rules of Arbitration is currently available in English and French. During 1998 it will become available in Arabic, Chinese, German, Italian, Spanish and other languages. Should you wish to receive the publication in a language other than English or French, please contact the Secretariat of the Court and the publication will be sent to you as soon as it is available. You can also consult our website (www.iccwbo.org) from which you can download both the English and French versions of the 1998 Rules.

Please also advise us if there are any corrections to be made in your mailing address.

Sincerely yours,
Horacio A. Grigera Naón
Secretary General of the International Court of Arbitration

Encl. 1

Appendix 4(b)

ICC COURT SECRETARIAT

October 1, 1995

NOTE CONCERNING THE APPOINTMENT OF ADMINISTRATIVE SECRETARIES BY
ARBITRAL TRIBUNALS

The ICC Rules of Arbitration do not contain any provisions concerning the appointment of administrative secretaries by arbitral tribunals. Arbitral tribunals do, however, occasionally wish to have the assistance of such a person to assist them with the administrative tasks of the tribunal.

This Note, which replaces the Secretariat's earlier Note on this subject, is intended to set forth the policies and practices of the ICC Court in respect of the use by arbitral tribunals of administrative secretaries.

APPOINTMENT

The arbitral tribunal may appoint an administrative secretary, but only if no party has an objection and the secretary's tasks do not exceed those described in this Note. Prior to making any such appointment, the arbitral tribunal must advise the parties of the person whom it wishes to appoint after having verified that such person satisfies the same requirements of *independence* as are laid down in the Rules for the arbitrators. The arbitral tribunal must also advise the parties of the *tasks* that the administrative secretary is to carry out. The arbitral tribunal shall immediately inform the Secretariat in writing of the appointment of an administrative secretary.

COST

The arbitral tribunal should inform the Secretariat and the parties as early as possible of the estimated *cost* of the administrative secretary so that this may be taken into account when the Court fixes the advance on costs for the arbitration.

It shall normally be the arbitral tribunal's responsibility, however, to pay the administrative secretary out *of the fees* awarded to the arbitrators by the Court, the amount of which shall be solely for the Court to decide in accordance with Article 20.2 of the ICC Rules. The fees of the administrative secretary shall therefore not normally be treated as expenses of the arbitral tribunal, although reasonable expenses of the administrative secretary *(e.g.,* for travel) shall be reimbursable as such.

In deciding upon the amount of the arbitrators' fees when an administrative secretary has been appointed, the Court will normally be concerned to ensure that the engagement of such person does not increase the cost of the arbitration to the parties. Indeed, the scale of arbitrators' fees set forth in Appendix III to the ICC Rules is intended to cover the arbitral tribunal's normal cost of carrying out the administrative tasks associated with the performance of the arbitral tribunal's work, with the exception of out-of-pocket disbursements *(e.g.,* for telephone, telefax, postage, special courier, photocopying and travel).

Arbitrators wishing to appoint an administrative secretary should therefore not normally assume that the fees awarded to them, after deduction of any amounts payable to the administrative secretary, will be equivalent to those that they might have received if they were not so assisted.

The Court can, however, be expected to take into account exceptional circumstances that may warrant greater compensation in some cases.

DUTIES

The duties of the administrative secretary must be strictly limited to *administrative tasks.* The choice of this person is important. Such person must not influence in any manner whatsoever the decisions of the arbitral tribunal.

In particular, the administrative secretary must not assume the functions of an arbitrator, notably by becoming involved in the decision-making process of the tribunal or expressing opinions or conclusions with respect to the issues in dispute.

The Chairman of the arbitral tribunal or the sole arbitrator, as the case may be, bears full *responsibility* for the behaviour and activities of the administrative secretary, and the ICC Court cannot in any case be held responsible for the payment of such secretary's social security charges or taxes or for other obligations or any errors committed by such person.

Appendix 4(c)

ICC COURT SECRETARIAT

January 1, 1993

Revised notice to the arbitrators:

PERSONAL AND ARBITRAL TRIBUNAL EXPENSES
(This replaces the notice, dated November 10, 1990)

Please be advised that an arbitrator's personal expenses and expenses of the arbitral tribunal which are incurred on or after January 1, 1993 will be reimbursed by the Secretariat of the ICC International Court of Arbitration from the advance on costs made by the parties on the following basis:

1. A flat US$ 400 *per diem* allowance is to be paid to an arbitrator for each day and night that the arbitrator is required to spend on ICC arbitration business out of his or her town of residence if hotel accommodations for the night are utilized.

2. Alternatively, a *per diem* allowance *up to* a maximum of US$ 500 is to be paid for each day and night the arbitrator is required to spend on ICC arbitration business out of his or her town of residence, during which period hotel accommodations for the night are utilized, *provided all expenses are justified by invoices* or *receipts* and subject to point 4 below.

3. A flat US$ 165 *per diem* allowance for each day the arbitrator spends on ICC arbitration business out of his or her town of residence, during which period hotel accommodations for the night are *not* utilized.

4. Expenses to be covered by the *per diem* allowance are those directly related to out-of-pocket personal living expenses, that is:
   - Hotel accommodations (except under point 3 above)
   - Meals/Snacks
   - Laundry/Pressing
   - Inner-city transport (including taxis)
   - Telephone calls, telefacsimiles or other communications
   - Tips.

Expenses may *not* include such items as entertainment (theater tickets, etc.), luxury restaurants or accompanying guests, nor payment of covered items for another arbitrator receiving an ICC *per diem.* In addition, only limited and reasonable telephone, telefacsimile or other communications charges may be included.

5. As the *per diem* allowance (whether a flat rate or a higher allowance justified by invoices or receipts) is considered as covering all items listed in point 4 above, these items cannot be taken into consideration in addition to the *per diem* rate.

6. An arbitrator may be reimbursed for actual expenses (justified by invoices or receipts) for meals and inner-city transport incurred *within* his or her town of residence which are directly related to the ICC arbitration in question, subject to the limitations described in point 4 above, to the extent relevant.

7. If required to travel for the purpose of an ICC arbitration, an arbitrator will be reimbursed for his or her actual cost of transportation, as justified by invoices and/or ticket stubs, provided that the amount of the reimbursable costs shall not exceed the relevant business class air fare in the case of flights of up to six hours. The cost of first class air travel will be reimbursable for longer flights. In addition, taxi fares for transportation to and from the airport will be reimbursed.

8. All expenses related to tribunal activities such as clerical secretary (typist), equipment, telex, telefacsimiles, phone calls, meeting room reservations, etc. are to be paid under "tribunal arbitration expenses" and *not* to be imputed to *"per diem"* living expenses

9. Arbitrators may request advance payment on *per diem* allowances and transportation costs, but must submit afterwards pertinent supporting documentation, including transportation tickets and a statement of working days and nights spent out of town on arbitration business.

10. Requests for reimbursement of tribunal expenses and *per diem* allowances must be presented to the Secretariat in a readily comprehensible form both in order to permit the Secretariat to carry out its accounting responsibilities and because the parties occasionally request the Secretariat to provide them with a statement of the expenses incurred by the arbitral tribunal.

11. In order to ensure that the advance on costs made by the parties is adequate to meet the costs of the arbitration, arbitrators are urged to submit to the Secretariat their requests for reimbursement of tribunal expenses and *per diem* allowances, together with any required justifications, on a continuous basis as such expenses are incurred. *All* requests for reimbursement *of tribunal expenses and per diem allowances relating to the period prior and up to the submission of the draft award* are due at the latest along with the submission of such draft to the Secretariat. *After this date no further requests for reimbursements of such expenses and allowances can be taken into consideration.*
    Where there is a three-member tribunal, the coarbitrators and the chairman should co-ordinate their submission of bills of tribunal expenses and *per diem* allowances in order to ensure that they reach the Secretariat no later than the draft of the final award

Appendix 5

Case no. _____

ARBITRATOR'S DECLARATION OF ACCEPTANCE AND STATEMENT OF
INDEPENDENCE*

I, the undersigned,

Name _____   First Name _____

❏ hereby declare that *I accept* to serve as arbitrator under the ICC Rules of
Arbitration in the instant case. In so declaring, I confirm that I have familiar-
ized myself with the requirements of the ICC Rules of Arbitration and am able
and available to serve as an arbitrator in accordance with all of the requirements of those Rules and accept to be remunerated in accordance therewith.

*(If this box is checked, please also check one of the two following boxes. The
choice of which box to check will be determined after you have taken into
account, inter alia, whether there exists any past or present relationship,
direct or indirect, with any of the parties, their counsel, whether financial,
professional or of another kind and whether the nature of any such relationship is such that disclosure is called for pursuant to the criteria set out below.
Any doubt should be resolved in favor of disclosure.)*

❏ I am independent of each of the parties and intend to remain so; to the best
of my knowledge, there are no facts or circumstances, past or present, that
need be disclosed because they might be of such nature as to call into question my independence in the eyes of any of the parties.

❏ I am independent of each of the parties and intend to remain so; however, in
consideration of Article 7, paragraph 2 & 3 of the ICC Rules of Arbitration**,
I wish to call your attention to the following facts or circumstances which I

---

* Please mark the relevant box or boxes.

** Article 7 (2):
"Before appointment or confirmation, a prospective arbitrator shall sign a statement of independence and disclose in writing to the Secretariat any facts or circumstances which might be
of such a nature as to call into question the arbitrator's independence in the eyes of the parties. The Secretariat shall provide such information to the parties in writing and fix a time
limit for any comments from them.
** Article 7 (3)
An arbitrator shall immediately disclose in writing to the Secretariat and to the parties any
facts or circumstances of a similar nature which may arise during the arbitration."

hereafter disclose because they might be of such a nature as to call into question my independence in the eyes of any of the parties. (Use separate sheet if necessary.)

❏ hereby declare that *I decline* to serve as arbitrator in the subject case. (If you wish to state the reasons for checking this box, please do so.)

Place: _____ Date: _____ Signature: _____

Appendix 6

ICC ARBITRATION STATISTICS FOR 1997

Number of Requests for Arbitration				
Year	*Number*	*Year*	*Number*	
1980	250	1990	365	
1981	262	1991	333	
1982	267	1992	337	
1983	291	1993	352	
1984	296	1994	384	
1985	339	1995	427	
1986	334	1996	433	
1987	285	1997	452	
1988	304			
1989	309			

Amounts in Dispute in new cases set in motion in 1997

Amount in US$	% of Cases
Over 1 BIL	0%
100 MIL - 1 BIL	2.2%
50 MIL - 100 MIL	2.2%
10 MIL - 50 MIL	11.4%
1 MIL - 10 MIL	32.1%
500,000 - 1 MIL	7.7%
200,000 - 500,000	11.2%
50,000 - 200,000	15.9%
under 50,000	2.9%
Not quantified	14.4%
TOTAL	100%

Status of Arbitrations

	1992	*1993*	*1994*	*1995*	*1996*	*1997*
Requests for arbitration filed	337	352	384	427	433	452
Cases set in motion by the ICC Court	257	287	277	368	370	376
Cases withdrawn	179	180	182	216	220	–
– Prior to the communication of the file to the Arbitral Tribunal	108	128	116	140	147	–
– After communication of the file to the Arbitral Tribunal and before the Terms of Reference have become operative	46	29	40	55	59	–
– After the Terms of Reference have become operative and before the final award	25	23	26	21	14	–
Awards by consent	22	18	20	20	19	33
Final awards	116	112	123	140	166	169
Cases pending as of December 31	745	764	801	855	881	935

Places of Arbitration
Fixed by the parties or the Court in 1997 (Number of selections)

	Agreed by the Parties	*Decided by the Court*	*TOTAL*	*%*
Argentina	2	0	2	0.54%
Australia	1	0	1	0.27%
Austria	12	1	13	3.49%
Bahrain	1	0	1	0.27%
Belgium	3	0	3	0.80%
Canada	5	1	6	1.61%
Denmark	0	1	1	0.27%
Ecuador	1	0	1	0.27%
France	90	20*	110	29.49%
Germany	7	1	8	2.14%
Hong Kong	6	0	6	1.61%
India	6	0	6	1.61%
Indonesia	2	0	2	0.54%
Ireland	0	1	1	0.27%
Italy	3	3	6	1.61%
Japan	1	1	2	0.54%
Korea Rep. of	2	0	2	0.54%
Luxembourg	1	4	5	1.34%
Mexico	1	1	2	0.27%
Netherlands	4	1	5	1.34%
Norway	1	0	1	0.27%
Pakistan	1	1	2	0.54%
Portugal	1	0	1	0.27%
Romania	1	0	1	0.27%
Saudi Arabia	1	0	1	0.27%
Singapore	10	2	12	3.22%
Spain	3	0	3	0.80%
Sri Lanka	1	0	1	0.27%
Sweden	9	1	10	2.68%
Switzerland	67	10	77	20.64%
Turkey	1	0	1	0.27%
U.A.E.	1	0	1	0.27%
United Kingdom	37	4	41	10.99%
U.S.A.	35	2	37	9.92%
Vanuatu	1	0	1	0.27%
TOTAL	*318*	*55*	*373*	
%	*85.25%*	*14.75%*	*(100.00%)*	

*   In 15 cases, the Court decided that Paris was the place of arbitration where there was disagreement of the parties concerning the interpretation of clauses providing for "ICC arbitration in Paris," "of Paris," *etc. See supra*, notes 418-19, and accompanying text.

Origins of Arbitrators
Confirmed in 1997

	Co-Arbitrators	Sole Arbitrators/ Chairmen	TOTAL
Algeria	4	0	4
Angola	1	0	1
Argentina	4	0	4
Australia	4	3	7
Austria	11	20	31
Bahrain	1	0	1
Bangladesh	1	0	1
Belarus	1	0	1
Belgium	6	17	23
Benin	1	0	1
Bulgaria	1	0	1
Canada	16	23	39
China	2	0	2
Colombia	0	1	1
Czech Rep.	1	0	1
Denmark	2	2	4
Ecuador	1	0	1
Egypt	5	0	5
Ethiopia	2	0	2
Finland	0	3	3
France	47	45	92
Germany	21	24	45
Greece	5	1	6
Hungary	2	1	3
India	8	4	12
Indonesia	1	0	1
Iran	2	0	2
Ireland	2	4	6
Israel	1	1	2
Italy	N/A	N/A	40
Japan	2	2	4
Kuwait	0	1	1
Latvia	1	0	1
Lebanon	1	1	2
Luxembourg	0	1	1
Malaysia	0	1	1
Mexico	2	6	8
Morocco	2	0	2
Netherlands	7	8	15
New Zealand	1	1	2

Origins of Arbitrators
Continued

	Co-Arbitrators	Sole Arbitrators/ Chairmen	TOTAL
Norway	0	2	2
Panama	0	1	1
Peru	0	1	1
Philippines	1	0	1
Portugal	2	2	4
Romania	4	1	5
Russian Fed.	5	0	5
Saudi Arabia	1	0	1
Senegal	1	0	1
Singapore	3	5	8
Slovenia	1	0	1
South Africa	1	0	1
Spain	5	3	8
Sweden	5	10	15
Switzerland	46	75	121
Taiwan	0	1	1
Tunisia	N/A	N/A	2
Turkey	5	1	6
United Kingdom	46	50	96
Uruguay	1	0	1
U.S.A.	56	24	80
Yugoslavia	4	1	5
TOTAL			745

Number of Arbitrators (in cases submitted to the ICC Court in 1997)

	Sole Arbitrator		Three Arbitrators	
Contained in contractual provisions	43	(11.5%)	114	(30.4%)
By parties' subsequent agreement	63	(16.8%)	61	(16.3%)
By ICC Court's decisions	74	(19.7%)	20	(5.3%)
TOTAL	180	(48.0%)	195	(52.0%)

Origins of Parties
in cases submitted to the ICC in 1997

Western Europe

	Claimant	Respondent	TOTAL	% of all
Andorra	1	0	1	0.08%
Austria	10	8	18	1.40%
Belgium	13	13	26	2.02%
Cyprus	2	2	4	0.31%
Denmark	10	2	12	0.93%
Finland	5	5	10	0.78%
France	94	60	154	11.94%
Germany	38	44	82	6.36%
Gibraltar	0	1	1	0.08%
Greece	7	6	13	1.01%
Iceland	0	1	1	0.08%
Ireland	4	3	7	0.54%
Italy	32	24	56	4.34%
Liechtenstein	1	1	2	0.16%
Luxembourg	4	4	8	0.62%
Malta	0	1	1	0.08%
Netherlands	19	21	40	3.10%
Norway	5	8	13	1.01%
Portugal	3	2	5	0.39%
Spain	9	23	32	2.48%
Sweden	11	10	21	1.63%
Switzerland	22	16	38	2.95%
Turkey	6	9	15	1.16%
United Kingdom	34	43	77	5.97%
TOTAL	*330*	*307*	*637*	*49.38%*

Origins of Parties
Continued

Central and Eastern Europe

	Claimant	Respondent	TOTAL	% of all
Belarus	1	0	1	0.08%
Bosnia-Herzegovina	1	0	1	0.08%
Bulgaria	3	4	7	0.54%
Croatia	1	0	1	0.08%
Czech Rep.	2	12	14	1.09%
Hungary	2	7	9	0.70%
Kazakhstan	2	0	2	0.16%
Latvia	1	2	3	0.23%
Lithuania	0	1	1	0.08%
Poland	3	6	9	0.70%
Romania	9	5	14	1.09%
Russian Fed.	3	21	24	1.86%
Slovak Rep.	0	2	2	0.16%
Slovenia	1	2	3	0.23%
Turkmenistan	0	6	6	0.47%
Ukraine	0	2	2	0.16%
Yugoslavia	6	1	7	0.54%
TOTAL	*35*	*71*	*106*	*8.22%*

Middle East

	Claimant	Respondent	TOTAL	% of all
Iran	1	3	4	0.31%
Israel	3	2	5	0.39%
Jordan	0	4	4	0.31%
Kuwait	1	1	2	0.16%
Lebanon	1	3	4	0.31%
Oman	0	2	2	0.16%
Saudi Arabia	2	3	5	0.39%
Syria	1	1	2	0.16%
U.A.E.	5	3	8	0.62%
TOTAL	*14*	*22*	*36*	*2.79%*

Origins of Parties
Continued

North Africa

	Claimant	Respondent	TOTAL	% of all
Algeria	3	3	6	0.47%
Egypt	1	7	8	0.62%
Morocco	1	4	5	0.39%
Tunisia	1	3	4	0.31%
TOTAL	*6*	*17*	*23*	*1.78%*

Sub-Saharan Africa

	Claimant	Respondent	TOTAL	% of all
Angola	0	1	1	0.08%
Cameroon	0	1	1	0.08%
Ethiopia	1	2	3	0.23%
Gabon	2	0	2	0.16%
Guinea	0	1	1	0.08%
Ivory Coast	3	2	5	0.39%
Liberia	4	1	5	0.39%
Mali	0	1	1	0.08%
Mauritius	1	1	2	0.16%
Nigeria	1	1	2	0.16%
South Africa	1	3	4	0.31%
Uganda	1	2	3	0.23%
Zimbabwe	1	0	1	0.08%
TOTAL	*15*	*16*	*31*	*2.40%*

Origins of Parties
Continued

South Asia and Far East Asia

	Claimant	Respondent	TOTAL	% of all
China	6	11	17	1.32%
Hong Kong	10	5	15	1.16%
India	18	27	45	3.49%
Indonesia	3	5	8	0.62%
Japan	13	14	27	2.09%
Korea Rep. of	12	8	20	1.55%
Malaysia	1	14	15	1.16%
Pakistan	3	3	6	0.47%
Philippines	3	5	8	0.62%
Singapore	7	6	13	1.01%
Sri Lanka	2	3	5	0.39%
Taiwan	2	4	6	0.47%
Thailand	2	6	8	0.62%
Vietnam	0	2	2	0.16%
TOTAL	*82*	*113*	*195*	*15.12%*

Oceania

	Claimant	Respondent	TOTAL	% of all
Australia	6	11	17	1.32%
Cook Islands	1	0	1	0.08%
New Zealand	1	1	2	0.16%
Vanuatu	2	0	2	0.16%
TOTAL	*10*	*12*	*22*	*1.71%*

North America

	Claimant	Respondent	TOTAL	% of all
Canada	8	11	19	1.47
U.S.A.	47	67	114	8.84
TOTAL	*55*	*78*	*133*	*10.31%*

Origins of Parties
Continued

Latin America & Caribbean

	Claimant	Respondent	TOTAL	% of all
Argentina	7	8	15	1.16%
Bahamas	2	1	3	0.23%
Barbados	1	0	1	0.08%
Bermuda	1	2	3	0.23%
Brazil	3	9	12	0.93%
British Virgin Islands	2	1	3	0.23%
Cayman Islands	1	1	2	0.16%
Colombia	0	1	1	0.08%
Ecuador	1	2	3	0.23%
Guatemala	0	3	3	0.23%
Mexico	2	6	8	0.62%
Netherlands Antilles	0	2	2	0.16%
Panama	26	5	31	2.40%
Peru	1	1	2	0.16%
Puerto Rico	15	0	15	1.16%
Venezuela	0	3	3	0.23%
TOTAL	*62*	*45*	*107*	*8.29%*

ALL REGIONS

Claimant	Respondent	TOTAL	% of all
609	*681*	*1290*	*100%*

Appendix 7

ICC Rules of Arbitration
(in force as from January 1, 1998)

The ICC Rules set forth herein have been translated in many different languages. However, the English and French versions are the only authoritative texts.

Printed in August 1997
International Chamber of Commerce
38, Cours Albert 1er
75008 Paris – France
Tel: +33 1 49 53 28 28
Telefax: +33 1 49 53 29 33

ICC Publication N° 581
ISBN 98.842.1239.1

Foreword

During the last quarter of the twentieth century, international commercial arbitration has gained worldwide acceptance as the normal means of resolving international commercial disputes. National laws on arbitration have been modernised on all continents. International treaties on arbitration have been signed or adhered to with impressive success. Arbitration has become part of the curriculum of large numbers of law schools. With the gradual removal of political and trade barriers and the rapid globalisation of the world economy, new challenges have been created for arbitration institutions in response to the growing demand of parties for certainty and predictability, greater rapidity and flexibility as well as neutrality and efficacy in the resolution of international disputes. There has been a substantial increase not only in the number of cases, their complexity, the amounts in dispute and the diversity of the parties, but also in the demands made on the process by the parties.

Since the International Court of Arbitration was established in 1923, ICC arbitration has been constantly nourished by the experience gathered by the ICC International Court of Arbitration in the course of administering some ten thousand international arbitration cases, now involving each year parties and arbitrators from over 100 countries and from a diversity of legal, economic, cultural and linguistic backgrounds.

The present ICC Rules of Arbitration, in effect as of January 1, 1998, constitute the first major revision of the Rules in more than 20 years, following an intensive, worldwide consultation process. The changes made are designed to reduce delays and ambiguities and to fill certain gaps, taking into account the evolution of arbitration practice. The basic features of the ICC arbitration system have not been altered, however, notably its universality and flexibility, as well as the central role played by the International Court of Arbitration in the administration of arbitral cases.

Every ICC arbitration is conducted by an arbitral tribunal with responsibility for examining the merits of the case and rendering a final award. Each year, ICC arbitrations are held in some 40 countries, in several languages and with arbitrators of some 60 different nationalities. The work of those arbitral tribunals is monitored by the ICC International Court of Arbitration, which meets at least three (and often four) times a month all year round. Presently composed of some 65 members from over 55 countries, the Court's function is to organise and supervise arbitrations held under the ICC Rules of Arbitration. The Court must remain constantly alert to changes in the law and the practice of arbitration in all parts of the world and must adapt its working methods to the evolving needs of parties and arbitrators. For the day-to-day management of cases in several languages, the ICC Court is supported by a Secretariat based at the headquarters of the International Chamber of Commerce, in Paris.

Although the ICC Rules of Arbitration have been especially designed for arbitrations in an international context, they may also be used for non-international cases.

The ICC Rules of Optional Conciliation

The current ICC Rules of Conciliation entered into force on January 1, 1988. Conciliation is a process independent of arbitration. It remains entirely optional unless the parties have otherwise agreed. The ICC Rules of Arbitration do not require the parties to attempt conciliation prior to commencing an arbitration. So, too, the Rules permit conciliation to be attempted without requiring that the dispute be referred to arbitration thereafter if the conciliation effort is unsuccessful.

STANDARD ICC ARBITRATION CLAUSE

The ICC recommends that all parties wishing to make reference to ICC arbitration in their contracts use the following standard clause.

Parties are reminded that it may be desirable for them to stipulate in the arbitration clause itself the law governing the contract, the number of arbitrators and the place and language of the arbitration. The parties' free choice of the law governing the contract and of the place and language of the arbitration is not limited by the ICC Rules of Arbitration.

Attention is called to the fact that the laws of certain countries require that parties to contracts expressly accept arbitration clauses, sometimes in a precise and particular manner.

English

"All disputes arising out of or in connection with the present contract shall be finally settled under the Rules of Arbitration of the International Chamber of Commerce by one or more arbitrators appointed in accordance with the said Rules."

French

"Tous différends découlant du présent contrat ou en relation avec celui-ci seront tranchés définitivement suivant le Réglement d'Arbitrage de la Chambre de Commerce Internationale par un ou plusieurs arbitres nommés conformément à ce Réglement."

German

"Alle aus oder in Zusammenhang mit dem gegenwärtigen Vertrag sich ergebenden Streitigkeiten werden nach der Schiedsgerichtsordnung der Internationalen Handels-kammer von einem oder mehreren gemäß dieser Ordnung ernannten Schiedsrichtern endgültig entschieden."

Italian

"Tutte le controversie derivanti dal presente contratto o in relazione con lo stesso saranno risolte in via definitiva secondo il Regolamento d'arbitrato della Camera di Commercio Internazionale, da uno o più arbitri nominati in conformità di detto Regolamento."

Spanish

"Todas las desavenencias que deriven de este contrato o que guarden relación con éste serán resueltas definitivamente de acuerdo con el Reglamento de Arbitraje de la Cámara de Comercio Internacional por uno ó más árbitros nombrados conforme a este Reglamento."

RULES OF ARBITRATION OF THE INTERNATIONAL CHAMBER OF COMMERCE

INTRODUCTORY PROVISIONS

ARTICLE 1
International Court of Arbitration

1

The International Court of Arbitration (the "Court") of the International Chamber of Commerce (the "ICC") is the arbitration body attached to the ICC. The statutes of the Court are set forth in Appendix I. Members of the Court are appointed by the Council of the ICC. The function of the Court is to provide for the settlement by arbitration of business disputes of an international character in accordance with the Rules of Arbitration of the International Chamber of Commerce (the "Rules"). If so empowered by an arbitration agreement, the Court shall also provide for the settlement by arbitration in accordance with these Rules of business disputes not of an international character.

2

The Court does not itself settle disputes. It has the function of ensuring the application of these Rules. It draws up its own Internal Rules (Appendix II).

3

The Chairman of the Court, or, in the Chairman's absence or otherwise at his request, one of its Vice-Chairmen shall have the power to take urgent decisions on behalf of the Court, provided that any such decision is reported to the Court at its next session.

4

As provided for in its Internal Rules, the Court may delegate to one or more committees composed of its members the power to take certain decisions, provided that any such decision is reported to the Court at its next session.

5

The Secretariat of the Court (the "Secretariat") under the direction of its Secretary General (the "Secretary General") shall have its seat at the headquarters of the ICC.

ARTICLE 2
Definitions

In these Rules:
(i)   "Arbitral Tribunal" includes one or more arbitrators.
(ii) "Claimant" includes one or more claimants and "Respondent" includes one or more respondents.
(iii) "Award" includes, *inter alia*, an interim, partial or final Award.

ARTICLE 3
Written Notifications or Communications; Time Limits

1
All pleadings and other written communications submitted by any party, as well as all documents annexed thereto, shall be supplied in a number of copies sufficient to provide one copy for each party, plus one for each arbitrator, and one for the Secretariat. A copy of any communication from the Arbitral Tribunal to the parties shall be sent to the Secretariat.

2
All notifications or communications from the Secretariat and the Arbitral Tribunal shall be made to the last address of the party or its representative for whom the same are intended, as notified either by the party in question or by the other party. Such notification or communication may be made by delivery against receipt, registered post, courier, facsimile transmission, telex, telegram or any other means of telecommunication that provides a record of the sending thereof.

3
A notification or communication shall be deemed to have been made on the day it was received by the party itself or by its representative, or would have been received if made in accordance with the preceding paragraph.

4
Periods of time specified in, or fixed under the present Rules, shall start to run on the day following the date a notification or communication is deemed to have been made in accordance with the preceding paragraph. When the day next following such date is an official holiday, or a non-business day in the country where the notification or communication is deemed to have been made, the period of time shall commence on the first following business day. Official holidays and non-business days are included in the calculation of the period of time. If the last day of the relevant period of time granted is an official holiday or a non-business day in the country where the notification or communication is deemed to have been made, the period of time shall expire at the end of the first following business day.

COMMENCING THE ARBITRATION

ARTICLE 4
Request for Arbitration

1

A party wishing to have recourse to arbitration under these Rules shall submit its Request for Arbitration (the "Request") to the Secretariat, which shall notify the Claimant and Respondent of the receipt of the Request and the date of such receipt.

2

The date on which the Request is received by the Secretariat shall, for all purposes, be deemed to be the date of the commencement of the arbitral proceedings.

3

The Request shall, *inter alia,* contain the following information:
a) the name in full, description and address of each of the parties;
b) a description of the nature and circumstances of the dispute giving rise to the claims;
c) a statement of the relief sought, including, to the extent possible, an indication of any amount(s) claimed;
d) the relevant agreements and, in particular, the arbitration agreement;
e) all relevant particulars concerning the number of arbitrators and their choice in accordance with the provisions of Articles 8, 9 and 10, and any nomination of an arbitrator required thereby; and
f) any comments as to the place of arbitration, the applicable rules of law and the language of the arbitration.

4

Together with the Request, the Claimant shall submit the number of copies thereof required by Article 3(1) and shall make the advance payment on administrative expenses required by Appendix III ("Arbitration Costs and Fees") in force on the date the Request is submitted. In the event that the Claimant fails to comply with either of these requirements, the Secretariat may fix a time limit within which the Claimant must comply, failing which the file shall be closed without prejudice to the right of the Claimant to submit the same claims at a later date in another Request.

5

The Secretariat shall send a copy of the Request and the documents annexed thereto to the Respondent for its Answer to the Request once the Secretariat has sufficient copies of the Request and the required advance payment.

6

When a party submits a Request in connection with a legal relationship in respect of which arbitration proceedings between the same parties are already pending under these Rules, the Court may, at the request of a party, decide to include the claims contained in the Request in the pending proceedings provided that the Terms of Reference have not been signed or approved by the Court. Once the Terms of Reference have been signed or approved by the Court, claims may only be included in the pending proceedings subject to the provisions of Article 19.

ARTICLE 5

Answer to the Request; Counterclaims

1

Within 30 days from the receipt of the Request from the Secretariat, the Respondent shall file an Answer (the "Answer") which shall, *inter alia,* contain the following information:

a) its name in full, description and address;
b) its comments as to the nature and circumstances of the dispute giving rise to the claim(s);
c) its response to the relief sought;
d) any comments concerning the number of arbitrators and their choice in light of the Claimant's proposals and in accordance with the provisions of Articles 8, 9 and 10, and any nomination of an arbitrator required thereby; and
e) any comments as to the place of arbitration, the applicable rules of law and the language of the arbitration.

2

The Secretariat may grant the Respondent an extension of the time for filing the Answer, provided the application for such an extension contains the Respondent's comments concerning the number of arbitrators and their choice, and, where required by Articles 8, 9 and 10, the nomination of an arbitrator. If the Respondent fails to do so, the Court shall proceed in accordance with these Rules.

3

The Answer shall be supplied to the Secretariat in the number of copies specified by Article 3(1).

4

A copy of the Answer and the documents annexed thereto shall be communicated by the Secretariat to the Claimant.

5

Any counterclaim(s) made by the Respondent shall be filed with its Answer and shall provide :

a) a description of the nature and circumstances of the dispute giving rise to the counterclaim(s); and

b) a statement of the relief sought, including, to the extent possible, an indication of any amount(s) counter-claimed.

6

The Claimant shall file a Reply to any counterclaim within 30 days from the date of receipt of the counterclaim(s) communicated by the Secretariat. The Secretariat may grant the Claimant an extension of time for filing the Reply.

ARTICLE 6
Effect of the Arbitration Agreement

1

Where the parties have agreed to submit to arbitration under the Rules, they shall be deemed to have submitted *ipso facto* to the Rules in effect on the date of commencement of the arbitration proceedings unless they have agreed to submit to the Rules in effect on the date of their arbitration agreement.

2

If the Respondent does not file an Answer, as provided by Article 5, or if any party raises one or more pleas concerning the existence, validity or scope of the arbitration agreement, the Court may decide, without prejudice to the admissibility or merits of the plea or pleas, that the arbitration shall proceed if it is *prima facie* satisfied that an arbitration agreement under the Rules may exist. In such a case, any decision as to the jurisdiction of the Arbitral Tribunal shall be taken by the Arbitral Tribunal itself. If the Court is not so satisfied, the parties shall be notified that the arbitration cannot proceed. In such a case, any party retains the right to ask any court having jurisdiction whether or not there is a binding arbitration agreement.

3

If any of the parties refuses or fails to take part in the arbitration or any stage thereof, the arbitration shall proceed notwithstanding such refusal or failure.

4

Unless otherwise agreed, the Arbitral Tribunal shall not cease to have jurisdiction by reason of any claim that the contract is null and void or allegation that it is non-existent provided that the Arbitral Tribunal upholds the validity of the arbitration agreement. The Arbitral Tribunal shall continue to have jurisdiction to determine the respective rights of the parties and to adjudicate their claims and pleas even though the contract itself may be non-existent or null and void.

THE ARBITRAL TRIBUNAL

ARTICLE 7
General Provisions

1

Every arbitrator must be and remain independent of the parties involved in the arbitration.

2

Before appointment or confirmation, a prospective arbitrator shall sign a statement of independence and disclose in writing to the Secretariat any facts or circumstances which might be of such a nature as to call into question the arbitrator's independence in the eyes of the parties. The Secretariat shall provide such information to the parties in writing and fix a time limit for any comments from them.

3

An arbitrator shall immediately disclose in writing to the Secretariat and to the parties any facts or circumstances of a similar nature which may arise during the arbitration.

4

The decisions of the Court as to the appointment, confirmation, challenge or replacement of an arbitrator shall be final and the reasons for such decisions shall not be communicated.

5

By accepting to serve, every arbitrator undertakes to carry out his responsibilities in accordance with these Rules.

6

Insofar as the parties have not provided otherwise, the Arbitral Tribunal shall be constituted in accordance with the provisions of Articles 8, 9 and 10.

ARTICLE 8
Number of Arbitrators

1

The disputes shall be decided by a sole arbitrator or by three arbitrators.

2

Where the parties have not agreed upon the number of arbitrators, the Court shall appoint a sole arbitrator, save where it appears to the Court that the dispute is such as to warrant the appointment of three arbitrators. In such case, the Claimant shall nominate an arbitrator within a period of 15 days from the receipt of the notification of the decision of the Court, and the Respondent shall nominate an arbitrator within a period of 15 days from the receipt of the notification of the nomination made by the Claimant.

3

Where the parties have agreed that the dispute shall be settled by a sole arbitrator, they may, by agreement, nominate the sole arbitrator for confirmation. If the parties fail to nominate a sole arbitrator within 30 days from the date when the Claimant's Request for Arbitration has been received by the other party, or within such additional time as may be allowed by the Secretariat, the sole arbitrator shall be appointed by the Court.

4

Where the dispute is to be referred to three arbitrators, each party shall nominate in the Request and the Answer, respectively, one arbitrator for confirmation by the Court. If a party fails to nominate an arbitrator, the appointment shall be made by the Court. The third arbitrator, who will act as chairman of the Arbitral Tribunal, shall be appointed by the Court, unless the parties have agreed upon another procedure for such appointment, in which case the nomination will be subject to confirmation pursuant to Article 9. Should such procedure not result in a nomination within the time limit fixed by the parties or the Court, the third arbitrator shall be appointed by the Court.

ARTICLE 9

Appointment and Confirmation of the Arbitrators

1

In confirming or appointing arbitrators, the Court shall consider the prospective arbitrator's nationality, residence and other relationships with the countries of which the parties or the other arbitrators are nationals and the prospective arbitrator's availability and ability to conduct the arbitration in accordance with these Rules. The same shall apply where the Secretary General confirms arbitrators pursuant to Article 9(2).

2

The Secretary General may confirm as co-arbitrators, sole arbitrators and chairmen of Arbitral Tribunals persons nominated by the parties or pursuant to their particular agreements, provided they have filed a statement of independence without qualification or a qualified statement of independence has not given rise to objections. Such confirmation shall be reported to the Court at its next session. If the Secretary General considers that a co-arbitrator, sole arbitrator or chairman of an Arbitral Tribunal should not be confirmed, the matter shall be submitted to the Court.

3
Where the Court is to appoint a sole arbitrator or the chairman of an Arbitral Tribunal, it shall make the appointment upon a proposal of a National Committee of the ICC that it considers to be appropriate. If the Court does not accept the proposal made, or if the National Committee fails to make the proposal requested within the time limit fixed by the Court, the Court may repeat its request or may request a proposal from another National Committee that it considers to be appropriate.

4
Where the Court considers that the circumstances so demand, it may choose the sole arbitrator or the chairman of the Arbitral Tribunal from a country where there is no National Committee, provided that neither of the parties objects within the time limit fixed by the Court.

5
The sole arbitrator or the chairman of the Arbitral Tribunal shall be of a nationality other than those of the parties. However, in suitable circumstances and provided that neither of the parties objects within the time limit fixed by the Court, the sole arbitrator or the chairman of the Arbitral Tribunal may be chosen from a country of which any of the parties is a national.

6
Where the Court is to appoint an arbitrator on behalf of a party which has failed to nominate one, it shall make the appointment upon a proposal of the National Committee of the country of which that party is a national. If the Court does not accept the proposal made, or if the National Committee fails to make the proposal requested within the time limit fixed by the Court, or if the country of which the said party is a national has no National Committee, the Court shall be at liberty to choose any person whom it regards as suitable. The Secretariat shall inform the National Committee, if one exists, of the country of which such person is a national.

ARTICLE 10
Multiple Parties

1
Where there are multiple parties, whether as Claimant or as Respondent, and where the dispute is to be referred to three arbitrators, the multiple Claimants, jointly, and the multiple Respondents, jointly, shall nominate an arbitrator for confirmation pursuant to Article 9.

2

In the absence of such a joint nomination and where all parties are unable to agree to a method for the constitution of the Arbitral Tribunal, the Court may appoint each member of the Arbitral Tribunal and shall designate one of them to act as chairman. In such case, the Court shall be at liberty to choose any person it regards as suitable to act as arbitrator, applying Article 9 when it considers this appropriate.

ARTICLE 11
Challenge of Arbitrators

1

A challenge of an arbitrator, whether for an alleged lack of independence or otherwise, shall be made by the submission to the Secretariat of a written statement specifying the facts and circumstances on which the challenge is based.

2

For a challenge to be admissible, it must be sent by a party either within 30 days from receipt by that party of the notification of the appointment or confirmation of the arbitrator, or within 30 days from the date when the party making the challenge was informed of the facts and circumstances on which the challenge is based if such date is subsequent to the receipt of such notification.

3

The Court shall decide on the admissibility, and, at the same time, if necessary, on the merits of a challenge after the Secretariat has afforded an opportunity for the arbitrator concerned, the other party or parties and any other members of the Arbitral Tribunal, to comment in writing within a suitable period of time. Such comments shall be communicated to the parties and to the arbitrators.

ARTICLE 12
Replacement of Arbitrators

1

An arbitrator shall be replaced upon his death, upon the acceptance by the Court of the arbitrator's resignation, upon acceptance by the Court of a challenge or upon the request of all the parties.

2

An arbitrator shall also be replaced on the Court's own initiative when it decides that he is prevented *de jure* or *de facto* from fulfilling his functions, or that he is not fulfilling his functions in accordance with the Rules or within the prescribed time limits.

3

When, on the basis of information that has come to its attention, the Court considers applying Article 12(2), it shall decide on the matter after the arbitrator concerned, the parties and any other members of the Arbitral Tribunal have had an opportunity to comment in writing within a suitable period of time. Such comments shall be communicated to the parties and to the arbitrators.

4

When an arbitrator is to be replaced, the Court has discretion to decide whether or not to follow the original nominating process. Once reconstituted, and after having invited the parties to comment, the Arbitral Tribunal shall determine if and to what extent prior proceedings shall be repeated before the reconstituted Arbitral Tribunal.

5

Subsequent to the closing of the proceedings, instead of replacing an arbitrator who has died or been removed by the Court pursuant to Articles 12(1) and 12(2), the Court may decide, when it considers it appropriate, that the remaining arbitrators shall continue the arbitration. In making such determination, the Court shall take into account the views of the remaining arbitrators and of the parties and such other matters that it considers appropriate in the circumstances.

THE ARBITRAL PROCEEDINGS

ARTICLE 13
Transmission of the File to the Arbitral Tribunal

The Secretariat shall transmit the file to the Arbitral Tribunal as soon as it has been constituted, provided the advance on costs requested by the Secretariat at this stage has been paid.

ARTICLE 14
Place of the Arbitration

1

The place of the arbitration shall be fixed by the Court unless agreed upon by the parties.

2

The Arbitral Tribunal may, after consultation with the parties, conduct hearings and meetings at any location it considers appropriate unless otherwise agreed by the parties.

3

The Arbitral Tribunal may deliberate at any location it considers appropriate.

ARTICLE 15
Rules Governing the Proceedings

1

The proceedings before the Arbitral Tribunal shall be governed by these Rules, and, where these Rules are silent, by any rules which the parties or, failing them, the Arbitral Tribunal may settle on, whether or not reference is thereby made to the rules of procedure of a national law to be applied to the arbitration.

2

In all cases, the Arbitral Tribunal shall act fairly and impartially and ensure that each party has a reasonable opportunity to present its case.

ARTICLE 16
Language of the Arbitration

In the absence of an agreement by the parties, the Arbitral Tribunal shall determine the language or languages of the arbitration, due regard being given to all relevant circumstances, including the language of the contract.

ARTICLE 17
Applicable Rules of Law

1

The parties shall be free to agree upon the rules of law to be applied by the Arbitral Tribunal to the merits of the dispute. In the absence of any such agreement, the Arbitral Tribunal shall apply the rules of law which it determines to be appropriate.

2

In all cases the Arbitral Tribunal shall take account of the provisions of the contract and the relevant trade usages.

3

The Arbitral Tribunal shall assume the powers of an *amiable compositeur* or decide *ex aequo et bono* only if the parties have agreed to give it such powers.

ARTICLE 18
Terms of Reference; Procedural Timetable

1

As soon as it has received the file from the Secretariat, the Arbitral Tribunal shall draw up, on the basis of documents or in the presence of the parties and in the light of their most recent submissions, a document defining its Terms of Reference. This document shall include the following particulars:

a) the full names and descriptions of the parties;

b) the addresses of the parties to which notifications and communications arising in the course of the arbitration may be made;

c) a summary of the parties' respective claims and of the relief sought by each party, with an indication to the extent possible of the amounts claimed or counterclaimed;

d) unless the Arbitral Tribunal considers it inappropriate, a list of issues to be determined;

e) the full names, descriptions and addresses of the arbitrators;

f) the place of the arbitration; and

g) particulars of the applicable procedural rules and, if such is the case, reference to the power conferred upon the Arbitral Tribunal to act as *amiable compositeur* or to decide *ex aequo et bono*.

2

The Terms of Reference shall be signed by the parties and the Arbitral Tribunal. Within two months of the date on which the file has been transmitted to it, the Arbitral Tribunal shall transmit to the Court the Terms of Reference signed by it and by the parties. The Court may extend this time limit pursuant to a reasoned request from the Arbitral Tribunal or on its own initiative if it decides it is necessary to do so.

3

If any of the parties refuses to take part in the drawing up of the Terms of Reference or to sign the same, they shall be submitted to the Court for approval. When the Terms of Reference are signed in accordance with Article 18(2) or approved by the Court, the arbitration shall proceed.

4

When drawing up the Terms of Reference, or as soon as possible thereafter, the Arbitral Tribunal, after having consulted the parties, shall establish in a separate document a provisional timetable that it intends to follow for the conduct of the arbitration and shall communicate it to the Court and the parties. Any subsequent modifications of the provisional timetable shall be communicated to the Court and the parties.

ARTICLE 19
New Claims

After the Terms of Reference have been signed or approved by the Court, no party shall make new claims or counterclaims which fall outside the limits of the Terms of Reference unless it has been authorized to do so by the Arbitral Tribunal, which shall consider the nature of such new claims or counterclaims, the stage of the arbitration and other relevant circumstances.

ARTICLE 20
Establishing the Facts of the Case

1
The Arbitral Tribunal shall proceed within as short a time as possible to establish the facts of the case by all appropriate means.

2
After studying the written submissions of the parties and all documents relied upon, the Arbitral Tribunal shall hear the parties together in person if any of them so requests or, failing such a request, it may of its own motion decide to hear them.

3
The Arbitral Tribunal may decide to hear witnesses, experts appointed by the parties or any other person, in the presence of the parties, or in their absence provided they have been duly summoned.

4
The Arbitral Tribunal, after having consulted the parties, may appoint one or more experts, define their terms of reference and receive their reports. At the request of a party, the parties shall be given the opportunity to question at a hearing any such expert appointed by the Tribunal.

5
At any time during the proceedings, the Arbitral Tribunal may summon any party to provide additional evidence.

6
The Arbitral Tribunal may decide the case solely on the documents submitted by the parties unless any of the parties requests a hearing.

7
The Arbitral Tribunal may take measures for protecting trade secrets and confidential information.

ARTICLE 21
Hearings

1
When a hearing is to be held, the Arbitral Tribunal, giving reasonable notice, shall summon the parties to appear before it on the day and at the place fixed by it.

2
If any of the parties, although duly summoned, fails to appear without valid excuse, the Arbitral Tribunal shall have the power to proceed with the hearing.

3
The Arbitral Tribunal shall be in full charge of the hearings, at which all the parties shall be entitled to be present. Save with the approval of the Arbitral Tribunal and the parties, persons not involved in the proceedings shall not be admitted.

4
The parties may appear in person or through duly authorized representatives. In addition, they may be assisted by advisers.

ARTICLE 22
Closing of the Proceedings

1
When it is satisfied that the parties have had a reasonable opportunity to present their cases, the Arbitral Tribunal shall declare the proceedings closed. Thereafter, no further submission or argument may be made, or evidence produced, unless requested or authorized by the Arbitral Tribunal.

2
When the Arbitral Tribunal has declared the proceedings closed, it shall indicate to the Secretariat an approximate date by which the draft Award will be submitted to the Court for approval pursuant to Article 27. Any postponement of that date shall be communicated to the Secretariat by the Arbitral Tribunal.

ARTICLE 23
Conservatory and Interim Measures

1
Unless the parties have otherwise agreed, as soon as the file has been transmitted to it, the Arbitral Tribunal may, at the request of a party, order any interim or conservatory measure it deems appropriate. The Arbitral Tribunal may make the granting of any such measure subject to appropriate security being furnished by

the requesting party. Any such measure shall take the form of an order, giving reasons, or of an Award, as the Arbitral Tribunal considers appropriate.

2

Before the file is transmitted to the Arbitral Tribunal, and in appropriate circumstances even thereafter, the parties may apply to any competent judicial authority for interim or conservatory measures. The application of a party to a judicial authority for such measures or for the implementation of any such measures ordered by an Arbitral Tribunal shall not be deemed to be an infringement or a waiver of the arbitration agreement and shall not affect the relevant powers reserved to the Arbitral Tribunal. Any such application and any measures taken by the judicial authority must be notified without delay to the Secretariat. The Secretariat shall inform the Arbitral Tribunal thereof.

AWARDS

ARTICLE 24
Time Limit for the Award

1

The time limit within which the Arbitral Tribunal must render its final Award is six months. Such time limit shall start to run from the date of the last signature by the Arbitral Tribunal or of the parties of the Terms of Reference, or, in the case of application of Article 18(3), the date of the notification to the Arbitral Tribunal by the Secretariat of the approval of the Terms of Reference by the Court.

2

The Court may extend this time limit pursuant to a reasoned request from the Arbitral Tribunal or on its own initiative if it decides it is necessary to do so.

ARTICLE 25
Making of the Award

1

When the Arbitral Tribunal is composed of more than one arbitrator, an Award is given by a majority decision. If there be no majority, the Award shall be made by the chairman of the Arbitral Tribunal alone.

2

The Award shall state the reasons upon which it is based.

3

The Award shall be deemed to be made at the place of the arbitration and on the date stated therein.

ARTICLE 26
Award by Consent

If the parties reach a settlement after the file has been transmitted to the Arbitral Tribunal in accordance with Article 13, the settlement shall be recorded in the form of an Award made by consent of the parties if so requested by the parties and if the Arbitral Tribunal agrees to do so.

ARTICLE 27
Scrutiny of the Award by the Court

Before signing any Award, the Arbitral Tribunal shall submit it in draft form to the Court. The Court may lay down modifications as to the form of the Award and, without affecting the Arbitral Tribunal's liberty of decision, may also draw its attention to points of substance. No Award shall be rendered by the Arbitral Tribunal until it has been approved by the Court as to its form.

ARTICLE 28
Notification, Deposit and Enforceability of the Award

1

Once an Award has been made, the Secretariat shall notify to the parties the text signed by the Arbitral Tribunal, provided always that the costs of the arbitration have been fully paid to the ICC by the parties or by one of them.

2

Additional copies certified true by the Secretary General shall be made available on request and at any time to the parties, but to no one else.

3

By virtue of the notification made in accordance with Paragraph 1 of this Article, the parties waive any other form of notification or deposit on the part of the Arbitral Tribunal.

4

An original of each Award made in accordance with the present Rules shall be deposited with the Secretariat.

5

The Arbitral Tribunal and the Secretariat shall assist the parties in complying with whatever further formalities may be necessary.

6

Every Award shall be binding on the parties. By submitting the dispute to arbitration under these Rules, the parties undertake to carry out any Award without delay and shall be deemed to have waived their right to any form of recourse insofar as such waiver can validly be made.

ARTICLE 29
Correction and Interpretation of the Award

1

On its own initiative, the Arbitral Tribunal may correct a clerical, computational or typographical error, or any errors of similar nature contained in an Award, provided such correction is submitted for approval to the Court within 30 days of the date of such Award.

2

Any application of a party for the correction of an error of the kind referred to in Article 29(1), or for the interpretation of an Award, must be made to the Secretariat within 30 days of the receipt of the Award by such party, in a number of copies as stated in Article 3(1). After transmittal of the application to the Arbitral Tribunal, it shall grant the other party a short time limit, normally not exceeding 30 days, from the receipt of the application by that party to submit any comments thereon. If the Arbitral Tribunal decides to correct or interpret the Award, it shall submit its decision in draft form to the Court not later than 30 days following the expiration of the time limit for the receipt of any comments from the other party or within such other period as the Court may decide.

3

The decision to correct or to interpret the Award shall take the form of an addendum and shall constitute part of the Award. The provisions of Articles 25, 27 and 28 shall apply *mutatis mutandis.*

COSTS

ARTICLE 30
Advance to Cover the Costs of the Arbitration

1

After receipt of the Request, the Secretary General may request the Claimant to pay a provisional advance in an amount intended to cover the costs of arbitration until the Terms of Reference have been drawn up.

2

As soon as practicable, the Court shall fix the advance on costs in an amount likely to cover the fees and expenses of the arbitrators and the ICC administrative costs for the claims and counterclaims which have been referred to it by the parties. This amount may be subject to readjustment at any time during the arbitration. Where, apart from the claims, counterclaims are submitted, the Court may fix separate advances on costs for the claims and the counterclaims.

3

The advance on costs fixed by the Court shall be payable in equal shares by the Claimant and the Respondent. Any provisional advance paid on the basis of Article 30(1) will be considered as a partial payment thereof. However, any party shall be free to pay the whole of the advance on costs in respect of the principal claim or the counterclaim should the other party fail to pay its share. When the Court has set separate advances on costs in accordance with Article 30(2), each of the parties shall pay the advance on costs corresponding to its claims.

4

When a request for an advance on costs has not been complied with, and after consultation with the Arbitral Tribunal, the Secretary General may direct the Arbitral Tribunal to suspend its work and set a time limit, which must be not less than 15 days, on the expiry of which the relevant claims, or counterclaims, shall be considered as withdrawn. Should the party in question wish to object to this measure it must make a request within the aforementioned period for the matter to be decided by the Court. Such party shall not be prevented on the ground of such withdrawal from reintroducing the same claims or counterclaims at a later date in another proceeding.

5

If one of the parties claims a right to a set-off with regard to either claims or counterclaims, such set-off shall be taken into account in determining the advance to cover the costs of arbitration in the same way as a separate claim insofar as it may require the Arbitral Tribunal to consider additional matters.

ARTICLE 31
Decision as to the Costs of the Arbitration

1
The costs of the arbitration shall include the fees and expenses of the arbitrators and the ICC administrative costs fixed by the Court, in accordance with the scale in force at the time of the commencement of the arbitral proceedings, as well as the fees and expenses of any experts appointed by the Arbitral Tribunal and the reasonable legal and other costs incurred by the parties for the arbitration.

2
The Court may fix the fees of the arbitrators at a figure higher or lower than that which would result from the application of the relevant scale should this be deemed necessary due to the exceptional circumstances of the case. Decisions on costs other than those fixed by the Court may be taken by the Arbitral Tribunal at any time during the proceedings.

3
The final Award shall fix the costs of the arbitration and decide which of the parties shall bear them or in what proportion they shall be borne by the parties.

MISCELLANEOUS

ARTICLE 32
Modified Time Limits

1
The parties may agree to shorten the various time limits set out in these Rules. Any such agreement entered into subsequent to the constitution of an Arbitral Tribunal shall become effective only upon the approval of the Arbitral Tribunal.

2
The Court, on its own initiative, may extend any time limit which has been modified pursuant to Article 32(1) if it decides that it is necessary to do so in order that the Arbitral Tribunal or the Court may fulfil their responsibilities in accordance with these Rules.

ARTICLE 33
Waiver

A party which proceeds with the arbitration without raising its objection to a failure to comply with any provision of these Rules, or of any other rules applicable to the proceedings, any direction given by the Arbitral Tribunal, or any requirement under the arbitration agreement relating to the constitution of the Arbitral Tribunal, or to the conduct of the proceedings, shall be deemed to have waived its right to object.

ARTICLE 34
Exclusion of Liability

Neither the arbitrators, nor the Court and its members, nor the ICC and its employees, nor the ICC National Committees shall be liable to any person for any act or omission in connection with the arbitration.

ARTICLE 35
General Rule

In all matters not expressly provided for in these Rules, the Court and the Arbitral Tribunal shall act in the spirit of these Rules and shall make every effort to make sure that the Award is enforceable at law.

APPENDIX I

STATUTES OF THE INTERNATIONAL COURT OF ARBITRATION OF THE ICC

ARTICLE 1
Function

1

The function of the International Court of Arbitration of the International Chamber of Commerce (the Court) is to ensure the application of the Rules of Arbitration and the Rules of Conciliation of the International Chamber of Commerce, and it has all the necessary powers for that purpose.

2

As an autonomous body, it carries out these functions in complete independence from the ICC and its organs.

3

Its members are independent from the ICC National Committees.

ARTICLE 2
Composition of the Court

The Court shall consist of a Chairman, Vice-Chairmen, and members and alternate members (collectively designated as members). In its work it is assisted by its Secretariat (Secretariat of the Court).

ARTICLE 3
Appointment

1

The Chairman is elected by the ICC Council upon recommendation of the Executive Board of the ICC.

2

The ICC Council appoints the Vice-Chairmen of the Court from among the members of the Court or otherwise.

3

Its members are appointed by the ICC Council on the proposal of National Committees, one member for each Committee.

4

On the proposal of the Chairman of the Court, the Council may appoint alternate members.

5

The term of office of all members is three years. If a member is no longer in a position to exercise his functions, his successor is appointed by the Council for the remainder of the term.

ARTICLE 4

Plenary Session of the Court

The Plenary Sessions of the Court are presided over by the Chairman, or, in his absence, by one of the Vice-Chairmen designated by him. The deliberations shall be valid when at least six members are present. Decisions are taken by a majority vote, the Chairman having a casting vote in the event of a tie.

ARTICLE 5

Committees

The Court may set up one or more Committees and establish the functions and organization of such Committees.

ARTICLE 6

Confidentiality

The work of the Court is of a confidential nature and must be respected by everyone who participates in that work in whatever capacity. The Court lays down the rules regarding the persons who can attend the meetings of the Court and its Committees and who are entitled to have access to the materials submitted to the Court and its Secretariat.

ARTICLE 7

Modification of the Rules of Arbitration

Any proposal of the Court for a modification of the Rules is laid before the Commission on International Arbitration before submission to the Executive Board and the Council of the ICC for approval.

APPENDIX II

INTERNAL RULES OF THE INTERNATIONAL COURT OF ARBITRATION OF THE ICC

ARTICLE 1
Confidential Character of the Work of the International Court of Arbitration

1
The sessions of the Court, whether plenary or those of a Committee of the Court, are open only to its members and to the Secretariat.

2
However, in exceptional circumstances, the Chairman of the Court may invite other persons to attend. Such persons must respect the confidential nature of the work of the Court.

3
The documents submitted to the Court, or drawn up by it in the course of its proceedings, are communicated only to the members of the Court and to the Secretariat and to persons authorized by the Chairman to attend Court sessions.

4
The Chairman or the Secretary General of the Court may authorize researchers undertaking work of a scientific nature on international trade law to acquaint themselves with awards and other documents of general interest, with the exception of memoranda, notes, statements and documents remitted by the parties within the framework of arbitration proceedings.

5
Such authorization shall not be given unless the beneficiary has undertaken to respect the confidential character of the documents made available and to refrain from any publication in their respect without having previously submitted the text for approval to the Secretary General of the Court.

6
The Secretariat will in each case submitted to arbitration under the Rules retain in the archives of the Court all awards, terms of reference, and decisions of the Court as well as copies of the pertinent correspondence of the Secretariat.

7
Any documents, communications or correspondence submitted by the parties or the arbitrators may be destroyed unless a party or an arbitrator requests in writing within a period fixed by the Secretariat the return of such documents. All

related costs and expenses for the return of those documents shall be paid by such party or arbitrator.

ARTICLE 2
Participation of Members of the International Court of Arbitration in ICC Arbitration

1
The Chairman and the members of the Secretariat of the Court may not act as arbitrators or as counsel in cases submitted to ICC arbitration.

2
The Court shall not appoint Vice-Chairmen or members of the Court as arbitrators. They may, however, be proposed for such duties by one or more of the parties, or, pursuant to any other procedure agreed upon by the parties, subject to confirmation by the Court.

3
When the Chairman, a Vice-Chairman or a member of the Court or of the Secretariat is involved in any capacity whatsoever in proceedings pending before the Court, such person must inform the Secretary General of the Court upon becoming aware of such involvement.

4
Such person must refrain from participating in the discussions or in the decisions of the Court concerning the proceedings and must be absent from the courtroom whenever the matter is considered.

5
Such person will not receive any material documentation or information pertaining to such proceedings.

ARTICLE 3
Relations between the Members of the Court and the ICC National Committees

1
By virtue of their capacity, the members of the Court are independent of the ICC National Committees which proposed them for appointment by the ICC Council.

2
Furthermore, they must regard as confidential, vis-à-vis the said National Committees, any information concerning individual cases with which they have

become acquainted in their capacity as members of the Court, except when they have been requested by the Chairman of the Court or by its Secretary General to communicate specific information to their respective National Committee.

<h1 style="text-align:center">ARTICLE 4</h1>
<h2 style="text-align:center">Committee of the Court</h2>

1

In accordance with the provisions of Article 1 (4) of the Rules and Article 5 of its Statutes (Appendix I), the Court hereby establishes a Committee of the Court.

2

The members of the Committee consist of a Chairman and at least two other members. The Chairman of the Court acts as the Chairman of the Committee. If absent, the Chairman may designate a Vice-Chairman of the Court or, in exceptional circumstances, another member of the Court as Chairman of the Committee.

3

The other two members of the Committee are appointed by the Court from among the Vice-Chairmen or the other members of the Court. At each Plenary Session the Court appoints the members who are to attend the meetings of the Committee to be held before the next Plenary Session.

4

The Committee meets when convened by its Chairman. Two members constitute a quorum.

5
(a)   The Court shall determine the decisions that may be taken by the Committee.
(b)   The decisions of the Committee are taken unanimously.
(c)   When the Committee cannot reach a decision or deems it preferable to abstain, it transfers the case to the next Plenary Session, making any suggestions it deems appropriate.
(d)   The Committee's decisions are brought to the notice of the Court at its next Plenary Session.

<h1 style="text-align:center">ARTICLE 5</h1>
<h2 style="text-align:center">Court Secretariat</h2>

1

In case of absence, the Secretary General may delegate to the General Counsel and Deputy Secretary General the authority to confirm arbitrators, to certify true copies of awards and to request the payment of a provisional advance, respectively provided for in Articles 9(2), 28(2) and 30(1) of the Rules.

2

The Secretariat may, with the approval of the Court, issue notes and other documents for the information of the parties and the arbitrators, or as necessary for the proper conduct of the arbitral proceedings.

ARTICLE 6
Scrutiny of Arbitral Awards

When the Court scrutinizes draft awards in accordance with Article 27 of the Rules, it considers, to the extent practicable, the requirements of mandatory law at the place of arbitration.

APPENDIX III

ARBITRATION COSTS AND FEES

ARTICLE 1
Advance on Costs

1

Each request to commence an arbitration pursuant to the Rules must be accompanied by an advance payment of US $ 2 500 on the administrative expenses. Such payment is nonrefundable, and shall be credited to the Claimant's portion of the advance on costs.

2

The provisional advance on costs fixed by the Secretary General according to Article 30(1) of the Rules shall normally not exceed the amount obtained by adding together the administrative expenses, the minimum of the fees (as set out in the scale hereinafter) based upon the amount of the claim and the expected reimbursable expenses of the Arbitral Tribunal incurred with respect to the drafting of the Terms of Reference. If such amount is not quantified, the provisional advance shall be fixed at the discretion of the Secretary General. Payment by the Claimant shall be credited to its share of the advance on costs fixed by the Court.

3

In general, after the Terms of Reference have been signed or approved by the Court and the provisional timetable has been established, the Arbitral Tribunal shall, in accordance with Article 30(4) of the Rules, proceed only with respect to those claims or counterclaims in regard to which the whole of the advance on costs has been paid.

4

The advance on costs fixed by the Court according to Article 30(2) of the Rules comprises the fees of the arbitrator or arbitrators (hereinafter referred to as "arbitrator"), any arbitration-related expenses of the arbitrator and the administrative expenses.

5

Each party shall pay in cash its share of the total advance on costs. However, if its share exceeds an amount fixed from time to time by the Court, a party may post a bank guarantee for this additional amount.

6

A party that has already paid in full its share of the advance on costs fixed by the Court may, in accordance with Article 30(3) of the Rules, pay the unpaid portion of the advance owed by the defaulting party by posting a bank guarantee.

7
When the Court has fixed separate advances on costs pursuant to Article 30(2) of the Rules, the Secretariat shall invite each party to pay the amount of the advance corresponding to its respective claims.

8
When, as a result of the fixing of separate advances on costs, the separate advance fixed for the claim of either party exceeds one-half of such global advance as was previously fixed (in respect of the same claims and counterclaims that are the object of separate advances), a bank guarantee may be posted to cover any such excess amount. In the event that the amount of the separate advance is subsequently increased, at least one-half of the increase shall be paid in cash.

9
The Secretariat shall establish the terms governing all bank guarantees which the parties may post pursuant to the above provisions.

10
As provided in Article 30(2) of the Rules, the advance on costs may be subject to readjustment at any time during the arbitration, in particular to take into account fluctuations in the amount in dispute, changes in the amount of the estimated expenses of the arbitrator, or the evolving difficulty or complexity of arbitration proceedings.

11
Before any expertise ordered by the Arbitral Tribunal can be commenced, the parties, or one of them, shall pay an advance on costs fixed by the Arbitral Tribunal sufficient to cover the expected fees and expenses of the expert as determined by the Arbitral Tribunal. The Arbitral Tribunal shall be responsible for ensuring the payment by the parties of such fees and expenses.

ARTICLE 2
Costs and Fees

1
Subject to Article 31(2) of the Rules, the Court shall fix the fees of the arbitrator in accordance with the scale hereinafter set out, or, where the sum in dispute is not stated, at its discretion.

2

In setting the arbitrator's fees, the Court shall take into consideration the diligence of the arbitrator, the time spent, the rapidity of the proceedings, and the complexity of the dispute so as to arrive at a figure within the limits specified, or, in exceptional circumstances (Article 31(2) of the Rules), at a figure higher or lower than those limits.

3

When a case is submitted to more than one arbitrator, the Court, at its discretion, shall have the right to increase the total fees up to a maximum which shall normally not exceed three times the fees of one arbitrator.

4

The arbitrator's fees and expenses shall be fixed exclusively by the Court as required by the Rules. Separate fee arrangements between the parties and the arbitrator are contrary to the Rules.

5

The Court shall fix the administrative expenses of each arbitration in accordance with the scale hereinafter set out, or, where the sum in dispute is not stated, at its discretion. In exceptional circumstances, the Court may fix the administrative expenses at a lower or higher figure than that which would result from the application of such scale, provided that such expenses shall normally not exceed the maximum amount of the scale. Further, the Court may require the payment of administrative expenses in addition to those provided in the scale of administrative expenses as a condition to holding an arbitration in abeyance at the request of the parties or of one of them with the acquiescence of the other.

6

If an arbitration terminates before the rendering of a final award, the Court shall fix the costs of the arbitration at its discretion, taking into account the stage attained by the arbitral proceedings and any other relevant circumstances.

7

In the case of an application under Article 29(2) of the Rules, the Court may fix an advance to cover additional fees and expenses of the Arbitral Tribunal and may subordinate the transmission of such application to the Arbitral Tribunal to the prior cash payment in full to the ICC of such advance. The Court shall fix at its discretion any possible fees of the arbitrator when approving the decision of the Arbitral Tribunal.

8

When an arbitration is preceded by attempted conciliation, one-half of the administrative expenses paid for such conciliation shall be credited to the administrative expenses of the arbitration.

9

Amounts paid to the arbitrator do not include any possible value-added taxes (VAT) or other taxes or charges and imposts applicable to the arbitrator's fees. Parties are expected to pay any such taxes or charges; however, the recovery of any such charges or taxes is a matter solely between the arbitrator and the parties.

ARTICLE 3

Appointment of Arbitrators

1

A registration fee normally not exceeding US $ 2 500 is payable by the requesting party in respect of each request made to the ICC to appoint an arbitrator for any arbitration not conducted under the Rules. No request for appointment of an arbitrator will be considered unless accompanied by the said fee, which is not recoverable and becomes the property of the ICC.

2

The said fee shall cover any additional services rendered by the ICC regarding the appointment, such as decisions on a challenge of an arbitrator and the appointment of a substitute arbitrator.

ARTICLE 4

Scales of Administrative Expenses and of Arbitrator's Fees

1

The Scales of Administrative Expenses and Arbitrator's Fees set forth below shall be effective as of January 1, 1998 in respect of all arbitrations commenced on or after such date, irrespective of the version of the Rules applying to such arbitrations.

2

To calculate the administrative expenses and the arbitrator's fees, the amounts calculated for each successive slice of the sum in dispute must be added together, except that where the sum in dispute is over US $ 80 million, a flat amount of US $ 75 800 shall constitute the entirety of the administrative expenses.

A. Administrative Expenses

Sum in dispute (in US Dollars)				Administrative expenses(*)
up to	50 000			$ 2 500
from	50 001	to	100 000	3.50%
from	100 001	to	500 000	1.70%
from	500 001	to	1 000 000	1.15%
from	1 000 001	to	2 000 000	0.60%
from	2 000 001	to	5 000 000	0.20%
from	5 000 001	to	10 000 000	0.10%
from	10 000 001	to	50 000 000	0.06%
from	50 000 001	to	80 000 000	0.06%
over	80 000 000			$ 75 800

(*) For illustrative purposes only, the table on the following page indicates the resulting administrative expenses in US $ when the proper calculations have been made.

B. Arbitrator's Fees

Sum in dispute (in US Dollars)				Fees(**)	
				minimum	*maximum*
up to	50 000			$ 2 500	17.00%
from	50 001	to	100 000	2.00%	11.00%
from	100 001	to	500 000	1.00%	5.50%
from	500 001	to	1 000 000	0.75%	3.50%
from	1 000 001	to	2 000 000	0.50%	2.50%
from	2 000 001	to	5 000 000	0.25%	1.00%
from	5 000 001	to	10 000 000	0.10%	0.55%
from	10 000 001	to	50 000 000	0.05%	0.17%
from	50 000 001	to	80 000 000	0.03%	0.12%
from	80 000 001	to	100 000 000	0.02%	0.10%
over	100 000 000			0.01%	0.05%

(**) For illustrative purposes only, the table on the following page indicates the resulting range of fees when the proper calculations have been made.

Sum in dispute (in US Dollars)	A. Administrative Expenses(*) (in US Dollars)	B. Arbitrator's Fees(**) (in US Dollars)	
		Minimum	*Maximum*
up to 50 000	2 500	2 500	17.00% of amount in dispute
from 50 001 to 100 000	2 500 + 3.50% of amt. over 50 000	2 500 + 2.00% of amt. over 50 000	8 500 + 11.00% of amt. over 50 000
from 100 001 to 500 000	4 250 + 1.70% of amt. over 100 000	3 500 + 1.00% of amt. over 100 000	14 000 + 5.50% of amt. over 100 000
from 500 001 to 1 000 000	11 050 + 1.15% of amt. over 500 000	7 500 + 0.75% of amt. over 500 000	36 000 + 3.50% of amt. over 500 000
from 1 000 001 to 2 000 000	16 800 + 0.60% of amt. over 1 000 000	11 250 + 0.50% of amt. over 1 000 000	53 500 + 2.50% of amt. over 1 000 000
from 2 000 001 to 5 000 000	22 800 + 0.20% of amt. over 2 000 000	16 250 + 0.25% of amt. over 2 000 000	78 500 + 1.00% of amt. over 2 000 000
from 5 000 001 to 10 000 000	28 800 + 0.10% of amt. over 5 000 000	23 750 + 0.10% of amt. over 5 000 000	108 500 + 0.55% of amt. over 5 000 000
from 10 000 001 to 50 000 000	33 800 + 0.06% of amt. over 10 000 000	28 750 + 0.05% of amt. over 10 000 000	136 000 + 0.17% of amt. over 10 000 000
from 50 000 001 to 80 000 000	57 800 + 0.06% of amt. over 50 000 000	48 750 + 0.03% of amt. over 50 000 000	204 000 + 0.12% of amt. over 50 000 000
from 80 000 001 to 100 000 000	75 800	57 750 + 0.02% of amt. over 80 000 000	240 000 + 0.10% of amt. over 80 000 000
over 100 000 000	75 800	61 750 + 0.01% of amt. over 100 000 000	260 000 + 0.05% of amt. over 100 000 000

(*)(**) See preceding page

Appendix 8

ICC RULES OF OPTIONAL CONCILIATION
(in force as from January 1, 1988)

PREAMBLE

Settlement is a desirable solution for business disputes of an international character. The International Chamber of Commerce therefore sets out these Rules of Optional Conciliation in order to facilitate the amicable settlement of such disputes.

ARTICLE 1

All business disputes of an international character may be submitted to conciliation by a sole conciliator appointed by the International Chamber of Commerce.

ARTICLE 2

The party requesting conciliation shall apply to the Secretariat of the International Court of Arbitration of the International Chamber of Commerce setting out succinctly the purpose of the request and accompanying it with the fee required to open the file, as set out in the Appendix hereto.

ARTICLE 3

The Secretariat of the International Court of Arbitration shall, as soon as possible, inform the other party of the request for conciliation. That party will be given a period of 15 days to inform the Secretariat whether it agrees or declines to participate in the attempt to conciliate.

If the other party agrees to participate in the attempt to conciliate it shall so inform the Secretariat within such period.

In the absence of any reply within such period or in the case of a negative reply the request for conciliation shall be deemed to have been declined. The Secretariat shall, as soon as possible, so inform the party which had requested conciliation.

ARTICLE 4

Upon receipt of an agreement to attempt conciliation, the Secretary General of the International Court of Arbitration shall appoint a conciliator as soon as possible. The conciliator shall inform the parties of his appointment and set a time-limit for the parties to present their respective arguments to him.

ARTICLE 5

The conciliator shall conduct the conciliation process as he thinks fit, guided by the principles of impartiality, equity and justice.

With the agreement of the parties, the conciliator shall fix the place for conciliation.

The conciliator may at any time during the conciliation process request a party to submit to him such additional information as he deems necessary.

The parties may, if they so wish, be assisted by counsel of their choice.

ARTICLE 6

The confidential nature of the conciliation process shall be respected by every person who is involved in it in whatever capacity.

ARTICLE 7

The conciliation process shall come to an end:
(a)   Upon the parties signing an agreement. The parties shall be bound by such agreement. The agreement shall remain confidential unless and to the extent that its execution or application require disclosure.
(b)   Upon the production by the conciliator of a report recording that the attempt to conciliate has not been successful. Such report shall not contain reasons.
(c)   Upon notification to the conciliator by one or more parties at any time during the conciliation process of an intention no longer to pursue the conciliation process.

ARTICLE 8

Upon termination of the conciliation, the conciliator shall provide the Secretariat of the International Court of Arbitration with the settlement agreement signed by the parties or with his report of lack of success or with a notice from one or more parties of the intention no longer to pursue the conciliation process.

ARTICLE 9

Upon the file being opened, the Secretariat of the International Court of Arbitration shall fix the sum required to permit the process to proceed, taking into consideration the nature and importance of the dispute. Such sum shall be paid in equal shares by the parties.

This sum shall cover the estimated fees of the conciliator, expenses of the conciliation, and the administrative expenses as set out in the Appendix hereto.

In any case where, in the course of the conciliation process, the Secretariat of the Court shall decide that the sum originally paid is insufficient to cover the likely costs of the conciliation, the Secretariat shall require the provision of an additional amount which shall be paid in equal shares by the parties.

Upon termination of the conciliation, the Secretariat shall settle the total costs of the process and advise the parties in writing.

All above costs shall be borne in equal shares by the parties except and insofar as a settlement agreement provides otherwise.

A party's other expenditures shall remain the responsibility of that party.

ARTICLE 10

Unless the parties agree otherwise, a conciliator shall not act in any judicial or arbitration proceeding relating to the dispute which has been the subject of the conciliation process whether as an arbitrator, representative or counsel of a party.

The parties mutually undertake not to call the conciliator as a witness in any such proceedings, unless otherwise agreed between them.

ARTICLE 11

The parties agree not to introduce in any judicial or arbitration proceeding as evidence or in any manner whatsoever:

(a)   any views expressed or suggestions made by any party with regard to the possible settlement of the dispute;

(b)   any proposals put forward by the conciliator;

(c)   the fact that a party had indicated that it was ready to accept some proposal for a settlement put forward by the conciliator.

APPENDIX

SCHEDULE OF CONCILIATION COSTS

(a)   Each party to a dispute submitted to conciliation under the ICC Rules of Optional Conciliation is required to make an advance payment of US $500 on the administrative expenses. No request for conciliation shall be entertained unless accompanied by the appropriate payment. This payment is not recoverable and becomes the property of the ICC. Such payment by a party shall be credited to the portion of the administrative expenses for the conciliation of such party.

(b) The administrative expenses for a conciliation procedure shall be fixed at one-quarter of the amount calculated in accordance with the scale of administrative expenses as set out in Appendix III of the ICC Rules of Arbitration. Where the sum in dispute in a conciliation procedure is not stated, the Secretary General of the International Court of Arbitration (the "Court") shall fix the administrative expenses at his discretion.

(c) The fee of the conciliator to be paid by the parties shall be fixed by the Secretary General of the Court. Such fee shall be reasonable in amount, taking into consideration the time spent, the complexity of the dispute and any other relevant circumstances.

(d) Amounts paid to the conciliator do not include any possible value-added taxes (VAT) or other taxes or charges and imposts applicable to the conciliatior's fees. Parties are expected to pay any such taxes or charges; however, the recovery of any such charges or taxes is a matter solely between the conciliator and the parties.

Appendix 9

ICC Rules for Expertise
(in force as from January 1, 1993)

SECTION I
General provisions

ARTICLE 1
The International Centre for Expertise

1

The International Centre for Expertise which was established by the International Chamber of Commerce (ICC) has for its function the appointment or the proposal of experts in connection with international business transactions.

2

The Centre consists of a Standing Committee and a Secretariat. The Standing Committee is composed of five members (a chairman and four members) of different nationalities all of whom are appointed by the ICC for a three-year renewable term. The Secretariat of the Centre is assumed by the ICC.

ARTICLE 2
Recourse to the International Centre for Expertise

1

Any request for the appointment or proposal of an expert shall be submitted to the ICC International Centre for Expertise, at the ICC Headquarters in Paris.

2

The Request shall contain *inter alia* the following information:
– names, description and addresses of the parties involved;
– where applicable, a copy of the parties' agreement to have recourse to the ICC International Centre for Expertise;
– any relevant indications concerning the choice of an expert;
– a descriptive summary of the expert's brief.

ARTICLE 3
Manner in Which an Expert is Chosen

Any appointment or proposal of an expert as well as any decision on the replacement of an expert, in accordance with Articles 4, 5, and 7, shall be made as

quickly as possible by the Chairman of the Standing Committee after consultation with members of the Standing Committee.

SECTION II
Proposal of an Expert

ARTICLE 4

At the request of an arbitral tribunal or any person, the Chairman of the Standing
Committee may propose the name(s) of one or more experts. The Centre's intervention ends on notification of the proposal.

SECTION III
Appointment of an Expert and Expertise Procedure

ARTICLE 5
Appointment of an Expert

1
Where the parties have agreed to have recourse to the ICC International Centre
for Expertise, one or more parties may request the Centre to appoint an expert.
If the request for appointment is not made jointly by all the parties to the agreement, the Secretariat of the Centre shall send a copy of the request to the other
party or parties who may make representations within a time limit fixed by the
Secretariat according to the circumstances of the case.

2
Subject to Article 6, the Chairman of the Standing Committee shall confirm the
choice of the expert nominated by the parties by mutual consent. Failing such an
agreement, the Chairman shall appoint an expert.

ARTICLE 6
The Expert's Independence

Prior to an appointment, the Centre shall invite the prospective expert to submit
a declaration confirming his independence of the parties.

ARTICLE 7
Replacement of an Expert

1

The Chairman of the Standing Committee shall decide on the replacement of an expert who has died or resigns or is unable to carry out his functions.

The Chairman may replace the expert, after having considered his observations, if any, where objections are made by one of the parties concerning the person appointed as expert.

2

The Chairman may also replace the expert if he should find, after having considered the expert's observations, if any, that the expert is not fulfilling his functions in accordance with the Rules or within any prescribed time limits.

ARTICLE 8
The Expert's Brief

1

a) The expert is empowered to make findings within the limits set by the request for expertise, after giving the parties an opportunity to make submissions.

b) The expert may also be empowered, by express agreement between the parties, either in a prior agreement or in their request for the appointment of an expert, to:
–   recommend, as needed, those measures which he deems most appropriate for the performance of the contract and/or those which would be necessary in order to safeguard the subject matter;
–   supervise the carrying out of the contractual operations.

2

In agreeing to the application of these Rules the parties undertake to provide the expert with all facilities in order to implement his Brief and, in particular, to make available all documents he may consider necessary and also to grant him free access to any place where the expertise operations are being carried out. The information given to the expert will be used only for the purpose of the expertise and shall remain confidential.

3

Unless otherwise agreed the findings or recommendations of the expert shall not be binding upon the parties.

ARTICLE 9
Notification of the Expert's Report

The expert shall send his report to the Centre in as many copies as there are parties plus one for the Centre. Thereafter, the Centre shall notify the expert's report to the parties.

SECTION IV
Costs of the Expertise

ARTICLE 10
Costs where an Expert is Proposed

Each request for the proposal of an expert shall be accompanied by an amount of US$ 1,000. This amount represents the total administrative costs for any proposal of experts.

ARTICLE 11
Costs where an Expert is Appointed

1
Each request for the appointment of an expert shall be accompanied by an amount of US$ 1,000. This amount, which is not refundable, shall be credited to the Centre's administrative costs.

2
a) The costs of the expertise, where an expert is appointed under these Rules, comprise the expert's fees and expenses, and the administrative cost of the ICC International Centre for Expertise.

b) Before the appointment of the expert, the Chairman of the Standing Committee, following consultation with the expert and the requesting party(ies) shall determine the basis upon which the expert's fees and expenses are to be calculated.

c) The Chairman of the Standing Committee shall determine the amount of the administrative costs which in any case shall be neither greater than 15 per cent of the expert's fees nor less than US$ 1,000.

3
The estimated costs for the expertise as fixed by the Chairman of the Standing Committee are payable to the Centre by the party or parties requesting the appointment prior to the commencement of the expertise operations. This estimated amount may be readjusted by the Chairman of the Standing Committee in the course of the expertise.

4

The total amount of costs shall be fixed by the Chairman of the Standing Committee upon conclusion of the expertise operations and the balance, if any, shall be payable before the notification of the Report to the parties.

Appendix 10

ICC R<small>ULES FOR A</small> P<small>RE</small>-A<small>RBITRAL</small> R<small>EFEREE</small> P<small>ROCEDURE</small>
(in force as from January 1, 1990)

F<small>OREWORD</small>

The present ICC Rules for a Pre-arbitral Referee Procedure provide the business world with a new procedure through which rapid action may be taken when certain difficulties arise in the course of a contractual relationship. These Rules are designed to meet a specific need: that of having recourse at very short notice to a third person – the "Referee" – who is empowered to order provisional measures needed as a matter of urgency.

It should be stressed that these Rules may be resorted to only on the basis of a written agreement between the parties to that effect. Such an agreement may either be part of the relevant contract or may be made thereafter.

The Referee may be selected by the parties themselves or be appointed by the Chairman of the International Court of Arbitration of the ICC in the absence of such a selection. The Referee is invested with the power to make a wide range of appropriate orders which are characterized by their provisional and binding nature.

The main features of the ICC Pre-Arbitral Referee Procedure can thus be summarized as follows: it is a contractual process, particularly appropriate where urgent measures are required; it is rapid and the measures which are ordered are binding until the Referee or the competent jurisdiction (court or arbitral tribunal) has decided otherwise. In this respect it is useful to place the Pre-arbitral Referee Procedure in the context of other ICC procedures with which it may play a complementary role:

- The ICC Rules for Technical Expertise offer a method of quickly identifying, before the evidence is obliterated, whether technical problems in fact exist and, if so, their cause(s). The parties are thus provided with an objective statement of facts by an independent expert which may serve either as an aide to reaching an amicable settlement or else as reliable first-hand evidence in subsequent court or arbitral proceedings;
- The ICC Rules for Optional Conciliation provide for the appointment of a conciliator who can suggest terms of settlement to the parties who in turn may accept or reject them;
- The ICC Arbitration Rules serve to organize a procedure by which one or several arbitrators issue a final and binding award on the merits of a dispute.

Thus, depending on the circumstances, it may be desirable to be able to have recourse to the Prearbitral Referee Procedure as well as to one or more of the above procedures.

The present Rules have been developed at the request of many practitioners of different legal backgrounds, and were realized thanks to a collective effort under the aegis of the ICC Commission on International Arbitration.

The extent to which the Pre-arbitral Referee Rules are recognized and accepted may vary from one country to another depending on the applicable law(s). Parties wishing to have recourse to these Rules should ensure that they conform with the law(s) applicable to each case.

Further information on the Pre-arbitral Referee Procedure may be obtained at the following address:

The Secretariat
ICC International Court of Arbitration   Tel: (33 1) 49 53 28 28
38, Cours Albert 1e   Telex 640003 ICCARBIF
75008 – Paris, France   Telefax (33 1) 42 25 97 40

INTRODUCTION

During the course of many contracts, especially those made for long-term transactions, problems can arise which require an urgent response. It is frequently not possible to obtain in the time required a final decision from an arbitral tribunal or from a court.

Accordingly, the International Chamber of Commerce (ICC) has set out the following Rules for a Pre-arbitral Referee Procedure in order to enable parties which have so agreed to have rapid recourse to a person (called a "Referee") empowered to make an order designed to meet the urgent problem in issue, including the power to order the preservation or recording of evidence. The order should therefore provide a temporary resolution of the dispute and may lay the foundations for its final settlement either by agreement or otherwise.

Use of the Pre-arbitral Referee Procedure does not usurp the jurisdiction of any entity (whether arbitral tribunal or national court) that is ultimately responsible for deciding the merits of any underlying dispute.

STANDARD CLAUSE FOR AN ICC PRE-ARBITRAL REFEREE PROCEDURE

The ICC recommends that all parties wishing to make reference to the ICC Rules for a Pre-arbitral Referee Procedure use the following clause in their contracts:

English
   "Any party to this contract shall have the right to have recourse to and shall be bound by the Pre-arbitral Referee Procedure of the International Chamber of Commerce in accordance with its Rules."

French

> *"Toute partie au présent contrat peut recourir au Règlement de Référé pré-arbitral de la Chambre de Commerce Internationale, les parties se déclarant liées par les dispositions du dit Règlement."*

German

> *"Die Vertragsparteien vereinbaren die ICC Verfahrensordnung für aus-serschiedsgerichtliche vorläufige Massnahmen durch einen Référé. Jede Partei ist berechtigt das Verfahren in Anspruch zu nehmen."*

Parties are reminded that if they wish to have recourse to ICC Arbitration as well as to the ICC Prearbitral Referee Procedure, a specific reference to both procedures should be stipulated. For that purpose the following clause is recommended:

> "Any party to this contract shall have the right to have recourse to and shall be bound by the Pre-arbitral Referee Procedure of the International Chamber of Commerce in accordance with its Rules.
> "All disputes arising in connection with the present contract shall be finally settled under the Rules of Conciliation and Arbitration of the International Chamber of Commerce by one or more arbitrators appointed in accordance with the said Rules."

RULES FOR A PRE-ARBITRAL REFEREE PROCEDURE

ARTICLE 1
Definitions

1.1. These Rules concern a procedure called the "Pre-arbitral Referee Procedure" which provides for the immediate appointment of a person (the "Referee") who has the power to make certain orders prior to the arbitral tribunal or national court competent to deal with the case (the "competent jurisdiction") being seized of it.

1.2. The Secretariat of the ICC International Court of Arbitration (the "Secretariat") shall act as the Secretariat of the Pre-arbitral Referee Procedure.

1.3. (a) In these Rules any reference to a party includes a party's employees or agents. (b) Any reference to the "Chairman" means the Chairman of the ICC International Court of Arbitration or includes, in his absence, a Vice-Chairman.

ARTICLE 2
Powers of the Referee

2.1. The powers of the Referee are:
(a)   To order any conservatory measures or any measures of restoration that are urgently necessary to prevent either immediate damage or irreparable loss and so to safeguard any of the rights or property of one of the parties;
(b)   To order a party to make to any other party or to another person any payment which ought to be made;
(c)   To order a party to take any step which ought to be taken according to the contract between the parties, including the signing or delivery of any document or the procuring by a party of the signature or delivery of a document;
(d)   To order any measures necessary to preserve or establish evidence.

2.1.1. These powers may be altered by express written agreement between the parties.

2.2. The Referee shall not have power to make any order other than that requested by any party in accordance with Article 3.

2.3. Unless the parties otherwise agree in writing, a Referee appointed in accordance with these Rules shall not act as arbitrator in any subsequent proceedings between those parties or in any other proceedings in which there is any issue or question which is the same as or connected with any which had been raised in the proceedings before the Referee.

2.4. If the competent jurisdiction becomes seized of the case after the appointment of the Referee, the Referee shall nevertheless retain the power to make an order within the time provided by Article 6.2 unless the parties otherwise agree or the competent jurisdiction orders otherwise.

2.4.1. Except as provided in Article 2.4 above or by the relevant rules of the competent jurisdiction, once the competent jurisdiction becomes seized of the case it alone may order any further provisional or conservatory measures that it considers necessary. For such purpose the competent jurisdiction, if its rules so permit, shall be deemed to have been authorised by the parties to exercise the powers conferred on the Referee by Article 2.1.

ARTICLE 3
Request for Referee and Answer

3.1. An agreement to use the Pre-arbitral Referee Procedure must be in writing.

3.2. A party who requires the appointment of a Referee must send two copies of its Request and of any annexed documents to the Secretariat. Such party must at the same time notify the other party or parties of the Request by the quickest method of delivery available, including telefax.

3.2.1. Each such Request must be accompanied by the amount required to open the file, as set out in Article B.1 of the Appendix to these Rules.

3.2.2. The Request must be drawn up in whatever language may have been agreed upon in writing by the parties or, in the absence of any such agreement, in the same language as the agreement to use the Prearbitral Referee Procedure. If this language is not English, French or German, a translation of the Request into one of these languages must accompany the Request. The annexed documents may be submitted in their original language without translation except where it is necessary in order to understand the Request. The Request shall be in writing and shall contain in particular:
(a) the names and addresses of the parties to the agreement together with a brief description of the legal relationships between the parties;
(b) a copy of the agreement on which the Request is based;
(c) the order or orders requested and an explanation of the grounds relied on so as to show that the Request falls within Article 2.1;
(d) as the case may be, the name of the Referee chosen by agreement of the parties;
(e) any information concerning the choice of the Referee required to be appointed, including, as appropriate, technical or professional qualifications, nationality and language requirements;
(f) confirmation that the request has been sent to every other party, stating the means by which this has been done and enclosing proof of transmission, such as postal registration form, receipt from a private courier, or telefax receipt.

3.3. The requesting party shall, if required by the Secretariat, establish when a copy of the Request was received by each party to whom it was sent or when it should be treated as having been received by said party.

3.4. The other party or parties must submit to the Secretariat in writing an Answer to the Request within 8 days from receipt of the copy of the Request sent in accordance with Article 3.2 above, and must send at the same time a copy to the requesting party and to any other party, using the quickest method of delivery available, including telefax. The Answer must state any order requested by that party or parties.

ARTICLE 4
Appointment of the Referee and Transmission of File

4.1. The Referee may be chosen by the parties by agreement before or after a Request is made pursuant to Article 3, in which case the name and address of the Referee shall be sent immediately to the Secretariat. Upon receipt of the Answer or upon the expiry of the time limit set out in Article 3.4, whichever is sooner, and having verified the *prima facie* existence of the agreement of the parties, the Chairman shall appoint the Referee agreed upon.

4.2. If a Referee is to be appointed under Article 3.2.2 (e), the Chairman shall, upon the expiry of the time limit set out in Article 3.4, appoint the Referee in the shortest time possible, taking account of his technical or professional qualifications, his nationality, residence, other relationships with the countries in which the parties are established or with which they are otherwise connected, and any submissions of any party concerning the choice of a Referee.

4.3. Once the Referee has been appointed, the Secretariat shall so notify the parties and shall transmit the file to him. Thereafter all documentation from the parties must be sent directly to the Referee with a copy to the Secretariat. All documentation from the Referee to the parties must be copied to the Secretariat.

4.4. Any party may challenge a Referee appointed under Article 4.2. In such case the Chairman, after giving the other party and the Referee an opportunity to comment, shall take within the shortest time possible a final decision as to the validity of the challenge. His decision shall be within his sole discretion and shall not itself be subject to challenge or appeal by any party.

4.5. Another person shall be appointed (a) where a Referee dies or is prevented or unable to carry out his functions, or (b) it is decided under Article 4.4. that a challenge is valid or (c) if the Chairman decides, after giving the Referee an opportunity to comment, that he is not fulfilling his functions in accordance with the Rules or within any applicable time limit. Such an appointment shall be made in accordance with Article 4.2 (but subject to Article 4.4). In such case the new Referee shall proceed afresh.

4.6. The reasons for any decision about an appointment, challenge or replacement of any Referee shall not be disclosed.

ARTICLE 5
The Proceedings

5.1. If any party shall not have presented an Answer by the time the file has been transmitted to the Referee then the requesting party may be required by the Referee to establish to his satisfaction that a copy of the Request was received or should be treated as having been received by that party before he proceeds further. If the Referee is not so satisfied he shall notify the relevant party of his right to submit an Answer and shall set a time limit within which the Answer shall be submitted. Any such action by the arbitral Referee shall not affect the validity of his appointment.

5.2. Any decision as to the Referee's jurisdiction shall be taken by the Referee.

5.3. Within the limits of the powers conferred on him by Article 2.1. and subject to any agreement of the parties the Referee shall conduct the proceedings in the manner which he considers appropriate for the purpose for which he was appointed including:
– considering the written documents submitted by the parties,
– informing the parties of any further investigation or inquiry that he may consider necessary,
– making such further investigation or inquiry, which may include him visiting any place where the contract is being carried out or the establishments of the parties or any other relevant place, obtaining the report of an expert, and hearing any person he chooses in connection with the dispute, either in the presence of the parties or, if they have been duly convened, in their absence. The results of these investigations and inquiries shall be communicated to the parties for comment.

5.4. In acceding to these Rules the parties undertake to provide the Referee with every facility to implement his terms of reference and, in particular, to make available to him all documents which he may consider necessary and also to grant free access to any place for the purpose of any investigation or inquiry. The information given to the Referee shall remain confidential between the parties and the Referee.

5.5. The Referee may convene the parties to appear before him within the shortest time limit possible on a date and at a place fixed by him.

5.6. If one of the parties does not make a submission, comment or appear as required by the Referee, and the Referee is satisfied that the party concerned has received or should have received the relevant communication he may nonetheless continue with the proceedings and may make his order.

ARTICLE 6
The Order

6.1. The decisions taken by the Referee shall be sent by him to the Secretariat in the form of an order giving reasons.

6.2. The Referee shall make and send the order within 30 days from the date on which the file was transmitted to him. This time limit may be extended by the Chairman upon a reasoned request from the Referee or on his own initiative if he thinks it is necessary to do so.

6.3. The Referee's order does not pre-judge the substance of the case nor shall it bind any competent jurisdiction which may hear any question, issue or dispute in respect of which the order has been made. The order of the Referee shall however remain in force unless and until the Referee or the competent jurisdiction has decided otherwise.

6.4. The Referee may make the carrying out of his order subject to such conditions as he thinks fit including (a) that a party shall commence proceedings before the competent jurisdiction on the substance of the case within a specified period, (b) that a party for whose benefit an order is made shall provide adequate security.

6.5. The Secretariat shall notify the parties of the order of the Referee provided that it shall have received the full amount of the advance on costs fixed by the Secretariat. Only orders so notified are binding upon the parties.

6.6. The parties agree to carry out the Referee's order without delay and waive their right to all means of appeal or recourse or opposition to a request to a Court or to any other authority to implement the order, insofar as such waiver can validly be made.

6.7. Unless otherwise agreed between the parties and subject to any mandatory order, any submissions, communications or documents (other than the order) established or made solely for the purposes of the Pre-arbitral Referee Procedure shall be confidential and shall not be given to the competent jurisdiction.

6.8. The Referee shall not be obliged to explain or give further additional reasons for any order after it has been notified by the Secretariat under Article 6.5. Neither the ICC nor any of its employees or persons acting as Chairman or Vice-Chairman, nor any person acting as Referee shall be liable to any person for any loss or damage arising out of any act or omission in connection with the Rules except that the Referee may be liable for the consequences of conscious and deliberate wrongdoing.

6.8.1. The competent jurisdiction may determine whether any party who refuses or fails to carry out an order of the Referee is liable to any other party for loss or damage caused by such refusal or failure.

6.8.2. The competent jurisdiction may determine whether a party who requested the Referee to issue an order the carrying out of which caused damage to another party is liable to such other party.

ARTICLE 7
Costs

7.1. The costs of the Pre-arbitral Referee Procedure comprise: (a) an administrative charge as set out in the Appendix to these Rules, (b) the fees and expenses of the Referee to be determined as set out in the Appendix and (c) the costs of any expert. The Referee's order shall state who shall bear the costs of the Pre-arbitral Referee Procedure and in what proportion. A party who made an advance or other payment in respect of costs which it was not liable to have made under the Referee's order shall be entitled to recover the amount paid from the party who ought to have made the payment.

7.2. The costs of and payment for any procedure under these Rules are as set out in the Appendix hereto.

APPENDIX

COSTS AND PAYMENT FOR THE ICC
PRE-ARBITRAL REFEREE PROCEDURE

A. Costs

1. An administrative charge of US$1,500 is payable by the requesting party in respect of each request made to the ICC to appoint a Referee or to administer a Prearbitral Referee Procedure.

The charge covers all services rendered by the ICC that may be required by the Rules, but not any services required by alterations to or extensions of the Procedure. The administrative charge is not refundable and becomes the property of the ICC.

2. The amount of the fees and expenses of the Referee shall be fixed by the Secretary General of the ICC International Court of Arbitration. The amount shall be reasonable, taking into consideration the time spent, the complexity of the matter and any other relevant circumstances.

3. The costs of the procedure shall also include any fees and expenses of any expert.

B. Payment

1. The amount required to open the file (Article 3.2.1 of the Rules) is US$4,000 of which $1,500 constitutes the administrative charge as set out above and $2,500 constitutes an advance on the fees and expenses of the Referee and any expert. No request for the appointment of a Referee or for the administration of an ICC Pre-arbitral Referee Procedure will be entertained unless accompanied by this amount.

2. As soon as possible after the file has been sent to the Referee and after such consultation as is possible with the Referee and the parties, the Secretariat shall fix an advance on costs to cover the estimated costs of the Pre-arbitral Referee Procedure (Art. 7.1 of the Rules). Such advance on costs is subject to readjustment by the Secretariat.

The requesting party shall pay the whole of this advance on costs except insofar as the Secretariat may request the other party or parties to contribute to the advance on costs in the light of any request for an order by the Referee which any other party may have made.

3. No order of the Referee shall be notified by the Secretariat or be valid unless the advance on costs has been received (Art. 6.5). Where two or more parties have been asked to contribute to the advance on costs and have not paid their contribution, only the order requested by the party or parties who have fully paid the advance or contribution shall be notified and be valid.

Copyright © 1990
ICC Publishing S.A.
Publication N° 482
ISBN 92-842-1101-8

Table of Authorities

Jarvin and Derains, eds., *Collection of ICC Arbitral Awards 1974-1985* (ICC Publishing/Kluwer 1990).   **91, 94, 105, 211-12, 222, 224, 250, 277-78, 283**

Jarvin, Derains and Arnaldez, eds., *Collection of ICC Arbitral Awards 1986-1990* (ICC Publishing/Kluwer 1994).   **90-91, 105, 255, 285, 289, 354**

Kassis, *Réflexions sur le règlement d'arbitrage de la chambre de commerce internationale – Les déviations de l'arbitrage institutionnel* (LGDJ 1988).
64, 292

Lalive, Poudret and Reymond, *Le Droit de l'Arbitrage Interne et International en Suisse* (Payot 1989).   **37, 100, 105, 130, 321**

Lew, ed., *Contemporary Problems in International Arbitration* (Martinus Nijhoff 1987).   **95**

Loquin, *L'amiable composition en droit comparé et international* (Librairies Techniques 1980).   **226-27**

Multi-party Arbitration (ICC Publishing 1991).   **14**

Mustill and Boyd, *The Law and Practice of Commercial Arbitration in England*, 2d ed. (Butterworths 1989).   **182, 282, 332-33, 340**

Principles of International Commercial Contracts, International Institute for the Unification of Private Law (UNIDROIT) (Rome 1994).   **218-19, 225-26**

Redfern and Hunter, *Law and Practice of International Commercial Arbitration*, 2d ed. (Sweet & Maxwell 1991).   **119, 147-48, 150, 218, 251**

Schlosser, *Das Recht der Internationalen privaten schiedgeritchtsbarkeit* (1975).   **292**

Schwebel, *International Arbitration: Three Salient Problems* (Grotius Publications 1987).   **104**

Taking of Evidence in International Arbitral Proceedings (ICC Publishing 1990).   **251**

van den Berg, *The New York Arbitration Convention of 1958* (Kluwer 1981). **288**

van den Berg, ed., *ICCA Yearbook* (published annually since 1976 by the International Council for Commercial Arbitration (ICCA)).   **44, 76, 92, 96, 98, 108, 133, 141, 211, 216, 219, 225, 229, 250-51, 256, 270, 287, 294, 337, 349**

II. ARTICLES

Aguilar-Alvarez, "The Challenge of Arbitrators," *Arb. Int.*, Vol. 6, No. 3 (1990), p. 203.   **175**

Aksen, "The Law Applicable in International Arbitration: Relevance of Reference to Trade Usages," *ICCA Congress Series No. 7* (Kluwer 1996), p. 471.   **225**

Amoussou-Guenou *et al.*, "International Fast-Track Commercial Arbitration," *Comparative Law Yearbook of International Arbitration*, Special Issue (Graham & Trotman/Nijhoff 1994), p. 357.   **346**

Arnaldez, "*L'acte déterminant la mission de l'arbitre,*" *Etudes offertes à Pierre Bellet* (Litec 1991), p. 1.   **228, 239, 250**

"Note," ICC Case No. 6653 (1993), *ICC Arbitral Awards 1991-1995*, p. 525.
229, 353

"Note," ICC Case No. 6670 (1992), *ICC Arbitral Awards 1991-1995*, p. 447.
263
"Note," ICC Case No. 6719 (1991), *ICC Arbitral Awards 1991-1995*, p. 567.
64
"Note," *Société Farhat Trading Company c/ société Daewoo Industrial Company Ltd, Cour de cassation* (March 6, 1996), *Rev. arb.* (1997), p. 69. **234**
"*Réflexions sur l'autonomie et le caractère international du Règlement d'arbitrage de la CCI,*" *Clunet* (1993), p. 857. **129, 132**
Arnaldez and Jakandé, "*Les Amendements Apportés au Règlement d'Arbitrage de la Chambre de Commerce Internationale (C.C.I.),*" *Rev. arb.* (1988), p. 67.
158, 188, 191
Batiffol, "*L'arbitrage et les conflits de lois,*" *Rev. arb.* (1957), p. 111. **222**
Bedjaoui, "*Des fortes vérités de Cassandre aux modestes correctifs de Némésis (ou le souci communément partagé de voir la liberté fondamentale de choisir un arbitre n'être ni un danger ni en danger),*" *Etudes de Droit International en l'Honneur de Pierre Lalive* (Helbing & Lichtenhahn 1993), p. 385. **118**
Bellet, Intervention in Minoli, "*Relations entre partie et arbitre,*" *Rev. arb.* (1970), p. 221. **111**
"Note," *Ben Nasser et autre c/ BNP et Crédit Lyonnais, Cour d'appel de Paris* (October 14, 1993), *Rev. arb.* (1994), p. 380. **118**
"Note," *KFTCIC c/ Icori Estero, Cour d'appel de Paris* (June 28, 1991), *Rev. arb.* (1992), p. 568. **116**
"Note," *Sociétés BKMI et Siemens c/ Dutco construction, Cour d'appel de Paris* (May 5, 1989), *Rev. arb.* (1989), p. 723. **168**
Benglia, "Inaccurate Reference to the ICC," *ICC Ct. Bull.*, Vol. 7, No. 2 (1996), p. 11. **90**
Bernard, "Note," *Société Ripolin Georget Freitag c/ société Henry Clarks & Sons, Cour de cassation* (April 27, 1981), *Rev. arb.* (1983), p. 105. **282**
Bernardini, "The Powers of the Arbitrator," *Conservatory and Provisional Measures in International Arbitration* (ICC Publishing 1993), p. 21. **274**
Blessing, "Arbitrability of Intellectual Property Disputes," *Arb. Int.*, Vol. 12, No. 2 (1996), p. 191. **264**
"The ICC Arbitral Procedure Under the New ICC Rules – What Has Changed?" *ICC Ct. Bull.*, Vol. 8, No. 2 (1997), p. 16. **103, 217-18, 272**
"The Procedure before the Arbitral Tribunal," *ICC Ct. Bull.*, Vol. 3, No. 2 (1992), p. 18. **252, 254, 256, 262**
"Regulations in Arbitration Rules on Choice of Law," *ICCA Congress Series No. 7* (Kluwer 1996), p. 391. **218**
Böckstiegel, "Experience as an Arbitrator Using the UNCITRAL Arbitration Rules," *Etudes de Droit International en l'Honneur de Pierre Lalive* (Helbing & Lichtenhahn 1993), p. 423. **285**
"The Legal Rules Applicable in International Commercial Arbitration Involving States or State-controlled Enterprises," *60 Years of ICC Arbitration* (ICC Publishing 1984), p. 34. **95**

Byrne, "Payment of Advances on Fees to Arbitrators in ICC Proceedings," *ICC Ct. Bull.,* Vol. 7, No. 2 (1996), p. 84. **332**

Cadiet, *"La renonciation à se prévaloir des irrégularités de la procédure arbitrale,"* *Rev. arb.* (1996), p. 3. **130, 349, 351**

Cahier, "The Strengths and Weaknesses of International Arbitration Involving a State as a Party," *Contemporary Problems in International Arbitration* (Martinus Nijhoff 1987), p. 241. **95**

Carter, "Living with the Party-Appointed Arbitrator: Judicial Confusion, Ethical Codes and Practical Advice," *Am. Rev. Int. Arb.,* Vol. 3 (1992), p. 153. **111, 120, 141**

Chambreuil, *"Arbitrage international et garanties bancaires,"* *Rev. arb.* (1991), p. 33. **94**

Charrin, "The ICC International Centre for Expertise – Realities and Prospects," *ICC Ct. Bull.,* Vol. 6, No. 2 (1995), p. 33. **260**

Christie, "Amiable Composition in French and English Law," *Arbitration*, Vol. 58, No. 4 (1992), p. 259. **226-27**

Cohen, *"Arbitrage et Groupes de Contrats,"* *Rev. arb.* (1997), p. 471. **98**

Coulson, "An American Critique of the IBA's Ethics for International Arbitrators," *J. Arb. Int.,* Vol. 4, No. 2 (1987), p. 103. **108**

Craig, "Some Trends and Developments in the Laws and Practice of International Commercial Arbitration," *Texas International Law Journal*, Vol. 30, No. 1 (1995), p. 1. **200**

Darling and Ramsay, "Powers and Jurisdiction of the Arbitral Tribunal," *International and ICC Arbitration* (King's College 1990), p. 104. **353**

Davis, "Fast-Track Arbitration: Different Perspectives – The Case Viewed by a Counsel at the ICC Court's Secretariat," *ICC Ct. Bull.,* Vol. 3, No. 2 (1992), p. 4. **28, 346, 349**

"The ICC's Pre-Arbitral Referee Procedure in Context with Technical Expertise, Conciliation and Arbitration," *International Construction Law Review*, Vol. 9 (1992), p. 218. **14**

"Pathological Clauses: Frédéric Eisemann's still Vital Criteria," *Arb. Int.,* Vol. 7, No. 4 (1991), p. 365. **356**

Davis *et al.*, "When Doctrines Meet – Fast Track Arbitration and the ICC Experience," *J. Arb. Int.,* Vol. 10, No. 4 (1993), p. 69. **346**

Delaume, "The Proper Law of State Contracts and the *Lex Mercatoria*: A Reappraisal," *ICSID Review – Foreign Investment Law Journal*, No. 3 (1988), p. 79. **219**

Delvolvé, *"L'arbitrage multipartite en 1992,"* *ASA Bull.,* No. 2 (1992), p. 152. **172**

Derains, *"Attente légitime des parties et droit applicable au fond en matière d'arbitrage commercial international,"* *Travaux du Comité Français du Droit International Privé, 1984-1985*, p. 81. **223**

"Choice of the Law Applicable to the Contract and International Arbitration," *ICC Ct. Bull.,* Vol. 6, No. 1 (1996), p. 10. **220**

"Expertise Technique et Référé Arbitral," *Rev. arb.* (1982), p. 239. **275**

Sarre, "ICC United Kingdom and Its Role in Arbitration," *International and ICC Arbitration* (King's College 1990), p. 58.   **157**

"Security for Costs in ICC Arbitration in England – The *Ken-Ren* Cases," *International Commercial Arbitration in Europe, ICC Ct. Bull.*, Special Supplement (1994), p. 58.   **273**

Schäfer, "Terms of Reference in the Past and at Present," *ICC Ct. Bull.*, Vol. 3, No. 1 (1992), p. 8.   **228**

Schneider, "The Terms of Reference," *The New 1998 ICC Rules of Arbitration, ICC Ct. Bull.,* Special Supplement (1997), p. 26.   **228, 234-35**

Schwartz, "Arbitration Awards – Challenge and Enforcement," *Globalization and Harmonization of Basic Notions in International Arbitration* (IFCAI 1996), p. 141.   **293**

"The Costs of ICC Arbitration," *ICC Ct. Bull.*, Vol. 4, No. 1 (1993), p. 8.   **303, 311**

"Going astray in Bordelais: a comment on a recent decision of the Court of Appeal of Bordeaux," *The Arbitration and Dispute Resolution Law Journal*, Part 2 (1997), p. 91.   **23**

"The ICC Arbitration Rules and the UNCITRAL Model Law," *Arb. Int.,* Vol. 9, No. 3 (1993), p. 231.   **186**

"International Conciliation and the ICC," *ICC Ct. Bull.,* Vol. 5, No. 2 (1994), p. 5.   **25**

"Multi-Party Arbitration and the ICC: In the Wake of *Dutco," J. Arb. Int.*, Vol. 10, No. 3 (1993), p. 5.   **170**

"The Practices and Experience of the ICC Court," *Conservatory and Provisional Measures in International Arbitration* (ICC Publishing 1993), p. 45.   **273, 275-76**

"Reply," *ASA Bull.,* No. 1 (1996), p. 32.   **335**

"The Rights and Duties of ICC Arbitrators," *The Status of the Arbitrator* (ICC Publishing 1995), p. 67.   **176**

Schwebel, "The Validity of an Arbitral Award Rendered by a Truncated Tribunal," *ICC Ct. Bull.,* Vol. 6, No. 2 (1995), p. 19.   **193**

Schweizer, "Note," *Westland Helicopters Limited c/ The Arab British Helicopter Company, Tribunal fédéral suisse* (April 19, 1994), *ASA Bull.* (1995), p. 191.   **239**

Seppala and Gogek, "Multi-party Arbitration under ICC Rules," *International Financial Law Review* (November 1989), p. 32.   **168**

H. Smit, "Confidentiality in Arbitration," *Arb. Int.,* Vol. 11, No. 3 (1995), p. 337.   **13**

"Managing an International Arbitration: An Arbitrator's View," *Am. Rev. Int. Arb.*, Vol. 5 (1994), p. 129.   **184**

"The New International Arbitration Rules of the American Arbitration Association," *Am. Rev. Int. Arb.*, Vol. 2 (1991), p. 1.   **25, 143, 191, 288, 319**

R. Smit, "An Inside View of the ICC Court," *Arb. Int.*, Vol. 10, No. 1 (1994), p. 53.   **19, 122, 158**

Smith, "Impartiality of the Party-appointed Arbitrator," *Arbitration*, Vol. 58, No. 1 (1992), p. 30.   **108**

Solhchi, "The Validity of Truncated Tribunal Proceedings and Awards," *Arb. Int.*, Vol. 9, No. 3 (1993), p. 303.   **193**

Sutton, "Discovery and Production of Evidence in Arbitral Proceedings: the US and England Distinguished," *Taking of Evidence in International Arbitral Proceedings* (ICC Publishing 1990), p. 57.   **262**

Tekinay, "Turkey's Adhesion to the Geneva and New York Conventions," *ICC Ct. Bull.*, Vol. 3, No. 1 (1992), p. 14.   **294**

Tschanz, "The Chamber of Commerce and Industry of Geneva's Arbitration Rules and their Expedited Procedure," *J. Arb. Int.*, Vol. 10, No. 4 (1993), p. 51.   **348**

"Note," *Clear Star Limited c/ Centrala Morska Importoura-Eksportova "Contromor" et Centromor SA, Tribunal fédéral suisse* (April 9, 1991), *Rev. arb.* (1991), p. 709.   **298**

Tupman, "Challenge and Disqualification of Arbitrators in International Commercial Arbitration," *International Comparative Law Quarterly*, Vol. 38 (1989), p. 26.   **127**

van den Berg, "Consolidated Commentary" (on cases relating to Article V(1)(b) of New York Convention), *ICCA Yearbook* XXI (1996), p. 394.   **44, 294, 297**

Veeder, "Laws and Court Decisions in Common Law Countries and the UNCITRAL Model Law," *ICCA Congress Series No. 5* (Kluwer 1991), p. 277.   **182**

"National Report – England," *ICCA Handbook on Commercial Arbitration*, Supplement 23 (Kluwer 1997), p. 27.   **110, 193**

"Towards a Possible Solution: Limitation, Interest and Assignment in London and Paris," *ICCA Congress Series No. 7* (Kluwer 1996), p. 268.   **106**

Verbist, "The Practice of the ICC International Court of Arbitration with Regard to the Fixing of the Place of Arbitration," *Arb. Int.*, Vol. 12, No. 3 (1996), p. 347.   **201**

Wallace, "Consolidated Arbitration in the United States," *J. Arb. Int.*, Vol. 10, No. 4 (1993), p. 5.   **62**

Werner, "Remuneration of Arbitrators by the International Chamber of Commerce," *J. Arb. Int.*, Vol. 5, No. 3 (1988), p. 135.   **305, 332**

Wetter, "Ethical Guidelines," *Yearbook of the Arbitration Institute of the Stockholm Chamber of Commerce* (1993), p. 99.   **125**

"The ICC in the Context of International Arbitration," *International and ICC Arbitration* (King's College 1990), p. 40.   **127**

"The Present Status of the International Court of Arbitration of the ICC: An Appraisal," *Am. Rev. Int. Arb.*, Vol. 1, No. 1 (1990), p. 91.   **7, 229, 305**

Wetter and Priem, "Costs and their Allocation in International Commercial Arbitration," *Am. Rev. Int. Arb.*, Vol. 2 (1991), p. 249.**321-22, 324, 332, 336-37, 340-41, 343**

III.   ICC ARBITRAL TRIBUNAL AWARDS AND ORDERS

Awards

Orders

IV. National and International Court Decisions

Australia

Austria

England

European Court of Justice

France

Germany

Hong Kong

Spain

Sweden

Switzerland

Syria

Turkey

United States of America

V. Miscellaneous

"Rules of Ethics for International Arbitrators" (IBA 1987), *ICCA Yearbook* XII (1987), p. 199.   **108, 115, 120, 122, 141**

"The Standards and Burden of Proof in International Arbitration," *Arb. Int.,* Vol. 10, No. 3 (1994), p. 317.   **251**

"Supplementary Rules Governing the Presentation and Reception of Evidence in International Commercial Arbitration" (International Bar Association 1983), *ICCA Yearbook* X (1985), p. 145.   **251, 257, 262**

"Terms of Reference under the 1988 ICC Arbitration Rules – A Practical Guide" ICC Commission on International Arbitration Working Party (S. Lazareff, Chairman), *ICC Ct. Bull.*, Vol. 3, No. 1 (1992), p. 24.**228, 230, 232-34, 237-39, 241-42, 245, 250**

Index